# TYPES OF CONTEMPORARY DRAMA

# CONTINENTAL PLAYS

## *VOLUME TWO*

SELECTED AND EDITED BY

## THOMAS H. DICKINSON

*Editor, Chief Contemporary Dramatists, First, Second, and Third Series, etc.*
*Author, An Outline of Contemporary Drama, Contemporary Drama*
*of England, The Case of American Drama, etc.*

# HOUGHTON MIFFLIN COMPANY

BOSTON · NEW YORK · CHICAGO
DALLAS · ATLANTA · SAN FRANCISCO

The Riverside Press Cambridge

The Riverside Press
CAMBRIDGE · MASSACHUSETTS
PRINTED IN THE U.S.A.

# CONTENTS

# TYPES OF
# CONTEMPORARY DRAMA

THIS is the second volume in a series of contemporary drama which differs from preceding collections in several important respects. Apart from their handy size and great economy, which are matters of book-making, the volumes in this series offer an entirely new approach in the critical principles governing the inclusion of plays.

In previous collections plays have been included for two principal reasons: (1) they were the outstanding plays of the period judged by merit and historical significance; (2) they were plays that served well in the classroom. These two principles must still operate in any collection of plays, and they have been kept in mind in the present series. But there are other principles of selection, not heretofore employed, which should no longer be ignored.

These principles derive from the fact that contemporary plays are by no means all alike, that they differ widely in *form*, that they are of various *types*. If we are to understand contemporary drama, we must not consider it by content alone. We must consider it in its wide variety of forms. As we learn in the General Introduction to this series, many of these forms go back to the earliest history of drama. Only by considering the content of the play in the light of its form can the real significance of the author's work be grasped.

It is the purpose of this series to present the great representative plays of the period in their significant variety of forms. Each volume will be complete in itself, and each volume will contain the widest possible variety of play forms.

To find place in this series, each play has had to satisfy three standards of judgment: (1) it must be an outstanding play of the period by merit and historical significance; (2) it must satisfy the classroom demands of teachers throughout the United States; (3) finally, it must be a typical example of one of the many important *forms* or *types* in which contemporary drama has been composed.

THE EDITOR

# FIFTY YEARS OF EUROPEAN DRAMA

THIS is the second volume of a series of Types of Contemporary Drama. As it is the purpose of these volumes to represent the chief forms of playwriting of the last fifty years in Europe, it may be appropriate to inquire into the qualities that mark this period.

The outstanding figure in the theater of Europe at the beginning of the period covered by this book was Henrik Ibsen. This does not mean that Ibsen was the most popular dramatist. Ibsen always occupied a position outside the main current of European drama, from which he could exercise the extraordinary influence derived from the vigor of his opinions and the mastery of his craftsmanship.

For long Ibsen was given credit for the destruction of the "well-made" play. Closer study does not confirm this opinion. Ibsen did indeed introduce sincerity into the spirit of drama and substance into its theme. But he did this rather by adapting the forms of his contemporaries to his own purposes than by changing these forms. He was a romanticist whose plays revealed a great deal of artifice, an artifice which was impelled by didactic motive rather than by the desire to amuse.

During a large part of our period serious plays were characterized by what might be called "didactic romanticism." It is to this class of plays that the term "naturalism" is usually applied. Today we know that the term "naturalism" covers no single type of play, that it has indeed little meaning when applied to the form of a play. Naturalism covers the whole class of plays which seeks to treat seriously the problems of life, which discards the incentive of entertainment for the incentives of clear observation and progress. But there is no single pattern or principle of naturalism. Under naturalism there are grouped plays of the most exaggerated artifice, such as *The Red Robe* by Brieux, and plays upon which care had been lavished to conceal artifice, such as *The Lower Depths* by Gorky, both of which are included in this book. The quality that covered them all was one of outlook or animus rather than one of form.

Such was the situation in the early years of the present century. Revolt had long been the slogan of the European theater, but it was a revolt which had little to do with the theater itself. It was a revolt on the part of men who were using the theater for their own purposes. In their hands the forms of plays were changing very little. What was changing was content and social spirit. If the writers of these plays had been told that they were driving people from the theater, and were preparing the way for some strange revenges in the theater itself, they would have been surprised. But this is the case.

We now come to the second outstanding feature of the period under review in this book. This was the revolt on the part of the men of the theater themselves against some of the forces that had been constraining their art. Strange to say this did not appear first among the writers of plays. Its first appearance was among the producing workers of the theater, the directors, designers, and actors, who, recognizing the increasing imaginative aridity of the plays offered to them for interpretation, began to demand that the theater be returned to its ancient uses through the enrichment of its appeals to emotion and sensation. Thence came the universal requirement that the theater be "retheatricalized." Only after these practical workers in the theater had carried far the movement of retheatricalization were they joined by the authors themselves.

Perhaps the first of the consequences of this revolt among the playwrights was the conviction that the logical and naturalistic form of play was no longer an appropriate medium for their art. Some playwrights, notably Rostand in France and D'Annunzio in Italy, both of whom are represented in this series, had clung to the romantic form even in unfriendly times. Other poetic dramatists turned away from the romantic form to the more regular forms of neo-classicism. Still others, for example Claudel in *The Tidings Brought to Mary*, and Andreyev in *The Life of Man*, found their inspiration in the dramas of the medieval church.

But playwrights were not content merely to turn back to the older forms. Some of them sought to create new forms based upon a reinterpretation of the forces of modern life. Repudiating the cult of intellectualism, Wedekind seeks to isolate in his drama the more primitive strains in human life which he identifies with the "earth spirit." Now that the playwrights are aspiring for new worlds to conquer, questions of form assume an unwonted importance, beyond story-telling, characterization or message. In such plays as *A Dream Play* by Strindberg, and *The Coral* by Kaiser, both of which are found in this book, the playwrights seek by means of experiment in form to set forward the boundaries of the imaginative world. In two other plays found in this volume, *The Great Galeoto* by Echegaray, and *Six Characters in Search of an Author* by Pirandello, the absorption of the modern author in the mysteries of form is revealed in an interesting manner. Both of these are "plays in the making," and reveal the playwright standing in some uncertainty before the perplexities of his craft in a world of changing symbols. Finally, as the last play in this collection we have the resources of the theater employed with an exquisite economy for the achieving of the effects of mood which are usually sought in music rather than in drama.

# THE GREAT GALEOTO
## (EL GRAN GALEOTO)

### A PLAY IN THREE ACTS AND A PROLOGUE
### By JOSÉ ECHEGARAY

*Translated from the Spanish by ELEANOR BONTECOU*

## JOSÉ ECHEGARAY y EIZAGUIRRE

BEFORE he became famous as a playwright, José Echegaray was a mathematician, economist, and revolutionary statesman. Born in Madrid in 1832, he graduated in the School of Engineers at Madrid, and after a period in the field returned to his Alma Mater in 1858, and was for ten years Professor of Mechanics and Mathematics, publishing books on geometry and physics. He was admitted to the Academy of Natural Sciences in 1866. Having aided the revolutionary cause, he held positions in the revolutionary government of Spain of 1868–1871. His first play was *La hija naturel*, written in 1867. He wrote his first successful play, *El libro talonario*, in one act, in Paris during the existence of the short-lived republic of Castelar, 1873. With its production in 1874, Echegaray turned his attention almost entirely to the stage. He wrote sixty plays in the next twenty-five years. A man of strong convictions, passionate energy, and gloomy intensity, Echegaray lacked artistic restraint. The majority of his plays are melodramatic and machine-made. He finds place in this book because of an innovating quality of social vision which he frequently turns on the themes of his playwriting, a quality which, however, does not free him from the restraints of some of the cruder dramatic conventions. Echegaray died in 1916.

# THE GREAT GALEOTO

THIS is the first of two plays in this volume which might be called "Plays in the making," the second being Pirandello's *Six Characters in Search of an Author*. The problem faced by the author of *The Great Galeoto* is clearly stated in the introductory scenes of the play. Briefly the author revolts against the limitations of dramatic form which have hitherto restricted him to the treatment of man in his individual capacity. He would put the mass of society on the stage, and he would seek for dramatic motivations, not in clearly indicated personal impulses, but in the vaguer and more irresponsible impulses that arise in large groups. Other dramatists, notably Gorky and Hauptmann, have sought to give the impression of the mass upon the stage in a naturalistic manner. Though Echegaray is modern in this objective, he is ancient in his social conventions and in his standards of playwriting. His theme is based upon characters who are representative of a passing order, an order that, even while he wrote, had its existence in literary convention rather than in life itself. And the plot complex is the product of the type of "well-made" play which was the characteristic drama of artifice of the mid-nineteenth century.

Plays on the potency of rumor and gossip have been written, among others, by Beaumarchais, Scribe, Hervieu, Henry Arthur Jones, and Lady Gregory. None has been more suggestive than Echegaray's *El gran galeoto*, produced at the Teatro Español, March 19, 1881. The play was dedicated to "Everyone," public and actors. The play has been translated into all European languages. It was translated into English by Hannah Lynch, London, 1895; Jacob S. Fassett, Boston, 1914; and Eleanor Bontecou, New York, 1917. An adaptation entitled *The World and his Wife* was made by Charles F. Nirdlinger in 1908 and later produced.

# CHARACTERS

TEODORA

DON JULIAN, *her husband*

DOÑA MERCEDES

DON SEVERO, *her husband*

PEPITO, *her son*

ERNESTO

A BYSTANDER

A SERVANT

ANOTHER SERVANT

# PROLOGUE

ERNESTO's *study. To the left, a French window; to the right, a door. Nearly in the center, a table on which are books, papers, and a lighted lamp. To the right is a sofa. It is evening.* ERNESTO *is seated at the table, as though about to write.*

ERNESTO. There's no use. I can't do it. It is impossible. I am simply contending with the impossible. The idea is here; it is stirring in my brain; I can feel it. Sometimes a light from within illumines it and I see it with its shifting form and vague contours, and suddenly there sound in the hidden depths voices that give it life; cries of grief, sighs of love, sardonic, mocking laughter — a whole world of living, struggling passions. They break from me, and spread out, and fill the air all about me! Then, then, I say to myself, the moment has come, and I take up my pen, and with eyes gazing into space, with straining ears, with fast-beating heart, I bend over my paper.— But oh, the irony of impotence! The contours become blurred, the vision disappears, the shouts and sighs die away, and nothingness, nothingness surrounds me! The desolation of empty space, of meaningless thought, of deadly weariness! More than all that, the desolation of an idle pen and a barren page — a page bereft of all life-giving thought. Ah, how many forms has nothingness, and how it mocks, dark and silent, at creatures of my sort! Many, many forms: — the colorless canvas, the shapeless piece of marble, the discordant sound, but none more irritating, more mocking, more blighting than this worthless pen and this blank paper. Ah, I cannot cover you, but I can destroy you, vile accomplice in my wrecked ambitions and my everlasting humiliation! — So, so — smaller, still smaller. (*Tearing the paper — then, a pause.*) Well, it's fortunate that no one saw me, for at best such ranting is foolish, and it's all wrong. No — I will not give in; I will think harder, harder, until I conquer or blow up in a thousand pieces. No,

I will never admit I am beaten.   Come, let's see whether now ——

(*Enter* Don Julian, *right, wearing a frock coat and carrying his overcoat on his arm.   He looks in at the door but doesn't come in.*)

JULIAN.   Hello, Ernesto!

ERNESTO.   Don Julian!

JULIAN.   Still working?   Am I disturbing you?

ERNESTO.   Disturbing me?   Indeed, no.   Come in, come in, Don Julian.   Where's Teodora?

JULIAN.   We've just come from the opera.   She went up to the third floor with my brother and his wife to see some purchases of Mercedes, and I was on my way to my own room, when I saw a light in yours and looked in to say good night.

ERNESTO.   Were there many people there?

JULIAN.   A good many — as usual.   All my friends were asking for you.   They were surprised at your not going.

ERNESTO.   How kind of them!

JULIAN.   Not so very, considering all that you deserve.   But how about you?   Have you made good use of these three hours of solitude and inspiration?

ERNESTO.   Solitude, yes; inspiration, no.   That would not come to me, though I called upon it desperately and with passion.

JULIAN.   It wouldn't obey the summons?

ERNESTO.   No, and this was not the first time.   But I did make a profitable discovery, though I accomplished nothing.

JULIAN.   What?

ERNESTO.   Simply this — that I am a poor good-for-nothing.

JULIAN.   Good-for-nothing!   Well, that's a profitable discovery, indeed.

ERNESTO.   Precisely.

JULIAN.   And why so disgusted with yourself?   Isn't the play you told about the other day going well?

ERNESTO.   I'm the one who is going — out of my mind!

JULIAN.   And what is all this trouble that inspiration and the play together are making for my Ernesto?

ERNESTO.   The trouble is this; when I conceived it I thought the idea a good one; but when I give it form and dress it out in the proper stage trappings the result is extraordinary; contrary to all laws of the drama; utterly impossible.

JULIAN. But why impossible? Come, tell me about it. I am curious.

ERNESTO. Imagine, then, that the principal character, the one who creates the drama, who develops, who animates it, who brings about the catastrophe, and who thrives upon that catastrophe and revels in it — that person cannot appear on the stage.

JULIAN. Is he so ugly? Or so repulsive? Or so wicked?

ERNESTO. It's not that. He is no uglier than anyone else — than you or I. Nor is he bad. Neither bad nor good. Repulsive? No indeed. I am not such a sceptic, nor such a misanthrope, nor so at odds with the world that I would say such a thing or commit such an injustice.

JULIAN. Well, then, what is the reason?

ERNESTO. Don Julian, the reason is that there probably wouldn't be room on the stage for the character in question.

JULIAN. Good heavens, listen to the man! Is this a mythological play, then, and do Titans appear on the stage?

ERNESTO. They are Titans; but a modern variety.

JULIAN. In short?

ERNESTO. In short this character is — *Everybody*.

JULIAN. *Everybody!* Well, you are right! There's not room in the theater for everybody. That is an indisputable fact that has often been demonstrated.

ERNESTO. Now you see how right I was.

JULIAN. Not altogether. *Everybody* can be condensed into a certain number of types, or characters. I don't understand these things myself, but I have heard that authors have done it more than once.

ERNESTO. Yes, but in my case, that is, in my play, it can't be done.

JULIAN. Why not?

ERNESTO. For many reasons that it would take too long to explain; especially at this time of night.

JULIAN. Never mind, let's have some of them.

ERNESTO. Well then, each part of this vast whole, each head of this thousand-headed monster, of this Titan of today whom I call *Everybody*, takes part in my play only for the briefest instant, speaks one word and no more, gives one glance; perhaps his entire action consists in the suggestion of one smile; he appears for a moment and goes away again; he works without passion, without guile, without malice, indifferently, and absently — often *by* his very abstraction.

JULIAN. And what then?

ERNESTO. From those words, from those fleeting glances, from those indifferent smiles, from all those little whispers, from all those peccadilloes; from all these things that we might call insignificant rays of dramatic light, when brought to a focus in one family, result the spark and the explosion, the struggle and the victims. If I represent the whole of mankind by a given number of types or symbolic characters, I have to ascribe to each one that which is really distributed among many, with the result that a certain number of characters must appear who are made repulsive by vices that lack verisimilitude, whose crimes have no object. And, as an additional result, there is the danger that people will believe I am trying to paint society as evil, corrupt, and cruel, when I only want to show that not even the most insignificant acts are really insignificant or impotent for good or evil; for, gathered together by the mysterious agencies of modern life, they may succeed in producing tremendous results.

JULIAN. Come, stop, stop! That is all dreadfully metaphysical. I get a glimmering, but the clouds are pretty thick. In fact, you understand more than I do about these things. Now, if it were a question of drafts, of notes, of letters of credit, of discount, it would be another matter.

ERNESTO. Oh, no, you have common-sense, which is the main thing.

JULIAN. Thanks, Ernesto, you are very kind.

ERNESTO. But are you convinced?

JULIAN. No, I'm not. There must be some way of getting round the difficulty.

ERNESTO. If only there were!

JULIAN. Is there something more?

ERNESTO. I should say so! Tell me, what is the moving force of the drama?

JULIAN. I don't know exactly what you mean by the moving force of the drama, but I will say that I don't find any pleasure in plays in which there are no love-affairs; preferably unhappy love-affairs, for I have plenty of happy love-making in my own house with my Teodora.

ERNESTO. Good. Splendid! Well, in my play there is hardly any love-making at all.

JULIAN. Bad, very bad indeed, I say. Listen, I don't know what your play is about, but I am afraid that it won't interest anybody.

ERNESTO. That's just what I told you. Still, love-making might be put in, and even a little jealousy.

JULIAN. Well, with that, with an interesting and well-developed intrigue, with some really striking situation....

ERNESTO. No, señor, certainly not that. Everything must be quite commonplace, almost vulgar. This drama can have no outward manifestation. It goes on in the hearts and minds of the characters; it progresses slowly; today it is a question of a thought; tomorrow of a heartbeat; gradually the will is undermined....

JULIAN. But how is all this shown? How are these inner struggles expressed? Who tells the audience about them? Where are they seen? Are we to spend the whole evening in pursuit of a glance, a sigh, a gesture, a word? My dear boy, that is no sort of amusement. When a man wants to meddle with such abstractions he studies philosophy.

ERNESTO. That's it, exactly. You repeat my thoughts like an echo.

JULIAN. I don't want to discourage you, however. You probably know what you are doing. And, even though the play may be a little colorless, even though it may seem a bit heavy and uninteresting, so long as it has a fine climax and the catastrophe ... eh?

ERNESTO. Catastrophe — climax! They have hardly come when the curtain falls.

JULIAN. You mean that the play begins when the play ends?

ERNESTO. I'm afraid so — though, of course, I shall try to put a little warmth into it.

JULIAN. Come now, what you ought to do is write the second play, the one that begins when the first ends; for the first, judging by what you say, isn't worth the trouble — and plenty of trouble it's bound to give you.

ERNESTO. I was convinced of that.

JULIAN. And now we both are — thanks to your cleverness and the force of your logic. What is the title?

ERNESTO. Title! Why, that's another thing. It has no title.

JULIAN. What! What did you say? No title, either?

ERNESTO. No, señor.

JULIAN. Well, Ernesto, you must have been asleep when I came in — you were having a nightmare and now you are telling me your dreams.

ERNESTO. Dreaming? Yes. A nightmare? Perhaps. And I am telling you my dreams, good and bad. You have common-sense, and you always guess right in everything.

JULIAN. It didn't take much penetration to guess right in this case. A play in which the principal character doesn't appear, in which there is almost no love-making, in which nothing happens that doesn't happen every day, which begins as the curtain falls on the last act, and which has no title.— Well, I don't see how it can be written, how it can be acted, or how anyone can be found to listen to it — or, indeed, how it is a play at all.

ERNESTO. Ah, but it is a play. The only trouble is that I must give it form, and *that* I don't know how to do.

JULIAN. Do you want my advice?

ERNESTO. Your advice? The advice of my friend, my benefactor, my second father! Oh, Don Julian!

JULIAN. Come, come, Ernesto, let us not have a little sentimental play of our own here in place of yours which we have pronounced impossible. I only asked you whether you want d to know my advice.

ERNESTO. And I said, Yes.

JULIAN. Well, forget all about plays — go to bed — go to sleep — go shooting with me tomorrow, kill any number of partridges instead of killing two characters, and perhaps having the audience kill you — and when all is said and done, you'll be thankful to me.

ERNESTO. That can't be: I must write the play.

JULIAN. But, my dear fellow, you must have thought of it by way of penance for your sins.

ERNESTO. I don't know why it happened, but think of it I did. I feel it stirring in my mind, it begs for life in the outer world, and I am bound to give it that.

JULIAN. Can't you find some other plot?

ERNESTO. But what about this idea?

JULIAN. Let the devil take care of it.

ERNESTO. Ah, Don Julian, do you think that when an idea has been hammered out in our minds, we can destroy it and bring it to naught whenever we choose? I should like to think of another play, but this accursed one won't let me until it has been born into the world.

JULIAN. There's no use talking, then. I only hope you get some light on the subject.

ERNESTO. That is the question, as Hamlet says.

JULIAN (*in a low voice, with mock mystery*). Couldn't you put it in the literary orphanage for anonymous works?

ERNESTO. Don Julian, I am a man of conscience. My children, good or bad, are legitimate, and shall bear my name.

JULIAN. I'll say no more. It must be — it is written.

ERNESTO. I only wish it were. Unfortunately it is not written; but no matter, if I don't write it, someone else will.

JULIAN. Well, to work! Good luck, and don't let anyone get ahead of you.

TEODORA (*without*). Julian! Julian!

JULIAN. There's Teodora!

TEODORA. Are you here, Julian?

JULIAN. Yes, here I am. Come in!

### (*Enter* TEODORA.)

TEODORA. Good evening, Ernesto.

ERNESTO. Good evening, Teodora. Did they sing well?

TEODORA. As usual. Have you done a lot of work?

ERNESTO. As usual; nothing.

TEODORA. Why, you might better have gone with us. All my friends were asking for you.

ERNESTO. It seems that everybody is taking an interest in me.

JULIAN. I should say so; since you are going to make *Everybody* the principal character in your play, naturally it is to his interest to have you for his friend.

TEODORA. A play?

JULIAN. Hush, it's a great mystery; you mustn't ask anything about it. It has no title, no actors, no action, no catastrophe! Oh, how sublime! Good night, Ernesto.— Come, Teodora.

ERNESTO. Good-bye, Julian.

TEODORA. Until tomorrow.

ERNESTO. Good night.

TEODORA (*to* JULIAN). How preoccupied Mercedes seemed!

JULIAN. And Severo was in a rage.

TEODORA. I wonder why.

JULIAN. I'm sure I don't know. Pepito, on the other hand, was lively enough for both.

TEODORA. He always is — and speaking ill of everyone.

JULIAN. A character for Ernesto's play.

(TEODORA *and* JULIAN *go out, right.*)

ERNESTO. Let Julian say what he likes, I am not going to give up my undertaking. It would be rank cowardice. No, I will not retreat. Forward! (*He rises and walks up and down in agitation. Then he goes over to the French window.*) Night, lend me your protection, for against your blackness the luminous outlines of my inspiration are defined more clearly than against the blue cloak of day. Lift up your roofs, ye thousands of houses in this mighty city; for surely you should do as much for a poet in distress as for that crooked devil who mischievously lifted your tops off. Let me see the men and women coming back to your rooms to rest after the busy hours of pleasure-seeking. As my ears become more sensitive, let them distinguish the many words of those who were asking Julian and Teodora about me; and as a great light is made from scattered rays when they are gathered into a crystal lens, as the mountains are formed from grains of sand and the sea from drops of water, so from your chance words, your stray smiles, your idle glances, from a thousand trivial thoughts which you have left scattered in cafés, in theaters, in ballrooms, and which are now floating in the air, I shall shape my drama, and the crystal of my mind shall be the lens that brings to a focus the lights and shadows, so that from them shall result the dramatic spark and the tragic explosion. My drama is taking shape. Now it has a title, for there in the lamplight I see the work of the immortal Florentine poet, and in Italian it has given me the name which it would be madness or folly to write or speak in plain Spanish. Paolo and Francesca, may your love help me! (*Sitting down at the table and beginning to write.*) The play! the play begins! The first page is no longer blank. (*Writing.*) Now it has a title. (*Writes madly.*) *The Great Galeoto!*

CURTAIN

## ACT I

*A room in* DON JULIAN'S *house. At the back a large door. Beyond it, a little passage, at the very end of which is the dining-room door. This door is closed until the end of the act. To the left of the audience, towards the front, a French window. To the right, two doors. In front, at the right, a sofa. To the left a small table and an arm-chair. Everything is expensive and luxurious. It is late afternoon.* TEODORA *is looking out of the French window.* JULIAN *sits on the sofa, lost in thought.*

TEODORA. What a beautiful sunset! Such glorious colors, such clouds! If the future is printed on those azure pages, as poets say and our fathers believed; if the mysterious secret of human destiny is written on the sapphire sphere in stars of fire, and if this glorious sky is the page that tells of our fate, what joys await us, how the future smiles upon us! But what are you thinking of? Come, Julian, look out here. Why don't you say something?

JULIAN (*absent-mindedly*). What is it?

TEODORA (*going to him*). Weren't you listening to me?

JULIAN. My heart is always with you, for you are its goal and its loadstone; but sometimes my mind is distracted by importunate cares, by business affairs ——

TEODORA. Which I detest, since they rob me of my husband's attention, if not of his affection. But what is it, Julian? Something is worrying you, and it must be serious, because you have been sitting there for a long time, sadly, without speaking. Are you in trouble, Julian dear? Then my heart demands a share in it, for if my joys are yours I want your sorrows to be mine.

JULIAN. In trouble? When you are happy! Sorrows? When in my Teodora I have the sum of all joys? While your cheeks show those two roses and your eyes that fire which is the light of the soul, shining in twin heavens, while I know that I alone am master of your heart, what sorrows or troubles or afflictions could keep me from being the happiest man in the whole world?

TEODORA. And you have no business worries, either?

JULIAN. Money has never yet made me lose sleep or appetite. Though I have no aversion to it, I've always been perfectly indifferent, so it has always come running into my coffers as meek as a lamb. I've always been rich and I am rich now, and until I die of old age, thanks to God and his own good fortune, Don Julian de Garagarza will have the best credit, though perhaps not the largest fortune, of any banker in Madrid, Cadiz, or El Puerto.

TEODORA. Well, then, why were you so preoccupied a few minutes ago?

JULIAN. I was thinking — thinking of something nice.

TEODORA. That's not strange, Julian, since the thought was yours.

JULIAN. Flatterer, don't try to wheedle me!

TEODORA. But tell me what it was.

JULIAN. I wanted to close up a promising little deal.

TEODORA. Something about the new works?

JULIAN. Oh, it's not a question of works of stone and iron.

TEODORA. Of what, then?

JULIAN. Of works of charity and good-will in connection with a sacred debt of long standing.

TEODORA (*with natural and spontaneous joy*). Oh, I know!

JULIAN. Really?

TEODORA. You were thinking of Ernesto.

JULIAN. You have guessed right.

TEODORA. Poor lad, you do well to think of him. He is so good, so noble, so generous!

JULIAN. Exactly like his father, the very pattern of honor and chivalry!

TEODORA. So he is! And so talented! Twenty-six years old...
and so scholarly! He knows everything! Why, he is an
absolute prodigy!

JULIAN. A scholar, you say? Well, that doesn't help much.
Indeed, that's just the trouble, for I'm afraid that as he goes
about with his head in the clouds, he'll never learn to get on
in this world, which is prosaic and treacherous, and never
pays any tribute to genius until some three hundred years after
it has hounded it to death.

TEODORA. But with you for a guide... for surely, Julian, you are
not thinking of deserting him?

JULIAN. Desert him! I should be ungrateful indeed if I could
forget what I owe his father. For my sake Don Juan de Acedo
risked name, fortune, even honor. If this young man wants
the blood in my veins he need only ask for it, for it is ever ready
to pay my debt of honor.

TEODORA. Bravo, Julian! Spoken like yourself!

JULIAN. You yourself saw how it was. When they told me about
a year ago that Don Juan was dead and that his son was left
in poverty, I couldn't take the Gerona train fast enough. I
fairly dragged him away by main force, brought him here with
me, led him into the middle of the room, and said to him,
"Everything I own is at your disposal, for it is really yours.
I owe it all to your father. If you like, you shall be master of
this house. At least, look upon me as a second father. Though
I can't equal the first in goodness, I shall strive to be a close
second, and as for loving you.... Well, we shall see who is best
at that!"

TEODORA. It's true!... Those were your very words; and the
poor boy — he is so good — burst out crying like a child, and
threw his arms about your neck.

JULIAN. You're right, he is a child. And we must think of him
and of his future. And now you know why you saw me looking
grave and preoccupied a while ago. I was trying to think
of some way to do for him all I should like to, while you were
chattering to me about a beautiful view and a glorious sky
and a red sun, for which I have no use at all, since two far
brighter suns shine for me in our own heaven.

TEODORA. But I don't understand? What would you like to do for Ernesto?

JULIAN. That's what I said.

TEODORA. But how can you possibly do more than you have done? For a year now he has been living here with us like one of the family. Why, if he were your own son you couldn't show greater love for him, nor could I feel more affection for him if he were my own brother.

JULIAN. That's all very well, but it's not enough.

TEODORA. Not enough? Why, I believe...

JULIAN. You are thinking of the present, and I of the future.

TEODORA. The future.— Oh, I can arrange that very easily.— Listen! He will live in this house as long as he likes — oh, for years — just as though it were his own. That's quite simple. Then, in due course, as is right and natural, he will fall in love and marry. Then, honorably discharging your debts, you will hand over to him a large part of your fortune. From the church, *he* and *she* will go to his own house — for, as the saying goes, "To be head of a household one needs a house." But we shall not forget him, nor shall we love him any the less because he doesn't live here. And now everything is quite clear. Of course, they are happy; we are more so. — They have children — undoubtedly — we have more. At any rate we have a daughter. She and Ernesto's son fall in love with each other.— They get married....

JULIAN (*laughing*). But, good heavens, where does all this end?

TEODORA. You were talking about the future, and this is the future that I offer you. If you have any other, Julian, I don't like it, and I won't accept it.

JULIAN. Oh, mine is like yours, Teodora, but...

TEODORA. Mercy on us, here's a *but* already...

JULIAN. Listen, Teodora; in taking care of this unfortunate young man we are paying our debts as we should — and to the duty we owe the son of Acedo are added the demands of the affection we feel for him for his own sake. But complications enter into every act of man. There are always two points of view; the shield always has a reverse. By which I mean, Teodora, that in this case, giving help and receiving it are not simply opposites, but are entirely different things, and that I am afraid in the end he may consider my gifts a humiliation. He is high-minded, and he is extremely proud. We must find some way out of the situation for him, Teodora. We must do still more for him and pretend that we are doing less.

TEODORA. How?

JULIAN. You shall see. But here he comes.

TEODORA. Not a word!

(ERNESTO *enters and stands at the back.*)

JULIAN. Welcome!

ERNESTO. Don Julian — Teodora.

(*He greets them absent-mindedly and sits down by the table, lost in thought.*)

JULIAN (*going up to him*). What's the matter?

ERNESTO. Nothing.

JULIAN. I see something in your eyes, and your uneasiness betrays you. Are you unhappy?

ERNESTO. Nonsense.

JULIAN. Are you worried about something?

ERNESTO. Not at all.

JULIAN. Perhaps I am importunate?

ERNESTO. You importunate! Good gracious! (*Rising and going up to him. Effusively.*) No indeed, your affection moves you, your friendship gives you the right, and you read my very heart when you look into my eyes. Yes, señor, there is something wrong. But I will tell you all about it. Don Julian, forgive me, and you, too, I beg of you — (*to* TEODORA). I'm foolish and childish and ungrateful. Indeed, I don't deserve your kindness, I don't deserve your affection. I ought to be happy with such a father and such a sister, and not think of the morrow — and yet I must think of it. This explanation makes me blush; but don't you both understand? Yes, yes, you must understand that my position here is a false one (*vehemently*), that I am living here on charity.

TEODORA. That word...

ERNESTO. Teodora!

TEODORA. Is displeasing to us.

ERNESTO. Yes, señora, I have spoken awkwardly, but it is the truth.

JULIAN. And I tell you, it is not true. If anyone in this house lives on charity, and no mean charity at that, it is not you, but I.

ERNESTO. I know, señor, the story of two loyal friends, and of a great fortune of which I have no recollection. That noble act did honor to my father, but I should stain that honor if I demanded payment for his kindness. I am a young man, Don Julian, and although I am not good for much, I can certainly do something to earn my bread. Is this pride or madness? I don't know, and I have lost the ability to judge — but I have not forgotten that my father used to say to me, "What you can do yourself, entrust to no man; for what you can earn yourself, be indebted to no one."

JULIAN. So my favors humiliate you and are a burden to you — your friends seem importunate creditors?

TEODORA. Your argument is fallacious. You know a great deal, Ernesto, but in this case the heart knows more.

JULIAN. My father didn't show any such haughty disdain for yours....

TEODORA. Friendship, it seems, was a different thing in those days.

ERNESTO. Teodora!

TEODORA (to JULIAN). It's his idealism.

ERNESTO. It's true. I am ungracious.... I know it. And foolish, too. Forgive me, Don Julian.                    (Deeply moved.)

JULIAN (to TEODORA). He's raving mad.

TEODORA. Why, he doesn't live on this earth at all.

JULIAN. You're right, wise man and philosopher though he may be.... And he is drowning himself in a puddle of water.

ERNESTO. You say I know nothing of the world and can't make my way in it. It's true. But I can see that way dimly, and I tremble, I know not why. I'm drowning in the puddles of life as though in the deep sea! They frighten me more, I don't deny it, much more than the vast ocean. The sea stretches out to the boundaries set for it by the wide sands; the puddle sends its emanations throughout all space. Strong arms may struggle against the waves of the sea; there is no way to struggle against treacherous infections. And if I am destined to be defeated, I pray only that in the end, defeat may not dishonor me. I ask only to see before me — and this shall suffice — the sea that is waiting to engulf me, the sword that shall pierce me, or the rock that shall crush me; to recognize my enemy, to realize his strength and his fury, and to scorn him as I fall, to scorn him as I die. Let me not gradually breathe in from the atmosphere all about me the poison that shall slowly destroy me.

JULIAN. Didn't I tell you? He's out of his senses.

TEODORA. But, Ernesto, what does all this mean?

JULIAN. What has all this to do with the subject we were discussing?

ERNESTO. It means, señor, that I believe that when people see me living here under your protection, they think the same things about me that I have been thinking about myself, when I ride with you in the park, when I go out with Teodora or Mercedes in the morning, when I sit in your box at the opera, when I hunt in your coverts, when, day after day, I take the same place at your table. The fact is, señor — though your goodness may not let you believe it — that people say to each other, "Who is this man? Some relation of his? Not at all. His secretary, then? No, not that, either. His companion. — He doesn't add much to the company." That is what they are whispering.

JULIAN. Nobody thinks that. You are dreaming.

ERNESTO. Pardon me...

JULIAN. Well, let's have a name, then.

ERNESTO. Señor...

JULIAN. I'll be satisfied with just one.

ERNESTO. Then there is someone near at hand. The man lives in the third floor.

JULIAN. And his name is?

ERNESTO. Don Severo.

JULIAN. My brother?

ERNESTO. Exactly, your brother. If that isn't enough, Doña Mercedes, his wife. Another? Pepito. And now what have you to say?

JULIAN. Then I say — and I stick to it, and make no mistake

about it — that Severo is a martinet; that she doesn't know what she is talking about; and that the boy is a puppy.

ERNESTO. They only repeat what they hear.

JULIAN. Enough, these are foolish scruples. Where there are honest intentions, upright people need pay little heed to what the world may say. The louder the whispering the more deep-seated the scorn.

ERNESTO. That is honorable, and that is how every generous man would feel. But I have learned that what people say, either with or without malice, begins by being false and ends by being true. Does spreading gossip reveal to us hidden sin, and is it a reflection of the past, or does it invent the evil and lay a foundation for it? Does it brand with the seal of shame the fault which already exists, or does it engender vice and give opportunity for crime? Are gossiping tongues infamous, or avenging? Are they accomplices, or heralds? Executioners, or tempters? Do they strike down, or do they cause us to stumble? Do they wound in malice, or in sorrow? Do they condemn justly, or wantonly? I don't know, Don Julian. Perhaps they are two-edged. But time and opportunity and the event will show.

JULIAN. See here, I don't understand a word of that. It's all philosophy, or madness rather, with which you smother your natural good sense. But, to be brief, I don't want to distress or annoy you. You want, Ernesto, to earn for yourself, independently and by your own efforts, an honorable position. Isn't that it?

ERNESTO. Don Julian ——

JULIAN. Answer me.

ERNESTO (*joyfully*). Yes.

JULIAN. Then you have succeeded already. I happen to be without a secretary. I have been negotiating for one from London (*in a tone of affectionate reproach*), but I don't want anyone but an eccentric person who would rather have poverty, hard work, and a fixed salary like everyone else, than be the son of a man who loves him as if he were his own child.

ERNESTO. Don Julian...

JULIAN (*in a tone of mock severity*). But I am exacting and very business-like, and I don't pay good wages to people for nothing. I shall get all I can out of you, and in my house you will have to earn your salt. You will be at your desk ten hours a day. I wake up at daybreak, and I am going to be sterner with you than Severo. (*Unable to control himself any longer, and changing his tone and opening his arms.*) That's how we shall be before the world, you the victim of my selfishness.— But, Ernesto, in the bottom of my heart, I shall feel the same love for you!

ERNESTO. Don Julian ——

JULIAN. Do you accept the offer?

ERNESTO. Yes. Do what you like with me.

TEODORA. At last you have tamed the wild beast.

ERNESTO. I will do anything for you.

JULIAN. That's right. That's the way I like to see you. Now I shall write to my kind correspondent. I shall thank him and tell him that I realize the unusual merits of the Englishman he recommends, but that he is too late, as I already have a secretary. (*Turning towards the first door to the right.*) This will do for the present — later we shall see! (*Turning around and pretending to be very mysterious.*) Perhaps a companion — then!

TEODORA. For pity's sake, be still. Don't you see that you are frightening him!

(*Exit* DON JULIAN, *right, laughing and looking good-naturedly at* ERNESTO. *During the scene, daylight has been gradually dying away, so that by now the room is quite dark.*)

ERNESTO. His kindness overwhelms me! How can I ever repay him?

(*He sinks down on the sofa, deeply moved.* TEODORA *goes and stands beside him.*)

TEODORA. By resolutely putting aside all waywardness and distrust; by being reasonable and realizing that we really love you, and that we are not going to change. In short, Ernesto, by understanding that Julian does not make empty promises, but that he keeps his word, with the result that you have in him a father, and in me a sister.

DOÑA MERCEDES *and* DON SEVERO *appear in the background, and remain there. The room is quite dark, except for a little light from the French window, to which* TEODORA *and* ERNESTO *go.*

ERNESTO. Ah, how good you both are!

TEODORA. And what a child you are! After today you must never be unhappy again.

ERNESTO. Never.

MERCEDES (*in low tone*). How dark it is!

SEVERO. Come, Mercedes.

MERCEDES. There is no one here.                    (*Coming forward.*)

SEVERO (*stopping her*). There *is* someone there.

                         (*They both stand at the back, watching.*)

ERNESTO. Teodora, I would gladly give my life, and more, too, in return for the benefits I have received from you. You must think that I am unfeeling. I don't like to make protestations of affection, but I can love, and I can hate, too. Everyone may find in my heart a reflection of the emotion he chooses to arouse there.

MERCEDES. What are they saying?

SEVERO. Strange things.— I can't hear very well.

    (TEODORA *and* ERNESTO *remain at the window, talking in low tones.*)

MERCEDES. It certainly is Ernesto.

SEVERO. And she! It is she, of course.

MERCEDES. Teodora!

SEVERO. The same tricks, and always together! I have no patience with it! And those words... Why do I wait?

MERCEDES. You're right. Come, Severo, it has become a matter of duty. Everybody is saying...

SEVERO (*coming forward*). I must speak plainly to Julian today.

MERCEDES. Poor girl, she is such a child. I'll speak to her myself.

TEODORA. Go to some other house? No! Leave us? A fine idea, indeed! Julian would never consent to it.

SEVERO. Nor I, by heaven. (*To* MERCEDES — *aloud.*) Oh, Teodora, didn't you see me? Is this the way you receive people?

TEODORA (*coming away from the window*). Don Severo, how glad I am to see you!

MERCEDES. Not at dinner? Isn't it time yet?

TEODORA. Ah, Mercedes.

SEVERO (*aside*). How well she acts.

TEODORA. I'll ring for lights. (*Touching a bell on the table.*)

SEVERO. Good, one likes to be able to see something.

SERVANT (*appearing in the doorway*). Señora.

TEODORA. Lights, Genero. (*The servant goes out.*)

SEVERO. Those who tread the narrow path of duty and honor, and are always what they seem, need never be afraid or ashamed of any amount of light.

(*Servants come in with lights; the room is brilliantly illuminated.*)

TEODORA (*after a little pause, laughs and speaks quite naturally*). That applies to me and to someone else. (*Going to* MERCEDES.)

MERCEDES. Of course.

SEVERO. Hello, hello, Don Ernesto. (*Meaningly.*) So you were here with Teodora when I came in?

ERNESTO (*coldly*). As you see — apparently.

SEVERO. No, indeed, not apparently, for in the darkness one couldn't see you. (*Going up to him, taking his hand, and looking at him fixedly.* TEODORA *and* MERCEDES *talk aside.* SEVERO *says to himself.*) He is flushed and seems to have been weeping. Only children and lovers weep in this world. (*Aloud.*) And where is Julian?

TEODORA. He went off to write a letter.

SEVERO (*aside*). Be as patient as I may, this man upsets me. (*Aloud.*) I am going to speak to him. (*To* TEODORA.) Is there time before dinner?

TEODORA. Plenty of time.

SEVERO (*aside, rubbing his hands and looking at* ERNESTO *and* TEODORA). Good. To work, then. (*Aloud.*) Au revoir.

TEODORA. Au revoir.

SEVERO (*aside, looking at them angrily as he goes out the door*). Upon my word!

(MERCEDES *and* TEODORA *remain. They are seated on the sofa.* ERNESTO *is standing.*)

MERCEDES (*to* ERNESTO). You haven't been to see us today.

ERNESTO. No.

MERCEDES. Nor Pepito, either.

ERNESTO. No, señora.

MERCEDES. He is all alone up there.

ERNESTO (*aside*). Let him stay so!

MERCEDES (*to* TEODORA, *gravely and mysteriously*). I wish he'd go
away. I want to speak to you.

TEODORA. You?

MERCEDES (*in the same tone*). Yes, on a very grave matter.

TEODORA. Speak then.

MERCEDES. If this man doesn't go...

TEODORA (*in a low tone*). I don't understand?

MERCEDES. Courage! (*Takes her hand and strokes it affectionately.*
TEODORA *looks at her in astonishment, not understanding at all.*)
Get rid of him quickly.

TEODORA. Since you insist. (*Aloud.*) Ernesto, will you do me a
favor?

ERNESTO. I'd love to.

MERCEDES (*aside*). Ah, there's too much love about it.

TEODORA. Then go upstairs to Pepito — but perhaps I am bothering you with this errand?

ERNESTO. Indeed, no.

MERCEDES. How affectionate they are!

TEODORA. Ask him... if he renewed the subscription for our
box at the opera as I told him to. He knows about it.

ERNESTO. With pleasure.— I'll go at once.

TEODORA. Thanks, Ernesto. I appreciate ——

ERNESTO. Not at all.

TEODORA. Good-bye. (ERNESTO *goes out.*) A grave matter?
You frighten me, Mercedes. This tone, this mysterious air!
What is it?

MERCEDES. Something very serious.

TEODORA. But whom is it about?

MERCEDES. About all of you.

TEODORA. About us?

MERCEDES. About Julian and Ernesto and you. Now you understand.

TEODORA. About all three?

MERCEDES. Yes, you three.

TEODORA (*looks at* MERCEDES *in astonishment. A short pause*). But
tell me quickly.

MERCEDES (*aside*). I dislike doing it, but I mustn't falter. It's
an ugly business. (*Aloud.*) Listen, Teodora: after all, my

husband and yours are brothers, and we have all become one family, so that in life and in death, for better, for worse, we ought to support and aid and advise each other. So I gladly offer you my protection, and tomorrow, if need should arise, I should not be ashamed to ask help of you.

TEODORA. And you might count upon us, Mercedes. But, quick, tell me ——

MERCEDES. Until now I was unwilling to take this step, Teodora, but today Severo said to me, "I cannot suffer this any longer. I value my brother's honor as highly as anyone, and when I see certain things, I groan with shame and sorrow. Always making sly allusions, always watching for meaningful smiles, always lowering their eyes, always shunning other people! These disgraceful actions must end, for I cannot endure the things that are being said in Madrid."

TEODORA. Go on, go on.

MERCEDES. Listen, then.

(*A pause.* MERCEDES *looks fixedly at* TEODORA.)

TEODORA. Tell us; what do they say?

MERCEDES. Where there is smoke, there is fire ——

TEODORA. I don't know anything about smoke or anything about fire. I only know that I am going mad.

MERCEDES (*aside*). Poor child, it grieves me! (*Aloud.*) But don't you understand, then?

TEODORA. I? No.

MERCEDES (*aside*). She's dull, too. (*Aloud — emphatically.*) He is a laughing-stock!

TEODORA. Who?

MERCEDES. Who would it be? Your husband.

TEODORA (*rising, impetuously*). Julian? It's a lie. The person who said that was a scoundrel. Ah, if only Julian were face to face with him!

MERCEDES (*soothing her and making her sit down beside her again*). He would have to face a great many people, for unless rumor is mistaken, everyone is of the same opinion.

TEODORA. But tell me, then, what is this scandal? This great mystery? What is the world saying?

MERCEDES. So it makes you angry?

TEODORA. Makes me angry! But what is it?

MERCEDES. Listen, Teodora. You are very young. At your age one does many thoughtless things, without meaning any harm... and then later come many tears. Come, don't you understand me yet?

TEODORA. No. Why should I understand you, unless this story is about me?

MERCEDES. It is the story of a wretch, and it is the story of a lady.

TEODORA (*anxiously*). And her name?

MERCEDES. Her name is...

TEODORA (*stopping her*). What difference does it make what her name is?

> (TEODORA *moves away from* MERCEDES *without getting up from the sofa.* MERCEDES *draws nearer to her as she speaks. The contrast between* TEODORA'S *movement of repulsion and* MERCEDES' *of protection and insistence is very marked.*)

MERCEDES. Some men are worthless and treacherous, and in return for one hour of pleasure they condemn a woman to a life of sorrow. To her are left only the dishonor of her husband, the destruction of her family, and the seal of shame beneath which her head is bowed; the scorn of others is the penance imposed by society, and God's still greater punishment: the voice of conscience. (*Now they are at opposite ends of the sofa.* TEODORA *leans back and covers her face with her hands, understanding at last.*) Come to me, Teodora. (*Aside.*) Poor little girl, I pity her! (*Aloud.*) This man doesn't deserve you.

TEODORA. Where is your blind folly leading you, señora? I feel neither fear nor horror. There are no tears in my eyes, only blazing anger. About whom did you hear what I have just heard? Who is this man? He is — ? It is — ?

MERCEDES. Ernesto.

TEODORA. Ah! (*A pause.*) And I am the woman? (MERCEDES *makes a sign of assent, and* TEODORA *rises.*) Then listen to me, even though I make you angry. I don't know which is more vile, the world that invented this story, or you who repeat it to me. A curse on the slanderous tongue that first gave form to such a thought, and a curse on the knave or the fool who believes it! So vile, so deadly is it that whether I blot it from my memory, or whether I keep it there, I become guilty. Good heavens, I wouldn't have thought it! I never would have believed it! I saw him so unhappy that I loved him as a brother. Julian played Providence to him. And he is so generous, so noble... (*checking herself, watching* MERCEDES, *and turning her head.* — *Aside.*) How she looks at me! I mustn't praise him before her. So now I must play a part!

(*Visibly trying to control herself.*)

MERCEDES. Come, be calm.

TEODORA (*aloud*). I feel such anguish, such sorrow, such coldness in my very soul. To think that my honor should be stained by public gossip. Oh, mother, dear mother! Oh, Julian, dearest.

(*She sinks, sobbing, into the chair at the left.* MERCEDES *tries to console her.*)

MERCEDES. I didn't suppose... Oh, forgive me... don't cry! I didn't believe there was anything serious. Of course, I knew your past exonerated you. But even so, you yourself must admit that everyone might say with justice that you and Julian are very imprudent in letting people think the worst. You, a young girl of twenty, and Julian in the forties, and Ernesto with his head full of fantastic ideas; your husband wrapped up in his business, and the other man in his dreams. You with nothing to occupy your mind; every day a thousand opportunities for meeting.... The people who see you in the park, in the theater, have evil minds to think such evil, but, Teodora, to be just, I believe that in all that has happened, the world is in the wrong, but you have given it the opportunity. Let me tell you that the sin that modern society punishes most relentlessly and cruelly and with the greatest ingenuity — in man or in woman — is — don't be frightened, Teodora — rash confidence — indiscretion.

TEODORA (*turning to* MERCEDES, *but paying no attention to what she is saying*). And you say that Julian ——

MERCEDES. Yes, he is the laughing-stock of the city. And you ——

TEODORA. Oh, never mind about me. But Julian... he is so good, and so sensitive! When he knows ——

MERCEDES. He probably does know. Severo is doubtless talking to him this very minute.

TEODORA. What!

JULIAN (*without*). Enough!

TEODORA. Good heavens!

JULIAN. Leave me alone!

TEODORA. Oh, dear, let's go out quickly.

MERCEDES (*after looking out through the first door to the right*). Yes, quickly! He's beside himself.

(TEODORA *and* MERCEDES *go toward the left.*)

TEODORA (*stopping*). But what for? It will seem as though I am guilty. This vile slander does more than soil, it debases one. So deadly, so treacherous is it, that in spite of all evidence against it, it works its way into one's consciousness with its tang of guilt. Why should I be paralyzed in the deadly bonds of a senseless terror? (*At this moment,* DON JULIAN *appears in the doorway to the right, with* DON SEVERO *behind him.*) Julian!

JULIAN. Teodora! (*She runs to him and he presses her to his heart, passionately.*) Come to me!... This is your post of honor. (*To* SEVERO.) Come in; but, by heaven, be careful not to go too far. I swear, and I mean it, that if anyone stains this cheek with tears again, he shall never more cross my threshold, even if he is my own brother!

(*A pause.* DON JULIAN *caresses and comforts* TEODORA.)

SEVERO. I only repeat what people are saying about you, Julian.

JULIAN. Libel!

SEVERO. Maybe ——

JULIAN. It is!

SEVERO. But at least let me tell you what everyone knows.

JULIAN. Slanders, lies, filth!

SEVERO. I simply wanted to tell you.

JULIAN. There can be no need for doing so. (*A short pause.*)

SEVERO. You are wrong.

JULIAN. Right, and to spare! Would you track the mud of the streets into my salon?

SEVERO. It may be necessary.

JULIAN. Well, then, it must not be necessary.

SEVERO. My name is the same as yours.

JULIAN. No more!

SEVERO. And your honor ——

JULIAN. Remember that you are in the presence of my wife.
(*A pause.*)

SEVERO (*to* JULIAN, *in an undertone*). If our father could see you!

JULIAN. What! Severo — what do you mean?

MERCEDES. Hush! Ernesto is coming.

TEODORA (*aside*). How dreadful! If he should know.

(TEODORA *turns away and hangs her head.* JULIAN *looks at her fixedly.*)

ERNESTO (*looking at* TEODORA *and* DON JULIAN *for a minute. Aside*). He and she.— This can't be all imagination! If what I feared should happen? Then what I have just heard from this fool (*looking at* PEPITO, *who enters at this moment*) wasn't all made up by him.

PEPITO (*looking in surprise from one side to the other*). Greeting, and a good appetite to you. It's almost dinner-time. Here's the ticket, Teodora — Don Julian!

TEODORA (*mechanically taking the ticket*). Thanks, Pepito.

ERNESTO (*in an undertone to* DON JULIAN). What's the matter with Teodora?

JULIAN. Nothing.

ERNESTO (*as before*). She's pale, and she's been crying.

JULIAN (*unable to control himself*). Don't worry about my wife.
(*A pause.* DON JULIAN *and* ERNESTO *look at each other.*)

ERNESTO (*aside*). Poor souls, this has quite upset them.

PEPITO (*to his mother, aside, pointing to* ERNESTO). Mad as a hatter just because I joked about Teodora with him. My! My! He wanted to kill me on the spot!

ERNESTO (*aloud. Sadly, but resolutely*). Don Julian, I have been thinking over your generous offer, and although I have an awkward tongue that stumbles and blunders, and I know that I am imposing upon your kindness.— In short, señor, I must refuse the position you offered me.

JULIAN. Why?

ERNESTO. Because I am made that way. I am a poet, a dreamer. My father never could make a success of me, señor. I must travel. I am restless and rebellious. I can't settle down like other people to vegetate in one spot. I am filled with the spirit of adventure; I see myself as some new Columbus. In short, let Don Severo say whether I am right or not.

SEVERO. You speak like a man of understanding, like the very fount of wisdom. I have been thinking the same thing for a long, long time.

JULIAN. And so you feel a craving for travel, seeing the world? So you want to leave us? But how about the necessary funds?

SEVERO. He — is going away — to some place that will be more to his liking. Of course, for the rest he must depend upon you. Anything that he wants. I don't suppose he has saved any money at all?

ERNESTO (to DON SEVERO). I neither spread scandal nor receive alms! (A pause.) But indeed this must be. And as the parting must be sad — since perhaps I may never see you again — we had better embrace now... and break this bond... and — forgive my selfishness. (Deeply moved.)

SEVERO (aside). How strangely they both look at me!

TEODORA (aside). How fine he is!

ERNESTO. Don Julian, why hesitate? This is a last farewell.

(He goes to DON JULIAN with open arms. DON JULIAN takes him in his arms and they embrace tenderly.)

JULIAN. No, all things considered, it is neither the last nor the first. It is simply the sincere embrace of two honorable men. I don't want to hear anything more about this foolish plan.

SEVERO. But isn't he going away?

JULIAN. Never. I don't change with every wind, nor do I give up my cherished plans for the whim of a boy or the ravings of a madman. It would be a still greater blot on my honor to regulate my conduct by the foolish gossip of this most high-minded city!

SEVERO. Julian!

JULIAN. Enough. Dinner is ready ——

ERNESTO. My dear father! I can't ——

JULIAN. But I trust that you can. Or is my authority burdensome to you?

ERNESTO. I beg you!

JULIAN. Come, then, it is time to go. Give Teodora your arm and take her in to dinner.

ERNESTO. Teodora! (*Looking at her and drawing back.*)

JULIAN. Yes — as usual. (*A movement of doubt and hesitation from both. Finally ERNESTO goes up to TEODORA and she leans on his arm, but they do not look at each other, and seem agitated. To PEPITO.*) Give your mother your arm. (PEPITO *offers his arm to MERCEDES.*) And, Severo, my dear brother, you come with me, (*Leaning on his arm for a minute.*) Now we shall dine *en famille,* and our cup of happiness will overflow. You say people are whispering about us? All right. Let them whisper, or let them shout. I don't care a fig what they say. I wish I lived in a palace with glass walls, so that all those who are making free with our names might look in and see Ernesto and Teodora, so that they might realize how much importance I attach to their vile calumnies. Let every man go his own way.

(*A servant appears in conventional dress.*)

SERVANT. Dinner is served.

(*He opens the dining-room door. One can see the table, chairs, chandeliers, etc. Everything is very luxurious.*)

JULIAN. Well, let's attend to the things of this life and leave them to see to our funeral. Come. (*Urging them to go in.*)

TEODORA. Mercedes.

MERCEDES. Teodora.

TEODORA. You ——

MERCEDES. You first.

TEODORA. No, go first, Mercedes.

(MERCEDES *and* PEPITO *go ahead and walk slowly toward the dining-room. TEODORA and ERNESTO stand still, as though lost in thought. ERNESTO fixes his eyes on her.*)

JULIAN (*aside*). He is looking at her, and she is weeping. (*They slowly follow MERCEDES. TEODORA hesitates, tries to pull herself together and control her tears.— Aside to SEVERO.*) Are they whispering to each other?

SEVERO. I don't know; I suppose so.

(ERNESTO *and* TEODORA *stop and look around furtively, then proceed.*)

JULIAN. Why do they both look back? Why —— ?

SEVERO. Now you are coming to your senses.

JULIAN. Say, rather, I am catching your madness. Ah, scandal
has a sure aim! It goes straight to the heart.

*(He and* SEVERO *go into the dining-room.)*

CURTAIN

# ACT II

*A small room furnished with extreme simplicity; it is almost poverty-
stricken. At the back, a door; to the right of the audience, another door;
to the left, a French window. A little pine bookcase with a few books
in it, a table, an armchair. The table is at the left. On it is a framed
picture of* DON JULIAN. *On the other end, a frame, like the first, but
without a picture. Both are rather small. There are also on the table,
an unlighted lamp, a copy of Dante's "Divine Comedy," opened at the
incident of Francesca, and a half-burned piece of paper; in addition,
some loose papers and the manuscript of a play. A few chairs. This is
all the furniture.* DON JULIAN, DON SEVERO, *and a servant enter
at the back.*

SEVERO. Isn't your master in?

SERVANT. No, señor. He went out very early.

SEVERO. Never mind, we'll wait. I suppose Don Ernesto is
sure to return soon?

SERVANT. Probably. The master is most punctual and exact.

SEVERO. Good. You may go.

SERVANT. Yes, señor. If you want anything, I'll be at hand.

*(The servant goes out at the back.)*

SEVERO *(looking about the room)*. What simplicity!

JULIAN. What poverty, you'd better say!

SEVERO *(looking through the door at the right, then through the one at
the back)*. Well, this is a splendid apartment! A little alcove,
the anteroom, this study, and there you have it all.

JULIAN. And the devil has all he wants of human ingratitude
and unworthy thoughts, of despicable passion, of base calumny.
A nice little pile it is.

SEVERO. It was simply chance that brought it about.

JULIAN. That's not the right name, brother. It was brought about by... Well, I know whom ——

SEVERO. Who was it, then? I, perhaps?

JULIAN. Partly you. And before you, the idle fools who gossiped shamelessly about my honor and my wife. And then I myself who, like a coward, a jealous fool, a low scoundrel, let this young man leave my house after he had proved himself as noble as I was base — base and ungrateful! Think of the splendor and luxury in which I live, the magnificence of my salon, my stable, the credit of my firm, the wealth I enjoy. Well, do you know where every bit of it came from?

SEVERO. I have quite forgotten.

JULIAN. There you have it. Forgetfulness — the reward of mankind for every generous act, for every great sacrifice that one man makes for another, if he do it modestly, with no blare of trumpets and shouting of heralds — simply out of love and respect.

SEVERO. You are unjust to yourself. Your gratitude carried you to such lengths that you almost sacrificed honor, and even happiness to it. What more could anyone ask? What more could a saint do? There is a limit to all things, good and bad. He is proud; he insisted, though you opposed him. Of course, he is his own master. He controls his own person and his own acts; and one fine morning he left the palace in which you live because he wanted to; and in despair he betook himself to this garret. It is all very sad; but, my dear fellow, who could help it?

JULIAN. Everybody, if everybody had attended to his own affairs instead of throwing mud at other people, wagging his tongue, and gossiping about them, and pointing at them! Tell me, what business of theirs was it that, performing a sacred duty, I looked upon Ernesto as a son, and she regarded him as a brother? If they once see a beautiful girl and a handsome young man together at my table, or out walking, or at the opera, do they immediately think vile thoughts and imagine scandals? Are we to suppose that in this world an impure love is the one sure bond between men and women? Are there no such things as friendship, gratitude, sympathy, and are we so made that youth and beauty can meet only in the mud? And suppose even that what they thought were true, why should the fools feel called upon to avenge my wrongs? I have eyes to see with, and I have a sword, a heart, and hands to guard my own interests, and to avenge insults.

SEVERO. Well, granted that perhaps the people who went about gossiping were in the wrong, should I, who am your own flesh and blood, who bear your name — should I have been silent?

JULIAN. No, by heaven! but you should have been careful. You should have spoken cautiously to me alone, and not have kindled a volcano in my household.

SEVERO. I sinned through excess of affection. But if I acknowledge my guilt; if I admit that the world and I have done the harm — it, by inventing the slander, I, by stupidly lending ear to the thousand echoes of gossip, you, at least, Julian, are pure and free from sin. So dismiss your scruples and be light-hearted.

JULIAN. I can't be light-hearted, for in my heart I have sheltered the very thing that my reason and my lips repudiate. I reject indignantly the slanders of the world. "They lie," I cry aloud, and under my breath I repeat, "But what if they do not lie, but are right, after all!" So, in the struggle between two conflicting impulses, I am at the same time judge and accomplice. And so I am distracted; I am fighting with myself. Suspicion grows and spreads; my wounded heart cries out in anger; a blood-red mist spreads about me.

SEVERO. You are raving.

JULIAN. No, I am not raving. I am laying bare my soul to you, brother. Do you by any chance think that Ernesto would have left my house if I had stood in his way with the firm intention of intervening and preventing him? He went away because in the depths of my troubled soul a treacherous voice was sounding, saying to me: "Leave the door open that he may pass out freely, and then close it tightly after him. In the fortress of honor the trusting man is a poor steward." One wish was in my heart and another on my lips. Aloud, I said, "Come back, Ernesto," and under my breath, "Don't come back." When I seemed to be frank with him, I was a hypocrite and a coward, a knave and an ingrate.   No, Severo, that was not the action of an honorable man.

(*He sinks into the armchair, near the table, greatly moved.*)

SEVERO.   It was the action of a man who was protecting a young, high-spirited, and radiantly beautiful wife.

JULIAN.   Don't speak so of Teodora.   She is a mirror that we sully with our breath when we rashly try to come too near it. She reflected the sunlight, until the thousand viper-heads of the angry world came near to look at her.   Now they seem to be swarming in the crystal inside the divine frame.   But they are fleshless spectres.   A wave of my hand will surely drive them away and you will see again the clear-blue sky.

SEVERO.   So much the better.

JULIAN.   No.

SEVERO.   What's the trouble?

JULIAN.   Trouble enough.   I tell you, this inner struggle I described to you has warped my character.   Now my wife always finds me sad and morose.   I am not as I used to be.   I try in vain to seem so.   And as she notices this change she is bound to ask herself, "Where is Julian?   Where is my dear husband? What have I done to lose his confidence?   What evil thoughts preoccupy him and keep him from my arms?   And so, a shadow is coming between us which divides us and, slowly, step by step, drives us farther apart.   We have no more sweet confidences, no more quiet talks.   Our smiles are frozen; our tones bitter.   I harbor unjust suspicion; she is in tears.   I am wounded in my love; she is wounded — and by me — in her womanly dignity and her affection.   That's how we stand.

SEVERO.   Then you're on the road to destruction.   If you see so clearly what's wrong, why don't you find a remedy?

JULIAN.   I've tried in vain.   I know I am wrong to doubt her. More than that, I don't doubt her for the present.   But in the end as, little by little I lose ground, and little by little he gains, who can be sure that what we call a lie today may not be true tomorrow?   (*Seizing* DON SEVERO *by the arm and speaking to him with restrained passion and ill-concealed eagerness.*) I, jealous, morose, unjust; I, the tyrant; and he, noble, great-hearted, always gentle and resigned!   With the halo of martyrdom which in every woman's eyes becomes so well a handsome and gallant young man, it's clear that he gets the better part in this unjust assignment of rôles; that he gains what I lose, while I am powerless to help. This is the truth; and the result is that meanwhile the world with its idle talk plays traitor to them both, while now they are saying quite truthfully, "But indeed, we're not in love with each other," and as the latter words re-echo they may become reality.

SEVERO. Look here, Julian, if you feel this way, I think the wisest thing to do is to let Ernesto carry out his plans.

JULIAN. But that's what I've come here to prevent.

SEVERO. Then you're mad. Isn't he thinking of going to Buenos Ayres? Then why worry about it? Just wish him fair winds and a full sail.

JULIAN. Do you want me to seem cruel and mean and jealous in Teodora's eyes? Don't you know, my dear brother, that a woman may despise a man and still want him for a lover; but never for a husband? Do you want my wife to follow this unhappy exile across the seas with sad memories? Don't you know that if I saw so much as the trace of a tear on her cheek, and thought that it was a tear for Ernesto, I would strangle her with my own hands? (*With concentrated fury.*)

SEVERO. What are we to do then?

JULIAN. Suffer. The world must find a dénouement for this drama, which it created simply by looking at us — so potent is its glance for good and evil.

SEVERO (*going back*). I think someone is coming.

SERVANT (*without*). My master can't be long now.

(*Enter* PEPITO.)

SEVERO. You here?

PEPITO (*aside*). Phew, they've found it out already. I've over-reached myself. (*Aloud.*) So we're all here. Good-day, Uncle. Good-day, Papa. (*Aside.*) There's no use. They know what's up. (*Aloud.*) And so you — I suppose, of course, you've come to look for Ernesto?

SEVERO. For whom else in this house?

JULIAN. And I suppose you know all that this madman is planning?

PEPITO. All what? Oh, of course — a little —— I know — what everyone knows.

SEVERO. And is it tomorrow that —— ?

PEPITO. No. Tomorrow he's going away, so he has to settle this today.

JULIAN (*with amazement*). What did you say?

PEPITO. I? What Pepe Ucedo told me last night at the casino door. And he is the Viscount Nebreda's second, so if he doesn't know —— But how queer you look! Is it possible you don't know?

JULIAN. We know everything.

(*Resolutely forestalling a movement on his brother's part.*)

SEVERO. We ——

JULIAN (*aside*). Be quiet, Severo. (*Aloud.*) We heard that he is going away tomorrow — and that today he stakes his life. And we came, naturally, to prevent the duel and the departure.

(*Throughout this scene* DON JULIAN *pretends that he has been informed of the affair, so as to learn the facts from* PEPITO, *though it is evident that he came only on account of* ERNESTO'S *voyage.*)

SEVERO (*aside to* JULIAN). What is this duel?

JULIAN (*aside to* SEVERO). I don't know, but we'll find out.

PEPITO (*aside*). Come, I wasn't such a fool after all.

JULIAN. I know that a viscount ——

PEPITO. Exactly.

JULIAN. Is to fight a duel with Ernesto. Someone who knew about it at the time told us. They say it's a very serious affair —— (*Sign of assent from* PEPITO.) A scandalous quarrel; a great many people standing about.— "You lie!" "You say that I lie!" Then words, thick and fast.

PEPITO (*interrupting with the eagerness and pleasure of one who knows more.*) Words! A blow that would fell an ox.

SEVERO. Who struck whom?

PEPITO. Ernesto struck the other man.

JULIAN. Ernesto. Didn't you hear about it? This viscount exhausted his patience completely — put him in a perfect passion. Well, the poor boy broke loose ——

PEPITO. Exactly.

JULIAN. I told you we knew all about it. And is the affair very serious?

PEPITO. Very serious. I'm sorry to have to say so, but I might as well be frank with you.

JULIAN. What are the conditions?

PEPITO. It's to the death. And the viscount isn't afraid, and doesn't shrink. He's a wonderful swordsman.

JULIAN. And the quarrel? What was it about? They blame it on Nebreda?

PEPITO. Why, it wasn't exactly a quarrel. I'll tell you how it happened. Ernesto was planning to leave Madrid tomorrow so as to reach Cadiz in time to sail in the "Cid," and Luis Alcaraz had promised him a letter of introduction, which he said would serve as a good recommendation. So the poor boy went to the café to get it, with the best intentions in the world. The other man wasn't there; he waited for him. No one then recognized him and they go on with their pleasant game of tearing people to pieces, without noticing his threatening face and set teeth. One by one people are mentioned, and one by one they fall. A heavy hand and a sharp tongue. Every poor dog in the city passes in review. And right there in that miserable tavern, belching out more smoke than a train, in the midst of wine-glasses and cigar ashes, and scattered lumps of sugar, they set up a dissecting-table. With each draught of fine old wine, a woman's reputation gone. At every cutting lash, a roar of laughter. With four slashes of the scissors those fellows left reputations in tatters, women torn to pieces. But, after all, what does that sort of thing amount to? Echoes of society at the café table. I don't say this myself, and of course I don't think so, but that's what Ernesto said when he told me about it all.

JULIAN. Go on. Will you never get to the point?

PEPITO. Finally, in the midst of all these names, someone mentioned a certain man, and Ernesto couldn't control himself any longer. "Who dares besmirch the name of an honorable man?" he cries out, and they answer, "The lady." With flashing eyes he throws himself upon Nebreda. The poor viscount is completely bowled over; the public room becomes a

field of argument.  There you have a synopsis of the first act.
Today comes the duel with swords in some salon — I don't
know where.

JULIAN (*furiously seizing his arm*).  And the man was I?

PEPITO.  Señor ——

JULIAN.  And Teodora the woman?  And they have dragged her
and my name and my love to such depths?

SEVERO (*aside to* PEPITO).  Fool, what have you done?

PEPITO.  Didn't he say he knew about it?  Why I — Of course —
I thought.

JULIAN.  Disgraced, disgraced!

SEVERO (*going up to him, affectionately*).  Julian!

JULIAN.  True.  I know I must be calm.  But oh, if I lose faith,
I lose heart.  Great heavens! why should they slander us so?
What right have they to turn upon us and throw mud at us?
No matter.  I know how to act as befits a gentleman.  Can I
count on you, Severo?

SEVERO.  Count on me?  To the death!          (*They clasp hands.*)

JULIAN (*to* PEPITO).  The duel?

PEPITO.  At three.

JULIAN (*aside*).  I'm going to kill him.  Yes, I shall kill him.
(*To* SEVERO.)  Let's be going.

SEVERO.  Where?

JULIAN.  To find this viscount.

SEVERO.  Are you going to —— ?

JULIAN.  I am going to do what I can to avenge the insult to
my honor and to save the life of Juan Acedo's son.  (*To* PEPITO.)
Who are the seconds?

PEPITO.  Two — Alcaras and Ruedo.

JULIAN.  I know them.  (*Pointing to* PEPITO.)  He can stay here
in case of emergency.  And if Ernesto should come back ——

SEVERO.  I understand.

JULIAN.  Try, without arousing suspicion, to find out where the
duel is to be.

SEVERO.  You hear?

JULIAN.  Come!

SEVERO.  Julian, what possesses you?

JULIAN.  Joy such as I have not known for a long time.

SEVERO. What the devil, are you mad? Joy?

JULIAN. At the prospect of meeting this young man.

SEVERO. Nebreda?

JULIAN. Yes. Remember. Until now, calumny was intangible and I could not see its face. And now at last I know where it is hiding. At last it has taken human form, and is visibly before me in the guise of a viscount. For three months I have been eating gall and wormwood. And now, just think, I am face to face with him. (SEVERO *and* JULIAN *go out.*)

PEPITO. Well, here's a mess; and a useless mess, too. Just the same, no matter what my uncle may say, it was sheer madness to have a young girl as beautiful as the sun under the same roof, in almost continual contact with Ernesto, who is a handsome fellow with a soul all of fire, and a head full of romance. He swears there is nothing between them but the purest sort of friendship, that he loves her like a sister, and that my uncle is a father to him. But I'm pretty sharp, and though I am young, I know a thing or two about this world, and I don't put much faith in this brother-and-sister business; particularly where the brother is so young, and the relationship fictitious. But suppose this affection is all they say it is, how are other people to know that? Have they signed any pledge always to think well of everyone? Don't they see them together all the time — in the theater — in the park? Well, the person who saw them, saw them, and when he saw them, he told about it. Ernesto swore to me, "*No.*" They had *almost never* gone about in that way. Did he go once? Well, that's enough. If a hundred people saw them that day, they might as well have appeared in public not once, but a hundred different times. Are people bound to examine their witnesses and compare their dates to find out whether it was many times or only once that they went out together, she with her innocent sympathy, and he with his brotherly affection? Such a demand would be undignified and unjust — altogether ridiculous. They all tell what they've seen, and they're not lying when they tell it. "I saw them once. I saw them as well." One and one make two. There's no way out. "And I saw them, too." There you have three already. And this man, four; and that one, five. And so, adding up in all good faith, you go on indefinitely. And they saw because they looked. In short, because naturally one uses one's senses and doesn't stop to ask permission. So let him look after himself and remember that nowadays he who avoids the appearance of evil, avoids the slander and the danger. (*A little pause.*) And notice, I am admitting the purity of their affection; and that is a very important point; for, between ourselves, I must admit that to be near Teodora and not to love her, one must be as steady as a rock. He may be a scholar, and a philosopher, and a mathematician, and a physicist; but he's human, and she's divine; and that's enough. If only these walls could speak. If Ernesto's private thought scattered about here could only take visible form! Let's see. That frame, for example, is empty, while in the other is Don Julian's face. Teodora used to be there as a mate to my uncle. I wonder why her photograph has disappeared? To avoid temptation? If that's the reason, it's pretty bad! But it's still worse if she's left the frame for a better place; to find shelter near his heart! Let's see, make out your case against him, little devils who fly through the air, spinning invisible webs! Have no pity on this mystic, this philosopher! (*Looking at the table and seeing Dante's "Inferno."*) And here's another sign. I've never been to see Ernesto that I haven't found this beautiful book open on his table. (*Reading.*) Dante's *Divine Comedy*, his favorite poem. And apparently he never gets beyond this passage about Francesca. There are two possible explanations for this. Either Ernesto never reads, or else he always reads the same thing. But here's a spot; just as if a tear had fallen. What mystery, what deep secret have we here! How hard it must be for a married man to live in peace —— A paper burned to ashes? (*Taking it up from the table.*) No, there are still some traces of writing left.

(*Gets up and goes to the window, trying to read what is writte[n] on the paper. At this moment* ERNESTO *enters and, seei[ng] him, stops.*)

ERNESTO. What are you looking at?

PEPITO. Ah, Ernesto. Why, a piece of paper that was lying h[ere.] The breeze was blowing it about.

ERNESTO (*taking it and returning it to him after a minute's inspection*).
I don't remember what this is.

PEPITO. They were verses. You probably know about it. (*Reading with difficulty.*) "I am prey to a consuming fire." (*Aside.* Ah, the next line rhymes with Teodora.

ERNESTO. Oh, some trifle.

PEPITO (*stops reading*). Yes, that's all.

ERNESTO. This worthless paper is symbolic of our lives. A few cries of pain, a few flakes of ash.

PEPITO. Then they were verses?

ERNESTO. Yes, sometimes I don't know what I'm doing; I let my pen run on. And last night I wrote those.

PEPITO. And to help this divine afflatus, and to get yourself in the right spirit you were seeking inspiration in the book of the Master?

ERNESTO. It seems to me ——

PEPITO. Oh, you needn't say anything. It's a marvelous work. (*Pointing at the book.*) The episode of Francesca ——

ERNESTO (*ironically and impatiently*). It seems you've turned detective today?

PEPITO. Oh, I'm not entirely successful at it. Here, where the book's open, it says something I don't understand and that you must explain to me. It says that, reading a tale of love by way of pastime, Paolo and Francesca came to the place where the author, showing himself no fool, tells so freely of the love of Lancelot and Queen Guinevere. That was like flint triking fire. He pressed a kiss upon the book, and she, mad ith love, kissed him upon the lips. And at this point the rentine poet says, oddly enough, but with masterly con- ess, these words which are written here, and which I can- nderstand: "The book they read was Galeoto, and they othing else." They read nothing else? Of course, mple enough. But this Galeoto, tell me, where did he n and who was he? (*Pointing at some papers that are he play.*) You certainly ought to know. It's the play you've written that is to make you so famous. e. (*Takes up the play and examines it.*) to was the go-between for Lancelot and the

queen. And in all love-affairs the third person may be called
Galeoto by way of pseudonym. Especially if it is desirable
to avoid a more unpleasant name that brings trouble in its wake.

PEPITO. All right. I see that. But isn't there any appropriate
and convenient Spanish name?

ERNESTO. Very appropriate and very expressive. This business
which turns men's lusts into ready money, which plays upon
men's passions and grows fat on their amours has a name and
I know it; but I would shackle myself if I were to say in so
many words what, after all, I am not going to say. (*He snatches
the book from* PEPITO *and scatters its pages over the table.*) In each
particular case I find a particular person, but sometimes
Galeoto is all society. Then he works without any realization
of the office he is fulfilling, but such cunning has he in under-
mining honor and virtue, that a greater Galeoto never has
been seen, and never will be. A man and woman are living
happily and peacefully, doing their duty with all their hearts.
No one pays any attention to them and everything is as it should
be. But, by heaven, in this great city such a state of affairs
doesn't last long. Some fine morning someone looks squarely
at them, and from that time, either through stupidity or through
malice, all men cling to the belief that they are concealing an
impure love. Then there is nothing more to say; the matter is
settled. No reasoning can convince them, nor does the man
exist who can make them waver. The most upright man
finds his reputation of no avail. And the most horrible part
of it all is that in the beginning, people had no just grounds, and
in the end perhaps they have. So impenetrable an atmosphere surrounds the poor victims, such a torrent sweeps in
upon them, such pressure is brought to bear, that without
realizing it, they are forced upon one another, against their
will. They are drawn together, in their fall they become one
and, dying, they adore each other. The world has been the
battering-ram that breaks down virtue; it has prepared the
way for sin; it has been Galeoto and —— (*Aside.*) Away, away,
devilish thought — your fire consumes me!

PEPITO (*aside*). If Teodora reasons this way, heaven help Don
Julian! (*Aloud.*) And perhaps your verses last night were
on this subject?

ERNESTO. Exactly.

PEPITO. Is it possible that any man can calmly waste his time and be like this — so serene, so unconcerned, when he is about to cross swords with Nebreda, who, with a foil in his hand, is a match for any man? Wouldn't it be more sensible and more profitable for you to be practicing a straight thrust or a parry, instead of wearing out your brain with halting verses of rebel heroics? Now, really, don't you think it rather a serious matter to be meeting the viscount?

ERNESTO. No; and I have good grounds for my opinion. If I kill him, the world profits; if he kills me, the profit is mine.

PEPITO. Good. That's better.

ERNESTO. Let us not talk any more about it.

PEPITO (aside). Now, I'll be very clever about pumping him. (Going up to him, in a lower tone.) Will it take place today?

ERNESTO. Yes, today.

PEPITO. Will it be out-of-doors?

ERNESTO. No. That wouldn't be possible at such an hour. An affair that everyone knows about.

PEPITO. In some house?

ERNESTO. That's what I proposed.

PEPITO. Where?

ERNESTO. Upstairs. (Coldly and indifferently.) There's an empty apartment with a large salon, where the light comes in from the side. For a handful of silver we get a far better place for this business than any mountain-side, and no one will be any the wiser.

PEPITO. So now the only thing necessary —— ?

ERNESTO. A sword.

PEPITO (going back). There are voices outside. Someone is coming. The seconds?

ERNESTO. Perhaps.

PEPITO. It sounds like a woman's voice. (Looking out of the door.)

ERNESTO. But why doesn't he show them in? (A servant enters.)

SERVANT (mysteriously). Someone wants to see the master.

PEPITO. Who is it?

SERVANT. A lady.

ERNESTO. That's strange.

PEPITO (*in a low voice, to the servant*). Is she very insistent?

SERVANT. She's crying.

PEPITO. Is she young?

SERVANT. Well, I can't exactly say. The anteroom is very dark, and the lady is trying to cover her face, so that it certainly is hard to see her. And she speaks so softly, oh, so softly, I can hardly hear her.

ERNESTO. Who can it be?

PEPITO. Someone who wants to see you.

ERNESTO. I can't imagine ——

PEPITO (*aside*). He seems perplexed. (*Aloud.*) See here; I'll go and leave you to yourself. Good-bye, and good luck to you. (*Kissing him, and taking his hat. To the* SERVANT.) What are you waiting for, stupid?

SERVANT. For the master to tell me to show her in.

PEPITO. In affairs of this sort you should divine his intentions; then, until the mysterious lady has gone, don't dare to open the door for anyone, though the heavens fall.

SERVANT. Shall I tell her to come in, then?

ERNESTO (*to* PEPITO, *who is still in the doorway*). Good-bye.

PEPITO. Good-bye, Ernesto.

(PEPITO *and the servant go out at the back.*)

ERNESTO. A lady? Upon what pretext or for what reason? (*A pause.* TEODORA *appears in the doorway, and stops, covering her face with her veil.*) Here she is. (TEODORA *remains at the back, not daring to come forward. He is in front, facing her.*) You wished to speak to me? If you will be so kind, señora? (*Inviting her to come in.*)

TEODORA (*raising her veil*). Forgive me, Ernesto.

ERNESTO. Teodora!

TEODORA. I am doing wrong, I suppose.

ERNESTO (*abruptly, stammering*). I — don't know. For I don't know to what I owe so great an honor. But what am I saying? Why, in my house you are bound to meet with such respect as could be surpassed nowhere. Why, señora, should you fear there might be any harm in it?

TEODORA. There's no reason why. And there was a time, Ernesto — it has gone forever — when I would neither have doubted nor feared; when any woman you know might have come into your room without a blush, without fear; when, if you were going away from here, as they say you are going to America tomorrow — I myself — yes, since those who go away may never come back, and since it is so sad to lose a friend — before Julian — before all the world — would have given you a parting embrace without any thought of harm.

ERNESTO (*makes a movement, then checks himself*). Ah, Teodora!

TEODORA. But now — I suppose it is not the same. There is a gulf between us.

ERNESTO. You're right, señora. Now we cannot love each other, not even as brother and sister. Now our hands are stained if they touch when we meet. The past is over. We must conquer ourselves; we must hate each other.

TEODORA (*ingenuously*). Hate each other? Why?

ERNESTO. I hate you? Did I say that to you, poor child?

TEODORA. Yes.

ERNESTO. Never mind what I say. If the occasion arises, if you need my life, ask for it, Teodora. (*Passionately.*) To give my life for you would be (*controlling himself and changing his tone*) simply to do my duty. (*A slight pause.*) Hate! If my lips spoke such a word it was because I was thinking of the wrong. I was thinking of the injury I have involuntarily done to one who has been so good to me. You, Teodora, ought to hate me — I — no ——

TEODORA (*sadly*). Ah, they have made me weep much. You are right about that. (*Very sweetly.*) But you — you, Ernesto. I cannot accuse you. Nor would anyone blame you who was not blinded by passion. How are you to blame for the whisperings and spite of an evil-minded world, or for poor Julian's black mood; for the anger that tortures him, for his tones that wound me, for the agony that is killing him because he doubts my love?

ERNESTO. That I cannot understand; in him, least of all. (*With profound anger.*) The thing that puts one in a fury, that deserves no mercy, for which there is no possible excuse, is that any man should doubt a woman like you.

TEODORA. My poor Julian is paying dear for his cruel doubt.

ERNESTO (*frightened at having accused* JULIAN *before* TEODORA). What am I saying? (*Hastening to exculpate* JULIAN *and to kill the effect of what he has said.*) Do I blame him? No. He doubted as anyone would doubt. As everyone who loves, doubts. There is no such thing as love without jealousy. Why, there are people who even doubt the good God, Teodora. It's our earthly egotism. The owner of a treasure guards his gold just because it is gold, and he fears for it. I myself, if by some superhuman effort I succeeded in making a woman mine, *I* would be jealous. I would be suspicious even of my own brother! (*He speaks with increasing exultation. Suddenly he stops, seeing that he is about to fall again from another side into the abyss from which he has just escaped.* TEODORA *hears voices in the direction of the door at the back, and goes toward it.— Aside.*) Where are you leading me, my heart? What are my inmost feelings? You say the world speaks base slanders and then you justify them!

TEODORA. Listen, someone is coming.

ERNESTO. Hardly two o'clock. I wonder who it is?

TEODORA (*with a certain terror*). That's Julian's voice. He's probably coming in.

ERNESTO. No. He's stopping.

TEODORA (*all in the same tone, as if questioning* ERNESTO). If it is Julian——

(*Makes a movement in the direction of the door on the right.* ERNESTO *detains her, respectfully but firmly.*)

ERNESTO. If it is he, stay here. Our innocence protects us. If it is — those suspicious people, go in there. (*Pointing to the door at the right.— Listening.*) It's nothing, nothing.

TEODORA. How my heart beats!

ERNESTO. You needn't be afraid. Whoever wanted to come in has gone away — or else it was an illusion. (*Coming forward.*) Teodora!

TEODORA. I had to speak to you, Ernesto, and the time is going so fast!

ERNESTO. Teodora, forgive me — but — perhaps it's not wise. If anyone should come — and someone probably is coming——

TEODORA. That's just why I came — to prevent it.

ERNESTO. You mean —— ?

TEODORA. I mean that I know all. And the thought of the blood that you want to shed for me terrifies me. It sets my own blood on fire. I feel it rising — here.

(*Putting her hand on her heart.*)

ERNESTO. Because it is outraged by the shame and disgrace you must suffer until I have taken the viscount's life with my own hand. He wanted mud. Let him have the mud made by his own blood.

TEODORA (*frightened*). Is it to the death?

ERNESTO. Yes. (*Checking a gesture of supplication from* TEODORA.) You can lead me where you will, you can do anything with me, anything with one exception. May the time never come when, remembering that insult, I can have compassion on Nebreda.

TEODORA (*tearfully and supplicating*). And on me?

ERNESTO. On you?

TEODORA. Yes. It will be a terrible scandal.

ERNESTO. Perhaps.

TEODORA. Perhaps? You say it like that and don't try to prevent it, even when I myself plead with you?

ERNESTO. I can't prevent it, but I can make him pay for it. This is what I think, and this is what I say; this is what keeps running through my mind. Others have sought the affront, but I shall seek the punishment.

TEODORA (*going up to him, and speaking in an undertone, as if afraid of her words*). And Julian?

ERNESTO. Julian? Well?

TEODORA. If he should know?

ERNESTO. He probably does know.

TEODORA. And what will he say?

ERNESTO. What will he say?

TEODORA. That in my defence, who should show his courage except my husband who loves me?

ERNESTO. In defence of a woman? Any man of honor, without knowing her, without being relation, friend, or lover! It's enough to hear a woman insulted. You ask why I am going to fight this duel, why I defend her? Because I heard the slander and I am the man I am. Who would refuse to take up the cudgel in such a cause, or who would give up his right to do so? Wasn't I there? Then I was simply the first man on the spot.

TEODORA (*who has listened to him attentively, as though dominated by his vigor, approaches him and presses his hand with great emotion*). That is honorable, noble, and worthy of you, Ernesto. (*Checks herself, goes away from* ERNESTO, *and says sadly.*) But this is humiliating to my poor Julian!

ERNESTO. Humiliating?

TEODORA. Yes, indeed.

ERNESTO. Why?

TEODORA. Because...

ERNESTO. Who says so?

TEODORA. Everyone will think so.

ERNESTO. But why?

TEODORA. When people hear that I have been insulted, and that it was not my husband who chastised the offender, and that (*lowering her voice, hanging her head, and avoiding* ERNESTO'S *eyes*) it was you who took his place, scandal will be heaped upon scandal.

ERNESTO (*convinced, but protesting*). Good heavens, if we have to think what people are going to say about everything that we do, life isn't worth living at all.

TEODORA. But I am right.

ERNESTO. You're right. But it's horrible.

TEODORA. You yield, then?

ERNESTO. Impossible.

TEODORA. I beg you!

ERNESTO. No. It is more important than ever, Teodora, that I meet Nebreda, come what may. The truth is that the viscount makes up for his lack of honor by his skill in swordsmanship.

TEODORA (*somewhat hurt by the rather humiliating protection that* ERNESTO *is offering to* DON JULIAN). My husband is brave, too.

ERNESTO. The deuce! Either I don't make myself very clear, or you are very slow of understanding: I realize his courage. But when one man has foully insulted the name or honor of another and satisfaction is sought, no one can guess what will happen: which will kill, which be killed. If this man, therefore, is to win in the deadly combat there can be no doubt as to whether it is better for him to have Don Julian or Ernesto for an opponent. (*Sincerely but sadly.*)

TEODORA (*in real distress*). You? Oh, no. Not that.

ERNESTO. Why not? If that is my fate, my death will be no loss to anyone, and I myself will lose but little.

TEODORA (*hardly able to restrain her tears*). Don't say that.

ERNESTO. Well, what do I leave behind in the world? What friendship? What love? What woman will follow my body weeping tears of love?

TEODORA (*unable to control her tears*). All last night I was praying for you. And you say that no one — Oh, I don't want you to die!

ERNESTO. Ah, a woman may pray for anyone — (*passionately*) but she weeps for one man only!

TEODORA (*strangely*). Ernesto!

ERNESTO (*frightened at his own words*). Yes?

TEODORA (*drawing away from him*). Nothing.

ERNESTO (*timidly. Hanging his head and avoiding* TEODORA's *eyes*). If I spoke as I did a little while ago — I am beside myself. Pay no heed to me.

(*A pause. They stand, silent, thinking, at a distance from each other, and not daring to look at each other.*)

TEODORA (*pointing to the back*). Again!

ERNESTO. Someone has come.

TEODORA (*going back and listening*). And they want to come in.

ERNESTO. It must be they. In there, Teodora.

(*Pointing to the room.*)

TEODORA. My innocence protects me.

ERNESTO. But this is not your husband.

TEODORA. It's not Julian!

ERNESTO. No. (*Leading her to the right.*)

TEODORA. I hoped — (*Stopping near the door, beseechingly.*) Oh, give up this duel.

ERNESTO. Good heavens! Why, I struck him in the face!

TEODORA (*despairing, but realizing that any settlement is impossible*). I didn't know that. Then flee ——

ERNESTO. I flee?

TEODORA. For my sake — for his. In heaven's name ——

ERNESTO. I can bear to be hated, but not to be despised.

TEODORA. Just one more thing. Are they coming for you?

ERNESTO. It's not time yet.

TEODORA. You swear it?

ERNESTO. Yes, Teodora. Do you hate me?

TEODORA. Never!

PEPITO (*without*). It's no use. I must see him.

ERNESTO. Quick.

TEODORA. Yes.                                        (*Goes out, right.*)

PEPITO. No one shall stop me.

ERNESTO. Ah, slander justifies itself and makes the sin come true!

(*Enter* PEPITO *at the back, hatless, and much excited.*)

PEPITO. To the devil with you! I will go in. Ernesto, Ernesto!

ERNESTO. What's the matter?

PEPITO. I don't know how to tell you about it, but I must.

ERNESTO. Speak, man!

PEPITO. My head's in a whirl. Dear me, dear me! Who would
have thought —— !

ERNESTO. Quick! What has happened?

PEPITO. What has happened? A terrible calamity. Don Julian
found out about the duel. He came here to look for you.
You weren't here. He went to see your seconds. They all
met at the viscount's house ——

ERNESTO. At Nebreda's? But how?

PEPITO. Don Julian arranged it. He was like a whirlwind sweeping all before him, plans, conventions, everything, everything.

ERNESTO. Go on. What happened?

PEPITO. They're coming up now.

ERNESTO. Who?

PEPITO. Why, they. They are carrying him in their arms.

ERNESTO. You frighten me. Go on — quick.

                    (*Seizing him violently and dragging him forward.*)

PEPITO. He forced Nebreda to fight with him; would listen to no
excuse. So the viscount said, "With both, then." Don
Julian came up here. Your servant barred the door and swore

you were engaged with a lady and that no one was to come in;
no one ——

ERNESTO. And then?

PEPITO. Don Julian came down, saying, "So much the better.
I'll manage the whole affair." And he, Nebreda, the seconds,
my father, and I, who arrived after them all.— Well, the rest
is plain.

ERNESTO. They fought?

PEPITO. Madly, furiously. Like two men striving to fix upon
the sword's point a heart that they hated.

ERNESTO. And Don Julian? No, it's a lie!

PEPITO. They're here already.

ERNESTO. Hush! Hush! Tell me who it is — and speak softly.

PEPITO. See there.

(DON JULIAN, DON SEVERO, and RUEDA *appear at the back. They
are carrying* DON JULIAN, *who is badly wounded.*)

ERNESTO. God help me! Don Julian, my benefactor, my friend,
my father!                                    (*Rushes to him, weeping.*)

JULIAN (*in a weak voice*). Ernesto.

ERNESTO. What a wretch I am!

SEVERO. Come, be quick.

ERNESTO. Father!

SEVERO. The pain is killing him.

ERNESTO. You did this for my sake. Forgive me.

   (*Taking* JULIAN'S *right hand, kneeling beside him, and leaning
   over him.*)

JULIAN. There's no need. You did your duty. I have done mine.

SEVERO. A bed!    (*He releases* JULIAN, *and* PEPITO *takes his place.*)

PEPITO. Let's go in there.    (*Pointing to the door at the right.*)

ERNESTO (*in a terrible voice*). Nebreda ——

SEVERO. No more of this folly. Do you want to finish killing him?

ERNESTO (*in a frenzy*). Folly! We shall see. Oh, let them both come.

PEPITO. We'll put him in your bed in the alcove.

                               (ERNESTO *stops, terrified.*)

ERNESTO. Where?

SEVERO. In there.

PEPITO. Yes!

ERNESTO. No.

(*He rushes up and stands in front of the door. The group, leading the half-fainting* JULIAN, *stops in astonishment.*)

SEVERO. You refuse to let him?

PEPITO. You are mad!

SEVERO. Stand aside! Don't you see he's dying?

JULIAN. What does he mean? He doesn't want me?

(*Pulling himself together and looking at* ERNESTO *with mingled horror and astonishment.*)

RUEDA. I don't understand.

PEPITO. Nor I.

ERNESTO. He is dying, and he beseeches me and he doubts me. Father!

SEVERO. We must. (*The door opens.* TEODORA *appears.*)

ERNESTO. Good God!

SEVERO *and* PEPITO. She!

RUEDA. A woman!

TEODORA (*rushing up to* JULIAN *and embracing him*). Julian!

JULIAN (*drawing away to look at her, rising by a violent effort, rejecting all help*). Who is it? Teodora!

(*He falls to the floor, unconscious.*)

CURTAIN

# ACT III

*The same setting as Act I, except there is a settle instead of a sofa. It is evening. A lighted lamp is on the table.*

PEPITO. At last the crisis is over; at least I can't hear anything. Poor Don Julian. Very serious, very serious. His life is in the balance. On the one side death awaits him; on the other, another death. Two gulfs deeper than a hopeless love. The devil! With all these tragedies going on in the house I'm turning more romantic than *he* with his rhymes and his plots. Why, my head's a regular kaleidoscope of scandals, duels, deaths, treachery and infamy! Heavens, what a day and what a night! And the worst is yet to come. (*A little pause.*)

It was rank imprudence to pick him up and carry him off in such a condition. But, the deuce! Who can oppose my uncle when he sets his jaws, and frowns like that? And you must admit that he was right. No honorable man, so long as there was a breath of life in him, would have stayed in that house in such a situation. And he's a proud and sensitive man. (*Going back.*) Who's coming? Why, it's my mother.

(*Enter* MERCEDES.)

MERCEDES. How is Severo?

PEPITO. He won't leave his brother for a single instant. I knew he was devoted to him, but I had no idea he loved him as much as all this. I only hope that things won't turn out as I fear.

MERCEDES. And your uncle?

PEPITO. He suffers in silence. Sometimes he cries out "Teodora" in a harsh and anguished tone. At other times he cries, "Ernesto," and clutches the sheet between his fingers. Then he lies motionless as a statue, gazing fixedly into empty space, and the cold sweat of death bathes his brow. Suddenly fever gives him strength; he raises himself up in his bed, and listens eagerly, and says that *he* and *she* are waiting for him. He gets up and wants to go out, and my father resorts to tears and supplications to calm his anxiety. Calm it? He can't do it. His burning blood is carrying the anger of his heart and the tears of his soul through all his veins. Let's go, mother, it's heart-rending to see the bitter distortion of his mouth, to see his hands drawn up like two claws, his hair all in disorder, and his distended pupils eagerly searching every shadow flickering in the room.

MERCEDES. And when your father sees him?

PEPITO. He groans and swears that he will be avenged; and he, too, says "Teodora"; he, too, cries "Ernesto." Heaven forbid that he should meet them, for if he does, nothing can appease his anger, nothing can control his fury.

MERCEDES. Your father is very good.

PEPITO. Yes, with a temper — phew!

MERCEDES. It's true. He very seldom gets angry; but when he does ——

PEPITO. With all due respect, he is as fierce as a tiger.

MERCEDES. He always has just cause.

PEPITO. I don't know about that, but he undoubtedly has plenty of reason this time. But how is Teodora?

MERCEDES. She's upstairs. She wanted to come down.— And she was weeping. A veritable Magdalen.

PEPITO. Of course. Repentant or sinning?

MERCEDES. Don't talk that way. Why, she's only a child.

PEPITO. Who, innocent, spotless, sweet, pure, gentle little thing that she is, has killed Don Julian. If you're right and she is only a child, and she does such things when she's hardly out of the cradle, heaven help us a few years from now!

MERCEDES. She is hardly to blame. Your fine friend with his play — the poet, the dreamer — has been the cause of all this.

PEPITO. Well, I don't deny it.

MERCEDES. What does he gain by it?

PEPITO. Well, at present Ernesto is walking the streets, fleeing from his conscience, which he can't escape.

MERCEDES. Has he any?

PEPITO. He may have.

MERCEDES. How sad it is!

PEPITO. A terrible misfortune.

MERCEDES. How we have been deceived!

PEPITO. Cruelly!

MERCEDES. What treachery!

PEPITO. Staggering.

MERCEDES. What a scandal!

PEPITO. Unequalled!

MERCEDES. Poor Julian!

PEPITO. A bitter blow!

(*Enter a* SERVANT.)

SERVANT. Don Ernesto.

MERCEDES. How dare he!

PEPITO. What audacity!

SERVANT. I thought ——

PEPITO. You thought wrong.

SERVANT. He is just stopping in on his way. He said to the coachman, "I'll be right out. Wait here." So ——

PEPITO (*consulting his mother*). What shall we do?

MERCEDES. Let him come in.          (*The* SERVANT *goes out.*)

PEPITO. I'll get rid of him.

MERCEDES. Be tactful.

(MERCEDES *sits on the settle;* PEPITO *stands on the other side of the stage. Neither turns to greet* ERNESTO, *who enters through second wing.*)

ERNESTO (*aside*). Scorn, unfriendly silence! It bodes ill. From now on I shall be a monster of wickedness and insolence, even though I am entirely blameless. Everyone thinks so; they all despise me.

PEPITO (*turning to him, and speaking in harsh tones*). Look here, Ernesto.

ERNESTO. What is it?

PEPITO. I want to tell you ——

ERNESTO. To get out of here?

PEPITO (*changing his tone*). Goodness, what an idea! It was — I just wanted to ask — if it is true — (*as if hunting for his words*) that afterwards, the viscount ——

ERNESTO (*gloomily, hanging his head*). Yes.

PEPITO. With your own hands?

ERNESTO. When I went out of the house I was beside myself. They were coming down.— I stopped them.— We went up again.— I shut the door. Two men, two witnesses — two swords — then — I don't know how — two blades crossing.— A cry — a blow — a sob — blood flowing — a murderer standing there — and a man lying on the ground.

PEPITO. The devil! You have a good aim. Did you hear, mother?

MERCEDES. Still more blood!

PEPITO. Nebreda deserved it!

ERNESTO. Mercedes, I beg of you — just one word! Don Julian? Don Julian? If you only realized my anxiety, my grief. What do they say?

MERCEDES. That his wound is mortal, and that it grows more dangerous the nearer you come to his bed of death and sorrow. Leave this house.

ERNESTO. I want to see him.

MERCEDES. Go at once!

ERNESTO. No!

PEPITO. Such insolence!

ERNESTO. Is quite worthy of me! (*To* MERCEDES, *respectfully.*) Forgive me, señora, I am what others make me.

MERCEDES. For heaven's sake, Ernesto!

ERNESTO. Listen, Mercedes. When a man like me is trampled upon and is called infamous without reason, and is forced and dragged into sin, the struggle that results is dangerous — for all, but not for me; for in this fierce struggle with invisible beings, I have lost honor, affection, love, and there is nothing left for me to lose but the sad tatters of an insipid and monotonous existence. I came only to find out if there is any hope — that's all. Well, why do you deny me that consolation? (*Beseeching* MERCEDES.) Just one word!

MERCEDES. Well — they say — that he is better.

ERNESTO. But the truth? They're not deceiving me? It's true? They're sure of it? Ah, you are compassionate! You are good! Can it be true? Good God! can it be true? O Lord, save him! Don't let him die! Let him be happy once more! Let him forgive me! Let him embrace me again! Let me live to see it!

(*He sinks into the chair nearest to the table and hides his face in his hands, sobbing.* MERCEDES *and* PEPITO *go over to* ERNESTO.)

MERCEDES. If your father hears — if your father comes — ! (*To* ERNESTO.) Courage!

PEPITO. A man crying! (*Aside.*) These nervous people are terrible. One minute they weep, and the next they kill someone.

ERNESTO. If I cry, if my throat is torn by hysterical sobs, if I am as weak as a woman or a child, don't think it's for my own sake. It's for him, for her, for their lost happiness; for their good name, stained forever; for the injury I have done them in return for their love and their favors! I don't weep for my misfortunes, for *my* dark lot! And, by heaven! if the sad past could be wiped out with tears, I'd turn all my blood into tears and not leave a drop in my veins!

MERCEDES. Be still, for pity's sake!

PEPITO. We'll talk of tears and sorrow later.

ERNESTO. If everyone else is talking now, why shouldn't we talk, too? The whole town is a seething, boiling whirlpool that sucks in and absorbs and devours and utterly destroys the honor, the good name, the very being of three people, and carries them away on the spray of laughter through the canal of human misery to the social abyss of shame, and there drowns forever the future, the fair name, and the memory, of these unhappy beings.

MERCEDES. Speak lower, Ernesto.

ERNESTO. No; they aren't whispering; they're shouting aloud. Why, the air fairly resounds! There isn't a person who doesn't know the tragic story, but everyone tells it his own way. Wonder of wonders, people always know everything; but, sad to say, never the truth. (ERNESTO *is standing up now, and* MERCEDES *and* PEPITO *are listening eagerly to hear what is being said in the town.*) Some say that Teodora was surprised by her husband in my house, and that I rushed at him, blind with fury, and plunged my cowardly dagger into his breast; *others*, my friends apparently, give me a higher rank than that of a vulgar assassin: I killed him, but in an honorable fight, a properly arranged duel. There *are* some, of course, who know more of the details, and *they* say that Julian took my place in the affair that had been arranged with Nebreda.... I arrived too late... on purpose, or through cowardice, or because I was in the arms of... No, the vile words burn my lips; my brain is on fire! Think of the filthiest, the lowest, vilest, most infamous thing imaginable: dregs of the heart, ashes of the soul, evil scourings of unclean minds; cast it to the breezes blowing through the streets, salt all lips and tongues with it, and you'll have the story, and you will learn then what remains of two honorable men and a woman, when their reputations are bandied about the town!

MERCEDES. I don't deny that it's all most unfortunate. But perhaps we can't altogether blame these people for the conclusions they draw.

PEPITO. Teodora went to your house... she was there ——

ERNESTO.  To prevent the duel with Nebreda.

PEPITO.  Then why did she hide?

ERNESTO.  Because we were afraid her presence there would look suspicious.

PEPITO.  The explanation is easy and simple enough.  The difficulty, Ernesto, is to make people believe it.  There's another one that is still easier, and simpler ——

ERNESTO.  And more shameful! — so that is the best one.

PEPITO.  Grant at least that Teodora was indiscreet, though she was not guilty.

ERNESTO.  Guilt is wily and cautious.  On the other hand, how rash is innocence!

PEPITO.  That's all very well for saints and angels, but when you apply that rule to everyone ——

ERNESTO.  Oh, well, you're right.  Of what value or importance are such calumnies?  Why worry about them?  The horrible part is that one's very thoughts are tainted by the fatal contact with this fatal idea!  If one ever thinks of crime, it becomes familiar to one's consciousness.  One looks on it with fear and loathing — *but one looks on it* — at night, in the darkness!  That's how it is!  (*Aside.*)  But what's the matter?  Why do they look at me so strangely as they listen?  (*Aloud.*)  You know me; I bear an honorable name!... If I killed Nebreda simply because he lied, what would I not do if by my own guilt I turned his slanders into truth!

PEPITO (*aside to* MERCEDES).  And he denied it!  It's plain as day!

MERCEDES.  This is madness!

PEPITO.  The one thing that's plain is that he confesses!

MERCEDES (*aloud*).  Leave us, Ernesto.

ERNESTO.  Impossible.  If I were far from his bed tonight I should go mad.

MERCEDES.  But if Severo comes and sees you?

ERNESTO.  What difference will that make to me?  He's an honorable man.  All the better!  Let him come.  He who fears runs away, and he fears who has deceived, so it's not likely that I shall either run from him or fear him.

PEPITO (*listening*).  Someone is coming.

MERCEDES.  It's he.

PEPITO. It's not he.  Teodora!

ERNESTO. It's Teodora!... Teodora!... I want to see her!

MERCEDES (*sternly*). Ernesto!

PEPITO. Ernesto!

ERNESTO. Yes, to ask her to forgive me.

MERCEDES. You don't realize ——

ERNESTO. I realize everything, and I understand.  We two
together?  Oh, no — Enough!  You needn't be afraid.  I
may give my blood for her, give my life, my future, my honor,
and my conscience.... But see each other!  Never... It's no
longer possible — a blood-red cloud separates us!

(*He goes out, left.*)

MERCEDES. Leave me alone with her.  Go in with your father.
I want to search the very bottom of her heart.  I know too
well that my words will be like daggers to her.

PEPITO. Well, I leave you together.

MERCEDES. Good-bye.

PEPITO. Good-bye.                    (*He goes out, right.*)

MERCEDES. Now, to work!  (TEODORA *enters timidly, and stops by*
JULIAN'S *door.  She listens anxiously, stifling her sobs with her handker-*
*chief.*)  Teodora...

TEODORA. Is that you?

MERCEDES. Courage!  What good will it do to weep?

TEODORA. How is he?  How is he?  The truth!

MERCEDES. Much better.

TEODORA. Will he recover?

MERCEDES. I think so.

TEODORA. O God, take my life for his!

MERCEDES (*brings her forward affectionately*).  And then... then I
trust in your judgment, for I see by your tears and your anxiety
that you are repentant.

TEODORA. Yes.  (MERCEDES *sits down and watches her suspiciously.*)
It's quite true I did very wrong to go and see him.  (MERCEDES,
*seeing that this is not the kind of repentance that she meant, shows her*
*disapproval.*)  But last night you told me about the insult and
the duel.... I'm grateful for your kindness, though you can't
realize, and I wouldn't know how to explain to you the harm
you have done me.  What a night!  Groaning and raving!

Dear Julian's anger! the scandal! the insult!... the
the terrible struggle!... It all passed before my ey
poor Ernesto, too, perhaps dying for me.... Why do
at me that way? What harm is there in that? Don't you
believe me? Do you think as the rest do?

MERCEDES (*dryly*). I think you needn't have feared for this young
man's life.

TEODORA. No? Nebreda is a famous swordsman! You see —
my Julian ——

MERCEDES. In brief, your Julian is avenged and the duellist is
laid low with a wound in his heart, so your doubts and fears
were unfounded. (*Coldly and meaningly.*)

TEODORA (*with interest*). Did Ernesto do it?

MERCEDES. Yes, Ernesto.

TEODORA. He met the viscount?

MERCEDES. Face to face!

TEODORA (*unable to control herself*). Ah, how brave and noble!

MERCEDES. Teodora!

TEODORA. What is it? Tell me.

MERCEDES. I can read your thoughts.

TEODORA. My thoughts?

MERCEDES. Yes.

TEODORA. What thoughts?

MERCEDES. You know very well!

TEODORA. I did wrong to show my happiness at seeing Julian
avenged; but it was an impulse from my heart that I couldn't
control.

MERCEDES. That's not what you were thinking.

TEODORA. Then you must know more about it than I do?

MERCEDES (*meaningly*). Listen, when the heart admires greatly
it is on the road to love.

TEODORA. You say I admire something?

MERCEDES. This young man's courage.

TEODORA. His goodness.

MERCEDES. It's all one, that is the beginning.

TEODORA. These are the ravings of madness.

MERCEDES. It is madness... on your part.

TEODORA. Will you never understand!... Always this terrible
idea? Why, I feel only infinite pity!

MERCEDES. For whom?

TEODORA. For whom would it be? For Julian!

MERCEDES. Have you never heard that pity and forgetfulness go hand in hand in women.

TEODORA. Be still, for mercy's sake!

MERCEDES. I want to awaken your conscience with the voice of my experience and the light of truth.                    (*A pause.*)

TEODORA. I am listening to you, and as I listen you seem to me not like a mother, a sister, or a friend; your words sound to me as though Satan were counselling you and inspiring you and speaking through your lips. Why do you want to convince me that my love for my husband is a lie — a lie of the soul — and that a rival love is foully growing there, whose flame consumes and defiles? Why, I love him as I have always loved him. I would give the very last drop of the blood that runs through my veins and sets me on fire, for a single instant of life for that man from whom they separate me. I would go in there this very minute if your husband would let me. And I would clasp Julian in my arms and would bathe him with my tears, with such tender love and such passion that his doubts would be consumed by the fire of our souls. But just because I adore Julian, must I be so ungrateful as to hate the noble and generous man who risked his life for me? And if I don't hate him, must I love him? Heaven help me! The world thinks such things. I hear such strange stories, I see such sad things happen, I have such slanders heaped upon me, that sometimes I begin to doubt myself and I ask myself in horror: Am I, perhaps, what they all say I am? Do I nourish an unlawful passion in the very depths of my being, consuming me without my knowledge, and will the evil flame break out some sad and ill-omened hour and overpower my will and my senses?

MERCEDES. Are you telling me the truth?

TEODORA. The absolute truth.

MERCEDES. You don't love him?

TEODORA. Listen, Mercedes. I don't know how to convince you. Any other time such a question would make my blood boil; yet now, as you see, I am calmly discussing the question whether or not I am an honest woman. Can that mean that I really am one? At the bottom of my heart? No; to endure the humiliation is to deserve the shame.

(*She hides her face in her hands and sinks down on the settle.*)

MERCEDES. Don't cry. Come, I believe you. Don't cry, Teodora. Enough. No more of this. Just one word more, Teodora, and then I have finished. Ernesto is not what you think him: he doesn't deserve your confidence.

TEODORA. He is good, Mercedes.

MERCEDES. No.

TEODORA. He loves Julian.

MERCEDES. He is deceiving him.

TEODORA. Again! Good heavens!

MERCEDES. I don't say that you would listen to his declarations. I only say... I only say that *he loves you.*

TEODORA (*in horror, rising*). He loves me?

MERCEDES. Everyone knows it. A little while ago in this very room, before me, before my son... now, you see.

TEODORA (*anxiously*). Well, go on. What was it?

MERCEDES. He confessed it openly, and in impassioned words swore that for you he would give life, honor, conscience, and soul. And when you came he wanted to see you, and it was only by urgent insistence that I persuaded him to go in there. I am on pins and needles now for fear Severo may find him, and his anger break out! Now what do you say?

TEODORA (*in spite of herself she has followed this speech with a strange, indefinable mixture of interest, honor, and fear*). Good heavens! Can such infamy be? And I grieved for him! I professed such sincere affection for him!

MERCEDES. Are you crying again?

TEODORA. Can the soul help weeping at the disillusionments of this unhappy life? A man so noble, so pure... to see him fallen and defiled! You say he is in there! He! Ernesto! Holy Virgin! Listen, Mercedes — Mercedes — he must leave this house!

MERCEDES (*with real joy*). That is what I want. Your vehemence delights me. Forgive me. Now I believe you.

TEODORA. But you didn't before?

MERCEDES. Hush! Be still! He is coming!

TEODORA (*impatiently*). I won't see him! You tell him.... Julian is waiting for me.          (*Turning to the right.*)

MERCEDES. Impossible.... You know it now.... And he won't obey me. Now that I fully understand your feelings, I want him to see in you the scorn which he met with before in my words.

TEODORA. Let me go.

(*Enter* ERNESTO.)

ERNESTO (*stopping at the entrance*). Teodora!

MERCEDES (*aside to* TEODORA). It's too late. Do your duty and that will be enough. (*Aloud to* ERNESTO.) Teodora, as mistress of this house, is going to repeat to you the command that you heard from my lips a little while ago.

TEODORA (*in a low voice to* MERCEDES). Don't leave me.

MERCEDES. Are you afraid of something?

TEODORA. I afraid! I fear nothing!

(*Signs to her to go. She goes out, right.*)

ERNESTO. The command was... that I should go away. (*A pause. They are both silent and do not dare look at each other.*) And you... do you repeat it now? (TEODORA *makes a sign of assent, but does not meet his eye.*) Then don't be afraid, Teodora. I obey, I respect your commands. (*Sadly and respectfully.*) The others shan't make me obey, little as it pleases them. (*Harshly.*) But from you — even though you hurt — from you I can suffer all things.

TEODORA. Hurt you, Ernesto! No. Do you think that I...?

ERNESTO. I don't think so.          (*Another pause.*)

TEODORA (*without turning round or looking at him*). Good-bye. I wish you all happiness.

ERNESTO. Good-bye, Teodora. (*He pauses a moment, but she does not turn, or look at him, or put out her hand. Finally he starts to go. Then he turns and goes up to her.* TEODORA *feels him coming, but does not turn her eyes toward him.*) If I could wipe out now by my death all the harm I have done you in spite of myself, because of my unhappy fate, I give you my word of honor that soon not even a shadow of the past would remain, not a sigh of agony, nor that sad pallor, (TEODORA *raises her head and looks at him in terror*) nor that look that frightens me, not a sob in your throat, (TEODORA *does indeed stifle a sob*) not a tear on your cheek.

TEODORA (*aside, drawing away from* ERNESTO). Mercedes told the truth, and I, blind, heedless ——

ERNESTO. Give me just one word of farewell — just one, I beg.

TEODORA. Good-bye. Yes.... I forgive the wrong you have done us.

ERNESTO. That I have done, I, Teodora!

TEODORA. Yes.

ERNESTO. That look, that tone!

TEODORA. No more, Ernesto, please!

ERNESTO. What have I done to deserve this?

TEODORA. It is as though I had never existed. All is over between us.

ERNESTO. These scornful words!

TEODORA (*hoarsely, pointing to the door*). Go!

ERNESTO. You tell me to go — like that!

TEODORA. My husband is dying in there... and I am dying here, too.

    (*She totters, and has to support herself by the arm of the chair so as not to fall.*)

ERNESTO (*hurrying to help her*). Teodora!

TEODORA (*repulsing him violently*). Don't touch me. Leave me alone! (*A pause.*) Oh, my heart is breaking!

    (*She tries to take a few steps, her strength fails her, and* ERNESTO *again tries to support her. She repulses him and draws away.*)

ERNESTO. Why won't you let me?

TEODORA (*harshly*). Because you defile me.

ERNESTO. You say — I defile you?

TEODORA. Certainly.

ERNESTO (*a pause*). Good heavens, what is she saying? She, too! Impossible!... Death would be better than this!... It's not true! I'm going mad!... Say it's not so, Teodora! In Heaven's name, speak one word of forgiveness, or comfort, or pity, señora! I agree to leave you and never see you again, though it breaks my heart — it is killing me! But I do this on the condition that your affection and your esteem shall follow me in my solitude, together with your forgiveness... at least your pity! I must believe that you believe I am faithful and honorable, that I neither defile nor have defiled, that I neither wrong nor will wrong you! I care little for the world. I scorn its curses, and its anger fills me with profound contempt. Even though it hits me cruelly, wantonly; though it whispers about what I have been, it can never think as ill of me as I think of it. But you — the purest being imaginable — you, for whom I swear I would gladly give a thousand times not only my life on earth, but my place in heaven — for you to think me capable of treachery! Oh, not that, Teodora, not that!

TEODORA. You don't understand. We must separate, Ernesto.

ERNESTO. It is impossible.

TEODORA. At once. I implore you. (*Pointing to the door.*) Julian is suffering.

ERNESTO. I know it.

TEODORA. Then we mustn't forget it.

ERNESTO. No, but I'm suffering, too.

TEODORA. You, Ernesto? Why?

ERNESTO. Because you despise me.

TEODORA. Oh, I don't.

ERNESTO. You said so.

TEODORA. I lied.

ERNESTO. No, you meant it. So we are not suffering equally. In this eternal struggle, in this relentless warfare, he suffers as men suffer on earth, and I as they do in hell.

TEODORA. Good heavens, my brain is on fire!

ERNESTO. My heart is breaking.

TEODORA. Stop, Ernesto. Have some pity.

ERNESTO. That's all *I* ask.

TEODORA. Pity?

ERNESTO. Yes, pity. What is it that you fear from me — or think of me?

TEODORA. Forgive me, if I have hurt you.

ERNESTO. Hurt! No. The truth. I want the truth! I ask it on bended knees, with tears in my eyes.

*(He kneels before* TEODORA *and takes her hand. At this point* SEVERO *appears in the doorway of* JULIAN'S *room and stands there.)*

SEVERA *(aside).* The wretches!

TEODORA. Don Severo!

*(ERNESTO leaves TEODORA and goes to the right. SEVERO comes forward between him and TEODORA.)*

SEVERO *(to ERNESTO, with concentrated fury, but in a low tone, so that* JULIAN *may not hear).* Since I can find no words to express my anger and my contempt, I shall have to content myself with saying, "You are a scoundrel. Go at once!"

ERNESTO. Out of respect to Teodora and to this house, because of him who is suffering on that bed, I shall have to content myself with answering... by silence.

SEVERO *(ironically, thinking that he is going).* To be silent and obey is the part of prudence.

ERNESTO. You misunderstood. I don't obey.

SEVERO. You are going to stay here?

ERNESTO. Provided that Teodora does not confirm your command, I stay here. A few minutes ago I was about to leave, but God or the devil detained me. You came, you tried to throw me out, and at once, just as though your harsh words were some devil's spell, I felt roots shooting out from the soles of my feet and taking firm hold in the ground.

SEVERO. I'll try calling the servants to see whether they can tear them out by force.

ERNESTO. Try.

*(He takes a step toward SEVERO with a threatening air. TEODORA rushes between them and restrains him.)*

TEODORA. Ernesto. *(Then turning to her uncle, with spirit and dignity.)* You forget, doubtless, that in my house, while my husband, its master, is living, we, and we alone, have the right and the authority to command. *(To ERNESTO, sweetly.)* Not for his sake — but for mine — because I am in trouble.

*(ERNESTO cannot conceal his joy that TEODORA is defending him.)*

ERNESTO. Teodora, do you wish it?

TEODORA. I ask this of you.

*(ERNESTO bows respectfully and turns to go.)*

SEVERO. Your audacity amazes and horrifies me as much — no, far more than Ernesto's. (*He approaches* TEODORA *with a threatening look.* ERNESTO, *who has taken several steps, stops; then, making an effort to control himself, goes on.*) Do you dare lift up your head, unhappy woman, and before me, too! Bow your head to the dust. (ERNESTO *makes the same movements as before, but more markedly.*) Where did you, poor, trembling little coward, find those spirited words to defend him? Passion is eloquent! (ERNESTO, *now at the back, stops.*) But you forget that before throwing him out, Severo knew enough to turn you out of this house, which you have stained with Julian's blood. Why have you come back?

(*He seizes her brutally by the arm and gradually gets nearer and nearer to her.*)

ERNESTO. Oh, I can't! No! (*He rushes up to* SEVERO *and* TEODORA *and separates them.*) Let go of her, you scoundrel!

SEVERO. Again!

ERNESTO. Again!

SEVERO. You come back!

ERNESTO. Since you dare harm Teodora, what can I do but (*he has lost all control of himself*) come back, come back and punish your insolence, and call you a coward to your face?

SEVERO. Me!

ERNESTO. Yes!

TEODORA. No!

ERNESTO. He brought it on himself. I saw him lay hands on you in anger. On you — on you! Like this.

(*He seizes* SEVERO *violently by the arm.*)

SEVERO. Insolent!

ERNESTO. True. But I'm not going to let go. Did you ever have a mother? Yes. Did you love her very much? Did you respect her still more? Well, you are to respect Teodora as much, and you are to humble yourself before the terrible grief of this woman! Of this woman, purer and more honorable than your mother, you hound!

SEVERO. You dare say these things to me?

ERNESTO. Yes, and I've not finished yet.

SEVERO. You shall pay for this with your life.

ERNESTO. With my life. But now… (TEODORA *tries to separate them, but he puts her gently aside with one hand*). You probably believe in a God. You must… a creator… a future hope! Good! Well, just as you bend your sluggish knees before the altar of God in heaven, you must bend them now before Teodora. Now, at once! Down! Into the dust!

TEODORA. Oh, have pity!

ERNESTO. To the ground!

(*He forces* SEVERO *to kneel before* TEODORA.)

TEODORA. Stop! Ernesto!

SEVERO. The devil!

ERNESTO. At her feet.

SEVERO. *You* dare!

ERNESTO. I!

SEVERO. Before *her!*

ERNESTO. Yes.

TEODORA. Stop! Silence!

(TEODORA, *terrified, points to* JULIAN'S *room.* ERNESTO *lets go his prisoner.* SEVERO *rises and goes back toward the right.* TEODORA *goes to the back, toward* ERNESTO. *In this way he and she form a separate group.*)

JULIAN (*without*). Let me go.

MERCEDES. No.

JULIAN. It is they. Come!

TEODORA (*to* ERNESTO). Go!

SEVERO (*to* ERNESTO). My revenge!

ERNESTO. I admit it.

(*At this moment* JULIAN *appears, pale, haggard, half-dying, supported by* MERCEDES.)

JULIAN. Together! Where are they going? Stop them! They're running away from me. Traitors!

(*He tries to throw himself upon them, but his strength fails him, and he totters.*)

SEVERO (*rushing up to support him*). No!

JULIAN. Severo, they deceived me… they lied. Wretches!

(*As he is talking,* MERCEDES *and* SEVERO *lead him over to the settle.*)

Over there! Look! Both of them — she and Ernesto! Why are they together?

TEODORA *and* ERNESTO (*drawing away from each other*). No!

JULIAN. Why don't they come here? Teodora!

TEODORA (*stretching out her arms, but not going any nearer*). Dear Julian.

JULIAN. Come to me! (TEODORA *rushes into* JULIAN'S *arms and he embraces her violently. A pause.*) Do you see? Now, do you see? (*To his brother.*) I know they are deceiving me and I clasp her in my arms and hold her there... and I could kill her!... And she deserves it!... And I look at her.... *I look at her*, and I cannot!

TEODORA. Julian!

JULIAN. And that man? (*Pointing to* ERNESTO.)

ERNESTO. Señor ——

JULIAN. And I loved him! Be still, and come here! (ERNESTO *goes up to him. He holds* TEODORA.) I am still her master!

TEODORA. I am yours! I am yours!

JULIAN. Don't pretend! Don't lie to me.

MERCEDES (*trying to calm him*). Please!

SEVERO. Julian!

JULIAN (*to both*). Hush; be still! (*To* TEODORA.) I've found you out. I know that you love him. (TEODORA *and* ERNESTO *try to protest, but he will not let them.*) Why, Madrid knows it! All Madrid!

ERNESTO. No, father.

TEODORA. No.

JULIAN. They deny it; they still deny it. Why, I have evidence. I feel it in my very being. This fever that is burning me up lightens my mind with its flame.

ERNESTO. These stories are all the children of the fever in your blood, of your deliriums. Listen, señor!

JULIAN. You're going to lie to me!

ERNESTO (*pointing to* TEODORA). She is innocent.

JULIAN. I don't believe you.

ERNESTO. By the memory of my father, señor ——

JULIAN. Don't profane his name and his memory.

ERNESTO. By my mother's last kiss ——

JULIAN. Her last kiss is no longer on your forehead.

ERNESTO. Then by anything you wish, dear father, I will swear it, I will swear it.

JULIAN. No oaths, no lying words or protestations!

ERNESTO. Then what will satisfy you?

JULIAN. Deeds!

ERNESTO. What does he want, Teodora? What is he asking us to do?

TEODORA. I don't know. What shall we do? What shall we do, Ernesto?

JULIAN (*who is watching them with feverish eyes full of instinctive distrust*). Ah, you're planning deceits before my very eyes. Wretches! You're plotting together. I see you.

ERNESTO. You see with your fever, not with your eyes.

JULIAN. Yes, with my fever. My fever's a flame that has consumed the veil that you two drew in front of my eyes, and at last I see. Why do you look at each other now? Why, traitors? Why do your eyes shine? Speak, Ernesto. It's not the shining of tears. Come closer, closer! (*He forces them to come near, makes him bow his head, and at last kneel before him. JULIAN now is between TEODORA, who is beside him, and ERNESTO, who is at his feet. In this position he passes his hand over ERNESTO's eyes.*) Do you see? It's not tears; they're quite dry.

ERNESTO. Forgive me, forgive me!

JULIAN. Why, if you ask forgiveness, you confess your sin!

ERNESTO. No!

JULIAN. Yes!

ERNESTO. It's not true.

JULIAN. Then let your eyes meet before me.

SEVERO. Julian!

MERCEDES. Señor!

JULIAN (*to TEODORA and ERNESTO*). Perhaps you're afraid? Don't you love each other like brother and sister? Then prove it. Let your souls look out of your wide pupils, and let the rays of their chaste light mingle before me so that when I look very closely I may see whether those rays are *light* or *fire*. You, too, Teodora! Come, you must! Do it, both of you!
    (*He makes TEODORA kneel before him, faces them near together, and makes them look at each other.*)

TEODORA (*drawing away with a violent effort*). Ah, no!

ERNESTO (*tries to free himself, but JULIAN holds him*). I cannot.

JULIAN. You love each other, you love each other! I saw it clearly! (*To* ERNESTO.) You shall pay for this with your life!

ERNESTO. Yes.

JULIAN. With your blood!

ERNESTO. With every drop!

JULIAN. Be still.

TEODORA (*trying to calm him*). Julian!

JULIAN. Do *you* defend him? Defend him?

TEODORA. It's not for his sake!

SEVERO. By heaven!

JULIAN (*to* SEVERO). Silence! (*To* ERNESTO.) Unnatural son!

ERNESTO. Father!

JULIAN. Deceiver! traitor!

ERNESTO. No: father!

JULIAN. Today I am going to put the brand of shame upon your cheek with my hand!... later with my sword!

(*With a supreme effort he rises and strikes* ERNESTO *in the face.* ERNESTO *gives a terrible cry and goes away to the left, covering his face.*)

ERNESTO. Ah!

SEVERO (*pointing to* ERNESTO). A just punishment!

TEODORA. My God!

(*She hides her face in her hands and sinks into a chair.*)

MERCEDES (*to* ERNESTO, *as though excusing* JULIAN). It was delirium. (*These four cries are in quick succession, then come a few moments of stupefaction.* JULIAN *stands looking at* ERNESTO. MERCEDES *and* SEVERO *support him.*)

JULIAN. Delirium? No: punishment! Wretch, what did you expect?

MERCEDES. Let's go, let's go.

SEVERO. Come, Julian.

JULIAN. Yes. I'm coming.

(*He walks painfully to his room, supported by* SEVERO *and* MERCEDES, *but stops from time to time to look at* ERNESTO *and* TEODORA.)

MERCEDES. Quick, Severo!

JULIAN. Look at them, the wretches... It was justice! Isn't that true? Isn't that true? I think so.

SEVERO. Julian, for my sake!

JULIAN. You alone! You alone! You loved me.

(*Embracing him.*)

SEVERO. I? Of course.

JULIAN (*stops in the doorway and looks at them again*). And she is weeping for him, and she doesn't follow me! She doesn't even look at me! She doesn't see... that I'm dying! Yes, dying!

SEVERO. Julian!

JULIAN. Wait, wait! Shame for shame; good-bye, Ernesto.

(JULIAN, SEVERO, *and* MERCEDES *go out, right.* ERNESTO *sinks into the chair by the table.* TEODORA *remains standing. A pause.*)

ERNESTO (*aside*). What good is loyalty?

TEODORA. What good is innocence?

ERNESTO. My conscience is troubled.

TEODORA. Have mercy, God, have mercy!

ERNESTO. Poor child!

TEODORA. Poor Ernesto!

SEVERO (*without, in great anguish*). Brother!

MERCEDES. Help!

PEPITO. Quick!

TEODORA. Cries of grief!

ERNESTO. Of death!

TEODORA. Let's go at once!

ERNESTO. Where?

TEODORA. In there!

ERNESTO (*checking her*). We can't.

TEODORA. Why not? (*Anxiously.*) I want him to live.

ERNESTO. And I, but I can't —— (*Pointing to* JULIAN'S *room.*)

TEODORA. I can. (*Rushing to the door.*)

(SEVERO *comes out a moment after* PEPITO, *and blocks* TEODORA'S *way.*)

SEVERO. Where are you going?

TEODORA (*desperately*). I want to see him.

PEPITO. It's impossible.

SEVERO. Don't let her in. Is that woman in my house! Quick — put her out, without pity. Immediately.

ERNESTO. What is he saying?

TEODORA. I am going mad!

SEVERO. Even if your mother shields her, you must obey my commands, son. If she begs — if she implores — if she weeps... Let her weep. (*With concentrated anger.*) Get her far away, or I shall kill her.

TEODORA. Are those Julian's orders?

PEPITO. Yes, Julian's!

ERNESTO. Her husband's? Impossible!

TEODORA. I must see him!

SEVERO. Well, you shall see him, and then leave this house.

PEPITO (*as though wishing to oppose him*). Father ——— !

SEVERO. Let me be!

TEODORA. It can't be true?

PEPITO. It's terrible.

TEODORA. A lie!

SEVERO. Come, Teodora... come and see!

> (*He seizes her by the arms, drags her to the door of* JULIAN's *room and points inside.*)

TEODORA. He! Julian! My dear Julian! Dead!

> (*She falls, fainting.*)

ERNESTO. Father!

> (*He hides his face. A pause.* SEVERO *watches them in anger.*)

SEVERO (*to his son*). Put her out!

PEPITO (*hesitating*). Señor ——— ?

SEVERO. I command it. Do you hesitate?

ERNESTO. Have some pity.

SEVERO. Pity. Yes. As she had for *him*.

ERNESTO. Oh, my blood boils! — I'll leave Spain.

SEVERO. Very well.

ERNESTO. I'll die!

SEVERO. Life is short.

ERNESTO. For the last time ———

SEVERO. No.

ERNESTO. She's innocent, I tell you. I swear she is.

PEPITO (*trying to intercede*). Father ———

SEVERO (*pointing scornfully at* ERNESTO). He lies.

ERNESTO. So you turn me out to sink or swim? Well, I won't struggle. I'll go with the current. What she will think of the world, and of the wrong you have done, I can't guess, for her lips are mute and her mind is asleep, but I am going to tell you what I think.

SEVERO. It's useless. (*Starting to go to* TEODORA.) You can't keep me from ——

PEPITO (*restraining him*). Father!

ERNESTO. No! (*A pause.*) Let no one come near this woman. She is mine. The world decreed it; I accept its judgment. I carry her away in my arms. Come, Teodora. (*He lifts her up.*) You turn her out of here! We obey!

SEVERO. At last. Scoundrel!

PEPITO. Rascal!

ERNESTO. Yes, I am all that! Now you are right. Now I admit it! Do you want passion? Well, here is passion, madness! Do you want love? Here is love immeasurable! Do you want more? Then I'll give more! I'm not afraid. You thought of the plot. I only pick up my cue! Now tell all about it, tell all about it. Waken the echoes with this fine bit of news! But if anyone asks you who was the infamous accomplice in this infamous affair, say to him, "You yourself; though you didn't know it. You and the tongues of other fools!" Come, Teodora, my mother's spirit is watching over you. Good-bye. She belongs to me now! And in due time may heaven judge between you and me!

CURTAIN

# ERDGEIST
## (EARTH–SPIRIT)

### A TRAGEDY IN FOUR ACTS

### By FRANK WEDEKIND

*Translated by SAMUEL A. ELIOT, JR.*

I was created out of ranker stuff
By Nature, and to the earth by Lust am drawn.
Unto the spirit of evil, not of good,
The earth belongs.   What deities send to us
From heaven are only universal goods;
Their light gives gladness, but makes no man rich;
And in their state possession not obtains.
Therefore, the stone of price, all-treasured gold,
Must from the powers of falsehood be enticed,
The evil race that dwells beneath the day.
Not without sacrifice their favor is gained,
And no man liveth who from serving them
Hath extricated undefiled his soul.

# FRANK WEDEKIND

THE father of Frank Wedekind was an ardent republican, a doctor of Hanover, who left Germany in '48 and settled in San Francisco. On a journey to Valparaiso he met a young German singer, married her, and after making a comfortable position returned to Germany in 1864. In this year Frank Wedekind was born. In 1872 his father purchased the old château of Lenzburg near Aaran; there the young man, who had been baptized Franklin and himself suppressed the last syllable of his given name, was well educated, but in a sketchy manner. He was a great reader, his interests always turning away from the social and political preoccupations of the time to problems of abnormal psychology. At various times, in Zurich, Paris, London and Munich, he engaged in a variety of activities, was a publicity man, the secretary of a circus, a contributor to *Simplicissimus*, in which rôle he was prosecuted for lèse majeste. Starting as a reciter in Switzerland under the name of Cornelius Minehaha, he made himself an actor in order to produce the effects that he required in his plays. His plays were early recognized among a narrow circle but it was only gradually that they came to production. For his later recognition he owes most to Albert Langen, founder of *Simplicissimus*, Karl Heine who first produced *Erdgeist* and *Die Kammersänger* at Leipzig, and particularly to Max Reinhardt who gave him consistent support. His play *Such is Life* is autobiographic. In 1906 *Frühlings Erwachen*, written fifteen years before, was first produced; in the same year he married Tilly Niemen the actress. He died in Munich in 1918.

WEDEKIND is sometimes mistakenly classed as a representative of the naturalistic movement. In fact he was one of the first to revolt against naturalism, not as a reactionary back to the older forms but as an innovator seeking to find new symbols for essentially contemporary values. He therefore takes his place beside Strindberg as one of the radical reformers of modern dramatic art. Among his plays none better represents his spirit than *Erdgeist*. Holding that naturalism is a hard mistress that makes us forget man he seeks for a moral symbolism by which the essential biological roots of humanity may be represented. Speaking for himself as dramatist in the person of an animal-trainer he reminds us that human society is not a mechanism. It is a domesticated zoo. To meet this conception he creates a new type of play drawing upon the unconscious and suppressed emotion and couched in broken and unrestrained speech. There is a quality of lyric moralism in Wedekind that goes back to his German compatriots Büchner and Grabbe. The present play *Erdgeist*, *Earth-Spirit*, is a part of a play written between 1892 and 1895 called *Die Büchse der Pandora*, *eine Monstretragödie* in five acts. On account of its length and the difficulties of censorship it was divided into two parts, the first part entitled *Earth-Spirit* after Goethe, the second, *The Box of Pandora*. In the first there was interpolated a new third act. To the second part two acts were introduced at the beginning. *Earth-Spirit* was produced for the first time at Leipzig in 1898; it was then produced by Max Reinhardt at Berlin in 1902. It was in the entr'actes of this production that an orchestra introduced the refrain "Ta-ra-ra-boom-de-ay." Wedekind insisted that the figure of Lulu was not a character. It was a symbol, an abstraction. Lulu is the personification of instinct who does evil without willing it. She is not a prostitute; she does not live from love; love is her life. The part has been variously played by many of the leading actresses of Germany, including Gertrude Eysoldt, Maria Orska, and Madame Tilly Wedekind. The second part of the play, *The Box of Pandora*, dealing with Lulu's downfall, was not permitted on the stage until after 1919.

# CHARACTERS

DR. SCHÖN, *newspaper owner and editor.*

ALVA, *his son, a writer.*

DR. GOLL, M.D.

SCHWARZ, *an artist.*

PRINCE ESCERNY, *an African explorer.*

ESCHERICH, *a reporter.*

SCHIGOLCH, *a beggar.*

RODRIGO, *an acrobat.*

HUGENBERG, *a schoolboy* (*played by a girl*).

FERDINAND, *a coachman.*

LULU.

COUNTESS GESCHWITZ.

HENRIETTE, *a servant.*

# PROLOGUE

*At rise, is seen the entrance to a tent, out of which steps an animal-tamer, with long, black curls, dressed in a white cravat, a vermilion dresscoat, white trousers and white topboots. He carries in his left hand a dog-whip and in his right a loaded revolver, and enters to the sound of cymbals and kettledrums.*

> Walk in!   Walk in to the menagery,
> Proud gentlemen and ladies lively and merry!
> With avid lust or cold disgust, the very
> Beast without Soul bound and made secondary
> To human genius, to stay and see!
> Walk in, the show'll begin! — As customary,
> One child to each two persons comes in free.

> Here battle man and brute in narrow cages
> Where one in haught disdain his long whip lashes
> And one, with growls as when the thunder rages,
> Against the man's throat murderously dashes —
> Where now the crafty conquers, now the strong,
> Now man, now beast, lies cowed the floor along;
> The animal rears — the human on all fours!
> One ice-cold look of dominance —
> The beast submissive bows before that glance,
> And the proud heel upon his neck adores.

> Bad are the times!   Ladies and gentlemen
> Who once before my cage in thronging crescents
> Crowded, now honor operas, and then
> Ibsen, with their so highly valued presence.
> My boarders here are so in want of fodder
> That they reciprocally devour each other.
> How well off at the theater is a player,
> Sure of the meat upon his ribs, albeit
> His frightful hunger may tear him and he it
> And colleagues' inner cupboards be quite bare! —

Greatness in art we struggle to inherit,
Although the salary never match the merit.

What see you, whether in light or sombre plays?
House-animals, whose morals all must praise,
Who wreak pale spites in vegetarian ways,
And revel in an easy cry or fret,
Just like those others — down in the parquet.
This hero has a head by one dram swirled;
That is in doubt whether his love be right;
A third you hear despairing of the world —
Full five acts long you hear him wail his plight,
And no man ends him with a merciful sleight!
But the real beast, the beautiful, wild beast,
Your eyes on that, *I*, ladies, only feast!

You see the Tiger, that habitually
Devours whatever falls before his bound;
The Bear, so ravenous originally,
Who at a late night-meal sinks dead to ground;
You see the Monkey, little and amusing,
From sheer ennui his petty powers abusing —
He has some talent, of all greatness scant,
So, impudently, coquettes with his own want!
Upon my soul, within my tent's a mammal,
See, right behind the curtain, here — a Camel!
And all my creatures fawn about my feet
When my revolver cracks —

                              (*He shoots into the audience.*)
                         Behold!
Brutes tremble all around me. I am cold:
The man stays cold — you, with respect, to greet.

Walk in! — You hardly trust yourselves in here? —
Then very well, judge for yourselves! Each sphere
Has sent its crawling creatures to your telling:
Chameleons and serpents, crocodiles,
Dragons, and salamanders chasm-dwelling —

I know, of course, you're full of quiet smiles
And don't believe a syllable I say.—

> *(He lifts the entrance-flap and calls into the tent.)*

Hi, Charlie! — bring our Serpent just this way!

*(A stage-hand with a big paunch carries out the actress of* LULU *in her Pierrot costume, and sets her down before the animal-tamer.)*

She was created to incite to sin,
To lure, seduce, poison — yea, murder, in
A manner no man knows.— My pretty beast,

> *(Tickling* LULU's *chin.)*

Only be unaffected, and not pieced
Out with distorted, artificial folly,
Even if the critics praise thee for 't less wholly.
Thou hast no right to spoil the shape most fitting,
Most true, of woman, with meows and spitting!
And mind, all foolery and making faces
The childish simpleness of Vice disgraces.
Thou shouldst — today I speak emphatically —
Speak naturally and not unnaturally,
  For the first principle in every art,
Since earliest times, was True and Plain, not Smart!

> *(To the public.)*

There's nothing special now to see in her,
But wait and watch what later will occur!
Her strength about the Tiger she coils stricter:
He roars and groans! — Who'll be the final victor? —
Hop, Charlie, march! Carry her to her place,

*(The stage-hand carries* LULU *in his arms; the animal-tamer pats her on the hips.)*

Sweet innocence — my dearest treasure-case!

> *(The stage-hand carries* LULU *back into the tent.)*

And now I'll tell the best thing in the day:
My poll between the teeth of a beast of prey!
Walk in! Though to be sure the show's not new,
Yet everyone takes pleasure in its view!

Wrench open this wild animal's jaws I dare,
And he to bite dares not! My pate's so fair,
So wild, so gaily decked, it wins respect!
I offer it him with confidence unchecked.
One joke, and my two temples crack! — but, lo,
The lightning of my eyes I will forego,
Staking my life against a joke! and throw
My whip, my weapons, down. I am in my skin!
I yield me to this beast! — His name do ye know?
— The honored public! that has just walked in!

(*The animal-tamer steps back into the tent, accompanied by cymbals and kettledrums.*)

## ACT I

*A roomy studio. Entrance door at the rear, left. Another door at lower left to the bedroom. At center, a platform for the model, with a Spanish screen behind it and a Smyrna rug in front. Two easels at lower right. On the upper one is the picture of a young girl's head and shoulders. Against the other leans a reversed canvas. Below these, toward center, an ottoman, with a tigerskin on it. Two chairs along the left wall. In the background, right, a stepladder.*

SCHÖN *sits on the foot of the ottoman, inspecting critically the picture on the further easel.* SCHWARZ *stands behind the ottoman, his palette and brushes in his hands.*

SCHÖN. Do you know, I'm getting acquainted with a brand new side of the lady.

SCHWARZ. I have never painted anyone whose expression changed so continuously. I could hardly keep a single feature the same two days running.

SCHÖN (*pointing to the picture and observing him*). Do you find that in it?

SCHWARZ. I have done everything imaginable to call forth some sort of quiet in her mood by my conversation during the sittings.

SCHÖN. Then I understand the difference. (SCHWARZ *dips his brush in the oil and draws it over the features of the face.*) Do you think that makes it look more like her?

SCHWARZ. We can only work with art as scientifically as possible.

SCHÖN. Tell me ——

SCHWARZ (*stepping back*). The color had sunk in pretty well, too.

SCHÖN (*looking at him*). Have you ever loved a woman in your life?

SCHWARZ (*goes to the easel, puts a color on it, and steps back on the other side*). The dress isn't made to stand out enough yet. We don't see the living body under it.

SCHÖN. I make no doubt that the workmanship is good.

SCHWARZ. If you'll step this way....

SCHÖN (*rising*). You must have told her regular ghost-stories.

SCHWARZ. As far back as you can.

SCHÖN (*stepping back, knocks down the canvas that was leaning against the lower easel*). Excuse me ——

SCHWARZ (*picking it up*). That's all right.

SCHÖN (*surprised*). What is that?

SCHWARZ. Do you know her?

SCHÖN. No.  (SCHWARZ *sets the picture on the easel. It is of a lady dressed as Pierrot with a long shepherd's crook in her hand.*)

SCHWARZ. A costume-picture.

SCHÖN. But, really, you've succeeded with her.

SCHWARZ. You know her?

SCHÖN. No.  And in that costume —— ?

SCHWARZ. It isn't nearly finished yet.  (SCHÖN *nods.*)  What would you have?  While she is posing for me I have the pleasure of entertaining her husband.

SCHÖN. What?

SCHWARZ. We talk about art, of course — to complete my good fortune!

SCHÖN. But how did you make such a charming acquaintance?

SCHWARZ. As they're generally made.  An ancient, tottering little man drops in on me here to know if I can paint his wife. Why, of course, were she as wrinkled as Mother Earth!  Next day at ten prompt the doors fly open, and the fat-belly drives this little beauty in before him.  I can feel even now how my knees shook.  Then comes a sap-green lackey, stiff as a ramrod, with a package under his arm.  Where is the dressing-room? Imagine my plight.  I open the door there (*pointing left*).  Just luck that everything was in order.  The sweet thing vanishes

into it, and the old fellow posts himself outside as a bastion.
Two minutes later out she steps in this Pierrot. (*Shaking his
head.*) I never saw anything like it.

(*He goes left and stares in at the bedroom.*)

SCHÖN (*who has followed him with his eyes*). And the fat-belly stands
guard?

SCHWARZ (*turning round*). The whole body in harmony with that
impossible costume as if it had come into the world in it!
Her way of burying her elbows in her pockets, of lifting her
little feet from the rug — the blood often shoots to my head....

SCHÖN. One can see that in the picture.

SCHWARZ (*shaking his head*). People like us, you know ——

SCHÖN. Here the model is mistress of the conversation.

SCHWARZ. She has never yet opened her mouth.

SCHÖN. Is it possible?

SCHWARZ. Allow me to show the costume to you. (*Goes out left.*)

SCHÖN (*before the Pierrot*). A devilish beauty. (*Before the other
picture.*) There's more depth here. (*Coming down stage.*) He
is still rather young for his age.

(SCHWARZ *comes back with a white satin costume.*)

SCHWARZ. What sort of material is that?

SCHÖN (*feeling it*). Satin.

SCHWARZ. And all in one piece.

SCHÖN. How does one get into it then?

SCHWARZ. That I can't tell you.

SCHÖN (*taking the costume by the legs*). What enormous trouser-legs!

SCHWARZ. The left one she pulls up.

SCHÖN (*looking at the picture*). Above the knee!

SCHWARZ. She does that entrancingly!

SCHÖN. And transparent stockings?

SCHWARZ. Those have got to be painted, specially.

SCHÖN. Oh, you can do that.

SCHWARZ. And with it all a coquetry!

SCHÖN. What brought you to that horrible suspicion?

SCHWARZ. There are things that our school-philosophy lets
itself never dream of.

(*He takes the costume back into his bedroom.*)

SCHÖN (*alone*). When we sleep....

SCHWARZ (*comes back; looks at his watch*). If you wish to make her acquaintance too ——

SCHÖN. No.

SCHWARZ. They must be here in a moment.

SCHÖN. How much longer will the lady have to sit?

SCHWARZ. I shall probably have to bear the pains of Tantalus three months longer.

SCHÖN. I mean the other one.

SCHWARZ. I beg your pardon. Three times more at most. (*Going to the door with him.*) If the lady will just leave me the upper part of the dress then....

SCHÖN. With pleasure. Let us see you at my house again soon. For Heaven's sake! (*As he collides in the doorway with* DR. GOLL *and* LULU.)

SCHWARZ. May I introduce...

DR. GOLL (*to* SCHÖN). What are you doing here?

LULU (*as* SCHÖN *kisses her hand in greeting*). You're not going already?

DR. GOLL. But what wind blows you here?

SCHÖN. I've been looking at the picture of my bride.

LULU (*coming forward*). Your bride is here?

DR GOLL. So you're having work done here, too?

LULU (*before the upper picture*). Look at it! Enchanting! Entrancing!

DR. GOLL (*looking round him*). Have you got her hidden somewhere round here?

LULU. So that is the sweet young prodigy who's made a new person out of you....

SCHÖN. She sits in the afternoon mostly.

DR. GOLL. And you don't tell anyone about it?

LULU (*turning round*). Is she really so solemn?

SCHÖN. Probably the after-effects of the seminary still, dear lady.

DR. GOLL (*before the picture*). One can see that you have been transformed profoundly.

LULU. But now you mustn't let her wait any longer.

SCHÖN. In a fortnight I think the engagement will come out.

DR. GOLL (*to* LULU). Let's lose no time. Hop!

LULU (*to* SCHÖN). Just think, we came at a trot over the new bridge. I was driving, myself.

DR. GOLL (*as* SCHÖN *prepares to leave*). No, no. We two will talk some more later. Get along, Nellie. Hop!

LULU. Now you're going to talk about me!

DR. GOLL. Our Apelles is already wiping his brushes.

LULU. I had imagined it would be much more amusing.

SCHÖN. But you have always the satisfaction of preparing for us the greatest and rarest pleasure.

LULU (*going left*). Oh, just wait!

SCHWARZ (*before the bedroom door*). If madame will be so kind....
(*Shuts the door after her and stands in front of it.*)

DR. GOLL. I christened her Nellie, you know, in our marriage-contract.

SCHÖN. Did you? — Yes.

DR. GOLL. What do you think of it?

SCHÖN. Why not call her rather Mignon?

DR. GOLL. That would have been good, too. I didn't think of that.

SCHÖN. Do you consider the name so important?

DR. GOLL. Hm.... You know, I have no children.

SCHÖN. But you've only been married a couple of months.

DR. GOLL. Thanks, I don't want any.

SCHÖN (*having taken out his cigarette-case*). Have a cigarette?

DR. GOLL (*helps himself*). I've plenty to do with this one. (*To* SCHWARZ.) Say, what's your little danseuse doing now?

SCHÖN (*turning round on* SCHWARZ). You and a danseuse?

SCHWARZ. The lady was sitting for me at that time only as a favor. I made her acquaintance on a flying trip of the Cecilia Society.

DR. GOLL (*to* SCHÖN). Hm.... I think we're getting a change of weather.

SCHÖN. The toilet isn't going so quickly, is it?

DR. GOLL. It's going like lightning! Woman has got to be a virtuoso in her job. So must we all, each in his job, if life isn't to turn to beggary. (*Calls.*) Hop, Nellie!

LULU (*inside*). Just a second!

DR. GOLL (*to* SCHÖN). I can't get onto these blockheads.
(*Referring to* SCHWARZ.)

SCHÖN. I can't help envying them. These blockheads know

nothing holier than an altar-cloth, and feel richer than you
and me with 30,000-mark incomes. Besides, you can't be
judge of a man who from childhood has lived from palette to
mouth. Try to get at his finances: it's an arithmetic example!
I haven't the moral courage, and one can easily burn one's
fingers at it, too.

LULU (*as Pierrot, steps out of the bedroom*). Here I am!

SCHÖN (*turns; after a pause*). Superb!

LULU (*nearer*). Well?

SCHÖN. You put shame on the boldest fancy.

LULU. How do you like me?

SCHÖN. A picture before which art must despair.

DR. GOLL. Don't you think so, too?

SCHÖN (*to* LULU). Have you any notion what you do?

LULU. I'm perfectly possessed of myself!

SCHÖN. Then you might be a little more discreet.

LULU. But I'm only doing what's my duty.

SCHÖN. You are powdered?

LULU. What do you take me for!

DR. GOLL. I've never seen such a white skin as she's got. I've
told our Raphael here, too, to do just as little with the flesh
tints as possible. For once, I can't get enthusiastic about the
modern art-nonsense.

SCHWARZ (*by the easels, preparing his paints*). At any rate, it's thanks
to impressionism that present-day art can stand up beside the
old masters without blushing.

DR. GOLL. Oh, it can do quite well for a bit of butcher's work.

SCHÖN. For Heaven's sake don't get excited!

(LULU *falls on* GOLL's *neck and kisses him.*)

DR. GOLL. They can see your undershirt. You must pull it
lower.

LULU. I would soonest have left it off. It only bothers me.

DR. GOLL. He should be able to paint it out.

LULU (*taking the shepherd's crook that leans against the Spanish screen,
and mounting the platform, to* SCHÖN). What would you say now,
if you had to stand at attention for two hours?

SCHÖN. I'd sell my soul to the devil for the chance to exchange
with you.

DR. GOLL (*sitting, left*). Come over here. Here is my post of observation.

LULU (*plucking her left trouser-leg up to the knee, to* SCHWARZ). So?

SCHWARZ. Yes....

LULU (*plucking it a thought higher*). So?

SCHWARZ. Yes, yes....

DR. GOLL (*to* SCHÖN *who has seated himself on the chair next him, with a gesture*). From this place I find her still more attractive.

LULU (*without stirring*). I beg pardon! I am equally attractive on all sides.

SCHWARZ (*to* LULU). The right knee further forward, please.

SCHÖN (*with a gesture*). The body does show finer lines perhaps.

SCHWARZ. The light today can be borne at least half way.

DR. GOLL. Oh, you must throw on lots of it! Hold your brush a bit longer.

SCHWARZ. Certainly, Dr. Goll.

DR. GOLL. Treat her as a piece of still-life.

SCHWARZ. Certainly, Doctor. (*To* LULU.) You used to hold your head a wee mite higher, Mrs. Goll.

LULU (*raising her head*). Paint my lips a little open.

SCHÖN. Paint snow on ice. If you get warm doing that, then instantly your art gets inartistic!

SCHWARZ. Certainly, Doctor.

DR. GOLL. Art, you know, must so reproduce nature that one can find at least some spiritual enjoyment in it!

LULU (*opening her mouth a little, to* SCHWARZ). So — look. I'll hold it half opened, so.

SCHWARZ. As soon as the sun comes, the wall opposite throws warm reflections in here.

DR. GOLL (*to* LULU). You must keep your position just as if our Velasquez here didn't exist at all.

LULU. Well, a painter isn't a man at all, anyway.

SCHÖN. I don't think you ought to judge the whole profession by just one famous exception.

SCHWARZ (*stepping back from the easel*). I should have liked to have had to hire a different studio last fall.

SCHÖN (*to* GOLL). What I wanted to ask you — have you seen the little Murphy girl yet as a Peruvian pearl-fisher?

DR. GOLL. I see her tomorrow for the fourth time. Prince Polossov took me. His hair has already got dark yellow again with delight.

SCHÖN. So you find her quite fabulous too.

DR. GOLL. Whoever wants to judge of that beforehand?

LULU. I think someone knocked.

SCHWARZ. Pardon me a moment. (*Goes and opens the door.*)

DR. GOLL (*to* LULU). You can safely smile at him with less bashfulness!

SCHÖN. He makes nothing of it.

DR. GOLL. And if he did! — What are we two sitting here for?

ALVA SCHÖN (*entering, still behind the Spanish screen*). May one come in?

SCHÖN. My son!

LULU. Oh! It's Mr. Alva!

DR. GOLL. Don't mind. Just come along in.

ALVA (*stepping forward, shakes hands with* SCHÖN *and* GOLL). Glad to see you. (*Turning toward* LULU.) Do I see a-right? Oh, if only I could engage you for my title part!

LULU. I don't think I could dance nearly well enough for your show!

ALVA. But you do have a dancing-master such as cannot be found on any stage in Europe.

SCHÖN. But what brings you here?

DR. GOLL. Maybe you're having somebody or other painted here, too, in secret!

ALVA (*to* SCHÖN). I wanted to take you to the dress rehearsal.

DR. GOLL (*as* SCHÖN *rises*). Do you have 'em dance today in full costume?

ALVA. Of course. Come along, too. In five minutes I must be on the stage. (*To* LULU.) Unfortunately.

DR. GOLL. I've forgotten — what's the name of your ballet?

ALVA. Dalailama.

DR. GOLL. I thought he was in a madhouse.

SCHÖN. You're thinking of Nietzsche, Doctor.

DR. GOLL. You're right; I got 'em mixed up.

ALVA. I have helped Buddhism to its legs.

DR. GOLL. By his legs is the stage-poet known.

ALVA. Corticelli dances the youthful Buddha as though she had seen the light of the world by the Ganges.

SCHÖN. So long as her mother lived, she danced with her legs.

ALVA. Then when she got free she danced with her intelligence.

DR. GOLL. Now she dances with her heart.

ALVA. If you'd like to see her —— ?

DR. GOLL. Thank you.

ALVA. Come along with us!

DR. GOLL. Impossible.

SCHÖN. Anyway, we have no time to lose.

ALVA. Come with us, doctor. In the third act you see Dalailama in his cloister, with his monks ——

DR. GOLL. The only thing I care about is the young Buddha.

ALVA. Well, what's hindering you?

DR. GOLL. I can't. I can't do it.

ALVA. We're going to Peter's, after it. There you can express your admiration.

DR. GOLL. Don't press it on me, please.

ALVA. You'll see the tame monkey, the two Brahmans, the little girls....

DR. GOLL. For heaven's sake, just keep away from me with your little girls!

LULU. Reserve one of the proscenium boxes for us on Monday, Mr. Alva.

ALVA. How could you doubt that I would, dear lady!

DR. GOLL. When I come back the whole picture will be spoilt on me.

ALVA. Well, it could be painted over.

DR. GOLL. If I don't explain to this Caravacci every stroke of his brush ——

SCHÖN. Your fears are unfounded, I think....

DR. GOLL. Next time, gentlemen!

ALVA. The Brahmans are getting impatient. The daughters of Nirvana are shivering in their tights.

DR. GOLL. Damned enchantment!

SCHÖN. They'll quarrel with us, if we don't bring you with us.

DR. GOLL. In five minutes I'll be with you. (*Stands down right, behind* SCHWARZ *and compares the picture with* LULU.)

ALVA (*to* LULU). Duty calls me, gracious lady!

DR. GOLL (*to* SCHWARZ). You must model it a bit more here. The hair is bad. You aren't paying enough attention to your business!

ALVA. Come on.

DR. GOLL. Now, just hop it! Ten horses will not drag me to Peter's.

SCHÖN (*following* ALVA *and* GOLL). We'll take my carriage. It's waiting downstairs. (*Exeunt.*)

SCHWARZ (*leans over to the right, and spits*). Pack! As if that were all of life! The bread-basket! — paunch and mug! My artist's soul boils. (*After a look at* LULU.) This company! — (*Gets up, goes up left, observes* LULU *from all sides, and sits again at his easel.*) It would be hard to choose between them. If I may request Mrs. Goll to raise the right hand a little higher.

LULU (*grasps the crook as high as she can reach; to herself*). Who would have thought that was possible!

SCHWARZ. I am quite ridiculous, you think?

LULU. He's coming right back.

SCHWARZ. I can do nothing but paint.

LULU. There he is!

SCHWARZ (*rising*). Well?

LULU. Don't you hear?

SCHWARZ. Someone is coming....

LULU. I knew it.

SCHWARZ. It's the janitor. He's sweeping the stairs.

LULU. Thank heaven!

SCHWARZ. Do you perhaps accompany the doctor to his patients?

LULU. Everything but that.

SCHWARZ. Because, you are not accustomed to being alone.

LULU. We have a housekeeper at home.

SCHWARZ. She keeps you company?

LULU. She has a lot of taste.

SCHWARZ. What for?

LULU. She dresses me.

SCHWARZ. Do you go much to balls?

LULU. Never.

SCHWARZ. Then what do you need the dresses for?

LULU. For dancing.

SCHWARZ. You really dance?

LULU. Czardas... Samaqueca... Skirt-dance.

SCHWARZ. Doesn't — that — disgust you, then?

LULU. You find me ugly?

SCHWARZ. You don't understand me. But who gives you lessons then?

LULU. Him.

SCHWARZ. Who?

LULU. Him.

SCHWARZ. He?

LULU. He plays the violin ——

SCHWARZ. Every day one learns something new of the world!

LULU. I learned in Paris. I took lessons from Eugenie Fougère. She let me copy her costumes, too.

SCHWARZ. What are they like?

LULU. A little green lace skirt to the knee, all in ruffles, low-necked, of course, very low-necked and awfully tight-laced. Bright green petticoat, then brighter and brighter. Snow-white underclothes with a hand's-breadth of lace....

SCHWARZ. I can no longer ——

LULU. Then paint!

SCHWARZ (*scraping the canvas*). Aren't you cold at all?

LULU. God forbid! No. What made you ask? Are you so cold?

SCHWARZ. Not today. No.

LULU. Praise God, one can breathe!

SCHWARZ. How so?... (LULU *takes a deep breath*.) Don't do that, please! (*Springs up, throws away his palette and brushes, walks up and down.*) The bootblack only attends to her feet! His color doesn't eat into his money, either. If I go without supper tomorrow, no little society lady will ask me if I know anything about oyster-patties!

LULU. Is he going out of his head?

SCHWARZ (*takes up his work again*). Whatever drove the fellow to this test!

LULU. I'd like it better, too, if he had stayed here.

SCHWARZ. We are truly the martyrs of our calling!

LULU. I didn't wish to cause you pain.

SCHWARZ (*hesitating, to* LULU). If you — the left trouser-leg — a little higher ——

LULU. Here?

SCHWARZ (*steps to the platform*). Permit me....

LULU. What do you want?

SCHWARZ. I'll show you.

LULU. You mustn't.

SCHWARZ. You are nervous... (*Tries to seize her hand.*)

LULU (*throws the crook in his face*). Let me alone! (*Hurries to the entrance door.*) You don't get me for a long time yet.

SCHWARZ. You can't understand a joke.

LULU. Oh, yes I can. I understand everything. Just you leave me be. You'll get nothing at all from me by force. Go to your work. You have no right to molest me. (*Flees behind the ottoman.*) Sit down behind your easel!

SCHWARZ (*trying to get around the ottoman*). As soon as I've punished you — you wayward, capricious ——

LULU. But you must have me, first! Go away. You can't catch me. In long clothes I'd have fallen into your clutches long ago — but in the Pierrot! ——

SCHWARZ (*throwing himself across the ottoman*). I've got you!

LULU (*hurls the tiger-skin over his head*). Good-night! (*Jumps over the platform and climbs up the stepladder.*) I can see away over all the cities of the earth.

SCHWARZ (*unrolling himself from the rug*). This old skin!!

LULU. I reach up into heaven, and stick the stars in my hair.

SCHWARZ (*clambering after her*). I'll shake it till you fall off!

LULU. If you don't stop, I'll throw the ladder down. (*Climbing higher.*) Will you let go of my legs? God save the Poles! (*Makes the ladder fall over, jumps onto the platform, and as* SCHWARZ *picks himself up from the floor, throws the Spanish screen down on his head. Hastening down-stage, by the easels.*) I told you that you weren't going to get me.

SCHWARZ (*coming forward*). Let us make peace. (*Tries to embrace her.*)

LULU. Keep away from me, or —— (*She throws the easel with the finished picture at him, so that both fall crashing to the floor.*)

SCHWARZ (*screams*). Merciful Heaven!

LULU (*up-stage, right*). You knocked the hole in it yourself!

SCHWARZ. I am ruined! Ten weeks' work, my journey, my exhibition! Now there is nothing more to lose! (*Plunges after her.*)

LULU (*springs over the ottoman, over the fallen stepladder, and over the platform, down-stage*). A grave! Don't fall into it! (*She stamps through the picture on the floor.*) She made a new man out of him!

(*Falls forward.*)

SCHWARZ (*stumbling over the Spanish screen*). I am merciless now!

LULU (*up-stage*). Leave me in peace now. I'm getting dizzy. O Gott! O Gott!...

(*Comes forward and sinks down on the ottoman. SCHWARZ locks the door; then seats himself next her, grasps her hand, and covers it with kisses — then pauses, struggling with himself. LULU opens her eyes wide.*)

LULU. He may come back.

SCHWARZ. How d'you feel?

LULU. As if I had fallen into the water....

SCHWARZ. I love you.

LULU. One time, I loved a student.

SCHWARZ. Nellie ——

LULU. With four-and-twenty scars ——

SCHWARZ. I love you, Nellie.

LULU. My name isn't Nellie. (SCHWARZ *kisses her.*) It's Lulu.

SCHWARZ. I would call you Eve.

LULU. Do you know what time it is?

SCHWARZ (*looking at his watch*). Half-past ten. (LULU *takes the watch and opens the case.*) You don't love me.

LULU. Yes I do.... It's five minutes after half-past ten.

SCHWARZ. Give me a kiss, Eve!

LULU (*takes him by the chin and kisses him. Throws the watch in the air and catches it.*) You smell of tobacco.

SCHWARZ. Why so distant?

LULU. It would be uncomfortable to ——

SCHWARZ. You're just making believe!

LULU. You're making believe yourself, it seems to me. *I* make believe? What makes you think that? I never needed to do that.

SCHWARZ (*rises, disconcerted, passing his hand over his forehead*). God in Heaven! The world is strange to me — !

LULU (*screams*). Only don't kill me!

SCHWARZ (*instantly whirling round*). Thou hast never yet loved!

LULU (*half raising herself*). You have never yet loved…!

DR. GOLL (*outside*). Open the door!

LULU (*already sprung to her feet*). Hide me! O God, hide me!

DR. GOLL (*pounding on the door*). Open the door!

LULU (*holding back* SCHWARZ *as he goes toward the door*). He will strike me dead!

DR. GOLL (*hammering*). Open the door!

LULU (*sunk down before* SCHWARZ, *gripping his knees*). He'll beat me to death! He'll beat me to death!

SCHWARZ. Stand up.…

> (*The door falls crashing into the studio.* DR. GOLL *with blood-shot eyes rushes upon* SCHWARZ *and* LULU, *brandishing his stick.*)

DR. GOLL. You dogs! You…!

> (*Pants, struggles for breath a few seconds, and falls headlong to the ground.* SCHWARZ's *knees tremble.* LULU *has fled to the door. Pause.*)

SCHWARZ. Mister — Doctor — Doc — Doctor Goll ——

LULU (*in the door*). Please, though, first put the studio in order.

SCHWARZ. Dr. Goll! (*Leans over.*) Doc —— (*Steps back.*) He's cut his forehead. Help me to lay him on the ottoman.

LULU (*shudders backward in terror*). No. No..

SCHWARZ (*trying to turn him over*). Dr. Goll.

LULU. He doesn't hear.

SCHWARZ. But you, help me, please.

LULU. The two of us together couldn't lift him.

SCHWARZ (*straightening up*). We must send for a doctor.

LULU. He is fearfully heavy.

SCHWARZ (*getting his hat*). Please, though, be so good as to put the place a little to rights while I'm away. (*He goes out.*)

LULU. He'll spring up all at once. (*Intensely.*) Bussi! He just won't notice anything. (*Comes down-stage in a wide circle.*) He sees my feet, and watches every step I take. He has his eye on me everywhere. (*Touches him with her toe.*) Bussi! (*Flinching, backward.*) It's serious with him. The dance is over. He'll send me to prison. What shall I do? (*Leans over, to the*

*floor*.)    A strange, wild face!    (*Getting up*.)    And no one to do
him the last services — isn't that sad!    (SCHWARZ *returns*.)

SCHWARZ. Still not come to himself?

LULU (*down right*). What shall I do?

SCHWARZ (*bending over* GOLL). Doctor Goll.

LULU. I almost think it's serious.

SCHWARZ. Talk decently!

LULU. He wouldn't say that to me.    He makes me dance for
him when he doesn't feel well.

SCHWARZ. The doctor will be here in a moment.

LULU. Doctoring won't help him.

SCHWARZ. But people do what they can, in such cases!

LULU. He doesn't think so.

SCHWARZ. Then won't you at least — get dressed?

LULU. Yes — right off.

SCHWARZ. What are you waiting for?

LULU. Please...

SCHWARZ. What is it?

LULU. Shut his eyes.

SCHWARZ. You make me shiver.

LULU. Not nearly so much as you make me!

SCHWARZ. I?

LULU. You're a born criminal.

SCHWARZ. Doesn't this moment touch you at all, then?

LULU. It hits me, too, some.

SCHWARZ. Please, just you keep still now!

LULU. It hits you some, too.

SCHWARZ. You really didn't need to say that to a man, in such a
moment.

LULU. Please... !

SCHWARZ. Do what you think necessary.    I don't know how.

LULU (*left of* GOLL). He's looking at me.

SCHWARZ (*right of* GOLL). And at me, too.

LULU. You're a coward!

SCHWARZ (*shuts* GOLL'*s eyes with his handkerchief*). It's the first time
in my life that anyone has called me that.

LULU. Didn't you do it to your mother?

SCHWARZ (*nervously*). No.

LULU. You were away, perhaps.

SCHWARZ. No!

LULU. Or else you were afraid?

SCHWARZ (*violently*). No!

LULU (*shivering, backward*). I didn't mean to insult you.

SCHWARZ. She's still alive.

LULU. Then you still have somebody.

SCHWARZ. She's as poor as a beggar.

LULU. I know what that is.

SCHWARZ. Don't laugh at me!

LULU. Now I am rich ——

SCHWARZ. It gives me cold shudders —— (*Goes right.*) She can't help it!

LULU (*to herself*). What'll I do?

SCHWARZ (*to himself*). Absolutely depraved! (*They look at each other mistrustfully.* SCHWARZ *goes over to her and grips her hand.*) Look me in the eyes!

LULU (*apprehensively*). What do you want?

SCHWARZ (*takes her to the ottoman and makes her sit next to him*). Look me in the eyes.

LULU. I see myself in them as Pierrot.

SCHWARZ (*shoves her from him*). Confounded dancer-ing!

LULU. I must change my clothes ——

SCHWARZ (*holds her back*). One question ——

LULU. I can't answer it.

SCHWARZ. Can you speak the truth?

LULU. I don't know.

SCHWARZ. Do you believe in a Creator?

LULU. I don't know.

SCHWARZ. Can you swear on anything?

LULU. I don't know. Leave me alone. You're mad.

SCHWARZ. What do you believe in, then?

LULU. I don't know.

SCHWARZ. Have you no soul, then?

LULU. I don't know.

SCHWARZ. Have you ever once loved —— ?

LULU. I don't know.

SCHWARZ (*gets up, goes right, to himself*). She doesn't know!

LULU (*without moving*). I don't know.
SCHWARZ (*glancing at* GOLL). He knows.
LULU (*nearer him*). What do you want to know?
SCHWARZ (*angrily*). Go, get dressed! (LULU *goes into the bedroom.
To* GOLL.) Would I could change with you, you dead man!
I give her back to you. I give my youth to you, too. I lack
the courage and the faith. I've had to wait patiently too long.
It's too late for me. I haven't grown up big enough for happiness. I have a hellish fear of it. Wake up! I didn't touch
her. He opens his mouth. Mouth open and eyes shut, like
the children. With me it's the other way round. Wake up,
wake up! (*Kneels down and binds his handkerchief round the dead
man's head.*) Here I beseech Heaven to make me able to be
happy — to give me the strength and the freedom of soul to be
just a weeny mite happy! For her sake, only for her sake.
    (LULU *comes out of the bedroom, completely dressed, her hat on,
    and her right hand under her left arm.*)
LULU (*raising her left arm, to* SCHWARZ). Would you hook me up
here? My hand trembles.

CURTAIN

# ACT II

*A very ornamental parlor. Entrance-door rear, left. Curtained en-
trances right and left, steps leading up to the right one. On the back wall
over the fireplace,* LULU's *picture as Pierrot in a magnificent frame. Right,
a tall mirror; a couch in front of it. Left, an ebony writing-table. Center,
a few chairs around a little Chinese table.*

LULU *stands motionless before the mirror, in a green silk morning-
dress. She frowns, passes a hand over her forehead, feels her cheeks, and
draws back from the mirror with a discouraged, almost angry, look.
Frequently turning round, she goes left, opens a casket on the writing-
table, lights herself a cigarette, looks for a book among those that are
lying on the table, takes one, and lies down on the couch opposite the mirror.
After reading a moment, she lets the book sink, and nods seriously to
herself in the glass; then resumes reading.* SCHWARZ *enters, left, palette*

*and brushes in hand, and bends over* LULU, *kisses her on the forehead, and goes up the steps, right.*

SCHWARZ (*turning in the doorway*). Eve!

LULU (*smiling*). At your orders?

SCHWARZ. Seems to me you look extra charming today.

LULU (*with a glance at the mirror*). Depends on what you expect.

SCHWARZ. Your hair breathes out a morning freshness....

LULU. I've just come out of the water.

SCHWARZ (*approaching her*). I've an awful lot to do today.

LULU. That's what you say to yourself.

SCHWARZ (*lays his palette and brushes down on the carpet, and sits on the edge of the couch*). What are you reading?

LULU (*reads*). "Suddenly she heard an anchor of refuge come nodding up the stairs."

SCHWARZ. Who under the sun writes so absorbingly?

LULU (*reading*). "It was the postman with a money-order." (HENRIETTE, *the servant, comes in, upper left, with a hat-box on her arm and a little tray of letters which she puts on the table.*)

HENRIETTE. The mail. I'm going to take your hat to the milliner, madam. Anything else?

LULU. No. (SCHWARZ *signs to her to go out, which she does, slyly smiling.*)

SCHWARZ. What was it you dreamt all last night?

LULU. You've asked me that twice already, today.

SCHWARZ (*rises, takes up the letters*). I tremble for news. Every day I fear the world may go to pieces. (*Giving* LULU *a letter.*) For you.

LULU (*sniffs at the paper*). Madame Corticelli. (*Hides it in her bosom.*)

SCHWARZ (*skimming a letter*). My Samaqueca-dancer sold — for fifty thousand marks!

LULU. Who says that?

SCHWARZ. Sedelmeier in Paris. That's the third picture since our marriage. I hardly know how to save myself from my luck!

LULU (*pointing to the letters*). There are more there.

SCHWARZ (*opening an engagement announcement*). See.

(*Gives it to* LULU.)

LULU (*reads*). Sir Henry von Zarnikow has the honor to announce the engagement of his daughter, Charlotte Marie Adelaide, to Doctor Ludwig Schön.

SCHWARZ (*as he opens another letter*). At last!  He's been an eternal
   while evading a public engagement.  I can't understand it —
   a man of his standing and influence.  What can be in the way
   of his marriage?

LULU.  What is that you're reading?

SCHWARZ.  An invitation to take part in the international exhibition at St. Petersburg.  I have no idea what to paint for it.

LULU.  Some entrancing girl or other, of course.

SCHWARZ.  Will you be willing to pose for it?

LULU.  God knows there are other pretty girls enough in existence!

SCHWARZ.  But with any other model — though she be as racy as
   hell — I can't get such a full display of my powers.

LULU.  Then I must, I suppose.  Wouldn't it go as well lying down?

SCHWARZ.  Really, I'd liefest have your taste arrange it for me.
   (*Folding up the letters.*)  Don't let's forget to congratulate Schön
   today, anyway.

               (*Goes left and shuts the letters in the writing-table.*)

LULU.  But we did that a long time ago.

SCHWARZ.  For his bride's sake.

LULU.  You can write to him again if you want.

SCHWARZ.  And now to work!  (*Takes up his brushes and palette,
   kisses* LULU, *goes up the steps, right, and turns around in the doorway.*)
   Eve!

LULU (*lets her book sink, smiling*).  Your pleasure?

SCHWARZ (*approaching her*).  I feel every day as if I were seeing
   you for the very first time.

LULU.  You're a terror.

SCHWARZ.  The fault is yours.

           (*He sinks on his knees by the couch and caresses her hand.*)

LULU (*stroking his hair*).  You're wasting me.

SCHWARZ.  You are mine.  But you are never more ensnaring
   than when you ought for God's sake to be, just once, real
   ugly for a couple of hours!  Since I've had you, I have had
   nothing more.  I'm entirely lost to myself.

LULU.  Not so excited!                        (*Bell rings in the corridor.*)

SCHWARZ (*pulling himself together*).  Confound it!

LULU.  No one at home!

SCHWARZ.  Perhaps it's the art-dealer ——

LULU. And if it's the Chinese Emperor!

SCHWARZ. One moment.                                    (*Exit.*)

LULU (*visionary*). Thou?    Thou?                    (*Closes her eyes.*)

SCHWARZ (*coming back*). A beggar, who says he was in the war.
  I have no small change on me. (*Taking up his palette and brushes.*)
  It's high time, too, that I should finally go to work.

                                                (*Goes out, right.*)

(LULU *touches herself up before the glass, strokes back her hair, and goes
  out, returning leading in* SCHIGOLCH.)

SCHIGOLCH. I'd thought he was more of a swell — a little more
  glory to him.  He's sort of embarrassed.  He quaked a little
  in the knees when he saw me in front of him.

LULU (*shoving a chair round for him*). How can you beg from him,
  too?

SCHIGOLCH. That's why I've dragged my seventy-seven summers
  just here.  You told me he kept at his painting in the mornings.

LULU. He hadn't got quite awake yet.  How much do you need?

SCHIGOLCH. Two hundred, if you have that much handy.  Personally, I'd like three hundred.  Some of my clients have
  evaporated.

LULU (*goes to the writing-table and rummages in the drawer*). Whew,
  I'm tired!

SCHIGOLCH (*looking round him*). That's just what brought me, too.
  I've been wanting a long time to see how things were looking
  now with you.

LULU. Well?

SCHIGOLCH. It just sweeps over you.    (*Looking up.*)  Like with me
  fifty years ago.  Devil, but you've brought it pretty far!
  (*Scuffing.*) Carpets....

LULU (*giving him two bills*). I like best to walk on them barefooted.

SCHIGOLCH (*scanning* LULU'S *portrait*). Is that you?

LULU (*winking*). Pretty fine?

SCHIGOLCH. If all that's genuine.

LULU. Have something sweet?

SCHIGOLCH. What?

LULU (*getting up*). Elixir de Spaa.

SCHIGOLCH. That doesn't help me —— Does he drink?

LULU (*taking a decanter and glasses from a cupboard near the fireplace*).

Not yet.    (*Coming down-stage.*)    The cordial has such various
effects!

SCHIGOLCH.  He comes to blows?

LULU.  He goes to sleep.          (*She fills the two glasses.*)

SCHIGOLCH.  When he's drunk, you can see right into his insides.

LULU.  I'd rather not.  (*Sits opposite* SCHIGOLCH.)   Tell me about it.

SCHIGOLCH.  The streets keep on getting longer, and my legs
shorter.

LULU.  And your harmonica?

SCHIGOLCH.  Has bad air, like me with my asthma.  I just keep
a-thinking it isn't worth the trouble to make it better.

(*They clink glasses.*)

LULU (*emptying her glass*).  I thought you'd come to an end a long
time ago ——

SCHIGLOCH.  To an end — already up and away?   I thought so,
too.   But no matter how early the sun goes down, still we
aren't let lie quiet.   I'm hoping for winter.   Perhaps then my
(*coughing*) — my — my asthma will invent some opportunity
to carry me off.

LULU (*filling the glasses*).  Do you think they could have forgotten
you on the other side?

SCHIGOLCH.  Would be possible, for it certainly isn't going like it
usually does.   (*Stroking her knee.*)   Now you tell — not seen
you a long time — my little Lulu.

LULU (*jerking back, smiling*).  Life is beyond me!

SCHIGOLCH.  What do you know about it?   You're still so young!

LULU.  That you call me Lulu.

SCHIGOLCH.  Lulu, isn't it?  Have I ever called you anything else?

LULU.  In the memory of man my name has no longer been Lulu.

SCHIGOLCH.  Another way of naming?

LULU.  Lulu sounds to me quite ante-diluvian.

SCHIGOLCH.  Children!  Children!

LULU.  My name now is ——

SCHIGOLCH.  As if the principle wasn't always the same!

LULU.  You mean —— ?

SCHIGOLCH.  What is it now?

LULU.  Eve.

SCHIGOLCH.  Lept, hopped, skipped, jumped....

LULU. I'm listening.

SCHIGOLCH (*gazing round*). This is the way I dreamt of it for you. You've aimed straight for it. (*Seeing* LULU *sprinkling herself with perfume.*) What's that?

LULU. Heliotrope.

SCHIGOLCH. Does that smell better than you?

LULU (*sprinkling him*). That needn't bother you any more.

SCHIGOLCH. Who would have dreamt of this royal luxury before!

LULU. When I think back — Ugh!

SCHIGOLCH (*stroking her knee*). How's it going with you, then? You still keep at the French?

LULU. I lie and sleep.

SCHIGOLCH. That's genteel. That always looks like something. And afterwards?

LULU. I stretch — till it cracks.

SCHIGOLCH. And when it has cracked?

LULU. What do you mind about that?

SCHIGOLCH. What do I mind about that? What do I mind? I'd rather live till the last trump and renounce all heavenly joys than leave my Lulu deprived of anything down here behind me. What do I mind about that? It's my sympathy. To be sure, my better self is already transfigured — but I still have some sense for this world.

LULU. I haven't.

SCHIGOLCH. You're too well off.

LULU (*shuddering*). Idiot....

SCHIGOLCH. Better than with the old dancing-bear?

LULU (*sadly*). I don't dance any more.

SCHIGOLCH. For him it was time, too.

LULU. Now I am —— (*Stops.*)

SCHIGOLCH. Speak how it is with you, child! I believed in you when there was no more to be seen in you than your two big eyes. What are you now?

LULU. A beast....

SCHIGOLCH. That you —— ! And what kind of a beast? A fine beast! An elegant beast! A glorified beast! Then I'll let them bury me. We're through with prejudices — even with the one against the corpse-washer.

LULU. You needn't be afraid that you will be washed once more.

SCHIGOLCH. Doesn't matter, either. One gets dirty again.

LULU (*sprinkling him*). It would call you back to life again!

SCHIGOLCH. We are mud.

LULU. I beg your pardon! I rub grease into myself every day and then powder on top of it.

SCHIGOLCH. Probably worth while, too, on the dressed-up mucker's account.

LULU. It makes the skin like satin.

SCHIGOLCH. As if it weren't just dirt all the same!

LULU. Thank you. I wish to be worth biting at!

SCHIGOLCH. We are. Give a big dinner down below there pretty soon. Keep open house.

LULU. Your guests will hardly overeat themselves at it.

SCHIGOLCH. Patience, girl! Your worshippers won't put you in alcohol, either. It's "schöne Melusine" as long as things go well. Afterwards? (*Rising.*)

LULU (*getting up*). Have you had enough?

SCHIGOLCH. There's still enough left over to plant a juniper on my grave. I'll find my own way out. (*Exit.* LULU *follows him, and presently returns with* DR. SCHÖN.)

SCHÖN. What's your father doing here?

LULU. What's the matter?

SCHÖN. If I were your husband that man would never come over my threshold.

LULU. You can speak intimately. He's not here. (*Referring to* SCHWARZ.)

SCHÖN. Thank you, I'd rather not.

LULU. I don't understand.

SCHÖN. I know that. (*Offering her a seat.*) I should like to speak with you on that very subject.

LULU (*sitting down uncertainly*). Why didn't you tell me so yesterday, then?

SCHÖN. Please, nothing now about yesterday. I did tell you two years ago.

LULU (*nervously*). Oh, yes — Hm!

SCHÖN. Please be kind enough to cease your visits to my house.

LULU. May I offer you an elixir ——

SCHÖN. Thanks. No elixir. Have you understood me? (LULU *shakes her head.*) Good. You have the choice. You force me to the most extreme measures: — either act in accordance with your station ——

LULU. Or?

SCHÖN. Or — you compel me — I should have to turn to that person who is responsible for your behavior.

LULU. What makes you imagine that?

SCHÖN. I shall request your husband, himself to watch over your ways. (LULU *rises, goes up the steps, right.*) Where are you going?

LULU (*calls through the curtains*). Walter!

SCHÖN (*springing up*). Are you mad?

LULU (*turning round*). Aha!

SCHÖN. I have made the most superhuman efforts to raise you in society. You can be ten times as proud of your name as of your intimacy with me.

LULU (*comes down the steps and puts her arm around* SCHÖN's *neck*). Why are you still afraid, now that you're at the zenith of your hopes?

SCHÖN. No comedy! The zenith of my hopes? I am at last engaged: I have now the hope of bringing my bride into a clean house.

LULU (*sitting*). She has developed delightfully in the two years!

SCHÖN. She no longer looks through one so earnestly.

LULU. She is now, for the first time, a woman. We can meet each other wherever it seems suitable to you.

SCHÖN. We shall meet each other nowhere but in the presence of your husband!

LULU. You don't believe yourself what you say.

SCHÖN. Then he must believe it. Go on and call him! Through his marriage to you, through all that I've done for him, he has become my friend.

LULU (*rising*). Mine, too.

SCHÖN. Then I'll cut down the sword over my head.

LULU. You have, indeed, chained me up. But I owe my happiness to you. You will get friends by the crowd as soon as you have a pretty young wife again.

schön. You judge women by yourself! He's got the sense of a child or he would have tracked out your doublings and windings long ago.

lulu. I only wish he would! Then, at last he'd get out of his swaddling-clothes. He puts his trust in the marriage contract he has in his pocket. Trouble is past and gone. One can now give oneself and let oneself go as if one were at home. That isn't the sense of a child! It's banal! He has no education; he sees nothing; he sees neither me nor himself; he is blind, blind, blind....

schön (*half to himself*). When his eyes open!!

lulu. Open his eyes for him! I'm going to ruin. I'm neglecting myself. He doesn't know me at all. What am I to him? He calls me darling and little devil. He would say the same to any piano-teacher. He makes no pretensions. Everything is all right, to him. That comes from his never in his life having felt the need of intercourse with women.

schön. If that's true!

lulu. He admits it perfectly openly.

schön. A man who has painted them, rags and tags and velvet gowns, since he was fourteen.

lulu. Women make him anxious. He trembles for his health and comfort. But he isn't afraid of me!

schön. How many girls would deem themselves God knows how blessed in your situation.

lulu (*softly pleading*). Seduce him. Corrupt him. You know how. Take him into bad company — you know the people. I am nothing to him but a woman, just woman. He makes me feel so ridiculous. He will be prouder of me. He doesn't know any differences. I'm thinking my head off, day and night, how to shake him up. In my despair I dance the can-can. He yawns; and drivels something about obscenity.

schön. Nonsense. He is an artist, though.

lulu. At least he believes he is.

schön. That's the chief thing!

lulu. When *I* pose for him.... He believes, too, that he's a famous man.

schön. We have made him one.

LULU. He believes everything. He's as mistrustful as a thief, and lets himself be lied to, till one loses all respect! When we first knew each other I informed him I had never yet loved — (SCHÖN *falls into an easy-chair.*) Otherwise he would really have taken me for a fallen woman!

SCHÖN. You make God knows what exorbitant demands on legitimate relations!

LULU. I make no exorbitant demands. Often I even dream still of Goll.

SCHÖN. He was, at any rate, not banal!

LULU. He is there, as if he had never been away. Only he walks as though in his socks. He isn't angry with me; he's awfully sad. And then he is fearful, as though he were there without the permission of the police. Otherwise, he feels at ease with us. Only he can't quite get over my having thrown away so much money since —

SCHÖN. You yearn for the whip once more?

LULU. Maybe. I don't dance any more.

SCHÖN. Teach him to do it.

LULU. A waste of trouble.

SCHÖN. Out of a hundred women, ninety educate their husbands to suit themselves.

LULU. He loves me.

SCHÖN. That's fatal, of course.

LULU. He loves me ——

SCHÖN. That is an unbridgeable abyss.

LULU. He doesn't know me, but he loves me! If he had anything like a correct idea of me, he'd tie a stone around my neck and sink me in the sea where it's deepest.

SCHÖN. Let's finish this!                    (*He gets up.*)

LULU. As you say.

SCHÖN. I've married you off. Twice I have married you off. You live in luxury. I've created a position for your husband. If that doesn't satisfy you, and he laughs in his sleeve at it, I don't pretend to meet ideal claims; but — leave me out of the game, out of it!

LULU (*resolutely*). If I belong to any person on this earth, I belong to you. Without you I'd be — I won't say where. You took me by the hand, gave me food to eat, had me dressed — when I was going to steal your watch. Do you think that can be forgotten? Anybody else would have called the police. You sent me to school, and had me learn manners. Who but you in the whole world has ever thought anything of me? I've danced and posed, and was glad to be able to earn my living that way. But love at command, I can't!

SCHÖN (*raising his voice*). Leave me out! Do what you will. I'm not coming to make scandal; I'm coming to shake the scandal from my neck. My engagement is costing me sacrifices enough! I had imagined that with a healthy young man, than whom a woman of your years can wish herself no better, you would, at last, have been contented. If you are under obligations to me, don't throw yourself a third time in my way! Am I to wait yet longer before putting my pile in security? Am I to risk the whole success of my patents falling into the water again after two years? What good is it to me to be your married-man, when you can be seen going in and out of my house at every hour of the day? Why the devil didn't Dr. Goll stay alive just one year more! With him you were in safe keeping. Then I'd have had my wife long since under my roof!

LULU. And what would you have had then? The kid gets on your nerves. The child is too uncorrupted for you. She's been much too carefully brought up. What should I have against your marriage? But you are deceived about yourself if you think that on account of your impending marriage you may express your contempt to me.

SCHÖN. Contempt? If anything is contemptible, it's your intrigues!

LULU (*laughing*). Am I jealous of the child? That never once entered my head.

SCHÖN. Then why talk about the child? The child is not even a whole year younger than you are. Leave me my freedom to live what life I still have. No matter how the child's been brought up, she's got her five senses just like you....

(SCHWARZ *appears, right, brush in hand.*)

SCHWARZ. What's the matter here?

LULU (*to* SCHÖN). Well? Go on. Talk.

SCHWARZ. What's the matter with you two?

LULU. Nothing that touches you ——

SCHÖN (*sharply*). Quiet!

LULU. He's had enough of me.

(SCHWARZ *leads her off, to the right.*)

SCHÖN (*turning over the leaves in one of the books on the table*). It had to come out — I must have my hands free at last!

SCHWARZ (*coming back*). Is that a way to jest?

SCHÖN (*pointing to a chair*). Please.

SCHWARZ. What is it?

SCHÖN. Please.

SCHWARZ (*seating himself*). Well?

SCHÖN (*seating himself*). You have married half a million....

SCHWARZ. Explain to me the peculiar scene....

SCHÖN. You have married half a million ——

SCHWARZ. No one can make a crime of that.

SCHÖN. You have created a name for yourself. You can work unmolested. You need to deny yourself no wish ——

SCHWARZ. What have you two got against me?

SCHÖN. For six months you've been revelling in all the heavens. You have a wife whom the world envies you, and she deserves a man whom she can respect ——

SCHWARZ. Doesn't she respect me?

SCHÖN. No.

SCHWARZ (*depressed*). I come from the dark depths of society. She is above me. I cherish no more ardent wish than to become her equal. (*Offers* SCHÖN *his hand.*) Thank you.

SCHÖN (*pressing it, half embarrassed*). Don't mention it.

SCHWARZ (*with determination*). Speak!

SCHÖN. Keep a little more watch on her.

SCHWARZ. I — on her?

SCHÖN. We are not children! We don't trifle! She demands that she be taken seriously. Her value gives her a perfect right to be.

SCHWARZ. What does she do, then?

SCHÖN. You have married half a million!

SCHWARZ (*rises; beside himself*). She ——?

SCHÖN (*takes him by the shoulder*). No, that's not the way! (*Forces *him to sit.*)   We must speak with each other very seriously here.

SCHWARZ.  What does she do?

SCHÖN.  First count on your fingers what you have to thank her for, and then ——

SCHWARZ.  What does she do — man!!

SCHÖN.  And then make yourself responsible for your faults, and no one else.

SCHWARZ.  With whom?  With whom?

SCHÖN.  If we should shoot each other ——

SCHWARZ.  Since when, then?

SCHÖN (*evasive*).  — I don't come here to make scandal, I come to save you from the scandal.

SCHWARZ.  You have misunderstood her.

SCHÖN (*embarrassed*).  That will not do for me.  I can't see you go on living in blindness.  The girl deserves to be a respectable woman.  Since I have known her she has improved as she developed.

SCHWARZ.  Since you have known her?  Since when have you known her then?

SCHÖN.  Since about her twelfth year.

SCHWARZ (*bewildered*).  She told me nothing about that.

SCHÖN.  She sold flowers in front of the Alhambra Café.  Every evening between twelve and two she pressed in among the guests, bare-footed.

SCHWARZ.  She told me nothing of that.

SCHÖN.  She did right there.  I'm telling you, so you may see that you have not to do with moral degeneracy.  The girl is, on the contrary, of extraordinarily good disposition.

SCHWARZ.  She said she had grown up with an aunt.

SCHÖN.  That was the woman I gave her to.  She was her best pupil.  The mothers used to make her an example to their children.  She has the feeling for duty.  It is simply and solely your mistake if you have till now neglected to take her on her best sides.

SCHWARZ (*sobbing*).  O God! ——

SCHÖN (*with emphasis*).  No O God!!  Nothing of the happiness you have cost can be changed.  Done is done.  You over-rate yourself against your better knowledge if you persuade yourself you will lose. You stand to gain. But with "O God" nothing is gained. A greater friendliness I have not yet shown you: I speak plainly and offer you my help. Don't show yourself unworthy of it!

SCHWARZ (*from now on more and more broken up*). When I first knew her, she told me she had never loved.

SCHÖN. When a widow says that ——! It does her credit that she chose you for a husband. Make the same claims on yourself and your happiness is without a blot.

SCHWARZ. She says he made her wear short dresses.

SCHÖN. But he married her! That was her master-stroke. How she brought the man to it is beyond me. You really must know it now: you are enjoying the fruits of her diplomacy.

SCHWARZ. How did she get to know Dr. Goll then?

SCHÖN. Through me! It was after my wife's death, when I was making the first advances to my present fiancée. She stuck herself in between. She had fixed her mind on becoming my wife.

SCHWARZ (*as if seized with a horrible suspicion*). And then when her husband died?

SCHÖN. You married half a million!!

SCHWARZ (*wailing*). O, to have stayed where I was! To have died of hunger!

SCHÖN (*superior*). Do you think, then, that *I* make no compromises? Who is there that does not compromise? You have married half a million. You are today one of the foremost artists. That can't be done without money. You are not the man to sit in judgment on her. You can't possibly treat an origin like Mignon's according to the notions of bourgeois society.

SCHWARZ (*quite distraught*). Who are you speaking of?

SCHÖN. Of her father! You're an artist, I say: your ideals are on a different plane from those of a wage-worker.

SCHWARZ. I don't understand a word of all that.

SCHÖN. I am speaking of the inhuman conditions out of which, thanks to her good management, the girl has developed into what she is!

SCHWARZ. Who?

SCHÖN. Who? Your wife.

SCHWARZ. Eve?

SCHÖN. I called her Mignon.

SCHWARZ. I thought her name was Nellie?

SCHÖN. Dr. Goll called her so.

SCHWARZ. I called her Eve ——

SCHÖN. What her real name is I don't know.

SCHWARZ (*absently*). Perhaps she knows.

SCHÖN. With a father like hers, she is, with all her faults, a miracle. I don't understand you ——

SCHWARZ. He died in a madhouse ——?

SCHÖN. He was here just now!

SCHWARZ. Who was here?

SCHÖN. Her father.

SCHWARZ. Here — in my house?

SCHÖN. He squeezed by me as I came in. And there are the two glasses still.

SCHWARZ. She says he died in the madhouse.

SCHÖN. Let her feel she's in authority —! She craves nothing but the compulsion to unconditional obedience. With Dr. Goll she was in heaven, and with him there was no joking.

SCHWARZ (*shaking his head*). She said she had never loved ——

SCHÖN. But you, make a beginning with yourself. Pull yourself together!

SCHWARZ. She has sworn ——!

SCHÖN. You can't demand a sense of duty in her before you know your own task.

SCHWARZ. By her mother's grave!

SCHÖN. She never knew her mother, let alone the grave. Her mother hasn't got a grave.

SCHWARZ. I don't fit in society.          (*He is in desperation.*)

SCHÖN. What's the matter?

SCHWARZ. Pain — horrible pain!

SCHÖN (*gets up, steps back; after a pause*). Guard her for yourself: she's yours. The moment is decisive. Tomorrow she may be lost to you.

SCHWARZ (*pointing to his breast*). Here, here.

SCHÖN. You have married half — (*Reflecting.*) She is lost to you if you let this moment slip!

SCHWARZ. If I could weep! Oh, if I could cry out!

SCHÖN (*with a hand on his shoulder*). You're suffering ——

SCHWARZ (*getting up, apparently quiet*). You are right, quite right.

SCHÖN (*gripping his hand*). Where are you going?

SCHWARZ. To speak with her.

SCHÖN. Right! (*Accompanies him to the door, left. Coming back.*) That was tough work. (*After a pause, looking right.*) He had taken her into the studio before though? (*A fearful groan, left. He hurries to the door and finds it locked.*) Open! Open the door!

LULU (*stepping through the hangings, right*). What's ——

SCHÖN. Open it!

LULU (*comes down the steps*). That is horrible.

SCHÖN. Have you an ax in the kitchen?

LULU. He'll open it right off ——

SCHÖN. I can't kick it down.

LULU. When he's had his cry out.

SCHÖN (*kicking the door*). Open! (*To Lulu.*) Bring me an ax.

LULU. Send for the doctor ——

SCHÖN. You are not yourself.

LULU. It serves you right.

> (*Bell rings in the corridor. SCHÖN and LULU stare at each other. Then SCHÖN slips up-stage and stands in the doorway.*)

SCHÖN. I mustn't let myself be seen here.

LULU. Perhaps it's the art-dealer. (*The bell rings again.*)

SCHÖN. But if we don't answer it ——

LULU. (*Steals toward the door; but SCHÖN holds her.*) ——

SCHÖN. Stop. It sometimes happens that one is not just at hand —— (*He goes out on tip-toes. LULU turns back to the locked door and listens. SCHÖN returns with ALVA.*) Please be quiet.

ALVA (*very excited*). A revolution has broken out in Paris!

SCHÖN. Be quiet.

ALVA (*to Lulu*). You're as pale as death.

SCHÖN (*rattling at the door*). Walter! Walter!

> (*A death-rattle heard behind the door.*)

LULU. God pity you.

SCHÖN. Haven't you brought an ax?

LULU. If there's one there —— *(Goes slowly out, upper left.)*

ALVA. He's just keeping us in suspense.

SCHÖN. A revolution has broken out in Paris?

ALVA. In the editors' room they're beating their heads against the wall. No one knows what he ought to write.

*(The bell rings in the corridor.)*

SCHÖN *(kicking against the door)*. Walter!

ALVA. Shall I force it in?

SCHÖN. I can do that. Who is it coming now? *(Standing up.)* To enjoy life and let others be responsible for it ——

LULU *(coming back with a kitchen ax)*. Henriette has come home.

SCHÖN. Shut the door behind you.

ALVA. Give it here.

*(Takes the ax and pounds with it between the jamb and the lock.)*

SCHÖN. You must hold it nearer the end.

ALVA. It's cracking ——

*(The lock gives; ALVA lets the ax fall and staggers back.)    (Pause.)*

LULU *(to SCHÖN pointing to the door.)* After you. *(SCHÖN flinches, drops back.)* Are you getting — dizzy?

*(SCHÖN wipes the sweat from his forehead and goes in.)*

ALVA *(from the couch)*. Ghastly!

LULU *(stopping in the door-way, finger on lips, cries out sharply)*. Oh! Oh! *(Hurries to ALVA.)* I can't stay here.

ALVA. Horrible!

LULU *(taking his hand)*. Come.

ALVA. Where to?

LULU. I can't be alone. *(Goes out with ALVA, right.)*

*(SCHÖN comes back, a bunch of keys in his hand, which shows blood. He pulls the door to, behind him, goes to the writing-table, opens it, and writes two notes.)*

ALVA *(coming back, right)*. She's changing her clothes.

SCHÖN. She has gone?

ALVA. To her room. She's changing her clothes.

*(SCHÖN rings. HENRIETTE comes in.)*

SCHÖN. You know where Dr. Bernstein lives?

HENRIETTE. Of course, Doctor. Right next door.

SCHÖN *(giving her one note)*. Take that over to him, please.

HENRIETTE. In case the doctor is not at home?

SCHÖN. He is at home. (*Giving her the other note.*) And take this
   to police headquarters. Take a cab. (HENRIETTE *goes out.*)
   I am judged!

ALVA. My blood is cold.

SCHÖN (*toward the left*). The fool!

ALVA. He waked up to something, perhaps?

SCHÖN. He has been too absorbed with himself.

   (LULU *appears on the steps, right, in dust-coat and hat.*)

ALVA. Where are you going now?

LULU. Out. I see it on all the walls.

SCHÖN. Where are his papers?

LULU. In the desk.

SCHÖN (*at the desk*). Where?

LULU. Lower right-hand drawer. (*She kneels and opens the drawer,*
   *emptying the papers on the floor.*) Here. There is nothing to fear.
   He had no secrets.

SCHÖN. Now I can just withdraw from the world.

LULU (*still kneeling*). Write a pamphlet about him. Call him
   Michelangelo.

SCHÖN. What good'll that do? (*Pointing left.*) There lies my
   engagement.

ALVA. That's the curse of your game!

SCHÖN. Shout it through the streets!!

ALVA (*pointing to* LULU). If you had treated that girl fairly and
   justly when my mother died ——

SCHÖN. My engagement is bleeding to death there!

LULU (*getting up*). I shan't stay here any longer.

SCHÖN. In an hour they'll be selling extras. I dare not go across
   the street!

LULU. Why, what can you do to help it?

SCHÖN. That's just it! They'll stone me for it!

ALVA. You must get away — travel.

SCHÖN. To leave the scandal a free field!

LULU (*by the couch*). Ten minutes ago he was lying here.

SCHÖN. This is the reward for all I've done for him! In one second
   he wrecks my whole life for me!

ALVA. Control yourself, please!

LULU (*on the couch*). There's no one but ourselves here.

ALVA. But our position?

SCHÖN (*to* LULU). What will you say to the police?

LULU. Nothing.

ALVA. He didn't want to remain a debtor to his destiny.

LULU. He always thought of death immediately.

SCHÖN. He thought what a human being can only dream of.

LULU. He has paid dearly for it.

ALVA. He had what we don't have!

SCHÖN (*suddenly violent*). I know your reasons! I have no cause to consider you! If you try every means to prevent having any brothers and sisters, that's all the more reason why I should get more children.

ALVA. You've a poor knowledge of men.

LULU. You get out an extra yourself!

SCHÖN (*with passionate indignation*). He had no moral sense! (*Suddenly controlling himself again.*) Paris in revolution ———?

ALVA. Our editors act as though they'd been struck. Everything has stopped dead.

SCHÖN. That's got to help me over this! Now if only the police would come. The minutes are worth more than gold.

(*The bell rings in the corridor.*)

ALVA. There they are ———

(SCHÖN *starts to the door.* LULU *jumps up.*)

LULU. Wait, you've got blood ———

SCHÖN. Where?

LULU. Wait, I'll wipe it.

(*Sprinkles her handkerchief with heliotrope and wipes the blood from* SCHÖN's *hand.*)

SCHÖN. It's your husband's blood.

LULU. It leaves no trace.

SCHÖN. Monster!

LULU. You will marry me, though. (*The bell rings in the corridor.*) Only have patience, children.

(SCHÖN *goes out and returns with* ESCHERICH, *a reporter.*)

ESCHERICH (*breathless*). Allow me to — to introduce myself ——

SCHÖN. You've run?

ESCHERICH (*giving him his card*). From police headquarters. A suicide, I understand.

SCHÖN (*reads*).    Fritz Escherich, correspondent of the "News and Novelties."    Come along.

ESCHERICH.    One moment.    (*Takes out his note-book and pencil, looks around the parlor, writes a few words, bows to* LULU, *writes, turns to the broken door, writes.*)    A kitchen-ax.                    (*Starts to lift it.*)

SCHÖN (*holding him back*).    Excuse me.

ESCHERICH (*writing*).    Door broken open with a kitchen-ax.
                                                (*Examines the lock.*)

SCHÖN (*his hand on the door*).    Look before you, my dear sir.

ESCHERICH.    Now if you will have the kindness to open the door ——
    (SCHÖN *opens it.*    ESCHERICH *lets book and pencil fall, clutches at his hair.*)    Merciful Heaven!    God!!

SCHÖN.    Look it all over carefully.

ESCHERICH.    I can't look at it!

SCHÖN (*snorting scornfully*).    Then what did you come here for?

ESCHERICH.    To — to cut up — to cut up his throat with a razor!

SCHÖN.    Have you seen it all?

ESCHERICH.    That must feel ——

SCHÖN (*draws the door to, steps to the writing-table*).    Sit down.    Here is paper and pen.    Write.

ESCHERICH (*mechanically taking his seat*).    I can't write ——

SCHÖN (*behind his chair*).    Write!    Persecution — mania....

ESCHERICH (*writes*).    Per-secu-tion — mania.
                                                (*The bell rings in the corridor.*)

CURTAIN


# ACT III

*A theatrical dressing-room, hung with red.    Door upper right.    Across upper left corner, a Spanish screen.    Center, a table set endwise, on which dance costumes lie.    Chair on each side of this table.    Lower right, a smaller table with a chair.    Lower left, a high, very wide, old-fashioned arm-chair.    Above it, a tall mirror, with a make-up stand before it holding puff, rouge, etc., etc.*

ALVA *is at lower right, filling two glasses with red wine and champagne.*

ALVA:    Never since I began to work for the stage have I seen a public so uncontrolled in enthusiasm.

LULU (*voice from behind the screen*). Don't give me too much red wine. Will he see me today?

ALVA. Father?

LULU. Yes.

ALVA. I don't know if he's in the theater.

LULU. Doesn't he want to see me at all?

ALVA. He has so little time.

LULU. His bride occupies him.

ALVA. Speculations. He gives himself no rest. (SCHÖN *enters.*) You? We're just speaking of you.

LULU. Is he there?

SCHÖN. You're changing?

LULU (*peeping over the Spanish screen, to* SCHÖN). You write in all the papers that I'm the most gifted danseuse who ever trod the stage, a second Taglioni and I don't know what else — and you haven't once found me gifted enough to convince yourself of the fact.

SCHÖN. I have so much to write. You see, I was right: there were hardly any seats left. You must keep rather more in the proscenium.

LULU. I must first accustom myself to the light.

ALVA. She has kept herself strictly to her part.

SCHÖN (*to* ALVA). You must get more out of your performers! You don't know enough yet about the technique. (*To* LULU.) What do you come as now?

LULU. As a flower-girl.

SCHÖN (*to* ALVA). In tights?

ALVA. No. In a skirt to the ankles.

SCHÖN. It would have been better if you hadn't ventured on symbolism.

ALVA. I look at a dancer's feet.

SCHÖN. The point is, what the public looks at. An apparition like her has no need, thank heaven, of your symbolic mummery.

ALVA. The public doesn't look as if it was bored!

SCHÖN. Of course not; because I have been working for her success in the press for six months. Has the prince been here?

ALVA. Nobody's been here.

SCHÖN. Who lets a dancer come on through two acts in raincoats?

ALVA. Who is the prince?

SCHÖN. Shall we see each other afterwards?

ALVA. Are you alone?

SCHÖN. With acquaintances. At Peter's?

ALVA. At twelve?

SCHÖN. At twelve. (*Exit.*)

LULU. I'd given up hoping he'd ever come.

ALVA. Don't let yourself be misled by his grumpy growls. If you'll only be careful not to spend your strength before the last number begins ——

> (LULU *steps out in a classical, sleeveless dress, white with a red border, a bright wreath in her hair and a basket of flowers in her hands.*)

LULU. He doesn't seem to have noticed at all how cleverly you have used your performers.

ALVA. I won't blow in sun, moon and stars in the first act!

LULU (*sipping*). You disclose me by degrees.

ALVA. I knew, though, that you knew all about changing costumes.

LULU. If I'd wanted to sell my flowers this way before the Alhambra café, they'd have had me behind lock and key right off the very first night.

ALVA. Why? You were a child!

LULU. Do you remember me when I entered your room the first time?

ALVA. You wore a dark blue dress with black velvet.

LULU. They had to stick me somewhere and didn't know where.

ALVA. My mother had been lying sick two years then.

LULU. You were playing theater, and asked me if I wanted to play too.

ALVA. To be sure! We played theater!

LULU. I see you still — the way you shoved the figures back and forth.

ALVA. For a long time my most terrible memory was when all at once I saw clearly into your relations ——

LULU. You got icy curt towards me then.

ALVA. Oh, God — I saw in you something so infinitely far above me. I had perhaps a higher devotion to you than to my mother. Think — when my mother died — I was seventeen — I went and stood before my father and demanded that he make you his wife on the spot or we'd have to fight a duel.

LULU. He told me that at the time.

ALVA. Since I've grown older, I can only pity him. He will never comprehend me. There he is making up a story for himself about a little diplomatic game that puts me in the rôle of laboring against his marriage with the Countess.

LULU. Does she still look as innocently as ever at the world?

ALVA. She loves him. I'm convinced of that. Her family has tried everything to make her turn back. I don't think any sacrifice in the world would be too great for her for his sake.

LULU (holds out her glass to him). A little more, please.

ALVA (giving it to her). You're drinking too much.

LULU. He shall learn to believe in my success! He doesn't believe in any art. He believes only in papers.

ALVA. He believes in nothing.

LULU. He brought me into the theater in order that someone might eventually be found rich enough to marry me.

ALVA. Well, all right. Why need that troubleus?

LULU. I am to be glad if I can dance myself into a millionaire's heart.

ALVA. God defend that anyone should take you from us!

LULU. You've composed the music for it, though.

ALVA. You know that it was always my wish to write a piece for you.

LULU. I am not at all made for the stage, however.

ALVA. You came into the world a dancer!

LULU. Why don't you write your things at least as interesting as life is?

ALVA. Because if we did no man would believe us.

LULU. If I didn't know more about acting than the people on the stage do, what might not have happened to me?

ALVA. I've provided your part with all the impossibilities imaginable, though.

LULU. With hocus-pocus like that no dog is lured from the stove in the real world.

ALVA. It's enough for me that the public finds itself most tremendously stirred.

LULU. But *I*'d like to find myself most tremendously stirred.

(*Drinks.*)

ALVA. You don't seem to be in need of much more for that.

LULU. No one of them realizes anything about the others. Each thinks that he alone is the unhappy victim.

ALVA. But how can you feel that?

LULU. There runs up one's body such an icy shudder.

ALVA. You are incredible. (*An electric bell rings over the door.*)

LULU. My cape.... I shall keep in the proscenium!

ALVA (*putting a wide shawl round her shoulders*). Here is your cape.

LULU. He shall have nothing more to fear for his shameless boosting.

ALVA. Keep yourself under control!

LULU. God grant that I dance the last sparks of intelligence out of their heads. (*Exit.*)

ALVA. Yes, a more interesting piece could be written about her. (*Sits, right, and takes out his note-book. Writes. Looks up.*) First act: Dr. Goll. Rotten already! I can call up Dr. Goll from purgatory or wherever else he's doing penance for his orgies, but I'll be made responsible for his sins. (*Long-continued but much deadened applause and bravos outside.*) They rage there as in a menagery when the meat appears at the cage. Second act: Walter Schwarz. Still more impossible! How our souls do strip off their last coverings in the light of such lightning-strokes! Third act? Is it really to go on this way? (*The attendant opens the door from outside and lets Escerny enter. He acts as though he were at home, and without greeting* ALVA *takes the chair near the mirror.* ALVA *continues, not heeding him.*) It cannot go on this way in the third act!

ESCERNY. Up to the middle of the third act it didn't seem to go so well today as usual.

ALVA. I was not on the stage.

ESCERNY. Now she's in full career again.

ALVA. She's lengthening each number.

ESCERNY. I once had the pleasure of meeting the artiste at Schön's.

ALVA. My father has brought her before the public by some critiques in his paper.

ESCERNY (*bowing slightly*). I was conferring with Dr. Schön about the publication of my discoveries at Lake Tanganika.

ALVA (*bowing slightly*). His remarks leave no doubt that he takes the liveliest interest in your work.

ESCERNY. It's a very good thing in the artiste that the public does not exist for her at all.

ALVA. As a child she learned the quick changing of clothes; but I was surprised to discover such an expressive dancer in her.

ESCERNY. When she dances her solo she is intoxicated with her own beauty, with which she herself seems to be mortally in love.

ALVA. Here she comes. (*Gets up and opens the door.*)

(*Enter* LULU.)

LULU (*without wreath or basket, to* ALVA). You're called for. I was three times before the curtain. (*To* ESCERNY.) Dr. Schön is not in your box?

ESCERNY. Not in mine.

ALVA (*to* LULU). Didn't you see him?

LULU. He is probably away again.

ESCERNY. He has the last parquet-box on the left.

LULU. It seems he is ashamed of me!

ALVA. There wasn't a good seat left for him.

LULU (*to* ALVA). Ask him, though, if he likes me better now.

ALVA. I'll send him up.

ESCERNY. He applauded.

LULU. Did he really?

ALVA. Give yourself some rest. (*Exit.*)

LULU. I've got to change again now.

ESCERNY. But your maid isn't here?

LULU. I can do it quicker alone. Where did you say Dr. Schön was sitting?

ESCERNY. I saw him in the left parquet-box farthest back.

LULU. I've still five costumes before me now; dancing-girl, ballerina, queen of the night, Ariel, and Lascaris....

(*She goes behind the Spanish screen.*)

ESCERNY. Would you think it possible that at our first meeting I expected nothing more than to make the acquaintance of a young lady of the literary world?... (*He sits at the left of the center table, and remains there to the end of the scene*.) Have I perhaps erred in my judgment of your nature, or did I rightly interpret the smile which the thundering storms of applause called forth on your lips? That you are secretly pained at the necessity of profaning your art before people of doubtful disinterestedness? (LULU *makes no answer*.) That you would gladly exchange at any moment the shimmer of publicity for a quiet, sunny happiness in distinguished seclusion? (LULU *makes no answer*.) That you feel in yourself enough dignity and high rank to fetter a man to your feet — in order to enjoy his utter helplessness?... (LULU *makes no answer*.) That in a comfortable, richly furnished villa you would feel in a more fitting place than here — with unlimited means, to live completely as your own mistress?

 (LULU *steps forth in a short, bright, pleated petticoat and white satin bodice, black shoes and stockings, and spurs with bells at her heels*.)

LULU (*busy with the lacing of her bodice*). If there's just one evening I don't go on, I dream the whole night that I'm dancing and feel the next day as if I'd been racked.

ESCERNY. But what difference could it make to you to see before you instead of this mob one spectator, specially elect?

LULU. That would make no difference. I don't see anybody anyway.

ESCERNY. A lighted summer-house — the splashing of the water near at hand.... I am forced in my exploring-trips to the practice of a quite inhuman tyranny ——

LULU (*putting on a pearl necklace before the mirror*). A good school!

ESCERNY. And if I now long to deliver myself unreservedly into the power of a woman, that is a natural need for relaxation.... Can you imagine a greater life-happiness for a woman than to have a man entirely in her power?

LULU (*jingling her heels*). Oh yes!

ESCERNY (*disconcerted*). Among cultured men you will find not one who doesn't lose his head over you.

LULU. Your wishes, however, no one will fulfill without deceiving you.

ESCERNY. To be deceived by a girl like you must be ten times more enrapturing than to be uprightly loved by anybody else.

LULU. You have never in your life been uprightly loved by a girl!

(*Turning her back to him and pointing.*)   Would you undo this knot
for me?   I've laced myself too tight.   I am always so excited
getting dressed.

ESCERNY (*after repeated efforts*).   I'm sorry; I can't.

LULU.  Then leave it.   Perhaps I can.                    (*Goes left.*)

ESCERNY.  I confess that I am lacking in deftness.   Maybe I was
not docile enough with women.

LULU.  And probably you don't have much opportunity to be so in
Africa, either?

ESCERNY (*seriously*).   Let me openly admit to you that my loneliness in the world embitters many hours.

LULU.  The knot is almost done....

ESCERNY.  What draws me to you is not your dancing.   It's your
physical and mental refinement, as it is revealed in every one of
your movements.   Anyone who is so much interested in art as
I am could not be deceived in that.   For ten evenings I've been
studying your spiritual life in your dance, until today when you
entered as the flower-girl I became perfectly clear.   Yours is
a grand nature — unselfish; you can see no one suffer; you em-
body the joy of life.   As a wife you will make a man happy above
all things.... You are all open-heartedness.   You would be
a poor actor.                                   (*The bell rings again.*)

LULU (*having somewhat loosened her laces, takes a deep breath and jingles
her spurs*).   Now I can breathe again.   The curtain is going up.
(*She takes from the center table a skirt-dance costume — of bright yellow
silk, without a waist, closed at the neck, reaching to the ankles, with
wide, loose sleeves — and throws it over her.*)   I must dance.

ESCERNY (*raises and kisses her hand*).   Allow me to remain here a
little while longer.

LULU.  Please, stay.

ESCERNY.  I need some solitude.   (*LULU goes out.*)   What is to be
aristocratic?   To be eccentric, like me?   Or to be perfect in
body and mind, like this girl?   (*Applause and bravos outside.*)   He
who gives me back my faith in men, gives me back my life.
Should not the children of this woman be more princely, body
and soul, than the children whose mother has no more vitality
in her than I have felt in me until today?   (*Sitting, right; ecstatically.*)   The dance has ennobled her body....

(ALVA *enters.*)

ALVA. One is never sure a moment that some miserable chance may not throw the whole performance out for good.

> (*He throws himself into the big chair, left, so that the two men are in exactly reversed positions from their former ones. Both converse somewhat boredly and apathetically.*)

ESCERNY. But the public has never yet shown itself so grateful.

ALVA. She's finished the skirt-dance.

ESCERNY. I hear her coming....

ALVA. She isn't coming. She has no time. She changes her costume in the wings.

ESCERNY. She has two ballet-costumes, if I'm not mistaken.

ALVA. I find the white one more becoming to her than the rose.

ESCERNY. Do you?

ALVA. Don't you?

ESCERNY. I find she looks too body-less in the white tulle.

ALVA. I find she looks too animal in the rose tulle.

ESCERNY. I don't find that.

ALVA. The white tulle expresses more the child-like in her nature.

ESCERNY. The rose tulle expresses more the female in her nature.

> (*The electric bell rings over the door. ALVA jumps up.*)

ALVA. For heaven's sake, what is wrong?

ESCERNY (*getting up too*). What's the matter?

> (*The electric bell goes on ringing to the close of the dialogue.*)

ALVA. Something's gone wrong there ——

ESCERNY. How can you get so suddenly frightened?

ALVA. That must be a hellish confusion!

> (*He runs out. ESCERNY follows him. The door remains open. Faint dance-music heard. Pause. LULU enters in a long cloak, and shuts the door to behind her. She wears a rose-colored ballet costume with flower garlands. She walks across the stage and sits down in the big arm-chair near the mirror. After a pause ALVA returns.*)

ALVA. You had a faint?

LULU. Please lock the door.

ALVA. At least come down to the stage.

LULU. Did you see him?

ALVA. See whom?

LULU. With his bride?

ALVA. With his —— (*To* SCHÖN, *who enters.*)   You might have spared yourself that jest!

SCHÖN. What's the matter with her?   (*To* LULU.)   How can you play the scene straight at me!

LULU. I feel as if I'd been whipped.

SCHÖN (*after bolting the door*).   You will dance — as sure as I've taken the responsibility for you!

LULU. Before your bride?

SCHÖN. Have you a right to trouble yourself before whom?   You've been engaged here.   You receive your salary...

LULU. Is that your affair?

SCHÖN. You dance for anyone who buys a ticket.   Whom I sit with in my box has nothing to do with your business!

ALVA. I wish you'd stayed sitting in your box!   (*To* LULU.)   Tell me, please, what I am to do.   (*A knock at the door.*)   There is the manager.   (*Calls.*)   Yes, in a moment!   (*To* LULU.)   You won't compel us to break off the performance?

SCHÖN (*to* LULU).   Onto the stage with you!

LULU. Let me have just a moment!   I can't now.   I'm utterly miserable.

ALVA. The devil take the whole theater crowd!

LULU. Put in the next number.   No one will notice if I dance now or in five minutes.   There's no strength in my feet.

ALVA. But you will dance then?

LULU. As well as I can.

ALVA. As badly as you like.   (*A knock at the door again.*)   I'm coming.

LULU (*when* ALVA *is gone*).   You are right to show me where my place is.   You couldn't do it better than by letting me dance the skirt-dance before your fiancée....   You do me the greatest service when you point out where I belong.

SCHÖN (*sardonically*).   For you with your origin it's incomparable luck to still have the chance of entering before respectable people!

LULU. Even when my shamelessness makes them not know where to look.

SCHÖN. Nonsense! — Shamelessness? — Don't make a necessity

of virtue! Your shamelessness is balanced with gold for you at every step. One cries "bravo," another "fie" — it's all the same to you! Can you wish for a more brilliant triumph than when a respectable girl can hardly be kept in the box? Has your life any other aim? As long as you still have a spark of self-respect, you are no perfect dancer. The more terribly you make people shudder, the higher you stand in your profession!

LULU. But it is absolutely indifferent to me what they think of me. I don't, in the least, want to be any better than I am. I'm content with myself.

SCHÖN (*in moral indignation*). That is your true nature. I call that straightforward! A corruption!!

LULU. I wouldn't have known that I had a spark of self-respect ——

SCHÖN (*suddenly distrustful*). No harlequinading ——

LULU. O Lord — I know very well what I'd have become if you hadn't saved me from it.

SCHÖN. Are you then, perhaps, something different today?

LULU. God be thanked, no!

SCHÖN. That is right!

LULU (*laughs*). And how awfully glad I am about it.

SCHÖN (*spits*). Will you dance now?

LULU. In anything, before anyone!

SCHÖN. Then down to the stage!

LULU (*begging like a child*). Just a minute more! Please! I can't stand up straight yet. They'll ring.

SCHÖN. You have become what you are in spite of everything I sacrificed for your education and your welfare.

LULU. Had you overrated your ennobling influence?

SCHÖN. Spare me your witticisms.

LULU. The prince was here.

SCHÖN. Well?

LULU. He takes me with him to Africa.

SCHÖN. Africa?

LULU. Why not? Didn't you make me a dancer just so that some-one might come and take me away with him?

SCHÖN. But not to Africa, though!

LULU. Then why didn't you let me fall quietly in a faint, and silently thank heaven for it?

schön. Because, more's the pity, I had no reason for believing in your faint!

lulu (*making fun of him*). You couldn't bear it any longer out there?

schön. Because I had to bring home to you what you are and to whom you are not to look up.

lulu. You were afraid, though, that my legs might have been seriously injured?

schön. I know too well you are indestructible.

lulu. So you know that?

schön (*bursting out*). Don't look at me so impudently!

lulu. No one is keeping you here.

schön. I'm going as soon as the bell rings.

lulu. As soon as you have the energy! Where is your energy? You have been engaged three years. Why don't you marry? You recognize no obstacles. Why do you want to put the blame on me? You ordered me to marry Dr. Goll: I forced Dr. Goll to marry me. You ordered me to marry the painter: I made the best of a bad bargain. Artists are your creatures, princes your protegés. Why don't you marry?

schön (*raging*). Do you imagine you stand in the way?

lulu (*from here to the end of the act triumphant*). If you knew how happy your rage is making me! How proud I am that you should humble me by every means in your power! You debase me as deep — as deep as a woman can be debased, for you hope you can then jump over me easier. But you have suffered unspeakably yourself from everything you just said to me. I see it in you. Already you are near the end of your self-command. Go! For your innocent fiancée's sake, leave me alone! One minute more, your mood will change around and you'll make a scene with me of another kind, that you can't answer for now.

schön. I fear you no longer.

lulu. Me? Fear yourself! I do not need you. I beg you to go! Don't give me the blame. You know I don't need to faint to destroy your future. You have unlimited confidence in my honorableness. You believe not only that I'm an ensnaring daughter of Eve; you believe, too, that I'm a very good-natured creature. I am neither the one nor the other. Your misfortune is only that you think I am.

SCHÖN (*desperate*). Leave my thoughts alone! You have two men under the sod. Take the prince, dance him into the earth! I am through with you. I know when the angel in you stops off and the devil begins. If I take the world as it's made, the Creator must be responsible, not I! To me life is not an amusement!

LULU. And, therefore, you make claims on life greater than anyone can make. Tell me, who of us two is more full of claims and demands, you or I?

SCHÖN. Be silent! I don't know how or what I think. When I hear you, I don't think any more. In a week I'll be married. I conjure you, by the angel that is in you, during that time come no more to my sight!

LULU. I will lock my doors.

SCHÖN. Go on and boast! God knows since I've been wrestling with the world and with life I have cursed no one like you!

LULU. That comes from my lowly origin.

SCHÖN. From your depravity!

LULU. With a thousand pleasures I take the blame on myself! You must feel clean now; you must think yourself a model of austerity now, a paragon of unflinching principle! Otherwise you could never marry the child in her boundless inexperience ——

SCHÖN. Do you want me to grab you and ——

LULU. Yes! What must I say to make you? Not for the world would I change with the innocent kid now! Though the girl loves you as no woman has ever loved you yet!

SCHÖN. Silence, beast! Silence!

LULU. Marry her — and then she'll dance in her childish wretchedness before my eyes, instead of I before hers!

SCHÖN (*raising his fists*). God forgive me ——

LULU. Strike me! Where is your riding-whip? Strike me on the legs ——

SCHÖN (*grasping his temples*). Away, away! (*Rushes to the door, recollects himself, turns around.*) Can I go before the girl now, this way? Home!

LULU. Be a man! Look yourself in the face once — you have no trace of a conscience; you are frightened at no wickedness; in the most cold-blooded way you mean to make the girl that loves you unhappy; you conquer half the world; you do what you please; — and you know as well as I that ——

SCHÖN (*sunk in the chair, right center, utterly exhausted*). Stop!

LULU. That you are too weak — to tear yourself away from me.

SCHÖN (*groaning*). Oh! Oh! You make me weep.

LULU. This moment makes me I cannot tell you how glad.

SCHÖN. My age! My position!

LULU. He cries like a child — the terrible man of might! Now go so to your bride and tell her what kind of a girl I am at heart — not a bit jealous!

SCHÖN (*sobbing*). The child! The innocent child!

LULU. How can the incarnate devil get so weak all of a sudden! But now go, please. You are nothing more now to me.

SCHÖN. I cannot go to her.

LULU. Out with you. Come back to me when you have regained your strength again.

SCHÖN. Tell me in God's name what I must do.

LULU (*gets up; her cloak remains on the chair. Shoving aside the costumes on the center table*). Here is writing-paper ——

SCHÖN. I can't write....

LULU (*upright behind him, her arm on the back of his chair*). Write! "My dear young lady...."

SCHÖN (*hesitating*). I call her Adelheid...

LULU (*with emphasis*). "My dear young lady..."

SCHÖN. My sentence of death! (*He writes.*)

LULU. "Take back your promise. I cannot reconcile it with my conscience ——" (SCHÖN *drops the pen and glances up at her entreatingly.*) Write conscience! — "to fasten you to my unhappy lot...."

SCHÖN (*writing*). You are right. You are right.

LULU. "I give you my word that I am unworthy of your love ——" (SCHÖN *turns round again.*) Write love! "These lines are the proof of it. For three years I have tried to tear myself loose; I have not the strength. I am writing you by the side of the woman that commands me. Forget me. Dr. Ludwig Schön."

SCHÖN (*groaning*). O God!

LULU (*half startled*). No, no O God! (*With emphasis.*) "Dr. Ludwig Schön." Postscript: "Do not attempt to save me."

SCHÖN (*having written to the end, quite collapses*). Now — comes the — execution.

CURTAIN

## ACT IV

*A splendid hall in German Renaissance style, with a thick floor of oak-blocks. The lower half of the walls of dark carved wood; the upper half on both sides hung with faded Gobelins. At rear, a curtained gallery from which a monumental staircase leads, right, half-way down the stage. At center, under the gallery, the entrance-door with twisted posts and pediment. At left, a high and spacious fireplace with a Chinese folding screen before it. Further down, left, a French window onto a balcony, with heavy curtains, closed. Down right, door hung with Genoese velvet. Near it, a broad ottoman, with a chair on its left. Behind, near the foot of the stairs, LULU's Pierrot-picture on a decorative stand and in a gold frame made to look antique. In the center of the hall, a heavy square table, with three high-backed upholstered chairs round it and a vase of white flowers on it.*

*COUNTESS GESCHWITZ sits on the ottoman, in a soldier-like, fur-trimmed waist, high, upright collar, enormous cuff-links, a veil over her face and her hands clasped convulsively in her muff. SCHÖN stands down right. LULU, in a big-flowered morning-dress, her hair in a simple knot in a golden circlet, sits in the armchair left of the ottoman.*

GESCHWITZ. You can't think how glad I shall be to see you at our artists' ball. (*To* LULU.)

SCHÖN. Is there no sort of possibility of a person like me smuggling in?

GESCHWITZ. It would be high treason if any of us lent herself to such an intrigue.

SCHÖN (*crossing to the center table, behind the ottoman*). The glorious flowers!

LULU. Fräulein von Geschwitz brought me those.

GESCHWITZ. Don't mention it.   Oh, you'll be in man's costume, won't you?

LULU. Do you think that becomes me?

GESCHWITZ. You're a dream here.        (*Signifying the picture.*)

LULU. My husband doesn't like it.

GESCHWITZ. Is it by a local man?

LULU. You will hardly have known him.

GESCHWITZ. No longer living?

SCHÖN (*down left, with a deep voice*). He had enough.

LULU. You're in bad temper.        (SCHÖN *controls himself.*)

GESCHWITZ (*getting up*). I must go, Mrs. Schön.   I can't stay any longer.   This evening we have life-class, and I have still so much to get ready for the ball.   Good-bye, Dr. Schön.

    (*Exit, up-stage.* LULU *accompanies her.* SCHÖN *looks around him.*)

SCHÖN. Pure Augean stable.   That, the end of my life.   They ought to show me a corner that's still clean.   The pest in the house.   The poorest day-laborer has his tidy nest.   Thirty years' work, and this my family circle, the circle of my people —— (*Glancing round.*)   God knows who is overhearing me again now! (*Draws a revolver from his breast pocket.*) Man is, indeed, uncertain of his life!   (*The cocked revolver in his right hand, he goes left and speaks at the closed window curtains.*)   That, my family circle! The fellow still has courage!   Shall I not rather shoot myself in the head?   Against deadly enemies one fights, but the —— (*Throws up the curtains, but finds no one hidden behind them.*)   The dirt — the dirt.... (*Shakes his head and crosses right.*)   Insanity has already conquered my reason, or else — exceptions prove the rule!

    (*Hearing* LULU *coming he puts the revolver back in his pocket.* LULU *comes down right.*)

LULU. Couldn't you get away for this afternoon?

SCHÖN. Just what did that Countess want?

LULU. I don't know.   She wants to paint me.

SCHÖN. Misfortune in human guise, that waits upon one.

LULU. Couldn't you get away, then?   I would so like to drive through the grounds with you.

SCHÖN. Just the day when I must be at the exchange.   You

know that I'm not free today. All my property is drifting on the waves.

LULU. I'd sooner be dead and buried than let my life be embittered so by my property.

SCHÖN. Who takes life lightly does not take death hard.

LULU. As a child I always had the most horrible fear of death.

SCHÖN. That is just why I married you.

LULU (with her arms round his neck). You're in bad humor. You give yourself too much work. For weeks and months I've seen nothing of you.

SCHÖN (stroking her hair). Your light-heartedness should cheer up my old days.

LULU. Indeed, you didn't marry me at all.

SCHÖN. Whom else did I marry then?

LULU. I married you!

SCHÖN. How does that alter anything?

LULU. I was always afraid it would alter a great deal.

SCHÖN. It has, indeed, crushed a great deal underfoot.

LULU. But not one thing, praise God!

SCHÖN. Of that I should be covetous.

LULU. Your love for me.

(SCHÖN's face twitches, he signs to her to go out in front of him. Both exeunt lower right. COUNTESS GESCHWITZ cautiously opens the rear door, ventures forth, and listens. Hearing voices approaching in the gallery above her, she starts suddenly.)

GESCHWITZ. Oh dear, there's somebody ——
(Hides behind the fire-screen.)

SCHIGOLCH (steps out from the curtains onto the stairs, turns back). Has the youngster left his heart behind him in the "Nightlight" café?

RODRIGO (between the curtains). He is still too small for the great world, and can't walk so far on foot yet. (He disappears.)

SCHIGOLCH (coming down the stairs). God be thanked we're home again at last! What damned skunk has waxed the stairs again? If I have to have my joints set in plaster again before being called home, she can just present me between the palms here to her relations as the Venus de' Medici. Nothing but steep rocks and stumbling blocks!

RODRIGO (comes down the stairs, carrying HUGENBERG in his arms).

This thing has a royal police-captain for a father and not as much courage in his body as the raggedest hobo!

HUGENBERG. If there was nothing more to it than life and death, then you'd soon learn to know me!

RODRIGO. Even with his lover's woe, little brother don't weigh more than sixty kilos. I'll let myself be hung on that statement any time.

SCHIGOLCH. Throw him up to the ceiling and catch him by the feet. That'll whip his young blood into the proper rhythm right from the start.

HUGENBERG (*kicking his legs*). Hooray, hooray, I shall be expelled from school!

RODRIGO (*setting him down at the foot of the stairs*). You've never been to any sensible school at all yet.

SCHIGOLCH. Here many a man has already won his spurs. Only, no timidity! First, I'll set before you a drop of what can't be had anywhere for money. (*Opens a cupboard under the stairs.*)

HUGENBERG. Now if she doesn't come dancing in on the instant, I'll wallop you two so you'll still rub your tails in the hereafter.

RODRIGO (*seated left of the table*). The strongest man in the world little brother will wallop! Let mamma put long trousers on you first. (HUGENBERG *sits opposite him.*)

HUGENBERG. I'd rather you lent me your mustache.

RODRIGO. Maybe you want her to throw you out of the door straight off?

HUGENBERG. If I only knew now what the devil I was going to say to her!

RODRIGO. That she knows best herself.

SCHIGOLCH (*putting two bottles and three glasses on the table*). I started in on one of them yesterday. (*Fills the glasses.*)

RODRIGO (*guarding* HUGENBERG's). Don't give him too much, or we'll both have to pay for it.

SCHIGOLCH (*supporting himself with both hands on the table-top*). Will the gentlemen smoke?

HUGENBERG (*opening his cigarette case*). Havana-imported!

RODRIGO (*helping himself*). From papa police-captain?

SCHIGOLCH (*sitting*). Everything in the house is mine. You only need to ask.

HUGENBERG. I made a poem to her yesterday.

RODRIGO. What did you make to her?

SCHIGOLCH. What did he make to her?

HUGENBERG. A poem.

RODRIGO (to SCHIGOLCH). A poem.

SCHIGOLCH. He's promised me a dollar if I can spy out where he can meet her alone.

HUGENBERG. Just who does live here?

RODRIGO. Here we live!

SCHIGOLCH. Jour fix — every stock-market day! Our health. (They clink.)

HUGENBERG. Should I read it to her first, maybe?

SCHIGOLCH (to RODRIGO). What's he mean?

RODRIGO. His poem. He'd like to stretch her out and torture her a little first.

SCHIGOLCH (staring at HUGENBERG). His eyes! His eyes!

RODRIGO. His eyes, yes. They've robbed her of sleep for a week.

SCHIGOLCH (to RODRIGO). You can have yourself pickled.

RODRIGO. We can both have ourselves pickled! Our health, gossip Death!

SCHIGOLCH (clinking with him). Health, jack-in-the-box! If it's still better later on, I'm ready for departure at any moment; but — but —— (LULU enters right, in an elegant Parisian ball dress, much décolleté, with flowers in breast and hair.)

LULU. But children, children, I expect company!

SCHIGOLCH. But I can tell you what, those things must cost something over there!

(HUGENBERG has risen. LULU sits on the arm of his chair.)

LULU. You've fallen into pretty company! I expect visitors, children!

SCHIGOLCH. I guess I've got to stick something in there, too. (He searches among the flowers on the table.)

LULU. Do I look well?

SCHIGOLCH. What are those you've got there?

LULU. Orchids. (Bending over HUGENBERG.) Smell.

RODRIGO. Do you expect Prince Escerny?

LULU (shaking her head). God forbid!

RODRIGO. So somebody else again —— !

LULU. The prince has gone traveling.

RODRIGO. To put his kingdom up for auction?

LULU. He's spying out a fresh tribe in the neighborhood of Africa.
            (*Rises, hurries up the stairs, and steps into the gallery.*)

RODRIGO (*to* SCHIGOLCH). He wanted to marry her originally.

SCHIGOLCH (*sticking a lily in his buttonhole*). I, too, wanted to marry
    her originally.

RODRIGO. You wanted to marry her originally?

SCHIGOLCH. Didn't you, too, want to marry her originally?

RODRIGO. You bet I wanted to marry her originally!

SCHIGOLCH. Who has not wanted to marry her originally!!

RODRIGO. I would never have got a better!

SCHIGOLCH. She has let no one regret that he didn't marry her.

RODRIGO. Then she's not your child?

SCHIGOLCH. Never occurs to her.

HUGENBERG. What is her father's name then?

SCHIGOLCH. She has boasted of me!

HUGENBERG. What is her father's name then?

SCHIGOLCH. What's he say?

RODRIGO. What her father's name is.

SCHIGOLCH. She never had one.

LULU (*comes down from the gallery and sits again on* HUGENBERG'S
    *chair-arm*). What have I never had?

ALL THREE. A father.

LULU. Yes, sure — I'm a wonder-child. (*To* HUGENBERG.) How
    are you getting along with your father?

RODRIGO. He smokes a respectable cigar, anyway, the police-
    captain.

SCHIGOLCH. Have you locked up upstairs?

LULU. There is the key.

SCHIGOLCH. Better have left it in the lock.

LULU. Why?

SCHIGOLCH. So no one can unlock it from outside.

RODRIGO. Isn't he at the stock-exchange?

LULU. Oh, yes, but he suffers from persecution-mania.

RODRIGO. I take him by the feet, and yup! — there he stays stick-
    ing to the roof.

LULU. He hunts you into a mouse-hole with the corner of his eye.

RODRIGO. What does he hunt?  Who does he hunt?  (*Baring his arm.*)  Just look at this biceps!

LULU. Show me.  (*Goes left.*)

RODRIGO (*hitting himself on the muscle*). Granite.  Wrought-iron!

LULU (*feeling by turns* RODRIGO's *arm and her own*). If you only didn't have such long ears ——

FERDINAND (*entering, rear-center*). Doctor Schön!

RODRIGO. The rogue!  (*Jumps up, starts behind the fire-screen, recoils.*)  God preserve me!  (*Hides, lower left, behind the curtains.*)

SCHIGOLCH. Give me the key!

(*Takes it and drags himself up the stairs.*)

LULU (HUGENBERG *having slid under the table*). Show him in!

HUGENBERG (*under the front edge of the tablecloth, listening; to himself*).  If he doesn't stay — we'll be alone.

LULU (*poking him with her toe*). Sh!

(HUGENBERG *disappears.* ALVA *is shown in by* FERDINAND.)

ALVA (*in evening dress*). Methinks the matinee will take place with burning lamps.  I've —— (*Notices* SCHIGOLCH *painfully climbing the stairs.*)  What the —— is that?

LULU. An old friend of your father's.

ALVA. Wholly unknown to me.

LULU. They were in the campaign together.  He's awfully badly ——

ALVA. Is my father here then?

LULU. He drank a glass with him.  He had to go to the stock market.  We'll have lunch before we go, won't we?

ALVA. When does it begin?

LULU. After two.  (ALVA *still follows* SCHIGOLCH *with his eyes.*)  How do you like me?  (SCHIGOLCH *disappears through the gallery.*)

ALVA. Had I not better be silent to you on that point?

LULU. I only mean my appearance.

ALVA. Your dressmaker manifestly knows you better than I may permit myself to know you.

LULU. When I saw myself in the glass I could have wished to be a man — my man! ——

ALVA. You seem to envy your man the joy you offer to him.  (LULU *is at the right,* ALVA *at the left, of the center table.  He regards her with shy satisfaction.* FERDINAND *enters, rear, covers the table*

*and lays two plates, etc., a bottle of Pommery, and hors d'oeuvres.*)
Have you a toothache?

LULU (*across to* ALVA). Don't.

FERDINAND. Doctor Schön... ?

ALVA. He seems so puckered-up and tearful today.

FERDINAND (*through his teeth*). One is only a man after all. (*Exit.*)

LULU (*when both are seated*). What I always think most highly of in you is your firmness of character. You're so perfectly sure of yourself. Even when you must have been afraid of quarreling with your father about it, you always stood up for me like a brother just the same.

ALVA. Let's drop that. It's just my fate ——
(*Moves to lift up the tablecloth in front.*)

LULU (*quickly*). That was me.

ALVA. Impossible! It's just my fate, with the most frivolous ideas always to seize on the best.

LULU. You deceive yourself if you make yourself out worse than you are.

ALVA. Why do you flatter me so? It is true that perhaps there is no man living, so bad as I — who has brought about so much good.

LULU. In any case you're the only man in the world who's protected me without lowering me in my own eyes!

ALVA. Do you think that so easy? (SCHÖN *appears in the gallery cautiously parting the hangings between the middle pillars. He starts, and whispers, "My own son!"*) With gifts from God like yours, one turns those around one to criminals without ever dreaming of it. I, too, am only flesh and blood, and if we hadn't grown up with each other like brother and sister ——

LULU. That's why, too, I give myself to you alone quite without reserve. From you I have nothing to fear.

ALVA. I assure you there are moments when one expects to see one's whole inner self cave in. The more self-restraint a man loads onto himself, the easier he breaks down. Nothing will save him from that except —— (*Stops to look under the table.*)

LULU (*quickly*). What are you looking for?

ALVA. I conjure you, let me keep my confession of faith to myself! As an inviolable sanctity you were more to me than with all your gifts you could be to anyone else in your life!

LULU. How do you come to think on that so entirely differently from your father?

(FERDINAND *enters, rear, changes the plates and serves broiled chicken with salad.*)

ALVA (*to him*). Are you sick?

LULU (*to* ALVA). Let him be!

ALVA. He's trembling as if he had fever.

FERDINAND. I am not yet so used to waiting...

ALVA. You must have something prescribed for you.

FERDINAND (*through his teeth*). I'm a coachman usually —— (*Exit.*)

SCHÖN (*whispering from the gallery*). So, he too.

(*Seats himself behind the rail, able to cover himself with the hangings.*)

LULU. What sort of moments are those of which you spoke, where one expects to see his whole inner self tumble in?

ALVA. I didn't want to speak of them. I should not like to lose, in joking over a glass of champagne, what has been my highest happiness for ten years.

LULU. I have hurt you. I won't begin on that again.

ALVA. Do you promise me that for always?

LULU. My hand on it. (*Gives him her hand across the table. ALVA takes it hesitatingly, grips it in his, and presses it long and ardently to his lips.*) What are you doing? (RODRIGO *sticks his head out from the curtains, left. LULU darts an angry look at him across ALVA, and he draws back.*)

SCHÖN (*whispering from the gallery*). And there is still another!

ALVA (*holding the hand*). A soul — that in the hereafter rubs the sleep out of its eyes.... Oh, this hand....

LULU (*innocently*). What do you find in it?...

ALVA. An arm....

LULU. What do you find in it?...

ALVA. A body....

LULU (*guilelessly*). What do you find in it?...

ALVA (*stirred up*). Mignon!

LULU (*wholly ingenuously*). What do you find in it?...

ALVA (*passionately*). Mignon! Mignon!

LULU (*throws herself on the ottoman*). Don't look at me so — for God's sake! Let us go before it is too late. You're an infamous wretch!

ALVA. I told you, didn't I, I was the basest villain.

LULU. I see that!

ALVA. I have no sense of honor, no pride....

LULU. You think I am your equal!

ALVA. You? — you are as heavenly high above me as — as the sun is over the abyss! (*Kneeling.*) Destroy me! I beg you, put an end to me! Put an end to me!

LULU. Do you love me then?

ALVA. I will pay you with everything that was mine!

LULU. Do you love me?

ALVA. Do you love me — Mignon?

LULU. I? Not a soul.

ALVA. I love you. (*Hides his face in her lap.*)

LULU (*both hands in his hair*). I poisoned your mother —— (Ro-DRIGO *sticks his head out from the curtains, left, sees* SCHÖN *sitting in the gallery and signs to him to watch* LULU *and* ALVA. SCHÖN *points his revolver at* RODRIGO; RODRIGO *signs to him to point it at* ALVA. SCHÖN *cocks the revolver and takes aim.* RODRIGO *draws back behind the curtain.* LULU *sees him draw back, sees* SCHÖN *sitting in the gallery, and gets up.*) His father!

(SCHÖN *rises, lets the hangings fall before him.* ALVA *remains motionless on his knees. Pause.*)

SCHÖN (*holding a paper in his hand, takes* ALVA *by the shoulder*). Alva! (ALVA *gets up as though drunk with sleep.*) A revolution has broken out in Paris.

ALVA. To Paris... let me go to Paris ——

SCHÖN. In the editors' room they're beating their heads against the wall. No one knows what he ought to write.

(*He unfolds the paper and accompanies* ALVA *out, rear.* RODRIGO *rushes out from the curtains toward the stairs.*)

LULU (*barring his way*). You can't get out here.

RODRIGO. Let me through!

LULU. You'll run into his arms.

RODRIGO. He'll shoot me through the head!

LULU. He's coming.

RODRIGO (*stumbling back*). Devil, death and demons!

(*Lifts the tablecloth.*)

HUGENBERG. No room!

RODRIGO. Damned and done for!

> (*Looks around and hides in the doorway, right.*)

SCHÖN (*comes in, center; locks the door; and goes, revolver in hand, to the window down left, of which he throws up the curtains*). Where is he gone?

LULU (*on the lowest step*). Out.

SCHÖN. Down over the balcony?

LULU. He's an acrobat.

SCHÖN. That could not be foreseen. (*Turning against* LULU.) You who drag me through the muck of the streets to a tortured death!

LULU. Why did you not bring me up better?

SCHÖN. You destroying angel! You inexorable fate! To be a murderer without drowning in filth; to take me on board like a released convict, or hang me up over the morass! You joy of my old age! You hangman's noose!

LULU (*in cold blood*). Oh, shut up, and kill me!

SCHÖN. Everything I possess I have made over to you, and asked nothing but the respect that every servant pays to my house. Your credit is exhausted!

LULU. I can answer for my reckoning still for years. (*Coming forward from the stairs.*) How do you like my new gown?

SCHÖN. Away with you, or my brains will give way tomorrow and my son swim in his own blood! You infect me like an incurable pest in which I shall groan away the rest of my life. I will cure myself! Do you understand? (*Pressing the revolver on her.*) This is your physic. Don't break down; don't kneel! You yourself shall apply it. You or I — which is the weaker?

> (LULU, *her strength threatening to desert her, has sunk down on the couch. Turning the revolver this way and that.*)

LULU. It doesn't go off.

SCHÖN. Do you still remember how I tore you out of the clutches of the police?

LULU. You have much confidence ——

SCHÖN. Because I'm not afraid of a street-girl? Shall I guide your hand for you? Have you no mercy towards yourself? (LULU *points the revolver at him.*) No false alarms! (LULU *fires a shot into the ceiling.* RODRIGO *springs out of the portières, up the stairs and away through the gallery.*) What was that?

LULU (*innocently*). Nothing.

SCHÖN (*lifting the portières*). What flew out of here?

LULU. You're suffering from persecution-mania.

SCHÖN. Have you got still more men hidden here? (*Tearing the revolver from her.*) Is yet another man calling on you? (*Going left.*) I'll regale your men! (*Throws up the window curtains, flings the fire-screen back, grabs* COUNTESS GESCHWITZ *by the collar and drags her forward.*) Did you come down the chimney?

GESCHWITZ (*in deadly terror, to* LULU). Save me from him!

SCHÖN (*shaking her*). Or are you, too, an acrobat?

GESCHWITZ (*whimpering*). You hurt me.

SCHÖN (*shaking her*). Now you will have to stay to dinner. (*Drags her right, shoves her into the next room and locks the door after her.*) We want no town-criers. (*Sits next* LULU *and makes her take the revolver again.*) There's still enough for you in it. Look at me! I cannot assist the coachman in my house to decorate my forehead for me. Look at me! I pay my coachman. Look at me! Am I doing the coachman a favor when I can't stand the stable-stench?

LULU. Have the carriage got ready! Please! We're going to the opera.

SCHÖN. We're going to the devil! Now I am coachman. (*Turning the revolver in her hand from himself to* LULU's *breast.*) Think you we let ourselves be mistreated as you mistreat me, and hesitate between a galley-slave's shame at the end of life and the merit of freeing the world of you? (*Holds her down by the arm.*) Come, get through. It will be the gladdest remembrance of my life. Pull the trigger!

LULU. You can get a divorce.

SCHÖN. Only that was left! In order that tomorrow the next man may find his pastime where I have shuddered from cleft to chasm, suicide upon me and thou before me! You dare suggest that? That part of my life I have poured into you I am to see thrown before wild beasts? Do you see your bed with the sacrifice — the victim — on it? The boy is homesick for you. Did you let yourself be divorced? You trod him under your feet, knocked out his brains, caught up his blood in gold pieces. I let myself be divorced? Can one be divorced when two people have grown into each other and half the man must go, too. (*Reaching for the revolver.*) Give it here!

LULU. Don't!

SCHÖN. I'll spare you the trouble.

LULU (*tears herself loose, holding the revolver down; in a determined, self-possessed tone*). If men have killed themselves for my sake, that doesn't lower my value. You know as well why you made me your wife as I knew why I took you for husband. You had deceived your best friends with me; you could not well go on deceiving yourself with me. If you bring me the close of your life as a sacrifice, still you have had my whole youth for it. You understand ten times better than I do which is the more valuable. I have never in the world wished to seem to be anything different from what I am taken for, and I have never in the world been taken for anything different from what I am. You want to force me to fire a bullet into my heart. I'm not sixteen any more, but to fire a bullet in my heart I am still much too young!

SCHÖN (*pursuing her*). Down, murderess! Down with you! To your knees, murderess! (*Crowding her to the foot of the stairs.*) Down, and never dare to stand again! (*Raising his hand. LULU has sunk to her knees.*) Pray to God, murderess, that He give you strength. Sue to heaven that strength for it may be lent you!

> (HUGENBERG *jumps up from under the table, knocking a chair aside, and screams "Help!"* SCHÖN *whirls toward him, turning his back to* LULU *who instantly fires five shots into him and continues to pull the trigger.* SCHÖN, *tottering over, is caught by* HUGENBERG *and let down in the chair.*)

SCHÖN. And — there — is — one — more ——

LULU (*rushing to* SCHÖN). All merciful —— !

SCHÖN. Out of my sight! Alva!

LULU (*kneeling*). The one man I loved!

SCHÖN. Harlot! Murderess! Alva! Alva! Water!

LULU. Water; he's thirsty.

> (*Fills a glass with champagne and sets it to* SCHÖN's *lips.* ALVA *comes through the gallery, down the stairs.*)

ALVA. Father! O God, my father!

LULU. I shot him.

HUGENBERG. She is innocent!

SCHÖN (*to* ALVA). You! It miscarried.

ALVA (*tries to lift him*). You must go to bed; come.

SCHÖN. Don't take me so! I'm drying up. (LULU *comes with the champagne-cup; to her.*) You are still like yourself. (*After drinking.*) Don't let her escape. (*To* ALVA.) You are the next.

ALVA (*to* HUGENBERG). Help me carry him to bed.

SCHÖN. No, no, please, no. Wine, murderess ——

ALVA (*to* HUGENBERG). Take him up that side. (*Pointing right.*) Into the bedroom.

(*They lift* SCHÖN *upright and lead him right.* LULU *stays near the table, the glass in her hand.*)

SCHÖN (*groaning*). O God! O God! O God! (ALVA *finds the door locked, turns the key and opens it.* COUNTESS GESCHWITZ *steps out.* SCHÖN *at the sight of her straightens up, stiffly.*) The Devil. (*He falls backward onto the carpet.* LULU *throws herself down, takes his head in her lap, and kisses him.*)

LULU. He has got over it. (*Gets up and starts toward the stairs.*)

ALVA. Don't stir!

GESCHWITZ. I thought it was you.

LULU (*throwing herself before* ALVA). You can't give me up to the law! It is my head that is struck off. I shot him because he was about to shoot me. I have loved nobody in the world but him! Alva, demand what you will, only don't let me fall into the hands of justice. Take pity on me. I am still young. I will be true to you as long as I live. I will belong only to you. Look at me, Alva. Man, look at me! Look at me!!

(*Knocking on the door outside.*)

ALVA. The police. (*Goes to open it.*)

HUGENBERG. I shall be expelled from school.

**CURTAIN**

# CYRANO DE BERGERAC

## By EDMOND ROSTAND

*Translated from the French by GERTRUDE HALL*

# EDMOND ROSTAND

ROSTAND was born in Marseilles in 1868, the son of a renowned economist of artistic inclinations. A child of privilege his associations were with the old aristocracy. In his early twenties he married the granddaughter of a Maréchal of Napoleon. He passed his life without being touched by, or even aware of, the impulses and passions which were moving his contemporaries. That he was able to win the plaudits of millions of his fellows is a tribute to his technical skill and artistic subtlety. Edmond Rostand's first collection of verse, *Les Musardises*, published when he was twenty, displayed the qualities of preciosity and artifice, that were to be the hall-marks of his style throughout his life. His *The Romancers* was produced by the Comedie Française in 1894. In *Cyrano de Bergerac* he provided Coquelin with the most sensational success of the modern romantic stage. The plays after Cyrano show a flagging of energy and an excess of ornament. During the World War Rostand wrote poems which have been gathered into two volumes, *Le vol de la Marseillaise*, 1919, and *Le cantique d'aile*, 1922. Rostand died in 1918.

# CYRANO DE BERGERAC

THE appearance of *Cyrano de Bergerac* is essentially unique in the history of the contemporary theater. Since Victor Hugo there has been no other poetic play with comparable vitality. And the play is unique in the author's history. A man without vitality, but with matchless technical skill, particularly in versification, Rostand wore himself out in one of the most vigorous imaginative *tours de force* in the modern theater. A generation ago there was a disposition to emphasize the originality of Rostand's achievement. Today it is recognized that the work was made possible by an assiduous conning of all the lessons of the play craftsman, and by appeals for support to existing pillars of the Parisian boulevards. The play was written as a vehicle for the dean of the French theater, Constant Coquelin. At no point does its craftsmanship come either from life or from a reference to new or untried principles of imaginative expression. The characterization is of the theater, the plot structure is of the school of Sardou, the spirit is from Hugo's Preface to *Cromwell*. Only the magnificent embroidery of the verse is Rostand's own. The quality which made the play such a stupendous phenomenon in its youth, the quality of jocose irreverence at romance itself, has dated rapidly. The play was probably suggested by the farce *Roquelaure, ou l'homme le plus laid de France*, which had been written by de Leuveu, de Livry and Lhérie (1836). The chief character is derived from a Gascon swashbuckler of the name, born in Paris in 1619, a member of the regiment of Carbon de Castel-Jaloux, a braggart and wit who himself wrote a play, *Le Pédant joué*, which was used by Molière in his *Les Fourberies de Scapin*. He also wrote fantastic pieces about the geography of the moon and sun. *Cyrano de Bergerac* was produced at the Théâtre de la Porte Saint-Martin in Paris in 1897, the part of Cyrano being played by Constant Coquelin. The play was immediately translated into the chief languages of Europe and has been a recurrent feature on the stage of all western nations to this day. In America it has been played by Richard Mansfield and Walter Hampden. It has been frequently translated, by Charles Renault in 1899, by Gertrude Hall in 1898, H. T. Kingsbury in 1898, H. D. Norman, 1921, and by Brian Hooker, 1923.

# DRAMATIS PERSONÆ

Cyrano de Bergerac

Christian de Neuvillette

Comte de Guiche

Ragueneau

Le Bret

Captain Carbon de Castel-Jaloux

Lignière

De Valvert

Montfleury

Bellerose

Jodelet

Cuigy

Brissaille

A Bore

A Mousquetaire

Other Mousquetaire

A Spanish Officer

A Light-Cavalry Man

A Doorkeeper

A Burgher

His Son

A Pickpocket

A Spectator

A Watchman

Bertrandou the Fifer

A Capuchin

Two Musicians

Seven Cadets

Three Marquises

Poets

Pastrycooks

Roxane

Sister Martha

Lise

The Sweetmeat Vender

Mother Margaret

The Duenna

Sister Claire

An Actress

A Soubrette

A Flower-Girl

Pages

The crowd, bourgeois, marquises, mousquetaires, pickpockets, pastry-cooks, poets, Gascony Cadets, players, fiddlers, pages, children, Spanish soldiers, spectators, précieuses, actresses, bourgeoises, nuns, etc.

# ACT FIRST

### A PLAY AT THE HOTEL DE BOURGOGNE

*The great hall of the Hotel de Bourgogne, in 1640. A sort of tennis-court arranged and decorated for theatrical performances.*

*The hall is a long rectangle, seen obliquely, so that one side of it con-stitutes the background, which runs from the position of the front wing at the right, to the line of the furthest wing at the left, and forms an angle with the stage, which is equally seen obliquely.*

*This stage is furnished, on both sides, along the wings, with benches. The drop-curtain is composed of two tapestry hangings, which can be drawn apart. Above a harlequin cloak, the royal escutcheon. Broad steps lead from the raised platform of the stage into the house. On either side of these steps, the musicians' seats. A row of candles fills the office of footlights.*

*Two galleries run along the side; the lower one is divided into boxes. No seats in the pit, which is the stage proper. At the back of the pit, that is to say, at the right, in the front, a few seats raised like steps, one above the other; and, under a stairway which leads to the upper seats, and of which the lower end only is visible, a stand decked with small candelabra, jars full of flowers, flagons and glasses, dishes heaped with sweetmeats, etc.*

*In the center of the background, under the box-tier, the entrance to the theater, large door which half opens to let in the spectators. On the panels of this door, and in several corners, and above the sweetmeat stand, red playbills announcing* LA CLORISE.

*At the rise of the curtain, the house is nearly dark, and still empty. The chandeliers are let down in the middle of the pit, until time to light them.*

*The audience, arriving gradually. Cavaliers, burghers, lackeys, pages, fiddlers, etc.*

*A tumult of voices is heard beyond the door; enter brusquely a* CAVALIER.

DOORKEEPER (*running in after him*). Not so fast! Your fifteen pence!

CAVALIER. I come in admission free!

DOORKEEPER. And why?

CAVALIER. I belong to the king's light cavalry!

DOORKEEPER (*to another* CAVALIER *who has entered*). You?

SECOND CAVALIER. I do not pay!

DOORKEEPER. But...

SECOND CAVALIER. I belong to the mousquetaires!

FIRST CAVALIER (*to the* SECOND). It does not begin before two.
The floor is empty. Let us have a bout with foils.

(*They fence with foils they have brought.*)

A LACKEY (*entering*). Pst!... Flanquin!

OTHER LACKEY (*arrived a moment before*). Champagne?...

FIRST LACKEY (*taking a pack of cards from his doublet and showing it to*
SECOND LACKEY). Cards. Dice. (*Sits down on the floor.*) Let
us have a game.

SECOND LACKEY (*sitting down likewise*). You rascal, willingly!

FIRST LACKEY (*taking from his pocket a bit of candle which he lights
and sticks on the floor*). I prigged an eyeful of my master's light!

ONE OF THE WATCH (*to a* FLOWER-GIRL, *who comes forward*). It is
pleasant getting here before the lights.

(*Puts his arm around her waist.*)

ONE OF THE FENCERS (*taking a thrust*). Hit!

ONE OF THE GAMBLERS. Clubs!

THE WATCHMAN (*pursuing the girl*). A kiss!

THE FLOWER-GIRL (*repulsing him*). We shall be seen!

THE WATCHMAN (*drawing her into a dark corner*). No, we shall not!

A MAN (*sitting down on the floor with others who have brought provisions*).
By coming early, you get a comfortable chance to eat.

A BURGHER (*leading his son*). This should be a good place, my boy.
Let us stay here.

ONE OF THE GAMBLERS. Ace wins!

A MAN (*taking a bottle from under his cloak and sitting down*). A proper
toper, toping Burgundy (*drinks*), I say should tope it in Burgundy House!

THE BURGHER (*to his son*). Might one not suppose we had stumbled
into some house of evil fame? (*Points with his cane at the drunkard.*)
Guzzlers!... (*In breaking guard one of the fencers jostles him.*)
Brawlers!... (*He falls between the gamblers.*) Gamesters!...

THE WATCHMAN (*behind him, still teasing the flower-girl*). A kiss!

THE BURGHER (*dragging his son precipitately away*). Bless my soul!...

And to reflect that in this very house, my son, were given the plays of the great Rotrou!

THE YOUTH. And those of the great Corneille!

(*A band of* PAGES *holding hands rush in performing a farandole and singing.*)

PAGES. Tra la la la la la la la!...

DOORKEEPER (*severely to the* PAGES). Look, now!... you pages, you! none of your tricks!

FIRST PAGE (*with wounded dignity*). Sir!... this want of confidence...
(*As soon as the doorkeeper has turned away, briskly to the* SECOND PAGE.) Have you a string about you?

SECOND PAGE. With a fish-hook at the end!

FIRST PAGE. We will sit up there and angle for wigs!

A PICKPOCKET (*surrounded by a number of individuals of dubious appearance*). Come, now, my little hopefuls, and learn your A B C's of trade. Being as you're not used to hooking...

SECOND PAGE (*shouting to other* PAGES *who have already taken seats in the upper gallery*). Ho!... Did you bring any pea-shooters?

THIRD PAGE (*from above*). Yes!... And pease!...
(*Shoots down a volley of pease.*)

THE YOUTH (*to his father*). What are we going to see?

THE BURGHER. Clorise.

THE YOUTH. By whom?

THE BURGHER. By Balthazar Baro. Ah, what a play it is!...
(*Goes toward the back on his son's arm.*)

PICKPOCKET (*to his disciples*). Particularly the lace-ruffles at the knees,... you're to snip off carefully!

A SPECTATOR (*to another, pointing toward an upper seat*). Look! On the first night of the Cid, I was perched up there!

PICKPOCKET (*with pantomimic suggestion of spiriting away*). Watches...

THE BURGHER (*coming forward again with his son*). The actors you are about to see, my son, are among the most illustrious...

PICKPOCKET (*with show of subtracting with furtive little tugs*). Pocket-handkerchiefs...

THE BURGHER. Montfleury...

SOMEBODY (*shouting from the upper gallery*). Make haste, and light the chandeliers!

THE BURGHER. Bellerose, l'Épy, the Beaupré, Jodelet...

A PAGE (*in the pit*). Ah!... Here comes the goody-seller!

THE SWEETMEAT VENDER (*appearing behind the stand*). Oranges...
Milk... Raspberry cordial... citron-wine... (*Hubbub at the door.*)

FALSETTO VOICE (*outside*). Make room, ruffians!

ONE OF THE LACKEYS (*astonished*). The marquises... in the pit!

OTHER LACKEY. Oh, for an instant only!

(*Enter a band of foppish* YOUNG MARQUISES.)

ONE OF THE MARQUISES (*looking around the half-empty house*). What?...
We happen in like so many linen-drapers? Without disturbing
anybody? treading on any feet?... Too bad! too bad! too bad!
(*He finds himself near several other gentlemen, come in a moment before.*)
Cuigy, Brissaille!                               (*Effusive embraces.*)

CUIGY. We are of the faithful indeed. We are here before the
lights.

THE MARQUIS. Ah, do not speak of it!... It has put me in such a
humor!

OTHER MARQUIS. Be comforted, marquis... here comes the candle-
lighter!

THE AUDIENCE (*greeting the arrival of the candle-lighter*). Ah!...
      (*Many gather around the chandeliers while they are being lighted.
      A few have taken seats in the galleries.*)

(LIGNIÈRE *enters, arm in arm with* CHRISTIAN DE NEUVILLETTE.
  LIGNIÈRE, *in somewhat disordered apparel, appearance of gentle-
  manly drunkard.* CHRISTIAN, *becomingly dressed, but in clothes of a
  slightly obsolete elegance.*)

CUIGY. Lignière!

BRISSAILLE (*laughing*). Not tipsy yet?

LIGNIÈRE (*low to* CHRISTIAN). Shall I present you? (CHRISTIAN
*nods assent.*) Baron de Neuvillette...       (*Exchange of bows.*)

THE AUDIENCE (*cheering the ascent of the first lighted chandelier*). Ah!...

CUIGY (*to* BRISSAILLE, *looking at* CHRISTIAN). A charming head...
charming!

FIRST MARQUIS (*who has overheard*). Pooh!...

LIGNIÈRE (*presenting* CHRISTIAN). Messieurs de Cuigy... de
Brissaille...

CHRISTIAN (*bowing*). Delighted!...

FIRST MARQUIS (*to* SECOND). He is a pretty fellow enough, but is dressed in the fashion of some other year!

LIGNIÈRE (*to* CUIGY). Monsieur is lately arrived from Touraine.

CHRISTIAN. Yes, I have been in Paris not over twenty days. I enter the Guards tomorrow, the Cadets.

FIRST MARQUIS (*looking at those who appear in the boxes*). There comes the président Aubry!

SWEETMEAT VENDER. Oranges! Milk!

THE FIDDLERS (*tuning*). La... la...

CUIGY (*to* CHRISTIAN, *indicating the house which is filling*). A good house!...

CHRISTIAN. Yes, crowded.

FIRST MARQUIS. The whole of fashion!

(*They give the names of the women, as, very brilliantly attired, these enter the boxes. Exchange of bows and smiles.*)

SECOND MARQUIS. Mesdames de Guéménée...

CUIGY. De Bois-Dauphin...

FIRST MARQUIS. Whom... time was!... we loved!...

BRISSAILLE. ... de Chavigny...

SECOND MARQUIS. Who still plays havoc with our hearts!

LIGNIÈRE. *Tiens!* Monsieur de Corneille has come back from Rouen!

THE YOUTH (*to his father*). The Academy is present?

THE BURGHER. Yes... I perceive more than one member of it. Yonder are Boudu, Boissat and Cureau... Porchères, Colomby, Bourzeys, Bourdon, Arbaut... All names of which not one will be forgotten. What a beautiful thought it is!

FIRST MARQUIS. Attention! Our précieuses are coming into their seats... Barthénoide, Urimédonte, Cassandace, Félixérie...

SECOND MARQUIS. Ah, how exquisite are their surnames!... Marquis, can you tell them off, all of them?

FIRST MARQUIS. I can tell them off, all of them, marquis!

LIGNIÈRE (*drawing* CHRISTIAN *aside*). Dear fellow, I came in here to be of use to you. The lady does not come. I revert to my vice!

CHRISTIAN (*imploringly*). No! No!... You who turn into ditties Town and Court, stay by me; you will be able to tell me for whom it is I am dying of love!

THE LEADER OF THE VIOLINS (*rapping on his desk with his bow*). Gentlemen!...                                      (*He raises his bow.*)

SWEETMEAT VENDER. Macaroons... Citronade...

(*The fiddles begin playing.*)

CHRISTIAN. I fear... oh, I fear to find that she is fanciful and intricate!   I dare not speak to her, for I am of a simple wit. The language written and spoken in these days bewilders and baffles me.   I am a plain soldier... shy, to boot.— She is always at the right, there, the end: the empty box.

LIGNIÈRE (*with show of leaving*). I am going.

CHRISTIAN (*still attempting to detain him*). Oh, no!... Stay, I beseech you!

LIGNIÈRE. I cannot.   D'Assoucy is expecting me at the pot-house. Here is a mortal drought!

SWEETMEAT VENDER (*passing before him with a tray*). Orangeade?...

LIGNIÈRE. Ugh!

SWEETMEAT VENDER. Milk?...

LIGNIÈRE. Pah!...

SWEETMEAT VENDER. Lacrima?...

LIGNIÈRE. Stop!   (*To* CHRISTIAN.)   I will tarry a bit.... Let us see this lacrima?

(*Sits down at the sweetmeat stand.   The* VENDER *pours him a glass of lacrima.*)

(*Shouts among the audience at the entrance of a little, merry-faced, roly-poly man.*)

AUDIENCE. Ah, Ragueneau!...

LIGNIÈRE (*to* CHRISTIAN). Ragueneau, who keeps the great cook-shop.

RAGUENEAU (*attired like a pastrycook in his Sunday best, coming quickly toward* LIGNIÈRE). Monsieur, have you seen Monsieur de Cyrano?

LIGNIÈRE (*presenting* RAGUENEAU *to* CHRISTIAN). The pastrycook of poets and of players!

RAGUENEAU (*abashed*). Too much honor....

LIGNIÈRE. No modesty!... Mecænas!...

RAGUENEAU. It is true, those gentlemen are among my customers....

LIGNIÈRE. Debitors!... A considerable poet himself....

RAGUENEAU. It has been said!...

LIGNIÈRE. Daft on poetry!

RAGUENEAU. It is true that for an ode...

LIGNIÈRE. You are willing to give at any time a tart!

RAGUENEAU. ... let. A tart-let.

LIGNIÈRE. Kind soul, he tries to cheapen his charitable acts! And for a triolet were you not known to give...?

RAGUENEAU. Rolls. Just rolls.

LIGNIÈRE (*severely*). Buttered!... And the play, you are fond of the play?

RAGUENEAU. It is with me a passion!

LIGNIÈRE. And you settle for your entrance fee with a pastry currency. Come now, among ourselves, what did you have to give today for admittance here?

RAGUENEAU. Four custards... eighteen lady-fingers. (*He looks all around.*) Monsieur de Cyrano is not here. I wonder at it.

LIGNIÈRE. And why?

RAGUENEAU. Montfleury is billed to play.

LIGNIÈRE. So it is, indeed. That ton of man will today entrance us in the part of Phœdo... Phœdo!... But what is that to Cyrano?

RAGUENEAU. Have you not heard? He interdicted Montfleury, whom he has taken in aversion, from appearing for one month upon the stage.

LIGNIÈRE (*who is at his fourth glass*). Well?

RAGUENEAU. Montfleury is billed to play.

CUIGY (*who has drawn near with his companions*). He cannot be prevented.

RAGUENEAU. He cannot?... Well, I am here to see!

FIRST MARQUIS. What is this Cyrano?

CUIGY. A crack-brain!

SECOND MARQUIS. Of quality?

CUIGY. Enough for daily uses. He is a cadet in the Guards. (*Pointing out a gentleman who is coming and going about the pit, as if in search of somebody.*) But his friend Le Bret can tell you. (*Calling.*) Le Bret!... (LE BRET *comes toward them.*) You are looking for Bergerac?

LE BRET. Yes. I am uneasy.

CUIGY. Is it not a fact that he is a most uncommon fellow?

LE BRET (*affectionately*). The most exquisite being he is that walks beneath the moon!

RAGUENEAU. Poet!

CUIGY. Swordsman!

BRISSAILLE. Physicist!

LE BRET. Musician!

LIGNIÈRE. And what an extraordinary aspect he presents!

RAGUENEAU. I will not go so far as to say that I believe our grave Philippe de Champaigne will leave us a portrait of him; but, the bizarre, excessive, whimsical fellow that he is would certainly have furnished the late Jacques Callot with a type of madcap fighter for one of his masques. Hat with triple feather, doublet with twice-triple skirt, cloak which his interminable rapier lifts up behind, with pomp, like the insolent tail of a cock; prouder than all the Artabans that Gascony ever bred, he goes about in his stiff Punchinello ruff, airing a nose.... Ah, gentlemen, what a nose is that! One cannot look upon such a specimen of the nasigera without exclaiming, "No! truly, the man exaggerates."... After that, one smiles, one says: "He will take it off."... But Monsieur de Bergerac never takes it off at all.

LE BRET (*shaking his head*). He wears it always... and cuts down whoever breathes a syllable in comment.

RAGUENEAU (*proudly*). His blade is half the shears of Fate!

FIRST MARQUIS (*shrugging his shoulders*). He will not come!

RAGUENEAU. He will. I wager you a chicken à la Ragueneau.

FIRST MARQUIS (*laughing*). Very well!

(*Murmur of admiration in the house.* ROXANE *has appeared in her box. She takes a seat in the front, her duenna at the back.* CHRISTIAN, *engaged in paying the* SWEETMEAT VENDER, *does not look.*)

SECOND MARQUIS (*uttering a series of small squeals*). Ah, gentlemen, she is horrifically enticing!

FIRST MARQUIS. A strawberry set in a peach, and smiling!

SECOND MARQUIS. So fresh, that being near her, one might catch cold in his heart!

CHRISTIAN (*looks up, sees* ROXANE, *and, agitated, seizes* LIGNIÈRE *by the arm*). That is she!

LIGNIÈRE (*looking*). Ah, that is she!...

CHRISTIAN. Yes. Tell me at once.... Oh, I am afraid!...

LIGNIÈRE (*sipping his wine slowly*). Magdeleine Robin, surnamed
Roxane Subtle. Euphuistic.

CHRISTIAN. Alack-a-day!

LIGNIÈRE. Unmarried. An orphan. A cousin of Cyrano's... the
one of whom they were talking.

(*While he is speaking, a richly dressed nobleman, wearing the order of the
Holy Ghost on a blue ribbon across his breast, enters* ROXANE's *box,
and, without taking a seat, talks with her a moment.*)

CHRISTIAN (*starting*). That man?...

LIGNIÈRE (*who is beginning to be tipsy, winking*). Hé! Hé! Comte
de Guiche. Enamored of her. But married to the niece of
Armand de Richelieu. Wishes to manage a match between
Roxane and certain sorry lord, one Monsieur de Valvert,
vicomte and... easy. She does not subscribe to his views, but
De Guiche is powerful: he can persecute to some purpose a
simple commoner. But I have duly set forth his shady machina-
tions in a song which... Ho! he must bear me a grudge! The
end was wicked... Listen!...

(*He rises, staggering, and lifting his glass, is about to sing.*)

CHRISTIAN. No. Good evening.

LIGNIÈRE. You are going?...

CHRISTIAN. To find Monsieur de Valvert.

LIGNIÈRE. Have a care. You are the one who will get killed.
(*Indicating* ROXANE *by a glance.*) Stay. Someone is looking...

CHRISTIAN. It is true...

(*He remains absorbed in the contemplation of* ROXANE. *The
pickpockets, seeing his abstracted air, draw nearer to him.*)

LIGNIÈRE. Ah, you are going to stay. Well, I am going. I am
thirsty! And I am looked for... at all the public houses!
(*Exit unsteadily.*)

LE BRET (*who has made the circuit of the house, returning toward* RAGUE-
NEAU, *in a tone of relief*). Cyrano is not here.

RAGUENEAU. And yet...

LE BRET. I will trust to Fortune he has not seen the announcement.

THE AUDIENCE. Begin! Begin!

ONE OF THE MARQUISES (*watching* DE GUICHE, *who comes from*
ROXANE's *box, and crosses the pit, surrounded by obsequious satellites,*

*among whom the* VICOMTE DE VALVERT). Always a court about him, De Guiche!

OTHER MARQUIS. Pf!... Another Gascon!

FIRST MARQUIS. A Gascon, of the cold and supple sort. That sort succeeds. Believe me, it will be best to offer him our duty.

(*They approach* DE GUICHE.)

SECOND MARQUIS. These admirable ribbons! What color, Comte de Guiche? Should you call it Kiss-me-Sweet or... Expiring Fawn?

DE GUICHE. This shade is called Sick Spaniard.

FIRST MARQUIS. Appropriately called, for shortly, thanks to your valor, the Spaniard will be sick indeed, in Flanders!

DE GUICHE. I am going upon the stage. Are you coming? (*He walks toward the stage, followed by all the* MARQUISES *and men of quality. He turns and calls.*) Valvert, come!

CHRISTIAN (*who has been listening and watching them, starts on hearing that name*). The vicomte!... Ah, in his face... in his face I will fling my... (*He puts his hand to his pocket and finds the pickpocket's hand. He turns.*) Hein?

PICKPOCKET. Aï!

CHRISTIAN (*without letting him go*). I was looking for a glove.

PICKPOCKET (*with an abject smile*). And you found a hand. (*In a different tone, low and rapid.*) Let me go... I will tell you a secret.

CHRISTIAN (*without releasing him*). Well?

PICKPOCKET. Lignière who has just left you...

CHRISTIAN (*as above*). Yes?...

PICKPOCKET. Has not an hour to live. A song he made annoyed one of the great, and a hundred men — I am one of them — will be posted tonight...

CHRISTIAN. A hundred?... By whom?

PICKPOCKET. Honor...

CHRISTIAN (*shrugging his shoulders*). Oh!...

PICKPOCKET (*with great dignity*). Among rogues!

CHRISTIAN. Where will they be posted?

PICKPOCKET. At the Porte de Nesle, on his way home. Inform him.

CHRISTIAN (*letting him go*). But where can I find him.

PICKPOCKET. Go to all the taverns: the Golden Vat, the Pine-Apple, the Belt and Bosom, the Twin Torches, the Three Funnels, and in each one leave a scrap of writing warning him.

CHRISTIAN. Yes.  I will run!... Ah, the blackguards!  A hundred against one!... (*Looks lovingly toward* ROXANE.)  Leave her!... (*Furiously, looking toward* VALVERT.)  And him!... But Lignière must be prevented.                          (*Exit running.*)

>    (DE GUICHE, *the* MARQUISES, *all the gentry have disappeared behind the curtain, to place themselves on the stage-seats.  The pit is crowded.  There is not an empty seat in the boxes or the gallery.*)

THE AUDIENCE.  Begin!

A BURGHER (*whose wig goes sailing off at the end of a string held by one of the* PAGES *in the upper gallery*).  My wig!

SCREAMS OF DELIGHT.  He is bald!... The pages!... Well done!... Ha, ha, ha!...

THE BURGHER (*furious, shaking his fist*).  Imp of Satan!...

>    (*Laughter and screams, beginning very loud and decreasing suddenly.  Dead silence.*)

LE BRET (*astonished*).  This sudden hush?... (*One of the spectators whispers in his ear.*)  Ah?...

THE SPECTATOR.  I have it from a reliable quarter.

RUNNING MURMURS.  Hush!... Has he come?  No!... Yes, he has!  In the box with the grating.... The cardinal!... the cardinal!... the cardinal!...

ONE OF THE PAGES.  What a shame!... Now we shall have to behave!

>                     (*Knocking on the stage.  Complete stillness.  Pause.*)

VOICE OF ONE OF THE MARQUISES (*breaking the deep silence, behind the curtain*).  Snuff that candle!

OTHER MARQUIS (*thrusting his head out between the curtains*).  A chair!

>    (*A chair is passed from hand to hand, above the heads.  The* MARQUIS *takes it and disappears, after kissing his hand repeatedly toward the boxes.*)

A SPECTATOR.  Silence!

>    (*Once more, the three knocks.  The curtain opens.  Tableau.  The* MARQUISES *seated at the sides, in attitudes of languid haughtiness.  The stage-setting is the faint-colored bluish sort usual in a pastoral.  Four small crystal candelabra light the stage.  The violins play softly.*)

LE BRET (*to* RAGUENEAU, *under breath*).  Is Montfleury the first to appear?

RAGUENEAU (*likewise under breath*). Yes. The opening lines are his.

LE BRET. Cyrano is not here.

RAGUENEAU. I have lost my wager.

LE BRET. Let us be thankful. Let us be thankful.

(*A bagpipe is heard.* MONTFLEURY *appears upon the stage, enormous, in a conventional shepherd's costume, with a rose-wreathed hat set jauntily on the side of his head, breathing into a be-ribboned bagpipe.*)

THE PIT (*applauding*). Bravo, Montfleury! Montfleury!

MONTFLEURY (*after bowing, proceeds to play the part of* PHŒDO).

Happy the man who, freed from Fashion's fickle sway,
In exile self-prescribed whiles peaceful hours away;
Who when Zephyrus sighs amid the answering trees...

A VOICE (*from the middle of the pit*). Rogue! Did I not forbid you for one month? (*Consternation.* *Everyone looks around.* *Murmurs.*)

VARIOUS VOICES. *Hein?* What? What is the matter?

(*Many in the boxes rise to see.*)

CUIGY. It is he!

LE BRET (*alarmed*). Cyrano!

THE VOICE. King of the Obese! Incontinently vanish!...

THE WHOLE AUDIENCE (*indignant*). Oh!...

MONTFLEURY. But...

THE VOICE. You stop to muse upon the matter?

SEVERAL VOICES (*from the pit and the boxes*). Hush!... Enough!... Proceed, Montfleury.... Fear nothing!

MONTFLEURY (*in an unsteady voice*). Happy the man who, freed from Fashion's f——...

THE VOICE (*more threatening than before*). How is this? Shall I be constrained, Man of the Monster Belly, to enforce my regulation... regularly?

(*An arm holding a cane leaps above the level of the heads.*)

MONTFLEURY (*in a voice growing fainter and fainter*). Happy the man... (*The cane is wildly flourished.*)

THE VOICE. Leave the stage!

THE PIT. Oh!...

MONTFLEURY (*choking*). Happy the man who freed...

CYRANO (*appears above the audience, standing upon a chair, his arms *folded on his chest, his hat at a combative angle, his moustache on end, his nose terrifying).* Ah! I shall lose my temper!

(*Sensation at sight of him.*)

MONTFLEURY (*to the* MARQUISES). Messieurs, I appeal to you!

ONE OF THE MARQUISES (*languidly*). But go ahead!... Play!

CYRANO. Fat man, if you attempt it, I will dust the paint off you with this!

THE MARQUIS. Enough!

CYRANO. Let every little lordling keep silence in his seat, or I will ruffle his ribbons with my cane!

ALL THE MARQUISES (*rising*). This is too much!... Montfleury....

CYRANO. Let Montfleury go home, or stay, and, having cut his ears off, I will disembowel him!

A VOICE. But...

CYRANO. Let him go home, I said!

OTHER VOICE. But after all...

CYRANO. It is not yet done? (*With show of turning up his sleeves.*) Very well, upon that stage, as on a platter trimmed with green, you shall see me carve that mount of brawn...

MONTFLEURY (*calling up his whole dignity*). Monsieur, you cast indignity, in my person, upon the Muse!

CYRANO (*very civilly*). Monsieur, if that lady, with whom you have naught to do, had the pleasure of beholding you... just as you stand, there, like a decorated pot!... she could not live, I do protest, but she hurled her buskin at you!

THE PIT. Montfleury!... Montfleury!... Give us Baro's piece!

CYRANO (*to those shouting around him*). I beg you will show some regard for my scabbard: it is ready to give up the sword!

(*The space around him widens.*)

THE CROWD (*backing away*). Hey... softly, there!

CYRANO (*to* MONTFLEURY). Go off!

THE CROWD (*closing again, and grumbling*). Oh!... Oh!

CYRANO (*turning suddenly*). Has somebody objections?

(*The crowd again pushes away from him.*)

A VOICE (*at the back, singing*).

> Monsieur de Cyrano, one sees,
> Inclines to be tyrannical;
> In spite of that tyrannicle
> We shall see La Clorise!

THE WHOLE AUDIENCE (*catching up the tune*). La Clorise! La Clorise!

CYRANO. Let me hear that song again, and I will do you all to death with my stick!

A BURGHER. Samson come back!...

CYRANO. Lend me your jaw, good man!

A LADY (*in one of the boxes*). This is unheard of!

A MAN. It is scandalous!

A BURGHER. It is irritating, to say no more.

A PAGE. What fun it is!

THE PIT. Ksss!... Montfleury!... Cyrano!...

CYRANO. Be still!...

THE PIT (*in uproar*). Hee-haw!... Baaaaah!... Bow-wow!... Cockadoodledoooooo!

CYRANO. I will...

A PAGE. Meeeow!

CYRANO. I order you to hold your tongues!... I dare the floor collectively to utter another sound!... I challenge you, one and all!... I will take down your names... Step forward, budding heroes! Each in his turn. You shall be given numbers. Come, which one of you will open the joust with me? You, monsieur? No! You? No! The first that offers is promised all the mortuary honors due the brave. Let all who wish to die hold up their hands! (*Silence.*) It is modesty that makes you shrink from the sight of my naked sword? Not a name? Not a hand? — Very good. Then I proceed. (*Turning toward the stage where* MONTFLEURY *is waiting in terror.*) As I was saying, it is my wish to see the stage cured of this tumor. Otherwise... (*claps hand to his sword*) the lancet!

MONTFLEURY. I...

CYRANO (*gets down from his chair, and sits in the space that has become vacant around him, with the ease of one at home*). Thrice will I clap my hands, O plenilune! At the third clap... eclipse!

THE PIT (*diverted*). Ah!...

CYRANO (*clapping his hands*). One!...

MONTFLEURY. I...

A VOICE (*from one of the boxes*). Do not go!...

THE PIT. He will stay!... He will go!...

MONTFLEURY. Messieurs, I feel...

CYRANO. Two!...

MONTFLEURY. I feel it will perhaps be wiser...

CYRANO. Three!...

    (MONTFLEURY *disappears, as if through a trap-door.* **Storm of** *laughter, hissing, catcalls.*)

THE HOUSE. Hoo!... Hoo!... Milksop!... Come back!...

CYRANO (*beaming, leans back in his chair and crosses his legs*). Let him come back, if he dare!

A BURGHER. The spokesman of the company!

    (BELLEROSE *comes forward on the stage and bows.*)

THE BOXES. Ah, there comes Bellerose!

BELLEROSE (*with elegant bearing and diction*). Noble ladies and gentlemen...

THE PIT. No! No! Jodelet... We want Jodelet!...

JODELET (*comes forward, speaks through his nose*). Pack of swine!

THE PIT. That is right!... Well said!... Bravo!

JODELET. Don't bravo me!... The portly tragedian, whose paunch is your delight, felt sick!...

THE PIT. He is a poltroon!...

JODELET. He was obliged to leave...

THE PIT. Let him come back!

SOME. No!

OTHERS. Yes!...

A YOUTH (*to* CYRANO). But, when all is said, monsieur, what good grounds have you for hating Montfleury?

CYRANO (*amiably, sitting as before*). Young gosling, I have two, whereof each, singly, would be ample. Primo: He is an execrable actor, who bellows, and with grunts that would disgrace a water-carrier launches the verse that should go forth as if on pinions!... Secundo: is my secret.

THE OLD BURGHER (*behind* CYRANO). But without compunction you deprive us of hearing La Clorise. I am determined...

CYRANO (*turning his chair around so as to face the old gentleman; respectfully*). Venerable mule, old Baro's verses being what they are, I do it without compunction, as you say.

THE PRÉCIEUSES (*in the boxes*). Ha!... Ho!... Our own Baro!... My dear, did you hear that? How can such a thing be said?... Ha!... Ho!...

CYRANO (*turning his chair so as to face the boxes; gallantly*). Beautiful creatures, do you bloom and shine, be ministers of dreams, your smiles our anodyne. Inspire poets, but poems ... spare to judge!

BELLEROSE. But the money which must be given back at the door!

CYRANO (*turning his chair to face the stage*). Bellerose, you have said the only intelligent thing that has, as yet, been said! Far from me to wrong by so much as a fringe the worshipful mantle of Thespis.... (*He rises and flings a bag upon the stage.*)  Catch!... and keep quiet!

THE HOUSE (*dazzled*). Ah!... Oh!...

JODELET (*nimbly picking up the bag, weighing it with his hand*). For such a price, you are authorized, monsieur, to come and stop the performance every day!

THE HOUSE. Hoo!... Hoo!...

JODELET. Should we be hooted in a body!...

BELLEROSE. The house must be evacuated!

JODELET. Evacuate it!

    (*The audience begins to leave;* CYRANO *looking on with a satisfied air. The crowd, however, becoming interested in the following scene, the exodus is suspended. The women in the boxes who were already standing and had put on their wraps, stop to listen and end by resuming their seats.*)

LE BRET (*to* CYRANO). What you have done ... is mad!

A BORE. Montfleury!... the eminent actor!... What a scandal!... But the Duc de Candale is his patron!... Have you a patron, you?

CYRANO. No!

THE BORE. You have not?

CYRANO. No!

THE BORE. What? You are not protected by some great nobleman under the cover of whose name...

CYRANO (*exasperated*). No, I have told you twice. Must I say the same thing thrice? No, I have no protector... (*hand on sword*) but this will do.

THE BORE. Then, of course, you will leave town.

CYRANO. That will depend.

THE BORE. But the Duc de Candale has a long arm...

CYRANO. Not so long as mine... (*pointing to his sword*) pieced out with this!

THE BORE. But you cannot have the presumption...

CYRANO. I can, yes.

THE BORE. But...

CYRANO. And now,... face about!

THE BORE. But...

CYRANO. Face about, I say... or else, tell me why you are looking at my nose.

THE BORE (*bewildered*). I...

CYRANO (*advancing upon him*). In what is it unusual?

THE BORE (*backing*). Your worship is mistaken.

CYRANO (*same business as above*). Is it flabby and pendulous, like a proboscis?

THE BORE. I never said...

CYRANO. Or hooked like a hawk's beak?

THE BORE. I...

CYRANO. Do you discern a mole upon the tip?

THE BORE. But...

CYRANO. Or is a fly disporting himself thereon? What is there wonderful about it?

THE BORE. Oh...

CYRANO. Is it a freak of nature?

THE BORE. But I had refrained from casting so much as a glance at it!

CYRANO. And why, I pray, should you not look at it?

THE BORE. I had...

CYRANO. So it disgusts you?

THE BORE. Sir...

CYRANO. Its color strikes you as unwholesome?

THE BORE. Sir...

CYRANO. Its shape, unfortunate?

THE BORE. But far from it!

CYRANO. Then wherefore that depreciating air?... Perhaps monsieur thinks it a shade too large?

THE BORE. Indeed not. No, indeed. I think it small... small— I should have said, minute!

CYRANO. What? How? Charge me with such a ridiculous defect? Small, my nose? Ho!...

THE BORE. Heavens!

CYRANO. Enormous, my nose!... Contemptible stutterer, snub-nosed and flat-headed, be it known to you that I am proud, proud of such an appendage! inasmuch as a great nose is properly the index of an affable, kindly, courteous man, witty, liberal, brave, such as I am! and such as you are for evermore precluded from supposing yourself, deplorable rogue! For the inglorious surface my hand encounters above your ruff, is no less devoid —— *(Strikes him.)*

THE BORE. Aï, aï!...

CYRANO. Of pride, alacrity and sweep, of perception and of gift, of heavenly spark, of sumptuousness, to sum up all, of NOSE, than that *(turns him around by the shoulders and suits the action to the word)*, which stops my boot below your spine!

THE BORE *(running off.)* Help! The watch!...

CYRANO. Warning to the idle who might find entertainment in my organ of smell.... And if the facetious fellow be of birth, my custom is, before I let him go to chasten him, in front, and higher up, with steel, and not with hide!

DE GUICHE *(who has stepped down from the stage with the* MARQUISES*).* He is becoming tiresome!

VALVERT *(shrugging his shoulders).* It is empty bluster!

DE GUICHE. Will no one take him up?

VALVERT. No one?... Wait! I will have one of those shots at him! *(He approaches* CYRANO *who is watching him, and stops in front of him, in an attitude of silly swagger.)* Your... your nose is... errr ... Your nose... is very large!

CYRANO *(gravely).* Very.

VALVERT *(laughs).* Ha!...

CYRANO *(imperturbable).* Is that all?

VALVERT. But...

CYRANO. Ah, no, young man, that is not enough! You might have said, dear me, there are a thousand things... varying the tone... For instance... here you are: — Aggressive: "I, monsieur, if I had such a nose, nothing would serve but I must cut it off!" Amicable: "It must be in your way while drinking;

you ought to have a special beaker made!" Descriptive: "It is a crag!... a peak!... a promontory!... A promontory, did I say?... It is a peninsula!" Inquisitive: "What may the office be of that oblong receptacle? Is it an inkhorn or a scissor-case?" Mincing: "Do you so dote on birds, you have, fond as a father, been at pains to fit the little darlings with a roost?" Blunt: "Tell me, monsieur, you, when you smoke, is it possible you blow the vapor through your nose without a neighbor crying 'The chimney is afire'?" Anxious: "Go with caution. I beseech, lest your head, dragged over by that weight, should drag you over!" Tender: "Have a little sunshade made for it! It might get freckled!" Learned: "None but the beast, monsieur, mentioned by Aristophanes, the hippocampelephanto-camelos, can have borne beneath his forehead so much cartilage and bone!" Offhand: "What, comrade, is that sort of peg in style? Capital to hang one's hat upon!" Emphatic: "No wind can hope, O lordly nose, to give the whole of you a cold, but the Nor-Wester!" Dramatic: "It is the Red Sea when it bleeds!" Admiring: "What a sign for a perfumer's shop!" Lyrical: "Art thou a Triton, and is that thy conch?" Simple: "A monument! When is admission free?" Deferent: "Suffer, monsieur, that I should pay you my respects: that is what I call possessing a house of your own!" Rustic: "Hi, boys! Call that a nose? Ye don't gull me! It's either a prize carrot or else a stunted gourd!" Military: "Level against the cavalry!" Practical: "Will you put it up for raffle? Indubitably, sir, it will be the feature of the game!" And finally in parody of weeping Pyramus: "Behold, behold the nose that traitorously destroyed the beauty of its master! and is blushing for the same!" — That, my dear sir, or something not unlike, is what you would have said to me, had you the smallest leaven of letters or of wit; but of wit, O most pitiable of objects made by God, you never had a rudiment, and of letters, you have just those that are needed to spell "fool!" — But, had it been otherwise, and had you been possessed of the fertile fancy requisite to shower upon me, here, in this noble company, that volley of sprightly pleasantries, still should you not have delivered yourself of so much as a quarter of the tenth part of the beginning of the

first.... For I let off these good things at myself, and with
sufficient zest, but do not suffer another to let them off at
me!

DE GUICHE (*attempting to lead away the amazed vicomte*). Let be,
vicomte!

VALVERT. That insufferable haughty bearing!... A clodhopper
without... without so much as gloves... who goes abroad without points... or bowknots!...

CYRANO. My foppery is of the inner man. I do not trick myself
out like a popinjay, but I am more fastidious, if I am not so
showy. I would not sally forth, by any chance, not washed
quite clean of an affront; my conscience foggy about the eye,
my honor crumpled, my nicety black-rimmed. I walk with all
upon me furbished bright. I plume myself with independence
and straightforwardness. It is not a handsome figure, it is my
soul, I hold erect as in a brace. I go decked with exploits in
place of ribbon bows. I taper to a point my wit like a moustache. And at my passage through the crowd true sayings ring
like spurs!

VALVERT. But, sir...

CYRANO. I am without gloves?... a mighty matter! I only had
one left, of a very ancient pair, and even that became a burden
to me... I left it in somebody's face.

VALVERT. Villain, clod-poll, flat-foot, refuse of the earth!

CYRANO (*taking off his hat and bowing as if the* VICOMTE *had been
introducing himself*). Ah?... And mine, Cyrano-Savinien-Hercule
of Bergerac!

VALVERT (*exasperated*). Buffoon!

CYRANO (*giving a sudden cry, as if seized with a cramp*). Aï!...

VALVERT (*who had started toward the back, turning*). What is he saying
now?

CYRANO (*screwing his face as if in pain*). It must have leave to stir...
it has a cramp! It is bad for it to be kept still so long!

VALVERT. What is the matter?

CYRANO. My rapier prickles like a foot asleep!

VALVERT (*drawing*). So be it!

CYRANO. I shall give you a charming little hurt!

VALVERT (*contemptuous*). A poet!

CYRANO. Yes, a poet,... and to such an extent, that while we fence, I will, hop! extempore, compose you a ballade!

VALVERT. A ballade?

CYRANO. I fear you do not know what that is.

VALVERT. But...

CYRANO (*as if saying a lesson*). The ballade is composed of three stanzas of eight lines each...

VALVERT (*stamps with his feet*). Oh!...

CYRANO (*continuing*). And an envoi of four.

VALVERT. You...

CYRANO. I will with the same breath fight you and compose one. And at the last line, I will hit you.

VALVERT. Indeed you will not!

CYRANO. No?... (*Declaiming.*)

> Ballade of the duel which in Burgundy House
> Monsieur de Bergerac fought with a jackanapes.

VALVERT. And what is that, if you please?

CYRANO. That is the title.

THE AUDIENCE (*at the highest pitch of excitement*). Make room!... Good sport!... Stand aside!... Keep still!...

> (*Tableou. A ring, in the pit, of the interested; the MARQUISES and OFFICERS scattered among the BURGHERS and COMMON PEOPLE. The PAGES have climbed on the shoulders of various ones, the better to see. All the women are standing in the boxes. At the right, DE GUICHE and his attendant gentlemen. At left, LE BRET, RAGUENEAU, CUIGY, etc.*)

CYRANO (*closing his eyes a second*). Wait. I am settling upon the rhymes. There. I have them.

> (*In declaiming, he suits the action to the word.*)

> Of my broad felt made lighter,
> I cast my mantle broad,
> And stand, poet and fighter,
> To do and to record.
> I bow, I draw my sword...
> En garde! with steel and wit
> I play you at first abord...
> At the last line, I hit!

> (*They begin fencing.*)

You should have been politer;
Where had you best be gored?
The left side or the right — ah?
Or next your azure cord?
Or where the spleen is stored?
Or in the stomach pit?
Come we to quick accord...
At the last line, I hit!

You falter, you turn whiter?
You do so to afford
Your foe a rhyme in "iter"?...
You thrust at me — I ward —
And balance is restored.
Laridon! Look to your spit!...
No, you shall not be floored
Before my cue to hit!

(*He announces solemnly.*)

ENVOI

Prince, call upon the Lord!...
I skirmish... feint a bit...
I lunge!... I keep my word!
(*The* VICOMTE *staggers;* CYRANO *bows.*)
At the last line, I hit!

(*Acclamations. Applause from the boxes. Flowers and handkerchiefs are thrown. The* OFFICERS *surround and congratulate*
CYRANO. RAGUENEAU *dances with delight.* LE BRET *is
tearfully joyous and at the same time highly troubled. The
friends of the* VICOMTE *support him off the stage.*)

THE CROWD (*in a long shout*). Ah!...

A LIGHT-CAVALRY MAN. Superb!

A WOMAN. Sweet!

RAGUENEAU. Astounding!

A MARQUIS. Novel!

LE BRET. Insensate!

THE CROWD (*pressing around* CYRANO). Congratulations!... Well
done!... Bravo!...

A WOMAN'S VOICE. He is a hero!

A MOUSQUETAIRE (*striding swiftly toward* CYRANO, *with outstretched hand*). Monsieur, will you allow me? It was quite, quite excellently done, and I think I know whereof I speak. But, as a fact, I expressed my mind before, by making a huge noise....

(*He retires.*)

CYRANO (*to* CUIGY). Who may the gentleman be?

CUIGY. D'Artagnan.

LE BRET (*to* CYRANO, *taking his arm*). Come, I wish to talk with you.

CYRANO. Wait till the crowd has thinned. (*To* BELLEROSE.) I may remain?

BELLEROSE (*deferentially*). Why, certainly!...

(*Shouts are heard outside.*)

JODELET (*after looking*). They are hooting Montfleury.

BELLEROSE (*solemnly*). Sic transit!... (*In a different tone, to the doorkeeper and the candle snuffer.*) Sweep and close. Leave the lights. We shall come back, after eating, to rehearse a new farce for tomorrow.

(*Exeunt* JODELET *and* BELLEROSE, *after bowing very low to* CYRANO.)

THE DOORKEEPER (*to* CYRANO). Monsieur will not be going to dinner?

CYRANO. I?... No. (*The doorkeeper withdraws.*)

LE BRET (*to* CYRANO). And this, because?...

CYRANO (*proudly*). Because... (*In a different tone, having seen that the doorkeeper is too far to overhear.*) I have not a penny!

LE BRET (*making the motion of flinging a bag*). How is this? The bag of crowns...

CYRANO. Monthly remittance, thou lastedst but a day!

LE BRET. And to keep you the remainder of the month?...

CYRANO. Nothing is left!

LE BRET. But then, flinging that bag, what a child's prank!

CYRANO. But what a gesture!...

THE SWEETMEAT VENDER (*coughing behind her little counter*). Hm!... (CYRANO *and* LE BRET *turn toward her. She comes timidly forward.*) Monsieur, to know you have not eaten... makes my heart ache. (*Pointing to the sweetmeat-stand.*) I have there all that is needed... (*Impulsively.*) Help yourself!

CYRANO (*taking off his hat*). Dear child, despite my Gascon pride, which forbids that I should profit at your hand by the most inconsiderable of dainties, I fear too much lest a denial should grieve you: I will accept therefore... (*He goes to the stand and selects.*) Oh, a trifle!... A grape off this... (*She proffers the bunch, he takes a single grape.*) No... one! This glass of water... (*She starts to pour wine into it, he stops her.*) No... clear! And half a macaroon.

(*He breaks in two the macaroon, and returns half.*)

LE BRET. This comes near being silly!

SWEETMEAT VENDER. Oh, you will take something more!...

CYRANO. Yes. Your hand to kiss.

(*He kisses the hand she holds out to him, as if it were that of a princess.*)

SWEETMEAT VENDER. Monsieur, I thank you. (*Curtseys.*) Good-evening! (*Exit.*)

CYRANO (*to* LE BRET). I am listening. (*He establishes himself before the stand, sets the macaroon before him.*) Dinner! (*Does the same with the glass of water.*) Drink! (*And with the grape.*) Dessert! (*He sits down.*) La! let me begin! I was as hungry as a wolf! (*Eating.*) You were saying?

LE BRET. That if you listen to none but those great boobies and swashbucklers your judgment will become wholly perverted. Inquire, will you, of the sensible, concerning the effect produced today by your prowesses.

CYRANO (*finishing his macaroon*). Enormous!

LE BRET. The cardinal...

CYRANO (*beaming*). He was there, the cardinal?

LE BRET. Must have found what you did...

CYRANO. To a degree, original.

LE BRET. Still...

CYRANO. He is a poet. It cannot be distasteful to him wholly that one should deal confusion to a fellow-poet's play.

LE BRET. But, seriously, you make too many enemies!

CYRANO (*biting into the grape*). How many, thereabouts, should you think I made tonight?

LE BRET. Eight and forty. Not mentioning the women.

CYRANO. Come, tell them over!

LE BRET. Montfleury, the old merchant, De Guiche, the Vicomte, Baro, the whole Academy...

CYRANO. Enough! You steep me in bliss!

LE BRET. But whither will the road you follow lead you? What can your object be?

CYRANO. I was wandering aimlessly; too many roads were open... too many resolves, too complex, allowed of being taken. I took...

LE BRET. Which?

CYRANO. By far the simplest of them all. I decided to be, in every matter, always, admirable!

LE BRET (*shrugging his shoulders*). That will do.— But tell me, will you not, the motive — look, the true one! — of your dislike to Montfleury.

CYRANO (*rising*). That old Silenus, who has not seen his knees this many a year, still believes himself a delicate desperate danger to the fair. And as he struts and burrs upon the stage, makes sheep's-eyes at them with his moist frog's-eyes. And I have hated him... oh, properly!... since the night he was so daring as to cast his glance on her... her, who — Oh, I thought I saw a slug crawl over a flower!

LE BRET (*amazed*). Hey? What? Is it possible?...

CYRANO (*with a bitter laugh*). That I should love? (*In a different tone, seriously.*) I love.

LE BRET. And may one know?... You never told me...

CYRANO. Whom I love?... Come, think a little. The dream of being beloved, even by the beautiless, is made, to me, an empty dream indeed by this good nose, my forerunner ever by a quarter of an hour. Hence, whom should I love?... It seems superfluous to tell you!... I love... it was inevitable!... the most beautiful that breathes!

LE BRET. The most beautiful?...

CYRANO. No less, in the whole world! And the most resplendent, and the most delicate of wit, and among the golden-haired... (*With overwhelming despair.*) Still the superlative!

LE BRET. Dear me, what is this fair one?

CYRANO. All unawares, a deadly snare, exquisite without concern to be so. A snare of nature's own, a musk-rose, in which ambush Love lies low. Who has seen her smile remembers the ineffable! There is not a thing so common but she turns it into prettiness; and in the merest nod or beck she can make manifest all the attributes of a goddess. No, Venus! you cannot step into your iridescent shell, nor, Dian, you, walk through the blossoming groves, as she steps into her chair and walks in Paris!

LE BRET. Sapristi! I understand! It is clear!

CYRANO. It is pellucid.

LE BRET. Magdeleine Robin, your cousin?

CYRANO. Yes, Roxane.

LE BRET. But, what could be better? You love her? Tell her so! You covered yourself with glory in her sight a moment since.

CYRANO. Look well at me, dear friend, and tell me how much hope you think can be justly entertained with this protuberance. Oh, I foster no illusions!... Sometimes, indeed, yes, in the violet dusk, I yield, even I! to a dreamy mood. I penetrate some garden that lies sweetening the hour. With my poor great devil of a nose I sniff the April.... And as I follow with my eyes some woman passing with some cavalier, I think how dear would I hold having to walk beside me, linked like that, slowly, in the soft moonlight, such a one! I kindle — I forget — and then... then suddenly I see the shadow of my profile upon the garden-wall!

LE BRET (touched). My friend...

CYRANO. Friend, I experience a bad half hour sometimes, in feeling so unsightly... and alone.

LE BRET (in quick sympathy, taking his hand). You weep?

CYRANO. Ah, God forbid! That? Never! No, that would be unsightly to excess! That a tear should course the whole length of this nose! Never, so long as I am accountable, shall the divine loveliness of tears be implicated with so much gross ugliness! Mark me well, nothing is so holy as are tears, nothing! and never shall it be that, rousing mirth through me, a single one of them shall seem ridiculous!

LE BRET. Come, do not despond! Love is a lottery.

CYRANO (shaking his head). No! I love Cleopatra: do I resemble Caesar? I worship Berenice: do I put you in mind of Titus?

LE BRET. But your courage... and your wit! — The little girl who but a moment ago bestowed on you that very modest meal, her eyes, you must have seen as much, did not exactly hate you!

CYRANO (*impressed*). That is true!

LE BRET. You see? So, then! — But Roxane herself, in following your duel, went lily-pale.

CYRANO. Lily-pale?...

LE BRET. Her mind, her heart as well, are struck with wonder! Be bold, speak to her, in order that she may...

CYRANO. Laugh in my face!... No, there is but one thing upon earth I fear.... It is that.

THE DOORKEEPER (*admitting the* DUENNA *to* CYRANO). Monsieur, you are inquired for.

CYRANO (*seeing the* DUENNA). Ah, my God!... her duenna!

THE DUENNA (*with a great curtsey*). Somebody wishes to know of her valorous cousin where one may, in private, see him.

CYRANO (*upset*). See me?

THE DUENNA (*with curtsey*). See you. There are things for your ear.

CYRANO. There are... ?

THE DUENNA (*other curtsey*). Things.

CYRANO (*staggering*). Ah, my God!...

THE DUENNA. Somebody intends, tomorrow, at the earliest roses of the dawn, to hear Mass at Saint Roch.

CYRANO (*upholds himself by leaning on* LE BRET). Ah, my God!

THE DUENNA. That over, where might one step in a moment, have a little talk?

CYRANO (*losing his senses*). Where?... I... But... Ah, my God!

THE DUENNA. Expedition, if you please.

CYRANO. I am casting about...

THE DUENNA. Where?

CYRANO. At... at... at Ragueneau's... the pastrycook's.

THE DUENNA. He lodges?

CYRANO. In... In Rue... Ah, my God! my God!... St. Honoré.

THE DUENNA (*retiring*). We will be there. Do not fail. At seven.

CYRANO. I will not fail.                    (*Exit* DUENNA.)

CYRANO (*falling on* LE BRET's *neck*). To me... from her... a meeting!

LE BRET. Well, your gloom is dispelled?

CYRANO. Ah, to whatever end it may be, she is aware of my existence!

LE BRET. And now you will be calm?

CYRANO (*beside himself*). Now, I shall be fulminating and frenetical! I want an army all complete to put to rout! I have ten hearts and twenty arms... I cannot now be suited with felling dwarfs to earth.... (*At the top of his lungs.*)   Giants are what I want!

(*During the last lines, on the stage at the back, shadowy shapes of players have been moving about.   The rehearsal has begun; the fiddlers have resumed their places.*)

A VOICE (*from the stage*). Hey! Psst! Over there!   A little lower. We are trying to rehearse!

CYRANO (*laughing*). We are going!          (*He goes toward the back.*)

(*Through the street door, enter* CUIGY, BRISSAILLE, *several* OFFICERS *supporting* LIGNIÈRE *in a state of complete intoxication.*)

CUIGY. Cyrano!

CYRANO. What is this?

CUIGY. A *turdus vinaticus* we are bringing you.

CYRANO (*recognizing him*). Lignière!   Hey, what has happened to you?

CUIGY. He is looking for you.

BRISSAILLE. He cannot go home.

CYRANO. Why?

LIGNIÈRE (*in a thick voice, showing him a bit of crumpled paper*). This note bids me beware... A hundred men against me... on account of lampoon... Grave danger threatening me... Porte de Nesle... must pass it to get home.   Let me come and sleep under your roof.

CYRANO. A hundred, did you say? — You shall sleep at home!

LIGNIÈRE (*frightened*). But...

CYRANO (*in a terrible voice, pointing to the lighted lantern which the* DOORKEEPER *stands swinging as he listens to this scene*).   Take that lantern (LIGNIÈRE *hurriedly takes it*) and walk!... I swear to tuck you in your bed tonight myself.   (*To the* OFFICERS.)   You, follow at a distance.   You may look on!

CUIGY. But a hundred men...

CYRANO. Are not one man too many for my mood tonight!

(*The players, in their several costumes, have stepped down from the stage and come nearer.*)

LE BRET. But why take under your especial care...

CYRANO. Still Le Bret is not satisfied!

LE BRET. That most commonplace of sots?

CYRANO (*slapping* LIGNIÈRE *on the shoulder*). Because this sot, this cask of muscatel, this hogshead of rosolio, did once upon a time a wholly pretty thing. On leaving Mass, having seen her whom he loved take holy-water, as the rite prescribes, he, whom the sight of water puts to flight, ran to the holy-water bowl, and stooping over, drank it dry....

AN ACTRESS (*in the costume of soubrette*). *Tiens*, that was nice!

CYRANO. Was it not, soubrette?

THE SOUBRETTE (*to the others*). But why are they, a hundred, all against one poor poet?

CYRANO. Let us start! (*To the* OFFICERS.) And you, gentlemen, when you see me attack, whatever you may suppose to be my danger, do not stir to second me!

ANOTHER OF THE ACTRESSES (*jumping from the stage*). Oh, I will not miss seeing this!

CYRANO. Come!

ANOTHER ACTRESS (*likewise jumping from the stage, to an elderly actor*). Cassandre, will you not come?

CYRANO. Come, all of you! the Doctor, Isabel, Leander, all! and you shall lend, charming fantastic swarm, an air of Italian farce to the Spanish drama in view. Yes, you shall be a tinkling heard above a roar, like bells about a tambourine!

ALL THE WOMEN (*in great glee*). Bravo!... Hurry!... A mantle!... A hood!

JODELET. Let us go!

CYRANO (*to the fiddlers*). You will favor us with a tune, messieurs the violinists!

(*The fiddlers fall into the train. The lighted candles which furnished the footlights are seized and distributed. The procession becomes a torchlight procession.*)

CYRANO. Bravo! Officers, beauty in fancy dress, and, twenty steps ahead... (*he takes the position he describes*). I, by myself,

under the feather stuck, with her own hand, by Glory, in my
hat! Proud as a Scipio trebly Nasica! — It is understood?
Formal interdiction to interfere with me! — We are ready?
One! Two! Three! Doorkeeper, open the door!

(*The* DOORKEEPER *opens wide the folding door. A picturesque
corner of Old Paris appears, bathed in moonlight.*)

CYRANO. Ah!... Paris floats in dim nocturnal mist.... The sloping
bluish roofs are washed with moonlight ... A setting, exquisite
indeed, offers itself for the scene about to be enacted.... Yonder,
under silvery vapor wreathes, like a mysterious magic mirror,
glimmers the Seine.... And you shall see what you shall see!

ALL. To the Porte de Nesle!

CYRANO (*standing on the threshold*). To the Porte de Nesle! (*Before
crossing it, he turns to the* SOUBRETTE.) Were you not asking,
mademoiselle, why upon that solitary rhymster a hundred
men were set? (*He draws his sword, and tranquilly.*) Because
it was well known he is a friend of mine! (*Exit.*)

(*To the sound of the violins, by the flickering light of the candles,
the procession —* LIGNIÈRE *staggering at the head, the* ACTRESSES
*arm in arm with the* OFFICERS, *the players capering behind —
follows out into the night.*)

CURTAIN

# ACT SECOND

### THE COOKSHOP OF POETS

RAGUENEAU'S *shop, vast kitchen at the corner of Rue St. Honoré and
Rue de l'Arbre-Sec, which can be seen at the back, through the glass door,
gray in the early dawn.*

*At the left, in front, a counter overhung by a wrought-iron canopy
from which geese, ducks, white peacocks are hanging. In large china
jars, tall nosegays composed of the simpler flowers mainly sunflowers.
On the same side, in the middle distance, an enormous fireplace, in front
of which, between huge andirons, each of which supports a small iron pot,
roasting meats drip into appropriate pans.*

*At the right, door in the front wing. In the middle distance, a staircase
leading to a loft, the interior of which is seen through open shutters; a*

*spread table lighted by a small Flemish candelabrum, shows it to be an eating-room. A wooden gallery continuing the stairway, suggests other similar rooms to which it may lead.*

*In the center of the shop, an iron hoop — which can be lowered by means of a rope — to which large roasts are hooked.*

*In the shadow, under the stairway, ovens are glowing. Copper molds and saucepans are shining; spits turning, hams swinging, pastry pyramids showing fair. It is the early beginning of the workday. Bustling of hurried scullions, portly cooks and young cook's-assistants; swarming of caps decorated with hen feathers and guinea-fowl wings. Wicker crates and broad sheets of tin are brought in loaded with brioches and tarts.*

*There are tables covered with meats and cakes; others, surrounded by chairs, await customers. In a corner, a smaller table, littered with papers. At the rise of the curtain,* RAGUENEAU *is discovered seated at this table, writing with an inspired air, and counting upon his fingers.*

FIRST PASTRYCOOK (*bringing in a tall molded pudding*). Nougat of fruit!

SECOND PASTRYCOOK (*bringing in the dish he names*). Custard!

THIRD PASTRYCOOK (*bringing in a fowl roasted in its feathers*). Peacock!

FOURTH PASTRYCOOK (*bringing in a tray of cakes*). Mince-pies!

FIFTH PASTRYCOOK (*bringing in a deep earthen dish*). Beef stew!

RAGUENEAU (*laying down his pen, and looking up*). Daybreak already plates with silver the copper pans! Time, Ragueneau, to smother within thee the singing divinity! The hour of the lute will come anon — now is that of the ladle! (*He rises; speaking to one of the cooks.*) You, sir, be so good as to lengthen this gravy — it is too thick!

THE COOK. How much?

RAGUENEAU. Three feet. (*Goes farther.*)

THE COOK. What does he mean?

FIRST PASTRYCOOK. Let me have the tart!

SECOND PASTRYCOOK. The dumpling!

RAGUENEAU (*standing before the fireplace*). Spread thy wings, Muse, and fly further, that thy lovely eyes may not be reddened at the sordid kitchen fire! (*To one of the cooks, pointing at some small loaves of bread.*) You have improperly placed the cleft in those loaves; the cæsura belongs in the middle — between the hemistichs! (*To another of the* COOKS, *pointing at an unfinished pastry.*) This pastry palace requires a roof! (*To a young cook's apprentice, who, seated upon the floor, is putting fowls on a spit.*) And you, on that long spit, arrange, my son, in pleasing alternation, the modest pullet and the splendid turkey-cock — even as our wise Malherbe alternated of old the greater with the lesser lines, and so with roasted fowls compose a poem!

ANOTHER APPRENTICE (*coming forward with a platter covered by a napkin*). Master, in your honor, see what I have baked....I hope you are pleased with it!

RAGUENEAU (*ecstatic*). A lyre!

THE APPRENTICE. Of pie-crust!

RAGUENEAU (*touched*). With candied fruits!

THE APPRENTICE. And the strings, see — of spun sugar!

RAGUENEAU (*giving him money*). Go, drink my health! (*Catching sight of* LISE *who is entering.*) Hush! My wife!... Move on, and hide that money. (*To* LISE, *showing her the lyre, with a constrained air.*) Fine, is it not?

LISE. Ridiculous! (*She sets a pile of wrapping-paper on the counter.*)

RAGUENEAU. Paper bags? Good. Thanks. (*He examines them.*) Heavens! My beloved books! The masterpieces of my friends — dismembered — torn! — to fashion paper bags for penny pies! — Ah, the abominable case is re-enacted of Orpheus and the Mænads!

LISE (*drily*). And have I not an unquestionable right to make what use I can of the sole payment ever got from your paltry scribblers of uneven lines?

RAGUENEAU. Pismire! Forbear to insult those divine, melodious crickets!

LISE. Before frequenting that low crew, my friend, you did not use to call me a Mænad — no, nor yet a pismire!

RAGUENEAU. Put poems to such a use!

LISE. To that use and no other!

RAGUENEAU. If with poems you do this, I should like to know, Madame, what you do with prose!

(*Two children have come into the shop.*)

RAGUENEAU. What can I do for you, little ones?

FIRST CHILD. Three patties.

RAGUENEAU (*waiting on them*). There you are! Beautifully browned, and piping hot.

SECOND CHILD. Please, will you wrap them for us?

RAGUENEAU (*starting, aside*). There goes one of my bags! (*To the children.*) You want them wrapped, do you? (*He takes one of the paper bags, and as he is about to put in the patties, reads.*) "*No otherwise, Ulysses, from Penelope departing....*" Not this one! (*He lays it aside and takes another. At the moment of putting in the patties, he reads.*) "*Phœbus of the aureate locks...*" Not that one! (*Same business.*)

LISE (*out of patience*). Well, what are you waiting for?

RAGUENEAU. Here we are. Here we are. Here we are. (*He takes a third bag and resigns himself.*) The sonnet to Phyllis! ... It is hard, all the same.

LISE. It is lucky you made up your mind. (*Shrugging her shoulders.*) Nicodemus! (*She climbs on a chair and arranges dishes on a sideboard.*)

RAGUENEAU (*taking advantage of her back being turned, calls back the children who had already reached the door*). Psst!... Children! Give me back the sonnet to Phyllis, and you shall have six patties instead of three! (*The children give back the paper-bag, joyfully take the patties and exeunt.* RAGUENEAU *smooths out the crumpled paper and reads declaiming.*) "*Phyllis!* "... Upon that charming name, a grease-spot!... "*Phyllis!* "...

(*Enter brusquely* CYRANO.)

CYRANO. What time is it?

RAGUENEAU (*bowing with eager deference*). Six o'clock.

CYRANO (*with emotion*). In an hour! (*He comes and goes in the shop.*)

RAGUENEAU (*following him*). Bravo! I too was witness...

CYRANO. Of what?

RAGUENEAU. Your fight.

CYRANO. Which?

RAGUENEAU. At the Hotel de Bourgogne.

CYRANO (*with disdain*). Ah, the duel!

RAGUENEAU (*admiringly*). Yes — the duel in rhyme.

LISE. He can talk of nothing else.

CYRANO. Let him!... It does no harm.

RAGUENEAU (*thrusting with a spit he has seized*). "*At the last line, I hit!*"

"*At the last line I hit!*"—How fine that is!   (*With growing enthusiasm.*)   "*At the last line, I*"——

CYRANO.   What time, Ragueneau?

RAGUENEAU (*remaining fixed in the attitude of thrusting, while he looks at the clock*).   Five minutes past six.— "*I hit!*"   (*He recovers from his duelling posture.*)   Oh, to be able to make a ballade!

LISE (*to* CYRANO, *who in passing her counter has absentmindedly shaken hands with her*).   What ails your hand?

CYRANO.   Nothing.   A scratch.

RAGUENEAU.   You have been exposed to some danger?

CYRANO.   None whatever.

LISE (*shaking her finger at him*).   I fear that is a fib!

CYRANO.   From the swelling of my nose?   The fib in that case must have been good-sized.... (*In a different tone.*)   I am expecting someone.   You will leave us alone in here.

RAGUENEAU.   But how can I contrive it?   My poets shortly will be coming...

LISE (*ironically*).   For breakfast!

CYRANO.   When I sign to you, you will clear the place of them.— What time is it?

RAGUENEAU.   It is ten minutes past six.

CYRANO (*seating himself nervously at* RAGUENEAU's *table and helping himself to paper*).   A pen?

RAGUENEAU (*taking one from behind his ear, and offering it*).   A swan's quill.

A MOUSQUETAIRE (*with enormous moustachios, enters; in a stentorian voice*).   Good-morning!

(LISE *goes hurriedly to him, toward the back.*)

CYRANO (*turning*).   What is it?

RAGUENEAU.   A friend of my wife's — a warrior — terrible, from his own report.

CYRANO (*taking up the pen again, and waving* RAGUENEAU *away*).   Hush!... (*To himself.*)   Write to her, ... fold the letter, ... hand it to her, ... and make my escape.... (*Throwing down the pen.*)   Coward!... But may I perish if I have the courage to speak to her, ... to say a single word.... (*To* RAGUENEAU.)   What time is it?

RAGUENEAU.   A quarter past six.

CYRANO (*beating his breast*). A single word of all I carry here!...
Whereas in writing... (*He takes up the pen again.*) Come, let us
write it then, in very deed, the love-letter I have written in
thought so many times, I have but to lay my soul beside my
paper, and copy! (*He writes.*)

(*Beyond the glass door, shadowy lank hesitating shabby forms are
seen moving.*)

(*Enter the* POETS, *clad in black, with hanging hose, sadly mudsplashed.*)

LISE (*coming forward, to* RAGUENEAU). Here they come, your scare-
crows!

FIRST POET (*entering, to* RAGUENEAU). Brother in art!...

SECOND POET (*shaking both* RAGUENEAU'S *hands*). Dear fellow-
bard....

THIRD POET. Eagle of pastrycooks (*sniffs the air*), your eyrie smells
divine!

FOURTH POET. Phœbus turned baker!

FIFTH POET. Apollo master-cook!

RAGUENEAU (*surrounded, embraced, shaken by the hand*). How at his
ease a man feels at once with them!

FIRST POET. The reason we are late, is the crowd at the Porte de
Nesle!

SECOND POET. Eight ugly ruffians, ripped open with the sword, lie
weltering on the pavement.

CYRANO (*raising his head a second*). Eight? I thought there were
only seven. (*Goes out with his letter.*)

RAGUENEAU (*to* CYRANO). Do you happen to know who is the
hero of this event?

CYRANO (*negligently*). I?... No.

LISE (*to the* MOUSQUETAIRE). Do you?

THE MOUSQUETAIRE (*turning up the ends of his moustache*). Possibly!

CYRANO (*writing; from time to time he is heard murmuring a word or two*).
... "I love you..."

FIRST POET. A single man, we were told, put a whole gang to
flight!

SECOND POET. Oh, it was a rare sight! The ground was littered
with pikes, and cudgels...

CYRANO (*writing*).... "*Your eyes...*"

THIRD POET. Hats were strewn as far as the Goldsmiths' square!

FIRST POET. Sapristi! He must have been a madman of mettle....

CYRANO (*as above*). "*... your lips...*"

FIRST POET. An infuriate giant, the doer of that deed!

CYRANO (*same business*). "*... but when I see you, I come near to swooning with a tender dread...*"

SECOND POET (*snapping up a tart*). What have you lately written, Ragueneau?

CYRANO (*same business*). "*... who loves you devotedly...*" (*In the act of signing the letter, he stops, rises, and tucks it inside his doublet.*) No need to sign it. I deliver it myself.

RAGUENEAU (*to* SECOND POET). I have rhymed a recipe.

THIRD POET (*establishing himself beside a tray of cream puffs*). Let us hear this recipe!

FOURTH POET (*examining a brioche of which he has possessed himself*). It should not wear its cap so saucily on one side... it scarcely looks well!... (*Bites off the top.*)

FIRST POET. See, the spice-cake there, ogling a susceptible poet with eyes of almond under citron brows!... (*He takes the spice cake.*)

SECOND POET. We are listening!

THIRD POET (*slightly squeezing a cream puff between his fingers*). This puff creams at the mouth.... I water!

SECOND POET (*taking a bite out of the large pastry lyre*). For once the Lyre will have filled my stomach!

RAGUENEAU (*who has made ready to recite, has coughed, adjusted his cap, struck an attitude*). A recipe in rhyme!

SECOND POET (*to* FIRST POET, *nudging him*). Is it breakfast, with you?

FIRST POET (*to* SECOND POET). And with you, is it dinner?

RAGUENEAU. *How Almond Cheese-Cakes should be made.*

> Briskly beat to lightness due,
> > Eggs, a few;
> With the eggs so beaten, beat —
> Nicely strained for this same use —
> > Lemon-juice,
> Adding milk of almonds, sweet.

> With fine pastry dough, rolled flat,
>      After that,
> Line each little scalloped mold;
> Round the sides, light-fingered, spread
>      Marmalade;
> Pour the liquid eggy gold,
>
> Into each delicious pit;
>      Prison it
> In the oven — and, bye and bye,
> Almond cheese-cakes will in gay
>      Blond array
> Bless your nostril and your eye!

THE POETS (*their mouths full*).   Exquisite!... Delicious!

ONE OF THE POETS (*choking*).   Humph!

> (*They go toward the back, eating.   CYRANO, who has been
>      watching them, approaches RAGUENEAU.*)

CYRANO.  While you recite your works to them, have you a notion
how they stuff?

RAGUENEAU (*low, with a smile*).   Yes, I see them... without looking,
lest they should be abashed.   I get a double pleasure thus from
saying my verses over: I satisfy a harmless weakness of which
I stand convicted, at the same time as giving those who have
not fed a needed chance to feed!

CYRANO (*slapping him on the shoulder*).   You,... I like you!   (RA-
GUENEAU *joins his friends.   CYRANO looks after him; then, somewhat
sharply.*)   Hey, Lise!   (LISE, *absorbed in tender conversation with the
MOUSQUETAIRE, starts and comes forward toward CYRANO.*)   Is
that captain... laying siege to you?

LISE (*offended*).   My eyes, sir, have ever held in respect those who
meant hurt to my character....

CYRANO.  For eyes so resolute... I thought yours looked a little
lanquishing!

LISE (*choking with anger*).   But...

CYRANO (*bluntly*).   I like your husband.   Wherefore, Madame
Lise, I say he shall not be sc... horned!

LISE.  But...

CYRANO (*raising his voice so as to be heard by the* MOUSQUETAIRE). A word to the wise!

> (*He bows to the* MOUSQUETAIRE, *and after looking at the clock, goes to the door at the back and stands in watch.*)

LISE (*to the* MOUSQUETAIRE, *who has simply returned* CYRANO'S *bow*). Really... I am astonished at you.... Defy him... to his face!

THE MOUSQUETAIRE. To his face, indeed!... to his face!...

> (*He quickly moves off.* LISE *follows him.*)

CYRANO (*from the door at the back, signalling to* RAGUENEAU *that he should clear the room*). Pst!...

RAGUENEAU (*urging the* POETS *toward the door at the right*). We shall be much more comfortable in there....

CYRANO (*impatiently*). Pst!... Pst!...

RAGUENEAU (*driving along the* POETS). I want to read you a little thing of mine....

FIRST POET (*despairingly, his mouth full*). But the provisions....

SECOND POET. Shall not be parted from us!

> (*They follow* RAGUENEAU *in procession, after making a raid on the eatables.*)

CYRANO. If I feel that there is so much as a glimmer of hope... I will out with my letter!...

> (ROXANE, *masked, appears behind the glass door, followed by the* DUENNA.)

CYRANO (*instantly opening the door*). Welcome! (*Approaching the* DUENNA.) Madame, a word with you!

THE DUENNA. A dozen.

CYRANO. Are you fond of sweets?

THE DUENNA. To the point of indigestion!

CYRANO (*snatching some paper bags off the counter*). Good. Here are two sonnets of Benserade's...

THE DUENNA. Pooh!

CYRANO. Which I fill for you with grated almond drops.

THE DUENNA (*with a different expression*). Ha!

CYRANO. Do you look with favor upon the cate they call a trifle?

THE DUENNA. I affect it out of measure, when it has whipped cream inside.

CYRANO. Six shall be yours, thrown in with a poem by Saint-

Amant. And in these verses of Chapelain I place this wedge of fruit-cake, light by the side of them.... Oh! And do you like tarts... little jam ones... fresh?

THE DUENNA. I dream of them at night!

CYRANO (*loading her arms with crammed paper bags*). Do me the favor to go and eat these in the street.

THE DUENNA. But...

CYRANO (*pushing her out*). And do not come back till you have finished it! (*He closes the door upon her, comes forward toward* ROXANE, *and stands, bareheaded, at a respectful distance.*) Blessed forevermore among all hours the hour in which, remembering that so lowly a being still draws breath, you were so gracious as to come to tell me... to tell me?...

ROXANE (*who has removed her mask*). First of all, that I thank you. For that churl, that coxcomb yesterday, whom you taught manners with your sword, is the one whom a great nobleman, who fancies himself in love with me...

CYRANO. De Guiche?

ROXANE (*dropping her eyes*). Has tried to force upon me as a husband.

CYRANO. Honorary? (*Bowing.*) It appears, then, that I fought, and I am glad of it, not for my graceless nose, but your thrice-beautiful eyes.

ROXANE. Further than that... I wished... But, before I can make the confession I have in mind to make, I must find in you once more the... almost brother, with whom as a child I used to play, in the park — do you remember? — by the lake!

CYRANO. I have not forgotten. Yes... you came every summer to Bergerac.

ROXANE. You used to fashion lances out of reeds...

CYRANO. The silk of the tasselled corn furnished hair for your doll...

ROXANE. It was the time of long delightful games...

CYRANO. And somewhat sour berries...

ROXANE. The time when you did everything I bade you!

CYRANO. Roxane, wearing short frocks, was known as Magdeleine.

ROXANE. Was I pretty in those days?

CYRANO. You were not ill-looking.

ROXANE. Sometimes, in your venturesome climbings you used to hurt yourself. You would come running to me, your hand bleeding. And, playing at being your mamma, I would harden my voice and say... (*She takes his hand.*) "Will you never keep out of mischief?" (*She stops short, amazed.*) Oh, it is too much! Here you have done it again! (CYRANO *tries to draw back his hand.*) No! Let me look at it!... Aren't you ashamed? A great boy like you!... How did this happen, and where?

CYRANO. Oh, fun... near the Porte de Nesle.

ROXANE (*sitting down at a table and dipping her handkerchief into a glass of water*). Let me have it.

CYRANO (*sitting down too*). So prettily, so cheeringly maternal!

ROXANE. And tell me, while I wash this naughty blood away... with how many were you fighting?

CYRANO. Oh, not quite a hundred.

ROXANE. Tell me about it.

CYRANO. No. What does it matter? You tell me, you... what you were going to tell me before, and did not dare...

ROXANE (*without releasing his hand*). I do dare, now. I have breathed in courage with the perfume of the past. Oh, yes, now I dare. Here it is. There is someone whom I love.

CYRANO. Ah!...

ROXANE. Oh, he does not know it.

CYRANO. Ah!...

ROXANE. As yet.....

CYRANO. Ah!...

ROXANE. But if he does not know it, he soon will.

CYRANO. Ah!...

ROXANE. A poor boy who until now has loved me timidly, from a distance, without daring to speak....

CYRANO. Ah!...

ROXANE. No, leave me your hand. It is hot, this will cool it.... But I have read his heart in his face.

CYRANO. Ah!...

ROXANE (*completing the bandaging of his hand with her small pocket-handkerchief*). And, cousin, is it not a strange coincidence — that he should serve exactly in your regiment!

CYRANO. Ah!...

ROXANE (*laughing*). Yes. He is a cadet, in the same company!

CYRANO. Ah!...

ROXANE. He bears plain on his forehead the stamp of wit, of genius! He is proud, noble, young, brave, handsome....

CYRANO (*rising, pale*). Handsome!...

ROXANE. What... what is the matter?

CYRANO. With me?... Nothing!... It is... it is... (*Showing his hand, smiling.*) You know!... It smarts a little...

ROXANE. In short, I love him. I must tell you, however, that I have never seen him save at the play.

CYRANO. Then you have never spoken to each other?

ROXANE. Only with our eyes.

CYRANO. But, then... how can you know?...

ROXANE. Oh, under the lindens of Place Royale, people will talk. A trustworthy gossip told me many things!

CYRANO. A cadet, did you say?

ROXANE. A cadet, in your company.

CYRANO. His name?

ROXANE. Baron Christian de Neuvillette.

CYRANO. What? He is not in the cadets.

ROXANE. He is! He certainly is, since morning. Captain Carbon de Castel-Jaloux.

CYRANO. And quickly, quickly, she throws away her heart!... But my poor little girl...

THE DUENNA (*opening the door at the back*). Monsieur de Bergerac, I have eaten them, every one!

CYRANO. Now read the poetry printed upon the bags! (*The* DUENNA *disappears.*) My poor child, you who can endure none but the choicest language, who savor eloquence and wit,... if he should be a barbarian!

ROXANE. No! No!... He has hair like one of D'Urfé's heroes!

CYRANO. If he had on proof as homely a wit as he has pretty hair!

ROXANE. No! No!... I can see at a single glance, his utterances are fine, pointed...

CYRANO. Ah, yes! A man's utterances are invariably like his moustache!... Still, if he *were* a ninny?...

ROXANE (*stamping with her foot*). I should die, there!

CYRANO (*after a time*). You bade me come here that you might tell me this? I scarcely see the appropriateness, madame.

ROXANE. Ah, it was because someone yesterday let death into my soul by telling me that in your company you are all Gascons,... all!

CYRANO. And that we pick a quarrel with every impudent fledgling, not Gascon, admitted by favor to our thoroughbred Gascon ranks? That is what you heard?

ROXANE. Yes, and you can imagine how distracted I am for him!

CYRANO (*in his teeth*). You well may be!

ROXANE. But I thought, yesterday, when you towered up, great and invincible, giving his due to that miscreant, standing your ground against those caitiffs, I thought "Were he but willing, he of whom all are in awe..."

CYRANO. Very well, I will protect your little baron.

ROXANE. Ah, you will... you will protect him for me?... I have always felt for you the tenderest regard!

CYRANO. Yes, yes.

ROXANE. You will be his friend?

CYRANO. I will!

ROXANE. And never shall he have to fight a duel?

CYRANO. I swear it.

ROXANE. Oh, I quite love you!... Now I must go. (*She hurriedly resumes her mask, throws a veil over her head; says absentmindedly.*) But you have not yet told me about last night's encounter. It must have been amazing!... Tell him to write to me. (*She kisses her hand to him.*) I love you dearly!

CYRANO. Yes, yes.

ROXANE. A hundred men against you?... Well, adieu. We are fast friends.

CYRANO. Yes, yes.

ROXANE. Tell him to write me!... A hundred men! You shall tell me another time. I must not linger now... A hundred men! What a heroic thing to do!

CYRANO (*bowing*). Oh, I have done better since!...

(*Exit* ROXANE. CYRANO *stands motionless, staring at the ground. Silence. The door at the right opens.* RAGUENEAU *thrusts in his head.*)

RAGUENEAU. May we come back?

CYRANO (*without moving*). Yes...

(RAGUENEAU *beckons, his friends come in again. At the same time, in the doorway at the back, appears* CARBON DE CASTEL-JALOUX, *costume of a Captain of the Guards. On seeing* CYRANO, *he gesticulates exaggeratedly by way of signal to someone out of sight.*)

CARBON DE CASTEL-JALOUX. He is here!

CYRANO (*looking up*). Captain!

CARBON DE CASTEL-JALOUX (*exultant*). Hero! We know all!... About thirty of my cadets are out there!...

CYRANO (*drawing back*). But...

CARBON DE CASTEL-JALOUX (*trying to lead him off*). Come!... You are in request!

CYRANO. No!

CARBON DE CASTEL-JALOUX. They are drinking across the way, at the Cross of the Hilt.

CYRANO. I...

CARBON DE CASTEL-JALOUX (*going to the door and shouting toward the street corner, in a voice of thunder*). The hero refuses. He is not in the humor!

A VOICE (*outside*). Ah, *sandious!*...

>        (*Tumult outside, noise of clanking swords and of boots drawing nearer.*)

CARBON DE CASTEL-JALOUX (*rubbing his hands*). Here they come, across the street....

THE CADETS (*entering the cookshop*). *Mille dious!* ... *Capdedious!* ... *Mordious!* ... *Pocapdedious!* ...

RAGUENEAU (*backing in alarm*). Messieurs, are you all natives of Gascony?

THE CADETS. All!

ONE OF THE CADETS (*to* CYRANO). Bravo!

CYRANO. Baron!

OTHER CADET (*shaking both* CYRANO's *hands*). Vivat!

CYRANO. Baron!

THIRD CADET. Let me hug you to my heart!

CYRANO. Baron!

SEVERAL GASCONS. Let us hug him!

CYRANO (*not knowing which one to answer*).    Baron!... baron!...
your pardon!

RAGUENEAU.    Messieurs, are you all barons?

THE CADETS.    All!

RAGUENEAU.    Are they truly?

FIRST CADET.    Our coats of arms piled up would dwindle in the
clouds!

LE BRET (*entering, running to* CYRANO).    They are looking for you!
A crowd, gone mad as March, led by those who were with you
last night.

CYRANO (*alarmed*).    You never told them where to find me?...

LE BRET (*rubbing his hands*).    I did.

A BURGHER (*entering, followed by a number of others*).    Monsieur, the
Marais is coming in a body!

(*The street outside has filled with people.    Sedan-chairs, coaches
stop before the door.*)

LE BRET (*smiling, low to* CYRANO).    And Roxane?

CYRANO (*quickly*).    Be quiet!

THE CROWD (*outside*).    Cyrano!

(*A rabble bursts into the cookshop.    Confusion.    Shouting.*)

RAGUENEAU (*standing upon a table*).    My shop is invaded!    They are
breaking everything!    It is glorious!

PEOPLE (*pressing round* CYRANO).    My friend... my friend....

CYRANO.    I had not so many friends... yesterday!

LE BRET.    This is success!

A YOUNG MARQUIS (*running toward* CYRANO, *with outstretched hands*).
If you knew, my dear fellow...

CYRANO.    Dear?... Fellow?... Where was it we stood sentinel
together?

OTHER MARQUIS.    I wish to present you, sir, to several ladies, who
are outside in my coach....

CYRANO (*coldly*).    But you, to me, by whom will you first be
presented?

LE BRET (*astonished*).    But what is the matter with you?

CYRANO.    Be still!

A MAN OF LETTERS (*with an inkhorn*).    Will you kindly favor me with
the details of...

CYRANO.    No.

LE BRET (*nudging him*). That is Theophrastus Renaudot, the inventor of the gazette.

CYRANO. Enough!

LE BRET. A sheet close packed with various information! It is an idea, they say, likely to take firm root and flourish!

A POET (*coming forward*). Monsieur...

CYRANO. Another!

THE POET. I am anxious to make a pentacrostic on your name.

SOMEBODY ELSE (*likewise approaching* CYRANO). Monsieur...

CYRANO. Enough, I say!

(*At the gesture of impatience which* CYRANO *cannot repress, the crowd draws away.*)

(DE GUICHE *appears, escorted by officers; among them* CUIGY, BRISSAILLE, *those who followed* CYRANO *at the end of the first act.* CUIGY *hurries toward* CYRANO.)

CUIGY (*to* CYRANO). Monsieur de Guiche! (*Murmurs. Everyone draws back.*) He comes at the request of the Marshal de Gaussion.

DE GUICHE (*bowing to* CYRANO). Who wishes to express his admiration for your latest exploit, the fame of which has reached him.

THE CROWD. Bravo!

CYRANO (*bowing*). The Marshal is qualified to judge of courage.

DE GUICHE. He would scarcely have believed the report, had these gentlemen not been able to swear they had seen the deed performed.

CUIGY. With our own eyes!

LE BRET (*low to* CYRANO, *who wears on abstracted air*). But...

CYRANO. Be silent!

LE BRET. You appear to be suffering...

CYRANO (*starting, and straightening himself*). Before these people... (*His moustache bristles; he expands his chest.*) I... suffering?... You shall see!

DE GUICHE (*in whose ear* CUIGY *has been whispering*). But this is by no means the first gallant achievement marking your career. You serve in the madcap Gascon company, do you not?

CYRANO. In the cadets, yes.

ONE OF THE CADETS (*in a great voice*). Among his countrymen!

DE GUICHE (*considering the* GASCONS, *in line behind* CYRANO).    Ah,
    ha! — All these gentlemen then of the formidable aspect, are
    the famous...

CARBON DE CASTEL-JALOUX.    Cyrano!

CYRANO.    Captain?...

CARBON DE CASTEL-JALOUX.    My company, I believe, is here in
    total.    Be so obliging as to present it to the Count.

CYRANO (*taking a step toward* DE GUICHE, *and pointing at the* CADETS).

> They are the Gascony Cadets
>     Of Carbon de Castel-Jaloux;
> Famed fighters, liars, desperates,
>     They are the Gascony Cadets!
> All, better-born than pickpockets,
>     Talk couchant, rampant,... pendent, too!
> They are the Gascony Cadets
>     Of Carbon de Castel-Jaloux!
>
> Cat-whiskered, eyed like falconets,
>     Wolf-toothed and heron-legged, they hew
> The rabble down that snarls and threats...
>     Cat-whiskered, eyed like falconets!
> Great pomp of plume hides and offsets
>     Holes in those hats they wear askew...
> Cat-whiskered, eyed like falconets,
>     They drive the snarling mob, and hew!
>
> The mildest of their sobriquets
>     Are Crack-my-crown and Run-me-through,
> Mad drunk on glory Gascon gets!
>     These boasters of soft sobriquets
> Whenever rapier rapier whets
>     Are met in punctual rendezvous....
> The mildest of their sobriquets
>     Are Crack-my-crown and Run-me-through!
>
> They are the Gascony Cadets
>     That give the jealous spouse his due!
> Lean forth, adorable coquettes
>     They are the Gascony Cadets,

With plumes and scarfs and aigulets!
The husband gray may well look blue....
They are the Gascony Cadets
That give the jealous spouse his due!

DE GUICHE (*nonchalantly seated in an armchair which* RAGUENEAU *has hurriedly brought for him*). A gentleman provides himself today, by way of luxury, with a poet. May I look upon you as mine?

CYRANO. No, your lordship, as nobody's.

DE GUICHE. My uncle Richelieu yesterday found your spontaneity diverting. I shall be pleased to be of use to you with him.

LE BRET (*dazzled*). Great God!

DE GUICHE. I cannot think I am wrong in supposing that you have rhymed a tragedy?

LE BRET (*whispering to* CYRANO). My boy, your Agrippina will be played!

DE GUICHE. Take it to him....

CYRANO (*tempted and pleased*). Really...

DE GUICHE. He has taste in such matters. He will no more than, here and there, alter a word, recast a passage....

CYRANO (*whose face has instantly darkened*). Not to be considered, monsieur! My blood runs cold at the thought of a single comma added or suppressed.

DE GUICHE. On the other hand, my dear sir, when a verse finds favor with him, he pays for it handsomely.

CYRANO. He scarcely can pay me as I pay myself, when I have achieved a verse to my liking, by singing it over to myself!

DE GUICHE. You are proud.

CYRANO. You have observed it?

ONE OF THE CADETS (*coming in with a number of disreputable, draggled tattered hats threaded on his sword*). Look, Cyrano! at the remarkable feathered game we secured this morning near the Porte de Nesle! The hats of the fugitives!

CARBON DE CASTEL-JALOUX. *Spoliæ opimæ!*

ALL (*laughing*). Ha! Ha! Ha!...

CUIGY. The one who planned that military action, my word! must be proud of it today!

BRISSAILLE. Is it known who did it?

DE GUICHE. I! — (*The laughter stops short.*) They had instructions

to chastise — a matter one does not attend to in person —
a drunken scribbler.                    (*Constrained silence.*)

THE CADET (*under breath, to* CYRANO, *indicating the hats*).   What can
we do with them?   They are oily.... Make them into a hotch
pot?

CYRANO (*taking the sword with the hats, and bowing, as he shakes them
off at* DE GUICHE's *feet*).   Monsieur, if you should care to return
them to your friends?...

DE GUICHE (*rises, and in a curt tone*).   My chair and bearers, at once.
(*To* CYRANO, *violently.*)   As for you, sir...

A VOICE (*in the street, shouting*).   The chairmen of Monseigneur the
Comte de Guiche!

DE GUICHE (*who has recovered control over himself, with a smile*).   Have
you read Don Quixote?

CYRANO.   I have.   And at the name of that divine madman,
I uncover...

DE GUICHE.   My advice to you is to ponder...

A CHAIRMAN (*appearing at the back*).   The chair is at the door!

DE GUICHE.   The chapter of the wind mills.

CYRANO (*bowing*).   Chapter thirteen.

DE GUICHE.   For when a man attacks them, it often happens...

CYRANO.   I have attacked, am I to infer, a thing that veers with
every wind?

DE GUICHE.   That one of their far-reaching canvas arms pitches
him down into the mud!

CYRANO.   Or up among the stars!

(*Exit* DE GUICHE.   *He is seen getting into his chair.   The
gentlemen withdraw whispering.*   LE BRET *goes to the door
with them.   The crowd leaves.   The* CADETS *remain seated
at the right and left at tables where food and drink is brought
to them.*)

CYRANO (*bowing with a derisive air to those who leave without daring to
take leave of him*).   Gentlemen... gentlemen... gentlemen....

LE BRET (*coming forward, greatly distressed, lifting his hands to Heaven*).
Oh, in what a pretty pair of shoes...

CYRANO.   Oh, you!... I expect you to grumble!

LE BRET.   But yourself, you will agree with me that invariably to
cut the throat of opportunity becomes an exaggeration!...

CYRANO. Yes. I agree. I do exaggerate.

LE BRET (*triumphant*). You see, you admit it!...

CYRANO. But for the sake of principle, and of example, as well, I think it a good thing to exaggerate as I do!

LE BRET. Could you but leave apart, once in a while, your mousquetaire of a soul, fortune, undoubtedly, fame...

CYRANO. And what should a man do? Seek some grandee, take him for patron, and like the obscure creeper clasping a treetrunk, and licking the bark of that which props it up, attain to height by craft instead of strength? No, I thank you. Dedicate, as they all do, poems to financiers? Wear motley in the humble hope of seeing the lips of a minister distend for once in a smile not ominous of ill? No, I thank you. Eat every day a toad? Be threadbare at the belly with grovelling? Have his skin dirty soonest at the knees? Practice feats of dorsal elasticity? No, I thank you. With one hand stroke the goat while with the other he waters the cabbage? Make gifts of senna that counter-gifts of rhubarb may accrue, and indefatigably swing his censer in some beard? No, I thank you. Push himself from lap to lap, become a little great man in a great little circle, propel his ship with madrigals for oars and in his sails the sighs of the elderly ladies? No, I thank you. Get the good editor Sercy to print his verses at proper expense? No, I thank you. Contrive to be nominated Pope in conclaves held by imbeciles in wineshops? No, I thank you. Work to construct a name upon the basis of a sonnet, instead of constructing other sonnets? No, I thank you. Discover talent in tyros, and in them alone? Stand in terror of what gazettes may please to say, and say to himself, "At whatever cost, may I figure in the Paris Mercury!" No, I thank you. Calculate, cringe, peak, prefer making a call to a poem — petition, solicit, apply? No, I thank you! No, I thank you! No, I thank you! But... sing, dream, laugh, loaf, be single, be free, have eyes that look squarely, a voice with a ring; wear, if he chooses, his hat hindside afore; for a yes, for a no, fight a duel or turn a ditty!... Work, without concern of fortune or of glory, to accomplish the heart's-desired journey to the moon! Put forth nothing that has not its spring in the very heart, yet, modest, say to himself, "Old man, be satisfied with blossoms, fruits, yea, leaves alone, so they be gathered in your garden and not another man's!" Then, if it happen that to some small extent he triumph, be obliged to render of the glory, to Cæsar, not one jot, but honestly appropriate it all. In short, scorning to be the parasite, the creeper, if even failing to be the oak, rise, not perchance to a great height,... but rise alone!

LE BRET. Alone? Good! but not one against all! How the devil did you contract the mania that possesses you for making enemies, always, everywhere?

CYRANO. By seeing you make friends, and smile to those same flocks of friends with a mouth that takes for model an old purse! I wish not to be troubled to return bows in the street, and I exclaim with glee, "An enemy the more!"

LE BRET. This is mental aberration!

CYRANO. I do not dispute it. I am so framed. To displease is my pleasure. I love that one should hate me. Dear friend, if you but know how much better a man walks under the exciting fire of hostile eyes, and how amused he may become over the spots on his doublet, spattered by Envy and Cowardice!... You, the facile friendship wherewith you surround yourself, resembles those wide Italian collars, loose and easy, with a perforated pattern, in which the neck looks like a woman's. They are more comfortable, but of less high effect; for the brow not held in proud position by any constraint from them, falls to nodding this way and that.... But for me every day Hatred starches and flutes the ruff whose stiffness holds the head well in place. Every new enemy is another plait in it, adding compulsion, but adding, as well, a ray: for, similar in every point to the Spanish ruff, Hatred is a bondage,... but is a halo, too!

LE BRET (after a pause, slipping his arm through CYRANO's). To the hearing of all be proud and bitter,... but to me, below breath, say simply that she does not love you!

CYRANO (sharply). Not a word!

(CHRISTIAN has come in and mingled with the CADETS; they ignore him; he has finally gone to a little table by himself, where LISE waits on him.)

ONE OF THE CADETS (seated at a table at the back, glass in hand). Hey, Cyrano! (CYRANO turns toward him.) Your story!

CYRANO. Presently!

(*He goes toward the back on* LE BRET'*s arm.   They talk low.*)

THE CADET (*rising and coming toward the front*).   The account of your fight!   It will be the best lesson (*stopping in front of the table at which* CHRISTIAN *is sitting*) for this timorous novice!

CHRISTIAN (*looking up*).... Novice?

OTHER CADET. Yes, sickly product of the North!

CHRISTIAN. Sickly?

FIRST CADET (*impressively*).   Monsieur de Neuvillette, it is a good deed to warn you that there is a thing no more to be mentioned in our company than rope in the house of the hanged!

CHRISTIAN. And what is it?

OTHER CADET (*in a terrifying voice*).   Look at me!   (*Three times, darkly, he places his finger upon his nose.*)   You have understood?

CHRISTIAN. Ah, it is the...

OTHER CADET. Silence!... Never must you so much as breathe that word, or... (*He points toward* CYRANO *at the back talking with* LE BRET.)   You will have him, over there, to deal with!

OTHER CADET (*who while* CHRISTIAN *was turned toward the first, has noiselessly seated himself on the table behind him*).   Two persons were lately cut off in their pride by him for talking through their noses.   He thought it personal.

OTHER CADET (*in a cavernous voice, as he rises from under the table where he had slipped on all fours*).   Not the remotest allusion, ever, to the fatal cartilage,... unless you fancy an early grave!

OTHER CADET. A word will do the business!   What did I say?... A word?... A simple gesture!   Make use of your pocket-handkerchief, you will shortly have use for your shroud!

(*Silence.   All around* CHRISTIAN *watch him, with folded arms. He rises and goes to* CARBON DE CASTEL-JALOUX, *who in conversation with an officer, affects to notice nothing.*)

CHRISTIAN. Captain!

CARBON (*turning and looking him rather contemptuously up and down*). Monsieur?

CHRISTIAN. What is the proper course for a man when he finds gentlemen of the South too boastful?...

CARBON DE CASTEL-JALOUX. He must prove to them that one can be of the North, yet brave.   (*He turns his back upon him.*)

CHRISTIAN. I am much obliged.

FIRST CADET (*to* CYRANO). And now, the tale of your adventure!

ALL. Yes, yes, now let us hear!

CYRANO (*coming forward among them*). My adventure? (*All draw their stools nearer, and sit around him, with craned necks.* CHRISTIAN *sits astride a chair.*) Well, then, I was marching to meet them. The moon up in the skies was shining like a silver watch, when suddenly I know not what careful watch-maker having wrapped it in a cottony cloud, there occurred the blackest imaginable night; and, the streets being nowise lighted — *mordious!* — you could see no further than...

CHRISTIAN. Your nose.

> (*Silence. Every one slowly gets up; all look with terror at* CYRANO. *He has stopped short, amazed. Pause.*)

CYRANO. Who is that man?

ONE OF THE CADETS (*low*). He joined this morning.

CYRANO (*taking a step toward* CHRISTIAN). This morning?

CARBON DE CASTEL-JALOUX (*low*). His name is Baron de Neuvill...

CYRANO (*stopping short*). Ah, very well.... (*He turns pale, then red, gives evidence of another impulse to throw himself upon* CHRISTIAN.) I... (*He conquers it, and says in a stifled voice.*) Very well. (*He takes up his tale.*) As I was saying... (*with a burst of rage*) Mordious!... (*he continues in a natural tone*) one could not see in the very least. (*Consternation. All resume their seats, staring at one another.*) And I was walking along, reflecting that for a very insignificant rogue I was probably about to offend some great prince who would bear me a lasting grudge, that, in brief, I was about to thrust my...

CHRISTIAN. Nose...

> (*All get up.* CHRISTIAN *has tilted his chair and is rocking on the hind legs.*)

CYRANO (*choking*). Finger... between the tree and the bark; for the aforesaid prince might be of sufficient power to trip me and throw me...

CHRISTIAN. On my nose...

CYRANO (*wipes the sweat from his brow*). But, said I, "Gascony forward! Never falter when duty prompts! Forward, Cyrano!"

and, saying this, I advance — when suddenly, in the darkness,
I barely avoid a blow...

CHRISTIAN. Upon the nose...

CYRANO. I ward it... and thereupon find myself...

CHRISTIAN. Nose to nose...

CYRANO (*springing toward him*). *Ventre-Saint-Gris!* ... (*All the*
GASCONS *rush forward, to see;* CYRANO, *on reaching* CHRISTIAN,
*controls himself and proceeds*) ... with a hundred drunken brawlers,
smelling...

CHRISTIAN. To the nose's limit...

CYRANO (*deathly pale, and smiling*)... of garlic and of grease. I leap
forward, head lowered...

CHRISTIAN. Nose to the wind!...

CYRANO. And I charge them. I knock two breathless and run
a third through the body. One lets off at me: Paf! and I
retort...

CHRISTIAN. Pif!

CYRANO (*exploding*). Death and damnation! Go — all of you!
(*All the* CADETS *make for the door.*)

FIRST CADET. The tiger is roused at last!

CYRANO. All! and leave me with this man.

SECOND CADET. *Bigre!* When we see him again, it will be in the
shape of mince-meat!

RAGUENEAU. Mince-meat?...

OTHER CADET. In one of your pies.

RAGUENEAU. I feel myself grow white and flabby as a table-napkin!

CARBON DE CASTEL-JALOUX. Let us go!

OTHER CADET. Not a smudge of him will be left!

OTHER CADET. What these walls are about to behold gives me
gooseflesh to think upon!

OTHER CADET (*closing the door at the right*). Ghastly!... Ghastly!
(*All have left, by the back or the sides, a few up the stairway.*
CYRANO *and* CHRISTIAN *remain face to face, and look at each
other a moment.*)

CYRANO. Embrace me!

CHRISTIAN. Monsieur...

CYRANO. Brave fellow.

CHRISTIAN. But what does this...

CYRANO. Very brave fellow. I wish you to.

CHRISTIAN. Will you tell me?...

CYRANO. Embrace me, I am her brother.

CHRISTIAN. Whose?

CYRANO. Hers!

CHRISTIAN. What do you mean?

CYRANO. Roxane's!

CHRISTIAN (*running to him*). Heavens! You, her brother?

CYRANO. Or the same thing: her first cousin.

CHRISTIAN. And she has...

CYRANO. Told me everything!

CHRISTIAN. Does she love me?

CYRANO. Perhaps!

CHRISTIAN (*seizing his hands*). How happy I am, monsieur, to make your acquaintance!...

CYRANO. That is what I call a sudden sentiment!

CHRISTIAN. Forgive me!...

CYRANO (*looking at him, laying his hand upon his shoulder*). It is true that he is handsome, the rascal!

CHRISTIAN. If you but knew, monsieur, how greatly I admire you!...

CYRANO. But all those noses which you...

CHRISTIAN. I take them back!

CYRANO. Roxane expects a letter tonight...

CHRISTIAN. Alas!

CYRANO. What is the matter?

CHRISTIAN. I am lost if I cease to be dumb!

CYRANO. How is that?

CHRISTIAN. Alas! I am such a dunce that I could kill myself for shame!

CYRANO. But, no... no.... You are surely not a dunce, if you believe you are! Besides, you scarcely attacked me like a dunce.

CHRISTIAN. Oh, it is easy to find words in mounting to the assault! Indeed, I own to a certain cheap military readiness, but when I am before women, I have not a word to say.... Yet their eyes, when I pass by, express a kindness toward me...

CYRANO. And do their hearts not express the same when you stop beside them?

CHRISTIAN. No!... for I am of those — I recognize it, and am dismayed! — who do not know how to talk of love.

CYRANO. *Tiens!*... It seems to me that if Nature had taken more pains with my shape, I should have been of those who do know how to talk of it.

CHRISTIAN. Oh, to be able to express things gracefully!

CYRANO. Oh, to be a graceful little figure of a passing mousquetaire!

CHRISTIAN. Roxane is a précieuse,... there is no chance but that I shall be a disillusion to Roxane!

CYRANO (*looking at* CHRISTIAN). If I had, to express my soul, such an interpreter!...

CHRISTIAN (*desperately*). I ought to have eloquence!...

CYRANO (*abruptly*). Eloquence I will lend you!... And you, to me, shall lend all-conquering physical charm... and between us we will compose a hero of romance!

CHRISTIAN. What?

CYRANO. Should you be able to say, as your own, things which I day by day would teach you?

CHRISTIAN. You are suggesting?...

CYRANO. Roxane shall not have disillusions! Tell me, shall we win her heart, we two as one? Will you submit to feel, transmitted from my leather doublet into your doublet stitched with silk, the soul I wish to share?

CHRISTIAN. But Cyrano!...

CYRANO. Christian, will you?

CHRISTIAN. You frighten me!

CYRANO. Since you fear, left to yourself, to chill her heart, will you consent — and soon it will take fire, I vouch for it! — to contribute your lips to my phrases?

CHRISTIAN. Your eyes shine!...

CYRANO. Will you?

CHRISTIAN. What, would it please you so much?

CYRANO (*with rapture*). It would... (*remembering, and confining himself to expressing an artistic pleasure*)... amuse me! It is an experiment fit surely to tempt a poet. Will you complete me, and let me in exchange complete you? We will walk side by side: you in full light, I in your shadow.... I will be wit to you... you, to me, shall be good looks!

CHRISTIAN. But the letter, which should be sent to her without delay?... Never shall I be able...

CYRANO (*taking from his doublet the letter written in the first part of the act*). The letter? Here it is!

CHRISTIAN. How?...

CYRANO. It only wants the address.

CHRISTIAN. I...

CYRANO. You can send it without uneasiness. It is a good letter.

CHRISTIAN. You had?...

CYRANO. You shall never find us — poets! — without epistles in our pockets to the Chlorises... of our imagining! For we are those same that have for mistress a dream blown into the bubble of a name! Take — you shall convert this feigning into earnest; I was sending forth at random these confessions and laments: you shall make the wandering birds to settle... Take it! You shall see... I was as eloquent as if I had been sincere! Take, and have done!

CHRISTIAN. But will it not need to be altered in any part?... Written without object, will it fit Roxane?

CYRANO. Like a glove!

CHRISTIAN. But...

CYRANO. Trust to the blindness of love... and **vanity**! Roxane will never question that it was written for her.

CHRISTIAN. Ah, my friend!

(*He throws himself into* CYRANO's *arms. They stand embraced.*)

ONE OF THE CADETS (*opening the door a very little*). Nothing more... The stillness of death... I dare not look... (*He thrusts in his head.*) What is this?

ALL THE CADETS (*entering and seeing* CYRANO *and* CHRISTIAN *locked in each other's arms*). Ah!... Oh!...

ONE OF THE CADETS. This passes bounds! (*Consternation.*)

THE MOUSQUETAIRE (*impudent*). *Ouais?*

CARBON DE CASTEL-JALOUX. Our demon is waxen mild as an apostle; smitten upon one nostril, he turns the other also!

THE MOUSQUETAIRE. It is in order now to speak of his nose, is it? (*Calling* LISE, *with a swaggering air.*) Hey, Lise! now listen and look. (*Pointedly sniffing the air.*) Oh,... oh,... it is surprising!... what an odor! (*Going to* CYRANO.) But monsieur must have smelled it, too? Can you tell me what it is, so plain in the air?

CYRANO (*beating him*). Why, sundry blows!

(*Joyful antics of the* CADETS *in beholding* CYRANO *himself again.*)

CURTAIN

# ACT THIRD

ROXANE'S KISS

*A small square in the old Marais. Old-fashioned houses. Narrow streets seen in perspective. At the right,* ROXANE'S *house and the wall of her garden, above which spreading tree-tops. Over the house-door, a balcony and window. A bench beside the doorstep.*

*The wall is overclambered by ivy, the balcony wreathed with jasmine.*

*By means of the bench and projecting stones in the wall, the balcony can easily be scaled.*

*On the opposite side, old house in the same style of architecture, brick and stone, with entrance-door. The door-knocker is swaddled in linen.*

*At the rise of the curtain, the* DUENNA *is seated on the bench. The window on* ROXANE'S *balcony is wide open.*

RAGUENEAU, *in a sort of livery, stands near the* DUENNA; *he is finishing the tale of his misfortunes, drying his eyes.*

RAGUENEAU. And then, she eloped with a mousquetaire! Ruined, forsaken, I was hanging myself. I had already taken leave of earth, when Monsieur de Bergerac, happening along, unhanged me, and proposed me to his cousin as her steward....

THE DUENNA. But how did you fall into such disaster?

RAGUENEAU. Lise was fond of soldiers, I, of poets! Mars ate up all left over by Apollo. Under those circumstances, you conceive, the pantry soon was bare.

THE DUENNA (*rising and calling toward the open window*). Roxane, are you ready?... They are waiting for us!...

ROXANE'S VOICE (*through the window*). I am putting on my mantle!

THE DUENNA (*to* RAGUENEAU, *pointing at the door opposite*). It is over there, opposite, we are expected. At Clomire's. She holds a meeting in her little place. A disquisition upon the Softer Sentiments is to be read.

RAGUENEAU. Upon the Softer Sentiments?

THE DUENNA (*coyly*). Yes!... (*Calling toward the window.*) Roxane, you must make haste, or we shall miss the disquisition upon the Softer Sentiments!

ROXANE'S VOICE. I am coming!

(*A sound of string-instruments is heard, drawing nearer.*)

CYRANO'S VOICE (*singing in the wings*). La! la! la! la! la!...

THE DUENNA (*surprised*). We are to have music?

CYRANO (*enters followed by two* PAGES *with theorbos*). I tell you it is a demi-semi-quaver!... you demi-semi-noddle!

FIRST PAGE (*ironically*). Monsieur knows then about quavers, semi and demi?

CYRANO. I know music, as do all Gassendi's disciples!

THE PAGE (*playing and singing*). La! la!

CYRANO (*snatching the theorbo from him and continuing the musical phrase*). I can carry on the melody.... La, la, la, la,...

ROXANE (*appearing on the balcony*). It is you?

CYRANO (*singing upon the tune he is continuing*). I, indeed, who salute your lilies and present my respects to your ro-o-oses!...

ROXANE. I am coming down! (*She leaves the balcony.*)

THE DUENNA (*pointing at the* PAGES). What is the meaning of these two virtuosi?

CYRANO. A wager I won from D'Assoucy. We were disputing upon a question of grammar. Yes! No! Yes! No! Suddenly pointing at these two tall knaves, expert at clawing strings, by whom he constantly goes attended, he said, "I wager a day long of music!" He lost. Until therefore the next rise of the sun, I shall have dangling after me these archlute players, harmonious witnesses of all I do!... At first I liked it very well, but now it palls a little. (*To the musicians.*) Hey!... Go, from me, to Montfleury, and play him a pavane!... (*The* PAGES *go toward the back. To the* DUENNA.) I have come to inquire of Roxane, as I do every evening... (*To the* PAGES *who are leaving.*) Play a long time... and out of tune! (*To the* DUENNA.)... whether in the friend of her soul she can still detect no fault?

ROXANE (*coming out of the house*). Ah, how beautiful he is, what wit he has, how deeply I love him!

CYRANO (*smiling*). Christian has so much wit?...

ROXANE. Cousin, more than yourself!

CYRANO. I grant you.

ROXANE. There is not one alive, I truly believe, more apt at turning those pretty nothings which yet are everything.... Sometimes he is of an absent mood, his muse is wool-gathering, then, suddenly, he will say the most enchanting things!

CYRANO (*incredulous*). Come!...

ROXANE. Oh, it is too bad! Men are all alike, narrow, narrow: because he is handsome, he cannot possibly be witty!

CYRANO. So he talks of the heart in acceptable fashion?

ROXANE. Talks, cousin, is feeble.... He dissertates!

CYRANO. And writes?...

ROXANE. Still better! Listen now to this... (*Declaiming.*) "*The more of my heart you steal from me, the more heart I have!*" (*Triumphantly to* CYRANO.) Well?...

CYRANO. Pooh!

ROXANE. And to this: "*Since you have stolen my heart, and since I must suffer, to suffer with send me your own!*"

CYRANO. Now he has too much heart, now he has not enough,.... just what does he want, in the matter of quantity?

ROXANE. You vex me! You are eaten up with jealousy...

CYRANO (*starting*). *Hein?*

ROXANE. Author's jealousy! And this, could anything be more exquisitely tender? "*Unanimously, believe it, my heart cries out to you, and if kisses could be sent in writing, Love, you should read my letter with your lips...*"

CYRANO (*in spite of himself smiling with satisfaction*). Ha! Ha! Those particular lines seem to me... ho!... ho!... (*remembering himself, disdainfully*)... puny, pretty...

ROXANE. This, then...

CYRANO (*delighted*). You know his letters by heart?

ROXANE. All!

CYRANO. It is flattering, one cannot deny.

ROXANE. In this art of expressing love he is a master!

CYRANO (*modest*). Oh,... a master!

ROXANE (*peremptory*). A master!

CYRANO. As you please, then... a master!

THE DUENNA (*who had gone toward the back, coming quickly forward*).

Monsieur de Guiche!   (*To* CYRANO, *pushing him toward the house.*)   Go in!   It is perhaps better that he should not see you here! it might put him on the scent...

ROXANE (*to* CYRANO).   Yes, of my dear secret!   He loves me, he is powerful,... he must not find out!   He might cut in sunder our loves... with an axe!

CYRANO (*going into the house*).   Very well, very well.

### (DE GUICHE *appears.*)

ROXANE (*to* DE GUICHE, *with a curtsey*).   I was leaving the house.

DE GUICHE.   I have come to bid you farewell.

ROXANE.   You are going away?

DE GUICHE.   To war.

ROXANE.   Ah!

DE GUICHE.   I have my orders.   Arras is besieged.

ROXANE.   Ah!... it is besieged?

DE GUICHE.   Yes.... I see that my departure does not greatly affect you.

ROXANE.   Oh!...

DE GUICHE.   As for me, I own it wrings my heart.   Shall I see you again?... When?... You know that I am made commander-in-general?

ROXANE (*uninterested*).   I congratulate you.

DE GUICHE.   Of the Guards.

ROXANE (*starting*).   Ah,... of the Guards?

DE GUICHE.   Among whom your cousin serves,... the man of the boasts and tirades.   I shall have opportunity in plenty to retaliate upon him down there.

ROXANE (*suffocating*).   What?   The Guards are going down there?

DE GUICHE.   Surely.   It is my regiment.

ROXANE (*falls sitting upon the bench; aside*).   Christian!

DE GUICHE.   What is it troubles you?

ROXANE (*greatly moved*).   This departure... grieves me mortally. When one cares for a person... to know him away at the war!

DE GUICHE (*surprised and charmed*).   For the first time you utter a kind and feeling word, when I am leaving!

ROXANE (*in a different tone, fanning herself*).   So... you are thinking of revenge upon my cousin?

DE GUICHE (*smiling*).   You side with him?

ROXANE.  No... against him.

DE GUICHE.  Do you see much of him?

ROXANE.  Very little.

DE GUICHE.  He is everywhere to be met with one of the cadets...
    (*trying to remember*) that Neu... villen... viller...

ROXANE.  A tall man?

DE GUICHE.  Light-haired.

ROXANE.  Red-haired.

DE GUICHE.  Good-looking.

ROXANE.  Pooh!

DE GUICHE.  But a fool!

ROXANE.  He looks like one.   (*In a different tone.*)  Your vengeance
    upon Cyrano is then to place him within reach of shot, which is
    the thing of all he loves!... A miserable vengeance!... I know,
    I do, what would more seriously concern him!

DE GUICHE.  And that is?

ROXANE.  Why... that the regiment should march, and leave him
    behind, with his beloved cadets, arms folded, the whole war
    through, in Paris!   That is the only way to cast down a man like
    him.   You wish to punish him?   Deprive him of danger.

DE GUICHE.  A woman!   A woman!   None but a woman could
    devise a vengeance of the sort!

ROXANE.  His friends will gnaw their fists, and he his very soul,
    with chagrin at not being under fire; and you will be abundantly
    avenged!

DE GUICHE (*coming nearer*).   Then you do love me a little?   (Rox-
    ANE *smiles.*)   I wish to see in this fact of your espousing my
    grudge a proof of affection, Roxane...

ROXANE. ... You may!

DE GUICHE (*showing several folded papers*).   I have here upon me the
    orders to be transmitted at once to each of the companies...
    except... (*He takes one from among the others.*)  This one!... the
    company of the cadets... (*He puts it in his pocket.*)   This, I will
    keep.   (*Laughing.*)  Ah, ah, ah!   Cyrano!   his belligerent
    humor!... So you sometimes play tricks upon people, you?...

ROXANE.  Sometimes.

DE GUICHE (*very near her*).   I love you to distraction!   This evening

... listen,... it is true that I must be gone.   But to go when I feel that it is a matter for your caring!   Listen!... There is, not far from here, in Rue Orléans, a convent founded by the Capuchins.   Father Athanasius.   A layman may not enter. But the good fathers... I fear no difficulty with them!   They will hide me up their sleeve... their sleeve is wide.   They are the Capuchins that serve Richelieu at home.   Fearing the uncle, they proportionately fear the nephew.   I shall be thought to have left.   I will come to you masked.   Let me delay by a single day, wayward enchantress!

ROXANE.  But if it should transpire... your fame...

DE GUICHE.  Bah!

ROXANE.  But... the siege... Arras!...

DE GUICHE.  Must wait!   Allow me, I beg...

ROXANE.  No!

DE GUICHE.  I beseech!

ROXANE (*tenderly*).  No!   Love itself bids me forbid you!

DE GUICHE.  Ah!

ROXANE.  You must go!   (*Aside.*)   Christian will stay!   (*Aloud.*) For my sake, be heroic... Antony!

DE GUICHE.  Ah, heavenly word upon your lips!... Then you love the one who...

ROXANE.  Who shall have made me tremble for his sake...

DE GUICHE (*in a transport of joy*).  Ah, I will go!   (*He kisses her hand.*) Are you satisfied with me?

ROXANE.  My friend, I am.                                    (*Exit* DE GUICHE.)

THE DUENNA (*dropping a mocking curtsey toward his back*).   My friend, we are!

ROXANE (*to the* DUENNA).  Not a word of what I have done: Cyrano would never forgive me for defrauding him of his war! (*She calls toward the house.*)  Cousin!   (CYRANO *comes out.*) We are going to Clomire's.   (*She indicates the house opposite.*) Alcandre has engaged to speak, and so has Lysimon.

THE DUENNA (*putting her little finger to her ear*).  Yes, but my little finger tells me that we shall be too late to hear them!

CYRANO (*to* ROXANE).  Of all things do not miss the trained monkeys!                          (*They have reached* COLMIRE'S *door.*)

THE DUENNA.  See!... See! they have muffled the door-knocker!

(*To the door-knocker.*)  You have been gagged, that your voice should not disturb the beautiful lecture,... little brutal disturber!

(*She lifts it with infinite care and knocks softly.*)

ROXANE (*seeing the door open*).  Come!  (*From the threshold to* CYRANO.)  If Christian should come, as probably he will, say he must wait!

CYRANO (*hurriedly, as she is about to disappear*).  Ah!  (*She turns.*)  Upon what shall you, according to your custom, question him today?

ROXANE.  Upon...

CYRANO (*eagerly*).  Upon?...

ROXANE.  But you will be silent...

CYRANO.  As that wall!

ROXANE.  Upon nothing!  I will say: Forward!  Free rein!  No curb!  Improvise!  Talk of love!  Be magnificent!

CYRANO (*smiling*).  Good.

ROXANE.  Hush!

CYRANO.  Hush!

ROXANE.  Not a word!  (*She goes in and closes the door.*)

CYRANO (*bowing, when the door is closed*).  A thousand thanks!

(*The door opens again and* ROXANE *looks out.*)

ROXANE.  He might prepare his speeches...

CYRANO.  Ah, no!... the devil, no!

BOTH (*together*).  Hush!...  (*The door closes.*)

CYRANO (*calling*).  Christian!  (*Enter* CHRISTIAN.)  I know all that we need to.  Now make ready your memory.  This is your chance to cover yourself with glory.  Let us lose no time.  Do not look sullen, like that.  Quick!  Let us go to your lodgings and I will rehearse you...

CHRISTIAN.  No!

CYRANO.  What?

CHRISTIAN.  No, I will await Roxane here.

CYRANO.  What insanity possesses you?  Come quickly and learn...

CHRISTIAN.  No, I tell you!  I am weary of borrowing my letters, my words... of playing a part, and living in constant fear.... It was very well at first, but now I feel that she loves me.  I thank you heartily.  I am no longer afraid.  I will speak for myself...

CYRANO. *Ouais?*...

CHRISTIAN. And what tells you that I shall not know how? I am not such an utter blockhead, after all! You shall see! Your lessons have not been altogether wasted. I can shift to speak without your aid! And, that failing, by Heaven! I shall still know enough to take her in my arms! (*Catching sight of* ROXANE *who is coming out from* CLOMIRE'S.) She is coming! Cyrano, no, do not leave me!...

CYRANO (*bowing to him*). I will not meddle, monsieur.

(*He disappears behind the garden wall.*)

ROXANE (*coming from Clomire's house with a number of people from whom she is taking leave. Curtseys and farewells.*) Barthénoïde!... Alcandre!... Crémoine!...

THE DUENNA (*comically desperate*). We missed the disquisition upon the Softer Sentiments! (*She goes into* ROXANE'S *house.*)

ROXANE (*still taking leave of this one and that*). Urimédonte!... Good-bye!

(*All bow to* ROXANE, *to one another, separate and go off by the various streets.* ROXANE *sees* CHRISTIAN.)

ROXANE. You are here! (*She goes to him.*) Evening is closing round.... Wait!... They have all gone.... The air is so mild.... Not a passer in sight.... Let us sit here.... Talk!... I will listen.

CHRISTIAN (*sits beside her, on the bench. Silence*). I love you.

ROXANE (*closing her eyes*). Yes. Talk to me of love.

CHRISTIAN. I love you.

ROXANE. Yes. That is the theme. Play variations upon it.

CHRISTIAN. I love...

ROXANE. Variations!

CHRISTIAN. I love you so much...

ROXANE. I do not doubt it. What further?...

CHRISTIAN. And further... I should be so happy if you loved me! Tell me, Roxane, that you love me...

ROXANE (*pouting*). You proffer cider to me when I was hoping for champagne!... Now tell me a little *how* you love me?

CHRISTIAN. Why... very, very much.

ROXANE. Oh!... unravel, disentangle your sentiments!

CHRISTIAN. Your throat!... I want to kiss it!...

ROXANE. Christian!

CHRISTIAN. I love you!...

ROXANE (*attempting to rise*). Again!...

CHRISTIAN (*hastily, holding her back*). No, I do not love you!...

ROXANE (*sitting down again*). That is fortunate!

CHRISTIAN. I adore you!

ROXANE (*rising and moving away*). Oh!...

CHRISTIAN. Yes,... love makes me into a fool!

ROXANE (*drily*). And I am displeased at it! as I should be displeased at your no longer being handsome.

CHRISTIAN. But...

ROXANE. Go, and rally your routed eloquence!

CHRISTIAN. I...

ROXANE. You love me. I have heard it. Good-evening.

(*She goes toward the house.*)

CHRISTIAN. No, no, not yet!... I wish to tell you...

ROXANE (*pushing open the door to go in*). That you adore me. Yes, I know. No! No! Go away!... Go!... Go!...

CHRISTIAN. But I... (*She closes the door in his face.*)

CYRANO (*who has been on the scene a moment, unnoticed*). Unmistakably a success.

CHRISTIAN. Help me!

CYRANO. No, sir, no.

CHRISTIAN. I will go kill myself if I am not taken back into favor at once... at once!

CYRANO. And how can I... how, the devil?... make you learn on the spot...

CHRISTIAN (*seizing him by the arm*). Oh, there!... Look!... See!

(*Light has appeared in the balcony window.*)

CYRANO (*with emotion*). Her window!

CHRISTIAN. Oh, I shall die!

CYRANO. Not so loud!

CHRISTIAN (*in a whisper*). I shall die!

CYRANO. It is a dark night....

CHRISTIAN. Well?

CYRANO. All may be mended. But you do not deserve... There! stand there, miserable boy!... in front of the balcony! I will stand under it and prompt you.

CHRISTIAN. But...

CYRANO. Do as I bid you!

THE PAGES (*reappearing at the back, to* CYRANO). Hey!

CYRANO. Hush! (*He signs to them to lower their voices.*)

FIRST PAGE (*in a lower voice*). We have finished serenading Mont-fleury!

CYRANO (*low, quickly*). Go and stand out of sight. One at this street corner, the other at that; and if anyone comes near, play!...

SECOND PAGE. What sort of tune, Monsieur the Gassendist?

CYRANO. Merry if it be a woman, mournful if it be a man. (*The* PAGES *disappear, one at each street corner.* *To* CHRISTIAN.) Call her!

CHRISTIAN. Roxane!

CYRANO (*picking up pebbles and throwing them at the window-pane*). Wait! A few pebbles...

ROXANE (*opening the window*). Who is calling me?

CHRISTIAN. It is I...

ROXANE. Who is... I?

CHRISTIAN. Christian!

ROXANE (*disdainfully*). Oh, you!

CHRISTIAN. I wish to speak with you.

CYRANO (*under the balcony, to* CHRISTIAN). Speak low!...

ROXANE. No, your conversation is too common. You may go home!

CHRISTIAN. In mercy!...

ROXANE. No... you do not love me any more!

CHRISTIAN (*whom* CYRANO *is prompting*). You accuse me... just Heaven! of loving you no more... when I can love you no more!

ROXANE (*who was about to close her window, stopping*). Ah, that is a little better!

CHRISTIAN (*same business*). To what a... size has Love grown in my... sigh-rocked soul which the... cruel cherub has chosen for his cradle!

ROXANE (*stepping nearer to the edge of the balcony*). That is distinctly better!... But, since he is so cruel, this Cupid, you were unwise not to smother him in his cradle!

CHRISTIAN (*same business*): I tried to, but, madame, the... attempt was futile. This... new-born Love is... a little Hercules...

ROXANE. Much, much better!

CHRISTIAN (*same business*).... Who found it merest baby-play to... strangle the serpents... twain, Pride and... Mistrust.

ROXANE (*leaning her elbows on the balcony-rail*). Ah, that is very good indeed!... But why do you speak so slowly and stintedly? Has your imagination gout in its wings?

CYRANO (*drawing* CHRISTIAN *under the balcony, and taking his place*). Hush! It is becoming too difficult!

ROXANE. Tonight your words come falteringly.... Why is it?

CYRANO (*talking low like* CHRISTIAN). Because of the dark. They have to grope to find your ear.

ROXANE. My words do not find the same difficulty.

CYRANO. They reach their point at once? Of course they do! That is because I catch them with my heart. My heart, you see, is very large, your ear particularly small.... Besides, your words drop... that goes quickly; mine have to climb... and that takes longer!

ROXANE. They have been climbing more nimbly, however, in the last few minutes.

CYRANO. They are becoming used to this gymnastic feat!

ROXANE. It is true that I am talking with you from a very mountain top!

CYRANO. It is sure that a hard word dropped from such a height upon my heart would shatter it!

ROXANE (*with the motion of leaving*). I will come down.

CYRANO (*quickly*). Do not!

ROXANE (*pointing at the bench at the foot of the balcony*). Then do you get up on the seat!...

CYRANO (*drawing away in terror*). No!

ROXANE. How do you mean... No?

CYRANO (*with ever-increasing emotion*). Let us profit a little by this chance of talking softly together without seeing each other...

ROXANE. Without seeing each other?...

CYRANO. Yes, to my mind, delectable! Each guesses at the other, and no more. You discern but the trailing blackness of a mantle, and I a dawn-gray glimmer which is a summer gown. I am a shadow merely, a pearly phantom are you! You can never know what these moments are to me! If ever I was eloquent...

ROXANE. You were!

CYRANO. My words never till now surged from my very heart...

ROXANE. And why?

CYRANO. Because, till now, they must strain to reach you through...

ROXANE. What?

CYRANO. Why, the bewildering emotion a man feels who sees you, and whom you look upon!... But this evening, it seems to me that I am speaking to you for the first time!

ROXANE. It is true that your voice is altogether different.

CYRANO (*coming nearer, feverishly*). Yes, altogether different, because, protected by the dark, I dare at last to be myself. I dare ... (*He stops, and distractedly.*) What was I saying?... I do not know.... All this... forgive my incoherence!... is so delicious... is so new to me!

ROXANE. So new?...

CYRANO (*in extreme confusion, still trying to mend his expressions*). So new... yes, new, to be sincere; the fear of being mocked always constrains my heart...

ROXANE. Mocked... for what?

CYRANO. Why... for its impulses, its flights!... Yes, my heart always cowers behind the defence of my wit. I set forth to capture a star... and then, for dread of laughter, I stop and pick a flower... of rhetoric.

ROXANE. That sort of flower has its pleasing points...

CYRANO. But yet, tonight, let us scorn it!

ROXANE. Never before had you spoken as you are speaking!...

CYRANO. Ah, if far from Cupid-darts and quivers, we might seek a place of somewhat fresher things! If instead of drinking, flat sip by sip, from a chiselled golden thimble, drops distilled and dulcified, we might try the sensation of quenching the thirst of our souls by stooping to the level of the great river, and setting our lips to the stream!

ROXANE. But yet, wit... fancy... delicate conceits...

CYRANO. I gave my fancy leave to frame conceits, before, to make you linger,... but now it would be an affront to this balm-breathing night, to Nature and the hour, to talk like characters in a pastoral performed at Court!... Let us give Heaven leave, looking at us with all its earnest stars, to strip us of disguise and artifice: I fear,... oh, fear!... lest in our mistaken alchemy sentiment should be subtilized to evaporation; lest the life of the heart should waste in these empty pastimes, and the final refinement of the fine be the undoing of the refined!

ROXANE. But yet, wit,... aptness,... ingenuity...

CYRANO. I hate them in love! Criminal, when one loves, to prolong overmuch that paltry thrust and parry! The moment, however, comes inevitably — and I pity those for whom it never comes! — in which, we apprehending the noble depth of the love we harbor, a shallow word hurts us to utter!

ROXANE. If... if, then, that moment has come for us two, what words will you say to me?

CYRANO. All those, all those, all those that come to me! Not in formal nosegay order,... I will throw them you in a wild sheaf! I love you, choke with love, I love you, dear.... My brain feels, I can bear no more, it is too much.... Your name is in my heart the golden clapper in a bell; and as I know no rest, Roxane, always the heart is shaken, and ever rings your name!... Of you, I remember all, all have I loved! Last year, one day, the twelfth of May, in going out at morning you changed the fashion of your hair.... I have taken the light of your hair for my light, and as having stared too long at the sun, on everything one sees a scarlet wheel, on everything when I come from my chosen light, my dazzled eye sets swimming golden blots!...

ROXANE (*in a voice unsteady with emotion*). Yes... this is love...

CYRANO. Ah, verily! The feeling which invades me, terrible and jealous, is love... with all its mournful frenzy! It is love, yet self-forgetting more than the wont of love! Ah, for your happiness now readily would I give mine, though you should never know it, might I but, from a distance, sometimes, hear the happy laughter bought by my sacrifice! Every glance of yours breeds in me new strength, new valor! Are you beginning to understand? Tell me, do you grasp my love's measure? Does some little part of my soul make itself felt of you there in the darkness? ... Oh, what is happening to me this evening is too sweet, too deeply dear! I tell you all these things, and you listen to me, you! Not in my least modest hoping did I ever hope so much!

I have now only to die! It is because of words of mine that she is trembling among the dusky branches! For you are trembling, like a flower among leaves! Yes, you tremble,... for whether you will or no, I have felt the worshipped trembling of your hand all along this thrilled and blissful jasmine-bough!

*(He madly kisses the end of a pendent bough.)*

ROXANE. Yes, I tremble... and weep... and love you... and am yours!... For you have carried me away... away!...

CYRANO. Then, let death come! I have moved you, I!... There is but one thing more I ask...

CHRISTIAN *(under the balcony)*. A kiss!

ROXANE *(drawing hastily back)*. What?

CYRANO. Oh!

ROXANE. You ask?...

CYRANO. Yes... I... *(To CHRISTIAN.)* You are in too great haste!

CHRISTIAN. Since she is so moved, I must take advantage of it!

CYRANO *(to ROXANE)*. I... Yes, it is true I asked... but, merciful heavens!... I knew at once that I had been too bold.

ROXANE *(a shade disappointed)*. You insist no more than so?

CYRANO. Indeed, I insist... without insisting! Yes! yes! but your modesty shrinks!... I insist, but yet... the kiss I begged... refuse it me!

CHRISTIAN *(to CYRANO, pulling at his mantle)*. Why?

CYRANO. Hush, Christian!

ROXANE *(bending over the balcony-rail)*. What are you whispering?

CYRANO. Reproaches to myself for having gone too far; I was saying "Hush, Christian!" *(The theorbos are heard playing.)* Your pardon!... a second!... Someone is coming!

*(ROXANE closes the window. CYRANO listens to the theorbos, one of which plays a lively and, the other a lugubrious tune.)*

CYRANO. A dance?... A dirge?... What do they mean? Is it a man or a woman?... Ah, it is a monk!

*(Enter a CAPUCHIN MONK, who goes from house to house, with a lantern, examining the doors.)*

CYRANO *(to the CAPUCHIN)*. What are you looking for, Diogenes?

THE CAPUCHIN. I am looking for the house of Madame...

CHRISTIAN. He is in the way!

THE CAPUCHIN. Magdeleine Robin...

CYRANO (*pointing up one of the streets*). This way!... Straight ahead
... go straight ahead...

THE CAPUCHIN. I thank you. I will say ten Aves for your peace.

CYRANO. My good wishes speed your cowl! (*Exit.*)

(*He comes forward toward* CHRISTIAN.)

CHRISTIAN. Insist upon the kiss!...

CYRANO. No, I will not!

CHRISTIAN. Sooner or later...

CYRANO. It is true! It must come, the moment of inebriation
when your lips shall imperiously be impelled toward each other,
because the one is fledged with youthful gold and the other is so
soft a pink!... (*To himself.*) I had rather it should be because...

(*Sound of the window reopening;* CHRISTIAN *hides under the
balcony.*)

ROXANE (*stepping forward on the balcony*). Are you there? We were
speaking of... of... of a...

CYRANO. Kiss. The word is sweet. Why does your fair lip stop
at it? If the mere word burns it, what will be of the thing itself?
Do not make it into a fearful matter, and then fear! Did you
not a moment ago insensibly leave playfulness behind and slip
without trepidation from a smile to a sigh, from a sigh to a tear?
Slip but a little further in the same blessed direction: from a tear
to a kiss there is scarcely a dividing shiver!

ROXANE. Say no more!

CYRANO. A kiss! When all is said, what is a kiss? An oath of
allegiance taken in closer proximity, a promise more precise,
a seal on a confession, a rose-red dot upon the letter i in loving;
a secret which elects the mouth for ear; an instant of eternity
murmuring like a bee; balmy communion with a flavor of
flowers; a fashion of inhaling each other's heart, and of tasting,
on the brink of the lips, each other's soul!

ROXANE. Say no more... no more!

CYRANO. A kiss, madame, is a thing so noble that the Queen of
France, on the most fortunate of lords, bestowed one, did the
queen herself!

ROXANE. If that be so...

CYRANO (*with increasing fervor*). Like Buckingham I have suffered

in long silence, like him I worship a queen, like him I am sorrowful and unchanging...

ROXANE. Like him you enthrall through the eyes the heart that
follows you!

CYRANO (*to himself, sobered*). True, I am handsome... I had
forgotten!

ROXANE. Come then and gather it, the supreme flower...

CYRANO (*pushing* CHRISTIAN *toward the balcony*). Go!

ROXANE. ... tasting of the heart.

CYRANO. Go!...

ROXANE. ... murmuring like a bee...

CYRANO. Go!

CHRISTIAN (*hesitating*). But now I feel as if I ought not!

ROXANE. ... making Eternity an instant...

CYRANO (*pushing* CHRISTIAN). Scale the balcony, you donkey!

(CHRISTIAN *springs toward the balcony, and climbs by means of
bench, the vine, the posts and balusters.*)

CHRISTIAN. Ah, Roxane!

(*He clasps her to him, and bends over her lips.*)

CYRANO. Ha!... What a turn of the screw to my heart!... Kiss,
banquet of Love at which I am Lazarus, a crumb drops from
your table even to me, here in the shade.... Yes, in my outstretched heart a little falls, as I feel that upon the lip pressing
her lip Roxane kisses the words spoken by me!... (*The theorbos
are heard.*)   A merry tune... a mournful one... The monk!
(*He goes through the pretence of arriving on the spot at a run, as if from
a distance; calling.*)   Ho, there!

ROXANE. What is it?

CYRANO. It is I. I was passing this way. Is Christian there?

CHRISTIAN (*astonished*). Cyrano!

ROXANE. Good-evening, cousin!

CYRANO. Cousin, good-evening!

ROXANE. I will come down.          (ROXANE *disappears in the house.*)

(CAPUCHIN *re-enters at the back.*)

CHRISTIAN (*seeing him*). Oh, again!          (*He follows* ROXANE.)

THE CAPUCHIN. It is here she lives, I am certain... Magdeleine
Robin.

CYRANO.  You said Ro-lin.

THE CAPUCHIN.  No, bin,... b,i,n, bin!

ROXANE (*appearing upon the threshold, followed by* RAGUENEAU *carrying a lantern, and* CHRISTIAN).  What is it?

THE CAPUCHIN.  A letter.

CHRISTIAN.  What?

THE CAPUCHIN (*to* ROXANE).  Oh, the contents can be only of a sacred character!  It is from a worthy nobleman who...

ROXANE (*to* CHRISTIAN).  It is from De Guiche!

CHRISTIAN.  He dares to...?

ROXANE.  Oh, he will not trouble me much longer!  (*Opening the letter.*)  I love you, and if... (*By the light of* RAGUENEAU's *lantern she reads, aside, low.*)  Mademoiselle: The drums are beating. My regiment is buckling on its corselet.  It is about to leave. I am thought to have left already, but lag behind.  I am disobeying you.  I am in the convent here.  I am coming to you, and send you word by a friar, silly as a sheep, who has no suspicion of the import of this letter.  You smiled too sweetly upon me an hour ago: I must see you smile again.  Provide to be alone, and deign graciously to receive the audacious worshipper, forgiven already, I can but hope, who signs himself your — etc.... (*To the* CAPUCHIN.)  Father, this is what the letter tells me... Listen: (*All draw nearer; she reads aloud.*)  Mademoiselle: The wishes of the cardinal may not be disregarded, however hard compliance with them prove.  I have therefore chosen as bearer of this letter a most reverend, holy, and sagacious Capuchin; it is our wish that he should at once, in your own dwelling, pronounce the nuptial blessing over you.  Christian must secretly become your husband.  I send him to you.  You dislike him.  Bow to Heaven's will in resignation, and be sure that it will bless your zeal, and sure, likewise, mademoiselle, of the respect of him who is and will be ever your most humble and ... etc.

THE CAPUCHIN (*beaming*).  The worthy gentleman!... I knew it! You remember that I said so: The contents of that letter can be only of a sacred character!

ROXANE (*low, to* CHRISTIAN).  I am a fluent reader, am I not?

CHRISTIAN.  Hm!

ROXANE (*with feigned despair*). Ah... it is horrible!

THE CAPUCHIN (*who has turned the light of his lantern upon* CYRANO). You are the one?

CHRISTIAN. No, I am.

THE CAPUCHIN (*turning the light upon him, and as if his good looks aroused suspicion*). But...

ROXANE (*quickly*). Postscript: You will bestow upon the convent two hundred and fifty crowns.

THE CAPUCHIN. The worthy, worthy gentleman! (*To* ROXANE.) Be reconciled!

ROXANE (*with the expression of a martyr*). I will endeavor! (*While* RAGUENEAU *opens the door for the* CAPUCHIN, *whom* CHRISTIAN *is showing into the house,* ROXANE *says low to* CYRANO.) De Guiche is coming!... Keep him here! Do not let him enter until...

CYRANO. I understand! (*To the* CAPUCHIN.) How long will it take to marry them?

THE CAPUCHIN. A quarter of an hour.

CYRANO (*pushing all toward the house*). Go in! I shall be here!

ROXANE (*to* CHRISTIAN). Come! (*They go in.*)

CYRANO. How can I detain De Guiche for a quarter of an hour? (*He jumps upon the bench, climbs the wall toward the balcony-rail.*) So!... I climb up here!... I know what I will do!... (*The theorbos play a melancholy tune.*) Ho, it is a man! (*The tune quavers lugubriously.*) Ho, ho, this time there is no mistake! (*He is on the balcony; he pulls the brim of his hat over his eyes, takes off his sword, wraps his cloak about him, and bends over the balcony-rail.*) No, it is not too far! (*He climbs over the balcony-rail, and reaching for a long bough that projects beyond the garden wall, holds on to it with both hands, ready to let himself drop.*) I shall make a slight commotion in the atmosphere!

DE GUICHE (*enters masked, groping in the dark*). What can that thrice-damned Capuchin be about?

CYRANO. The devil! if he should recognize my voice? (*Letting go with one hand, he makes show of turning a key.*) Cric! crac! (*Solemnly.*) Cyrano, resume the accent of Bergerac!

DE GUICHE (*looking at* ROXANE's *house*). Yes, that is it. I can scarcely see. This mask bothers my eyes!

(*He is about to enter* ROXANE's *house;* CYRANO *swings from the balcony, holding on to the bough, which bends and lets him down between the door and* DE GUICHE. *He intentionally drops very heavily, to give the effect of dropping from a great height, and lies flattened upon the ground, motionless, as if stunned.)*

DE GUICHE. What is it? (*When he looks up, the bough has swung into place; he sees nothing but the sky.*) Where did this man drop from?

CYRANO (*rising to a sitting posture*). From the moon!

DE GUICHE. From the...?

CYRANO (*in a dreamy voice*). What time is it?

DE GUICHE. Is he mad?

CYRANO. What time? What country? What day? What season?

DE GUICHE. But...

CYRANO. I am dazed!

DE GUICHE. Monsieur...

CYRANO. I have dropped from the moon like a bomb!

DE GUICHE (*impatiently*). What are you babbling about?

CYRANO (*rising, in a terrible voice*). I tell you I have dropped from the moon!

DE GUICHE (*backing a step*). Very well. You have dropped from the moon!... He is perhaps a lunatic!

CYRANO (*walking up close to him*). Not metaphorically, mind that!

DE GUICHE. But...

CYRANO. A hundred years ago, or else a minute — for I have no conception how long I have been falling — I was up there, in that saffron-colored ball!

DE GUICHE (*shrugging his shoulders*). You were. Now, let me pass!

CYRANO (*standing in his way*). Where am I? Be frank with me! Keep nothing from me! In what region, among what people, have I been shot like an aerolite?

DE GUICHE. I wish to pass!

CYRANO. While falling I could not choose my way, and have no notion where I have fallen! Is it upon a moon, or is it upon an earth, I have been dragged by my posterior weight?

DE GUICHE. I tell you, sir...

CYRANO (*with a scream of terror at which* DE GUICHE *starts backward a step*). Great God!... In this country men's faces are soot-black!

DE GUICHE (*lifting his hand to his face*). What does he mean?

CYRANO (*still terrified*). Am I in Algeria? Are you a native?...

DE GUICHE (*who has felt his mask*). Ah, my mask!

CYRANO (*pretending to be easier*). So I am in Venice!... Or am I in Genoa?

DE GUICHE (*attempting to pass*). A lady is expecting me!

CYRANO (*completely reassured*). Ah, then I am in Paris.

DE GUICHE (*smiling in spite of himself*). The rogue is not far from amusing!

CYRANO. Ah, you are laughing!

DE GUICHE. I laugh... but intend to pass!

CYRANO (*beaming*). To think I should strike Paris! (*Quite at his ease, laughing, brushing himself, bowing.*) I arrived — pray, pardon my appearance! — by the last whirlwind. I am rather unpresentable — Travel, you know! My eyes are still full of star-dust. My spurs are clogged with bristles off a planet. (*Appearing to pick something off his sleeve.*) See, on my sleeve, a comet's hair! (*He makes a feint of blowing it away.*)

DE GUICHE (*beside himself*). Sir...

CYRANO (*as* DE GUICHE *is about to pass, stretching out his leg as if to show something on it, thereby stopping him*). Embedded in my calf, I have brought back one of the Great Bear's teeth... and as, falling too near the Trident, I strained aside to clear one of its prongs, I landed sitting in Libra,... yes, one of the scales!... and now my weight is registered up there! (*Quickly preventing* DE GUICHE *from passing, and taking hold of a button on his doublet.*) And if, monsieur, you should take my nose between your fingers and compress it... milk would result!

DE GUICHE. What are you saying? Milk?...

CYRANO. Of the Milky Way.

DE GUICHE. Go to the devil!

CYRANO. No! I am sent from Heaven, literally. (*Folding his arms.*) Will you believe — I discovered it in passing — that Sirius at night puts on a night-cap? (*Confidentially.*) The lesser Bear is too little yet to bite.... (*Laughing.*) I tumbled plump through Lyra, and snapped a string!... (*Magnificent.*) But I intend setting all this down in a book, and the golden stars I have brought back caught in my shaggy mantle, when the book is printed, will be seen serving as asterisks!

DE GUICHE. I have stood this long enough! I want...

CYRANO. I know perfectly what you want!

DE GUICHE. Man...

CYRANO. You want to know, from me, at first hand, what the moon is made of, and whether that monumental pumpkin is inhabited?

DE GUICHE (*shouting*). Not in the very least! I want...

CYRANO. To know how I got there? I got there by a method of my own invention.

DE GUICHE (*discouraged*). He is mad!... stark!

CYRANO (*disdainfully*). Do not imagine that I resorted to anything so absurd as Regiomontanus's eagle, or anything so lacking in enterprise as Archytas's pigeon!...

DE GUICHE. The madman is erudite...

CYRANO. I drew up nothing that had ever been thought of before! (DE GUICHE *has succeeded in getting past* CYRANO, *and is nearing* ROXANE's *door;* CYRANO *follows him, ready to buttonhole him.*) I invented no less than six ways of storming the blue fort of Heaven!

DE GUICHE (*turning around*). Six, did you say?

CYRANO (*volubly*). One way was to stand naked in the sunshine, in a harness thickly studded with glass phials, each filled with morning dew. The sun in drawing up the dew, you see, could not have helped drawing me up too!

DE GUICHE (*surprised, taking a step toward* CYRANO). True. That is one!

CYRANO (*taking a step backward, with a view to drawing* DE GUICHE *away from the door*). Or else, I could have let the wind into a cedar coffer, then rarefied the imprisoned element by means of cunningly adjusted burning-glasses, and soared up with it!

DE GUICHE (*taking another step toward* CYRANO). Two!

CYRANO (*backing*). Or else, mechanic as well as artificer, I could have fashioned a giant grasshopper, with steel joints, which, impelled by successive explosions of salt peter, would have hopped with me to the azure meadows where graze the starry flocks!

DE GUICHE (*unconsciously following* CYRANO, *and counting on his fingers*). That makes three!

CYRANO. Since smoke by its nature ascends, I could have blown into an appropriate globe a sufficient quantity to ascend **with** me!

DE GUICHE (*as above, more and more astonished*). Four!

CYRANO. Since Phoebe, the moon-goddess, when she is at wane, is greedy, O beeves! of your marrow,... with that marrow have besmeared myself!

DE GUICHE (*amazed*). Five!

CYRANO (*who while talking has backed, followed by* DE GUICHE, *to the further side of the square, near a bench*). Or else, I could have placed myself upon an iron plate, have taken a magnet of suitable size, and thrown it in the air! That way is a very good one! The magnet flies upward, the iron instantly after; the magnet no sooner overtaken than you fling it up again.... The rest is clear! You can go upward indefinitely.

DE GUICHE. Six!... But here are six excellent methods! Which of the six, my dear sir, did you select?

CYRANO. A seventh!

DE GUICHE. Did you, indeed? And what was that?

CYRANO. I give you a hundred guesses!

DE GUICHE. I must confess that I should like to know!

CYRANO (*imitating the noise of the surf, and making great mysterious gestures*). Hoo-ish! hoo-ish!

DE GUICHE. Well! What is that?

CYRANO. Cannot you guess?

DE GUICHE. No!

CYRANO. The tide!... At the hour in which the moon attracts the deep, I lay down upon the sands, after a sea-bath... and, my head being drawn up first — the reason of this, you see, that the hair will hold a quantity of water in its mop! — I rose in the air, straight, beautifully straight, like an angel. I rose... I rose softly... without an effort... when, suddenly, I felt a shock. Then...

DE GUICHE (*lured on by curiosity, taking a seat on the bench*). Well,... then?

CYRANO. Then... (*Resuming his natural voice.*) The time is up, monsieur, and I release you. They are married.

DE GUICHE (*getting to his feet with a leap*). I am dreaming or drunk! That voice? (*The door of* ROXANE'S *house opens; lackeys appear carrying lighted candelabra.* CYRANO *removes his hat.*) And that nose!... Cyrano!

CYRANO (*bowing*). Cyrano. They have exchanged rings within the quarter of the hour.

DE GUICHE. Who have? (*He turns round. Tableau. Behind the lackey stand* ROXANE *and* CHRISTIAN *holding hands. The* CAPUCHIN *follows them smiling.* RAGUENEAU *holds high a flambeau. The* DUENNA *closes the procession, bewildered, in her bedgown.*) Heavens! (*To* ROXANE.) You! (*Recognizing* CHRISTIAN *with amazement.*) He? (*Bowing to* ROXANE.) Your astuteness compels my admiration! (*To* CYRANO.) My compliments to you, ingenious inventor of flying machines. Your experiences would have beguiled a saint on the threshold of Paradise! Make a note of them.... They can be used again, with profit, in a book!

CYRANO (*bowing*). I will confidently follow your advice.

THE CAPUCHIN (*to* DE GUICHE, *pointing at the lovers, and wagging his great white beard with satisfaction*). A beautiful couple, my son, brought together by you!

DE GUICHE (*eyeing him frigidly*). As you say! (*To* ROXANE.) And now proceed, Madame, to take leave of your husband.

ROXANE. What?

DE GUICHE (*to* CHRISTIAN). The regiment is on the point of starting. You are to join it!

ROXANE. To go to war?

DE GUICHE. Of course!

ROXANE. But the cadets are not going!

DE GUICHE. They are! (*Taking out the paper which he had put in his pocket.*) Here is the order. (*To* CHRISTIAN.) I beg you will take it to the Captain, baron, yourself.

ROXANE (*throwing herself in* CHRISTIAN'S *arms*). Christian!

DE GUICHE (*to* CYRANO, *with a malignant laugh*). The wedding night is somewhat far as yet!

CYRANO (*aside*). He thinks that he is giving me great pain!

CHRISTIAN (*to* ROXANE). Oh, once more, dear!... Once more!

CYRANO. Be reasonable... Come!... Enough!

CHRISTIAN (*still clasping* ROXANE). Oh, it is hard to leave her.... You cannot know...

CYRANO (*trying to draw him away*). I know.

> (*Drums are heard in the distance sounding a march.*)

DE GUICHE (*at the back*). The regiment is on its way!

ROXANE (*to* CYRANO, *while she clings to* CHRISTIAN *whom he is trying to draw away*). Oh!... I entrust him to your care! Promise that under no circumstance shall his life be placed in danger!

CYRANO. I will endeavor... but obviously cannot promise...

ROXANE (*same business*). Promise that he will be careful of himself!

CYRANO. I will do my best, but...

ROXANE (*as above*). That during this terrible siege he shall not take harm from the cold!

CYRANO. I will try, but...

ROXANE (*as above*). That he will be true to me!

CYRANO. Of course, but yet, you see...

ROXANE (*as above*). That he will write to me often!

CYRANO (*stopping*). Ah, that... I promise freely!

CURTAIN

# ACT FOURTH

## THE GASCONY CADETS

*The post occupied at the siege of Arras by the company of* CARBON DE CASTEL-JALOUX. *At the back, across the whole stage, sloping earthwork. Beyond this is seen a plain stretching to the horizon; the country is covered with constructions relating to the siege. In the distance, against the sky, the outlines of the walls and roofs of Arras. Tents; scattered arms; drums, etc. It is shortly before sunrise. The East is yellow. Sentinels at even intervals. Camp-fires. The* GASCONY CADETS *lie asleep, rolled in their cloaks.* CARBON DE CASTEL-JALOUX *and* LE BRET *are watching. All are very pale and gaunt.* CHRISTIAN *lies sleeping among the others, in his military cape, in the foreground, his face lighted by one of the camp-fires. Silence.*

LE BRET. It is dreadful!

CARBON. Yes. Nothing left.

LE BRET. *Mordious!*

CARBON (*warning him by a gesture to speak lower*). Curse in a whisper!

You will wake them!... (*To the* CADETS.) Hush! Go to sleep!
(*To* LE BRET.) Who sleeps dines.

LE BRET. Who lies awake misses two good things... What a
situation! (*A few shots are heard in the distance.*)

CARBON. The devil take their popping! They will wake my
young ones!... (*To the* CADETS *who lift their heads.*) Go to sleep!
(*The* CADETS *lie down again. Other shots are heard, nearer.*)

ONE OF THE CADETS (*stirring*). The devil! Again?

CARBON. It is nothing. It is Cyrano getting home.
(*The heads which had started up, go down again.*)

A SENTINEL (*outside*). *Ventrebleu!* Who goes there?

CYRANO'S VOICE. Bergerac!

THE SENTINEL (*upon the embankment*). *Ventrebleu!* Who goes there?

CYRANO (*appearing at the top of the embankment*). Bergerac, blockhead!
(*He comes down.* LE BRET *goes to him, uneasy.*)

LE BRET. Ah, thank God!

CYRANO (*warning him by a sign to wake no one*). Hush!

LE BRET. Wounded?

CYRANO. Do you not know that it has become a habit with them
to miss me?

LE BRET. To me, it seems a little excessive that you should, every
morning, for the sake of taking a letter, risk...

CYRANO (*stopping in front of* CHRISTIAN). I promised that he would
write often. (*He looks at* CHRISTIAN.) He sleeps. He has
grown pale. If the poor little girl could know that he is starving.
... But handsome as ever!

LE BRET. Go at once and sleep.

CYRANO. Le Bret, do not grumble! Learn this: I nightly cross
the Spanish lines at a point where I know beforehand everyone
will be drunk.

LE BRET. You ought sometime to bring us back some victuals!

CYRANO. I must be lightly burdened to flit through!... But I
know that there will be events before the evening. The French,
unless I am much mistaken, will eat or die.

LE BRET. Oh, tell us!

CYRANO. No, I am not certain... You will see!

CARBON. What a shameful reversal of the order of things, that
the besieger should be starved!

LE BRET. Alas! never was more complicated siege than this of Arras: We besiege Arras, and, caught in a trap, are ourselves besieged by the Cardinal-prince of Spain....

CYRANO. Someone now ought to come and besiege him.

LE BRET. I am not joking!

CYRANO. Oh, oh!

LE BRET. To think, ungrateful boy, that every day you risk a life precious as yours, solely to carry... (CYRANO *goes toward one of the tents.*) Where are you going?

CYRANO. I am going to write another.

(*He lifts the canvas flap, and disappears in the tent. Daybreak has brightened. Rosy flush. The city of Arras at the horizon catches a golden light. The report of a cannon is heard, followed at once by a drum-call, very far away, at the left. Other drums beat, nearer. The drum-calls answer one another, come nearer, come very near, and go off, decreasing, dying in the distance, toward the right, having made the circuit of the camp. Noise of general awakening. Voices of officers in the distance.*)

CARBON (*with a sigh*). The réveillé... Ah, me!... (*The* CADETS *stir in their cloaks, stretch.*) An end to the succulent slumbers! I know but too well what their first word will be!

ONE OF THE CADETS (*sitting up*). I am famished!

OTHER CADET. I believe I am dying!

ALL. Oh!...

CARBON. Get up!

THIRD CADET. I cannot go a step!

FOURTH CADET. I have not strength to stir!

FIRST CADET (*looking at himself in a bit of armor*). My tongue is coated: it must be the weather that is indigestible!

OTHER CADET. Anyone who wants them, can have all my titles of nobility for a Chester cheese... or part of one!

OTHER CADET. If my stomach does not have something put into it to take up the attention of my gastric juice, I shall retire into my tent before long... like Achilles!

OTHER CADET. Yes, they ought to provide us with bread!

CARBON (*going to the tent into which* CYRANO *has retired; low*). Cyrano!

OTHER CADETS. We cannot stand this much longer!

CARBON (*as above, at the door of the tent*). To the rescue, Cyrano!

You who succeed so well always in cheering them, come and make them pluck up spirits!

SECOND CADET (*falling upon* FIRST CADET *who is chewing something*). What are you chewing, man?

FIRST CADET. A bit of gun-tow fried in axle-grease... using a burganet as frying pan. The suburbs of Arras are not precisely rich in game....

OTHER CADET (*entering*). I have been hunting!

OTHER CADET (*the same*). I have been fishing!

ALL (*rising and falling upon the newcomers*). What? — what did you catch? — A pheasant? — A carp? — Quick! quick!... Let us see!

THE HUNTSMAN. A sparrow!

THE ANGLER. A gudgeon!

ALL (*exasperated*). Enough of this! Let us revolt!

CARBON. To the rescue, Cyrano! (*It is now broad daylight.*)

CYRANO (*coming out of the tent, tranquil, a pen behind his ear, a book in his hand*). What is the matter? (*Silence. To* FIRST CADET.) Why do you go off like that, with that slouching gait?

THE CADET. I have something away down in my heels which inconveniences me.

CYRANO. And what is that?

THE CADET. My stomach.

CYRANO. That is where mine is, too.

THE CADET. Then you too must be inconvenienced.

CYRANO. No. The size of the hollow within me merely increases my sense of my size.

SECOND CADET. I happen to have teeth, long ones!

CYRANO. The better will you bite... in good time!

THIRD CADET. I reverberate like a drum!

CYRANO. You will be of use... to sound the charge!

OTHER CADET. I have a buzzing in my ears!

CYRANO. A mistake. Empty belly, no ears. You hear no buzzing.

OTHER CADET. Ah, a trifling article to eat... and a little oil upon it!

CYRANO (*taking off the* CADET's *morion and placing it in his hand*). That is seasoned.

OTHER CADET. What is there we could devour?

CYRANO (*tossing him the book he has been holding*). Try the Iliad!

OTHER CADET. The minister, in Paris, makes his four meals a day!

CYRANO. You feel it remiss in him not to send you a bit of partridge?

THE SAME. Why should he not? And some wine!

CYRANO. Richelieu, some Burgundy, if you please?

THE SAME. He might, by one of his Capuchins!

CYRANO. By his Eminence, perhaps, in sober gray?

OTHER CADET. No ogre was ever so hungry!

CYRANO. You may have your fill yet of humble-pie!

FIRST CADET (*shrugging his shoulders*). Forever jests!... puns!... *mots!*

CYRANO. *Le mot* forever, indeed! And I would wish to die, on a fine evening, under a rose-flushed sky, delivering myself of a good *mot* in a good cause!... Ah, yes, the best were indeed, far from fever-bed and potion, pierced with the only noble weapon, by an adversary worthy of oneself, to fall upon a glorious field, the point of a sword through his heart, the point of a jest on his lips!...

ALL (*in a wail*). I am hungry!

CYRANO (*folding his arms*). God ha' mercy! can you think of nothing but eating?... Come here, Bertrandou the fifer, once the shepherd! Take from the double case one of your fifes: breathe into it, play to this pack of guzzlers and of gluttons our homely melodies, of haunting rhythm, every note of which appeals like a little sister, through whose every strain are heard strains of beloved voices... mild melodies whose slowness brings to mind the slowness of the smoke upcurling from our native hamlet hearths... melodies that seem to speak to a man in his native dialect!... (*The old fifer sits down and makes ready his fife.*) Today let the fife, martial unwillingly, be reminded, while your fingers upon its slender stem flutter like birds in a delicate minuet, that before being ebony it was reed; surprise itself by what you make it sing,... let it feel restored to it the soul of its youth, rustic and peaceable! (*The old man begins playing Languedoc tunes.*) Listen, Gascons! It is no more, beneath his fingers, the shrill fife of the camp, but the soft flute of the woodland! It is no more, between his lips, the whistling note of battle, but the lowly lay of goatherds leading their flocks to feed!... Hark!... It sings of the valley, the heath, the forest!... of the little shepherd, sunburned under his crimson cap!... the green delight of evening on the river!... Hark, Gascons all!  It sings of Gascony!

(*Every head has drooped; all eyes have grown dreamy; tears are furtively brushed away with a sleeve, the hem of a cloak.*)

CARBON (*to* CYRANO, *low*).  You are making them weep!

CYRANO.  With homesickness!... a nobler pain than hunger... not physical: mental!  I am glad the seat of their suffering should have removed... that the gripe should now afflict their hearts!

CARBON.  But you weaken them, making them weep!

CYRANO (*beckoning to a drummer*).  Never fear!  The hero in their veins is quickly roused.  It is enough to...

(*He signs to the drummer who begins drumming.*)

ALL (*starting to their feet and snatching up their arms*).  Hein?... What? ... What is it?

CYRANO (*smiling*).  You see?... The sound of the drum was enough! Farewell dreams, regrets, old homestead, love... What comes with the fife with the drum may go...

ONE OF THE CADETS (*looking off at the back*).  Ah! ah... Here comes Monsieur de Guiche!

ALL THE CADETS (*grumbling*).  Hoo...

CYRANO (*smiling*).  Flattering murmur...

ONE OF THE CADETS.  He bores us!...

OTHER CADET.  Showing himself off, with his broad point collar on top of his armor!...

OTHER CADET.  As if lace were worn with steel!

FIRST CADET.  Convenient, if you have a boil on your neck to cover...

SECOND CADET.  There is another courtier for you!

OTHER CADET.  His uncle's own nephew!

CARBON.  He is a Gascon, nevertheless!

FIRST CADET.  Not genuine!... Never trust him.  For a Gascon, look you, must be something of a madman: nothing is so deadly to deal with as a Gascon who is completely rational!

LE BRET.  He is pale!

OTHER CADET.  He is hungry, as hungry as any poor devil of us! But his corselet being freely embellished with gilt studs, his stomach-ache is radiant in the sun!

CYRANO (*eagerly*). Let us not appear to suffer, either! You, your cards, your pipes, your dice... (*All briskly set themselves to playing with cards and dice, on the heads of drums, on stools, on cloaks spread over the ground. They light long tobacco pipes.*) And I will be reading Descartes....

    (*He walks to and fro, forward and backward, reading a small book which he has taken from his pocket. Tableau.*)

(*Enter* DE GUICHE. *Everyone appears absorbed and satisfied.* DE CUICHE *is very pale. He goes toward* CARBON.)

DE GUICHE (*to* CARBON). Ah, good-morning. (*They look at each other attentively. Aside, with satisfaction.*) He is pale as plaster.

CARBON (*same business*). His eyes are all that is left of him.

DE GUICHE (*looking at the* CADETS). So here are the wrongheaded rascals?... Yes, gentlemen, it is reported to me on every side that I am your scoff and derision; that the cadets, highland nobility, Béarn clodhoppers, Périgord baronets, cannot express sufficient contempt for their colonel; call me intriguer, courtier, find it irksome to their taste that I should wear, with my cuirass, a collar of Genoese point, and never cease to air their wondering indignation that a man should be a Gascon without being a vagabond! (*Silence. The* CADETS *continue smoking and playing.*) Shall I have you punished by your captain?... I do not like to.

CARBON. Did you otherwise, however,... I am free, and punish only...

DE GUICHE. Ah?...

CARBON. My company is paid by myself, belongs to me. I obey no orders but such as relate to war.

DE GUICHE. Ah, is it so? Enough, then. I will treat your taunts with simple scorn. My fashion of deporting myself under fire is well known. You are not unaware of the manner in which yesterday, at Bapaume, I forced back the columns of the Comte de Bucquoi; gathering my men together to plunge forward like an avalanche, three times I charged him....

CYRANO (*without lifting his nose from his book*). And your white scarf?

DE GUICHE (*surprised and self-satisfied*). You heard of that circumstance?... In fact, it happened that as I was wheeling about to collect my men for the third charge, I was caught in a stream

of fugitives which bore me onward to the edge of the enemy.
I was in danger of being captured and cut off with an arque-
buse, when I had the presence of mind to untie and let slip
to the ground the white scarf which proclaimed my military
grade. Thus was I enabled, undistinguished, to withdraw
from among the Spaniards, and thereupon returning with my
reinspirited men, to defeat them. Well?... What do you say
to the incident?

(*The* CADETS *have appeared not to be listening; at this point,
however, hands with cards and dice-boxes remain suspended in
the air; no pipe-smoke is ejected; all expresses expectation.*)

CYRANO. That never would Henry the Fourth, however great
the number of his opponents, have consented to diminish his
presence by the size of his white plume.

(*Silent joy. Cards fall, dice rattle, smoke upwreathes.*)

DE GUICHE. The trick was successful, however!

(*As before, expectation suspends gambling and smoking.*)

CYRANO. Very likely. But one should not resign the honor of
being a target. (*Cards, dice, smoke, fall, rattle, and upwreathe,
as before, in expression of increasing glee.*) Had I been at hand
when you allowed your scarf to drop — the quality of our
courage, monsieur, shows different in this — I would have
picked it up and worn it....

DE GUICHE. Ah, yes — more of your Gascon bragging!...

CYRANO. Bragging?... Lend me the scarf. I engage to mount,
ahead of all, to the assault, wearing it crosswise upon my breast!

DE GUICHE. A Gascon's offer, that too! You know that the
scarf was left in the enemy's camp, by the banks of the Scarpe,
where bullets since then have hailed... whence no one can
bring it back!

CYRANO (*taking a white scarf from his pocket and handing it to* DE
GUICHE). Here it is.

(*Silence. The* CADETS *smother their laughter behind cards and in
dice-boxes.* DE GUICHE *turns around, looks at them; instantly
they become grave; one of them, with an air of unconcern, whistles
the tune played earlier by the fifer.*)

DE GUICHE (*taking the scarf*). I thank you. I shall be able with
this shred of white to make a signal... which I was hesitating

to make.... *(He goes to the top of the bank and waves the scarf.)*

ALL. What now?... What is this?

THE SENTINEL *(at the top of the bank)*. A man... over there... running off...

DE GUICHE *(coming forward again)*. It is a supposed Spanish spy. He is very useful to us. The information he carries to the enemy is that which I give him — so that their decisions are influenced by us.

CYRANO. He is a scoundrel!

DE GUICHE *(coolly tying on his scarf)*. He is a convenience. We were saying?... Ah, I was about to tell you. Last night, having resolved upon a desperate stroke to obtain supplies, the Marshal secretly set out for Dourlens. The royal sutlers are encamped there. He expects to join them by way of the tilled fields; but, to provide against interference, he took with him troops in such number that, certainly, if we were now attacked, the enemy would find easy work. Half of the army is absent from the camp.

CARBON. If the Spaniards knew that, it might be serious. But they do not know.

DE GUICHE. They do. And are going to attack us.

CARBON. Ah!

DE GUICHE. My pretended spy came to warn me of their intention. He said, moreover: I can direct the attack. At what point shall it be? I will lead them to suppose it the least strong, and they will center their efforts against it. I answered: Very well. Go from the camp. Look down the line. Let them attack at the point I signal from.

CARBON *(to the CADETS)*. Gentlemen, get ready!

*(All get up. Noise of swords and belts being buckled on.)*

DE GUICHE. They will be here in an hour.

FIRST CADET. Oh!... if there is a whole hour!...

*(All sit down again, and go on with their games.)*

DE GUICHE *(to CARBON)*. The main object is to gain time. The Marshal is on his way back.

CARBON. And to gain time?

DE GUICHE. You will be so obliging as to keep them busy killing you.

CYRANO. Ah, this is your revenge!

DE GUICHE. I will not pretend that if I had been fond of you, I would have thus singled out you and yours; but, as your bravery is unquestionably beyond that of others, I am serving my King at the same time as my inclination.

CYRANO. Suffer me, monsieur, to express my gratitude.

DE GUICHE. I know that you affect fighting one against a hundred. You will not complain of lacking opportunity.

(*He goes toward the back with* CARBON.)

CYRANO (*to the* CADETS). We shall now be able, gentlemen, to add to the Gascon escutcheon, which bears, as it is, six chevrons, or and azure, the chevron that was wanting to complete it — blood-red!

(DE GUICHE *at the back speaks low with* CARBON. *Orders are given. All is made ready to repel an attack.* CYRANO *goes toward* CHRISTIAN, *who stands motionless, with folded arms.*)

CYRANO (*laying his hand on* CHRISTIAN's *shoulder*). Christian?

CHRISTIAN (*shaking his head*). Roxane!

CYRANO. Ah me!

CHRISTIAN. I wish I might at least put my whole heart's last blessing in a beautiful letter!

CYRANO. I mistrusted that it would come today... (*he takes a letter from his doublet*) and I have written your farewells.

CHRISTIAN. Let me see!

CYRANO. You wish to see it?...

CHRISTIAN (*taking the letter*). Yes! (*He opens the letter, begins to read, stops short.*) Ah?...

CYRANO. What?

CHRISTIAN. That little round blister?

CYRANO (*hurriedly taking back the letter, and looking at it with an artless air*). A blister?

CHRISTIAN. It is a tear!

CYRANO. It looks like one, does it not?... A poet, you see, is sometimes caught in his own snare — that is what constitutes the interest, the charm!... This letter, you must know, is very touching. In writing it I apparently made myself shed tears.

CHRISTIAN. Shed tears?...

CYRANO. Yes, because... well, to die is not terrible at all... but never to see her again... never!... that, you know, is horrible beyond all thinking.... And, things having taken the turn they have, I shall not see her... (CHRISTIAN *looks at him*) we shall not see her... (*hastily*) you will not see her....

CHRISTIAN (*snatching the letter from him*). Give me the letter!

(*Noise in the distance.*)

VOICE OF A SENTINEL. *Ventrebleu*, who goes there?

(*Shots. Noise of voices, tinkling of bells.*)

CARBON. What is it?

THE SENTINEL (*on the top of the bank*). A coach! (*All run to see.*) (*Noisy exclamations.*) What? — In the camp? — It is driving into the camp! — It comes from the direction of the enemy! The devil! Fire upon it! — No! the coachman is shouting something! — What does he say? — He shouts: Service of the King!

DE GUICHE. What? Service of the King?

(*All come down from the bank and fall into order.*)

CARBON. Hats off, all!

DE GUICHE (*at the corner*). Service of the King! Stand back, low rabble, and give it room to turn around with a handsome sweep!

(*The coach comes in at a trot. It is covered with mud and dust. The curtains are drawn. Two lackeys behind. It comes to a standstill.*)

CARBON (*shouting*). Salute!

(*Drums roll. All the CADETS uncover.*)

DE GUICHE. Let down the steps!

(*Two men hurry forward. The coach door opens.*)

ROXANE (*stepping from the carriage*). Good-morning!

(*At the sound of a feminine voice, all the men, in the act of bowing low, straighten themselves. Consternation.*)

DE GUICHE. Service of the King! You?

ROXANE. Of the only King!... of Love!

CYRANO. Ah, great God!

CHRISTIAN (*rushing to her*). You! Why are you here?

ROXANE. This siege lasted too long!

CHRISTIAN. Why have you come?

ROXANE. I will tell you!

CYRANO (*who at the sound of her voice has started, then stood **motionless**

*without venturing to look her way*). God!... can I trust myself to
look at her?

DE GUICHE. You cannot remain here.

ROXANE. But I can — I can, indeed! Will you favor me with a
drum? (*She seats herself upon a drum brought forward for her.*)
There! I thank you! (*She laughs.*) They fired upon my carriage. (*Proudly.*) A patrol! — It does look rather as if it were
made out of a pumpkin, does it not? like Cinderella's coach!
and the footmen made out of rats! (*Blowing a kiss to* CHRISTIAN.)
How do you do? (*Looking at them all.*) You do not look over-
joyed!... Arras is a long way from Paris, do you know it?
(*Catching sight of* CYRANO.) Cousin, delighted!

CYRANO (*coming toward her*). But how did you... ?

ROXANE. How did I find the army? Dear me, cousin, that was
simple: I followed straight along the line of devastation.... Ah,
I should never have believed in such horrors had I not seen
them! Gentlemen, if that is the service of your King, I like
mine better!

CYRANO. But this is mad!... By what way did you come?

ROXANE. Way?... I drove through the Spaniards' camp.

FIRST CADET. Ah, what will keep lovely woman from her way!

DE GUICHE. But how did you contrive to get through their
lines?

LE BRET. That must have been difficult...

ROXANE. No, not very. I simply drove through them, in my
coach, at a trot. If a hidalgo, with arrogant front, showed
likely to stop us, I put my face at the window, wearing my
sweetest smile, and, those gentlemen being — let the French
not grudge my saying so! — the most gallant in the world,... I
passed!

CARBON. Such a smile is a passport, certainly!... But you must
have been not unfrequently bidden to stand and deliver where
you were going?

ROXANE. Not unfrequently, you are right. Whereupon I would
say, "I am going to see my lover!" At once, the fiercest looking
Spaniard of them all would gravely close my carriage door;
and, with a gesture the King might emulate, motion aside the
musket-barrels levelled at me; and, superb at once for grace and

haughtiness, bringing his spurs together, and lifting his plumed
hat, bow low and say, "Pass, señorita, pass!"

CHRISTIAN. But, Roxane...

ROXANE. I said, "My lover!" yes, forgive me! — You see, if I had
said, "My husband!" they would never have let me by!

CHRISTIAN. But...

ROXANE. What troubles you?

DE GUICHE. You must leave at once.

ROXANE. I?

CYRANO. At once!

LE BRET. As fast as you can.

CHRISTIAN. Yes, you must.

ROXANE. But why?

CHRISTIAN (*embarrassed*). Because...

CYRANO (*embarrassed too*). In three quarters of an hour...

DE GUICHE (*the same*). Or an hour...

CARBON (*the same*). You had much better...

LE BRET (*the same*). You might...

ROXANE. I shall remain. You are going to fight.

ALL. Oh, no!... No!

ROXANE. He is my husband! (*She throws herself in* CHRISTIAN'S
*arms.*) Let me be killed with you!

CHRISTIAN. How your eyes shine!

ROXANE. I will tell you why they shine!

DE GUICHE (*desperately*). It is a post of horrible probabilities!

ROXANE (*turning toward him*). What — of horrible?...

CYRANO. In proof of which he appointed us to it!...

ROXANE. Ah, you wish me made a widow?

DE GUICHE. I swear to you...

ROXANE. No! Now I have lost all regard.... Now I will surely
not go.... Besides, I think it fun!

CYRANO. What? The précieuse contained a heroine?

ROXANE. Monsieur de Bergerac, I am a cousin of yours!

ONE OF THE CADETS. Never think but that we will take good care
of you!

ROXANE (*more and more excited*). I am sure you will, my friends!

OTHER CADET. The whole camp smells of iris!

ROXANE. By good fortune I put on a hat that will look well in battle! (*Glancing toward* DE GUICHE.) But perhaps it is time the Count should go.— The battle might begin.

DE GUICHE. Ah, it is intolerable! — I am going to inspect my guns, and coming back.— You still have time: think better of it!

ROXANE. Never! (*Exit* DE GUICHE.)

CHRISTIAN (*imploring*). Roxane!

ROXANE. No!

FIRST CADET. She is going to stay!

ALL (*hurrying about, pushing one another, snatching things from one another*). A comb! — Soap! — My jacket is torn, a needle! — A ribbon! — Lend me your pocket-mirror! — My cuffs! — Curling-irons! — A razor!

ROXANE (*to* CYRANO, *who is still pleading with her*). No! Nothing shall prevail upon me to stir from this spot!

CARBON (*after having, like the others, tightened his belt, dusted himself, brushed his hat, straightened his feather, pulled down his cuffs, approaches* ROXANE, *and ceremoniously*). It is, perhaps, proper, since you are going to stay, that I should present to you a few of the gentlemen about to have the honor of dying in your presence... (ROXANE *bows, and stands waiting, with her arm through* CHRISTIAN's.) Baron Peyrescous de Colignac!

THE CADET (*bowing*). Madame!

CARBON (*continuing to present the* CADETS). Baron de Casterac de Cahuzac — Vidame de Malgouyre Estressac Lesbas d'Escarabiot — Chevalier d'Antignac-Juzet — Baron Hillot de Blagnac-Saléchan de Castel Crabioules...

ROXANE. But how many names have you apiece?

BARON HILLOT. Innumerable!

CARBON (*to* ROXANE). Open your hand with the handkerchief!

ROXANE (*opens her hand; the handkerchief drops*). Why?

(*The whole company starts forward to pick it up.*)

CARBON (*instantly catching it*). My company had no flag! Now, my word, it will have the prettiest one in the army!

ROXANE (*smiling*). It is rather small!

CARBON (*fastening the handkerchief on the staff of his captain's spear*). But it is lace!

ONE OF THE CADETS (*to the others*). I could die without a murmur, having looked upon that beautiful face, if I had so much as a walnut inside me!...

CARBON (*who has overheard, indignant*). Shame!... to talk of food when an exquisite woman...

ROXANE. But the air of the camp is searching, and I myself am hungry: Patties, jellied meat, light wine... are what I should like best! Will you kindly bring me some?

(*Consternation.*)

ONE OF THE CADETS. Bring you some?

OTHER CADET. And where, great God, shall we get them?

ROXANE (*quietly*). In my coach.

ALL. What?

ROXANE. But there is much to be done, carving and boning and serving. Look more closely at my coachman, gentlemen, and you will recognize a precious individual: the sauces, if we wish, can be warmed over...

THE CADETS (*springing toward the coach*). It is Ragueneau! (*Cheers.*) Oh! Oh!

ROXANE (*watching them*). Poor fellows!

CYRANO (*kissing her hand*). Kind fairy!

RAGUENEAU (*standing upon the box-seat like a vender at a public fair*). Gentlemen! (*Enthusiasm.*)

THE CADETS. Bravo! Bravo!

RAGUENEAU. How should the Spaniards, when so much beauty passed, suspect the repast? (*Applause.*)

CYRANO (*low to* CHRISTIAN). Hm! Hm! Christian!

RAGUENEAU. Absorbed in gallantry, no heed took they... (*he takes a dish from the box-seat*)... of galantine!

(*Applause. The galantine is passed from hand to hand.*)

CYRANO (*low to* CHRISTIAN). A word with you....

RAGUENEAU. Venus kept their eyes fixed upon herself, while Diana slipped past with the... (*he brandishes a joint*) game!

(*Enthusiasm. The joint is seized by twenty hands at once.*)

CYRANO (*low to* CHRISTIAN). I must speak with you.

ROXANE (*to the* CADETS *who come forward, their arms full of provisions*). Spread it all upon the ground!

(*Assisted by the two imperturbable footmen who were on the back of the coach, she arranges everything on the grass.*)

ROXANE (*to* CHRISTIAN *whom* CYRANO *is trying to draw aside*). Make yourself useful, sir!

(CHRISTIAN *comes and helps her.* CYRANO *gives evidence of uneasiness.*)

RAGUENEAU. A truffled peacock!

FIRST CADET (*radiant, comes forward cutting a large slice of ham*). Praise the pigs, we shall not go to our last fight with nothing in our b... (*correcting himself at sight of* ROXANE) hm... stomachs!

RAGUENEAU (*flinging the carriage cushions*). The cushions are stuffed with snipe! (*Tumult. The cushions are ripped open. Laughter. Joy.*)

RAGUENEAU (*flinging bottles of red wine*). Molten ruby! (*Bottles of white wine.*) Fluid topaz!

ROXANE (*throwing a folded tablecloth to* CYRANO). Unfold the cloth: Hey!... be nimble!

RAGUENEAU (*waving one of the coach lanterns*). Each lantern is a little larder!

CYRANO (*low to* CHRISTIAN, *while together they spread the cloth*). I must speak with you before you speak with her...

RAGUENEAU. The handle of my whip, behold, is a sausage!

ROXANE (*pouring wine, dispensing it*). Since we are the ones to be killed, *morbleu*, we will not fret ourselves about the rest of the army! Everything for the Gascons!... And if De Guiche comes, nobody must invite him! (*Going from one to the other.*) Gently! You have time... You must not eat so fast! There, drink. What are you crying about?

FIRST CADET. It is too good!

ROXANE. Hush! White wine or red? — Bread for Monsieur de Carbon! — A knife! — Pass your plate! — You prefer crust? — A little more? — Let me help you.— Champagne? — A wing? —

CYRANO (*following* ROXANE, *his hands full of dishes, helping her*). I adore her!

ROXANE (*going to* CHRISTIAN). What will you take?

CHRISTIAN. Nothing!

ROXANE. Oh, but you must take something! This biscuit — in a little Muscatel — just a little?

CHRISTIAN (*trying to keep her from going*). Tell me what made you come?

ROXANE. I owe myself to those poor fellows... Be patient... By and by...

LE BRET (*who had gone toward the back to pass a loaf of bread on the end of a pike to the* SENTINEL *upon the earthwork*). De Guiche!

CYRANO. Presto! Vanish basket, flagon, platter and pan! Hurry! Let us look as if nothing were! (*To* RAGUENEAU.) Take a flying leap onto your box! — Is everything hidden?

(*In a wink, all the eatables have been pushed into the tents, or hidden under clothes, cloaks, hats.*)

(*Enter* DE GUICHE, *hurriedly; he stops short, sniffing the air. Silence.*)

DE GUICHE. What a good smell!

ONE OF THE CADETS (*singing, with effect of mental abstraction*). To lo lo lo....

DE GUICHE (*stopping and looking at him closely*). What is the matter with you — you, there? You are red as a crab.

THE CADET. I? Nothing... It is just my blood.... We are going to fight: it tells...

OTHER CADET. Poom... poom... poom...

DE GUICHE (*turning*). What is this?

THE CADET (*slightly intoxicated*). Nothing... A song... just a little song.

DE GUICHE. You look in good spirits, my boy!

THE CADET. Danger affects me that way!

DE GUICHE (*calling* CARBON DE CASTEL-JALOUX *to give an order*). Captain, I... (*He stops at sight of his face.*) Peste! You look in good spirits, too.

CARBON (*flushed, holding a bottle behind him; with an evasive gesture*). Oh!...

DE GUICHE. I had a cannon left over, which I have ordered them to place (*he points in the wing*) there, in that corner, and which your men can use, if necessary...

ONE OF THE CADETS (*swaying from one foot to the other*). Charming attention!

OTHER CADET (*smiling sugarily*). Our thanks for your gracious thoughtfulness!

DE GUICHE. Have they gone mad?... (*Drily.*) As you are not accustomed to handling a cannon, look out for its kicking...

FIRST CADET. Ah, pfft!...

DE GUICHE (*going toward him, furious*). But...

THE CADET. A cannon knows better than to kick a Gascon!

DE GUICHE (*seizing him by the arm and shaking him*). You are all tipsy: on what?

THE CADET (*magnificently*). The smell of powder!

DE GUICHE (*shrugs his shoulders, pushes aside the* CADET, *and goes rapidly toward* ROXANE). Quick, Madame! what have you condescended to decide?

ROXANE. I remain.

DE GUICHE. Retire, I beseech you

ROXANE. No.

DE GUICHE. If you are determined, then... Let me have a musket!

CARBON. What do you mean?

DE GUICHE. I, too, will remain.

CYRANO. At last, monsieur, an instance of pure and simple bravery!

FIRST CADET. Might you be a Gascon, lace collar notwithstanding?

DE GUICHE. I do not leave a woman in danger.

SECOND CADET (*to* FIRST CADET). Look here! I think he might be given something to eat! (*All the food reappears, as if by magic.*)

DE GUICHE (*his eyes brightening*). Provisions?

THIRD CADET. Under every waistcoat!

DE GUICHE (*mastering himself, haughtily*). Do you imagine that I will eat your leavings?

CYRANO (*bowing*). You are improving!

DE GUICHE (*proudly, falling at the last of the sentence into a slightly* GASCON *accent*). I will fight before I eat!

FIRST CADET (*exultant*). Fight! Eat!... He spoke with an accent!

DE GUICHE (*laughing*). I did?

THE CADET. He is one of us!          (*All fall to dancing.*)

CARBON (*who a moment before disappeared behind the earthworks, reappearing at the top*). I have placed my pikemen. They are a determined troop...

          (*He points at a line of pikes projecting above the bank.*)

DE GUICHE (*to* ROXANE, *bowing*). Will you accept my hand and pass them in review?

          (*She takes his hand; they go toward the bank. Everyone uncovers and follows.*)

CHRISTIAN (*going to* CYRANO, *quickly*). Speak! Be quick!

(*As* ROXANE *appears at the top of the bank, the pikes disappear, lowered in a salute, and a cheer goes up;* ROXANE *bows.*)

PIKEMEN (*outside*). Vivat!

CHRISTIAN. What did you want to tell me?

CYRANO. In case Roxane...

CHRISTIAN. Well?

CYRANO. Should speak to you of the letters...

CHRISTIAN. Yes, the letters. I know!

CYRANO. Do not commit the blunder of appearing surprised...

CHRISTIAN. At what?

CYRANO. I must tell you!... It is quite simple, and merely comes into my mind today because I see her. You have...

CHRISTIAN. Hurry!

CYRANO. You... you have written to her oftener than you suppose...

CHRISTIAN. Oh, have I?

CYRANO. Yes. It was my business, you see. I had undertaken to interpret your passion, and sometimes I wrote without having told you I should write.

CHRISTIAN. Ah?

CYRANO. It is very simple.

CHRISTIAN. But how did you succeed since we have been so closely surrounded, in... ?

CYRANO. Oh, before daybreak I could cross the lines...

CHRISTIAN (*folding his arms*). Ah, that is very simple, too?... And how many times a week have I been writing? Twice? Three times? Four?...

CYRANO. More.

CHRISTIAN. Every day?

CYRANO. Yes, every day... twice.

CHRISTIAN (*violently*). And you cared so much about it that you were willing to brave death....

CYRANO (*seeing* ROXANE *who returns*). Be still... Not before her!

(*He goes quickly into his tent.* CADETS *come and go at the back.* CARBON *and* DE GUICHE *give orders.*)

ROXANE (*running to* CHRISTIAN). And now, Christian...

CHRISTIAN (*taking her hands*). And now, you shall tell me why, over these fearful roads, through these ranks of rough soldiery, you risked your dear self to join me?

ROXANE. Because of the letters!

CHRISTIAN. The... ? What did you say?

ROXANE. It is through your fault that I have been exposed to such and so many dangers. It is your letters that have gone to my head! Ah, think how many you have written me in a month, each one more beautiful...

CHRISTIAN. What?... Because of a few little love letters...

ROXANE. Say nothing! You cannot understand! Listen: The truth is that I took to idolizing you one evening, when, below my window, in a voice I did not know before, your soul began to reveal itself.... Think then what the effect should be of your letters, which have been like your voice heard constantly for one month, your voice of that evening, so tender, caressing... You must bear it as you can, I have come to you! Prudent Penelope would not have stayed at home with her eternal tapestry, if Ulysses, her lord, had written as you write... but, impulsive as Helen, have tossed aside her yarns, and flown to join him!

CHRISTIAN. But...

ROXANE. I read them, I re-read them, in reading I grew faint... I became your own indeed! Each fluttering leaf was like a petal of your soul wafted to me... In every word of those letters, love is felt as a flame would be felt — love, compelling, sincere, profound...

CHRISTIAN. Ah, sincere, profound?... You say that it can be felt, Roxane?

ROXANE. He asks me!

CHRISTIAN. And so you came?...

ROXANE. I came — oh Christian, my own, my master! If I were to kneel at your feet you would lift me, I know. It is my soul therefore which kneels, and never can you lift it from that posture! — I came to implore your pardon — as it is fitting, for we are both perhaps about to die! — your pardon for having done you the wrong, at first, in my shallowness, of loving you... for mere looking!

CHRISTIAN (in alarm). Ah, Roxane!...

ROXANE. Later, dear one, grown less shallow — similar to a bird which flutters before it can fly — your gallant exterior appealing to me still, but your soul appealing equally, I loved you for both!...

CHRISTIAN. And now?

ROXANE. Now at last yourself are vanquished by yourself: I love you for your soul alone...

CHRISTIAN (*drawing away*). Ah, Roxane!

ROXANE. Rejoice! For to be loved for that wherewith we are clothed so fleetingly must put a noble heart to torture.... Your dear thought at last casts your dear face in shadow: the harmonious lineaments whereby at first you pleased me, I do not see them, now my eyes are open!

CHRISTIAN. Oh!

ROXANE. You question your own triumph?

CHRISTIAN (*sorrowfully*). Roxane!

ROXANE. I understand, you cannot conceive of such a love in me?

CHRISTIAN. I do not wish to be loved like that! I wish to be loved quite simply...

ROXANE. For that which other women till now have loved in you? Ah, let yourself be loved in a better way.

CHRISTIAN. No... I was happier before!...

ROXANE. Ah, you do not understand! It is now that I love you most, that I truly love you. It is that which makes you, you — can you not grasp it? — that I worship... And did you no longer walk our earth like a young martial Apollo...

CHRISTIAN. Say no more!

ROXANE. Still would I love you!... Yes, though a blight should have fallen upon your face and form...

CHRISTIAN. Do not say it!

ROXANE. But I do say it... I do!

CHRISTIAN. What? If I were ugly, distinctly, offensively?

ROXANE. If you were ugly, dear, I swear it!

CHRISTIAN. God!

ROXANE. And you are glad, profoundly glad?

CHRISTIAN (*in a smothered voice*). Yes...

ROXANE. What is it?

CHRISTIAN (*pushing her gently away*). Nothing. I have a word or two to say to someone: your leave, for a second...

ROXANE. But...

CHRISTIAN (*pointing at a group of* CADETS *at the back*). In my selfish love, I have kept you from those poor brothers.... Go, smile on them a little, before they die, dear... go!

ROXANE (*moved*). Dear Christian!

(*She goes toward the* GASCONS *at the back; they respectfully gather around her.*)

CHRISTIAN (*calling toward* CYRANO'S *tent*). Cyrano!

CYRANO (*appears, armed for battle*). What is it?... How pale you are!

CHRISTIAN. She does not love me any more!

CYRANO. What do you mean?

CHRISTIAN. She loves you.

CYRANO. No!

CHRISTIAN. She only loves my soul!

CYRANO. No!

CHRISTIAN. Yes! Therefore it is you she loves... and you love her...

CYRANO. I...!

CHRISTIAN. I know it!

CYRANO. It is true.

CHRISTIAN. To madness!

CYRANO. More.

CHRISTIAN. Tell her then.

CYRANO. No!

CHRISTIAN. Why not?

CYRANO. Look at me!

CHRISTIAN. She would love me grown ugly.

CYRANO. She told you so?

CHRISTIAN. With the utmost frankness!

CYRANO. Ah! I am glad she should have told you that! But, believe me, believe me, place no faith in such a mad asseveration! Dear God, I am glad such a thought should have come to her, and that she should have spoken it — but believe me, do not take her at her word: Never cease to be the handsome fellow you are.... She would not forgive me!

CHRISTIAN. That is what I wish to discover.

CYRANO. No! no!

CHRISTIAN. Let her choose between us! You shall tell her everything.

CYRANO. No... No... I refuse the ordeal!

CHRISTIAN. Shall I stand in the way of your happiness because my outside is not so much amiss?

CYRANO. And I? shall I destroy yours, because, thanks to the hazard that sets us upon earth, I have the gift of expressing ... what you perhaps feel?

CHRISTIAN. You shall tell her everything!

CYRANO. He persists in tempting me...It is a mistake...and cruel!

CHRISTIAN. I am weary of carrying about, in my own self, a rival!

CYRANO. Christian!

CHRISTIAN. Our marriage... contracted without witnesses... can be annulled... if we survive!

CYRANO. He persists!...

CHRISTIAN. Yes. I will be loved for my sole self, or not at all! — I am going to see what they are about. Look! I will walk to the end of the line and back... Tell her, and let her pronounce between us.

CYRANO. She will pronounce for you.

CHRISTIAN. I can but hope she will! (*Calling.*) Roxane!

CYRANO. No! No!

ROXANE (*coming forward*). What is it?

CHRISTIAN. Cyrano has something to tell you... something important! (ROXANE *goes hurriedly to* CYRANO. *Exit* CHRISTIAN.)

ROXANE. Something important?

CYRANO (*distractedly*). He is gone!... (*To* ROXANE.) Nothing whatever! He attaches — but you must know him of old! — he attaches importance to trifles...

ROXANE (*quickly*). He did not believe what I told him a moment ago?... I saw that he did not believe...

CYRANO (*taking her hand*). But did you in very truth tell him the truth?

ROXANE. Yes. Yes. I should love him even...

(*She hesitates a second.*)

CYRANO (*smiling sadly*). You do not like to say it before me?

ROXANE. But...

CYRANO. I shall not mind!... Even if he were ugly?

ROXANE. Yes... Ugly. (*Musket shots outside.*) They are firing!

CYRANO (*ardently*). Dreadfully ugly?

ROXANE. Dreadfully.

CYRANO. Disfigured?

ROXANE. Disfigured!

CYRANO. Grotesque?

ROXANE. Nothing could make him grotesque... to me.

CYRANO. You would love him still?

ROXANE. I believe that I should love him more... if that were possible!

CYRANO (*losing his head, aside*). My God, perhaps she means it... perhaps it is true... and that way is happiness! (*To* ROXANE.) I... Roxane... listen!

LE BRET (*comes in hurriedly; calls softly*). Cyrano!

CYRANO (*turning*). Hein?

LE BRET. Hush! (*He whispers a few words to* CYRANO.)

CYRANO (*letting* ROXANE's *hand drop, with a cry*). Ah!...

ROXANE. What ails you?

CYRANO (*to himself, in consternation*). It is finished! (*Musket reports.*)

ROXANE. What is it? What is happening? Who is firing?

(*She goes to the back to look off.*)

CYRANO. It is finished.... My lips are sealed forevermore!

(CADETS *come in, attempting to conceal something they carry among them; they surround it, preventing* ROXANE's *seeing it.*)

ROXANE. What has happened?

CYRANO (*quickly stopping her as she starts towards them*). Nothing!

ROXANE. These men?...

CYRANO (*drawing her away*). Pay no attention to them!

ROXANE. But what were you about to say to me before?

CYRANO. What was I about to say?... Oh, nothing!... Nothing whatever, I assure you. (*Solemnly.*) I swear that Christian's spirit, that his soul, were... (*in terror, correcting himself*) are the greatest that...

ROXANE. Were?... (*With a great cry.*) Ah!...

(*Runs to the group of* CADETS, *and thrusts them aside.*)

CYRANO. It is finished!

ROXANE (*seeing* CHRISTIAN *stretched out in his cloak*). Christian!

LE BRET (*to* CYRANO). At the enemy's first shot!

> (ROXANE *throws herself on* CHRISTIAN's *body.  Musket reports.
> Clashing of swords.  Tramping.  Drums.*)

CARBON (*sword in hand*). The attack!  To your muskets!

> (*Followed by the* CADETS *he goes to the further side of the earth-
> works.*)

ROXANE. Christian!

CARBON'S VOICE (*beyond the earthworks*). Make haste!

ROXANE. Christian!

CARBON. Fall into line!

ROXANE. Christian!

CARBON. Measure... match!

> (RAGUENEAU *has come running in with water in a steel cap.*)

CHRISTIAN (*in a dying voice*). Roxane!

CYRANO (*quick, low in* CHRISTIAN's *ear, while* ROXANE, *distracted,
dips into the water a fragment of linen torn from her breast to bind
his wound*).  I have told her everything!... You are still the one
she loves!  (CHRISTIAN *closes his eyes.*)

ROXANE. What, dear love?

CARBON. Muzzle... high!

ROXANE (*to* CYRANO). He is not dead?...

CARBON. Open charge... with teeth!

ROXANE. I feel his cheek grow cold against my own!

CARBON. Take aim!

ROXANE. A letter on his breast.... (*She opens it.*)  To me!

CYRANO (*aside*). My letter!

CARBON. Fire!  (*Musket shots.  Cries.  Roar of battle.*)

CYRANO (*trying to free his hand which* ROXANE *clasps kneeling*).  But,
Roxane, they are fighting.

ROXANE (*clinging*). No!... Stay with me a little!... He is dead.
You are the only one that truly knew him.... (*She cries subduedly.*)
Was he not an exquisite being... an exceptional, marvellous
being?...

CYRANO (*standing bareheaded*). Yes, Roxane.

ROXANE. A poet without his peer,... one verily to reverence?

CYRANO. Yes, Roxane.

ROXANE. A sublime spirit?

CYRANO. Yes, Roxane.

ROXANE. A profound heart, such as the profane could never have understood... a soul as noble as it was charming?...

CYRANO (*firmly*). Yes, Roxane.

ROXANE (*throwing herself on* CHRISTIAN's *body*). And he is dead!

CYRANO (*aside, drawing his sword*). And I have now only to die, since, without knowing it, she mourns my death in his!

(*Trumpets in the distance.*)

DE GUICHE (*reappears on the top of the bank, bareheaded, his forehead bloody; in a thundering voice*). The signal they promised! The flourish of trumpets!... The French are entering the camp with supplies!... Stand fast a little longer!

ROXANE. Upon his letter... blood,... tears!

A VOICE (*outside, shouting*). Surrender!

VOICES OF THE CADETS. No!

RAGUENEAU (*who from the top of the coach is watching the battle beyond the bank*). The conflict rages hotter!...

CYRANO (*to* DE GUICHE *pointing at* ROXANE). Take her away!... I am going to charge.

ROXANE (*kissing the letter, in a dying voice*). His blood!... his tears!

RAGUENEAU (*leaping from the coach and running to* ROXANE). She is fainting!

DE GUICHE (*at the top of the bank, to the* CADETS, *madly*). Stand fast!

VOICE (*outside*). Surrender!

VOICES OF THE CADETS. No!

CYRANO (*to* DE GUICHE). Your courage none will question... (*Pointing at* ROXANE.) Fly for the sake of saving her!

DE GUICHE (*runs to* ROXANE *and lifts her in his arms*). So be it! But we shall win the day if you can hold out a little longer...

CYRANO. We can. (*To* ROXANE, *whom* DE GUICHE, *helped by* RAGUENEAU, *is carrying off insensible.*) Good-bye, Roxane!

(*Tumult. Cries.* CADETS *reappear, wounded, and fall upon the stage.* CYRANO *dashing forward to join the combatants is stopped on the crest of the bank by* CARBON *covered with blood.*)

CARBON. We are losing ground... I have got two halberd wounds...

CYRANO (*yelling to the* GASCONS). Steadfast!... Never give them an

inch!... Brave boys! (*To* CARBON.) Fear nothing! I have
various deaths to avenge: Christian's and all my hopes'! (*They
come down.* CYRANO *brandishes the spear at the head of which*
ROXANE'S *handkerchief is fastened.*) Float free, little cobweb
flag, embroidered with her initials! (*He drives the spear-staff
into the earth; shouts to the* CADETS.) Fall on them, boys!...
Crush them! (*To the fifer.*) Fifer, play!

> (*The fifer plays. Some of the wounded get to their feet again.
> Some of the* CADETS, *coming down the bank, group themselves
> around* CYRANO *and the little flag. The coach, filled and
> covered with men, bristles with muskets and becomes a redoubt.*)

ONE OF THE CADETS (*appears upon the top of the bank backing while
he fights; he cries*). They are coming up the slope! (*Falls dead.*)
CYRANO. We will welcome them!

(*Above the bank suddenly rises a formidable array of enemies. The great
banners of the Imperial Army appear.*)

CYRANO. Fire! (*General discharge.*)
CRY (*among the hostile ranks*). Fire!
(*Shots returned.* CADETS *drop on every side.*)
A SPANISH OFFICER (*taking off his hat*). What are these men, so
determined all to be killed?
CYRANO (*declaiming, as he stands in the midst of flying bullets*).

> They are the Gascony Cadets
> Of Carbon de Castel-Jaloux;
> Famed fighters, liars, desperates...
> (*He leaps forward, followed by a handful of survivors.*)
> They are the Gascony Cadets!...
> (*The rest is lost in the confusion of battle.*)

**CURTAIN**

# ACT FIFTH

## CYRANO'S GAZETTE

*Fifteen years later*, 1655. *The park belonging to the convent of the Sisters of the Cross, in Paris.*

*Superb shade-trees. At the left, the house; several doors opening on to broad terrace with steps. In the center of the stage, huge trees standing alone in a clear oval space. At the right, first wing, a semicircular stone seat, surrounded by large box-trees.*

*All along the back of the stage, an avenue of chestnut-trees, which leads, at the right, fourth wing, to the door of a chapel seen through trees. Through the double row of trees overarching the avenue are seen lawns, other avenues, clumps of trees, the further recesses of the park, the sky.*

*The chapel opens by a small side-door into a colonnade, overrun by a scarlet creeper; the colonnade comes forward and is lost to sight behind the box-tree at the right.*

*It is Autumn. The leaves are turning, above the still fresh grass. Dark patches of evergreens, box and yew. Under each tree a mat of yellow leaves. Fallen leaves litter the whole stage, crackle underfoot, lie thick on the terrace and the seats.*

*Between the seat at the right and the tree in the center, a large embroidery frame, in front of which a small chair. Baskets full of wools, in skeins and balls. On the frame, a piece of tapestry, partly done.*

*At the rise of the curtain, nuns come and go in the park; a few are seated on the stone seat around an older nun; leaves are falling.*

SISTER MARTHA (*to* MOTHER MARGARET). Sister Claire, after putting on her cap went back to the mirror, to see herself again.

MOTHER MARGARET (*to* SISTER CLAIRE). It was unbecoming, my child.

SISTER CLAIRE. But Sister Martha, today, after finishing her portion, went back to the tart for a plum. I saw her!

MOTHER MARGARET (*to* SISTER MARTHA). My child, it was ill done.

SISTER CLAIRE. I merely glanced!...

SISTER MARTHA. The plum was about so big!...

MOTHER MARGARET. This evening, when Monsieur Cyrano comes, I will tell him.

SISTER CLAIRE (*alarmed*). No! He will laugh at us!

SISTER MARTHA. He will say that nuns are very vain!

SISTER CLAIRE. And very greedy!

MOTHER MARGARET. And really very good.

SISTER CLAIRE. Mother Margaret, is it not true that he has come here every Saturday in the last ten years?

MOTHER MARGARET. Longer! Ever since his cousin brought among our linen coifs her coif of crape, the worldly symbol of her mourning, which settled like a sable bird amidst our flock of white some fourteen years ago.

SISTER MARTHA. He alone, since she took her abode in our cloister, has art to dispel her never-lessening sorrow.

ALL THE NUNS. He is so droll! — It is merry when he comes! — He teases us! — He is delightful! — We are greatly attached to him! — We are making Angelica paste to offer him!

SISTER MARTHA. He is not, however, a very good Catholic!

SISTER CLAIRE. We will convert him.

THE NUNS. We will! We will!

MOTHER MARGARET. I forbid your renewing that attempt, my children. Do not trouble him: he might not come so often!

SISTER MARTHA. But... God!

MOTHER MARGARET. Set your hearts at rest: God must know him of old!

SISTER MARTHA. But every Saturday, when he comes, he says to me as soon as he sees me, "Sister, I ate meat, yesterday!"

MOTHER MARGARET. Ah, that is what he says?... Well, when he last said it, he had eaten nothing for two days.

SISTER MARTHA. Mother!

MOTHER MARGARET. He is poor.

SISTER MARTHA. Who told you?

MOTHER MARGARET. Monsieur Le Bret.

SISTER MARTHA. Does no one offer him assistance?

MOTHER MARGARET. No, he would take offence.

(*In one of the avenues at the back, appears* ROXANE, *in black, wearing a widow's coif and long mourning veil;* DE GUICHE, *markedly older, magnificently dressed, walks beside her. They go very slowly.* MOTHER MARGARET *gets up.*)

MOTHER MARGARET. Come, we must go within. Madame Magdeleine is walking in the park with a visitor.

SISTER MARTHA (*low to* SISTER CLAIRE). Is not that the Marshal-
duke de Grammont?

SISTER CLAIRE (*looking*). I think it is!

SISTER MARTHA. He has not been to see her in many months!

THE NUNS. He is much engaged! — The Court! — The Camp! ——

SISTER CLAIRE. Cares of this world!

(*Exeunt.* DE GUICHE *and* ROXANE *come forward silently,
and stop near the embroidery frame. A pause.*)

DE GUICHE. And so you live here, uselessly fair, always in mourning?

ROXANE. Always.

DE GUICHE. As faithful as of old?

ROXANE. As faithful.

DE GUICHE (*after a time*). Have you forgiven me?

ROXANE. Since I am here.          (*Other silence.*)

DE GUICHE. And he was really such a rare being?

ROXANE. To understand, one must have known him!

DE GUICHE. Ah, one must have known him!... Perhaps I did not
know him well enough. And his last letter, still and always,
against your heart?

ROXANE. I wear it on this velvet, as a more holy scapular.

DE GUICHE. Even dead, you love him?

ROXANE. It seems to me sometimes he is but half dead, that our
hearts have not been severed, that his love still wraps me
round, no less than ever living!

DE GUICHE (*after another silence*). Does Cyrano come here to see you?

ROXANE. Yes, often. That faithful friend fulfils by me the office
of gazette. His visits are regular. He comes: when the
weather is fine, his armchair is brought out under the trees.
I wait for him here with my work; the hour strikes; on the last
stroke, I hear — I do not even turn to see who comes! — his
cane upon the steps; he takes his seat; he rallies me upon my
never-ending tapestry; he tells off the events of the week, and...
(LE BRET *appears on the steps.*) Ah, Le Bret! (LE BRET *comes down
the steps.*) How does your friend?

LE BRET. Ill.

THE DUKE. Oh!

ROXANE. He exaggerates!...

LE BRET. All is come to pass as I foretold: neglect! poverty! his·

writings ever breeding him new enemies! Fraud he attacks in every embodiment: usurpers, pious pretenders, plagiarists, asses in lions' skins... all! He attacks all!

ROXANE. No one, however, but stands in profound respect of his sword. They will never succeed in silencing him.

DE GUICHE (*shaking his head*). Who knows?

LE BRET. What I fear is not the aggression of man; what I fear is loneliness and want and winter creeping upon him like stealthy wolves in his miserable attic; they are the insidious foes that will have him by the throat at last!... Every day he tightens his belt by an eyelet; his poor great nose is pinched, and turned the sallow of old ivory; the worn black serge you see him in is the only coat he has!

DE GUICHE. Ah, there is one who did not succeed!... Nevertheless, do not pity him too much.

LE BRET (*with a bitter smile*). Marshal!...

DE GUICHE. Do not pity him too much: he signed no bonds with the world; he has lived free in his thought as in his actions.

LE BRET (*as above*). Duke...

DE GUICHE (*haughtily*). I know, yes: I have everything, he has nothing.... But I should like to shake hands with him. (*Bowing to* ROXANE.) Good-bye.

ROXANE. I will go with you to the door.

(DE GUICHE *bows to* LE BRET *and goes with* ROXANE *toward the terrace steps.*)

DE GUICHE (*stopping, while she goes up the steps*). Yes, sometimes I envy him. You see, when a man has succeeded too well in life, he is not unlikely to feel — dear me! without having committed any very serious wrong! — a multitudinous disgust of himself, the sum of which does not constitute a real remorse, but an obscure uneasiness; and a ducal mantle, while it sweeps up the stairs of greatness, may trail in its furry lining a rustling of sere illusions and regrets, as, when you slowly climb toward those doors, your black gown trails the withered leaves.

ROXANE (*ironical*). Are you not unusually pensive?...

DE GUICHE. Ah, yes! (*As he is about to leave, abruptly.*) Monsieur Le Bret! (*To* ROXANE.) Will you allow me? A word. (*He goes to* LE BRET, *and lowering his voice.*) It is true that no one will dare overtly to attack your friend, but many have him in particular disrelish; and someone was saying to me yesterday, at the Queen's, "It seems not unlikely that this Cyrano will meet with an accident."

LE BRET. Ah?...

DE GUICHE. Yes. Let him keep indoors. Let him be cautious.

LE BRET (*lifting his arms toward Heaven*). Cautious!... He is coming here. I will warn him. Warn him!... Yes, but...

ROXANE (*who has been standing at the head of the steps, to a nun who comes toward her*). What is it?

THE NUN. Ragueneau begs to see you, Madame.

ROXANE. Let him come in. (*To* DE GUICHE *and* LE BRET.) He comes to plead distress. Having determined one day to be an author, he became in turn precentor...

LE BRET. Bath-house keeper...

ROXANE. Actor...

LE BRET. Beadle...

ROXANE. Barber...

LE BRET. Arch-lute teacher...

ROXANE. I wonder what he is now!

RAGUENEAU (*entering precipitately*). Ah, madame! (*He sees* LE BRET.) Monsieur!

ROXANE (*smiling*). Begin telling your misfortunes to Le Bret. I am coming back.

RAGUENEAU. But, madame...

(ROXANE *leaves without listening, with the* DUKE. RAGUENEAU *goes to* LE BRET.)

RAGUENEAU. It is better so. Since you are here, I had liefer not tell her! Less than half an hour ago, I was going to see your friend. I was not thirty feet from his door, when I saw him come out. I hurried to catch up with him. He was about to turn the corner. I started to run, when from a window below which he was passing — was it pure mischance? It may have been! — a lackey drops a block of wood...

LE BRET. Ah, the cowards!... Cyrano!

RAGUENEAU. I reach the spot, and find him...

LE BRET. Horrible!

RAGUENEAU. Our friend, monsieur, our poet, stretched upon the ground, with a great hole in his head!

LE BRET. He is dead?

RAGUENEAU. No, but... God have mercy! I carried him to his lodging... Ah, his lodging! You should see that lodging of his!

LE BRET. Is he in pain?

RAGUENEAU. No, monsieur, he is unconscious.

LE BRET. Has a doctor seen him?

RAGUENEAU. One came... out of good nature.

LE BRET. My poor, poor Cyrano!... We must not tell Roxane outright. And the doctor?...

RAGUENEAU. He talked... I hardly grasped... of fever... cerebral inflammation! Ah, if you should see him, with his head done up in cloths!... Let us hurry... No one is there to tend him... And he might die if he attempted to get up!

LE BRET (dragging RAGUENEAU off at the right). This way. Come, it is shorter through the chapel.

ROXANE (appearing at the head of the steps, catching sight of LE BRET hurrying off through the colonnade which leads to the chapel side-door). Monsieur Le Bret! (LE BRET and RAGUENEAU make their escape without answering.) Le Bret not turning back when he is called? ... Poor Ragueneau must be in some new trouble! (She comes down the steps.) How beautiful... how beautiful, this golden-hazy waning day of September at its wane! My sorrowful mood, which the exuberant gladness of April offends, Autumn, the dreamy and subdued, lures on to smile... (She sits down at her embroidery frame. Two NUNS come from the house bringing a large armchair which they place under the tree.) Ah, here comes the classic armchair in which my old friend always sits!

SISTER MARTHA. The best in the convent parlor!

ROXANE. I thank you, sister. (The nuns withdraw.) He will be here in a moment. (She adjusts the embroidery frame before her.) There! The clock is striking... My wools!... The clock has struck?... I wonder at this!... Is it possible that for the first time he is late?... It must be that the sister who keeps the door... my thimble? ah, here it is!... is detaining him to exhort him to repentance... (A pause.) She exhorts him at some length!... He cannot be much longer... A withered leaf! (She brushes *away the dead leaf which has dropped on the embroidery.*)  Surely nothing could keep... My scissors?... in my workbag!... could keep him from coming!

A NUN (*appearing at the head of the steps*). Monsieur de Bergerac!

ROXANE (*without turning round*). What was I saying?... (*She begins to embroider.  CYRANO appears, exceedingly pale, his hat drawn down over his eyes.  The NUN who has shown him into the garden, withdraws.  He comes down the steps very slowly, with evident difficulty to keep on his feet, leaning heavily on his cane.  ROXANE proceeds with her sewing.*)  Ah, these dull soft shades!... How shall I match them?  (*To CYRANO, in a tone of friendly chiding.*)  After fourteen years, for the first time you are late!

CYRANO (*who has reached the armchair and seated himself, in a jolly voice which contrasts with his face*).  Yes, it seems incredible!  I am savage at it.  I was detained, spite of all I could do!...

ROXANE.  By?...

CYRANO.  A somewhat inopportune call.

ROXANE (*absent-minded, sewing*).  Ah, yes... some troublesome fellow!

CYRANO.  Cousin, it was a troublesome Madam.

ROXANE.  You excused yourself?

CYRANO.  Yes.  I said, "Your pardon, but this is Saturday, on which day I am due in a certain dwelling.  On no account do I ever fail.  Come back in an hour!"

ROXANE (*lightly*).  Well, she will have to wait some time to see you. I shall not let you go before evening.

CYRANO.  Perhaps... I shall have to go a little earlier.

(*He closes his eyes and is silent a moment.  SISTER MARTHA is seen crossing the park from the chapel to the terrace.  ROXANE sees her and beckons to her by a slight motion of her head.*)

ROXANE (*to CYRANO*).  Are you not going to tease Sister Martha today?

CYRANO (*quickly, opening his eyes*).  I am indeed!  (*In a comically gruff voice.*)  Sister Martha, come nearer!  (*The NUN demurely comes toward him.*)  Ha! ha! ha!  Beautiful eyes, ever studying the ground!

SISTER MARTHA (*lifting her eyes and smiling*).  But... (*She sees his face and makes a gesture of surprise.*)  Oh!

CYRANO (*low, pointing at* ROXANE). Hush!... It is nothing! (*In a swaggering voice, aloud.*) Yesterday, I ate meat!

SISTER MARTHA. I am sure you did! (*Aside.*) That is why he is so pale! (*Quickly, low.*) Come to the refectory presently. I shall have ready for you there a good bowl of broth... You will come!

CYRANO. Yes, yes, yes.

SISTER MARTHA. Ah, you are more reasonable today?

ROXANE (*hearing them whisper*). She is trying to convert you?

SISTER MARTHA. Indeed I am not!

CYRANO. It is true, you, usually almost discursive in the holy cause, are reading me no sermon! You amaze me! (*With comical fury.*) I will amaze you, too! Listen, you are authorized... (*With the air of casting about in his mind, and finding the jest he wants.*) Ah, now I shall amaze you! to... pray for me, this evening... in the chapel.

ROXANE. Oh! oh!

CYRANO (*laughing*). Sister Martha... lost in amazement!

SISTER MARTHA (*gently*). I did not wait for your authorization.

(*She goes in.*)

CYRANO (*turning to* ROXANE, *who is bending over her embroidery*). The devil, tapestry... the devil, if I hope to live to see the end of you!

ROXANE. I was waiting for that jest.

(*A slight gust of wind makes the leaves fall.*)

CYRANO. The leaves!

ROXANE (*looking up from her work and gazing off toward the avenues*). They are the russet gold of a Venetian beauty's hair... Watch them fall!

CYRANO. How consummately they do it! In that brief fluttering from bough to ground, how they contrive still to put beauty! And though foredoomed to moulder upon the earth that draws them, they wish their fall invested with the grace of a free bird's flight!

ROXANE. Serious, you?

CYRANO (*remembering himself*). Not at all, Roxane!

ROXANE. Come, never mind the falling leaves! Tell me the news, instead... Where is my budget?

CYRANO. Here it is!

ROXANE. Ah!

CYRANO (*growing paler and paler, and struggling with pain*). Saturday, the nineteenth: The king having filled his dish eight times with Cette preserves, and emptied it, was taken with a fever; his distemper, for high treason, was condemned to be let blood, and now the royal pulse is rid of febriculosity! On Sunday: at the Queen's great ball, were burned seven hundred and sixty-three wax candles; our troops, it is said, defeated Austrian John; four sorcerers were hanged; Madame Athis's little dog had a distressing turn, the case called for a...

ROXANE. Monsieur de Bergerac, leave out the little dog!

CYRANO. Monday,... nothing, or next to it: Lygdamire took a fresh lover.

ROXANE. Oh!

CYRANO (*over whose face is coming a change more and more marked*). Tuesday: the whole Court assembled at Fontainebleau. Wednesday, the fair Monglat said to Count Fiesco "No!" Thursday, Mancini, Queen of France,... or little less. Twenty-fifth, the fair Monglat said to Count Fiesco "Yes!" And Saturday, the twenty-sixth...

(*He closes his eyes. His head drops on his breast. Silence.*)

ROXANE (*surprised at hearing nothing further, turns, looks at him and starts to her feet in alarm*). Has he fainted? (*She runs to him, calling.*) Cyrano!

CYRANO (*opening his eyes, in a faint voice*). What is it?... What is the matter! (*He sees ROXANE bending over him, hurriedly readjusts his hat, pulling it more closely over his head, and shrinks back in his armchair in terror.*) No! no! I assure you, it is nothing!... Do not mind me!

ROXANE. But surely...

CYRANO. It is merely the wound I received at Arras... Sometimes ... you know... even now...

ROXANE. Poor friend!

CYRANO. But it is nothing... It will pass... (*He smiles with effort.*) It has passed.

ROXANE. Each one of us has his wound: I too have mine. It is here, never to heal, that ancient wound... (*She places her hand on her breast.*)   It is here, beneath the yellowing letter on which are still faintly visible tear-drops and drops of blood!

(*The light is beginning to grow less.*)

CYRANO.   His letter?... Did you not once say that some day... you might show it to me?

ROXANE.   Ah!... Do you wish?... His letter?

CYRANO.   Yes... today... I wish to...

ROXANE (*handing him the little bag from her neck*).   Here!

CYRANO.   I may open it?

ROXANE.   Open it... read!

(*She goes back to her embroidery frame, folds it up, orders her wools.*)

CYRANO.   "Good-bye, Roxane!  I am going to die!"

ROXANE (*stopping in astonishment*).   You are reading it aloud?

CYRANO (*reading*).   "It is fated to come this evening, beloved, I believe!  My soul is heavy, oppressed with love it had not time to utter... and now Time is at end!  Never again, never again shall my worshipping eyes..."

ROXANE.   How strangely you read his letter!

CYRANO (*continuing*).   "... whose passionate revel it was, kiss in its fleeting grace your every gesture.  One, usual to you, of tucking back a little curl, comes to my mind... and I cannot refrain from crying out..."

ROXANE.   How strangely you read his letter!...

(*The darkness gradually increases.*)

CYRANO.   "and I cry out: Good-bye!"

ROXANE.   You read it...

CYRANO.   "my dearest, my darling,... my treasure..."

ROXANE.   ... in a voice...

CYRANO.   "... my love!..."

ROXANE.   ... in a voice... a voice which I am not hearing for the first time!

(ROXANE *comes quietly nearer to him, without his seeing it; she steps behind his armchair, bends noiselessly over his shoulder, looks at the letter.  The darkness deepens.*)

CYRANO.   "... My heart never desisted for a second from your side... and I am and shall be in the world that has no end, the one who loved you without measure, the one..."

ROXANE (*laying her hand on his shoulder*).   How can you go on reading? It is dark. (CYRANO *starts, and turns round; sees her close to him, makes a gesture of dismay and hangs his head. Then, in the darkness which has completely closed round them, she says slowly, clasping her hands.*) And he, for fourteen years, has played the part of the comical old friend who came to cheer me!

CYRANO. Roxane!

ROXANE. So it was you.

CYRANO. No, no, Roxane!

ROXANE. I ought to have divined it, if only by the way in which he speaks my name!

CYRANO. No, it was not I!

ROXANE. So it was you!

CYRANO. I swear to you...

ROXANE. Ah, I detect at last the whole generous imposture: The letters... were yours!

CYRANO. No!

ROXANE. The tender fancy, the dear folly... yours!

CYRANO. No!

ROXANE. The voice in the night, was yours!

CYRANO. I swear to you that it was not!

ROXANE. The soul... was yours!

CYRANO. I did not love you, no!

ROXANE. And you loved me!

CYRANO. Not I... it was the other!

ROXANE. You loved me!

CYRANO. No!

ROXANE. Already your denial comes more faintly!

CYRANO. No, no, my darling love, I did not love you!

ROXANE. Ah, how many things within the hour have died... how many have been born! Why, why have... been silent these long years, when on this letter, in which he had no part, the tears were yours?

CYRANO (*handing her the letter*). Because... the blood was his.

ROXANE. Then why let the sublime bond of this silence be loosed today?

CYRANO. Why?

(LE BRET *and* RAGUENEAU *enter running.*)

LE BRET. Madness! Monstrous madness!... Ah, I was sure of it! There he is!

CYRANO (*smiling and straightening himself*). *Tiens!* Where else?

LE BRET. Madame, he is likely to have got his death by getting out of bed!

ROXANE. Merciful God! A moment ago, then... that faintness ... that... ?

CYRANO. It is true. I had not finished telling you the news. And on Saturday, the twenty-sixth, an hour after sundown, Monsieur de Bergerac died of murder done upon him.

(*He takes off his hat; his head is seen wrapped in bandages.*)

ROXANE. What is he saying?... Cyrano?... Those bandages about his head?... Ah, what have they done to you?... Why?...

CYRANO. "Happy who falls, cut off by a hero, with an honest sword through his heart!" I am quoting from myself!... Fate will have his laugh at us!... Here am I killed, in a trap, from behind, by a lackey, with a log! Nothing could be completer! In my whole life I shall have not had anything I wanted... not even a decent death!

RAGUENEAU. Ah, monsieur!...

CYRANO. Ragueneau, do not sob like that! (*Holding out his hand to him.*) And what is the news with you, these latter days, fellow-poet?

RAGUENEAU (*through his tears*). I am candle-snuffer at Molière's theater.

CYRANO. Molière!

RAGUENEAU. But I intend to leave no later than tomorrow. Yes, I am indignant! Yesterday, they were giving Scapin, and I saw that he has appropriated a scene of yours.

LE BRET. A whole scene?

RAGUENEAU. Yes, monsieur. The one in which occurs the famous "What the devil was he doing in..."

LE BRET. Molière has taken that from you!

CYRANO. Hush! hush! He did well to take it! (*To* RAGUENEAU.) The scene was very effective, was it not?

RAGUENEAU. Ah, monsieur, the public laughed... laughed!

CYRANO. Yes, to the end, I shall have been the one who prompted

... and was forgotten! (*To* ROXANE.) Do you remember that evening on which Christian spoke to you from below the balcony? There was the epitome of my life: while I have stood below in darkness, others have climbed to gather the kiss and glory! It is well done, and on the brink of my grave I approve it: Molière has genius... Christian was a fine fellow! (*At this moment, the chapel bell having rung, the* NUNS *are seen passing at the back, along the avenue, on their way to service.*) Let them hasten to their prayers... the bell is summoning them...

ROXANE (*rising and calling*). Sister! Sister!

CYRANO (*holding her back*). No! No! do not leave me to fetch anybody! When you came back I might not be here to rejoice... (*The* NUNS *have gone into the chapel; the organ is heard.*) I longed for a little music... it comes in time!

ROXANE. I love you... you shall live!

CYRANO. No! for it is only in the fairy-tale that the shy and awkward prince when he hears the beloved say "I love you!" feels his ungainliness melt and drop from him in the sunshine of those words!... But you would always know full well, dear Heart, that there had taken place in your poor slave no beautifying change!

ROXANE. I have hurt you... I have wrecked your life, I!... I!

CYRANO. You?... The reverse! Woman's sweetness I had never known. My mother... thought me unflattering. I had no sister. Later, I shunned Love's crossroad in fear of mocking eyes. To you I owe having had, at least, among the gentle and fair, a friend. Thanks to you there has passed across my life the rustle of a woman's gown.

LE BRET (*calling his attention to the moonlight peering through the branches*). Your other friend, among the gentle and fair, is there... she comes to see you!

CYRANO (*smiling to the moon*). I see her!

ROXANE. I never loved but one... and twice I lose him!

CYRANO. Le Bret, I shall ascend into the opalescent moon, without need this time of a flying-machine!

ROXANE. What are you saying?

CYRANO. Yes, it is there, you may be sure, I shall be sent for my Paradise. More than one soul of those I have loved

must be apportioned there... There I shall find Socrates and
Galileo!

LE BRET (*in revolt*). No! No! It is too senseless, too cruel, too
unfair! So true a poet! So great a heart! To die... like this!
To die!...

CYRANO. As ever... Le Bret is grumbling!

LE BRET (*bursting into tears*). My friend! My friend!

CYRANO (*lifting himself, his eyes wild*). They are the Gascony Cadets!
... Man in the gross... Eh, yes!... the weakness of the weakest
point...

LE BRET. Learned... even in his delirium!...

CYRANO. Copernicus said...

ROXANE. Oh!

CYRANO. But what the devil was he doing... and what the devil
was he doing in that galley?

> Philosopher and physicist,
> Musician, rhymester, duellist,
> Explorer of the upper blue,
> Retorter apt with point and point,
> Lover as well — not for his peace!
> Here lies Hercule Savinien
> De Cyrano de Bergerac,
> Who was everything... but of account!

But your pardons, I must go... I wish to keep no one waiting...
See, a moonbeam, come to take me home! (*He has dropped in
his chair;* ROXANE's *weeping calls him back to reality; he looks at her
and gently stroking her mourning veil.*) I do not wish... indeed,
I do not wish... that you should sorrow less for Christian, the
comely and the kind! Only I wish that when the everlasting
cold shall have seized upon my fibres, this funereal veil should
have a twofold meaning, and the mourning you wear for him
be worn for me too... a little!

ROXANE. I promise...

CYRANO (*seized with a great shivering, starts to his feet*). Not there!
No! Not in an elbow-chair! (*All draw nearer to help him.*)
Let no one stay me! No one! (*He goes and stands against the tree.*)
Nothing but this tree! (*Silence.*) She comes, Mors, the in-

discriminate Madam!... Already I am booted with marble... gauntleted with lead! (*He stiffens himself.*) Ah, since she is on her way, I will await her standing... (*He draws his sword.*) Sword in hand!

LE BRET. Cyrano!

ROXANE (*swooning*). Cyrano! (*All start back, terrified.*)

CYRANO. I believe she is looking at me... that she dares to look at my nose, the bony baggage who has none! (*He raises his sword.*) What are you saying? That it is no use?... I know it! But one does not fight because there is hope of winning! No!... no!... it is much finer to fight when it is no use!... What are all those? You are a thousand strong?... Ah, I know you now ... all my ancient enemies!... Hypocrisy?... (*He beats with his sword, in the vacancy.*) Take this! and this! Ha! Ha! Compromises?... and Prejudices? and dastardly Expedients? (*He strikes.*) That I should come to terms, I?... Never! Never!... Ah, you are there too, you, bloated and pompous Silliness! I know full well that you will lay me low at last... No matter: whilst I have breath, I will fight you, I will fight you, I will fight you! (*He waves his sword in great sweeping circles, and stops, panting.*) Yes, you have wrested from me everything, laurel as well as rose... Work your wills!... Spite of your worst, something will still be left me to take whither I go... and tonight when I enter God's house, in saluting, broadly will I sweep the azure threshold with what despite of all I carry forth unblemished and unbent... (*he starts forward, with lifted sword*) and that is...

(*The sword falls from his hands, he staggers, drops in the arms of LE BRET and RAGUENEAU.*)

ROXANE (*bending over him and kissing his forehead*). That is?...

CYRANO (*opens his eyes again, recognizes her and says with a smile*). ... My plume!

**CURTAIN**

# THE RED ROBE
## LA ROBE ROUGE

### A PLAY IN FOUR ACTS
*Crowned by the French Academy*

### By EUGÈNE BRIEUX
#### OF THE FRENCH ACADEMY

*Translated by F. O. REED*

# EUGÈNE BRIEUX

BORN in Paris in 1859, the son of a carpenter, Brieux lacked the advantages of formal higher education. He turned early to journalism and as a young man was editor of the *Nouvelliste* at Rouen. He first wrote farces in collaboration with Gaston Salandri. It was Antoine at the Théâtre Libre who gave him his first recognition and turned his mind toward the forms of art with which his name is identified. Antoine produced *Ménages d'Artistes* in 1890 and *Blanchette* in 1892 with the latter achieving popular acclaim. The thesis play is old in France. Brieux gives the thesis play a new slant and a new emphasis. Among the writers of thesis dramas from Dumas fils to Hervieu the thesis drama was but an extension of the well-made play, seeking to save an artificial theatrical situation from banality by the addition of a modicum of social doctrine passionately declaimed. Brieux was a reformer and humanitarian radical expressing himself in the drama; he was not the purveyor of amusement turning his hand to the latest vogue of reform. His plays are social documents, as hard and out-spoken and as unmannered as memoranda. Few playwrights of our day have as highly developed the craft of characterization. Excellent as his characters are he seldom presents them for them-selves alone. They always stand as hard-bitten symbols of some issue greater than themselves. "My method," he writes to Barrett Clark, "consists in crying out against every abuse of power," and he insists that dramatists must have ideas in their plays taken from among the sufferings of their fellow beings. Naturally these principles greatly extend the scope of the subject matter of his plays; they also conduce to a certain shallowness in their treatment. Among the abuses against which Brieux has cried out are those incident to politics, philanthropy, science, marriage, venereal disease, the treatment of mothers, and the administration of justice. To the treatment of these themes Brieux brought a gift of concreteness and frankness that has been tonic to the theater. It is this gift of concreteness that in those rare occasions when he turns to comedy makes Brieux a playwright of first rank. In the tribute that he pays to the larger "human comedy" of Brieux it is now generally agreed that Shaw permitted himself the luxury of overstatement. The plays of Brieux are today little produced. He joined the French Academy in 1910 and died in 1932.

# THE RED ROBE

*The Red Robe* is often considered to be a naturalistic play. Due consideration of the principles of naturalism leads one to the conclusion that the element of didacticism is so strong in this play as to overcome any pretence it may make to present life naturalistically. Not alone are the actions and complications of the play manufactured for the part they may play in illustrating and emphasizing the author's thesis. The characters themselves are almost mathematical symbols fitly chosen to typify the various factors of the author's demonstration. The play is as much a vehicle of a message extending beyond its own structure as an allegory. The theme is not alone the failure of justice in a particular circle and particular action. It is the failure of society's institutions of justice. While setting himself such a difficult task Brieux limits himself strictly to the instruments of the most conscientious dramatist. He neither speaks for himself nor calls upon any character to speak for him; and this is more than can be said for Dumas, Augier and their successors, whose voices mingle more or less harmoniously with the voices of half their characters. Given the high and difficult extra-dramatic aim Brieux sets himself he achieves it with magnificent dramatic mastery and force. His characters are not symbols alone, they are men and women; his actions, theoretically covering the abstract case, are in practice possible and credible. The play wins the approval of the judgment through commanding sympathy and passionate self-identification. Notwithstanding its didactic motive *The Red Robe* is one of the great plays of modern times.

# PERSONS OF THE PLAY

MOUZON

VAGRET

ETCHEPARE

MONDOUBLEAU

LA BOUZULE

BUNERAT

ATTORNEY-GENERAL

PRESIDENT OF THE ASSIZES

DELORME

ARDEUIL

BRIDET

POLICE SERGEANT

CLERK

PLACAT

JANITOR OF THE COURT

YANETTA

ETCHEPARE'S MOTHER

MADAME VAGRET

MADAME BUNERAT

BERTHA

CATIALÉNA

*Time — the present, at Mauléon*

# ACT I

*A modest drawing-room in an old house at Mauléon.*

*As the curtain rises* MADAME VAGRET, *in evening dress, is arranging the position of the chairs in her drawing-room.*

(*Enter* BERTHA, *also in evening dress, holding a newspaper.*)

BERTHA. Here's the paper. I have had the *Record* taken to father. He is just back from court and is dressing.

MADAME VAGRET. Is the hearing over?

BERTHA. Not yet.

MADAME VAGRET (*taking the paper*). The paper is still full of it?

BERTHA. As usual.

MADAME VAGRET. It doesn't take long to find it.... Here it is in the headlines, in large letters: "THE IRISSARRY CRIME." They are after your father now! (*Reading.*) "M. Vagret, our prosecuting attorney..." (*Continuing to herself.*) And subheadings: "Murderer still at large." As if it were our fault!... "Justice asleep." Asleep, indeed! The idea of writing things like that when your father hasn't had a wink of sleep for two weeks! Hasn't he done his duty? Isn't Delorme, the examining magistrate, doing his? He has made himself sick over it, poor man!... Just day before yesterday he arrested another vagabond with scarcely a shred of evidence against him! Well, then! No, I tell you, these reporters are mad!

BERTHA. It seems there's going to be an article in the Basque paper too...

MADAME VAGRET. The *Eskual Herria!*

BERTHA. So the apothecary told me just now.

MADAME VAGRET. What do I care for a paper like that? The A.G. doesn't read it.

BERTHA. On the contrary, father was saying the other day that the Attorney-General has a translation sent him of all articles bearing on the magistracy.

MADAME VAGRET. Is that so? Then it's a pretty state of affairs! Well, we'll not talk of it any more.... How many of us will there be this evening? Have you the list?

BERTHA. Yes.... (*Getting it from the mantel and reading.*)    The
    Judge of the Assizes... the Judge of the Court...

MADAME VAGRET. All right, all right!... Nine in all, aren't there?

BERTHA. Yes, nine.

MADAME VAGRET. Nine!  To have nine people to dinner and not
    to know at what time they will come — that's the worst of
    these session-end dinners which we are obliged to give in honor
    of the Judge of the Assizes.... We dine after the hearing!...
    After the hearing!  Well!  Let us await the good pleasure of
    these gentlemen.... (*Sighing.*)   Well, my child?

BERTHA. Mamma?

MADAME VAGRET. Do you still want to marry a magistrate?

BERTHA (*decidedly*).   Oh, no!

MADAME VAGRET. To think that you had that idea two years ago!

BERTHA. I'm over it now!

MADAME VAGRET. Just look at us!  Consider your father.... Public
    Prosecutor — in a court of the third class, just because he is not
    a schemer, and has never known how to take advantage of
    politics.... Well — there's no use talking! he's an able man.
    Since he has been in office he has obtained three life-imprison-
    ments!  And in a district like this, where cases are hopelessly
    rare!  Isn't that doing pretty well?  Of course, he has just had
    two acquittals in this last session.  Granted!  But that was only
    bad luck.... And for defending Society as he does, what does
    he get?  Do you even know?

BERTHA. Oh, yes, I know.  You have told me often enough,
    mother.

MADAME VAGRET. And I'll tell you again.  Counting what is kept
    back for his pension, he gets in all, three hundred ninety-five
    francs and eighty-three centimes per month.... And we find
    ourselves obliged to give a dinner for nine to receive the coun-
    selor, Judge of the Assizes.... I hope everything is ready, at
    least.  Let us see.... Is my *Revue des Deux Mondes* there?...
    Yes.... Is my chair placed right?  (*Sitting down in it.*)   Yes....
    (*Bowing by way of rehearsal.*)  "Judge, be seated, I beg you..."
    I hope it will go off like that.... And to think that Dufour, who
    was a simple judge when we were at Castelnaudary, is today
    Judge of the second class at Douai after serving only at Brest!...

BERTHA. Really?

MADAME VAGRET (*getting a book from the mantel*). Look it up in the *Year Book.*

BERTHA. I'll take your word for it.

MADAME VAGRET. You well may! *The Year Book of the Magistracy,* I know that by heart!

BERTHA. But as father is going to receive his appointment as counselor almost any day...

MADAME VAGRET. It's been a long time coming — that counselor's appointment of his.

BERTHA. But it's all settled now. He is slated for the first vacancy — since the death of Lefèvre.

MADAME VAGRET. I hope to goodness you're right! If we miss it again this time, it's all up. We'll have to stay at Mauléon until we're pensioned. What a shame they can't lay hands on that accursed murderer! Such a beautiful crime!... This time we might hope for the death sentence — the very first!

BERTHA. Never mind, little mother, there is still a chance.

MADAME VAGRET. You take it lightly, I must say! You see that the papers are beginning to growl. They are attacking us for indolence. My child, I suppose you do *not* know that there is talk of sending to Paris for a member of the police! That would be disgrace itself! Everything promised so well.... You have no idea how excited your father was when they woke him up to tell him that an old man, eighty-seven years old, had just been murdered in his district! He had on his clothes in less than five minutes and he said to me, mastering his feelings, but vigorously pressing my hand: "I think I've got it this time, my appointment!" (*She sighs.*) And now here's everything going to smash through the fault of this good-for-nothing who refuses to be caught! (*She sighs again.*) What time is it?

BERTHA. It has just struck six.

MADAME VAGRET. Go make the menus... Don't forget that only the titles are put on: "Judge of the Assizes... Judge of the Court of Mauléon..." and so on.

BERTHA. That's a good deal to write.

MADAME VAGRET. There's no way to get out of it! Here's your father. Go take a look into the kitchen as if by accident....

(BERTHA *goes out.*)

*(Enter* VAGRET, *in evening dress.)*

MADAME VAGRET. Isn't the hearing over?

VAGRET. No. When I left, my Substitute was rising to demand the application of the penalty.

MADAME VAGRET. Anything new?

VAGRET. About the crime? Nothing....

MADAME VAGRET. And is Delorme, your examining magistrate, making thorough investigations?

VAGRET. He is doing all he can.

MADAME VAGRET. Oh! If *I* were in his place, it seems to me.... There! The examining magistrates ought to be women! *(Absent-mindedly.)* Nothing in the *Record*?

VAGRET *(annoyed)*. Yes.

MADAME VAGRET. And you didn't tell me.... Something for us?

VAGRET. No.... Nanteuil has been appointed Advocate-General.

MADAME VAGRET. Nanteuil?

VAGRET. Yes.

MADAME VAGRET. That's the last straw! He was Assistant Judge at Lunéville when you were Substitute there!

VAGRET. Yes, but he has a cousin who is a Deputy — you can't beat that combination!

*(Silence.* MADAME VAGRET *sits down and begins to cry.)*

MADAME VAGRET. We never have any luck!

VAGRET. Come, come! my dear, don't cry.

MADAME VAGRET *(still weeping)*. My poor dear, I know well enough it's not your fault... you do the best you can... the only trouble with you is that you are too honest, and I would be the last one to reproach you for it... only, what's the use of talking! Everybody gets ahead of us... before long you will be the oldest Prosecutor...

VAGRET. What! I? Where is the *Year Book*?

MADAME VAGRET *(still in tears)*. Look under *Length of Service* — farther over.

VAGRET *(throwing aside the Year Book)*. Don't cry like that! You know I have been picked out as Lefèvre's successor.

MADAME VAGRET. Yes, I know.

VAGRET. I am slated for advancement.

MADAME VAGRET. So is everybody else.

VAGRET. But I have the definite promise of the Attorney-General and of the Chief Justice.

MADAME VAGRET. It's the Deputy's you need.

VAGRET. Oh!

MADAME VAGRET. Certainly. Until now you have waited for advancement; you must meet it halfway, my dear. If you don't do as others do, you are only a simpleton.

VAGRET. A man of principle, you mean!

MADAME VAGRET. And for the very reason that you are a man of principle you ought to strive to attain to higher duties. If the independent and capable magistrates let the others outstrip them, what will be the future of the magistracy?

VAGRET. There is some truth in that...

MADAME VAGRET. Since you can better our situation through the influence of a Deputy, and still scrupulously retain your integrity, you would be wrong not to do so.... What do they want you to do in return, anyway? — to defend the Ministry...

VAGRET. As it happens, I am on that side anyway.

MADAME VAGRET. Hurry, then: a Ministry doesn't last long.... To defend the Ministry is to defend the Government, that is, the State, that is, Society. It is to do one's duty.

VAGRET. You are ambitious.

MADAME VAGRET. Ambitious! No, my dear... but really one must think of the future.... If you knew how hard it is for me to make both ends meet.... We ought to be getting Bertha married; our sons are going to cost us more every year; on account of our position we are constrained to certain useless expenditures which we could well dispense with, but we must keep up appearances, we must maintain our position. We want George to enter the Polytechnic, and that's going to take money! And then, there is Henry who is going to study law.... The better position you hold the better you will be able to help him.

VAGRET (*after a pause*). I haven't told you all.

MADAME VAGRET. What is it now?

VAGRET (*timidly*). Cortan has been appointed Counselor at Amiens.

MADAME VAGRET (*angrily*). What! That idiot Cortan?

VAGRET. Yes.

MADAME VAGRET. Worse than ever!

VAGRET. What did you expect? The new Keeper of the Seals is from his Department; you can't beat that combination!

MADAME VAGRET. There is always something.... Cortan! What a splurge she will make! — Madame Cortan! A woman who writes "judiciary" with an s.... I suppose she'll trot out that yellow hat! Don't you remember that yellow hat?

VAGRET. No.

MADAME VAGRET. It's the husband who should wear that color.

VAGRET. Rosa, you are unjust.

MADAME VAGRET (*nervously*). I know it, but it relieves me...

(*Enter* CATIALÉNA.)

CATIALÉNA. Madame, where shall I put that bundle that we took out of the linen-closet this morning?

MADAME VAGRET. What bundle?

CATIALÉNA. That bundle, you know — when we took the linen-closet for the cloak-room...

MADAME VAGRET (*suddenly*). Yes, yes... take it to my room.

CATIALÉNA. This way?

MADAME VAGRET. No; just leave it here. I will put it away myself.

CATIALÉNA. Very well, madame. (*Goes out.*)

MADAME VAGRET (*to herself, smelling of the bundle*). For all my moth-balls, it will be all worm-eaten before you ever get a chance to wear it.

VAGRET. What is it?

MADAME VAGRET (*putting the bundle on the table and opening the wrapper*). Look.

VAGRET. Ah, yes, my red robe... the one you bought me ahead of time two years ago.

MADAME VAGRET. Yes. That time it was Gamard who was chosen in your place.

VAGRET. How else could it be! Gamard was brother-in-law of a Deputy. You can't beat that combination! Of course, the Ministry has to assure itself of a majority.

MADAME VAGRET. And to think that in spite of all my hunting I have not been able to discover even among my cousins as much as an alderman!

VAGRET. Here, put it away. I don't like to look at it.... (*Giving back the robe which he has unfolded.*) Perhaps it wouldn't fit me now...

MADAME VAGRET. Oh, those things fit everyone!

VAGRET. Let's see. (*Takes off his coat.*)

MADAME VAGRET. And they bring you a thousand francs more a year!

VAGRET. It hasn't faded.

(*Enter* BERTHA; *he hides his red robe.*)

What is it?

BERTHA. It is I.

VAGRET. You frightened me.

BERTHA (*seeing the robe*). You are appointed! You are appointed!

VAGRET. Be quiet! Go lock the door!

BERTHA. Papa is appointed?

MADAME VAGRET. Do as you're told! No, he is not appointed.

VAGRET. It's just as good as new, isn't it? (*Putting on the robe.*)

MADAME VAGRET. Well, it ought to be! I got the best there was.

VAGRET. Ah, if I only had that on to demand the head of the Irissarry murderer! There's no use talking, the man who planned that costume was no fool. What an effect it does have on the jury! And just as much on the prisoner! I remember one fellow who did not take his eyes from the robe of the Prosecutor during a whole hearing. You feel stronger with it on, you have more dignity, a freer gesture.... "Gentlemen of the court, gentlemen of the jury!" Wouldn't my demand have an effect, though! "Gentlemen of the court, gentlemen of the jury; 'tis in the name of Society, which voices its vengeance through me, 'tis in the name of the sacred interests of humanity, in the name of the eternal principles, 'tis in the strength of my right and of my duty, that I rise — (*recommencing his gesture*) — that I rise to demand of you the head of the wretch who is before you..."

MADAME VAGRET. How well you speak!

(VAGRET, *after shrugging his shoulders, sighs, takes off his robe slowly in silence and gives it to his wife.*)

VAGRET. Here, put it away....

MADAME VAGRET. There's the bell.

BERTHA. Yes.

MADAME VAGRET (*to her daughter*). Here, take it!

BERTHA. Yes, mother.

(*Does up the bundle and starts to go out.*)

MADAME VAGRET. Bertha.

BERTHA. Mother?

MADAME VAGRET (*weeping*). Put some more mothballs in it, my
poor child!                                        (BERTHA *goes out.*)

(*Enter* CATIALÉNA.)

CATIALÉNA (*hands a note to* VAGRET). Someone just brought this
for you.                                              (*Goes out.*)

VAGRET. What is it? The Basque paper, the *Eskual Herria*... an
article marked with blue pencil. (*Reading.*) "Eskual herri
guzia, hamabartz égun huntan..." Just try to make something
out of that language of savages, will you!

MADAME VAGRET (*who has been reading over his shoulder*). It is something about you.

VAGRET. No!

MADAME VAGRET. Yes, there... "Vagret procuradoreak galdegin
..." Wait a minute. (*Calling at the door in the background.*)
Catialéna! Catialéna!

VAGRET. What are you doing?

MADAME VAGRET. Catialéna will translate it for us.... (*To* CATIA-
LÉNA *who has just entered.*) Here, Catialéna, read us this, will you?

CATIALÉNA. Yes, madame. (*Reading.*) "Eta gaitzegilea ozda
oraino gakopian Irissarryko."

VAGRET. What does that mean?

CATIALÉNA. That means that the Irissarry murderer has not been
arrested yet....

VAGRET. We know that. What else?

CATIALÉNA. "Baginakien yadanik dona Mauléano tribunala yuye
bourru arin edo tzarrendka ko béréchiazela"... that means
that at Mauléon there are only judges who have been driven
away from everywhere else and who don't know how to do anything... who haven't much sense.

VAGRET. Very well, that's enough...

MADAME VAGRET. No, no; go on, Catialéna.

CATIALÉNA. "Yaun hoyen Biribi…"

MADAME VAGRET. Biribi?

CATIALÉNA. Yes, madame.

MADAME VAGRET. What does that mean in Basque, — "Biribi?"

CATIALÉNA. I don't know.

MADAME VAGRET. You don't know? — You mean you don't want to say it? Is it a coarse word?

CATIALÉNA. Oh, madame, in that case I would understand it…

VAGRET. Biribi…

BERTHA. Perhaps it is a nickname they have given you…

MADAME VAGRET. Perhaps… (*A silence.* To CATIALÉNA.) Go on.

CATIALÉNA. It's about Monsieur Vagret.

MADAME VAGRET (*to her husband*). I told you so… (*To* CATIALÉNA.) Anything bad?

VAGRET. Enough of this, I tell you! (*Snatches the paper from* CATIALÉNA *and puts it in his pocket.*) Go to your kitchen, you! And be mighty quick about it!

CATIALÉNA. Sir, I swear I will not tell you the other words there…

VAGRET. Nobody wants you to. Go!

CATIALÉNA. I knew you would get angry… (*Starts to go out.*)

MADAME VAGRET. Catialéna!

CATIALÉNA. Madame?

MADAME VAGRET. So you really don't know what Biribi means?

CATIALÉNA. No, madame,… on my word…

MADAME VAGRET. All right. There's the bell. Go see what it is. (CATIALÉNA *goes out.*) That girl's going to get her week's notice — and no later than tomorrow.

VAGRET. Well, now…

CATIALÉNA (*returning*). It is Monsieur Delorme, sir.

MADAME VAGRET. Your examining magistrate?

VAGRET. Yes, he has come to give me his reply. (*To* CATIALÉNA.) Show him in.

MADAME VAGRET. What reply?

VAGRET. He has come to give up the case.

MADAME VAGRET. Give up the case…

VAGRET. Yes, I asked him to think it over until this evening.

MADAME VAGRET. Perhaps he has only come to dinner.

VAGRET. No, you know, of course, his health... Here he is. Leave us.

(*Enter* MONSIEUR DELORME.)

MADAME VAGRET (*amiably, going out*). Good-evening, Monsieur Delorme.

DELORME. Madame...

VAGRET. Well, my friend...

DELORME. It's no; that's final.

VAGRET. Why?

DELORME. I've already told you. (*A silence.*)

VAGRET. And the *alibi* of your prisoner?

DELORME. I have verified it.

VAGRET. It holds?

DELORME. Beyond the·shadow of a doubt.

VAGRET (*sadly*). Then you let the fellow go?

DELORME (*regretfully*). There was nothing else to do.

VAGRET (*still sad*). Of course. (*Pause.*) It's too bad, though.

DELORME. Yes.

VAGRET. And what, then?

DELORME. I wish you would give the case to someone else.

VAGRET. There's no appeal?

DELORME. I'm afraid not; you see, my dear Vagret, I am too old to adapt myself to the customs of the present day.... I am a magistrate of the old school, like yourself. I inherited from my father certain scruples which are no longer the fashion. These daily attacks in the papers are driving me wild.

VAGRET. They would stop soon enough at the news of an arrest.

DELORME. Precisely! The result would be that I would do something foolish — in fact, I have already: I would not have arrested that fellow if I hadn't been hounded as I was.

VAGRET. He was only a vagabond; you gave him shelter for a few days — there's no harm done.

DELORME. All the same...

VAGRET. You are too easily discouraged; this very evening or tomorrow some chance may put you on a new track.

DELORME. Even so... By the way, they say Placat, the Bordeaux attorney, will come to defend the accused.

VAGRET. I don't see what interest he can have in the matter.

DELORME. He expects to run at the next elections in our district and counts on his plea, in which he will not fail to lodge certain attacks, to work up a little popularity here.

VAGRET. What difference will that make?

DELORME. Don't you see? He will be able to be present at all the examinations of the prisoner — the law allows it — and, as he is thirsting for notoriety, he will communicate to the papers whatever he may wish and they will insult me every morning if my proceedings do not suit him.

VAGRET. You take it too seriously.

DELORME. Not a bit. Nowadays examinations aren't conducted by the magistrate, but by the public and by the newspapers.

VAGRET. That is true for the big criminals — in reality the new law is an advantage to no one else. You know as well as I that for the common run of offenders...

DELORME. Really, I must beg you to let me off.

VAGRET. Come, now, you do not imagine that Placat, who has a hundred cases to look after, will come to all your examinations. You know well enough what these fellows generally do.... He will send some subordinate — if, indeed, he sends any one at all.

DELORME. Please don't insist, my mind is made up.

VAGRET. In that case...

DELORME. Allow me to withdraw. I don't want to meet my colleagues who are dining here.

VAGRET. Until tomorrow, then... I am very sorry...

DELORME. Tomorrow.                                          (*Goes out.*)

(*Enter immediately* MADAME VAGRET *by another door.*)

MADAME VAGRET. Well, I was listening; he gives up the case.

VAGRET. Yes... his health... the papers...

MADAME VAGRET. Well?

VAGRET. Don't tell any one. No one suspects yet.

MADAME VAGRET. Never fear. (*Listens.*) This time it's our guests.

BERTHA (*entering*). Here they are.

MADAME VAGRET. Your work, Bertha! My *Revue des Deux Mondes*...
(*They settle down in their chairs. Silence.*)

BERTHA. They are taking their time...

MADAME VAGRET. It's that Madame Bunerat with her ceremony…

BUTLER. Judge of the Court and Madame Bunerat…

MADAME VAGRET. Good-evening, Madame…    (*Effusive greetings.*)

BUTLER. Judge La Bouzule…Judge Mouzon.

(*Deep bows.    They all take seats.*)

MADAME VAGRET (*to* MADAME BUNERAT).    Well, madame, there's one more session over.

MADAME BUNERAT. Yes, at last!

MADAME VAGRET. Your husband probably isn't sorry…

MADAME BUNERAT. Nor yours either, I am sure…

MADAME VAGRET. Isn't the judge of the Assizes coming?

BUNERAT. He will be a little late.   He expects to leave early to-morrow morning and he has a lot of things to sign.   You must remember the hearing is only just over…. When we saw that there was no end to it, we sent for our evening clothes while the jury was out, put them on, and then put our robes over them to pronounce the sentence…

MADAME VAGRET. What was it?

BUNERAT. Acquittal.

MADAME VAGRET. Another!   Jurors are such idiots!

VAGRET. Aren't you a little immoderate in your speech, my dear?

MADAME BUNERAT. Come, madame, don't take it so hard…

(*The two go together toward the rear of the stage.*)

BUNERAT (*to* VAGRET).    Yes, my dear attorney, an acquittal… that makes three for the session.

MOUZON (*forty years of age, side whiskers, handsome, but of coarse type*). Three prisoners released, all because we had no excuse for holding them any longer.

BUNERAT. A veritable run of black…

LA BOUZULE (*seventy years of age*).   No doubt, you would have preferred one of red, my dear colleagues…

BUNERAT. La Bouzule, you're a cynic.   I don't see how you have the heart to joke on such a subject.

LA BOUZULE. I wouldn't be joking if your prisoners had been convicted.

MOUZON. Never you mind the prisoners.   It's ourselves we have to think of.   If you think we shall receive congratulations from the Chancery, you are very much mistaken.

BUNERAT. A lot he cares whether the Mauléon court is in bad odor at Paris or not!

LA BOUZULE. You are right, Bunerat, I don't care a fig. I have nothing more to hope for. I am seventy years old next week and shall be retired on pension. Nothing more to hope for: I have the right to judge according to my conscience. I'm free! Oho! Oho! (*Executes a step.*) Don't get angry, I won't say anything more. I see the *Year Book* over there; I will look up the approaching vacancies for you. (*Sits down at the left.*)

BUNERAT. Go ahead! (*To* VAGRET.) The Judge of the Assizes is furious.

MOUZON. This won't help him any, either.

VAGRET. And my substitute?

BUNERAT. That's true...

MOUZON. It's all his fault.... He asked for extenuating circumstances.

BUNERAT. Where does the idiot come from?

VAGRET. He is far from an idiot, I assure you. He has been Secretary of the Conference at Paris, he is Doctor of Laws, and a very capable man.

BUNERAT. Capable?

VAGRET. Yes, capable — he has real oratorical gifts.

BUNERAT. Ah, we noticed it.

VAGRET. He is a very distinguished young man.

BUNERAT (*vehemently*). Yes, I suppose so! But when one has as much talent as that, he goes into practice, he does not enter the magistracy!

MADAME VAGRET (*to* LA BOUZULE, *who has come up to her*). So, really, Judge La Bouzule, it was the fault of the new substitute, it seems...

MADAME BUNERAT. Tell us all about it.

LA BOUZULE. It was like this...

> (*Goes toward the ladies and continues in a low voice.* BERTHA *has come in and has joined the group of which* VAGRET *also is a member.*)

MOUZON (*to* BUNERAT). All this is not going to hasten the appointment of poor Vagret...

BUNERAT (*with a smile*). The fact is, poor Vagret is playing in bad luck just now.

MOUZON. Is it true that he was seriously thought of when there is at the Mauléon court a man so much better qualified…

BUNERAT (*with an air of false modesty*). I don't see…. Whom have you in mind?

MOUZON. Yourself, Judge.

BUNERAT. In fact, I *have* been considered by the Ministry.

MOUZON. When you preside at the Assizes, the debates will be different from these lately…

BUNERAT. Why do you say that, Mouzon?

MOUZON. Because I have seen you preside at the police court.

(*Laughs.*)

BUNERAT. What are you laughing at?

MOUZON. Something you said comes to my mind — what you said the other day.

BUNERAT (*radiant*). I've forgotten…

MOUZON. So funny… (*Laughs.*)

BUNERAT. What was it? I said something funny? I don't remember…

MOUZON. I should say you did! A hundred times! You were in such spirits, that day. And what a face he made, the prisoner you know, the ragged fellow; his name was Fawcett…

BUNERAT. Oh, yes! When I said to him: "Fawcett, turn on the confession!"

MOUZON. That's it! That's it! And the witness for the prisoner, that idiot! Didn't you disconcert him, though! He couldn't finish, they laughed so hard, when you said to him: "If you wish to direct the hearing, say so! Do you want my place?"

BUNERAT. Oh, yes…. Ladies, Mouzon has just recalled to me a rather amusing incident. The other day at the police court…

BUTLER (*announcing*). Monsieur Gabriel Ardeuil, Substitute.

ARDEUIL (*to* MADAME VAGRET). Pray, pardon me, madame, for my tardiness. I was detained until just this minute.

MADAME VAGRET. Certainly, and the more readily in view of your success of today. They say it was enough to make all the lawyers of the district jealous. (*Leaves* ARDEUIL *by himself.*)

LA BOUZULE (*touching* ARDEUIL *on the shoulder*). Young man, sit down by me, please do!… You know, of course, that it would not take many hearings like that of today to get yourself recalled…

ARDEUIL. Do you mean to say they would recall me...

LA BOUZULE. Believe me, it doesn't do one any good to be considered odd!

ARDEUIL. Odd! But you — in spite of the secrecy of the deliberations, I know that you stand for independence and leniency.

LA BOUZULE. Yes, for some little time I have been indulging in that luxury.

ARDEUIL. For some little time?

LA BOUZULE. Yes, my young friend; for I have been recently cured of the malady which makes bad judges out of so many decent people. This malady is the madness for advancement. Look at those over there. If they had not been infected by this microbe, they would be kind and just men, instead of cruel and servile magistrates.

ARDEUIL. You are exaggerating, sir. The French magistracy is not...

LA BOUZULE. Is not venal, very true: among the four thousand magistrates, perhaps you would not find one — not one! Do you understand? — even among the poorest and most humble... especially among the poorest and most humble... who would accept money to modify his decision. That is the glory and the peculiar possession of the magistracy of our country. Let us pay it that respect! But a large number of them are ready to make concessions and to compromise if it is a matter of being agreeable either to the influential elector, or to the Deputy, or to the Ministry which dispenses places and favors. Universal suffrage is the God and the tyrant of magistrates. You are, therefore, right, and I am not wrong.

ARDEUIL. No one can rob us of our independence.

LA BOUZULE. True enough, but, as De Tocqueville said somewhere, we surrender it ourselves.

ARDEUIL. You are pessimistic. There are magistrates on whom no promise...

LA BOUZULE. Yes, there are some: — those without needs, or without ambition — certain obscure fellows who give up their whole lives without ever soliciting anything. But you may believe me, these are exceptions; and the Mauléon court which you have before your eyes represents a good average integrity of our magistrates. I exaggerate? Granted! Let's say that in France there are only fifty courts like this, only twenty; one would be too many! Ah, young man, what kind of an idea have you of the magistracy, anyway?

ARDEUIL. I am afraid of it.

LA BOUZULE. Are you serious?

ARDEUIL. Certainly.

LA BOUZULE. Then why are you Substitute?

ARDEUIL. Did I have any choice? My parents put me into this career.

LA BOUZULE. Yes, the magistracy is considered a career.... The main thing is to succeed!                    (*Pause.*)

ARDEUIL. It would be so wonderful to dispense justice, tempered with mercy!

LA BOUZULE. Yes, it would be wonderful. (*Pause.*) Do you want the advice of a man who has been for forty years a judge of the third class?

ARDEUIL. By all means.

LA BOUZULE. Hand in your resignation; you have chosen the wrong robe. Only in that of a priest could you attempt to put into practice the ideas which you are voicing.

ARDEUIL (*as if to himself*). Yes, but it would take a simple heart, capable of faith.

BUNERAT (*in the group*). If only we were lucky enough to have for Keeper of the Seals a Deputy from the Department — just for one week!

LA BOUZULE (*to* ARDEUIL). Those are the things you ought to be thinking about, my boy.

BUTLER (*entering*). From the Judge of the Assizes.

(*Gives a letter to* MADAME VAGRET.)

VAGRET. He's not coming?

MADAME VAGRET (*after reading*). No, he's not coming!

BUNERAT. I was almost expecting it...

MADAME VAGRET. He says he has a headache... He took the six-forty-nine train.

MOUZON. That means something.

MADAME BUNERAT. He couldn't have shown his displeasure more clearly.

BUNERAT. Three acquittals, too!

MADAME BUNERAT. If only they had had to deal with celebrated attorneys there might have been some excuse — but these local pettifoggers!

BUNERAT. Mere nobodies!

MADAME VAGRET (*to her daughter*). Oh, my poor child, what kind of report will he make!

BERTHA. What report?

MADAME VAGRET. Didn't you know that the Judge makes a report to the Minister at the end of each session?... Oh, my poor Madame Bunerat! (*The three women go and sit down at the rear.*)

MOUZON. Three acquittals... the Irissarry crime... a horrible showing.... We are in a pretty muddle!

BUNERAT. You know, my dear Vagret, I am an outspoken man; I am not accustomed to beating about the bush. When I hunt the boar I drive him hard. I am speaking to you frankly, with my heart on my sleeve — I am a peasant's son, and not ashamed of it, either! Well! In my opinion, your administration — of course you direct it with your characteristic integrity and honesty — but it seems to me — how shall I say it? — that it is losing its hold. Mouzon, you remember, we were just speaking of it, as we were looking over the statistics...

MOUZON. Yes, not much prospect for a good showing this year.

BUNERAT. You know, of course, that there was a question of making us an exception to the general rule and raising us one class.... Well, if the number of cases diminishes like this, Mauléon will certainly not be promoted from the third class to the second.

MOUZON. We must show that there is a great deal to do here.

BUNERAT. And many cases which you dismiss could very well furnish grounds for prosecution.

MOUZON. Just think! We imposed this year one hundred and eighteen years of imprisonment less than last year!

BUNERAT. And it's not the fault of the court, either. We defend the interests of Society with the utmost vigilance.

MOUZON. But, before we can convict, you must furnish us the accused.

VAGRET. It is only recently that I gave the strictest orders for the suppression of the smuggling that is so common in this region.

BUNERAT. A good idea, too. You understand, of course, our point of view... it is a question of public safety.

MOUZON. We are behind the other courts of the same class. Look here — I have worked it out. (*Draws a paper from his portfolio and accidentally drops other papers which* LA BOUZULE *picks up.*) See here!

LA BOUZULE. You are losing your papers, Mouzon.... Is this envelope yours? (*Reads:*) "Mr. Benoît, Officer of the Navy, Hôtel Terminal, Bordeaux..." perfumed.

MOUZON (*taking the envelope, embarrassed*). Yes, this letter belongs to one of my friends...

LA BOUZULE. And this? The Irissarry Crime...

MOUZON. Ah, yes, I will tell you about that.... It is... it is about the Irissarry crime — it is the translation which Bunerat gave me of the article which appeared in today's *Eskual Herria*.... It is very unkind. It says that Mauléon is the place of discipline for judges, something like the Coventry of the magistracy.

VAGRET. But I really can't invent this murderer, can I? — if he persists in not allowing himself to be caught. Delorme has sent to every center the description which was given us...

MOUZON. Delorme! Do you want me to tell you what I think! Well! Our colleague Delorme is wrong to persist in the idea that a vagabond is the criminal...

VAGRET. But there is a witness...

MOUZON. The witness is lying or is mistaken.

BUNERAT. A witness who saw some gypsies come out of the victim's house in the morning.

MOUZON. The witness is lying or is mistaken, I tell you.

VAGRET. How do you make that out?

MOUZON. I am sure of it.

VAGRET. How so?

MOUZON. Because I am convinced the murderer was not a gypsy.

VAGRET. I don't understand you.

MOUZON. Please don't insist, Vagret; I know too well my duties toward my colleague Delorme; I have said too much already.

VAGRET. No, you haven't! Go on!

BUNERAT. Yes, go on!

MOUZON. With the utmost delicacy I warned our colleague, who was kind enough to consult me frequently and show me the results of his investigations day by day — I warned him that he was on the wrong track. He wouldn't listen and persists in looking for his vagabond... let him look! There are fifty thousand vagabonds in France. After all, I am probably mistaken.... It would surprise me, though, if I were, for in the large cities where I have served as magistrate and where I came, not accidentally, but, so to speak, every day, face to face with difficulties of this sort, I succeeded in acquiring some little familiarity with criminal cases and some little insight into them.

VAGRET. Of course. Delorme, you know, has never had a chance to handle such a fine crime...

MOUZON. At Bordeaux, in the case of the fair Toulousaine, which made a good deal of talk, it was I who forced the prisoner to a confession which brought him to the guillotine.

BUNERAT (*admiringly*). Indeed?

VAGRET. My dear Mouzon, I am speaking most seriously, and if I insist, it is because I have grave reasons for so doing. Just between ourselves, I beg of you, tell us what are the grounds for your opinion.

MOUZON. Since you're so insistent, I will.

BUNERAT. We're all attention.

MOUZON. Let us recall the facts. In a house, isolated as are the majority of the Basque houses, there is found in his bed, one morning, an old man of eighty-seven, beaten to death. Servants sleeping in a neighboring building had heard nothing. The dogs hadn't barked; there was theft, it was true, but not simply of money, but also of family papers. Keep this point in mind. I will call your attention to another detail. It had rained the evening before. In the garden are found footprints, which are immediately attributed to the murderer, a man who was so badly shod that the big toe of his right foot protruded from his shoe. Delorme starts out on this clue; he receives evidence which encourages him and he declares that a vagabond was the murderer. All false, I tell you! The murderer was not a vagabond! The house of the crime is, indeed, an isolated one. It is known that within a radius of six to seven miles no tramp came to ask for food prior to the crime. Therefore, this tramp, if it was one, would have eaten and drunk at the scene of the murder, either before or after the deed. No evidence has been found to warrant the belief that this was the case. We have, therefore, a man who arrives worn out with fatigue. He asks for alms; he is refused; then he hides and, after nightfall, he kills and steals. There is wine there, bread, eatables of various kinds: he leaves without touching them. Is that likely? No! Don't tell me he was interrupted and fled. That won't do, since your witness himself declares that he saw him in the morning some few yards from the house — now the crime was committed before midnight. If Delorme, in addition to his other rare qualities, had also had experience in things of this sort, he would have known that empty bottles, glasses, remnants of eatables left on a table, constitute, so to speak, the signature which vagabond murderers leave on the scene of their crime.

BUNERAT. In fact, I knew that point.

LA BOUZULE (*in a low voice to* ARDEUIL). Mouzon would have a man convicted simply for looking intelligent.

VAGRET. Go on, go on...

MOUZON. Delorme might have known this also: there is, in the life of the vagabond, one pressing need, second in importance only to hunger, the need of shoes. This is so true that sometimes they use the subterfuge of appealing their case. Now the trip to the court of appeal is generally made on foot, and the State furnishes them with shoes for the journey. These they hardly wear during their detention and find them accordingly in good condition on their release. Now the foot of the alleged vagabond is about the same size as that of his victim. His shoes, as you say yourself, are in very bad condition. Well, gentlemen! This ill-shod vagabond did not take any of the stout, serviceable shoes which were there! I will add only one word more. If the crime was committed by a chance passer, by a professional beggar, will some one tell me what this strange murderer was doing on the road which passes before the house of the crime — a road devoid of attraction for beggars — on which the houses are several miles apart — when there is quite near at hand another road passing through villages and connecting numerous farmhouses where it is a tradition never to refuse hospitality to a fellow man? One word more — why, then, does this vagabond steal family papers which will identify him as the criminal at his first encounter with the police? No, gentlemen; the criminal is not a vagabond. If you wish to discover him, you must not look for him wandering on the highways; you must look for him right in the neighborhood of his victim; you must look for him among those who would profit by his death — relatives, friends, or debtors.

VAGRET. That is very true...

BUNERAT. There's logic and clearness for you!

MOUZON. You may take my word for it, the case is simple. If I were entrusted with the investigation, I guarantee that the culprit would be under lock and key within three days.

VAGRET. Well, my dear colleague, I have some news to impart to you. Delorme, whose health is very frail, gave up the case this afternoon and it devolves on you. It is you henceforth who are entrusted with the investigation of the Irissarry crime.

MOUZON. I don't need to say that I accept, my dear attorney. My duty is to obey. I retract nothing of what I have said; within three days the murderer will be arrested.

BUNERAT. Good for you!

VAGRET. In the name of all of us I thank you for this promise.... I must acknowledge that you have relieved me of a great burden. (*To his wife.*) Listen, my dear, M. Mouzon takes charge of the case and promises us the solution within three days...

MADAME VAGRET. We are very grateful to M. Mouzon...

MADAME BUNERAT. Very...

VAGRET. Bertha! Give the order to serve — and have some old Bordeaux wine brought up! I wish to drink to your success, Mouzon.

BUTLER. Madame is served.

(*The couples assemble, and all pass to the dining-room.*)

## ACT II

*Office of* MOUZON, *examining magistrate. Door in the background; also at the right. At the left, two desks. Files, armchairs, a chair. As the curtain rises the* CLERK, *sitting in the* JUDGE'S *armchair, is drinking his coffee.*

(*Enter the* JANITOR.)

CLERK. Well, Sir Janitor of the Court, what's the news?

JANITOR. Here's the old man.

CLERK. So soon?

JANITOR. He came back from Bordeaux yesterday evening. He seemed tired.

CLERK (*loftily*). A magistrate of Mauléon is always tired when he comes back from Bordeaux!

JANITOR. Why?

CLERK (*after a pause*). I don't know.

JANITOR. It is the Irissarry case which brings him so early.

CLERK. Probably. (*While speaking, he has put away his things — cup, saucer, coffee-pot, sugar-bowl — in a cabinet. Takes his own place at the desk in the rear. Enter* MOUZON. *The* JANITOR *puts on an air of dignity and goes out. The* CLERK *rises with effusive politeness.*) Good-morning, Judge.

MOUZON. Good-morning. You haven't summoned anyone, have you, except on the Irissarry case?

CLERK. I have summoned the police officer, the accused, and his wife.

MOUZON. I am tired out, Benoît... I have such a headache. No telegram for me?

CLERK. No, Judge.

MOUZON. Has the Prosecutor asked for me?

CLERK. No, sir... but I have something for you, though...

(*Gives him an envelope.*)

MOUZON (*opening the envelope*). Stamps for my collection! Ah, that's fine, that is, Benoît. Let us see what it is, let us see. (*Takes a stamp-album from the drawer of his desk which was locked.*) Uruguay... I have that, it will do to exchange... that one, too. Oh, Benoît, a George Albert, first issue!... Where *did* you get that, Benoît?

CLERK. A lawyer's clerk found it among some papers.

MOUZON. Beautiful!... I must stick it in at once.... Hand me the mucilage, will you. (*Trims the stamp delicately with the scissors and sticks it in with the greatest care, speaking all the while.*) It is rare, very rare! According to the *Stamp Collector* it will exchange for three Blue Amadeuses or for a canceled Khedive of '70. There! (*Running through his album.*) Now! That commences to look like something, eh! It's beginning to fill up, eh, friend? And do you know, I think I'm going to get that Haiti one? (*Gleefully.*) Look here! Here's a page full! All filled up! And such beautiful specimens. (*Closes the album and utters a sigh.*) Oh, Lord!

CLERK. Don't you feel well?

MOUZON. No, I had some annoyances at Bordeaux...

CLERK. In connection with stamps?

MOUZON. No. (*Sighs; then to himself.*) Accursed women, I really needed something like that! (*Takes up his album again.*) When I get that Haiti one I shall need only three to fill up this page... yes... (*Closes the album.*) What's in the mail? Ah, ha! here are the reports from Paris on the Etchepare woman and the court record of her husband.

(*Enter the JANITOR with a visiting card.*)

Who's coming to disturb me now? (*Mollified after having read it.*) Ah! (*To the* CLERK.) You may leave us, Benoît.

CLERK. Yes, sir. (*Goes out.*)

MOUZON (*to the* JANITOR). Show him in.

(*Hides his album, seizes a file of papers which he pretends to be reading with the greatest attention.*)

(*Enter MONDOUBLEAU.*)

MONDOUBLEAU (*Gascon accent*). I was passing by the court-house and I thought I would come in and shake hands with you. I hope I'm not intruding...

MOUZON (*smiling and closing his file of papers*). An examining magistrate, my dear Deputy, is always busy... but it is restful and agreeable to receive from time to time pleasant calls. Be seated, I beg you, please do...

MONDOUBLEAU. I will keep you but a moment.

MOUZON. I'm sorry.

MONDOUBLEAU. What's the news on the Irissarry crime?

MOUZON. Nothing, so far. I have heard the accused. He has a bad look and makes a poor defense. He denied everything, got angry, and I had to remand him to confinement without getting anything out of him.

MONDOUBLEAU. Are you really sure you have the right man?

MOUZON. Sure? No — but I would be surprised if I were mistaken.

MONDOUBLEAU. I saw Delorme yesterday; he is a little better.

MOUZON. I know. He still holds that the murderer is a vagabond. And in that connection, Deputy, I must call your attention to a peculiarity of us examining magistrates — it takes the devil himself to make us abandon the first idea which has come to our mind. I guard against this professional failing as much as I can. I am going to question Etchepare; I am awaiting the result of an investigation conducted by the police... if all that does not give me any results, I shall set him at liberty and shall look elsewhere... but I repeat, sir, I think I am on the right track.

MONDOUBLEAU. Delorme is an old magistrate, very clear-sighted, and, I confess, the reasons which he gave me...

MOUZON. I know my colleague is an able man. Notice, I do not claim that he is wrong.... We shall see. I have up to the present time only a moral certainty. I shall have a material certainty when I find out the antecedents of the accused and when I have established beyond question the motive for the deed. Just as you came in I was about to open my mail. Here is a letter from the court at Pau; it is the court record of the fellow. (*Takes a paper-cutter to open the envelope.*)

MONDOUBLEAU. You have a strange paper-cutter.

MONDOUBLEAU. You don't say so! Four convictions!

MOUZON. That? It is the knife-blade used in the murder of the fair Toulousaine at Bordeaux. Quite a weapon, eh? I had it made into a paper-cutter... (*Opens the envelope.*) There! Just it! Four convictions for assault and battery. See...

MOUZON. This is significant. Moreover, I have neglected nothing.
I have learned that his wife, Yanetta Etchepare...

MONDOUBLEAU. Is that the young woman I saw in the corridor a
moment ago?

MOUZON. Yes. I have summoned her as a witness. I am going
to examine her in a moment.

MONDOUBLEAU. She looks to me like a good sort.

MOUZON. Very likely. I learned, as I was saying, that she had
lived in Paris before her marriage. I sent for information and
here it is. (*Opens the envelope. Smiles.*) Well! This young
woman who "looks like a good sort" was once sentenced to a
month's imprisonment for complicity in theft.... We will now
listen to the police sergeant who is coming to report officially
the results of the examination which I entrusted to him and
which he will draw up formally this evening... I'll see...

MONDOUBLEAU. You think he brings something new?

MOUZON. If you are interested I will receive him in your presence.
(*Goes to the door and beckons. Returns and sits down.*) Bear in
mind that I am asserting nothing. It is very possible that my
colleague has been nearer right than I....

(*Enter the* POLICE OFFICER.)

OFFICER. Good-morning, your honor.

MOUZON. Good-morning, Sergeant. You may speak before this
gentleman.

OFFICER (*bowing*). Mr. Deputy...

MOUZON. Well?

OFFICER. You were right! It is he...

MOUZON (*after a look at* MONDOUBLEAU). Not so fast. On what do
you base your statement?

OFFICER. You will see. In the first place, he has been convicted
four times.

MOUZON. Yes, I know.

OFFICER. In the next place, fifteen years ago he bought of old
man Goyetche, the victim, a vineyard payable by annuity.

MOUZON. Good.

OFFICER. He claimed to have made a very bad bargain and used
to call old man Goyetche a robber.

MOUZON. Exactly.

OFFICER. Five years ago he sold this vineyard.

MOUZON. So that for five years he had been paying an annuity to the victim, although the vineyard no longer belonged to him.

OFFICER. Yes, your honor.

MOUZON. Go on.

OFFICER. After his arrest gossip started; the neighbors began to talk.

MOUZON. That's the way it always is.

OFFICER. To a certain girl, Gracieuse Mendione, whom I have examined as witness, Etchepare said: "What a nuisance to have to give money to that old rapscallion."

MOUZON. Wait a minute. You say Gracieuse...?

OFFICER. Mendione.

MOUZON (*writing*). "Mendione... what a nuisance... money... to that old rapscallion." Now I call that good! What next?

OFFICER. I have another witness, Piarrech Artola...

MOUZON (*writing*). "Piarrech Artola..."

OFFICER. About two months ago Etchepare said to him, speaking of old man Goyetche: "Did you ever hear anything like it! the Good Lord must have forgotten him."

MOUZON (*still writing*). "The Good Lord must have forgotten him." Excellent. Is that all you have?

OFFICER. About all, your honor.

MOUZON. When was the next annuity to old man Goyetche due?

OFFICER. A week after Ascension.

MOUZON. That is, about a week after the crime?

OFFICER. Yes, your honor!

MOUZON (*to* MONDOUBLEAU). Remarkable coincidence.... (*To the* OFFICER.) Was this Etchepare well off?

OFFICER. On the contrary, he was hard up. Three months ago he borrowed eight hundred francs from a Mauléon merchant.

MOUZON. And what do the neighbors say?

OFFICER. They say that Etchepare was tricky and miserly, and they are not surprised that he is the guilty party. On the other hand, they are all kindly disposed to the wife, Yanetta, and used to cite her as a model wife and mother.

MOUZON. How many children?

OFFICER. Two: George, and... I have forgotten the name of the other.

MOUZON. The morals of the woman?

OFFICER. Irreproachable.

MOUZON. Very well.

OFFICER. I almost forgot something.... One of my men, one of those sent to arrest Etchepare, told me that Etchepare, seeing him coming, said to his wife: "They've got me!"

MOUZON. "They've got me."... Well, that's rather important!

OFFICER. And he said to his wife in Basque: "Don't let on, for anything, that I was out last night."

MOUZON. He said that before the policeman?

OFFICER. No, your honor... the policeman was outside... by an open window. Etchepare didn't see him.

MOUZON. Have that man summoned.

OFFICER. Yes, your honor.... There is also that witness for the prisoner, Bridet.

MOUZON. Oh, yes.... I have read the deposition which he made before you — it doesn't amount to anything. However, if he is there, I will hear him. Thank you. So, then, draw up a very detailed report and procure summons for the witnesses.

OFFICER. Yes, your honor. (*Bows: goes out.*)

MONDOUBLEAU. Delorme is a fool.

MOUZON (*laughing*). *I* didn't say so, Deputy.

MONDOUBLEAU. A wonderful faculty of intuition you have!

MOUZON. Wonderful, no... I assure you...

MONDOUBLEAU. How did you come to suspect this Etchepare, anyhow?

MOUZON. There are, you know, Deputy, professional accomplishments. The search for a criminal is an art in itself. I mean that a good examining magistrate is less guided by the facts themselves than by a sort of inspiration.

MONDOUBLEAU. Wonderful! I repeat it, wonderful! And this witness for the prisoner?

MOUZON. He must be a false witness.

MONDOUBLEAU. What makes you think so?

MOUZON. He accuses gypsies of the crime! Besides that, he was in business relations with Etchepare. The Basques, you know, consider us still somewhat as enemies, as conquerors, and think nothing of perjuring themselves to us.

MONDOUBLEAU. So you have never been willing to accept the hypothesis of your predecessor...

MOUZON. Vagabonds... The unfortunate!... I know your love for the humble, Deputy, and I had the same feelings as you, in not directing my suspicions exclusively upon the outcast, homeless, and hungry.

MONDOUBLEAU. Good for you! I am delighted to see that you are not merely a capable judge, but that you hold political views which are not at variance with mine...

MOUZON. I am only too glad...

MONDOUBLEAU. I hope that henceforth the Basque paper will cease its attacks on you...

MOUZON. I hardly think...

MONDOUBLEAU. Come now...

MOUZON. How can it, Deputy? This paper is your enemy, and as I am not backward in supporting openly your candidacy, they make me pay as magistrate for my opinions as a citizen...

MONDOUBLEAU. I am overwhelmed... and I thank you, my dear friend, with all my heart. Continue, but be prudent, won't you? The Keeper of the Seals was saying just day before yesterday: "I am counting upon you to avoid for me all trouble in your district. No scandals; especially no scandals." I must tell you that Eugène is much attacked at this moment...

MOUZON. Are you on terms of such intimacy with the Keeper of the Seals?

MONDOUBLEAU (*with a wave of his hand, simply*). We fought together in the Commune.

MOUZON. I understand...

MONDOUBLEAU. By the way, tell me. What sort of a man is your Public Prosecutor?

MOUZON. Vagret?

MONDOUBLEAU. Yes.

MOUZON. Oh, he is a very conscientious magistrate, punctilious, even.

MONDOUBLEAU. No, I mean from the political point of view.

MOUZON. You ought not to bear him any ill-will, Deputy, for

being in the camp diametrically opposed to ours. Don't get the idea that he's a bad fellow, though.

MONDOUBLEAU. He's narrow-minded. (*For some little time he has been looking over the desk of* MOUZON.) I just happen to see on your desk the Labastide case... there's not enough in the case to whip a cat for. I know Labastide well; he is one of my best lieutenants, and I assure you he is incapable of committing the things of which he is accused. I have already told Vagret, but I see that he has gone ahead with the case just the same.

MOUZON. I can assure you of only one thing, Deputy. I will look into the Labastide case with particular care.

MONDOUBLEAU. I esteem you too highly, sir, to ask more. Well! I won't take any more of your time. Good luck!

MOUZON. Good-day. (DEPUTY *goes out.*) I think the Deputy won't have too bad an idea of me. (*Smiling.*) The fact is, I *was* pretty clever in suspecting Etchepare. Now, the point is to make him confess as soon as possible.

(*Enter* JANITOR *with a telegram.*)

MOUZON. A telegram for me?

JANITOR. Yes, your honor.

MOUZON. Give it to me. All right. (JANITOR *goes out. He reads:*) "Diana still in jail. Report of yesterday's affair sent Attorney-General. — Lucian." (*Aloud.*) That puts me in a pretty fix! (*Silence.*) Well! There's work to do. (*Goes to the door in the rear, calls his clerk.*) Benoît!

(*The* CLERK *enters.*)

MOUZON (*seated, gives a file of papers to the* CLERK). Draw up for me a discharge for this Labastide and a warrant for his immediate release. You can do that during the examination. Come, let's get started! It is already two o'clock and we have done nothing yet. Hurry up, won't you? What are you waiting for? Give me a list of the witnesses, don't you understand? What is the matter with you today? All right.... Well! Send in this famous witness for the prisoner so we can get rid of him. Is Etchepare here?

CLERK. Yes, Judge.

MOUZON. His wife, too?

CLERK. Yes, Judge.

MOUZON. Come, now! What are you looking at me like that for? Send him in...

CLERK. Who, Etchepare?

MOUZON. Of course not! The witness for the prisoner — the wit-ness for the pris-on-er! Do you understand?

CLERK (outside, angrily). Bridet! Come, Bridet, are you deaf? Come in. (Roughly.) Hurry up!

(Enter BRIDET.)

BRIDET. Your honor, I came to tell you...

MOUZON. Keep still. You can speak when you are spoken to. Name, given names, age, occupation, address...

BRIDET. Bridet, Jean-Pierre, thirty-eight, sandal manufacturer at Baïgorry.

MOUZON (without stopping to take breath). You swear to tell the truth, the whole truth, and nothing but the truth — say: I do. You are neither kith nor kin of the prisoner, you are not in his service nor he in yours. (To the CLERK.) Is he sworn?

CLERK. Yes, your honor.

MOUZON (to BRIDET). Speak. (Silence.) Speak, can't you!

BRIDET. I am waiting to be questioned.

MOUZON. A minute ago there was no keeping you still; now that I want you to speak, you don't find anything to say. What's your object in taking the defense of Etchepare?

BRIDET. My object?

MOUZON. Yes, your object. Don't you understand your own language?

BRIDET. Yes, sir.... Why, no object, sir.

MOUZON. No object? That's the truth, is it? Eh? No object? Well, I am willing to believe you. (Very sternly.) However, it is my duty to remind you that according to the Penal Code, Article 361, perjury is punishable by solitary confinement. Now that you understand the consequences of not telling the truth, I am willing to listen.

BRIDET (confused). I was going to tell you that old man Goyetche was murdered by some gypsies who crossed the frontier and who came down from the mountain.

MOUZON. Are you sure of that?

BRIDET. That's what I think.

MOUZON. You are not here to tell me what you think. Tell me what you have seen or heard. That is all that is required of you.

BRIDET. Why, you meet them all the time, these gypsies. Just the other day again they robbed a tobacco shop — there were three of them. Two went in — for I must tell you that they had examined the neighborhood in the day time.

MOUZON. Did you come here to make a jest of the law?

BRIDET. I? Why... sir...

MOUZON. I asked you if you came here to make a jest of the law.

BRIDET. No, sir.

MOUZON. You are wise, for that wouldn't be a safe thing to do. Do you understand?

BRIDET. Yes, sir.

MOUZON. Have you anything more to say?

BRIDET. Yes, sir.

MOUZON. Well, then! Say it! Lord Almighty! And don't make me waste my time like this. Do you think I have nothing else to do but listen to your gossip? If you have anything to say, say it!

BRIDET. It was like this; the day after Ascension, on a Monday — no, on a Friday...

MOUZON. Well, which was it?

BRIDET. On a Friday... I thought at first it was Monday, being the day after a holiday — anyway, the day after old man Goyetche was found murdered I saw a band of gypsies coming away from there.

MOUZON. Then you were close to the house?

BRIDET. No, I was going along the road...

MOUZON. Did they shut the door after them?

BRIDET. I don't know, sir.

MOUZON. Then, why do you say you saw them coming away?

BRIDET. I saw them coming from the field in front of the house.

MOUZON. Well?

BRIDET. That's all.

MOUZON (*lying back in his chair*). And is that all you came to disturb me for? Say! Is that all?

BRIDET. But, sir... I beg your pardon... I thought... I beg your pardon...

MOUZON. Wait a minute.... How many gypsies were there? Think hard, don't make any mistake...

BRIDET. Five.

MOUZON. Are you sure of it?

BRIDET. Yes, sir.

MOUZON. You are? Well, to the police officers you said there were five or six. So you are more sure of something a month after it happened than the day you saw it! On the other hand, you have forgotten whether the thing took place Monday or Friday, and whether the gypsies were coming out of the house or whether they were simply crossing the fields. (*Sternly.*) Tell me, you know the prisoner, Etchepare, don't you?

BRIDET. Yes, sir...

MOUZON. You have business dealings with him; you used to sell him sheep?

BRIDET. Yes, sir...

MOUZON. That's all I want of you. Go!

BRIDET. Yes, sir.

MOUZON. And you may call yourself lucky that I let you off so easy.

BRIDET. Yes, sir.

MOUZON. In future, before asking to appear as witness for the defense, I advise you to think twice.

BRIDET. You needn't worry, sir; you won't catch me again, I can tell you.

MOUZON. Sign your examination and go. If there were not so many simpletons and blunder-heads like you, there would not be so often occasion to complain of the delays and hesitations which justice is blamed for, but cannot help.

BRIDET. Yes, sir.

MOUZON (*to the* CLERK). Send Etchepare in.

CLERK (*returning immediately*). Sir...

MOUZON. Well?

CLERK. The counsel for the defense, M. Placat.

MOUZON. Is he there?

CLERK. Yes, your honor. He would like to see you before the examination.

MOUZON. Well, show him in, will you? What are you waiting for? Leave us; come back when I send for the prisoner.

(CLERK *goes out*.)

(*Enter* PLACAT.)

MOUZON. Good-afternoon, Placat. How goes it?

PLACAT. Quite well, thank you. How are you? I caught a glimpse of you at the Grand yesterday evening; you were with a very pretty woman.

MOUZON. Yes, in fact, I...

PLACAT. I didn't mean to be indiscreet.... By the way... I wanted to have a word with you about the Etchepare case.

MOUZON. If you are free now, we will proceed at once to the examination.

PLACAT. The fact is... I haven't a minute.

MOUZON. Would you like to have it put off until tomorrow?

PLACAT. No. I have just had a conversation with the prisoner. The case is without interest. He denies and denies, and that is all there is to it. He is willing to be examined without me. (*Laughing.*) I may as well tell you, of course, that I advised him to keep on denying. Well, good-day. If he asks for counsel later, let me know and I'll send one of my clerks.

MOUZON. All right. I'll see you soon...

(PLACAT *goes out.* MOUZON *comes back to his desk*.)

(*Enter the* CLERK; *then* ETCHEPARE *between two officers*.)

CLERK. Come forward.

MOUZON (*to the* CLERK). Take this down. (*Very hastily, mumbling.*) In the year eighteen hundred ninety-nine, etc.... before me, examining magistrate, aided by ... etc.... was brought Etchepare, Jean-Pierre, whose first appearance is recorded in the report of the... etc.... be it hereby attested that the prisoner, having consented to be examined without the presence of his counsel... (*To* ETCHEPARE.) You consent, don't you?

ETCHEPARE. I am innocent. I have no need of counsel.

MOUZON. All right. (*Continuing his mumbling.*) We proceeded. In consequence, we passed without delay as follows to the examination of the aforesaid Etchepare, Jean-Pierre. (*Speaking to* ETCHEPARE.) Etchepare, at the time of your first appearance, you refused to answer — a thing which was not very wise on your part, but within your rights. You became angry and I even had to recall to your mind the respect due the law. Will you speak today?

ETCHEPARE (*confused*). Yes, your honor.

MOUZON. So, my fine fellow! You are off your high horse now!

ETCHEPARE. Yes. I have thought it over and want to get out of this as soon as possible.

MOUZON. Well, for my part, I ask nothing better than to release you. So far we understand each other; let us hope it will last. Be seated. First of all, I advise you to abandon the line of defense which consists in laying the crime to a band of gypsies. A certain Bridet who is in business relations with you has tried, doubtless at your instigation, to have us accept this story.... I must tell you that he has not been successful.

ETCHEPARE. I have no idea what Bridet may have told you...

MOUZON. Ah! You do not acknowledge him? Very well, you are more clever than I thought. Is it you who murdered old man Goyetche?

ETCHEPARE. No, sir.

MOUZON. You had an interest in his death?

ETCHEPARE. No, sir.

MOUZON. Oh, really? I thought that you had to pay him an annuity.

ETCHEPARE (*after hesitating*). Yes, sir.

MOUZON. Then you did have an interest in his death? (*Silence.*) Well, you're not going to answer? Let's go on. You said to one witness... a certain... Mendione, Gracieuse Mendione: "What a nuisance to have to give money to that old rapscallion."

ETCHEPARE (*feebly*). That's not true.

MOUZON. Not true... the witness lies, eh?

ETCHEPARE. I don't know.

MOUZON. You don't know!... (*Silence.*) You thought it was time for old man Goyetche to die?

ETCHEPARE. No, sir...

MOUZON. No, sir.... Then why did you say to another witness, Piarrech Artola by name... why did you say to him, speaking of your creditor: "Did you ever hear anything like it? The Good Lord must have forgotten him"?

ETCHEPARE. I didn't say it...

MOUZON. You didn't.... That witness lies too.... Answer me, does he lie? (*Silence.*) You're not going to answer? It is just as well.... Come, Etchepare, what's the use? Isn't it clear? You are miserly, self-seeking, greedy for gain...

ETCHEPARE. It is so hard to earn one's living.

MOUZON. You are quick-tempered. You get drunk once in a while, and then you become dangerous. You have been convicted four times for assault and battery. You are quick with the knife. Isn't it all clear enough? You were tired of paying — without return — an annuity of considerable amount to the old man. This year's payment was approaching. You were short of funds. You thought it was time for old man Goyetche to die and you murdered him... You can't help seeing it, can you? Isn't it true?

ETCHEPARE (*gradually recovering his self-possession*). I didn't murder him.

MOUZON. Let's not trifle over words.... Did you pay someone else to kill him?

ETCHEPARE. I had nothing to do with his death. You say yourself that I was hard up. How could I have paid anyone to kill him?

MOUZON. Then you did it yourself...

ETCHEPARE. I did not.

MOUZON. Listen, Etchepare.... You will confess some day or other — your defense is already weakening...

ETCHEPARE. If I screamed it at you, you would say I was putting on...

MOUZON. Sooner or later, I tell you, you will make up your mind to confess. You already acknowledge facts which in themselves are serious charges against you.

ETCHEPARE. I say what is the truth without being concerned about the consequences.

MOUZON. Well! You ought to be concerned about the consequences because they may be particularly serious for you...

ETCHEPARE. I have no fear of death.

MOUZON. For others...

ETCHEPARE. Nor for myself.

MOUZON. So much the better. But you are Basque, you are Catholic. After death, there is hell...

ETCHEPARE. I have no fear of hell because I haven't done anything wrong.

MOUZON. There is the dishonor which will fall upon your children. You love them, your children, don't you? They ask for you... they love you because they don't know yet.

ETCHEPARE (*suddenly bursting into tears*). My poor little ones, my poor little ones!

MOUZON. Come, now! Not all good instincts are extinguished in you. Believe me, Etchepare, the jury will give you credit for your confession, your repentance. You will escape the severest penalty. You are still young... you have long years before you to expiate your crime. Good behavior may reduce your sentence, and perhaps you will again see your children, who will have forgiven you. Believe me, believe me, in your own interest, confess.... (MOUZON *has approached him during the preceding. Puts his hand on his shoulder. Continues with great kindness.*) Well, is it true? If you cannot speak, just nod your head, eh? It is true? I know it, anyway.... What? I don't hear what you say. It *was* you, wasn't it? It was you?

ETCHEPARE (*still weeping*). It wasn't I, sir! I swear to you I didn't do it. I swear it.

MOUZON (*back in his place: speaking sternly*). Oh, you don't need to swear; all you need to do is to tell me the truth.

ETCHEPARE. I am telling the truth, I *am*... but I can't say that I did it when I didn't!

MOUZON. Well! We'll get nothing out of him today. (*To the* CLERK.) Read him his examination and have him taken back to his cell.... Wait a minute, Etchepare.

ETCHEPARE. Yes, sir.

MOUZON. There is one way to prove your innocence, since you claim to be innocent. Prove in some way or other that you were somewhere else than at Irassarry the night of the crime and I will release you. Where were you?

ETCHEPARE. Where was I?

MOUZON. Yes; I want to know where you were the night of Ascension. Were you at home?

ETCHEPARE. Yes.

MOUZON. Is that really the truth?

ETCHEPARE. Yes.

MOUZON (*rising, somewhat theatrically with his finger pointed at* ETCHEPARE). Well! Etchepare. That convicts you. I happen to know that you were out. When you were arrested, you said to your wife: "Don't let on, for anything, that I was out last night." I may as well tell you all. Someone saw you, a maid. She has testified to the police that just as she was leaving a young man with whom she had been to a dance — at ten o'clock — she met you a few hundred yards from your house. Well?

ETCHEPARE. It is true. I went out.

MOUZON (*triumphantly*). Ah; — well, my good fellow, it is hard enough to make you say anything. But it shows on your face when you lie. It shows! I read it on your face as if it were written in letters as big as that! To prove it, no witness claims to have seen you go out, neither your own maid, nor any other, and still I would have sworn it with my head under the knife! Come, now, we have made some progress in the last few minutes. (*To the* CLERK.) You have his first confession down?... good! (*To* ETCHEPARE.) Collect yourself a moment... we are going on with our little talk....

(*Goes to the fireplace rubbing his hands, pours himself a glass of brandy, utters a sigh of satisfaction, returns and sits down at his place.*)

FIRST POLICEMAN (*to his companion*). That Judge is a wonder!

SECOND POLICEMAN. I should say so.

MOUZON. Let's go on; while you're at it, confess everything — why not? Look at those good policemen who are dying to go to supper. (POLICEMEN, CLERK, *and* MOUZON *laugh*.) You confess? No? Well, then, tell me, why did you persist in claiming that you were not out?

ETCHEPARE. Because I had said so to the police and didn't want to go back on what I had said.

MOUZON. But why did you say it to the police in the first place?

ETCHEPARE. Because I thought they had come to arrest me for smuggling.

MOUZON. Very well. Then you did not go to Irissarry that night?

ETCHEPARE. No.

MOUZON. Then, where did you go?

ETCHEPARE. To the mountain, to look for a horse that had run off the night before from a troop which we were bringing in from Spain.

MOUZON. Very well, fine! Not a bad thought. It is capable of defense. You went to look for a horse lost in the mountain, a horse which had escaped from a troop which you were smuggling in the night before — precisely. If it's the truth, it lies in your own power to be released at once. You will simply tell me to whom you sold this horse; we will send for the purchaser, and, if he confirms your statement, I shall at once sign your release. To whom did you sell it?

ETCHEPARE. I didn't sell it.

MOUZON. You gave it away.... You did *something* with it?

ETCHEPARE. No, I didn't find it.

MOUZON. Oh, you didn't find it! The devil, you didn't — that changes the situation. Anyway, we'll try another tack. You didn't go all alone to the mountain?

ETCHEPARE. Yes, all alone.

MOUZON. That's unfortunate. Next time, you see, you should take along a companion. Did you stay out long?

ETCHEPARE. All night. I came back at five o'clock in the morning.

MOUZON. That was a long time.

ETCHEPARE. We are not rich and for us a horse is a fortune.

MOUZON. Very well. But you didn't stay all night in the mountain without meeting a single soul — a shepherd, customs officers?

ETCHEPARE. It was raining torrents.

MOUZON. Then you met no one?

ETCHEPARE. No one.

MOUZON. I suspected it. (*In a tone of pouting reproach, with a show of pity.*) Tell me, Etchepare, do you take the jury for idiots? (*Silence.*) So this is all you have been able to think up, my poor man?... I was saying just a little while ago that you were clever — I take it back. What you're telling me is enough to put one to sleep standing up. Why, a child of eight would have done better. It's ridiculous, I tell you, ridiculous! The jury will shrug their shoulders when they hear it. Out all night in a driving rain-storm, looking for a horse which you don't find.... And without meeting a living soul, neither shepherds, nor customs officers — coming back at five o'clock in the morning... it is light this time of year and has been for some time — But no! No one saw you and you saw no one.... Everybody had become blind, eh? There was a miracle and everybody was blind that night.... You don't claim that? No? Why? It is just as plausible as the rest of your story.... Wasn't everybody blind? (*The* CLERK *bursts out laughing; the* POLICE-MEN *follow his example.*) You see what it's worth, your defense! It makes even the officers and my clerk laugh. Don't you agree that your new line of defense is ridiculous?

ETCHEPARE (*stupefied, half to himself*). I don't know.

MOUZON. If *you* don't, *we* do. Anyway, I have no advice to give you. Just repeat that at the hearing — you will see what an effect it will produce. But why not confess? Why not confess? I really don't understand your stubbornness.... I don't understand it, I tell you.

ETCHEPARE. Well, if I didn't do it, have I got to say, just the same, that I did?

MOUZON. Then you still persist in your phantom horse story, do you?

ETCHEPARE. How do I know? How do I know what to say? It would be better for me not to say anything. Everything I say turns against me!

MOUZON. It's because you invent stories which are altogether too ridiculous. It is because you think I am more stupid than I am that you believe I am going to take stock in such ridiculous inventions. I liked your first way better. You at least had two witnesses on your side — two witnesses without great weight,

to be sure, but still two witnesses.   You adopt a new plan...
that is your right.... Let's go after the lost horse....

ETCHEPARE.  Well?                                    (*A long silence.*)

MOUZON.  Come, now!  Out with it!

ETCHEPARE (*weakly, hesitatingly, looking at the clerk as if to read in
his eyes whether he is answering as he ought to*).  Well! I will tell
you, sir, you are right.... It is not the truth.... I did not go to
the mountain....I told the truth in the first place.  I didn't
leave the house.  Just a moment ago, I was confused.  In the
first place I denied everything, even what was true, I was so
afraid of you; then when you said to me... I have forgotten
what — because my head is getting weak — I have forgotten,
I have forgotten... I am sure that I'm innocent, though...
well, a moment ago, I almost wanted to acknowledge myself
guilty so you would leave me in peace.  What was I saying?
I have forgotten... Oh, yes, when you said to me... those things
which I can't remember... it seemed to me that it was better to
say that I had gone out... I lied... (*With earnestness.*)  But what
I swear to, though, is that I am not the criminal.... That I
swear to, I swear to you...

MOUZON.  I repeat that I ask nothing better than to believe it.
This time, we agree, you were at home?

ETCHEPARE.  Yes, sir.

MOUZON.  We will hear your wife.  You have no other witnesses
to bring forward?

ETCHEPARE.  No, sir.

MOUZON.  Very well.  Take away the prisoner... but stay in the
court-house.  I shall probably need him in a few moments to
face his wife.  His examination is not over yet.

                            (*The* POLICEMEN *take* ETCHEPARE *out.*)

MOUZON (*to the* CLERK).  What a rascal, eh?  You could have caught
him in the act with knife in hand and he would still have denied
it.   And he's a sly one, too!  He puts up an excellent defense!

CLERK.  I thought for a moment that your honor had him.

MOUZON.  When I spoke to him of his children?

CLERK.  Yes, it brought tears to one's eyes.  It made one want
to confess without having done anything.

MOUZON. Didn't it, though?  Ah, if I only didn't have this headache!  (*Silence.*)  I have just put my foot in it.

CLERK. Oh, your honor!

MOUZON. I did, just the same!  I was wrong to show him the
weakness of his new story.... It is so absurd that it would have
ruined him.  Whereas, if he continues to assert that he didn't
leave the house, if his maid persists, if his wife says the same
thing, it will be enough to cast a doubt in the mind of the jury...
he was well aware of it, the brute!  He perceived well enough
that of his two methods, the first was the better.  It is I who
was outwitted, Benoît....  (*To himself.*)  The question, now, is
how to repair the damage!  Let us reflect.... Etchepare committed the crime... of that there is no doubt.  I am as sure
of it as if I had seen him.  Therefore he was not at home the
night of the crime and his wife knows it.... After his hesitation
of a moment ago, if I succeed in making his wife confess that he
was out until morning, we get back the ridiculous story of the
lost horse — I'll catch him twice in a lie and I have him!...
Yes!  The thing to do now is to put the woman through the
third degree and it will be a wonder if I don't succeed.  (*To the*
CLERK.)  What did I do with the police report from Paris about
the Etchepare woman?

CLERK. You put it with the other papers.

MOUZON. Yes, here it is... the extract from her police record.
Bulletin number two, one month's imprisonment... complicity
... I suspected it!  Send her in.

(*The* CLERK *goes to the door and calls.*  YANETTA *comes in.*)

MOUZON. Come forward, madame.  I do not administer the oath
to you, since you are the wife of the prisoner.  But I must urge
you most earnestly to tell the truth.  I warn you that a lie on
your part might necessitate my accusing you of complicity
with your husband in the crime of which he is accused and make
me proceed to your immediate arrest.

YANETTA. I am not afraid.  I cannot be an accomplice of my
husband since he is not guilty.

MOUZON. I am not of your opinion, and, I may add, it is my
conviction that you know more about this matter than you are
willing to testify.

YANETTA. I? It's an outrage, sir!

MOUZON. Come, come! Don't get excited! I don't say you took part directly in the murder. I mean, it is very probable that you knew of it, perhaps advised it, and that you profited by it. That is enough to bring you to the bar of the Assizes beside your husband. On the frankness of your replies will depend my conduct toward you; and according as you tell the truth or not, I shall have you released or arrested. You can't say you have not been warned, can you? Now, be kind enough to inform me if you persist in your first declaration, namely, that Etchepare passed the night of Ascension Day at home.

YANETTA. I do.

MOUZON. Well, it is false!

YANETTA (*excitedly*). The night old man Goyetche was murdered my husband did not go out of the house.

MOUZON. It is false, I tell you.

YANETTA (*still excited*). The night old man Goyetche was murdered my husband did not leave the house.

MOUZON. You are so stubborn, you'll do nothing but repeat the same thing.

YANETTA. Yes, I shall do nothing but repeat the same thing.

MOUZON. Then we shall examine the worth of your testimony. Since your marriage... for ten years... your conduct has been above reproach. You are thrifty, faithful, industrious, honest...

YANETTA. What of it?

MOUZON. Don't interrupt. Wait. You have two children whom you adore. You are an excellent mother. People even talk of almost heroic deeds of devotion at the time your oldest boy — George, I think — was sick...

YANETTA. Yes, George... but what's that got to do with the charge against my husband?

MOUZON. Be patient; you'll see.

YANETTA. I'm waiting.

MOUZON. You are especially meritorious in being what you are in that your husband does not furnish an example of the same virtues. He drinks to excess occasionally.

YANETTA. He does not.

MOUZON. Come, now! Everybody knows it. He is quarrelsome.

YANETTA. He is not quarrelsome.

MOUZON. So much so that he has been convicted four times for assault and battery.

YANETTA. It is possible: evenings of holidays there are disputes. And, besides, that was a long time ago. Lately he has been gentler and I am very happy with him.

MOUZON. I am surprised...

YANETTA. Anyway, how does that prove that he killed old man Goyetche?

MOUZON. Your husband is very miserly.

YANETTA. The poor must be miserly, sir, or drop in their tracks of hunger.

MOUZON. You defend him well.

YANETTA. Did you think I was going to accuse him?

MOUZON. Haven't you ever been convicted in court?

YANETTA (embarrassed). I?

MOUZON. Yes, you.

YANETTA (weakly). No, I have never been convicted.

MOUZON. That is strange. There was, however, a girl with the same name who once served a month's imprisonment at Paris for complicity in theft.

YANETTA (weakly). For complicity...

MOUZON. You are not so confident. You seem embarrassed...

YANETTA (still weakly). No, no...

MOUZON. You are pale, you are trembling — are you faint? Give her a chair, Benoît. (The CLERK obeys.) Pull yourself together.

YANETTA. My God! How did you find that out?

MOUZON. The record which has been sent me reads as follows: "The herein mentioned Yanetta X. was brought to Paris at the age of sixteen as companion, or waiting-maid by the M—— family who took her into their employ at Saint-Jean-de-Luz." Is that correct?

YANETTA. Yes.

MOUZON. To continue: "It was not long before a love affair developed between the girl Yanetta and the son of the house, aged twenty-three. Two years later the lovers took flight, carrying with them eight thousand francs which young M—— had stolen from his father. On the complaint of this latter, Yanetta was arrested and sentenced to one month's imprisonment for complicity in the theft. After serving this sentence she disappeared. It is believed that she went back to her native district." I suppose you are the one?

YANETTA. Yes. My God! I thought that was so far off and so forgotten! It is all true, sir, but for ten years I have devoted every minute of my life to expiation, to an attempt to redeem myself.... Just now, sir, I answered you rudely.... I implore your pardon. You hold in your hands now not only my life, but my husband's life, and the honor of my children...

MOUZON. Your husband doesn't know?

YANETTA. No, sir. Oh! You won't tell him, will you! I beg you on my knees. It would be criminal, yes, criminal! Listen, listen to me! I came back home, I hid... I would have preferred to die... I didn't want to stay in Paris, you understand why. And then, after a little while, I lost mamma. Etchepare was in love with me and kept urging me to marry him. I refused... I had the courage to refuse for three years.... Then I was so lonely, so sad and he so unhappy, that I finally yielded. I ought to have told him everything. I wanted to, but I couldn't. He would have suffered too much. For he is good, sir, I swear it.... (*At a gesture of* MOUZON.) Yes, yes... sometimes, it is true, when he has been drinking, he is brutal... I was going to tell you. I won't lie to you any more, sir... but he does it less and less. (*Weeping.*) Oh! Don't let him know, sir, don't let him know! He would go away, he would leave me... he would take away my children. (*A shriek.*) Oh! He would take my children from me! I don't know what to say to you, but it can't be that you would tell him — now that you know all the harm it would do... Please don't! Of course I was to blame, but how was I to understand? Did I know? — I wasn't sixteen years old, sir, when I went to Paris. My employers had a son; he took me almost by force... and then I came to love him... and then he wanted to take me with him because his parents wanted to send him away. I did what he wanted me to.... That money — I didn't know he had stolen it... I swear, sir, that I didn't know it.

MOUZON. All right, calm yourself.

YANETTA. Yes, sir.

MOUZON. Let us drop that for a moment.

YANETTA. Yes, sir.

MOUZON. And return to your husband.

YANETTA. Yes, sir.

MOUZON (*bluntly*). Try to be brave, my poor woman. Your husband is guilty.

YANETTA. It can't be, it can't be!...

MOUZON (*with engaging frankness*). He hasn't confessed yet, himself, but very near it. I know, as a matter of fact, that he passed that night away from home.... I have witnesses to that effect...

YANETTA. No, sir! My God, my God! Witnesses, what witnesses? It isn't so!

MOUZON. Now, for your own sake, don't be so obstinate! Do you want me to tell you where you will come out? You will ruin your husband! If you persist, in the face of evidence, in your assertion that he spent the night at home, you will ruin him, I tell you.... On the other hand, if you tell me the truth, if he is not the murderer, he will tell us what he did do; he will tell us who his companions were.

YANETTA. He didn't have any.

MOUZON. Then he went out alone?

YANETTA. Yes.

MOUZON. At ten o'clock?

YANETTA. Yes.

MOUZON. And came back alone at five o'clock in the morning?

YANETTA. Yes, all alone.

MOUZON. But you may be mistaken in the evening. Are you sure that it was the evening of Ascension that he went out alone?...

YANETTA. Yes.

MOUZON. Have you got that down, Benoît?

CLERK. Yes, your honor...

MOUZON. Madame, I understand what your sorrow must be, but I beg of you to listen to me with the greatest attention. Your husband was short of funds, wasn't he?

YANETTA. No.

MOUZON. Yes, he was.

YANETTA. I tell you he wasn't.

MOUZON. Here's the proof of it. Three months ago he borrowed eight hundred francs from a Mauléon merchant.

YANETTA. He never told me anything about it...

MOUZON. Besides that, he was in debt for a considerable amount to old man Goyetche.

YANETTA. I never heard of it...

MOUZON. Here is a promise to pay written by your husband; I suppose it is his signature?

YANETTA. Yes, but I didn't know...

MOUZON. You didn't know of the existence of this debt... that supports still more what I know. Your husband went to Irissarry.

YANETTA. No, sir.

MOUZON. He told you that he was going to the mountain, but he went to Irissarry.

YANETTA. No, sir; he tells me everything he does.

MOUZON. You can see plainly that he does not, since you did not know of the existence of this debt. He went to Irissarry.... Don't you believe it?

YANETTA. Yes, sir, I believe it, but he never murdered a man for money; that is false, false, I tell you!

MOUZON. False? How do you expect me to see that? Your husband begins by denying everything, blindly; then he offers me in succession two methods of defense. You begin by false testimony yourself. All this, I repeat, is ruining him.

YANETTA. I don't know anything about that, but what I do know and what I shall keep on repeating as long as I live is that he never killed a man for money.

MOUZON. Well, after all.... Perhaps he is not as guilty as I thought a moment ago. Perhaps he acted without premeditation. It may have happened like this: Etchepare, somewhat under the influence of liquor, goes to Goyetche's to ask him to wait a little for the payment of the debt. A dispute ensues between the two men; old man Goyetche was still very vigorous; there may have been, on his part, provocation, and a struggle may have followed with the tragic end which you know. In this case the situation of your husband changes absolutely. He is no longer the criminal planning his crime in advance; and the penalty pronounced against him may be one of the very lightest. So you see, madame, how important it is for you to obtain from him a complete confession. If he persists in his denials I fear for him, at the hands of the jury, the greatest severity. That he killed old man Goyetche there is not the slightest doubt. Under what circumstances did he kill him? That is the whole question. If he persists in his attempt to make himself pass for entirely innocent, he runs the risk of being held more guilty than he is. Do you get my meaning?

YANETTA. Yes, sir.

MOUZON. Are you willing to speak to him from this point of view? Shall I send for him?

YANETTA. Yes, sir.

MOUZON (to the CLERK). Bring in the prisoner. Tell the officers I won't need them.

(*Enter* ETCHEPARE.)

YANETTA. Pierre! You! Is this the way I find you, my Pierre, in prison, like a thief!... My poor husband, my poor husband! Come, prove to him that you haven't done anything! Tell the Judge! Tell him the truth.... That will be the best way. I beg you, tell him the truth.

ETCHEPARE. What's the use now? I see well enough that I am lost. Nothing I could do, nothing I could say, would do any good. Every one of my words turns against me. The Judge will have it I am guilty. For him, I must be guilty. So then! ... How else can it be, my poor wife?... I am not strong enough to struggle against him. Let them do what they want with me — I shan't say anything more.

YANETTA. Oh, yes, do speak! You must speak, you must defend yourself. I beg you, Pierre, I implore you, defend yourself.

ETCHEPARE. What's the use?

YANETTA. I implore you in the name of your children... they know nothing yet, but they cry when they see me cry... because, you see, in spite of my hiding, in spite of my trying to control myself before them, I can't be gay, can I? Then, as they love me, they see it! And there are questions and more questions....

If you only knew! They ask for you... André was saying to me just this morning: "Where is papa? You'll go and get him, won't you? Say you will!" I said I would and ran off.... You see you must defend yourself, so you can come back to them as soon as possible.... If you have anything, the least little thing, to reproach yourself for, say so... you are rough sometimes; then, I don't know... if you went to Irissarry, say so.... Perhaps you got into a quarrel with the wretched man.... If that is it, say so, say so... perhaps you had a fight with him and... I say that... I don't know... you understand... you see, the Judge promised me a moment ago that, in that case, you wouldn't be punished, or not so much.... My God, what ought I to say to you? What ought I to do?

ETCHEPARE. So you believe me guilty, too, do you? You believe it too; do you?

YANETTA. I don't know what to think, I don't know...

ETCHEPARE (*to* MOUZON). Ah! So you have thought out another way, have you? You have thought that out, too! To have me tortured by my wife, and it is you who have prompted her to speak to me of my children.... I don't know what you may have told her, but you have almost convinced her that I am a scoundrel, and you hoped that she would succeed in having me sent to the guillotine in the name of my children by speaking to me of them, because you know that I adore them and because they are everything to me. You are right, perhaps there isn't a father in the world who loves his little ones as much as I love mine. (*To* YANETTA.) You know it, too, Yanetta! You know it! And you also know that, in spite of my faults, I am a good Christian, that I believe in God, in Almighty God.... Well! Listen; my two sons — my little George, my little André — I pray God to kill them both, if I am guilty!

YANETTA (*at the highest pitch of feeling*). He is innocent! He is innocent, I tell you! (*Pause.*) Ah! Now you may bring on your proofs and ten witnesses — a hundred if you want to, and you could tell me that you saw him do it and I would tell you, "It is not true. It's a lie!" Even if you should prove to me that he had confessed, I would still tell you, he is innocent. Oh, Judge, you must have felt it... you have a heart... you know how it is when one loves one's children.... So you must be sure now that he is innocent.... You are going to give him back to me, aren't you? It is all settled now, and you are going to give him back to me?

MOUZON. If he is innocent, why did he lie to me just a moment ago?

ETCHEPARE. It was you who lied! Yes, you! You told me that you had witnesses who saw me leave the house that evening... and you didn't have any!

MOUZON. If I didn't have any then, I do now. Yes, there is a witness who has testified that on the night of the crime you were not at home, and that witness — is your wife!

ETCHEPARE (*to* YANETTA). You?

MOUZON (*to the* CLERK). Give me her examination.

> (*While* MOUZON *is looking among his papers,* YANETTA *looks a long time at her husband and then at* MOUZON. *She reflects deeply. Finally she seems to have made up her mind.*)

MOUZON. There! Your wife has just testified that you went out at ten o'clock and didn't return until five in the morning.

YANETTA (*very short*). It's a lie, I didn't say any such thing.

MOUZON. You went on to testify that he returned alone at five o'clock in the morning.

YANETTA. I did not!

MOUZON. I will read you your examination. (*Reads.*) "*Question:* Then he went out alone? *Answer:* Yes. *Question:* At ten o'clock? *Answer:* Yes.*"

YANETTA. I never said it.

MOUZON. Come, now! I even took the trouble to be more exact and said to you: "But you may be mistaken in the evening. Are you sure that it was the evening of Ascension that he went out alone?" You answered: "Yes."

YANETTA. It's a lie!

MOUZON. But I have it down here in black and white.

YANETTA. You can put down anything you want to.

MOUZON. So, then, I am a liar! The clerk is a liar, too!

YANETTA. The night old man Goyetche was murdered my husband did not leave the house.

MOUZON. Sign this paper and be quick about it... it is your examination.

YANETTA. Everything in it is false! It is false, I tell you. (*With a shriek*.) The night old man Goyetche was murdered my husband did not leave the house... my husband did not leave the house!

MOUZON (*pale with wrath*). You'll pay for that! (*To the* CLERK.) Draw up for me at once an order for her detention; call the officers. (*To* YANETTA.) Yanetta Etchepare, I hereby put you under arrest on the charge of complicity in murder.... (*To the officers*.) The man you may take back to his cell; then come back and get the woman. (*The officers take* ETCHEPARE *out*.)

YANETTA. Ah! You are furious, aren't you, eh, not to have gained your point! Oh! You have done everything you could, though — except to have us burned with slow fire! You have pretended to be kind — you spoke gently! You wanted to have me send my husband to the scaffold! (MOUZON *has taken his file of papers and pretends to be running through them with indifference*.) It is your trade to furnish heads to be cut off... you must have victims! You must have them at any price. When a man has fallen into your claws he is lost. One enters here innocent, he must go out a criminal. It is your trade, it is your glory to succeed in it. You put questions which don't seem to be anything and which may send a man into the other world, and when you have forced the wretch to convict himself, you feel a cannibal's joy!

MOUZON (*to the officers*). Take her away; hurry up, can't you!

YANETTA. Yes! A cannibal's joy! That, justice? Is that what you call justice?... (*To the officers*.) You won't get me out so easy! No, you won't! (*Grasps a heavy piece of furniture*.) You are a torturer! You are as bloodthirsty as those of the olden days, who used to crush your bones to make you confess! (*The officers have torn her loose; she throws herself to the floor and roars out the following while the officers drag her to the door at the rear:*) Yes! Cruel! You don't even realize it and probably think yourself a decent man, but you are only a torturer...

MOUZON. Come, take her out, won't you! What! Can't the two of you rid me of that mad woman?

(*The officers put forth renewed efforts*.)

YANETTA. Hangman! Coward! Judas! Heartless! Yes, heartless! And still more false and still more cruel when you have to deal with poor people like us! (*At the door where she holds on.*) Oh! The brutes, they are breaking my fingers! Yes, the poorer people are, the worse you are to them! (*She is taken away. Her shrieks are still heard outside as the curtain falls.*) The poorer people are, the worse you are to them...

## ACT III

*The office of the Public Prosecutor. A door, on a cant, opening upon a corridor at the left. It opens inward allowing the sign to be read: "Public Prosecutor." Desk, chairs, files.*

*As the curtain goes up, the* CLERK *is collecting into a cardboard folder various papers which he is taking from the desk.*

(*Enter* LA BOUZULE.)

LA BOUZULE. Good afternoon, Benoît.

CLERK (*hesitating to take the hand which* LA BOUZULE *extends to him*). Sir, you do me too much honor...

LA BOUZULE. Come, come, Benoît, give me your hand. I ceased to be a magistrate this morning: my dignity no longer requires me to be impolite to my inferiors.... How far are they in the Etchepare case?

CLERK. The hearing so far has been entirely devoted to the demand for punishment and to the pleas...

LA BOUZULE. Will they get through today?

CLERK. Without a doubt.... Even if Monsieur Vagret should reply — seeing that the Judge of the Assizes is going hunting tomorrow morning.

LA BOUZULE. Are you looking for an acquittal, Benoît?

CLERK. I am inclined to, your honor. (*About to go out.*)

LA BOUZULE. Who is that old woman waiting in the corridor?

CLERK. Etchepare's mother, sir.

LA BOUZULE. Poor woman! She must be very anxious.

CLERK. Not at all. She is confident of the verdict. She hasn't the least concern. She spent all yesterday afternoon there and came back this morning as tranquil as you please... except that today she wanted at all odds to see the Prosecuting Attorney or a Substitute... Monsieur Ardeuil is away, and Monsieur Vagret...

LA BOUZULE. Is at the hearing...

CLERK. She seemed greatly disappointed not to be able to find anyone.

LA BOUZULE. Well, send her in; perhaps I can give her some good advice. Placat will speak for some little time yet, won't he?

CLERK. I think so.

LA BOUZULE. Then tell her to come and speak to me — this good woman. It won't disturb anybody, and perhaps will be of some help to her in her trouble.

CLERK. Very well, your honor.

(*Goes to the door at the right, beckons to* ETCHEPARE's *mother and goes out of the door at the rear.*)

LA BOUZULE (*alone*). It's remarkable how kindly disposed I've been feeling since this morning.

(*Enter* ETCHEPARE's *mother in the costume of the old Basque women.*)

LA BOUZULE. They tell me, madame, that you wish to see some member of the administration.

MOTHER. Yes, sir.

LA BOUZULE. You would like to attend the hearing?

MOTHER. No, sir.... I am so sure that my son cannot be convicted that I am not a bit interested in all they are saying inside there. I'm just waiting for him. I only came because we have been driven from our home.

LA BOUZULE. Driven from your home?

MOTHER. Some officers came.

LA BOUZULE. Your son had debts, then?

MOTHER. After he was arrested our men left us. We couldn't get the crops in, nor pay our debts. But I know they will make all that up to us as soon as my son is acquitted.

LA BOUZULE (*to himself*). Poor woman!

MOTHER. I am so glad to see the end of our troubles coming.... He will come back, he will go and get his house and lands again. He will have our cattle given back. That is why I wanted to see one of the magistrates.

LA BOUZULE. I don't understand.

MOTHER. Two weeks after the officers came to arrest my son, Monsieur Claudet had the water from his factory turned into the stream which flows through our land and where our cattle drink. That was also one of the causes of our ruin. If Etchepare sees that when he comes back, God knows what he will do! Justice must stop the wrong that is being done us.

LA BOUZULE. Justice! Ah, madame, how much better it would be for you if you could avoid recourse to it.

MOTHER. Why? Isn't it for everybody?

LA BOUZULE. Of course.

MOTHER. Does Monsieur Claudet have a right...

LA BOUZULE. Certainly not.

MOTHER. Then I come to ask the judges to make him stop.

LA BOUZULE. That is not so simple as you think, madame. You must first go to a bailiff.

MOTHER. All right, I will.

LA BOUZULE. He will authenticate your statement.

MOTHER. What does that mean?

LA BOUZULE. He will examine whether your water-course has been contaminated.

MOTHER. There is no use of bothering a bailiff, a child could see it.

LA BOUZULE. That is the law.

MOTHER. What next?

LA BOUZULE. Then you will have to go to a solicitor and get an opinion.

MOTHER. All right, if there is no other way...

LA BOUZULE. That is not all. If Claudet contests the facts the Judge will appoint an expert who will visit the spot and make a report. You would have to petition the judge to assign an early date in view of the urgency of the matter.... Your case once on the docket, it would be heard in its turn after the recess...

MOTHER. After the recess!

LA BOUZULE. And that is not all. Monsieur Claudet's attorney might make default, in which case you would have to take judgment by default. Then Monsieur Claudet might take issue or any sort of exceptions, require a decision on these exceptions, appeal from the decision before coming to a final issue... all that would cost a great deal.

MOTHER. Who would pay it?

LA BOUZULE. You, of course — and Claudet.

MOTHER. That would be nothing for him, he is rich; but for us, who have nothing now!...

LA BOUZULE. Then you will have to sue *in forma pauperis*.

MOTHER. Will that take still more time?

LA BOUZULE. A great deal...

MOTHER. But I always heard that justice was free in France.

LA BOUZULE. So it is, but the means to obtain it are sometimes expensive, that is all.

MOTHER. And how long would that take?

LA BOUZULE. If Monsieur Claudet appeals, it might take two years.

MOTHER. It can't be! Haven't I the right on my side, sir?

LA BOUZULE. My poor woman, it is not enough to have the right on your side... you need the law, too.

MOTHER. I understand. What is called justice — we poor know of it only when it swoops down on us — by the wrong it does us. Then we will have to go away, no matter where. Anyway, I shall not miss the place... they insult us everywhere.... Etchepare could never stand that.

LA BOUZULE. On that point the law protects you. Lodge a complaint and those who insult you will be punished.

MOTHER. I don't believe it.... I have already lodged one complaint, as you say... but they didn't do anything to the man who was hurting us... so he keeps on.

LA BOUZULE. Is it a man of your place?

MOTHER. Yes, a neighbor, Labastide, a friend of Monsieur Mondoubleau, the Deputy.

LA BOUZULE. Very well, I shall do all I can, I promise you....

MOTHER. I thank you sir.... (*A pause.*) Well, then, I will wait for them to give me back my son.

LA BOUZULE. That's right.                    (*She goes out slowly.*)

CLERK (*entering by the door in the rear*). The court has adjourned for a recess, your honor.

LA BOUZULE. Has Placat finished?

CLERK. In the midst of applause. Two jurors were seen to wipe their eyes. No one doubts an acquittal.

LA BOUZULE. I am glad of it.

CLERK. Does your honor know the great news?

LA BOUZULE. What news?

CLERK. The arrival of the Attorney-General.

LA BOUZULE. No, I hadn't heard.

CLERK. The Attorney-General has just arrived.... They say he is bringing the appointment of someone here as Counsellor at the Court of Appeal.

LA BOUZULE. Ah, ha! Benoît, in your opinion, who is going to capture the plum? Vagret?

CLERK. That was my opinion.... I hesitated a long time between the Prosecutor and the Judge, and had about decided for the Prosecutor, but I think I was wrong.

LA BOUZULE. Is it Bunerat?

CLERK. No, your honor, I am proud to say that I think it is my employer who has the honor...

LA BOUZULE. Mouzon!

CLERK. Yes, your honor.

LA BOUZULE. What makes you think that?

CLERK. The Attorney-General instructed me to ask Monsieur Mouzon to come and speak with him before the end of the hearing.

LA BOUZULE. My congratulations, Benoît.

#### (*Enter* MADAME BUNERAT.)

MADAME BUNERAT (*in tears*). Oh, my dear Monsieur La Bouzule...

LA BOUZULE. What has happened, Madame Bunerat?

MADAME BUNERAT. It was that lawyer! What talent! What feeling! What talent! I am overcome with emotion.

LA BOUZULE. An acquittal?

MADAME BUNERAT. It is hoped so....

MADAME VAGRET (*entering*). Well, my dear sir... did you hear that famous lawyer? What a clown!

LA BOUZULE. They say he had quite an effect on the jury — the prisoner will be acquitted.

MADAME VAGRET. I am afraid so.

#### (*Enter* BUNERAT, *in a black robe.*)

BUNERAT. Do you know what they tell me? The Attorney-General is here.

MADAME BUNERAT. Is that so?

MADAME VAGRET. Are you sure?

LA BOUZULE. Absolutely... he is bringing to Monsieur Mouzon his appointment at the Court of Pau...

BUNERAT. Mouzon!

MADAME BUNERAT *and* MADAME VAGRET. And my husband! We had a definite promise.

(*Enter the* JUDGE OF THE ASSIZES *in a red robe.*)

JUDGE OF THE ASSIZES. Good-afternoon, gentlemen.... You haven't seen the Attorney-General, have you?

LA BOUZULE. No, Judge... but if you wish to wait for him...

JUDGE OF THE ASSIZES. No... By the way, La Bouzule, you old veteran, were you at the hearing?

LA BOUZULE. I stayed until the lawyers began to talk.

JUDGE OF THE ASSIZES. You did not see me overlook any ground for appeal, did you?

LA BOUZULE. I can't say that I did...

JUDGE OF THE ASSIZES. That is my bogy... that's all I can think of during the whole hearing.... I always keep the Judge's Handbook wide open before me, but I am always afraid of forgetting some formality.... Think of the effect at the Chancery. My mind is not easy until the time of limitation has elapsed.... (*Pause.*) They tell me there were reporters from Toulouse and Bordeaux present.

LA BOUZULE. And one from Paris.

JUDGE OF THE ASSIZES. One from Paris? Are you sure?

LA BOUZULE. He was standing up near the prisoners' bench.

JUDGE OF THE ASSIZES. Standing up! A reporter from Paris, and he had to stand? (*Noticing the* CLERK.) You knew it, and didn't tell me? Is that the way you do your duty? Go at once and present him my regrets and find him a good place, you understand?

CLERK. Yes, Judge. (*Starts to go out.*)

JUDGE OF THE ASSIZES (*running after him*). Look here! (*In a low voice.*) Try to find out if he is displeased.

CLERK. Yes, Judge.

JUDGE OF THE ASSIZES. And then... (*Meeting* MADAME BUNERAT *at the door.*) I beg your pardon, madame.

(*Goes out running, holding up his robe.*)

LA BOUZULE. When I was at Montpelier, I knew an old tenor who had the same anxiety at the beginning of his third season.

(*Enter* MOUZON; *cool bows.*)

MADAME BUNERAT (*after a silence*). Is it true, Monsieur Mouzon?...

MADAME VAGRET. ... That the Attorney-General...

BUNERAT. ... Has arrived at Mauléon?

MOUZON (*loftily*). Precisely...

BUNERAT. They say that he is bringing a Counsellor's appointment...

MOUZON. So they say!

MADAME BUNERAT. And you don't know?

MADAME VAGRET. You don't know?

MOUZON. Haven't the slightest idea.

CLERK (*entering*). Here comes the Attorney-General...

MADAME BUNERAT. Goodness!...                    (*Arranges her hair.*)

(*Enter the* ATTORNEY-GENERAL; *handsome, dignified, impressive bearing.*)

ALL (*bowing low, in a murmur*). Attorney-General...

ATTORNEY-GENERAL. I think you may go on with the hearing, gentlemen. I am only passing through Mauléon. I am planning to return before long and receive you all...

ALL. Oh, Attorney-General...            (*They prepare to go out.*)

ATTORNEY-GENERAL. Mouzon, will you stay a moment?

(MOUZON *bows.*)

MADAME VAGRET (*going out*). My respects, I am very honored, Attorney...

ATTORNEY-GENERAL (*bowing*). Judge, madame, madame...

BUNERAT (*to his wife*). You were right!            (*They go out.*)

MOUZON (*to the* CLERK *who starts to go out*). Well, Benoît, I think that my appointment is assured.

CLERK. I am very glad, Counsellor.            (*Goes out.*)

MOUZON (*obsequiously*). Attorney-General...

ATTORNEY-GENERAL. Be seated. (MOUZON *takes a chair.*) There has come to my office at Bordeaux a certain report which concerns you, Judge. (*Looking in his portfolio.*) Here it is. (*Reading.*) *Case of Mouzon and the Pecquet Girl.* Do you know anything about it?

MOUZON (*not taking the matter seriously and trying to smile.  After a long silence*).  Yes, Attorney-General.

ATTORNEY-GENERAL.  I await your explanations.

MOUZON (*as before*).  You were young once yourself, Attorney...

ATTORNEY-GENERAL.  Not in that way, Judge.

MOUZON.  I did go a little beyond bounds, I confess.

ATTORNEY-GENERAL (*reading*).  "Under the influence of liquor accompanied by the Pecquet girl and two other women of immoral life in the same condition Monsieur Mouzon insulted and abused the officers, whom he threatened with discharge." (*Speaking.*)  Is that what you call going a little beyond bounds?

MOUZON.  To tell the truth, the expression is a little weak...

ATTORNEY-GENERAL.  And you allow the name of a magistrate to figure in a police record in conjunction with that of the Pecquet girl?

MOUZON.  She said her name was Diana de Montmorency.

ATTORNEY-GENERAL (*continuing*).  "Questioned by me, Police Commissioner, the next morning, about his disguise as officer in the navy which he had adopted..."

(*Looks at* MOUZON *again; continued silence.*)

MOUZON (*still smiling*).  Yes, on account of my sidewhiskers...

ATTORNEY-GENERAL.  Indeed?

MOUZON.  When I... that is... when I go to Bordeaux, I always go in the character of officer in the navy in order to safeguard the dignity of the magistracy.

ATTORNEY-GENERAL.  Your solicitude is a little tardy.

MOUZON.  I will beg you to observe, Attorney, that my solicitude dated from the very beginning, since I took care to leave the district, and even the jurisdiction...

ATTORNEY-GENERAL.  To continue... "Monsieur Mouzon revealed to me his real identity as examining magistrate.  He made use of this title to request us to drop further proceedings..."

MOUZON.  The idiot!  Did he put that in his report?  The idea!  Didn't he know any better than that?  That's not it; I tell you, it is a question of politics; the Police Commissioner is one of our opponents.  I asked him... Well, anyway, I wanted to avoid a scandal — anyone would have done the same in my place...

ATTORNEY-GENERAL. Have you anything more to say?...

MOUZON. Anything more to say? Certainly, sir, if you wish to insist in this conversation on the relations of superior and subordinate, I have nothing more to say. If, on the other hand, you would deign to allow me to forget for a moment your lofty position, if you would consent to speak with me as man to man, I would add that it was a youthful escapade, an unfortunate incident, of course, but explicable by the profound *ennui* which rises from the streets of Mauléon. I admit, I had dined too well... there are a lot of decent people who find themselves in the same situation every evening.... It is a trifling matter which does not compromise the character of anyone.

ATTORNEY-GENERAL. Sir, when one has the honor to be a magistrate, when one has accepted the responsibility of judging one's fellow-men, he is in duty bound to observe more decorum, more dignity than anyone else. A thing which does not compromise the character of the one judged, does compromise the character of the judge. Let that be said once for all.

MOUZON. In view of the fact, Attorney, that you do not deign to treat with me on any other than an official footing, I can do nothing but request you to inform me of your decision.

ATTORNEY-GENERAL. Have you no idea?

MOUZON. I am examining magistrate. You will degrade me to the rank of simple judge — a decrease of five hundred francs per year. I accept.

ATTORNEY-GENERAL. Unfortunately, this simple solution will not suffice. To speak more clearly, I have to inform you that Coire, director of the paper which is most open in its hostility toward us, is cognizant of all the facts of which you are accused, and consents to withhold them only on condition that you leave Mauléon before the end of the month. I find myself, therefore, under the painful necessity of requesting your resignation.

MOUZON. I shall not give it.

ATTORNEY-GENERAL. You won't give it!

MOUZON. It grieves me greatly to be unable to comply with one of your desires, Attorney, but my mind is made up; I shall not resign.

ATTORNEY-GENERAL. Well... but... are you not aware...

MOUZON. I am aware of everything.

ATTORNEY-GENERAL. Well, sir, we should let the law take its course.                                              (*Rises.*)

MOUZON. Pray do!

ATTORNEY-GENERAL. Have you considered the scandal which will devolve upon you from your appearance before the court, from your probable conviction?

MOUZON. My conviction is not so probable as you seem to think. I am quite able to defend myself and to choose my counsel. As for the scandal, it is not upon me that it will devolve; — I am a bachelor without a family. I know no one, so to speak, at Mauléon — which has been to me hardly more than an exile. My friends are all at Bordeaux; they belong to the gay set, and I would not be disgraced in their eyes by the proceedings in question. Even if I have to leave the magistracy, I have, fortunately, enough to live on, over and above the three thousand francs which the State allows me each year.

ATTORNEY-GENERAL. That is sufficient. You may go.

MOUZON. I wish you a very good day, sir.          (*Goes out.*)

JANITOR (*comes in*). Mr. Attorney-General, the Deputy... he says you are expecting him.

ATTORNEY-GENERAL. Yes, I am. Ask him to come in.

(*Enter* MONDOUBLEAU. *The* ATTORNEY-GENERAL *rises to greet him and grasps his hand.*)

MONDOUBLEAU. How do you do, Attorney?

ATTORNEY-GENERAL. Quite well, Deputy, thank you; how are you?

MONDOUBLEAU. Delighted to see you. I am just in from Paris. I took dinner yesterday with my friend, the Keeper of the Seals... the Cabinet is a little worried just for the moment...

ATTORNEY-GENERAL. How's that?

MONDOUBLEAU. They fear an interpellation — at any moment, so to speak. I'll tell you about it some time.... By the way, they say you have a young Substitute here who is making a little too much stir...

ATTORNEY-GENERAL. Ardeuil?

MONDOUBLEAU. Ardeuil, that's it. Eugène is so well posted...

ATTORNEY-GENERAL. Eugène?

MONDOUBLEAU. Yes, my friend, Eugène, the Keeper of the Seals. He said to me: "I am relying on the Attorney-General to do his duty."

ATTORNEY-GENERAL. I ask nothing better, provided someone will tell me in what it consists...

MONDOUBLEAU. That is just what they want to avoid... By the way, you certainly do know how to keep your own counsel, don't you?

ATTORNEY-GENERAL. I? What do you mean?

MONDOUBLEAU. You are asking to be transferred...

ATTORNEY-GENERAL. Who told you that?

MONDOUBLEAU. The only one who knows it, of course... who did you think?

ATTORNEY-GENERAL. Eu... (*Quickly.*) The Keeper of the Seals?

MONDOUBLEAU. You desire to be appointed at Orléans... Am I correctly informed?

ATTORNEY-GENERAL. To tell the truth, we *do* have family there.

MONDOUBLEAU. I believe you are already on the slate.

ATTORNEY-GENERAL. Are changes already in consideration?

MONDOUBLEAU. Yes. Speaking of Monsieur Ardeuil — the Minister confined himself to saying that he had confidence in your firmness and zeal.

ATTORNEY-GENERAL. The Keeper of the Seals may rely upon me. I have to do a little pruning here in several directions and shall lack neither firmness nor zeal, I assure you.

MONDOUBLEAU. All right, but, above all, have tact! Eugène repeated it ten times: "Especially no scandals! No scandals! Just now less than ever.... We are being watched.... So, perfect quiet!"

ATTORNEY-GENERAL. Be assured.... It is a question of Mouzon.

MONDOUBLEAU. Mouzon... Mouzon... the examining magistrate?

ATTORNEY-GENERAL. Yes.

MONDOUBLEAU. Of Mauléon?

ATTORNEY-GENERAL. Exactly.

MONDOUBLEAU. You can't mean it.... He's one of my best friends. ... Exceedingly favorable to us.... A thoroughly good fellow! An excellent magistrate, energetic and discerning.... Why, I have even spoken of him to Eugène for the Counsellor's vacancy.

ATTORNEY-GENERAL (*handing him the papers concerning* MOUZON). You certainly chose a good time! Here are some papers which concern him. Anyway, the place is promised to Vagret.

MONDOUBLEAU. What's the trouble?

ATTORNEY-GENERAL. Just this: I shall have to report him to the Superior Council of the Magistracy or bring suit against him before the Court of Appeal.

MONDOUBLEAU. What has he done? —

ATTORNEY-GENERAL. Read it.

MONDOUBLEAU (*after having glanced at the papers which have been handed him*). Yes, I see... a matter of no consequence. At all events, if you keep quiet nobody will know anything about it. No scandal! The enemies of the magistracy are too active now, anyway, without our furnishing them ammunition.

ATTORNEY-GENERAL. Unfortunately Coire is aware of the facts and threatens to publish them unless Mouzon is removed from Mauléon...

MONDOUBLEAU. The devil... (*Commences to laugh.*)

ATTORNEY-GENERAL. What are you laughing at?

MONDOUBLEAU. Nothing — a fantastic idea... just a joke... (*Laughs.*) Listen — now don't get angry, will you... it's just a joke...

ATTORNEY-GENERAL. What is it?

MONDOUBLEAU. I was thinking... just a strange idea, of course... after all, if you should propose Mouzon for Counsellor at Pau, everybody would be satisfied...

ATTORNEY-GENERAL. But, Deputy....

MONDOUBLEAU. I told you I was only joking... it's only a jest... and the funny thing about it all is that you would be satisfying Coire, myself, Mouzon, and Eugène, who doesn't want any scandal, all of us at the same time...

ATTORNEY-GENERAL. But that would be a scandal...

MONDOUBLEAU. You are wrong there. In politics there is no scandal until the scandal is out.

ATTORNEY-GENERAL. But still...

MONDOUBLEAU. I quite agree with you. I know perfectly well all that may be said... I told you I was only joking... and do you know that the curious part of it, really, when you think it over, is that this extravagant solution is the only one which does not have evident and serious objections.... Certainly, if you leave Mouzon here, Coire will tell everything. If you bring suit against him, you will give to a certain press an occasion to undermine one of the bases of Society which it will be only glad to have. Exactly! — they will confound the whole magistracy with Mouzon... it will not be Mouzon, who will be the ribald, it will be the tribunal, the Court of Pau... there will be mud on every gown.

ATTORNEY-GENERAL. But you cannot be asking seriously...

MONDOUBLEAU. I tell you what let's do... let's go and talk it over with Rollet, the Senator; he lives only a step away.

ATTORNEY-GENERAL. I assure you...

MONDOUBLEAU. Oh, come on! You will drop a word about Orléans at the same time... what do you risk? I tell you my solution is the best.... You will come to it, believe me! I will take you over.... (*Takes him by the arm.*)

ATTORNEY-GENERAL. Well, I *did* have a word to say to him.

### (*Enter* CLERK.)

ATTORNEY-GENERAL. How far have they got? To the verdict?

CLERK. Not yet... Monsieur Vagret has just replied...

ATTORNEY-GENERAL. Are the jury out?

CLERK. No, Attorney-General... they were just going when Monsieur Vagret asked for an intermission.

MONDOUBLEAU. That's a great idea... anyway, let's be going, friend, you will come around...

ATTORNEY-GENERAL (*weakly*). Never, never!

CLERK (*deeply moved*). Wonderful!

JANITOR (*half opening the door at the rear*). Benoît, what's the news?

CLERK. Wonderful! Our prosecutor has just been magnificent... and that Etchepare is the lowest of the low...

(*Enter* MADAME VAGRET, *deeply moved*. CLERK *goes to her;* JANITOR *disappears.*)

MADAME VAGRET. Oh, dear me!

CLERK. Madame Vagret, I am only a clerk, but allow me to say that it was wonderful!

MADAME VAGRET. Wonderful.

CLERK. How Monsieur Vagret did give it to that Bordeaux lawyer.

MADAME VAGRET. Didn't he, though?

CLERK. It's settled now, the death penalty....

MADAME VAGRET. Without any doubt.

CLERK. Madame, the jurors kept looking at that Etchepare, the scoundrel, in a way that made me afraid — as Monsieur Vagret went on speaking you could feel that they would have liked to settle his case, themselves, the wretch!

MADAME VAGRET. Yes, I saw it!

CLERK. I beg your pardon, madame, I am forgetting myself, but there are times when one is so happy, so happy that differences in station don't count.

MADAME VAGRET. You are right, my good Benoît.

(*Enter* JUDGE OF THE ASSIZES *and* BUNERAT.)

JUDGE OF THE ASSIZES. Oh, madame, let me congratulate you. We have it this time — the death penalty...

MADAME VAGRET. Yes, Judge, we have it at last, haven't we?

JUDGE OF THE ASSIZES. Beyond a doubt... but where is the victor? He was simply sublime... wasn't he, Bunerat?

BUNERAT. Yes, Judge, but you had prepared the way so well, by the way you presided...

JUDGE OF THE ASSIZES. Oh, of course, I don't mean I had nothing to do with the result, but Vagret must be given credit. (*To* MADAME VAGRET.) You ought to be happy, very happy and very proud, my dear madame...

MADAME VAGRET. Oh, yes, Judge...

JUDGE OF THE ASSIZES. But what kind of an idea was it, anyhow, to ask for a recess?... Is he sick?

MADAME VAGRET. Oh!

JUDGE OF THE ASSIZES. No, here he is.

(*Enter* VAGRET. *He looks worried.*)

MADAME VAGRET. Oh, my dear!

(*Takes his hand in hers. She can say nothing more, overcome by her feelings.*)

JUDGE OF THE ASSIZES. It was wonderful!

BUNERAT. I really must congratulate you, too!

VAGRET. Really, you overwhelm me... you deserve all the credit, Judge.

JUDGE OF THE ASSIZES. Not at all... do you know what carried everything before it?... (*Lights a cigarette.*)

VAGRET. No.

JUDGE OF THE ASSIZES. It was when you exclaimed: "Gentlemen of the jury, you have homes, farms, property; you have wives whom you love, you have daughters whom you have tenderly nurtured... beware..." At that point you were grand! (*Going on.*) "Beware, if you allow yourselves to be misled by the eloquent sentimentality of the defense; beware, I say, if you prove unfaithful to your lofty rôle of dispensers of justice, lest One on high pick up the glaive fallen from your feeble hands and shower upon you and yours the blood which you shall have left unavenged!" That was sublime, and it produced a tremendous effect!

BUNERAT. But it was you, my dear Judge, who moved them most when, recalling quite opportunely that the accused loved the sight of blood...

JUDGE OF THE ASSIZES. Oh, yes, that did have some effect...

ALL. What? What was it?

BUNERAT. The Judge puts this question: "The morning of the crime did you not kill two sheep?" "Yes," the prisoner replies... and then the Judge looking him straight in the face...

JUDGE OF THE ASSIZES. Yes, I said to him: "You were practicing, weren't you?"... (*To* VAGRET.) Anyhow, if I did have something to do with the result, it is to you that the greater part of the honor of the day will fall.

VAGRET. You are too kind.

JUDGE OF THE ASSIZES. By no means... and your conclusion! (*With an artist's curiosity.*) You were really under the influence of a powerful emotion, of a very powerful emotion, weren't you?

VAGRET (*soberly*). Yes, under the influence of a very powerful emotion.

JUDGE OF THE ASSIZES. You became very pale as you looked at the jury and you added with your voice sunk almost to a whisper... "Gentlemen, I demand of you the head of this man!"

VAGRET (*with staring eyes*). Yes.

JUDGE OF THE ASSIZES. Then you made a sign to the counsel for the defense.

VAGRET. Yes, I thought he might have something to add…

JUDGE OF THE ASSIZES. But why delay the verdict? You had won the victory.

VAGRET. That was just the trouble.

JUDGE OF THE ASSIZES. What do you mean?

VAGRET. During my demand for punishment something took place which troubled me…

JUDGE OF THE ASSIZES. Troubled you?

BUNERAT. What was it?

VAGRET. It wasn't exactly anything… but… in short… (*Pause.*) Excuse me, I am very tired…

JUDGE OF THE ASSIZES. I understand your emotion very well, Vagret. One always has it at the time one wins his first death penalty… but… you'll see… you'll get used to it. (*Going out; to* BUNERAT.) It is true, he does seem tired…

BUNERAT. I think he is too sentimental for his place…

VAGRET. As I left the courtroom, I met the Attorney-General and asked him urgently to give me a moment's conversation — I would like to speak alone with him… and with you, Judge.

BUNERAT. As you like.

MADAME VAGRET. I am afraid you are not well, my dear.…. I will stay outside here and will come back as soon as the gentlemen have gone.

VAGRET. All right.

MADAME BUNERAT (*going out, to her husband*). I know somebody who is going to make a blunder.

BUNERAT. What do we care? (*They go out.*)

JUDGE OF THE ASSIZES. Can it be that you noticed anything out of order on my part in the judicial procedure?

VAGRET. No, if there was anything wrong, I am to blame.

(*Enter* ATTORNEY-GENERAL.)

ATTORNEY-GENERAL. What is there so serious, my dear Attorney?

VAGRET. It is this… I am worried beyond all power of expression … I need the consciences of both of you to reassure me…

ATTORNEY-GENERAL. Explain yourself...

VAGRET. A whole array of facts, the attitude of the prisoner, certain details which had escaped me, have aroused in my mind a doubt as to the guilt of this man.

ATTORNEY-GENERAL. Was there any indication of these facts, of these details in the papers on the case?

VAGRET. Certainly.

ATTORNEY-GENERAL. Did the attorney for the defense have access to these papers?

VAGRET. Of course.

ATTORNEY-GENERAL. Well, then, why this concern of yours?

VAGRET. But, supposing this man were not guilty?

ATTORNEY-GENERAL. The jury will decide. We have nothing to do, any of us, but bow to their decision.

VAGRET. Allow me to tell you, Attorney-General, how my conviction was shaken.

ATTORNEY-GENERAL. I don't care to know. All that is only a matter between you and your conscience. You have the right to set forth your scruples to the jury. You know the proverb — the pen is servile, speech is free.

VAGRET. I shall follow your advice.

ATTORNEY-GENERAL. I am not giving any advice.

VAGRET. I shall set forth my doubts to the jury.

ATTORNEY-GENERAL. That means acquittal.

VAGRET. I can't help it.

ATTORNEY-GENERAL (angrily). Do anything you like; but I must tell you one thing, my dear sir. Anyone planning such revolutionary proceedings generally has the courage to carry them out alone, and to accept the undivided responsibility of the follies which he may commit.... You are shrewder and have succeeded in finding the means of forcing others to share the consequences of your doubts...

VAGRET. I, shrewd? How?

ATTORNEY-GENERAL. Come, come, now, we're no children; I see plainly enough the trap into which you have led me. You have laid your responsibilities on another. If you are criticized at the Chancery for your attitude, you will reply that you consulted your superior and it is I who will be the victim... and there I am in difficulties with the Chancery. What do you care for my interests or for a situation which doesn't affect you? You get some notion or other into your head and you make me responsible for it in spite of myself. Once more, it is very shrewd of you, I compliment you, but I am not grateful...

VAGRET. You misunderstand me, Attorney-General; I have not the slightest intention of unloading upon you any responsibilities which I may incur.... It is certainly not at the moment that I expect to receive a Counsellor's appointment that I would be guilty of such an error.... I am telling you my trouble and asking you for advice, that is all.

JUDGE OF THE ASSIZES. Have you any proof?

VAGRET. If I had proof I wouldn't be asking for advice, would I? (*Silence.*) If we only had a ground for appeal — a good one...

JUDGE OF THE ASSIZES (*wrathfully*). What's that! Ground for appeal! Based on an oversight or an error on my part, I suppose! Well, you are ingenious, my dear Attorney.... You arrive at some doubt or other, and in order to obtain peace with your morbidly sensitive conscience, you invite me to be kind enough to commit an error! Really, that would be convenient — to unload errors which you may have committed on others who have done their duty...

ATTORNEY-GENERAL (*again self-possessed*). I quite agree.

JUDGE OF THE ASSIZES. And at the Chancery, speaking of me, they will say: "What kind of a Counsellor is this, anyhow, who is not even capable of presiding over an Assize session at Mauléon!" A man we have had such trouble to convict, too! And to sacrifice me to such a scoundrel! Oh, no! Find some other way, my dear sir; this is not the one for you, take my word for it!

VAGRET. Then I shall find some other way, but I shall not leave the situation as it is.

ATTORNEY-GENERAL. I don't care what you do! Only don't forget that I have given you no advice one way or another.

VAGRET. I recognize that.

JUDGE OF THE ASSIZES. When you make up your mind to go on with the hearing, please let us know.

VAGRET. I will.

ATTORNEY-GENERAL (*to the* JUDGE *of the* ASSIZES). Shall we be going?... (*They go out.*)

MADAME VAGRET (*enters*). What's the trouble?

VAGRET. Nothing.

MADAME VAGRET. Nothing! Why are you so depressed in spite of a success which will mean so much in your career?

VAGRET. It's this very success that frightens me.

MADAME VAGRET. Frightens you?

VAGRET. Yes, I am afraid.

MADAME VAGRET. Of what?

VAGRET. Of having gone too far.

MADAME VAGRET. Too far! Doesn't he deserve death a hundred times, the murderer?

VAGRET (*after a silence*). Are you sure that he is a murderer?

MADAME VAGRET. Yes.

VAGRET (*in a low tone*). Well, I...

MADAME VAGRET. What?

VAGRET. For myself, I don't know what to think...

MADAME VAGRET. Good Heavens!

VAGRET. Yes, there occurred within me during the course of my demand for the penalty a terrible thing.... While I, representative of the State, while I, Official Prosecutor, was performing my duty, another judgment within me was examining the case with coolness; an inner voice was reproaching me for my violence and was insinuating into my mind a doubt which increased — there took place in my soul a grievous combat, a bitter combat, and a cruel one... that emotion as I closed of which the judge spoke, that low voice with which I demanded the penalty, was because I had reached the end of my strength; it was because, in this combat, my conscience was on the point of winning the day — and I hastened to finish because I was afraid that its voice would burst out in spite of me. When I saw the counsel for the defense remain seated without rising to say the things that I would have liked to have him say to the jury... then I was truly afraid of myself, afraid of my acts, of my words, of their horrible consequences, and I wanted to gain time...

MADAME VAGRET. But, my dear, you have done your duty; the

counsel for the defense has not done his — that is no concern of yours.

VAGRET. That same reply! If I were an honest man, in a few moments, at the reopening of the hearing, I would tell the jury of the doubt which has taken possession of me. I would explain how it arose in me.... I would call their attention to a point which I deliberately kept back because I thought that the prisoner's counsel would point it out to them.

MADAME VAGRET. You know, dear, how I respect your scruples, but I must call your attention to this fact: Etchepare will not be pronounced innocent or guilty by you, but by the jury. If anyone ought to be worried, it is Placat, not you...

VAGRET. I ought to represent justice!

MADAME VAGRET. Here you have a prisoner who comes before you with a record of previous convictions, with a whole mass of overwhelming circumstances which confirm his guilt. He is defended; by whom? By a leader in the profession, famous for his integrity as well as for his skill and oratorical talent. You expound the facts to the jury. If the jury decides in your favor, I don't see how your responsibility as a magistrate is compromised.

VAGRET. As a magistrate, perhaps not; as a man, certainly. No! I have no right to be silent... no right! I tell you, there is in this case a series of circumstances of which no one has spoken and of such a kind as to make me believe in the innocence of the accused.

MADAME VAGRET. But how is it you overlooked these circumstances until now?

VAGRET (with lowered head). Do you think that I did overlook them? In the name of Heaven, do I dare tell you all? I am not a wicked man; I wouldn't have anyone suffer through my fault, would I? Well... oh, how ashamed am I to confess it, to say it openly after having confessed it to myself! Well, as I studied the case, I had my mind so firmly made up in advance that Etchepare was guilty that when an argument in his favor presented itself to me, I rejected it with a shrug of the shoulders. As to the facts of which I am speaking, and from which my doubt rose... I at first simply tried to prove to myself that they were false, choosing in the depositions of the witnesses only what served to disprove them, repudiating all the rest with a horrible unquestioning simplicity in my bad faith... and at last, in order to dissipate my final scruples, I said to myself, as you are doing now — "It is the concern of the defense, not mine!" Listen! Just see to what extent the exercise of the profession of magistrate deforms us, makes us unjust and cruel: At first I had a feeling of joy when I saw the Judge in his examination leave all these little facts in the background! That's the trade! Do you understand, the trade! Oh, poor creatures that we are, poor creatures!

MADAME VAGRET. Perhaps the jury will not convict.

VAGRET. They will, though.

MADAME VAGRET. They may take into account extenuating circumstances.

VAGRET. No. I insisted too urgently on the contrary. How I insisted! How violent I was!

MADAME VAGRET. True.... Why did you speak with such passion?

VAGRET. Ah, why! why! For a long time before the hearing it was so well understood by everybody that the prisoner was guilty! And how they had turned my head, how they had intoxicated me! I was the voice of humanity, I was to make the public highways safe, make the family secure, and I don't know what. Then I felt that I must rise to what was expected of me. My first demand for the penalty had been comparatively moderate ... but when I saw the celebrated lawyer make the jurors weep, I thought I was lost; I felt that I was losing my grip on the accusation, and, contrary to my custom, I replied. When I rose the second time I was like a fighter who has caught a glimpse of defeat and who struggles with despair. From that moment Etchepare no longer existed for me, so to speak. I no longer was concerned with the defense of Society nor with the support of the accusation, I was struggling with the attorney; it was a contest of orators, a competition between comedians — I must come out victorious at any price. I must convince the jury, win it back again, wrest from them the two "Ayes" of the verdict. It was no longer a question of Etchepare, I tell you, it was a question of myself, of my vanity, of my reputation, of my honor, of my future.... It is shameful, I repeat, it is shameful!

At all hazards, I wished to prevent the acquittal which I felt was certain. And I was so afraid of not succeeding that I employed every argument, both good and bad, even to picturing to the terrified jury their houses in flames, their dear ones murdered... I spoke of the vengeance of God upon indulgent judges. And all that with a clear conscience — or rather absolutely unconsciously, in the heat of passion and in the heat of anger against the lawyer whom I hated then with all my power. My success went beyond my wishes; the jury is ready to obey me, and, my dear, I have allowed myself to be congratulated, I have taken the hands which were held out to me.... That's what a magistrate is!

MADAME VAGRET. Don't take it so seriously — there aren't, perhaps, ten men in France who would have done otherwise.

VAGRET. You are right. But, when you think of it, that is precisely what is so terrible.

CLERK (entering). Attorney, the Judge wants to know when the hearing may be resumed.

VAGRET. At once.

MADAME VAGRET. What are you going to do?

VAGRET. What a man of honor ought to do. (Prepares to go out.)

## ACT IV

### Setting as in Act II.

(BUNERAT, JUDGE OF THE ASSIZES, then VAGRET.)

BUNERAT. Well, there's another session over.

JUDGE OF THE ASSIZES (wearing a red gown). I was scared to death for fear those animals would make me miss my train... you see I am going hunting tomorrow on the Cambo lakes, and after this evening's train it's all off! (Looking at his watch.) Oh, I have still an hour and a half...

BUNERAT. What do you think of it, Judge?

JUDGE OF THE ASSIZES. Of what? The verdict? What do you suppose I care? In fact, I prefer it that way: I am sure that the defense will not dig up some unexpected error in procedure.... Where is my hat-box?

(Climbs on a chair to reach the hat-box which is on top of a wardrobe. BUNERAT anticipates him.)

BUNERAT. Allow me, Judge! You are our guest. (*From the chair.*) I'm afraid I'll have the pleasure of receiving you here again at the next session. (*Sighs, handing down the hat-box.*)

JUDGE OF THE ASSIZES. The pleasure will be mine....

(*Takes from the hat-box a small round hat.*)

BUNERAT. Do you want a brush?... There is Mouzon's... (*Sigh.*) Oh, Lord, when shall I ever leave Mauléon? I would so much like to live at Pau!

JUDGE OF THE ASSIZES. Pshaw! It is a much over-rated town, believe me....

BUNERAT. So, then, new duties don't take me there yet?

JUDGE OF THE ASSIZES. That's nothing! It is a good enough place in the winter... but the summers — goodness, what summers!

BUNERAT. So I did not get the appointment?

JUDGE OF THE ASSIZES. Ah, you know it already?

BUNERAT. Yes — I... that is, I did not know that it was official.

JUDGE OF THE ASSIZES (*brushing his hat and noticing a dent*). It is already dented. Nowadays, the hats they sell you for felt are nothing but pasteboard.

BUNERAT. That's so. No, I didn't know that it was official.... Mouzon is very fortunate....

(*Enter* VAGRET *in citizen's dress.*)

JUDGE OF THE ASSIZES. Well, well, here is Vagret. Already dressed! Yes, you are at home, while I must pack all this up.... Where in the devil is my robe-box? (BUNERAT *starts to get it for him, but stops.*) That's strange, what has become of it... in this wardrobe.... You haven't seen it, have you, Bunerat?

BUNERAT. No.

JUDGE OF THE ASSIZES. Ah, here it is... and my coat in it... (*Opens the box and takes out his cutaway which he puts beside the table.*) Well, you made them acquit him, my dear sir; are you satisfied?

VAGRET. Yes. I am very glad.

JUDGE OF THE ASSIZES. But suppose they were guilty?

VAGRET. I shall console myself with that saying from Berryer: "It is better to let ten guilty men go free than to punish one who is innocent."

JUDGE OF THE ASSIZES. You are sentimental.

VAGRET. Must one have a heart of stone to be a magistrate?

JUDGE OF THE ASSIZES (*tying up the box where he has put his judge's cap*). One must rise above the petty misfortunes of mankind.

VAGRET. That is, above the misfortunes of others...

JUDGE OF THE ASSIZES. Oh, well....

VAGRET. That's what I call selfishness.

JUDGE OF THE ASSIZES. Do you mean that for me?

VAGRET. For all three of us.

BUNERAT. Good-day, gentlemen... Good-day!

(*Shakes hands with both and goes out.*)

JUDGE OF THE ASSIZES (*taking off his robe*). My dear Attorney, I must ask you to be a little more careful in your choice of words.

VAGRET. I assure you, Judge, I am careful.... If I should speak out what is in my heart, you would hear some very disagreeable things.

JUDGE OF THE ASSIZES (*in his shirt-sleeves*). Do not forget to whom you are speaking. I am Counsellor at the Court, Mr. Attorney.

VAGRET. I am not speaking simply with reference to you, sir. The disagreeable things which I might say would condemn me also. I am thinking of those poor people...

JUDGE OF THE ASSIZES (*brushing his robe*). What poor people? The prisoners of this afternoon? Well, they are acquitted; what more do you want — give them pensions?

VAGRET. They were acquitted, it is true, but they have been sentenced for all that. They have been sentenced to misery for their natural lives...

JUDGE OF THE ASSIZES. What are you talking about?

VAGRET. And it was your fault, too, Judge.

JUDGE OF THE ASSIZES (*stopping in the midst of folding up his robe*). My fault?

VAGRET. And the worst of it is that you didn't even see the harm you did!

JUDGE OF THE ASSIZES. What harm have I done, pray?

VAGRET. Well, when you disclosed to Etchepare that his wife had once been convicted of complicity in theft and that she had been seduced before he married her... that was really too bad of you!

JUDGE OF THE ASSIZES. Don't be so quixotic! Do you think he didn't know it?

VAGRET. If you had seen his emotion when his wife replied "yes," when you asked if it were so, you would be as convinced as I that he didn't know anything about it.

JUDGE OF THE ASSIZES (*closing the box where he has put his robe*). Well, even so; you are ascribing to people like that feelings which they don't possess.

VAGRET. "People like that" have hearts as well as we, Judge.

JUDGE OF THE ASSIZES. Let's grant it.... Didn't my duty compel me to do what I did?

VAGRET. That's not for me to say.

JUDGE OF THE ASSIZES (*still in his shirt-sleeves*). Is the law at fault, then? Well, sir! If I did my duty, as I did, you are certainly not doing yours in attacking the law, whose faithful servant you are and which I am proud to represent.

VAGRET. You needn't be!

JUDGE OF THE ASSIZES. Sir!

VAGRET. It's an atrocity, I tell you, that it is permitted to throw up to a prisoner, innocent or guilty, a fault which he committed ten years before and which he has expiated. Yes, sir, it is revolting that after having punished, the law does not pardon.

JUDGE OF THE ASSIZES (*who has put on his coat and hat*). If you find that the law is bad, have it changed... run for Deputy at the next elections.

VAGRET. Alas!... If I were Deputy, I should probably do as the others do, and instead of thinking of that, I would be thinking of nothing but the probable duration of the Cabinet.

JUDGE OF THE ASSIZES (*with his box under his arm*). In that case, of course — is the janitor...

VAGRET (*ringing the bell*). He will be right here. — So Mouzon is appointed in my place?

JUDGE OF THE ASSIZES. Yes; Mouzon.

VAGRET. Because he is the henchman of a Deputy, of a Mondoubleau —

JUDGE OF THE ASSIZES. I shall not allow you to speak ill of Monsieur Mondoubleau before me...

VAGRET. You imagine you may need him...

JUDGE OF THE ASSIZES. Precisely. (JANITOR *appears*.) Will you carry that for me to my hotel, my good man? — the hotel near the station.... You will recognize it easily; my orderly is at the door... (*Gives him his boxes.*)　Good-day, Vagret — I don't bear you any grudge.

(*Goes out.* VAGRET *puts on his hat and also prepares to go out.*)

(*The* CLERK *comes in.*)

CLERK. You are going, sir?

VAGRET. Yes.

CLERK. Do you have any objections to my letting Etchepare come in here?　He is waiting, in the hall, for the formalities of release and complains of being exposed to public curiosity.

VAGRET. Let him come in, by all means.

CLERK. Shall I tell them to bring his wife here, too, when she comes from the office.

VAGRET. Certainly.

CLERK. I shall tell the officers, but the wife cannot be released immediately...

VAGRET. Why not?

CLERK. She is held on another complaint.　She is accused of insulting a magistrate in the exercise of his functions.

VAGRET. Mouzon?

CLERK. Yes, your honor.

VAGRET. I will try to arrange that.

CLERK. Good-day, your honor.

VAGRET. Good-day.　　　　　　　　　　　　　(*Goes out.*)

CLERK (*at the door*). Come in, Etchepare.　You will like it better here while you are waiting for your definite release... it won't be long.

ETCHEPARE. Thank you, sir.

CLERK. Well, at last you are acquitted, my poor man!　It is over at last.

ETCHEPARE. It is over as far as the trial is concerned, sir, but it is not over for me.　I am acquitted, it is true, but for me it's all up now!

CLERK. You didn't know?

ETCHEPARE. No, sir.

CLERK. It was so long ago... you will forgive her...

ETCHEPARE. A Basque never forgives those things... it was like a thunderbolt falling on my heart... and all our trouble has come to us because of her.... God has avenged himself... all is lost.

CLERK (*after a pause*). I feel for you from the bottom of my heart.

ETCHEPARE. Thank you, sir... (*A pause.*) Since you are so kind, sir, will you let my mother, who is waiting outside in the hall, come in and speak to me?

CLERK. I will send her in to you. Good-bye.

ETCHEPARE. Good-bye. (CLERK *goes out.*)

(*The* MOTHER *comes in.*)

ETCHEPARE (*pressing his mother's head to his breast*). My poor old mother, how the grief of these three months has changed you!...

MOTHER. My poor child, how you must have suffered!

ETCHEPARE. That woman!

MOTHER. Yes, they have just told me.

ETCHEPARE. For ten years I have lived with that thief... with that wench! How well she could lie! Ah! When I heard that Judge say to her: "You were sentenced for theft in complicity with your lover," and when before all the public she confessed... do you know, mother, I thought Heaven was falling on my head... and when she acknowledged that she had been the mistress of that man... I don't know what did happen after that! Nor whom I would have liked to kill — the Judge who was saying those things with such indifference; or her, who was acknowledging them with her head turned away from me... I almost felt like confessing myself guilty in spite of my innocence, in order not to know any more about it, in order to be freed... but I thought of you and the children!... (*A long silence.*) Come! We must decide what to do... did you leave them at home?

MOTHER. No, I had to send them away to our cousin at Bayonne; we have no home now, nor anything else, we are ruined... Anyway, it got so I couldn't stand it here... the women turned aside and crossed themselves when I met them; at church they left me all alone in the middle of an empty space.... Already I had been obliged to take the children out of school...

ETCHEPARE. Good God!

MOTHER. No one spoke to them any more. One day George

provoked the biggest boy in the school; they had a fight, and as George was the stronger, the other to get even called him a murderer's son.

ETCHEPARE. And George...

MOTHER. He came home crying and refused to go out of the house again. It is then that I sent them to Bayonne.

ETCHEPARE. I'll tell you what we will do. Go there and get them. Tomorrow or this evening I will meet you. There are emigration offices for America there. They will take the four of us and trust us for the tickets on account of the children.

MOTHER. And if they ask for their mother?

ETCHEPARE (*after a pause*). You will tell them, she is dead.

(*Enter* YANETTA *whom someone brings to the door.*)

YANETTA (*as the door is being closed*). Yes, sir.

MOTHER (*without looking at* YANETTA). Well, I am going.

ETCHEPARE (*also without looking at* YANETTA). Well, I shall meet you either here this evening or there tomorrow.

MOTHER. All right.

ETCHEPARE. As soon as you get there, you will inquire about the day and hour...

MOTHER. Very well.

ETCHEPARE. Until tomorrow.

MOTHER. All right. (*Goes out without a glance at* YANETTA.)

YANETTA (*takes a few steps toward her husband, falls on her knees and clasps her hands. In a low voice*). Forgive me!

ETCHEPARE. Never!

YANETTA. No, don't say that!

ETCHEPARE. Did the Judge lie?

YANETTA. No, the Judge did not lie.

ETCHEPARE. You are a bad woman!

YANETTA. Yes, I am a bad woman, forgive me!

ETCHEPARE. Forgive you! I would like to kill you!

YANETTA. Yes, yes, but forgive me!

ETCHEPARE. You are nothing but a wench, a Paris wench without shame or morals!

YANETTA. Yes, insult me, strike me!

ETCHEPARE. You have lived a lie to me for ten years!

YANETTA. Oh! How I wanted to tell you all! Oh! How many times I commenced that terrible confession! I never had the courage, Pierre; I was always afraid of your anger and of the pain I would cause you.... You were so happy!

ETCHEPARE. You came back fresh from vice, just out of prison, and took me for your victim...

YANETTA. And to think that he believes that, my God!

ETCHEPARE. You came to me — the leavings of a thief... and you stole in my house the place of a good woman.... Your lie has brought the curse of God on my family and you are the cause of it all. The misfortune which has just stricken us was caused by you, I tell you! You leper! Accursed! Damned! Don't talk to me any more! Don't talk to me any more!

YANETTA. Won't you have pity, Pierre? Do you think that I don't suffer!

ETCHEPARE. If you do you deserve it! What had I done to you that you should choose me for your victim? What have I done to suffer as I do? You have made a coward of me! You have degraded me almost to your own level; I ought already to have succeeded in putting you out of my head and my heart! And I cannot! And I suffer terribly... for I suffer in the love which I bore you... You! You have been all in my life for ten years... you have been all, all!... And I have nothing but one hope left — to forget you!

YANETTA. Forgive me!

ETCHEPARE. Never, never!

YANETTA. Don't say that... it is only God who has the right to say that. I will come back to your house; I shall only be the first of the servants... the most humble, if you wish! I shall not take my place at the fireside until you tell me to...

ETCHEPARE. We haven't any fireside, we haven't any home... we have nothing now! And I repeat it, it is all your fault... and it is because you used to sit there in the place of the mother, of my mother, you! false and faithless! that misfortune has fallen upon us!

YANETTA. I swear to you that I will make you forget all that by my humility, my devotion, and my repentance... and wherever you go I shall follow you; Pierre, reflect, your children still need me...

ETCHEPARE. My children! You shall never see them again! Nor speak to them! I won't have you kiss them, nor even touch them!

YANETTA (*changing her tone*). Not that! Not that! The children? You are mistaken there! Ah, no! Deprive me of all, condemn me to every shame, force me to beg my bread — I am quite willing! Don't even look at me, don't speak to me except to insult me... anything you like... but my children! My children! They belong to me: they came from my womb; they are still a part of me... and always, always will be my flesh and blood.... You can cut off one of my arms — it would be a dead thing and not a part of me... but you can't keep my children from being my children...

ETCHEPARE. You have made yourself unworthy of keeping them...

YANETTA. Unworthy! Don't talk that to me! Have I ever failed in my duties toward them? Have I been a bad mother? Answer! I haven't, have I? Well, if I haven't been a bad mother, my rights upon my children remain entire and absolute! Unworthy! I could be a thousand times more guilty! More unworthy, as you say, and still neither you, nor the law, nor priests, nor God would have the right to take them from me.... As a woman I may have been guilty — it is possible... as mother, nobody can accuse me of anything.... Well, then! Well, then! They cannot be stolen from me... and you who have this project... you are a scoundrel! Yes! Yes! To avenge yourself you wish to take them from me! You coward! You are only a man! Father! You don't know what the word means! You have no thought for your children.... Yes! Yes! You lie, I tell you! When you say that I am unworthy of bringing them up, you lie! Those are only words, words! You know it is not true; you know well enough that I have nourished them, cared for them, loved them, counseled them, and that I used to have them say their prayers every evening and that I would continue.... You know well that no woman could fill my place with them... but what do you care for all that! You forget them... you want to punish me and so you are going to take them from me.... I have the right to tell you that it is

cowardly and mean and is only a horrible vengeance! Ah! Ah!
The children! Now he wants to lug them in!! No! Take
them from me? Ah, just think, Pierre, it is impossible, what
you are saying!

ETCHEPARE. You have spoken truly — I am avenging myself!
What you say is impossible is already done. My mother has
taken the children and has gone off with them.

YANETTA. I will find them again.

ETCHEPARE. America is large.

YANETTA. I shall find them again!

ETCHEPARE. Then, I shall tell them why I took them from you.

YANETTA. Never! That, never! I will obey you, but swear to me…

(*Enter the* CLERK.)

CLERK. Come and sign your release, Etchepare. You will be
released at once.

YANETTA. Wait, sir, wait! (*To* ETCHEPARE.) I accept the separa-
tion since I must… I will disappear…. You will never hear of
me again. But, in return for this atrocious sacrifice, swear to
me a solemn oath that you will never tell them…

ETCHEPARE. I swear it…

YANETTA. You swear never to tell them a word which might
diminish their affection for me?

ETCHEPARE. I swear it…

YANETTA. Promise me also — I implore you, Pierre, in the name
of our happiness, and of my suffering — promise me to keep
alive in them the memory of their mother… you will have them
pray for me, won't you?

ETCHEPARE. I swear it to you…

YANETTA. Then go, my life is over….

ETCHEPARE. Good-bye.

(*Goes out with the* CLERK. *On the threshold of the door the latter
meets* MOUZON.)

CLERK (*to* ETCHEPARE). They will show you the way out…

CLERK. The Etchepare woman is here…

MOUZON. So she is here! Vagret has just spoken to me of her.
Well, I withdraw my complaint; I ask nothing better than to
release her. Now that I am Counsellor, I have no desire to

come back from Pau every week for the examination. Proceed with the necessary formalities. (*To* YANETTA.) Well, in consideration of the disciplinary confinement which you have undergone, I am willing to release you provisionally... perhaps I shall even withdraw my complaint if you apologize for having insulted me...

YANETTA. I do not regret having insulted you.

MOUZON. Do you want to go back to prison?

YANETTA. Ah, my poor man, if you only knew how little I care for your prison!

MOUZON. How so?

YANETTA. Because I have nothing left, neither house nor home, nor husband nor children. (*Looks at him.*) And it occurs to me, the more I think of it...

MOUZON. What?

YANETTA. That it is you who are the cause of all the trouble.

MOUZON. You have both of you been acquitted, haven't you? What more do you want?

YANETTA. Yes, we have been acquitted, it is true. But now, for my husband, for my children, for everybody, I am a bad woman just the same.

MOUZON. If anyone throws up to you your former conviction, if anyone makes allusion to your disciplinary detention, you have the right to prosecute the slanderer before the law. He will be punished.

YANETTA. Well! It is because someone has thrown up to me my conviction that my husband has taken away my children... this someone is a judge — can I have him sentenced?

MOUZON. No.

YANETTA. Why? Because he is a magistrate?

MOUZON. No. Because it is the law.

YANETTA. The law! (*Violently.*) Well! Your law is contemptible.

MOUZON. Come, now, no shrieks, nor insults, please. (*To the* CLERK.) Are you through? Then go to the office and get an order for her release.

YANETTA. For me I am not learned: I have not studied the law as you have out of books, and perhaps for that very reason I know what is just and what is not. And I have come to ask you simply this: How does the law propose to give me back my children and undo the wrong it has done me?

MOUZON. The law is not beholden to you.

YANETTA. Not beholden to me? Then what are you going to do about it? You, the judge?

MOUZON. A magistrate is not responsible.

YANETTA. Ah, you are not responsible! Then you could, just for a whim, arrest people, on a shadow of suspicion, even without suspicion; you might bring shame and dishonor on whole families, torture the unhappy, dig down deep into their existence, parade their misfortunes, bring to light forgotten and expiated faults, faults which go back ten years; you might, by your cunning, your tricks, your lies, and your cruelty, send a man to the foot of the scaffold, and what is worse, rob a mother of her little ones! And after that, like Pontius Pilate, you would say and would believe that you were not responsible! Not responsible! Before your law, you may not be responsible, as you say, but before justice itself, before the justice of decent people, before God's own justice, I swear to you that you are responsible and that is why I have come to bring you to account!

*(Sees upon the desk of* MOUZON, *whose back is turned, the dagger used as a paper-cutter. Seizes it and lays it down again.)*

MOUZON. I order you to go.

YANETTA. Listen to me... for the last time, I ask you what you are going to do to relieve me, to return to me all that I have lost through your fault; what are you going to do to lessen my anguish, and how do you propose to get my children back for me?

MOUZON. I have nothing to say to you; I owe you nothing.

YANETTA. You owe me nothing! You owe me more than life, more than everything... My children... I shall never see them... what you have taken from me is the happiness of every minute, it is their kisses every evening, it is the pride which I had in watching them grow. Never, never again, shall I hear them say mamma! It is as if they were dead! It is just the same as if you had killed them. *(Seizes the knife.)* Yes! Now look at your work, all you wicked judges: Of an innocent man you almost made a criminal, and of an honest woman, of a mother, you have made a murderess. *(Strikes him; he falls.)*

# A DREAM PLAY

## By AUGUST STRINDBERG

*Translated by C. D. LOCOCK*

*Reprinted by permission of The Anglo-Swedish Literary Foundation.*

# AUGUST STRINDBERG

ONE of the great geniuses of our time, a man whose imaginative force always hewed fresh paths, in whichever direction it might turn, August Strindberg, dramatist, novelist, poet, was born at Stockholm, Sweden, January 22, 1849. After a youth spent in poverty he managed to get some education at Upsala University and to enter upon the life of a teacher. Befriended by a doctor he then took a course in medicine but never practiced, turning rather to journalism at Stockholm, and in 1874 to work in the Royal Library. Strindberg's entire career is marked and clouded by pathological obsessions which become increasingly the fabric of his work itself. The first is associated with his humble heredity as the son of a serving-woman; the second is associated with an intense and perverse amativism. Strindberg wrote fifty-six plays of a great variety of types from one-acters to trilogies, including historical, biographical, fairy and religious plays, and plays of an extreme naturalism and didacticism. His first play, *Hermione*, written in 1869, was a tragedy in verse. *In Rome*, a play in one act, was performed in 1870. *Master Olof*, one of the great historical plays of modern times, was based on the life of the Swedish reformer, Petri. This was rewritten several times. Strindberg's later years were marked by mental aberration if not insanity. Many of his later plays, works of sheer originality and pure inspiration, were produced in the Intimate Theatre, established by August Falck. Strindberg became interested in this theatre and made it his own. As innovator, during his later years, in experimental types of dramatic composition, Strindberg exercised an influence that can not now be estimated. Strindberg died in 1912.

# A DREAM PLAY

THE concept of life as a dream is found in Calderon. Disjointed and dissolving scenes are found in Chinese and Hindu drama. Modern psychology has investigated the field of the subconscious and the unconscious. All these may have influenced Strindberg but it is safer to assume that *A Dream Play* is the product of his own genius. Obsessed as he was with persistent intangible forces Strindberg early seeks to dramatize these in his plays, at first introducing them as overtones and intimations in a naturalistic action. Eventually he centers all his interest in this other-worldly zone, seeking to interpret it by a dramaturgy that cuts itself off completely from the models of experience and convention. *A Dream Play* may perhaps serve as the most intelligible model among these essays into dramatic metaphysics. Repeating Prospero's lines,

> " These our actors,
> As I foretold you, were all spirits, and
> Are melted into air, into thin air;
> ...we are such stuff
> As dreams are made on, and our little life
> Is rounded with a sleep,"

Strindberg seeks to sum up in this play his own experience. He believes he is with Shakespeare not only in presenting life as a dream but in an adherence to the Buddhist philosophy. In the play there was only one central character, the Daughter of India, who descends to earth to live human existence and through whose perceptions the action is followed. The substance of the play is autobiographical. The Officer, prisoner in a chateau, is a figure from *The Son of a Servant* and from *The Road to Damascus*. He is the lover eternally deceived. The background is a panorama of the regions that Strindberg had visited. The critical commentary offers a transcript of institutional and scientific life seen through Strindberg's imagination. *A Dream Play* offers one of the supreme opportunities to the imagination of the producer. First presented at Stockholm in 1907, the play was produced at the Provincetown Theatre in New York in January, 1926, and by the new Scandinavian Theatre established in London in 1933.

## AUTHOR'S NOTE

IN THIS Dream Play, as in his earlier one *To Damascus*, the Author has tried to imitate the disjointed but apparently logical form of a dream. Anything may happen: everything is possible and probable. Time and space do not exist; on an insignificant groundwork of reality imagination spins and weaves new patterns: a mixture of memories, experiences, unfettered fancies, absurdities and improvisations.

The characters are split, doubled and multiplied: they evaporate and are condensed, are diffused and concentrated. But a single consciousness holds sway over them all — that of the dreamer; for him there are no secrets, no inconsequences, no scruples and no law. The dreamer neither condemns nor acquits: he merely relates; and since a dream is usually painful, less frequently cheerful, a tone of melancholy, of sympathy with all that lives, runs through the swaying narrative. Sleep, the liberator, often plays a painful part, but when the pain is at its fiercest comes the awakening to reconcile the sufferer with reality, which, however agonizing it be, is at that moment a joy compared with the excruciating dream.

# PROLOGUE

*The background represents cloud-domes resembling demolished slate-cliffs, with ruins of castles and fortresses.*

*The constellations Leo, Virgo and Libra are visible, and shining brightly among them is the planet Jupiter.*

(INDRA'S DAUGHTER *is standing on the topmost cloud.*)

INDRA'S VOICE (*from above*).   Where art thou, Daughter, where?
INDRA'S DAUGHTER.   Here, Father, here!
VOICE.   Thou'rt gone astray, my child; give heed, thou sinkest...
  How cam'st thou hither?
DAUGHTER.   From the high Ether on the lightning's track I came,
  A storm-cloud for my chariot...
  But the cloud sank, and now my course is downward...
  Tell me, O mighty Father, Indra, to what regions
  I now am come? so close the air,
  So hard to breathe!
VOICE.   Leaving the second sphere thou camest to the third.
  From Çucra, Star of Morning,
  Far art thou come, and enterest now
  Earth's atmosphere; there take thou note
  Of the Sun's Seventh House — 'tis called the Scales —
  Where the Day's Star presides at Autumn's weighing,
  And day and night are equal...
DAUGHTER.   Thou speakest of the Earth — is it that dark
  That ponderous world that's lighted by the moon?
VOICE.   Of all the globes through space that wander
  It is the heaviest and densest.
DAUGHTER.   And doth the Sun shine never there?
VOICE.   Yea, the Sun shines thereon, but not unceasing...
DAUGHTER.   A rift is in the cloud.   I see down there...
VOICE.   What see'st thou, child?
DAUGHTER.   I see... that Earth is fair... I see green forests,
  Blue waters and white peaks and yellow fields...
VOICE.   Yes, it is fair, as all that Brahma made...

Yet fairer still it was in the first dawn
Of Time; then something happened — maybe some
Displacement of the orbit, some revolt
Followed by crime, which could not pass unchecked...

DAUGHTER. Now I hear sounds arising thence...
What folk are they that have their dwelling there?

VOICE. Descend and see... Of Brahma's children I would speak
No ill, but what thou hearest is their language.

DAUGHTER. It sounds like... nay, it hath no cheerful ring.

VOICE. So I could well believe! their mother-tongue
Is called Complaint. Truly a discontented,
A thankless generation is this earthly...

DAUGHTER. Nay, say not so! for now come shouts of joy,
And shots and din, and lightning flashes,
And bells are ringing, fires are kindled;
And hark! a thousand thousand voices
Singing their praise and thanks to heaven...

(*A pause.*)

Thou art too hard on them, my Father...

VOICE. Descend and see, and hear; then come again
And tell me if this voice of their complaint
And lamentation has just cause...

DAUGHTER. So be it: I descend! but come with me!

VOICE. Nay, for I cannot breathe their air...

DAUGHTER. Now sinks the cloud: 'tis stifling, I feel choked...
It is not air, 'tis smoke and water that I breathe...
So dense, it drags me downward, downward:
Even now I can discern its lurching:
Surely this third of spheres is not the highest...

VOICE. The highest, nay! yet is it not the lowest;
Dust is it called, goes whirling round like all the others,
Whence dizziness at times infects its people,
Hovering 'twixt folly and the bounds of madness. —
Courage, my Daughter! this is but a trial.

DAUGHTER (*on her knees, while the cloud descends*). I sink!

*The background represents a forest of gigantic hollyhocks in flower:*
*white, pink, purple, sulphur-yellow, and violet. Above them*
*is seen the gilded roof of a castle, with a crown-shaped flower-*

*bud at the top. Under the walls of the castle heaps of straw are
seen lying about, covering disused stable litter which has been
cleared out. The wings, which remain unaltered throughout the
play, consist of conventional frescoes, which represent at the
same time interiors, architecture and landscape.*

(*Enter the* GLAZIER *and the* DAUGHTER.)

DAUGHTER. The castle keeps on growing out of the earth.... Do
you see how much it's grown since last year?

GLAZIER (*aside*). I've never seen that castle before... never heard
of a castle growing... still — (*To the* DAUGHTER, *with conviction.*)
Yes, it's grown six feet, but that's because they've manured it...
and if you look carefully you'll see a wing has come out on the
sunny side.

DAUGHTER. Oughtn't it to be flowering soon? It's past midsummer.

GLAZIER. Don't you see the flower up at the top there?

DAUGHTER. Yes, I see! (*Claps her hands.*) Tell me, Father: why
do flowers grow out of dirt?

GLAZIER (*innocently*). They don't feel at home in the dirt, so they
hurry up into the light as quickly as they can, to bloom and die!

DAUGHTER. Do you know who lives in that castle?

GLAZIER. I used to know, but I don't remember.

DAUGHTER. I believe there's a prisoner there... and I'm sure he's
waiting for me to set him free.

GLAZIER. But at what cost?

DAUGHTER. One doesn't bargain about what one *has* to do. Let's
go into the castle!...

GLAZIER. Yes, let's go!

(*They go towards the background, which is slowly drawn away
towards the sides. The scene is now a simple bare room with
a table and some chairs. On one of the chairs is sitting an*
OFFICER, *in a very unusual modern uniform. He is rocking
the chair, and striking the table with his sword.*)

DAUGHTER (*goes up to the* OFFICER *and takes the sword gently out of his
hand*). Don't do that! don't do that!

OFFICER. Agnes dear, let me keep my sword!

DAUGHTER. No, you're cutting the table to pieces! (*To her father.*)

Go down to the harness-room and put the pane in. We shall
meet later! (*The* GLAZIER *goes out.*)

DAUGHTER. You're a prisoner in your own rooms; I've come to
set you free!

OFFICER. Well, I've been waiting for that, but I wasn't sure you'd
be willing.

DAUGHTER. The castle is strong: it has seven walls, but — it shall
be done!... Do you wish it, or do you not?

OFFICER. To tell the truth — I don't know! I come off badly
either way! Every joy in life must be paid for with twice its
equivalent in sorrow. It's hard enough where I am; but if
I buy the sweets of freedom I shall have to suffer threefold. —
Agnes, I'd rather go through with it, if only I'm allowed to see
you!

DAUGHTER. What do you see in me?

OFFICER. The beautiful, which is the harmony of the universe. —
There are lines in your form which I find only in the orbits of
the solar system, in the beautiful resonance of strings, in the
vibrations of light. — You are a child of heaven...

DAUGHTER. You are that too!

OFFICER. Then why do I have to look after horses, mind stables
and see to the straw being removed?

DAUGHTER. So that you may long to get away from it all!

OFFICER. I do — but it's such a trouble to get free of it!

DAUGHTER. But it is a duty to seek freedom in the light!

OFFICER. A duty? Life has never recognized any duties towards
me!

DAUGHTER. You feel you've been wronged by life?

OFFICER. Yes! it hasn't been fair...

(*Voices are now heard from behind a screen, which is immediately
pulled away. The* OFFICER *and the* DAUGHTER *look in that
direction and become motionless in gesture and expression.*

*At a table is sitting the* MOTHER, *an invalid. Before her is burning
a tallow candle, which she trims from time to time with candle-
snuffers. On the table are lying heaps of shirts which she has
just sewn, and which she is marking with marking-ink and
a quill pen. On the left is a brown wardrobe.*)

FATHER (*gently, offering her a silk shawl*). Won't you have it?

MOTHER. A silk shawl for me, dear — what good'll that be when I'm going to die so soon?

FATHER. You believe what the Doctor says?

MOTHER. Yes, I believe him too; but most of all I believe in the voice which speaks here.

FATHER (*sadly*). It's really true then?... And your first and your last thoughts are for your children!

MOTHER. They were my life; my justification... my joy, and my sorrow...

FATHER. Kristin, forgive me... everything!

MOTHER. But what is there to forgive? Forgive *me*, dear! We have plagued each other — why? We don't know! We couldn't help it!... However, here's the children's new linen... See that they change twice a week, on Sundays and Wednesdays, and that Louisa washes them... all over... Are you going out?

FATHER. I have to be up at the masters' meeting — by eleven!

MOTHER. Ask Alfred to come in before you go!

FATHER (*pointing to the* OFFICER). Why, here he is, all the time!

MOTHER. Surely my sight's going too!... yes, it's getting dark... (*Snuffs the candle.*) Alfred! come here!

(*The* FATHER *goes out through the middle of the wall, nodding good-bye.*)

(*The* OFFICER *goes up to the* MOTHER.)

MOTHER. Who's that girl?

OFFICER (*whispers*). It's Agnes!

MOTHER. Oh, is that Agnes? Do you know what they say?... that she's the God Indra's daughter, who asked to be allowed to come down to earth so as to find out how it really is with human beings.... But don't say anything!...

OFFICER. A child of the gods!

MOTHER (*raising her voice*). Alfred dear, I shall soon be leaving you and your brothers and sisters.... Let me tell you one thing — to remember all your life!

OFFICER (*sadly*). Tell me, Mother!

MOTHER. Just one word: never quarrel with God!

OFFICER. What do you mean, Mother?

MOTHER. You mustn't go about feeling you've been wronged by life.

OFFICER. But if people treat me unjustly....

MOTHER. You're thinking of the time when you were unjustly punished for taking a penny which was afterwards found!

OFFICER. Yes! and that act of injustice gave a warped direction to the whole of my after-life....

MOTHER. Very well! But now go to that wardrobe there....

OFFICER (*ashamed*). So you know about that! It's...

MOTHER. "The Swiss Family Robinson"... which...

OFFICER. Don't say any more!...

MOTHER. Which your brother was punished for... and which *you* tore to pieces and hid!

OFFICER. Fancy that wardrobe still standing there after twenty years!... Think how often we've moved: and my mother died ten years ago!

MOTHER. And what of it? You keep on asking about everything, and so spoil the best part of your life!... Ah, there's Lina!

LINA (*coming in*). Thanks very much, ma'am, but I can't go to the christening....

MOTHER. Why not, child?

LINA. I've got nothing to wear!

MOTHER. You can borrow this shawl of mine!

LINA. Oh, ma'am! but that would never do!

MOTHER. I don't see why! I'm not likely to go to any more parties....

OFFICER. What will father say? Why, it's a present from him....

MOTHER. What small minds....

FATHER (*putting his head in*). Are you going to lend the girl my present?

MOTHER. Don't say that... remember, I've been a servant-girl myself.... Why should you hurt an innocent girl?

FATHER. Why should you hurt me, your husband....

MOTHER. Oh, this life! If one does anything nice there's always somebody who thinks it nasty... doing good to one person means doing harm to another. Oh, this life!

(*She snuffs the candle so that it goes out. The stage becomes dark and the screen is drawn forward again.*)

DAUGHTER. Men are pitiable creatures!

OFFICER. You find that!

DAUGHTER. Yes, life is hard, but love overcomes all! come and see!
         (*They go towards the background.*)

(*The background is drawn up and a new one appears, representing
a shabby old party-wall. In the middle of the wall is a gate
opening on to a passage which leads to a green open space, where
one sees an enormous blue monkshood (aconite). To the left of the
gate sits the* PORTRESS, *with a shawl over her head and shoulders,
crocheting a star-pattern coverlet. On the right is a notice-
board which the* BILLSTICKER *is washing; near him is a dip-net
with a green handle. Further to the right is a door with an
air-hole shaped like a four-leaved clover. To the left of the gate
stands a small linden-tree with coal-black stem and a few pale-
green leaves. Close to that is a cellar window.*)

DAUGHTER (*going up to the* PORTRESS). Isn't the star-coverlet
finished yet?

PORTRESS. No, dear; twenty-six years is nothing for such a piece of
work!

DAUGHTER. And your lover never came back?

PORTRESS. No, but it wasn't his fault. He *had* to go away... poor
boy; that was thirty years ago!

DAUGHTER (*to* BILLSTICKER). She was in the ballet, wasn't she?
Up there in the opera-house?

BILLSTICKER. She was number one there... but when *he* left it
seemed as if he took her dancing away with him like... and so
she never got any more parts....

DAUGHTER. They all complain, with their eyes at any rate, and
with their voices....

BILLSTICKER. I don't grumble so much now... not now I've got
my dip-net and my green fish-box!

DAUGHTER. And that makes you happy?

BILLSTICKER. Happy? — why 'twas the dream of my youth...
and now it's come true! I'm fifty now, you see....

DAUGHTER. Fifty years for a dip-net and a box....

BILLSTICKER. A *green* box, a green...

DAUGHTER (*to the* PORTRESS). Give me the shawl now: then I can
sit here and look on the children of men! You stand behind and
tell me about them! (*Puts on the shawl and sits down by the
gate.*)

PORTRESS. Today's the last day before the opera season ends...
now's the time they find out if they're engaged....

DAUGHTER. And those that aren't?

PORTRESS. O Lord, what a sight! I pull the shawl over my
head, I...

DAUGHTER. Poor creatures!

PORTRESS. Look, here's one coming!... She's not got an engagement... See how she's crying....

> (*The* SINGER *comes rushing out through the gate from the right,
> with her handkerchief to her eyes. She pauses for a moment in
> the passage beyond the gate and leans her head against the wall.
> Then goes out quickly.*)

DAUGHTER. Men are pitiable creatures!

PORTRESS. But look there! that's more like a happy one!

> (*The* OFFICER *comes in through the passage: in frock-coat and
> tall hat, with a bunch of roses in his hand. Looks radiantly
> happy.*)

PORTRESS. He's going to marry Madam Victoria!...

OFFICER (*down stage: looks up and sings*). Victoria!

PORTRESS. Madam will be here in a minute!

OFFICER. Good! the carriage is waiting, the table is laid and the
champagne is on ice.... Let me embrace you, ladies! (*Embraces the* DAUGHTER *and the* PORTRESS. *Sings.*) Victoria!

A WOMAN'S VOICE (*from above, sings*). I am here!

OFFICER (*beginning to walk about*). All right! I'm waiting!

DAUGHTER. Do you know me?

OFFICER. No, I know only one woman... Victoria! Seven years
have I come here to wait for her... at noon, when the sun
touched the chimneys, and in the evening, when the shadows of
night began to fall.... Look at the pavement here! can't you
see the track worn by the faithful lover! Hurrah! she's mine!
(*Sings.*) Victoria! (*No answer.*) Oh well, she's dressing now!
(*To the* BILLSTICKER.) There's the dip-net, I see! Everybody
at the opera is crazy about dip-nets... or rather about fishes!
dumb fishes, because they can't sing.... What does a thing like
that cost?

BILLSTICKER. Rather a lot!

OFFICER (*sings*). Victoria!... (*Shakes the linden-tree.*) Why it's

getting green again! for the eighth time!... (*Sings.*) Victoria!...
Now she's tidying her hair!... (*To the* DAUGHTER.) Now,
madam! let me go up and fetch my bride!...

PORTRESS. Nobody's allowed on the stage!

OFFICER. Seven years have I come here! Seven times three
hundred and sixty-five makes two thousand five hundred and
fifty-five! (*Stops and pokes at the door with the clover-shaped hole.*)...
To think that I've seen that door two thousand five hundred and
fifty-five times without finding out where it leads! And that
clover leaf for letting in the light... who does it let the light in
for? is there anyone inside? does anybody live there?

PORTRESS. I don't know! I've never seen it opened!...

OFFICER. It looks like a pantry door which I saw when I was four
years old, one Sunday afternoon when I went out with the maid.
We went to call on other maids, but I never got further than the
kitchen, where I sat between the water-barrel and the salt-box.
I've seen so many kitchens in my time, and the pantries were
invariably out on the landing, with round holes bored in the
door, and another like a clover leaf.... But the opera-house
can't have any pantry; they haven't even got a kitchen! (*Sings.*)
Victoria!... I say, madam! I suppose she can't be coming out
any other way?

PORTRESS. No, there is no other way!

OFFICER. Good! then I'm bound to meet her

(*The theatre people come running out, closely scanned by the*
OFFICER.)

OFFICER. She's sure to be here soon!... Madam! that blue monkshood out there! I've known it since I was a child... is it the
same one?... I remember at a country parsonage, when I was
seven... there were two doves, two blue doves under that hood...
but then there came a bee and found its way under the hood....
Now I have you! thought I, and grabbed hold of the flower.
But the bee stung through it, and I cried... but then the pastor's
wife came and put wet earth on the place... we had strawberries
and cream for supper afterwards!... I believe it's getting dark
already. — Where are you going, Billsticker?

BILLSTICKER. I'm going home to supper.

OFFICER (*rubbing his eyes*). Supper? this time of day? — Oh!

may I go in and telephone to the Growing Castle for one
moment?

DAUGHTER. What do you want there?

OFFICER. I'm going to tell the glazier to put double windows in.
It will be winter soon and I'm terribly cold!

(*Goes into the* PORTRESS's *lodge.*)

DAUGHTER. Who is Madam Victoria?

PORTRESS. She's his sweetheart!

DAUGHTER. A very good answer! What she is to us and other
people doesn't matter to him! Simply what she is to *him* —
that is what she *is!*...              (*It becomes dark quickly.*)

PORTRESS (*lighting the lantern*). It's getting dark quickly today!

DAUGHTER. To the gods a year is as a minute!

PORTRESS. And to human beings a minute may be as long as
a year!

OFFICER (*comes in again. He looks dusty; the roses are withered*).
Hasn't she come yet?

PORTRESS. No!

OFFICER. She'll certainly come... *she'll* come! (*Walks up and
down.*)... Still, perhaps it's best to give up that luncheon after
all!... as it's evening already... Yes, I'll do so!

(*Goes in and telephones.*)

PORTRESS (*to the* DAUGHTER). May I have my shawl now?

DAUGHTER. No, my friend: have a rest while I look after your
duties... I want to get to know mankind: to know life, to find
out whether it's as hard as it's said to be.

PORTRESS. But you can't go to sleep at your post here: never go to
sleep, night or day....

DAUGHTER. No sleep at night?

PORTRESS. Well, if you can get it, with the bell-string round your
arm... you see there are night-watchmen on the stage, and
they're changed every three hours....

DAUGHTER. But that's torture....

PORTRESS. So you think; but people like us are glad to get such
a job. If you only knew how envied I am....

DAUGHTER. Envied? Does one envy the tortured?

PORTRESS. Yes!... but I'll tell you what's worse than drudgery and night duty, and draughts and cold and damp — and that is having to listen to the secrets of all the unhappy people up there.... I'm the one they come to: and why? Perhaps they read in the lines of my face the runes which suffering writes, and which invite confidences... in that shawl, my dear, are hidden thirty years' agony, my own and that of others!...

DAUGHTER. It's heavy too, and it stings like nettles....

PORTRESS. Wear it if you like.... When it gets too heavy, call me and I'll come and relieve you!

DAUGHTER. Farewell! What you can bear, surely I can!

PORTRESS. We shall see!... But be kind now to my little friends and don't get tired of their complaints.

(*Disappears in the passage.*)

(*The stage becomes pitch-dark. Under cover of the darkness the scenery is changed. The linden is stripped of its leaves: the blue monkshood withers quickly: and when the stage is light again the green space in the distance beyond the passage has become an autumnal brown.*)

OFFICER (*comes in when it is light again. He has grey hair now and a grey beard. His clothes are shabby, his collar soiled and limp. The bunch of roses has fallen to pieces, so that only the bare stems are seen. He walks up and down*). To judge by all appearances summer is over and autumn is near. — I can tell that by the linden, and the monkshood!... (*Walks up and down.*) But autumn is *my* spring, for that is when the theatre opens again! and then she *must* come! Dear lady, will you let me sit on this chair for a little while?

DAUGHTER. Do, my friend! I can stand!

OFFICER (*sitting down*). If only I could manage to get a little sleep, then it might not be so bad!... (*He falls asleep for a moment: then starts up and begins walking again; stops by the door with the clover leaf and pokes at it.*) This door now — it gives me no peace.... What is there behind it? There must be something! (*Soft dance-music is heard from above.*) Ah, now they've begun the rehearsals! (*The stage is now lighted intermittently, as if by a lighthouse.*) What does this mean? (*Speaking in time with the blinking of the light.*) Light and dark — light and dark?

DAUGHTER (*imitating him*). Day and night — day and night!...

A merciful Providence seeks to shorten your time of waiting!
And that is why the days are flying, pursuing the nights!

(*The light on the stage is now constant. The* BILLSTICKER *comes in with his dip-net and implements.*)

OFFICER. Here comes the Billsticker, with his dip-net.... Has the fishing been good?

BILLSTICKER. Oh, quite! It's been a hot summer — a bit longer than usual... the net was good enough — not *quite* what I hoped for....

OFFICER (*accentuating the words*). Not quite what I hoped for!... an excellent phrase! Nothing ever is what I hoped for!... since the thought is more than the deed — greater than the thing....

(*Walks up and down, striking the rose stems against the walls till the last leaves fall off.*)

BILLSTICKER. Hasn't she come down yet?

OFFICER. No, not yet, but she'll soon be here!... Do you know what there is behind that door?

BILLSTICKER. No, I've never seen that door open.

OFFICER. I shall telephone for a locksmith to come and open it!

(*Goes into the lodge. The* BILLSTICKER *pastes up a bill and goes towards the door on the right.*)

DAUGHTER. What was wrong with the net?

BILLSTICKER. Wrong? Well, there wasn't really anything wrong... but it wasn't what I'd expected, and so I didn't get quite so much fun out of it....

DAUGHTER. What did you expect it to be like?

BILLSTICKER. Like?... Well, I can't exactly say....

DAUGHTER. Let me say then!... You expected it to be what it *wasn't!* It had to be green, but not that green!

BILLSTICKER. You know all about it, lady, you do! all about it — and that's why they all come to you with their worries.... If you'd only listen to me too, just for once....

DAUGHTER. I will, gladly.... Come in here and pour out your heart....

(*Goes into the lodge. The* BILLSTICKER *stands outside the window speaking to her.*)

(*It becomes pitch-dark again; then light, and now the linden becomes green again and the monkshood blooms. The sun shines*

> *on the greenery in the distance beyond the passage. The OFFICER*
> *comes on; he is old and white-haired now: ragged, with worn-*
> *out shoes. He carries the stems of the bunch of roses. Walks*
> *to and fro, slowly, like an old man. Then he reads the bill.*)

(*A BALLET GIRL comes in from the right.*)

OFFICER. Has Madam Victoria gone?

BALLET GIRL. No, she hasn't!

OFFICER. Then I'll wait! I suppose she'll be coming soon?

BALLET GIRL (*seriously*). Yes, she's sure to!

OFFICER. Don't go away now: then you'll be able to see what's behind that door. I've sent for the locksmith!

BALLET GIRL. It'll be awfully interesting to see that door opened. That door and the Growing Castle — have you ever heard of the Growing Castle?

OFFICER. Have I! — why, I've been a prisoner there!

BALLET GIRL. It was you, was it? But why did they keep such a lot of horses there?

OFFICER. It was a stable castle of course....

BALLET GIRL (*distressed*). How stupid of me! fancy my not seeing that!

(*A CHORUS SINGER comes in from the right.*)

OFFICER. Has Madam Victoria gone?

CHORUS SINGER (*seriously*). No, she hasn't gone! she never does go!

OFFICER. That's because she loves me!... Now don't go before the locksmith comes to open this door.

CHORUS SINGER. Oh? is the door going to be opened? How interesting!... I just want to ask the Portress something.

(*The PROMPTER comes in from the right.*)

OFFICER. Has Madam Victoria gone?

PROMPTER. Not so far as I know!

OFFICER. There! didn't I say she was waiting for me! — Don't go before the door's opened.

PROMPTER. Which door?

OFFICER. Is there more than one door?

PROMPTER. Now I understand: the one with the clover leaf!...

In that case I'll certainly stay! I'm just going to have a little chat with the Portress!

(*The* BALLET GIRL, *the* CHORUS SINGER *and the* PROMPTER *form a group with the* BILLSTICKER *outside the* PORTRESS'S *window, and speak in turn to the* DAUGHTER. *The* GLAZIER *comes in through the gate.*)

OFFICER. Are you the locksmith?

GLAZIER. No, the locksmith had visitors: I suppose a glazier's just as good.

OFFICER. Oh, certainly, certainly... but have you got your diamond with you?

GLAZIER. Of course I have! A glazier without his diamond! What good would that be?

OFFICER. None at all! — Let's get to work then!

(*Claps his hands. All the characters group themselves round the door.* CHORUS MEN *dressed as Mastersingers, and figurantes as the dancers in "Aida" come in from the right and join them.*)

OFFICER. Locksmith — or Glazier — do your duty! (*The* GLAZIER *comes forward with his diamond.*) A moment such as this seldom occurs twice in a lifetime. For this reason, my friends, I beg you... to consider carefully...

A POLICEMAN (*coming forward*). In the name of the law, I forbid the opening of this door!

OFFICER. Good Lord, what a fuss the moment one wants to do anything new and great!... But we'll go to law about it!... To the Lawyer then! Then we shall see whether the law still holds good! — To the Lawyer!

(*Without any lowering of the* CURTAIN *the scene changes to a lawyer's office, in the following manner. The gate remains, serving the purpose of a doorway in the railing which runs right across the stage. The Portress's lodge becomes the Lawyer's writing compartment, but is open in front. The linden, now leafless, has become a coat-and-hatstand. The notice-board is covered with proclamations and decrees of the court. The four-leaved clover door now belongs to a cupboard for documents.*

*The* LAWYER, *in evening dress, with white tie, is sitting accordingly to the left, inside the doorway, at a desk covered with papers. His appearance bears witness to indescribable sufferings; his face is chalk-white and furrowed, with violet shades. He is ugly, and his face mirrors all the various crimes and vices with which, from the nature of his business, he has necessarily come into contact.*

*One of his two clerks has lost an arm, the other an eye.*

*The people who had assembled to witness the "Opening of the door" are still present, but seem now to be waiting admission to the office, and look as if they had always been standing there.*

*The* DAUGHTER, *wearing the shawl, and the* OFFICER *are in front.*)

LAWYER (*going up to the* DAUGHTER). May I have that shawl, sister... I'll hang it up in here till I have a fire in the grate; and then I'll burn it, with all its griefs and miseries...

DAUGHTER. Not yet, brother; I want to get it quite full first, and I want especially to get all your own sufferings into it, all the confidences which you have received about crimes, vices, ill-gotten gains, slanders, abuse...

LAWYER. My little friend, your shawl would never hold all that! Look at these walls; doesn't the paper look as if it were stained by every kind of sin? Look at these papers on which I write tales of wrong; look at *me*... no human being ever comes here with a smile; nothing but angry looks, snarling lips, clenched fists... and all of them squirt their malice, their envy, their suspicions over me... Look! my hands are black, and can never be washed clean; see how they are cracked and bleeding... I can never keep clothes more than a few days — they stink of other people's crimes... sometimes I have the place fumigated with sulphur, but it doesn't help; I sleep close by, and I dream only of crimes.... Just now I have a murder case in court... that's not so bad, but do you know what is worse than anything? ... Separating married people! — Then a cry seems to come from heaven above and the earth beneath... a cry of treason against the primal power, against the source of good, against love.... Besides, after reams of paper have been filled with mutual accusations, if some kindly person eventually takes one of them apart, and with a pinch on the ear and a smile asks the simple question, What have you really got against your husband — or your wife? — well, he, or she, will stand speechless —

cannot think of any reason! On one occasion — oh, I think it was about a salad, another time about a word, usually about nothing. But the tortures, the suffering! These I have to bear!... Look at my face! Do you think that I, looking like a criminal as I do, could ever get a woman to return my love? Do you think anybody would care to be friends with a man who has to collect all the debts, all the money debts of the town?... It's misery to be a man!

DAUGHTER. Men are pitiable creatures!

LAWYER. They are indeed! And what people live on is a puzzle to me! They marry on an income of one hundred, when they need two hundred... they borrow, of course, they all borrow! They manage to rub along somehow, by the skin of their teeth, till they die... and then the estate is always in debt! Who has to pay in the end I really don't know!

DAUGHTER. He who feeds the birds!

LAWYER. Yes! but if He who feeds the birds would come down to this earth of His and see the plight of the poor children of men, perhaps compassion would come over Him...

DAUGHTER. Men are pitiable creatures!

LAWYER. Yes, that is the truth! — (*To the* OFFICER.) What do you want?

OFFICER. I just wanted to ask if Madam Victoria had gone!

LAWYER. No, she hasn't: you needn't worry about that... what are you poking at my cupboard for?

OFFICER. I thought the door was so like...

LAWYER. Oh, no, no! — Oh, no! (*Church bells are heard.*)

OFFICER. Is there a funeral in the town?

LAWYER. No, it's a graduation — a conferment of doctors' degrees. I myself am just going to take the degree of Doctor of Law. Perhaps you might feel inclined to graduate and receive a laurel wreath?

OFFICER. Yes, why not? It would be a little distraction anyhow...

LAWYER. Perhaps we ought to proceed at once to the solemn rite? — Hadn't you better go and change your clothes?

(*The* OFFICER *goes out; the stage is now darkened while the following changes take place. The railing remains, serving now as the chancel rail of a church; the notice-board is used for indicating*

> *the numbers of the hymns; the linden hatstand becomes a candela-*
> *brum; the lawyer's desk becomes the President's pulpit; and the*
> *four-leaved clover door now leads to the vestry.... The Chorus*
> *from "The Mastersingers" turn into ushers with staves, and the*
> *figurantes carry laurel wreaths.*
>
> *The rest of the people act as spectators.*
>
> *The backcloth is raised and the new one represents one huge organ,*
> *with the keyboards below and the mirror above.*
>
> *Music is heard. At the sides are seen the four Faculties, Philosophy,*
> *Theology, Medicine and Jurisprudence. The stage remains empty*
> *for a moment.*
>
> *The* USHERS *come forward from the right.*
>
> *The* FIGURANTES *follow, with laurel wreaths in their outstretched*
> *hands.*
>
> THREE CANDIDATES *come forward successively from the left, are*
> *crowned by the* FIGURANTES, *and go out to the right.*
>
> *The* LAWYER *comes forward to receive his wreath.*
>
> *The* FIGURANTES *turn away, refusing to crown him, and go out.*
> *The* LAWYER, *greatly agitated, leans against a pillar. All the*
> *others retire, and the* LAWYER *is left alone.*)

DAUGHTER (*comes in with a white veil over her head and shoulders*).
Look! I've washed the shawl... But why are you standing here?
Didn't you get your wreath?

LAWYER. No, I was not worthy.

DAUGHTER. Why? Because you defended the poor, put in a good
word for the wrongdoer, eased the burden of the guilty, obtained a respite for the condemned... alas for mankind!...
angels they are not, but they are pitiable nevertheless.

LAWYER. Speak no evil of mankind; after all, it's my business to
plead for them....

DAUGHTER (*leaning against the organ*). Why do they strike their
friends in the face?

LAWYER. They know no better!

DAUGHTER. Let us enlighten them! Will you? You and I
together!

LAWYER. Enlightenment they will not receive!... Oh, that our
complaint might reach the gods of heaven....

DAUGHTER. It shall reach the throne!... (*Turns round towards the organ.*) Do you know what I see in this mirror?... The world the right way up!... Yes, for by nature it's upside down!

LAWYER. How did it become upside down?

DAUGHTER. When the copy was made....

LAWYER. Yes, that's the word — copy! I always suspected it was a faulty copy... and when I began to remember the forms of the original I became dissatisfied with everything... People called it discontent, bits of the devil's glass in one's eye, and soon....

DAUGHTER. 'Tis a mad world truly! Look at these four faculties! ... The government which upholds society pays all four of them: theology, the science of religion, continually attacked and ridiculed by philosophy, which claims to be wisdom itself! And medicine, which is always giving the lie to philosophy, and does not count theology as one of the sciences, but calls it superstition.... And they sit together in the same council, whose function it is to teach young men respect — for the University. Why, it's a madhouse! And woe to him who first recovers his senses!

LAWYER. The first to get to know it are the theologians. For their preparatory studies they take philosophy, which teaches them that theology is nonsense; after that they learn from theology that philosophy is nonsense! Madmen, surely?

DAUGHTER. And then jurisprudence, which serves all but the servants!

LAWYER. Justice, which when it tries to be just, becomes its champion's ruin!... Right, which so often spells wrong!

DAUGHTER. How you have bungled it all, O children of men! Children! — Come, you shall have a wreath from me... one that will suit you better! (*Puts a crown of thorns on his head.*) Now I will play to you!

(*Seats herself at the organ and plays a Kyrie; but instead of organ-tones human voices are heard.*)

CHILDREN'S VOICES. O everlasting God! (*The last note is sustained.*)

WOMEN'S VOICES. Have mercy upon us! (*The last note is sustained.*)

MEN'S VOICES (*tenors*). Deliver us for Thy tender mercy's sake! (*The last note is sustained.*)

MEN'S VOICES (*basses*). Spare Thy children, O Lord, and be not bitter against us!

ALL. Have mercy upon us! hear us! Have compassion on us mortals! — O Eternal One, why art Thou so far?... Out of the depths we call, Be merciful, O Eternal One! Make not the burden too heavy for Thy children! Hear us! hear us!

(*The stage becomes dark. The* DAUGHTER *rises and comes near the* LAWYER. *By a change in the lighting the organ is changed into Fingal's Cave. The sea comes flooding in among the basalt pillars, producing a mingled harmony of waves and winds.*)

LAWYER. Where are we, sister?

DAUGHTER. What do you hear?

LAWYER. I hear drops falling...

DAUGHTER. They are the tears that men weep... What else do you hear?

LAWYER. Sighing... and whining... and wailing...

DAUGHTER. Thus far the complaint of mortals has come... no further. But why this endless complaining? Is there nothing in life to rejoice at?

LAWYER. Yes, the sweetest, which is also the bitterest — love! wife and home! the highest and the lowest!

DAUGHTER. May I try it!

LAWYER. With me?

DAUGHTER. With you! You know the rocks, the stones on which one stumbles. Let us avoid them!

LAWYER. I am poor!

DAUGHTER. What does that matter so long as we love each other? And a little beauty costs nothing!

LAWYER. I have dislikes which may be your likes.

DAUGHTER. They can be adjusted!

LAWYER. And if we get tired?

DAUGHTER. Then the child comes, bringing with it a distraction that is always new!

LAWYER. You, you will take me, poor and ugly, despised, rejected?

DAUGHTER. Yes! let us unite our destinies!

LAWYER. So be it then!

(*A very simple room inside the Lawyer's office. To the right is a large double bed with curtains; near it a window. To the left is a portable stove with cooking utensils.* KRISTIN *is pasting strips of paper on the inner windows. At the back is an open door leading to the office. Outside are seen some poor people waiting for admission.*)

KRISTIN. I paste, I paste!

DAUGHTER (*pale and worn, is sitting by the stove*). You're shutting out the air! I'm suffocating!

KRISTIN. Now there's only one tiny crack left!

DAUGHTER. Air, air! I can't breathe!

KRISTIN. I paste, I paste!

LAWYER. That's right, Kristin; heat is precious!

DAUGHTER. Oh, it's like having one's mouth glued up!

LAWYER (*standing in the doorway with a paper in his hand*). Is the child asleep?

DAUGHTER. Yes, at last!

LAWYER (*gently*). This crying frightens away my clients!

DAUGHTER (*pleasantly*). What can we do about it?

LAWYER. Nothing!

DAUGHTER. We must take a bigger flat!

LAWYER. We've got no money!

DAUGHTER. May I open the window? This foul air is choking me.

LAWYER. Then the warmth will escape and we shall freeze!

DAUGHTER. This is terrible!... Can we do some scrubbing in there then?

LAWYER. You aren't strong enough to do any scrubbing, nor I either; and Kristin must go on pasting; she must paste up the whole house, every crack, in ceiling, floor and walls!

DAUGHTER. Poverty I was prepared for, not dirt!

LAWYER. Poverty is always more or less dirty!

DAUGHTER. This is worse than I dreamt of!

LAWYER. Others are worse off! There's still food in the pot!

DAUGHTER. But what sort of food?...

LAWYER. Cabbage is cheap, nourishing and nice!

DAUGHTER. For those who like cabbage! To me it's disgusting!

LAWYER. Why didn't you say so?

DAUGHTER. Because I loved you! I was willing to sacrifice my taste!

LAWYER. Then I must sacrifice to you my taste for cabbage! sacrifices must be mutual!

DAUGHTER. What are we to eat then? Fish? but you hate fish.

LAWYER. And it's expensive!

DAUGHTER. Things are harder than I could have believed!

LAWYER (*kindly*). Yes, they are hard!... And the child, that should have been the link between us, and a blessing... becomes our ruin!

DAUGHTER. Dearest, I am dying in this air, in this room with its backyard outlook, with its baby cries through endless hours of sleeplessness: with those people out there, and their wailings and quarrels and accusations... Here I can only die!

LAWYER. Poor little flower — no light, no air....

DAUGHTER. And you say there are people worse off!

LAWYER. I am one of the envied ones among my neighbours here.

DAUGHTER. I could put up with all the rest if only I could have some beauty in my home!

LAWYER. I know you're thinking of some flower — a heliotrope in particular. But that costs one and sixpence — the price of six quarts of milk, or half a bushel of potatoes.

DAUGHTER. I would gladly go without food to have my flower.

LAWYER. There is a kind of beauty which costs nothing. Not to have it in one's home is sheer torture for any man with a sense of beauty!

DAUGHTER. What is that?

LAWYER. If I tell you you'll get angry!

DAUGHTER. We've agreed not to get angry!

LAWYER. We've agreed... we can put up with anything now, dear, except the short, hard accents... do you know those? Not yet!

DAUGHTER. They shall never be heard between us!

LAWYER. Not if it depends on me!

DAUGHTER. Tell me then!

LAWYER. Well, when I come into a house I look first of all to see how the curtains are draped... (*Goes up to the window curtain and puts it right.*)... If they hang like ropes or rags I soon go!... Then I have a look at the chairs... If they're arranged tidily, then I stay!... (*Puts a chair straight against the wall.*) After that I look at the candles in the candlesticks... If they're crooked, then the whole house is askew! (*Straightens a candle on the bureau.*)... That, my dear, is the beauty which costs nothing!

DAUGHTER (*sinks her head on her breast*). Not the short accents, dear!

LAWYER. They were not short!

DAUGHTER. Yes, they were!

LAWYER. What the devil...

DAUGHTER. What sort of language is that?

LAWYER. Forgive me, Agnes! But I have suffered as much from your untidiness as you do from the dirt! And I haven't dared help put things straight myself; you'd get furious, just as if I were finding fault with you... ugh! shall we stop now?

DAUGHTER. Married life is terribly hard... harder than anything! One has to be an angel, I think!

LAWYER. Yes, I think so too!

DAUGHTER. I feel I'm beginning to hate you after this!

LAWYER. Woe to us then!... But let's prevent hatred! I promise never to make any more remarks about untidiness... though it's torture to me!

DAUGHTER. And I'll eat cabbage, though it's torment to me!

LAWYER. Result — life together in torment! One's pleasure, the other's pain!

DAUGHTER. Men are pitiable creatures!

LAWYER. You realize that?

DAUGHTER. Yes! but in God's name let's avoid the rocks, now that we know them so well!

LAWYER. Let us do so! Surely we're humane, enlightened people; surely we can overlook and forgive!

DAUGHTER. Yes, and smile at trifles!

LAWYER. We, we only, can do so!... You know, I read in today's *Morning*... by the way, where is the paper?

DAUGHTER (*embarrassed*). What paper?

LAWYER (*harshly*). Do I take in more than one?

DAUGHTER. Smile now, and don't speak harshly... Your paper — I lit the fire with it....

LAWYER (*violently*). The devil you did!

DAUGHTER. Smile now!... I burnt it because it mocked at what to me is holy...

LAWYER. And to me unholy! tcha!... (*Claps his hands together, beside himself.*) I will smile, smile so that my back teeth show.... I'll be humane and swallow my opinions: say yes to everything, and cringe and play the hypocrite! So you've burnt my paper, have you? (*Tidies the bed-curtains.*) There! now I'm going to tidy the place again till you get angry.... Agnes, this is simply impossible!

DAUGHTER. Of course it is!

LAWYER. And yet we must hold out, not for our vows' sake, but for the child's!

DAUGHTER. Yes, that is true! for the child's sake! Oh! — oh!... we must hold out!

LAWYER. And now I must go and see my clients! Listen to them growling with impatience to rend one another, to get one another fined and imprisoned... poor lost souls...

DAUGHTER. Wretched, wretched creatures! And all this pasting!
 (*She bows her head on her breast in dumb despair.*)

KRISTIN. I paste, I paste!
 (*The* LAWYER *stands by the door, fingering the handle nervously.*)

DAUGHTER. Oh, how that handle does squeak! it feels as though you were twisting my heart-strings....

LAWYER. I twist, I twist...

DAUGHTER. Don't!

LAWYER. I twist...

DAUGHTER. No!

LAWYER. I...

OFFICER (*from inside the office, taking hold of the handle*). Permit me!

LAWYER (*letting go of the handle*). Certainly! since you've got your degree!

OFFICER. All life is now mine! every path lies open for me: I have set foot on Parnassus: the laurels are won: immortality, fame — all are mine!

LAWYER. What will you live on?

OFFICER. Live on?

LAWYER. I imagine you'll want a house, clothes, food?

OFFICER. That's always to be had, if only you've someone to love you!

LAWYER. Fancy that now!... fancy!... Paste, Kristin!... paste! till they can't breathe! (*Goes out backwards, nodding.*)

KRISTIN. I paste, I paste! till they can't breathe!

OFFICER. Are you coming with me now?

DAUGHTER. At once! but where?

OFFICER. To Fairhaven! It's summer there: there the sun is shining, there are youth, children and flowers: song and dance, feasting and revelry!

DAUGHTER. Then I'll go there!

OFFICER. Come!

LAWYER (*coming in again*). I shall go back now to my first hell... this one here was the second... and the worst! The sweetest hell is the worst.... There, she's gone and left her hairpins all over the floor again!... (*Picks some off the floor.*)

OFFICER. So he's discovered the hairpins too!

LAWYER. What do you mean by "too"?... Look at this one! two prongs, but only one pin! two, and yet one! If I straighten it out it becomes one single piece of wire! if I bend it, it becomes two, without ceasing to be one! In other words — the two are one! But if I break it in half — like this — then the two are two! (*Breaks the hairpin and throws away the pieces.*)

OFFICER. So he's seen all that!... But before you can break it the prongs must diverge! If they converge the thing holds together!

LAWYER. And if they are parallel — then they never meet: then it neither holds nor breaks.

OFFICER. The hairpin is the most perfect of all created things! a straight line which is equal to two parallel straight lines!

LAWYER. A lock that shuts when it's open!

OFFICER. Which shuts, when it is open, a plait of hair which remains loose while it is being bound....

LAWYER. It's like this door! When I close it, I open — the way out — for you, Agnes! (*Withdraws, closing the door.*)

DAUGHTER. Well?

> (*The scene changes: the bed with its curtains is transformed into a tent; the stove remains; the backcloth is raised; on the right, in the foreground, are seen burnt hill-sides with red heather and tree stumps that are black and white after a forest fire; red pigsties and outhouses. Below these an open-air establishment for mechanical treatment of the sick, where men and women are being exercised on machines resembling instruments of torture. On the left, in the foreground, some of the open sheds belonging to the quarantine station, with ovens, brick furnaces and rows of pipes. In the middle distance is a strait. The backcloth represents a*

*beautiful wooded shore, with flag-decorated landing-stages, where*
*white boats are moored, some with sails set, and some without.*
*Through the trees on the shore are seen little Italian villas, pa-*
*vilions, kiosks and marble statues.* The QUARANTINE OFFICER,
*got up as a blackamoor, is walking along the shore.*)

OFFICER (*goes up to him and shakes hands*). What, Ordström? You
here?

QUARANTINE OFFICER. Yes, I'm here!

OFFICER. Is this Fairhaven?

QUARANTINE OFFICER. No — over there; this is Foulstrand!

OFFICER. Then we've come all wrong!

QUARANTINE OFFICER. We? — Won't you introduce me?

OFFICER. No, that would hardly do! (*Half aloud.*) It's Indra's
own daughter!

QUARANTINE OFFICER. Indra's? I thought it must be Varuna himself!... Well, aren't you surprised to see me with my face all
black?

OFFICER. My son, I am past fifty; at that age one ceases to be
surprised! — I assumed at once that you were going to a fancy-
dress ball this afternoon!

QUARANTINE OFFICER. Quite correct! I hope you're coming too?

OFFICER. Certainly; you see, here... well, it doesn't look very
attractive!... What sort of people live here?

QUARANTINE OFFICER. The sick live here — over there the healthy!

OFFICER. Only poor people here then?

QUARANTINE OFFICER. No, my boy, it's here you have the rich!
Look at that man on the rack! He has eaten too much goose-
liver and truffles, and drunk so much Burgundy that his feet
have gone knobbly!

OFFICER. Knobbly?

QUARANTINE OFFICER. Yes, he's got knobbly feet!... And that one
lying on the guillotine; he's drunk so much Hennessy that his
backbone has to be mangled out!

OFFICER. There's always something wrong!

QUARANTINE OFFICER. Besides these you'll find on this side all those
who have some misery to conceal! Look at this one, for
instance!

(*An elderly fop in a Bath-chair is wheeled on to the stage. He is accompanied by a gaunt and hideous coquette of sixty, dressed in the latest fashion, and attended by the "friend," a man of forty.)*

OFFICER. Why, it's the Major! our schoolfellow!

QUARANTINE OFFICER. Don Juan! You see he's still in love with the spectre at his side. He doesn't see that she's grown old — that she's ugly, faithless, cruel.

OFFICER. There's real love for you! I should never have thought such a flighty fellow as he is would have been capable of loving so deeply and so earnestly!

QUARANTINE OFFICER. That's a nice way of looking at it, yours!

OFFICER. I've been in love myself, with Victoria... yes, I still walk about the corridor waiting for her....

QUARANTINE OFFICER. So you're the fellow who walks about the corridor?

OFFICER. Yes, I'm the man!

QUARANTINE OFFICER. Well, have you got that door opened yet?

OFFICER. No, we're still fighting the case.... The Billsticker is out with his dip-net, you see, which delays the taking of evidence.... Meanwhile the glazier has put in the panes in the castle, which has grown half a story.... It's been an unusually good year this year... warm and damp!

QUARANTINE OFFICER. All the same you've had nothing like the heat I've had here!

OFFICER. What's the temperature of your ovens then?

QUARANTINE OFFICER. A hundred and ninety degrees, when we're disinfecting cholera suspects.

OFFICER. Is cholera about again then?

QUARANTINE OFFICER. Didn't you know that?

OFFICER. Of course I knew it: but I so often forget what I know!

QUARANTINE OFFICER. I often wish I could forget things — especially myself. That's why I go in for masquerades, fancy dress and private theatricals.

OFFICER. What have you been doing then?

QUARANTINE OFFICER. If I speak about it, they say I'm bragging: if I don't, they call me a hypocrite!

OFFICER. Is that why you've blackened your face?

QUARANTINE OFFICER. Yes! a shade blacker than I really am!

OFFICER. Who's this coming?

QUARANTINE OFFICER. Oh, that's a poet! he's going to have his mud-bath!

(*The* POET *comes in, with his eyes raised to heaven, carrying a pail of mud.*)

OFFICER. Heavens! he ought to have light baths and air baths!

QUARANTINE OFFICER. No, he keeps so much to the upper air that he gets home-sick for the mud... it makes the skin hard to wallow in the mire, just as it does with pigs. After his bath he doesn't feel the gadflies sting!

OFFICER. It's a funny world — all contradictions!

POET (*ecstatically*). Out of clay the god Ptah fashioned man on a potter's wheel, a lathe — (*sceptically*) or any other damned thing!... (*Ecstatically.*) Out of clay the sculptor fashions his more or less immortal masterpieces — (*sceptically*). Usually rubbish! (*Ecstatically.*) Out of clay are formed those vessels, so indispensable in the pantry, which bear the generic name of pots and plates — (*sceptically*). As if I cared what they're called! (*Ecstatically.*) Such is clay! When clay is a thin fluid it's called mud — *c'est mon affaire!* (*Calls.*) Lina!

(LINA *comes in with a pail.*)

POET. Lina, show yourself to Miss Agnes! — She knew you ten years ago, when you were a young, happy and, let us say, pretty girl.... Look at her now! Five children, drudgery, squalling, hunger, blows! See how beauty has perished, how joy has vanished, in the fulfilment of duties which ought to have given the inward content that express itself in the harmonious lines of the face and the quiet shining of the eye....

QUARANTINE OFFICER (*putting his hand to the other's lips*). Shut up, shut up!

POET. That's what they all say! And then if one does keep silent they say "Speak!" How impossible people are!

DAUGHTER (*going up to* LINA). Tell me your grievances!

LINA. I daren't: I should only get it worse!

DAUGHTER. Who could be so cruel?

LINA. I daren't say: if I did I should get beaten!

POET. That's how it is! But I *will* talk about it, even if the blackamoor knocks my teeth out for me!... I will say that injustice does occur.... Agnes, daughter of the gods! Do you hear music and dancing up there on the hill? — Well, that's Lina's sister come home from the town, where she went astray, you understand.... Now they're killing the fatted calf, while Lina, who stayed at home, has to go about with the slop-pail and feed the pigs!...

DAUGHTER. There is joy in the house because the wanderer has left the evil ways, not merely because she has come home! Remember that!

POET. Then arrange a ball and supper every evening for that blameless servant who has never gone astray: do that! That they never do: when Lina's free she has to go to prayer meetings, to be reprimanded for not being perfect! Is that justice?

DAUGHTER. Your questions are so difficult to answer, because... there are so many unforeseen cases....

POET. Caliph Harun the Just perceived that too! — Sitting peacefully on his throne on high, he could never see the plight of those below! At last complaints reached his lofty ear. So he stepped down one fine day, disguised himself, and went unobserved among the crowds, to find out what sort of justice they were getting!

DAUGHTER. Surely you don't take me for Harun the Just?

OFFICER. Let's talk about something else!... Here come strangers!

(*A white boat, shaped like a dragon, with a light-blue silken sail on a gilt yard, and a gilded mast with a rose-red pennon, glides along the strait from the left. At the helm, with their arms round each other's waists, are sitting* HE *and* SHE.)

Behold, the perfect happiness, bliss without measure, the jubilation of young love! (*The stage becomes light.*)

HE (*stands up in the boat and sings*). Hail to thee, fairest bay,
Where I dwelt in my youth's first springtime,
Where I dreamed my earliest dreams,
My dreams of roses!
Behold me returning,
Not lonely as then!
Forests and havens,
Heaven and sea,
Send her greeting!

My love and my bride,
My sun, my life!

> (*The flags on the landing-stages of Fairhaven are dipped in salute;
> white handkerchiefs are waved from villas and shores, and the
> music of harps and violins sounds over the strait.*)

POET. See how they radiate light!  Hark to the music sounding
over the water! — Eros!

OFFICER. It's Victoria!

QUARANTINE OFFICER. What if it is?

OFFICER. It's *his* Victoria: I've got my own!  Mine, that none shall
ever see!... Now hoist the quarantine flag while I haul in the
net!  (*The* QUARANTINE OFFICER *waves a yellow flag.  The*
OFFICER *pulls in a line which causes the boat to turn in towards Foulstrand.*)  Hold on there!

> (HE *and* SHE *now become aware of the hideous landscape, and
> show their disgust.*)

QUARANTINE OFFICER. Well, well! it's very trying!  But all — all
who come from infected districts must stop here!

POET. Fancy being able to speak like that, to act like that, when
you see two human beings come together in love!  Touch them
not! lay not hands on love; that is high treason!... Alas, alas!
all that is fair must now go down, down into the mud!

> (HE *and* SHE *step ashore, looking sorrowful and ashamed.*)

HE. Alas! what have we done?

QUARANTINE OFFICER. It isn't necessary to have done anything
to meet life's little discomforts!

SHE. How brief is joy and happiness!

HE. How long do we have to stay here?

QUARANTINE OFFICER. Forty days and forty nights!

SHE. We'd rather go and drown ourselves!

HE. Live here, among burnt-up hills and pigsties?

POET. Love overcomes everything, even sulphur fumes and
carbolic acid!

QUARANTINE OFFICER (*lights the stove; blue sulphur fumes burst forth*).
I'm lighting the sulphur now!  Will you kindly step in?

SHE. Oh, my blue dress will lose its colour!

QUARANTINE OFFICER. And become white!  Your red roses will
also become white!

HE. And even your cheeks! Forty days!

SHE (*to the* OFFICER). That will please you!

OFFICER. No, it will not!... No doubt your happiness was the origin of my torment, but... it doesn't matter — I've got my degree now and a situation over there... heigh-ho! And in the autumn I shall get a post in a school... to teach the boys, the same lessons that I myself learnt throughout my childhood, throughout my youth, and shall now have to teach: the same lessons, throughout my manhood and in the end throughout my old age, the same lessons: what does twice two make? how many times will two go into four without remainder?... till I get a pension and have nothing to do but wait for meals and the papers — till at last I'm carried out to the crematorium and burnt to ashes.... Have you no old pensioner out here? It's probably the worst thing after "Twice two makes four"; to begin school again when one *has* taken one's degree; to go on asking the same questions till one dies....

(*An elderly man walks past with his hands behind his back.*) Look — there goes a pensioner, just waiting for the life to go out of him; probably a captain who failed to become a major, or a clerk who wasn't made an assessor. Many are called but few are chosen.... He walks about, waiting for breakfast....

PENSIONER. No, for the paper! the morning paper!

OFFICER. And he's only fifty-four; he may go on another twenty-five years waiting for meals and the paper.... Isn't it dreadful?

PENSIONER. What is *not* dreadful? Tell me that! tell me that!

OFFICER. Yes, let him tell who can!... Now I'm going to teach boys, Twice two makes four! How many times will two go into four without remainder? (*Clutches his head in despair.*) And Victoria, whom I loved, and wished the greatest of earthly happiness... now she has her happiness, the greatest she can know, and meanwhile I suffer,... suffer, suffer!

SHE. Do you think I can be happy when I see you suffer? How can you think so? Perhaps it lightens your pain to know I shall be a prisoner here forty days and nights? Tell me, does it lighten your pain?

OFFICER. Yes, and no! I can't be happy while I see you suffering! oh!

HE. And do you think my happiness can be built on your torments?

OFFICER. We are pitiable creatures — all of us!

ALL (*stretching out their hands to heaven, utter a cry of anguish like a dissonant chord*). Oh!

DAUGHTER. O God eternal, hear them! Life is evil! Men are pitiable creatures!

ALL (*as before*). Oh!

> (*The stage becomes pitch-dark for a moment, while all who are present either go out or take up new positions. When the stage is light again, Foulstrand is seen in the background, but in shadow. The strait lies in the middle distance and Fairhaven in the foreground, both fully lighted. To the right is a corner of the assembly rooms with open windows; inside it are seen couples dancing. On an empty box outside* THREE SERVANT GIRLS *are standing, clasping one another's waists and looking on at the dance. On the steps of the assembly rooms is a bench where* UGLY EDITH *is sitting, bareheaded and sad-looking, with long, dishevelled hair. In front of her is an open piano.*
>
> *To the left is a yellow wooden house.*
>
> *Two children in summer dress are playing ball outside.*
>
> *On the nearer side of the strait is a landing-stage with white boats, and flagstaffs with flags. A white warship is anchored in the strait, a brig with gun-ports. But the whole landscape is in winter dress, with snow on the leafless trees and on the ground.*)

(*The* DAUGHTER *and the* OFFICER *come in.*)

DAUGHTER. Here is peace and happiness in holiday time! Work has ceased; every day a festival; everybody in holiday clothes; music and dancing even in the morning. (*To the* SERVANT GIRLS.) Why don't you go in and dance, girls?

SERVANTS. We?

OFFICER. But they're servants!

DAUGHTER. That's true!... But why is Edith sitting there instead of dancing? (EDITH *hides her face in her hands.*)

OFFICER. Don't ask her! She's been sitting there three hours without being invited to dance....

(*Goes into the yellow house on the left.*)

DAUGHTER. What a cruel amusement!

MOTHER (*in a low-necked dress, comes out of the assembly rooms. She goes up to* EDITH). Why don't you go in as I told you?

EDITH. Because... I can't throw myself at people. I know I'm ugly, and that's why nobody cares to dance with me; but surely I needn't be reminded of the fact!

(*Begins to play on the piano Sebastian Bach's Toccata con Fuga, No.* 10):

(*The waltz from within the hall is heard faintly at first, but afterwards increases in volume as though it were fighting against the Toccata. But* EDITH *plays it down and reduces it to silence. Dancers appear in the doorway to listen to her playing; everybody on the stage stands reverently and listens.*)

A NAVAL OFFICER (*seizes* ALICE, *one of the dancers, by the waist and leads her down to the landing-stage*). Come, quick!

(EDITH *breaks off, rises and looks at them in despair. She remains standing, as if turned to stone.*)

(*The front wall of the yellow house is now removed, and three forms are seen, with boys sitting on them: among them the* OFFICER, *who looks worried and ill at ease. In front of them stands the* MASTER, *wearing spectacles, with chalk and cane.*)

MASTER (*to the* OFFICER). Now, my boy, can you tell me what twice two is?

(*The* OFFICER *remains seated, painfully searching his memory without finding the answer.*)

You should stand up when I ask you a question!

OFFICER (*rises, apprehensively*). Twice... two... let me see... That makes two twos!

MASTER. Oho! so you've not prepared your lesson!

OFFICER (*ashamed*). Yes, I have, but... I know what it is, but I can't say it....

MASTER. You're trying to shuffle! You know, but you can't say! Perhaps I can assist you! (*Pulls his hair.*)

OFFICER. Oh, this is dreadful, dreadful!

MASTER. Yes, it is dreadful: such a big boy, and no ambition....

OFFICER (*in anguish*). A big boy! yes, I am big — much bigger than the others here. I'm grown up: I've finished with school. ... (*As if waking up.*) Why, I've taken my degree!... Why am I sitting here then? Haven't I taken my degree?

MASTER. No doubt; but you've got to sit here and mature, you see. We must mature... isn't that so?

OFFICER (*clasping his head*). Yes, that is so: we must mature.... Twice two... is two, as I propose to demonstrate by analogy — the highest form of proof! Listen now!... Once one is one; therefore twice two is two! For that which applies to the one must also apply to the other!

MASTER. The proof is perfectly in accordance with the rules of logic; nevertheless the answer is incorrect!

OFFICER. Whatever is in accordance with the rules of logic cannot be incorrect! Let us test the case! One into one goes once: therefore two into two goes twice!

MASTER. Quite correct according to analogy. But how much is once three?

OFFICER. Three!

MASTER. Consequently twice three is also three!

OFFICER (*thoughtfully*). No, that cannot be right... it cannot be... for if so... (*Sits down in despair.*) No, I am not mature yet!

MASTER. No, you're very far from that....

OFFICER. How long shall I have to stay here then?

MASTER. How long? Do you believe that time and space exist?... Assuming that time does exist, then you ought to be able to tell us what time is! What is time?

OFFICER. Time? (*Considers.*) I can't say, though I know what it is: *ergo*, I may know what twice two is, without being able to say! Can you say yourself what time is?

MASTER. Of course I can!

ALL THE BOYS. Tell us then!

MASTER. Time?... Let me see! (*Remains standing motionless, with his finger on his nose.*) While we are speaking, time flies. Consequently time is something which flies while I am speaking!

A BOY (*getting up*). You're speaking now, sir, and while you're speaking, I fly; consequently I am time!    (*Flies.*)

MASTER. That is quite correct according to the rules of logic!

OFFICER. Then the rules of logic are absurd. Nils, who fled away then, cannot be time!

MASTER. That is also quite correct according to the rules of logic, even though it is absurd.

OFFICER. Then logic is absurd!

MASTER. It really seems so! But if logic is absurd, then the whole world is absurd... and I'll be damned if I sit here and teach you absurdities!... If there's anybody to stand us a drink we'll go and bathe!

OFFICER. That's a *posterus prius* — a world turned upside down! It's usual to bathe first and have one's drink afterwards! You old fossil!

MASTER. Don't be so stuck-up, Doctor!

OFFICER. Captain, if you please. I'm an Officer, and I don't understand why I should sit here to be insulted among a lot of schoolboys....

MASTER (*raising his finger*). We had to mature, you know!

QUARANTINE OFFICER (*coming in*). The quarantine is beginning!

OFFICER. Oh, there you are! Fancy this fellow making me sit on a school bench when I've taken my degree!

QUARANTINE OFFICER. Then why don't you go away?

OFFICER. Why indeed!... Go away? That's not so easy!

MASTER. So I should think! Just try!

OFFICER (*to the* QUARANTINE OFFICER). Save me! save me from his eye!

QUARANTINE OFFICER. Come now!... Come and help us dance.... We must dance before the plague breaks out! We really must!

OFFICER. Is the ship leaving then?

QUARANTINE OFFICER. The ship will leave first!... There'll be some tears shed of course!

OFFICER. Always tears: when she comes, and when she goes!... Let's go!

(*They go out. The* MASTER *continues his lesson in silence.*)
(*The* SERVANT GIRLS *who had been standing by the window of the dancing hall, walk sadly down to the landing-stage.*

EDITH, *who had been standing motionless at the piano, follows them.*)

DAUGHTER (*to the* OFFICER). Isn't there one single happy person in this paradise?

OFFICER. Yes, there's a newly married couple! Listen to them!

(*The newly married couple comes in.*)

HUSBAND (*to the* WIFE). My happiness is so unspeakable that I could gladly die....

WIFE. Why die?

HUSBAND. Because in the midst of happiness grows the seed of unhappiness; it consumes itself like a flame of fire.... It cannot burn for ever, but must die out; this presentiment of the end annihilates bliss at its very climax.

WIFE. Let us die together, now, now!

HUSBAND. Die? Let us die then! For I fear Fortune — the deceitful jade! (*They go towards the sea.*)

DAUGHTER (*to the* OFFICER). Life is evil! Men are pitiable creatures!

OFFICER. Look at that man coming now! He's the most envied mortal in the place!

(*The* BLIND MAN *is led in.*)

He's the owner of these hundred Italian villas; he owns all these bays, creeks, shores, woods, together with the fish in the water, the birds in the air, and the game in the woods. These thousand human beings are his tenants, and the sun rises over his sea, and sets over his lands....

DAUGHTER. Well, does he complain too?

OFFICER. Yes, and with good reason: he can't see!

QUARANTINE OFFICER. He's blind!...

DAUGHTER. The most envied of all!

OFFICER. Now he's going to see the ship go off, with his son on board!

BLIND MAN. I can't see, but I can hear! I hear the fluke of the anchor tearing the clay bottom, just as when the hook is drawn out of a fish, and the heart comes up with it through the gullet!... My son, my only child, is journeying across the wide ocean into alien lands; I can follow him only in thought;... now I can hear the chain rattling... and... there's something that goes flapping and snapping, like clothes drying on a line... wet handkerchiefs perhaps... and I can hear the sound of gasping and sobbing as if people were crying... is it the splashing of the little waves against the sides of the boat, or is it the girls on the shore... abandoned... comfortless?... I asked a child once why the sea was salt; the child, whose father was on a long voyage, replied at once, The sea is salt because sailors cry so much. But why do sailors cry so much?... Well, he said, because they're always having to go away... so they're always drying their handkerchiefs on the masts!... And why do people cry when they're sad? I asked.... Well, said he, that's because the glassy part of the eye must be washed sometimes so that one can see better!...

(*The brig has now set sail and is gliding away; the girls on the shore wave their handkerchiefs and dry their eyes alternately. And now on the fore-topmast is hoisted the signal "Yes" — a red ball on a white ground. ALICE waves triumphantly in reply.*)

DAUGHTER (*to the* OFFICER). What does that flag mean?

OFFICER. It means "Yes." It's the Lieutenant's "yes" in red — red as the heart's blood, inscribed on the blue canvas of the sky!

DAUGHTER. What does "no" look like then?

OFFICER. That is blue, like the tainted blood in blue veins... but look at Alice, how radiant she is!

DAUGHTER. And look how Edith is crying!...

BLIND MAN. Meet and part! part and meet! that is life! I met his mother! And then she went! Our boy was left me; now he is gone!

DAUGHTER. But he'll come back, won't he?...

BLIND MAN. Who is speaking to me? I have heard that voice before, in my dreams, in my youth, when the summer holidays began; in my newly married life, when my child was born; whenever life smiled I heard that voice, like the south wind's sighing, like a harp chord from above, like the angels' greeting as I feel it must be on Christmas Eve...

*(The* LAWYER *comes in, goes up to the* BLIND MAN *and whispers.)*

BLIND MAN. Really?

LAWYER. Yes, it's true! *(Goes to the* DAUGHTER.*)* Now you've seen most of it, but you haven't experienced the worst.

DAUGHTER. What can that be?

LAWYER. Reiterations... repetitions!... Going back! doing one's lessons over again.... Come!

DAUGHTER. Where?

LAWYER. To your duties!

DAUGHTER. What are they?

LAWYER. Everything you abominate most! everything you don't want to do, and yet must do! To abstain, to renounce, to go without, to leave behind... everything that is unpleasant, repulsive, painful...

DAUGHTER. Are there no such things as pleasant duties?

LAWYER. They become pleasant when they are fulfilled...

DAUGHTER. When they no longer exist.... Duty then is altogether unpleasant! What is pleasant then?

LAWYER. What is pleasant is sin.

DAUGHTER. Sin?

LAWYER. Yes, and punishment will follow! If I've had a pleasant day and evening, I suffer from hell's torments and an evil conscience next day.

DAUGHTER. How strange!

LAWYER. Yes, I wake up in the morning with a headache; and then begins the repetition, but a perverted repetition. For instance, everything that was pretty, pleasant and witty the night before, memory represents the next morning as ugly, repulsive and stupid. Pleasure seems to decay, and joy falls to pieces. What men call success is always a step towards the next failure. The successes I have had in life have been my ruin. Men have an instinctive horror of the prosperity of others; they think it unjust that fate should favour any one man, and they seek accordingly to restore the equilibrium by rolling stones on to the road. To possess talent is a mortal danger; one may so easily starve to death!... However, go back to your duties, or I shall take proceedings against you, and we'll go through all three courts, one, two, three!

DAUGHTER. Go back? to the stove and cabbage pot, and the baby-clothes...

LAWYER. Yes, yes! there's a big wash today; we have to wash all the handkerchiefs...

DAUGHTER. Oh, must I do that again?

LAWYER. All life consists in doing things again.... Look at the master in there.... He took his degree yesterday, with laurel wreath and gun salute, climbed Parnassus and was embraced by the monarch... and today he starts school again, asks how much twice two is, and will continue so doing till he dies.... However, come back to your home!

DAUGHTER. I'd rather kill myself!

LAWYER. Kill yourself? You can't do that! In the first place it's dishonourable — even one's dead body is insulted: and secondly, ... one is damned for it!... it's one of the deadly sins!

DAUGHTER. It is not easy — being a mortal!

ALL. Hear, hear!

DAUGHTER. I shall not go back with you to humiliation and dirt!... I would ascend to the place whence I came, but... the door must first be opened, so that I may know the secret... I insist on the door being opened!

LAWYER. Then you must retrace your steps, return the way you came; put up with all the horrors, the repetitions, the redraftings, the reiterations of the lawsuit....

DAUGHTER. Be that as it may, I must first go out into solitude and the wilderness, to find myself again! We shall meet later! (*To the* POET.) Come with me! (*A cry of lamentation far away beyond the background:* "Woe! woe! woe!") What was that?

LAWYER. The lost souls at Foulstrand!

DAUGHTER. Why do they complain today more than usual?

LAWYER. Because the sun is shining here — because there is music here, and dancing, and youth! That makes them feel their suffering so much more.

DAUGHTER. We must set them free!

LAWYER. Try! Once there came a liberator, but he was hanged on a cross!

DAUGHTER. By whom?

LAWYER. By all right-thinking men!

DAUGHTER. Who are they?

LAWYER. Don't you know who all right-thinking men are? You soon will, though!

DAUGHTER. Were they the ones who refused you your degree?

LAWYER. Yes!

DAUGHTER. Then I know them!

*(A sea-coast on the Mediterranean. To the left, in the foreground, is seen a white wall, above which appear branches of orange-trees with fruit. In the background are villas, and a Casino with a terrace. To the right is a large heap of coal and two wheelbarrows. In the background, to the right, a strip of blue sea.*

TWO COALHEAVERS, *naked to the waist, with their faces and hands black, and the naked parts of their bodies, are sitting in despair on their wheelbarrows. The* DAUGHTER *and the* LAWYER *are seen in the background.)*

DAUGHTER. This is Paradise!

FIRST COALHEAVER. This is hell!

SECOND COALHEAVER. A hundred and twenty in the shade!

FIRST COALHEAVER. Shall we go and bathe?

SECOND COALHEAVER. Then the police'll come! No bathing allowed here!

FIRST COALHEAVER. Couldn't we pick an orange off that tree?

SECOND COALHEAVER. No, the police would come.

FIRST COALHEAVER. But I can't work in this heat; I shall just throw up the job.

SECOND COALHEAVER. Then the police'll come and nab you!... *(A pause.)* Besides, you won't have anything to eat...

FIRST COALHEAVER. Nothing to eat? It's we that do the most work that get the least food; and the rich, who do nothing, get the most!... Couldn't one — without taking liberties with the truth — call this unfair?... What does the Daughter of the Gods say?

DAUGHTER. I cannot answer!... But tell me — what have you done to get so black and to have such a hard life?

FIRST COALHEAVER. What have we done? We've been born of poor and fairly bad parents.... Perhaps punished once or twice!

DAUGHTER. Punished?

FIRST COALHEAVER. Yes; the unpunished live up there in the Casino, dining on eight courses and wine.

DAUGHTER (*to the* LAWYER). Can this be true?

LAWYER. On the whole, yes!...

DAUGHTER. You mean that every human being at some time or other has deserved imprisonment?

LAWYER. Yes!

DAUGHTER. Even you?

LAWYER. Yes!

DAUGHTER. Is it true the wretched creatures aren't allowed to bathe in the sea here?

LAWYER. No, not even with their clothes on! Only those who attempt to drown themselves get off paying. And they probably get beaten, up at the police station!

DAUGHTER. Can't they go outside the town and bathe, out in the country?

LAWYER. There is no country: it's all fenced in!

DAUGHTER. In the free, open spaces, I mean!

LAWYER. There's nothing free: somebody owns it all!

DAUGHTER. Even the sea — the great wide...

LAWYER. Everything! You can't go in a boat on the sea and land anywhere without having it booked and paid for. It's fine!

DAUGHTER. This is not Paradise!

LAWYER. It certainly is not!

DAUGHTER. Why don't people do something to better their position....

LAWYER. Doubtless they do; but all who try that end in prison or the madhouse....

DAUGHTER. Who puts them in prison?

LAWYER. All right-thinking people, all decent...

DAUGHTER. Who puts them in the madhouse?

LAWYER. Their own despair, when they see that the struggle is hopeless!

DAUGHTER. Has it never occurred to anyone that there may be some mysterious reason for the present order of things?

LAWYER. Yes, those who are well off always think so!

DAUGHTER. That things are all right as they are?...

FIRST COALHEAVER. And yet we are the foundations of society. If you can't get coal the kitchen stove goes out, and the sitting-room fire, and the machines in the factory stop working; the

lights go out in street and shop and home; darkness and cold
are upon you... and that's why we sweat like hell, carrying the
black coal.... What do you give us in return?

LAWYER (*to the* DAUGHTER).   Help them... (*A pause.*)   I recognize
that things can't be quite the same for all: but need they differ
so much?

(*The* GENTLEMAN *and the* LADY *cross the stage.*)

LADY.  Are you coming to have a game with us?

GENTLEMAN.  No, I must take a little walk to get an appetite for
dinner!

FIRST COALHEAVER.  To *get* an appetite?

SECOND COALHEAVER.  To *get*...?

(*Some children come in; they shriek with horror when they catch sight
of the grimy workers.*)

FIRST COALHEAVER.  They shriek when they catch sight of us! they
shriek...

SECOND COALHEAVER.  God damn them!... I suppose we'll have
to get the scaffolds out soon and set to work on this rotten
body...

FIRST COALHEAVER.  God damn them, I say too!  Curses on them!

LAWYER (*to the* DAUGHTER).  It's all wrong!  People aren't so
bad... but...

DAUGHTER.  But...?

LAWYER.  But the Government...

DAUGHTER (*hides her face and goes out*).  This is not Paradise!

THE COALHEAVERS.  No, it's hell — just hell!

(*Fingal's Cave.   Long grey billows are rolling gently into the cave.
In the foreground a red-painted bell-buoy is rocking on the waves,
but does not give any sound till the place indicated.   Music of
the winds.   Music of the waves.*)

(*The* DAUGHTER *and the* POET.)

POET.  Where hast thou led me?

DAUGHTER.  Far from the hum and wailing of the children of men,
to the utmost bounds of Ocean, to that cave whose name is
"Indra's Ear," since here men say the King of Heaven listens
to the complaints of mortals!

POET. What — here?

DAUGHTER. See'st thou not how the cave is formed like a shell!
Yea, thou see'st it! Knowest thou not that thine ear is formed
like a shell? Thou knowest, but hast not thought thereon.
(*She picks up a shell from the shore.*) Hast thou never, as a child,
held a shell to thine ear and listened... listened to the murmur
of thy heart's blood, to the humming of thoughts in thy brain,
to the snapping of a thousand little worn-out threads in the
fabric of thy body?... All these canst thou hear in this little
shell; think then what may be heard in this great one!...

POET (*listening*). I hear nothing but the sighing of the wind....

DAUGHTER. Then I will be its interpreter! Listen! The Winds'
complaint! (*Recites to soft music.*)

> Born beneath the clouds of heaven,
> Hunted were we of Indra's lightning-fires
> Down to the dusty Earth...
> Soiled were our feet, drenched by the sodden acres;
> Dust of the country roads,
> Smoke from the cities,
> Evil draughts of breath,
> Of food and fumes of wine,
> Doomed were we to suffer...
> Over the ocean wide we winged our way,
> To fill our lungs with air,
> To flutter our wings in flight,
> To cleanse our muddied feet.
> Indra, Lord of the Heavens,
> Hear us!
> Hark to our sighing!
> Earth is all unclean,
> Life a worthless boon,
> Men nor good nor evil:
> Living as they can,
> From day to day.
> Sons of the dust,
> Through dust they wander,
> Born of the dust
> In dust they end.

Feet for tramping have they gained,
Wings possess not.
Soiled of the dust they grow —
Is the fault theirs,
Or thine?

POET. So heard I once awhile...

DAUGHTER. Hush! for the winds sing yet!    (*Recites to soft music.*)
We are the winds, children of air,
Bearers of mortal wailing.
Us thou hast heard
On autumn eves in the chimneys,
In stove-vents singing,
In panes of windows,
When the rain wept tears on the roof-plates;
Through the long winter nights,
In snowy woods of pine:
On the gusty ocean
Hast thou not heard the lament
In rigging and sail?...
'Twas we, the winds,
Children of air,
Who from mortal breasts
That ourselves had pierced
Had learnt these notes of torture...
In sick-room,
On battle-field,
In the nursery most,
Where the new-born cry,
Lamenting, shrieking,
From the pain of being alive.
It is we, we, the winds,
That wail and whistle
"Woe, woe, woe!"

POET. Methinks that once before...

DAUGHTER. Hush! the waves are singing.    (*Recites to soft music.*)
It is we, we, the waves,
That rock the winds
To rest!

> Green-hued cradles we waves:
> Wet we are, and salt;
> Like unto flames of fire —
> Wet flames are we.
> Quenching and burning,
> Cleansing and bathing,
> Breeding, engendering;
> We, we, the waves,
> That rock the winds
> To rest!

DAUGHTER. False waves and faithless; all on earth that is not burned is drowned — in the waves. — Look at this. (*Pointing to a heap of relics.*) Behold what the sea has stolen and shattered ... Of the sunken ships the figure-heads alone remain... and the names: Justice, Friendship, Golden Peace, Hope — that is all that is left of Hope... delusive Hope!... Spars, rullocks, bailers! And see! the lifebuoy, which saved itself, and let those in need perish!

POET (*searching in the heap*). Here is the name-board of the ship Justice: the same that left Fairhaven with the Blind Man's son on board. Sunk then! And on her too was Alice's sweetheart — Edith's hopeless love.

DAUGHTER. The Blind Man? Fairhaven? I must have dreamt it! And Alice's betrothed, ugly Edith, Foulstrand and the quarantine, the sulphur and carbolic acid, the conferment of degrees in the church, the Lawyer's office, the corridor and Victoria, the Growing Castle and the Officer... All these I have dreamt....

POET. I made a poem of them once!

DAUGHTER. Thou knowest then what poetry is....

POET. Nay, I know what dreaming is.... What is poetry?

DAUGHTER. Not reality, but more than reality... not dreaming, but waking dreams....

POET. And the children of men believe that we poets merely play ... that we devise and invent!

DAUGHTER. 'Tis well, my friend: or the world would lie desolate for lack of inspiration. All men would be lying on their backs, gazing up to heaven; none would touch plough or spade, plane or mattock.

POET. Speakest thou so, Daughter of Indra, thou who half belongest to heaven....

DAUGHTER. Rightly dost thou upbraid me; too long have I sojourned here below, bathing in the mud, even as thou... my thoughts can no longer fly; clay is on their wings... mould on their feet... and I myself — (*raising her arms*) — I sink, I sink... Help me, Father, God of Heaven! (*Silence.*) No longer do I hear His answer! the ether bears no more the sound from his lips to the shell of my ear... the silver thread is snapped... Woe is me, I am earthbound!

POET. Is it thy will to ascend... soon?

DAUGHTER. As soon as I have burnt this earthly element... the waters of the ocean cannot make me clean. Why askest thou?

POET. Because I have a prayer... a petition...

DAUGHTER. What kind of petition...

POET. A petition from humanity to the ruler of the universe, set forth by a dreamer!

DAUGHTER. To be presented by...?

POET. Indra's daughter....

DAUGHTER. Canst thou repeat thy poem?

POET. I can.

DAUGHTER. Speak it then!

POET. Rather thou!

DAUGHTER. Where can I read it?

POET. In my thoughts, or here! (*Gives her a roll of paper.*)

DAUGHTER. Well, I will speak it then!

(*Takes the paper, but recites the poem from memory.*)

DAUGHTER. "Wherefore art thou born in anguish,
Wherefore torturest thou thy mother,
Child of man, when thou art bringing
To her soul the joy maternal,
Joy all earthly joys excelling?
Wherefore must thy life's awakening,
Thy first greeting to the sunlight,
Be a cry of fury and of anguish?
Canst not greet thy life with smiling,
Child of man, since life's bestowal
Should be happiness itself?

Born are we like beasts that perish,
We, whose line descends from God and Man!
Meeter for the soul some nobler garment
Than this robe of filth and blood!
Must God's image change its teeth..."
Hush, too curious! let the work not blame the Master!
Life's great riddle none hath answered yet!...
"Then begin the years of wandering
Over stones and thorns and thistles;
Goes thy way along some beaten track,
Straightway read the sign 'Forbidden';
Dare to pluck a flower, and swift
Sounds the warning cry, 'It is another's';
Comes a field athwart thy pathway
On the road that thou must go,
Lo, thou spoilst another's harvest;
Others then shall trample thine,
So the balance may be equal!
Every joy that doth befall thee
Brings to all thy fellows woe;
Yet thy woe brings no man gladness,
So is woe still heaped on woe!
Travellest on till thou art dead:
Death for thee is others' bread!"

With such words as these thou thinkest,
Son of dust, to approach the Almighty...?
POET. How should son of dust discover
Words so light, so pure, so airy,
As might soar from Earth to Heaven?
Child of God, wilt thou interpret
Our lament into the speech
Comprehended by the Immortals?
DAUGHTER. I will!
POET (*pointing to the buoy*).  What is that floating there?... a
buoy?
DAUGHTER. Yes!

POET. It is like a lung with a windpipe!

DAUGHTER. It is the watchman of the sea. When danger is afoot it sings.

POET. Methinks the sea is rising and the waves begin to roll...

DAUGHTER. So it seems!

POET. Alas! What do I see? A ship... just off the rocks.

DAUGHTER. What ship can that be?

POET. I think it is the ghost-ship.

DAUGHTER. What is that?

POET. "The Flying Dutchman."

DAUGHTER. Is it he? Why is he punished so cruelly, and why does he not land?

POET. Because he had seven unfaithful wives.

DAUGHTER. Must he be punished for that?

POET. Yes! all right-thinking men condemned him....

DAUGHTER. A strange world!... How then can he be freed from the curse?

POET. Freed? Not lightly would one set free...

DAUGHTER. Why not?

POET. Because... No, it is not the Dutchman! it is a common ship in distress!... Why then does the buoy give no sound? Look! the sea is rising, the waves run high; soon we shall be imprisoned in the cave!... The ship's bell is ringing now! — Soon we shall have one more figure-head here.... Cry out, buoy! do thy duty, O watchman!... (*The buoy sings a four-part chord in fifths and sixths, like the sound of foghorns.*) The crew is waving to us... but we ourselves perish!

DAUGHTER. Dost thou not long for the liberation?

POET. Oh, yes, yes! but not now... and not by water!

THE CREW (*singing in four-part harmony*). Christ, Kyrie!

Christ ky - ri - e!

POET. They are calling now; and the sea calls! But none hears.

THE CREW (*as before*). Christ, Kyrie!

DAUGHTER. Who is that coming?

POET. Walking upon the water? There is only one who walks upon the water — not Peter, the solid rock, for he sank like a stone.... (*A white glow appears over the sea.*)

THE CREW. Christ, Kyrie!

DAUGHTER. Is that He?

POET. It is He, the Crucified...

DAUGHTER. Why — tell me — why was He crucified?

POET. Because He wished to free...

DAUGHTER. Who were they — I have forgotten — that crucified Him?

POET. All right-thinking men.

DAUGHTER. What a strange world!

POET. The sea is rising! Darkness is overtaking us.... The storm is growing... (*The CREW shriek aloud.*)

POET. The crew cry out in horror when they behold their Saviour ... And now... they leap overboard, fearing the Redeemer... (*The CREW utter another shriek.*)

Now they cry out because they are going to die! Crying when they are born, and crying when they die!

(*The mounting waves threaten to drown them in the cave.*)

DAUGHTER. If I were sure it was a ship...

POET. In truth I do not believe it is a ship... it is a two-storied house, with trees in front... and... a telephone tower... a tower that reaches up to the skies.... It is the modern tower of Babel, sending wires aloft — to tell those above...

DAUGHTER. Child, the thought of man needs no metal wire for its flight... the prayer of the righteous forces its way through the worlds.... Surely this is no tower of Babel; would'st thou storm the heaven, storm it with thy prayers!

POET. No, it is not a house... not a telephone tower... see'st thou there?

DAUGHTER. What see'st thou?

POET. I see a snow-clad heath, a parade ground.... The winter sun is shining behind a church on the hill, and the tower casts its long shadow on the snow.... And now a troop of soldiers comes marching along the heath; they march along the tower, up the spire; now they are on the cross, but I seem to know that the first to tread on the weather-cock must die.... Now they are near it... the corporal at their head... ha-ha! a cloud comes sailing over the heath, passing over the sun... and now all is gone... the moisture of the cloud has quenched the sun's fire! — the sunlight created the shadow-image of the tower, but the shadow-image of the cloud quenched the shadow-image of the tower....

(*During the above speech the scene has again changed to the corridor of the theatre.*)

DAUGHTER (*to the* PORTRESS). Has the Lord Chancellor arrived yet?

PORTRESS. No!

DAUGHTER. The Deans then?

PORTRESS. No!

DAUGHTER. Call them at once then: the door is going to be opened....

PORTRESS. Is it so urgent?

DAUGHTER. Yes. It is suspected that the solution of the world's riddle is stored up in there!... Summon the Lord Chancellor and the Deans of the four faculties then! (*The* PORTRESS *blows a whistle.*) And don't forget the Glazier and his diamond, or nothing can be done!

(*The stage people come in from the left, as at the beginning of the play.*)

OFFICER (*comes in at the back, in frock-coat and tall hat with a bunch of roses in his hand. Looks radiantly happy*). Victoria!

PORTRESS. Madam will be here in a minute!

OFFICER. Good! the carriage is waiting, the table is laid and the champagne is on ice.... Let me embrace you, madam. (*Embraces the* PORTRESS.) Victoria!

A WOMAN'S VOICE (*from above, sings*). I am here!

OFFICER (*beginning to walk about*). All right! I'm waiting.

POET. I seem to have lived through this before...

DAUGHTER. And I.

POET. Perhaps I have dreamt it?

DAUGHTER. Or made a poem of it perhaps?

POET. Or made a poem of it.

DAUGHTER. Then you know what poetry is.

POET. I know what dreaming is.

DAUGHTER. I feel as though we had spoken these words before, somewhere else.

POET. Then you will soon be able to work out for yourself what reality is!

DAUGHTER. Or dreaming!

POET. Or poetry!

(*The* LORD CHANCELLOR, *the* DEANS *of the Faculties of Theology, Philosophy, Medicine and Jurisprudence.*)

LORD CHANCELLOR. The question concerns the door, I understand! — What does the Dean of the Theological Faculty think about it?

DEAN OF THEOLOGY. I don't think — I believe... *credo*...

DEAN OF PHILOSOPHY. I regard...

DEAN OF MEDICINE. I know...

DEAN OF JURISPRUDENCE. I doubt, until I have heard evidence and witnesses!

LORD CHANCELLOR. Quarrelling again, are you?... Well, first of all, what does Theology believe?

DEAN OF THEOLOGY. I believe that this door ought not to be opened, because it conceals dangerous truths...

DEAN OF PHILOSOPHY. The truth is never dangerous.

DEAN OF MEDICINE. What is truth?

DEAN OF JURISPRUDENCE. Whatever can be proved by two witnesses.

DEAN OF THEOLOGY. Anything can be proved by two false witnesses — if you're a pettifogger.

DEAN OF PHILOSOPHY. Truth is wisdom; and wisdom, knowledge, is philosophy itself.... Philosophy is the science of sciences, the knowledge of knowledge; all other sciences are its servants.

DEAN OF MEDICINE. The only science is natural science: philosophy isn't science at all — just empty speculation.

DEAN OF THEOLOGY. Bravo!

DEAN OF PHILOSOPHY (*to* DEAN OF THEOLOGY). Bravo, you say! And what are you, may I ask? You are the hereditary foe of all knowledge, the antithesis of science; you are ignorance and darkness...

DEAN OF MEDICINE. Bravo!

DEAN OF THEOLOGY (*to* DEAN OF MEDICINE). And you say Bravo! you who can't see further than the length of your nose in a magnifying-glass: you who believe in nothing but your own delusive senses — in your sense of sight, for example, which may be long-sighted, short-sighted, blind, purblind, squinting, one-eyed, colour-blind, red-blind, green-blind...

DEAN OF MEDICINE. Blockhead!

DEAN OF THEOLOGY. Ass! (*They fight.*)

LORD CHANCELLOR. Peace! crows shouldn't pick each other's eyes out.

DEAN OF PHILOSOPHY. If I had to choose between those two, Theology and Medicine, I should choose — neither!

DEAN OF JURISPRUDENCE. And if I had to sit in judgment on you other three, I should condemn — you all!... You can't agree on one single point, and you never could! — Let's get back to the case once more! What are the Lord Chancellor's views as to this door and its opening?

LORD CHANCELLOR. Views? I have no views! I am merely appointed by the Government to see that you don't break one another's arms and legs in this court... while you are educating the young. Views? No, I take good care not to have any. There was a time when I had a few, but they were at once refuted. Views always are at once refuted — by one's opponents, of course!... Perhaps we can now have the door opened, even at the risk of its concealing dangerous truths?

DEAN OF JURISPRUDENCE. What is truth? what is the truth?

DEAN OF THEOLOGY. I am the truth and the life...

DEAN OF PHILOSOPHY. I am the knowledge of knowledge...

DEAN OF MEDICINE. I am the one exact knowledge...

DEAN OF JURISPRUDENCE. I doubt! (*They fight.*)

DAUGHTER. For shame, teachers of youth!

DEAN OF JURISPRUDENCE. Lord Chancellor, delegate of the Government, head of the body of teachers, denounce this woman's offence! She has cried shame on you, which is contumelious language; moreover in a derisive, ironical sense she has called you teachers of youth, and that is slander.

DAUGHTER. Poor youth!

DEAN OF JURISPRUDENCE. She pities youth — tantamount to accusing *us*. Lord Chancellor, denounce her offence!

DAUGHTER. Yes, I accuse you, all of you together, of sowing doubt and dissension in the minds of the young.

DEAN OF JURISPRUDENCE. Listen to her! She herself raises doubts in the young as to our authority, and then accuses *us* of raising doubts. I ask all right-thinking men — is that not a criminal act?

ALL RIGHT-THINKING MEN. Yes, it is criminal.

DEAN OF JURISPRUDENCE. All right-thinking men have condemned you! — Go in peace, with your gains! Or else...

DAUGHTER. My gains? — Or else? Else what?

DEAN OF JURISPRUDENCE. Or else you'll be stoned.

POET. Or crucified.

DAUGHTER. I will go. Come with me, and you shall learn the riddle!

POET. Which riddle?

DAUGHTER. What does he mean by "my gains"?

POET. Probably nothing. It's what we call nonsense. He was talking nonsense.

DAUGHTER. But that was what hurt me most!

POET. Do doubt that's why he said it... Men are like that.

ALL RIGHT-THINKING MEN. Hurrah! the door is opened!

LORD CHANCELLOR. What was concealed behind the door?

GLAZIER. I can't see anything.

LORD CHANCELLOR. He can't see anything: I can quite believe it! ... Deans! what was concealed behind the door?

DEAN OF THEOLOGY. Nothing! That is the solution of the world's riddle... Of nothing in the beginning God created the heaven and the earth.

DEAN OF PHILOSOPHY. From nothing proceeds nothing.

DEAN OF MEDICINE. Bosh! that is nothing.

DEAN OF JURISPRUDENCE. I doubt! Moreover there is some deception here. I appeal to all right-thinking men!

DAUGHTER (*to the* POET). Who are the right-thinking men?

POET. Yes, let him say who can! In most cases "all right-thinking men" consists of one person. Today it is I and mine, tomorrow you and yours. — One is nominated for the post: more correctly, one nominates oneself.

ALL RIGHT-THINKING MEN. We have been deceived!

LORD CHANCELLOR. Who has deceived you?

ALL RIGHT-THINKING MEN. The Daughter!

LORD CHANCELLOR. Will the Daughter be so good as to inform us what her idea was in having this door opened?

DAUGHTER. No, friends! If I told you, you wouldn't believe me.

DEAN OF MEDICINE. But there's nothing there.

DAUGHTER. You have said it. But you haven't understood!

DEAN OF MEDICINE. What she says is bosh.

ALL. Bosh!

DAUGHTER (to the POET). They are pitiable creatures.

POET. Do you mean that seriously?

DAUGHTER. Always seriously.

POET. And are right-thinking men also pitiable?

DAUGHTER. They perhaps most of all.

POET. And the four Faculties too?

DAUGHTER. They too, and by no means the least! Four heads, four minds, on one body! Who created that monster?

ALL. She doesn't answer!

LORD CHANCELLOR. Stone her then!

DAUGHTER. I have answered.

LORD CHANCELLOR. Listen! she is answering.

ALL. Stone her! she is answering.

DAUGHTER. Whether she answers, or doesn't answer — stone her! ... Come, thou Seer, and I will tell you the riddle — but far from here — out in the wilderness where none can hear us, none can see us! For...

LAWYER (comes forward and takes the DAUGHTER by the arm). Have you forgotten your duties?

DAUGHTER. Good heavens, no! But I have higher duties.

LAWYER. And your child?

DAUGHTER. My child! what of it?

LAWYER. Your child is calling for you.

DAUGHTER. My child! Alas, I am bound to earth!... And this torture in my breast, this anguish... what is it?

LAWYER. Don't you know?

DAUGHTER. No!

LAWYER. It is the pangs of conscience.

DAUGHTER. Are these the pangs of conscience?

LAWYER. Yes! and they come after every neglected duty, after every pleasure, even the most innocent — if there are such things as innocent pleasures, which is doubtful; and after every suffering inflicted on one's neighbour.

DAUGHTER. And there is no remedy?

LAWYER. Yes, but only one! To fulfil one's duty at once....

DAUGHTER. You look like a devil when you mention the word duty! — And when one has two duties to fulfil, as I have?

LAWYER. Fulfil first the one and then the other!

DAUGHTER. The highest first.... Look after my child, then, and I will do my duty....

LAWYER. Your child is suffering because it misses you.... Can you bear to know that a human being is suffering because of you?

DAUGHTER. Unrest now is in my soul... it has been rent in twain, and is pulled in two directions!

LAWYER. Life's little discords, you see!

DAUGHTER. Oh, how it pulls!

POET. If you only knew what sorrow and desolation I have spread in the exercise of my calling — yes, calling, which is the highest duty — you would not care to take me by the hand!

DAUGHTER. Why not?

POET. I had a father whose hopes were centred in me, as an only son who would carry on his affairs.... I ran away from the Commercial College.... My father worried himself to death.... My mother wanted me to be religious... I couldn't be that... she disowned me.... I had a friend who helped me through the hard times.... That friend behaved like a tyrant to those for whom I spoke and sang. I had to strike down my friend and benefactor in order to save my soul! Since then I have had no peace; men call me dishonourable, the scum of the earth. What help is it that my conscience tells me, "You have done right," when the next moment it says, "You have done wrong"? Such is life!

DAUGHTER. Come with me into the wilderness!

LAWYER. Your child!

DAUGHTER (*pointing to all present*). These are my children! Individually they are good, but they have only to get together to quarrel and turn into demons.... Farewell!

> (*Outside the castle. The same scenery as in Act I, Scene I. But the ground beneath the castle walls is now covered with flowers (blue monkshood, aconite). On the roof of the castle, at the very top of the lantern, is seen a chrysanthemum bud on the point of opening. The castle windows are illuminated with wax candles.*)

> (*The* DAUGHTER *and the* POET.)

DAUGHTER. The hour is at hand when, by the aid of fire, I shall ascend into the ether again... It is what you mortals call death — the death that you approach in fear.

POET. Fear of the unknown.

DAUGHTER. Which you know.

POET. Who knows it?

DAUGHTER. All men! Why do you not believe your prophets?

POET. Prophets have never been believed; why is that? And "If God hath spoken, why then do men not believe?" His convincing might should be irresistible!

DAUGHTER. Have you always doubted?

POET. No! Often I have had the certainty; but after a time it passed away, like a dream when one awakes!

DAUGHTER. It is not easy — being a mortal!

POET. You understand and admit that?...

DAUGHTER. Yes!

POET. Tell me: was it not Indra who once sent his son down to Earth to hear the complaints of mankind?

DAUGHTER. Yes: and how was he received?

POET. How did he fulfil his mission? — to answer with a question.

DAUGHTER. To answer with another... Was not the state of mankind better after his visit to Earth? Answer truthfully!

POET. Better?... Yes, a little! a very little!... But instead of asking questions, will you tell me the riddle?

DAUGHTER. Yes, but what good will it be — since you won't believe me?

POET. I shall believe *you*, for I know who you are!

DAUGHTER. Well then, I will tell you! In the dawn of time, before the sun shone, Brahma, the divine primeval force, let himself be enticed by Maya, mother of the world, to propagate himself. This mingling of the divine element with the earthly was Heaven's Fall. The world, life, and humanity are thus but a phantom, a semblance, a dream-image...

POET. My dream!

DAUGHTER. A dream come true! But in order to get free of the earthly element, Brahma's descendants seek privation and suffering.... Here you have suffering as the liberator.... But this yearning for suffering comes into conflict with the craving for enjoyment, which is love... and now you understand what love is, with its highest joys merged in the greatest sufferings, the sweetest in the bitterest! Do you understand now what woman is? Woman, through whom sin and death entered into life?

POET. I understand!... And the end?...

DAUGHTER. That you know... The conflict between the pain of enjoyment and the enjoyment of suffering... the pangs of the penitent and the pleasures of the sensualist...

POET. Conflict then?

DAUGHTER. Conflict between opposites gives birth to power, just as fire and water give steam-power....

POET. But peace? rest?

DAUGHTER. Hush! you must ask no more, and I must not answer! ... The altar is already adorned for the sacrifice... the flowers are keeping watch; the lights are kindled... white sheets before the windows... fir twigs in the porch....

POET. You speak as calmly as though suffering did not exist for you!

DAUGHTER. Not exist?... I have suffered all your sufferings; but a hundredfold, since my perceptions were finer....

POET. Tell me your sorrows!

DAUGHTER. Poet, could you tell me yours without a single discordant word? Could your speech ever approach your thought?

POET. No, you are right! In my own eyes I was deaf and dumb, and while the multitude listened in admiration to my song, to me it seemed mere bawling... thus when men paid me homage I was always ashamed!

DAUGHTER. And yet you wish me...?  Look me in the eyes!

POET. I cannot endure your glance....

DAUGHTER. How then will you endure my speech if I talk my own language?...

POET. But tell me before you go: what have you suffered most from, down here?

DAUGHTER. From — being alive; from feeling my vision weakened by having eyes, my hearing dulled by having ears; my bright and airy thought bound in labyrinthine coils of fat.  You have seen a brain... what crooked, crawling channels...

POET. Yes, and that's why all right-thinking men think crookedly!

DAUGHTER. Spiteful, always spiteful!  But that you all are!...

POET. How can one be otherwise?

DAUGHTER. And now, first of all, I will shake the dust off my feet... the earth, the clay...  (*Takes off her shoes and puts them in the fire.*)

PORTRESS (*comes in and puts her shawl in the fire*).  Perhaps I may burn my shawl too?                                    (*Goes out.*)

OFFICER (*comes in*).  And I my roses, of which only the thorns remain!                                              (*Goes out.*)

BILLSTICKER (*comes in*).  The bills can go, but the dip-net, never!
                                                        (*Goes out.*)

GLAZIER (*comes in*).  The diamond that opened the door! farewell!
                                                        (*Goes out.*)

LAWYER (*comes in*).  The report of the great suit touching the Pope's beard, or the diminishing water-supply in the sources of the Ganges.                                   (*Goes out.*)

QUARANTINE OFFICER (*comes in*).  A small contribution consisting of the black mask which turned me into a blackamoor against my will!                                          (*Goes out.*)

VICTORIA (*comes in*).  My beauty, my sorrow!        (*Goes out.*)

EDITH (*comes in*).  My ugliness, my sorrow!          (*Goes out.*)

BLIND MAN (*comes in and puts his hand in the fire*).  I give my hand for my eye!                                         (*Goes out.*)

(Don Juan *comes in in the Bath-chair.* She *and the* Friend.)

DON JUAN. Hurry, hurry!  Life is short!

                                        (*Goes out with the others.*)

POET. I have read that when life is nearing its end, everything and everybody throng past in a single stream... Is this the end?

DAUGHTER. Yes, it is mine! Farewell!

POET. Say one parting word!

DAUGHTER. No, I cannot! Do you think that your language could express our thoughts?

THE THEOLOGIAN (*comes in furiously*). I am disavowed by God, I am persecuted by men, abandoned by the Government and scorned by my colleagues! How shall I have faith when none else has... How defend a God who does not defend his own? It's bosh!

(*Throws a book on the fire and goes out.*)

POET (*snatching the book from the fire*). Do you know what that was? ... A Book of Martyrs: a calendar, with a martyr for every day of the year.

DAUGHTER. A martyr?

POET. Yes, one who was tortured and put to death for his faith! Tell me why! Do you believe that all who are tortured suffer? that all who are put to death feel pain? Surely suffering is redemption, and death liberation.

KRISTIN (*with her strips of paper*). I paste, I paste, till there's nothing left to paste....

POET. And if the very heavens cracked you'd try to paste them up... Go!

KRISTIN. Aren't there any double windows in the castle there?

POET. No, no — not there!

KRISTIN (*going out*). Well, I'll go then!

DAUGHTER. Our parting hour has come — the end draws nigh.
      Dreamer, farewell! farewell, thou mortal child,
      Thou bard who knowest best the way of life!
      Thou hoverest on light wings above the earth,
      Stooping at times to touch the clay beneath,
      To graze its surface, not to cling to it! —
      Now that I go... even in this parting hour
      Of separation from a friend, a place,
      How poignantly the loss of all we loved,
      And penitence for sin, rises anew...
      Have I not learned the anguish of all being —
      Learned what it is to be a mortal man?...

One misses even what one never prized,
Repenting deeds that one has never wrought...
Fain would we hence, and yet we long to stay...
So is the heart riven in twain, our feelings,
As between pulling horses, torn asunder
By contradiction, discord, irresolve...
Farewell!
Say to thy brethren that I think of them
There, where I go: and carry in thy name
Their lamentations to the throne of God.
Farewell!

(*She goes into the castle.   Music is heard.   The background is lit up by the burning castle, and now shows a wall of human faces, questioning, sorrowing, despairing.... While the castle is burning, the flower-bud on the roof blossoms forth into a giant chrysanthemum.*)

# THE LOWER DEPTHS

## By MAXIM GORKY

### *Translated by JENNIE COVAN*

*Reprinted by permission of Morris Gest*

# MAXIM GORKY

Born Alexy Maximovich Peshkov in 1868 at Nizhni-Novgorod, Maxim Gorky was orphaned at five, grew up with his grandfather, and was compelled to earn his living at nine years of age. Until he was twenty-five years of age he was a wanderer and jack of all trades. It was a period in which the revolutionary principles of Tolstoy, who was humanitarian rather than realist, who believed in the power of suffering to cleanse the social organism of sin, was giving way to the hard and realistic programs of Lenin. Maxim Gorky falls between these two. He had a grasp of underworld character more racy and immediate than that of Tolstoy, who always saw the underworld from above. At the same time he combined with his galleries of down-and-outers and tramps, figures like Luka, the sermonizer who had more than a hint of Tolstoy's Platon Karatayev in *War and Peace*. Managing to educate himself, Gorky published at Tiflis a story in a local newspaper to which he attached the pseudonym, meaning Very Bitter, by which he is now world-known. In 1895 a story was accepted at St. Petersburg. When his first book was published in 1897 Gorky became one of the first literary men in Russia. In 1899 he joined the Social Democratic Party. Like much of Russian narrative literature, Gorky's work lacks constructive quality. This lack is compensated by conviction and by observation. Gorky was encouraged in the writing of plays by Chekhov and by the Moscow Art Theatre. Though he has written many plays he is best known for *Na Dnye*, which has been translated under various titles as *In the Depths*, *Submerged*, and *A Night Refuge*.

# THE LOWER DEPTHS

No PLAY better illustrates the changing standards of criticism than does this one. Once hailed as one of the supreme works of pure naturalism, it was later held to be a vehicle of a special moral and romantic attitude toward life. Probably no play has better prepared the world for an understanding of the Russian Revolution, and yet the makers of the Revolution have set it aside as misrepresentative of the spirit that is forcing the new Russian order to a place in world affairs. By the forces of these contending critical opinions this play is established firmly in its proper place, namely as one of the most vital dramatic documents in all history. The Russian genius saves its pure naturalism for comedy. In serious drama it broods too much. Like Chekhov and Tolstoy, Gorky is something more than a naturalist. He is a naturalist with overtones. *Na Dnye* (literally, *At the Bottom*) was first produced at the Moscow Art Theatre, December 18 (Russian style), or December 31 (Western style), 1902. In the following February it was forbidden at the Imperial Theatres, but was done at St. Petersburg by the Art Theatre. The play went through 14 editions in 1903. Produced by Reinhardt in 1903 in Berlin, the play ran for two years. In the same year it was produced in the German version of *Nachtasyl* at the Irving Place Theatre in New York by Heinrich Conreid; on November 29 it was played in an English version by the London Stage Society at the Court Theatre under the direction of Laurence Irving. It was again produced at the Kingsway Theatre, London, in December, 1911; and in New York by Arthur Hopkins, December, 1919, the Moscow Art Theatre, in Russian, January 15, 1923, and by Leo Bulgakov, January 9, 1930. It has been translated as *In the Depths* by W. H. H. Chambers, in Bates's *The Drama*, London, 1903; *A Night's Lodging*, by Edwin Hopkins, *Poet Lore*, 1905; *The Lower Depths* by Laurence Irving, London, 1912, and by Jenny Covan, New York, 1923; *Submerged*, Boston, 1915; and *At the Bottom* by W. L. Lawrence, New York, 1930. It was translated in French as *Dans les bas-fonds* in *La Revue politique et littéraire*, Paris, 1903.

# CAST OF CHARACTERS

MIKHAIL IVANOFF KOSTILYOFF, *keeper of a night lodging*

VASSILISA KARPOVNA, *his wife*

NATASHA, *her sister*

MIEDVIEDIEFF, *her uncle, a policeman*

VASKA PEPEL, *a young thief*

ANDREI MITRITCH KLESHTCH, *a locksmith*

ANNA, *his wife*

NASTYA, *a street-walker*

KVASHNYA, *a vendor of meat-pies*

BUBNOFF, *a cap-maker*

THE BARON

SATINE

THE ACTOR

LUKA, *a pilgrim*

ALYOSHKA, *a shoemaker*

KRIVOY ZOB  &#125; *Porters*
THE TARTAR

NIGHT LODGERS, TRAMPS AND OTHERS

*The action takes place in a Night Lodging and in "The Waste," an area in its rear.*

# ACT ONE

*A cellar resembling a cave. The ceiling, which merges into stone walls, is low and grimy, and the plaster and paint are peeling off. There is a window, high up on the right wall, from which comes the light. The right corner, which constitutes* PEPEL'S *room, is partitioned off by thin boards. Close to the corner of this room is* BUBNOFF'S *wooden bunk. In the left corner stands a large Russian stove. In the stone wall, left, is a door leading to the kitchen where live* KVASHNYA, *the* BARON, *and* NASTYA. *Against the wall, between the stove and the door, is a large bed covered with dirty chintz. Bunks line the walls. In the foreground, by the left wall, is a block of wood with a vise and a small anvil fastened to it, and another smaller block of wood somewhat further towards the back.* KLESHTCH *is seated on the smaller block, trying keys into old locks. At his feet are two large bundles of various keys, wired together, also a battered tin samovar, a hammer, and pincers. In the center are a large table, two benches, and a stool, all of which are of dirty, unpainted wood. Behind the table* KVASHNYA *is busying herself with the samovar. The* BARON *sits chewing a piece of black bread, and* NASTYA *occupies the stool, leans her elbows on the table, and reads a tattered book. In the bed, behind curtains,* ANNA *lies coughing.* BUBNOFF *is seated on his bunk, attempting to shape a pair of old trousers with the help of an ancient hat shape which he holds between his knees. Scattered about him are pieces of buckram, oilcloth, and rags.* SATINE, *just awakened, lies in his bunk, grunting. On top of the stove, the* ACTOR, *invisible to the audience, tosses about and coughs.*

*It is an early Spring morning.*

THE BARON. And then?

KVASHNYA. No, my dear, said I, keep away from me with such proposals. I've been through it all, you see — and not for a hundred baked lobsters would I marry again!

BUBNOFF (*to* SATINE). What are you grunting about?

(SATINE *keeps on grunting.*)

KVASHNYA. Why should I, said I, a free woman, my own mistress, enter my name into somebody else's passport and sell myself into slavery — no! Why — I wouldn't marry a man even if he were an American prince!

KLESHTCH. You lie!

KVASHNYA. Wha-at?

KLESHTCH. You lie! You're going to marry Abramka....

THE BARON (*snatching the book out of* NASTYA's *hand and reading the title*). "Fatal Love"... (*Laughs.*)

NASTYA (*stretching out her hand*). Give it back — give it back! Stop fooling! (*The* BARON *looks at her and waves the book in the air.*)

KVASHNYA (*to* KLESHTCH). You crimson goat, you — calling me a liar! How dare you be so rude to me?

THE BARON (*hitting* NASTYA *on the head with the book*). Nastya, you little fool!

NASTYA (*reaching for the book*). Give it back!

KLESHTCH. Oh — what a great lady... but you'll marry Abramka just the same — that's all you're waiting for...

KVASHNYA. Sure! Anything else? You nearly beat your wife to death!

KLESHTCH. Shut up, you old bitch! It's none of your business!

KVASHNYA. Ho-ho! can't stand the truth, can you?

THE BARON. They're off again! Nastya, where are you?

NASTYA (*without lifting her head*). Hey — go away!

ANNA (*putting her head through the curtains*). The day has started. For God's sake, don't row!

KLESHTCH. Whining again!

ANNA. Every blessed day... let me die in peace, can't you?

BUBNOFF. Noise won't keep you from dying.

KVASHNYA (*walking up to* ANNA). Little mother, how did you ever manage to live with this wretch?

ANNA. Leave me alone — get away from me....

KVASHNYA. Well, well! You poor soul... how's the pain in the chest — any better?

THE BARON. Kvashnya! Time to go to market....

KVASHNYA. We'll go presently. (*To* ANNA.) Like some hot dumplings?

ANNA. No, thanks. Why should I eat?

KVASHNYA. You must eat. Hot food — good for you! I'll leave you some in a cup. Eat them when you feel like it. Come on, sir! (*To* KLESHTCH.) You evil spirit!

(*Goes into kitchen.*)

ANNA (*coughing*). Lord, Lord...

THE BARON (*painfully pushing forward* NASTYA's *head*). Throw it away — little fool!

NASTYA (*muttering*). Leave me alone — I don't bother you...

(*The* BARON *follows* KVASHNYA, *whistling*.)

SATINE (*sitting up in his bunk*). Who beat me up yesterday?

BUBNOFF. Does it make any difference who?

SATINE. Suppose they did — but why did they?

BUBNOFF. Were you playing cards?

SATINE. Yes!

BUBNOFF. That's why they beat you.

SATINE. Scoundrels!

THE ACTOR (*raising his head from the top of the stove*). One of these days they'll beat you to death!

SATINE. You're a jackass!

THE ACTOR. Why?

SATINE. Because a man can die only once!

THE ACTOR (*after a silence*). I don't understand ——

KLESHTCH. Say! You crawl from that stove — and start cleaning house! Don't play the delicate primrose!

THE ACTOR. None of your business!

KLESHTCH. Wait till Vassilisa comes — she'll show you whose business it is!

THE ACTOR. To hell with Vassilisa! Today is the Baron's turn to clean.... Baron!    (*The* BARON *comes from the kitchen.*)

THE BARON. I've no time to clean... I'm going to market with Kvashnya.

THE ACTOR. That doesn't concern me. Go to the gallows if you like. It's your turn to sweep the floor just the same — I'm not going to do other people's work...

THE BARON. Go to blazes! Nastya will do it. Hey there — fatal love! Wake up!    (*Takes the book away from* NASTYA.)

NASTYA (*getting up*). What do you want? Give it back to me! You scoundrel! And that's a nobleman for you!

THE BARON (*returning the book to her*). Nastya! Sweep the floor for me — will you?

NASTYA (*goes to kitchen*). Not so's you'll notice it!

KVASHNYA (*to the* BARON *through kitchen door*). Come on — you!

They don't need you! Actor! You were asked to do it, and now you go ahead and attend to it — it won't kill you...

THE ACTOR. It's always I... I don't understand why....

(*The* BARON *comes from the kitchen, across his shoulders a wooden beam from which hang earthen pots covered with rags.*)

THE BARON. Heavier than ever!

SATINE. It paid you to be born a Baron, eh?

KVASHNYA (*to* ACTOR). See to it that you sweep up!

(*Crosses to outer door, letting the* BARON *pass ahead.*)

THE ACTOR (*climbing down from the stove*). It's bad for me to inhale dust. (*With pride.*) My organism is poisoned with alcohol.

(*Sits down on a bunk, meditating.*)

SATINE. Organism — organon....

ANNA. Andrei Mitritch....

KLESHTCH. What now?

ANNA. Kvashnya left me some dumplings over there — you eat them!

KLESHTCH (*coming over to her*). And you — don't you want any?

ANNA. No. Why should I eat? You're a workman — you need it.

KLESHTCH. Frightened, are you? Don't be! You'll get all right!

ANNA. Go and eat! It's hard on me.... I suppose very soon...

KLESHTCH (*walking away*). Never mind — maybe you'll get well — you can never tell! (*Goes into kitchen.*)

THE ACTOR (*loud, as if he had suddenly awakened*). Yesterday the doctor in the hospital said to me: "Your organism," he said, "is entirely poisoned with alcohol..."

SATINE (*smiling*). Organon...

THE ACTOR (*stubbornly*). Not organon — organism!

SATINE. Sibylline....

THE ACTOR (*shaking his fist at him*). Nonsense! I'm telling you seriously... if the organism is poisoned... that means it's bad for me to sweep the floor — to inhale the dust...

SATINE. Macrobistic... hah!

BUBNOFF. What are you muttering?

SATINE. Words — and here's another one for you — transcendentalistic...

BUBNOFF. What does it mean?

SATINE. Don't know — I forgot...

BUBNOFF. Then why did you say it?

SATINE. Just so! I'm bored, brother, with human words — all our words. Bored! I've heard each one of them a thousand times surely.

THE ACTOR. In Hamlet they say: "Words, words, words!" It's a good play. I played the grave-digger in it once....

(KLESHTCH *comes from the kitchen.*)

KLESHTCH. Will you start playing with the broom?

THE ACTOR. None of your business. (*Striking his chest.*) Ophelia! O — remember me in thy prayers!

(*Back stage is heard a dull murmur, cries, and a police whistle. KLESHTCH sits down to work, filing screechily.*)

SATINE. I love unintelligible, obsolete words. When I was a youngster — and worked as a telegraph operator — I read heaps of books....

BUBNOFF. Were you really a telegrapher?

SATINE. I was. There are some excellent books — and lots of curious words... Once I was an educated man, do you know?

BUBNOFF. I've heard it a hundred times. Well, so you were! That isn't very important! Me — well — once I was a furrier. I had my own shop — what with dyeing the fur all day long, my arms were yellow up to the elbows, brother. I thought I'd never be able ever to get clean again — that I'd go to my grave, all yellow! But look at my hands now — they're plain dirty — that's what!

SATINE. Well, and what then?

BUBNOFF. That's all!

SATINE. What are you trying to prove?

BUBNOFF. Oh, well — just matching thoughts — no matter how much dye you get on yourself, it all comes off in the end — yes, yes ——

SATINE. Oh — my bones ache!

THE ACTOR (*sits, nursing his knees*). Education is all rot. Talent is the thing. I knew an actor — who read his parts by heart, syllable by syllable — but he played heroes in a way that... why — the whole theater would rock with ecstasy!

SATINE. Bubnoff, give me five kopecks.

BUBNOFF. I only have two ——

THE ACTOR. I say — talent, that's what you need to play heroes. And talent is nothing but faith in yourself, in your own powers —

SATINE. Give me five kopecks and I'll have faith that you're a hero, a crocodile, or a police inspector — Kleshtch, give me five kopecks.

KLESHTCH. Go to hell! All of you!

SATINE. What are you cursing for? I know you haven't a kopeck in the world!

ANNA. Andrei Mitritch — I'm suffocating — I can't breathe ——

KLESHTCH. What shall I do?

BUBNOFF. Open the door into the hall.

KLESHTCH. All right. You're sitting on the bunk, I on the floor. You change places with me, and I'll let you open the door. I have a cold as it is.

BUBNOFF (*unconcernedly*). I don't care if you open the door — it's your wife who's asking ——

KLESHTCH (*morosely*). I don't care who's asking ——

SATINE. My head buzzes — ah — why do people have to hit each other over the heads?

BUBNOFF. They don't only hit you over the head, but over the rest of the body as well. (*Rises.*) I must go and buy some thread — our bosses are late today — seems as if they've croaked. (*Exit.*)

(ANNA *coughs:* SATINE *is lying down motionless, his hands folded behind his head.*)

THE ACTOR (*looks about him morosely, then goes to* ANNA). Feeling bad, eh?

ANNA. I'm choking ——

THE ACTOR. If you wish, I'll take you into the hallway. Get up, then, come! (*He helps her to rise, wraps some sort of a rag about her shoulders, and supports her toward the hall.*) It isn't easy. I'm sick myself — poisoned with alcohol...

(KOSTILYOFF *appears in the doorway.*)

KOSTILYOFF. Going for a stroll? What a nice couple — the gallant cavalier and the lady fair!

THE ACTOR. Step aside, you — don't you see that we're invalids?

KOSTILYOFF. Pass on, please! (*Hums a religious tune, glances about him suspiciously, and bends his head to the left as if listening to what is happening in* PEPEL'S *room.* KLESHTCH *is jangling his keys and scraping away with his file, and looks askance at the other.*) Filing?

KLESHTCH. What?

KOSTILYOFF. I say, are you filing? (*Pause.*) What did I want to ask? (*Quick and low.*) Hasn't my wife been here?

KLESHTCH. I didn't see her.

KOSTILYOFF (*carefully moving toward* PEPEL'S *room*). You take up a whole lot of room for your two rubles a month. The bed — and your bench — yes — you take up five rubles' worth of space, so help me God! I'll have to put another half ruble to your rent ——

KLESHTCH. You'll put a noose around my neck and choke me... you'll croak soon enough, and still all you think of is half rubles ——

KOSTILYOFF. Why should I choke you? What would be the use? God be with you — live and prosper! But I'll have to raise you half a ruble — I'll buy oil for the ikon lamp, and my offering will atone for my sins, and for yours as well. You don't think much of your sins — not much! Oh, Andrushka, you're a wicked man! Your wife is dying because of your wickedness — no one loves you, no one respects you — your work is squeaky, jarring on everyone.

KLESHTCH (*shouts*). What do you come here for — just to annoy me? (SATINE *grunts loudly.*)

KOSTILYOFF (*with a start*). God, what a noise!

(*The* ACTOR *enters.*)

THE ACTOR. I've put her down in the hall and wrapped her up.

KOSTILYOFF. You're a kindly fellow. That's good. Some day you'll be rewarded for it.

THE ACTOR. When?

KOSTILYOFF. In the Beyond, little brother — there all our deeds will be reckoned up.

THE ACTOR. Suppose you reward me right now?

KOSTILYOFF. How can I do that?

THE ACTOR. Wipe out half my debt.

KOSTILYOFF. He-ho! You're always jesting, darling — always poking fun... can kindliness of heart be repaid with gold? Kindliness — it's above all other qualities. But your debt to me — remains a debt. And so you'll have to pay me back. You ought to be kind to me, an old man, without seeking for reward!

THE ACTOR. You're a swindler, old man!    (*Goes into kitchen.*)

(KLESHTCH *rises and goes into the hall.*)

KOSTILYOFF (*to* SATINE). See that squeaker ——? He ran away — he doesn't like me!

SATINE. Does anybody like you besides the Devil?

KOSTILYOFF (*laughing*). Oh — you're so quarrelsome! But I like you all — I understand you all, my unfortunate down-trodden, useless brethren... (*Suddenly, rapidly.*) Is Vaska home?

SATINE. See for yourself ——

KOSTILYOFF (*goes to the door and knocks*). Vaska!

(*The* ACTOR *appears at the kitchen door, chewing something.*)

PEPEL. Who is it?

KOSTILYOFF. It's I — I, Vaska!

PEPEL. What do you want?

KOSTILYOFF (*stepping aside*). Open!

SATINE (*without looking at* KOSTILYOFF). He'll open — and she's there ——    (*The* ACTOR *makes a grimace.*)

KOSTILYOFF (*in a low, anxious tone*). Eh? Who's there? What?

SATINE. Speaking to me?

KOSTILYOFF. What did you say?

SATINE. Oh — nothing — I was just talking to myself ——

KOSTILYOFF. Take care, brother. Don't carry your joking too far! (*Knocks loudly at door.*) Vassily!

PEPEL (*opening door*). Well? What are you disturbing me for?

KOSTILYOFF (*peering into room*). I — you see ——

PEPEL. Did you bring the money?

KOSTILYOFF. I've something to tell you ——

PEPEL. Did you bring the money?

KOSTILYOFF. What money? Wait ——

PEPEL. Why — the seven rubles for the watch — well?

KOSTILYOFF. What watch, Vaska? Oh, you ——

PEPEL. Look here. Yesterday, before witnesses, I sold you a

watch for ten rubles, you gave me three — now let me have the other seven. What are you blinking for? You hang around here — you disturb people — and don't seem to know yourself what you're after.

KOSTILYOFF. Sh-h! Don't be angry, Vaska. The watch — it is ——

SATINE. Stolen!

KOSTILYOFF (sternly). I do not accept stolen goods — how can you imagine ——

PEPEL (taking him by the shoulder). What did you disturb me for? What do you want?

KOSTILYOFF. I don't want — anything. I'll go — if you're in such a state ——

PEPEL. Be off, and bring the money!

KOSTILYOFF. What ruffians! I — I ——                    (Exit.)

THE ACTOR. What a farce!

SATINE. That's fine — I like it.

PEPEL. What did he come here for?

SATINE (laughing). Don't you understand? He's looking for his wife. Why don't you beat him up once and for all, Vaska?

PEPEL. Why should I let such trash interfere with my life?

SATINE. Show some brains! And then you can marry Vassilisa — and become our boss ——

PEPEL. Heavenly bliss! And you'd smash up my household and, because I'm a soft-hearted fool, you'll drink up everything I possess. (Sits on a bunk.) Old devil — woke me up — I was having such a pleasant dream. I dreamed I was fishing — and I caught an enormous trout — such a trout as you only see in dreams! I was playing him — and I was so afraid the line would snap. I had just got out the gaff — and I thought to myself — in a moment ——

SATINE. It wasn't a trout, it was Vassilisa ——

THE ACTOR. He caught Vassilisa a long time ago.

PEPEL (angrily). You can all go to the devil — and Vassilisa with you ——                    (KLESHTCH comes from the hall.)

KLESHTCH. Devilishly cold!

THE ACTOR. Why didn't you bring Anna back? She'll freeze, out there ——

KLESHTCH. Natasha took her into the kitchen ——

THE ACTOR. The old man will kick her out ——

KLESHTCH (*sitting down to his work*). Well — Natasha will bring her in here ——

SATINE. Vassily — give me five kopecks!

THE ACTOR (*to* SATINE). Oh, you — always five kopecks — Vassya — give us twenty kopecks ——

PEPEL. I'd better give it to them now before they ask for a ruble. Here you are!

SATINE. Gibraltar! There are no kindlier people in the world than thieves!

KLESHTCH (*morosely*). They earn their money easily — they don't work ——

SATINE. Many earn it easily, but not many part with it so easily. Work? Make work pleasant — and maybe I'll work too. Yes — maybe. When work's a pleasure, life's, too. When it's toil, then life is a drudge. (*To the* ACTOR.) You, Sardanapalus! Come on!

THE ACTOR. Let's go, Nebuchadnezzar! I'll get as drunk as forty thousand topers! (*They leave.*)

PEPEL (*yawning*). Well, how's your wife?

KLESHTCH. It seems as if soon —— (*Pause.*)

PEPEL. Now I look at you — seems to me all that filing and scraping of yours is useless.

KLESHTCH. Well — what else can I do?

PEPEL. Nothing.

KLESHTCH. How can I live?

PEPEL. People manage, somehow.

KLESHTCH. Them? Call them people? Muck and dregs — that's what they are! I'm a workman — I'm ashamed even to look at them. I've slaved since I was a child.... D'you think I shan't be able to tear myself away from here? I'll crawl out of here, even if I have to leave my skin behind — but crawl out I will! Just wait... my wife'll die... I've lived here six months, and it seems like six years.

PEPEL. Nobody here's any worse off than you... say what you like...

KLESHTCH. No worse is right. They've neither honor nor conscience.

PEPEL (*indifferently*). What good does it do — honor or conscience? Can you get them on their feet instead of on their uppers — through honor and conscience? Honor and conscience are needed only by those who have power and energy...

BUBNOFF (*coming back*). Oh — I'm frozen...

PEPEL. Bubnoff! Got a conscience?

BUBNOFF. What? A conscience?

PEPEL. Exactly!

BUBNOFF. What do I need a conscience for? I'm not rich.

PEPEL. Just what I said: honor and conscience are for the rich — right! And Kleshtch is upbraiding us because we haven't any!

BUBNOFF. Why — did he want to borrow some of it?

PEPEL. No — he has plenty of his own...

BUBNOFF. Oh — are you selling it? You won't sell much around here. But if you had some old boxes, I'd buy them — on credit...

PEPEL (*didactically*). You're a jackass, Andrushka! On the subject of conscience you ought to hear Satine — or the Baron...

KLESHTCH. I've nothing to talk to them about!

PEPEL. They have more brains than you — even if they're drunkards...

BUBNOFF. He who can be drunk and wise at the same time is doubly blessed...

PEPEL. Satine says every man expects his neighbor to have a conscience, but — you see — it isn't to anyone's advantage to have one — that's a fact.

(NATASHA *enters, followed by* LUKA *who carries a stick in his hand, a bundle on his back, a kettle and a teapot slung from his belt.*)

LUKA. How are you, honest folks?

PEPEL (*twisting his mustache*). Aha — Natasha!

BUBNOFF (*to* LUKA). I was honest — up to spring before last.

NATASHA. Here's a new lodger...

LUKA. Oh, it's all the same to me. Crooks — I don't mind them, either. For my part there's no bad flea — they're all black — and they all jump —... Well, dearie, show me where I can stow myself.

NATASHA (*pointing to kitchen door*). Go in there, grand-dad.

LUKA. Thanks, girlie! One place is like another — as long as an old fellow keeps warm, he keeps happy...

PEPEL. What an amusing old codger you brought in, Natasha!

NATASHA. A hanged sight more interesting than you!... Andrei, your wife's in the kitchen with us — come and fetch her after a while...

KLESHTCH. All right — I will...

NATASHA. And be a little more kind to her — you know she won't last much longer.

KLESHTCH. I know...

NATASHA. Knowing won't do any good — it's terrible — dying — don't you understand?

PEPEL. Well — look at me — I'm not afraid...

NATASHA. Oh — you're a wonder, aren't you?

BUBNOFF (*whistling*). Oh — this thread's rotten...

PEPEL. Honestly, I'm not afraid! I'm ready to die right now. Knife me to the heart — and I'll die without making a sound... even gladly — from such a pure hand...

NATASHA (*going out*). Spin that yarn for someone else!

BUBNOFF. Oh — that thread is rotten — rotten ——

NATASHA (*at hallway door*). Don't forget your wife, Andrei!

KLESHTCH. All right.

PEPEL. She's a wonderful girl!

BUBNOFF. She's all right.

PEPEL. What makes her so curt with me? Anyway — she'll come to no good here...

BUBNOFF. Through you — sure!

PEPEL. Why through me? I feel sorry for her...

BUBNOFF. As the wolf for the lamb!

PEPEL. You lie! I feel very sorry for her... very... very sorry! She has a tough life here — I can see that...

KLESHTCH. Just wait till Vassilisa catches you talking to her!

BUBNOFF. Vassilisa? She won't give up so easily what belongs to her — she's a cruel woman!

PEPEL (*stretching himself on the bunk*). You two prophets can go to hell!

KLESHTCH. Just wait — you'll see!

LUKA (*singing in the kitchen*). "In the dark of the night the way is black..."

KLESHTCH. Another one who yelps!

PEPEL. It's dreary! Why do I feel so dreary? You live — and everything seems all right. But suddenly a cold chill goes through you — and then everything gets dreary...

BUBNOFF. Dreary? Hm-hm ——

PEPEL. Yes — yes ——

LUKA (*sings*). "The way is black..."

PEPEL. Old fellow! Hey there!

LUKA (*looking from kitchen door*). You call me?

PEPEL. Yes. Don't sing!

LUKA (*coming in*). You don't like it?

PEPEL. When people sing well I like it ——

LUKA. In other words — I don't sing well?

PEPEL. Evidently!

LUKA. Well, well — and I thought I sang well. That's always the way: a man imagines there's one thing he can do well, and suddenly he finds out that other people don't think so...

PEPEL (*laughs*). That's right...

BUBNOFF. First you say you feel dreary — and then you laugh!

PEPEL. None of your business, raven!

LUKA. Who do they say feels dreary?

PEPEL. I do.

(*The* BARON *enters.*)

LUKA. Well, well — out there in the kitchen there's a girl reading and crying! That's so! Her eyes are wet with tears... I say to her: "What's the matter, darling?" And she says: "It's so sad!" "What's so sad?" say I. "The book!" says she.— And that's how people spend their time. Just because they're bored...

THE BARON. She's a fool!

PEPEL. Have you had tea, Baron?

THE BARON. Yes. Go on!

PEPEL. Well — want me to open a bottle?

THE BARON. Of course. Go on!

PEPEL. Drop on all fours, and bark like a dog!

THE BARON. Fool! What's the matter with you? Are you drunk?

PEPEL. Go on — bark a little! It'll amuse me. You're an aristocrat. You didn't even consider us human formerly, did you?

THE BARON. Go on!

PEPEL. Well — and now I am making you bark like a dog — and you will bark, won't you?

THE BARON. All right. I will. You jackass! What pleasure can you derive from it since I myself know that I have sunk almost lower than you. You should have made me drop on all fours in the days when I was still above you.

BUBNOFF. That's right...

LUKA. I say so, too!

BUBNOFF. What's over, is over. Remain only trivialities. We know no class distinctions here. We've shed all pride and self-respect. Blood and bone — man — just plain man — that's what we are!

LUKA. In other words, we're an equal... and you, friend, were you really a Baron?

THE BARON. Who are you? A ghost?

LUKA (laughing). I've seen counts and princes in my day — this is the first time I meet a baron — and one who's decaying — at that!

PEPEL (laughing). Baron, I blush for you!

THE BARON. It's time you knew better, Vassily...

LUKA. Hey-hey — I look at you, brothers — the life you're leading...

BUBNOFF. Such a life! As soon as the sun rises, our voices rise, too — in quarrels!

THE BARON. We've all seen better days — yes! I used to wake up in the morning and drink my coffee in bed — coffee — with cream! Yes ——

LUKA. And yet we're all human beings. Pretend all you want to, put on all the airs you wish, but man you were born, and man you must die. And as I watch I see that the wiser people get, the busier they get — and though from bad to worse, they still strive to improve — stubbornly ——

THE BARON. Who are you, old fellow? Where do you come from?

LUKA. I?

THE BARON. Are you a tramp?

LUKA. We're all of us tramps — why — I've heard said that the very earth we walk on is nothing but a tramp in the universe.

THE BARON (*severely*). Perhaps. But have you a passport?

LUKA (*after a short pause*). And what are you — a police inspector?

PEPEL (*delighted*). You scored, old fellow! Well, Barosha, you got it this time!

BUBNOFF. Yes — our little aristocrat got his!

THE BARON (*embarrassed*). What's the matter? I was only joking, old man. Why, brother, I haven't a passport, either.

BUBNOFF. You lie!

THE BARON. Oh — well — I have some sort of papers — but they have no value ——

LUKA. They're papers just the same — and no papers are any good ——

PEPEL. Baron — come on to the saloon with me ——

THE BARON. I'm ready. Good-bye, old man — you old scamp ——

LUKA. Maybe I am one, brother ——

PEPEL (*near doorway*). Come on — come on!

(*Leaves,* BARON *following him quickly*.)

LUKA. Was he really once a Baron?

BUBNOFF. Who knows? A gentleman — ? Yes. That much he's even now. Occasionally it sticks out. He never got rid of the habit.

LUKA. Nobility is like smallpox. A man may get over it — but it leaves marks...

BUBNOFF. He's all right all the same — occasionally he kicks — as he did about your passport...

(ALYOSHKA *comes in, slightly drunk, with a concertina in his hand, whistling.*)

ALYOSHKA. Hey there, lodgers!

BUBNOFF. What are you yelling for?

ALYOSHKA. Excuse me — I beg your pardon! I'm a well-bred man ——

BUBNOFF. On a spree again?

ALYOSHKA. Right you are! A moment ago Medyakin, the precinct captain, threw me out of the police station and said:

"Look here — I don't want as much as a smell of you to stay in the streets — d'you hear?" I'm a man of principles, and the boss croaks at me — and what's a boss anyway — pah! — it's all bosh — the boss is a drunkard. I don't make any demands on life. I want nothing — that's all. Offer me one ruble, offer me twenty — it doesn't affect me. (NASTYA *comes from the kitchen.*) Offer me a million — I won't take it! And to think that I, a respectable man, should be ordered about by a pal of mine — and he a drunkard! I won't have it — I won't!

(NASTYA *stands in the doorway, shaking her head at* ALYOSHKA.)

LUKA (*good-naturedly*). Well, boy, you're a bit confused ——

BUBNOFF. Aren't men fools!

ALYOSHKA (*stretches out on the floor*). Here, eat me up alive — and I don't want anything. I'm a desperate man. Show me one better! Why am I worse than others? There! Medyakin said: "If you show yourself on the streets I smash your face!" And yet I shall go out — I'll go — and stretch out in the middle of the street — let them choke me — I don't want a thing!

NASTYA. Poor fellow — only a boy — and he's already putting on such airs ——

ALYOSHKA (*kneeling before her*). Lady! Mademoiselle! *Parlez français — ? Prix courrant ?* I'm on a spree ——

NASTYA (*in a loud whisper*). Vassilisa!

VASSILISA (*opens door quickly; to* ALYOSHKA). You here again?

ALYOSHKA. How do you do — ? Come in — you're welcome ——

VASSILISA. I told you, young puppy, that not a shadow of you should stick around here — and you're back — eh?

ALYOSHKA. Vassilisa Karpovna... shall I tune up a funeral march for you?

VASSILISA (*seizing him by the shoulders*). Get out!

ALYOSHKA (*moving towards the door*). Wait — you can't put me out this way! I learned this funeral march a little while ago! It's refreshing music... wait — you can't put me out like that!

VASSILISA. I'll show whether I can or not. I'll rouse the whole street against you — you foul-mouthed creature — you're too young to bark about me ——

ALYOSHKA (*running out*). All right — I'll go ——

VASSILISA. Look out — I'll get you yet!

ALYOSHKA (*opens the door and shouts*). Vassilisa Karpovna — I'm not afraid of you —— (*Hides.*)

(LUKA *laughs.*)

VASSILISA. Who are you?

LUKA. A passer-by — a traveler...

VASSILISA. Stopping for the night or going to stay here?

LUKA. I'll see.

VASSILISA. Have you a passport?

LUKA. Yes.

VASSILISA. Give it to me.

LUKA. I'll bring it over to your house ——

VASSILISA. Call yourself a traveler? If you'd say a tramp — that would be nearer the truth ——

LUKA (*sighing*). You're not very kindly, mother!

(VASSILISA *goes to door that leads to* PEPEL'S *room.* ALYOSHKA *pokes his head through the kitchen door.*)

ALYOSHKA. Has she left?

VASSILISA (*turning around*). Are you still here?

(ALYOSHKA *disappears, whistling.* NASTYA *and* LUKA *laugh.*)

BUBNOFF (*to* VASSILISA). He isn't here ——

VASSILISA. Who?

BUBNOFF. Vaska.

VASSILISA. Did I ask you about him?

BUBNOFF. I noticed you were looking around ——

VASSILISA. I am looking to see if things are in order, you see? Why aren't the floors swept yet? How often did I give orders to keep the house clean?

BUBNOFF. It's the actor's turn to sweep ——

VASSILISA. Never mind whose turn it is! If the health inspector comes and fines me, I'll throw out the lot of you ——

BUBNOFF (*calmly*). Then how are you going to earn your living?

VASSILISA. I don't want a speck of dirt! (*Goes to kitchen; to* NASTYA.) What are you hanging round here for? Why's your face all swollen up? Why are you standing there like a dummy? Go on — sweep the floor! Did you see Natalia? Was she here?

NASTYA. I don't know — I haven't seen her...

VASSILISA. Bubnoff! Was my sister here?

BUBNOFF. She brought him along.

VASSILISA. That one — was he home?

BUBNOFF. Vassily? Yes — Natalia was here talking to Kleshtch ——

VASSILISA. I'm not asking you whom she talked to. Dirt every-where — filth — oh, you swine! Mop it all up — do you hear?
(*Exit rapidly.*)

BUBNOFF. What a savage beast she is!

LUKA. She's a lady that means business!

NASTYA. You grow to be an animal, leading such a life — any human being tied to such a husband as hers...

BUBNOFF. Well — that tie isn't worrying her any ——

LUKA. Does she always have these fits?

BUBNOFF. Always. You see, she came to find her lover — but he isn't home ——

LUKA. I guess she was hurt. Oh-ho! Everybody is trying to be boss — and is threatening everybody else with all kinds of punishment — and still there's no order in life... and no cleanliness ——

BUBNOFF. All the world likes order — but some people's brains aren't fit for it. All the same — the room should be swept — Nastya — you ought to get busy!

NASTYA. Oh, certainly? Anything else? Think I'm your servant?
(*Silence.*) I'm going to get drunk tonight — dead-drunk!

BUBNOFF. Fine business!

LUKA. Why do you want to get drunk, girlie? A while ago you were crying — and now you say you'll get drunk ——

NASTYA (*defiantly*). I'll drink — then I cry again — that's all there's to it!

BUBNOFF. That's nothing!

LUKA. But for what reason — tell me! Every pimple has a cause!
(NASTYA *remains silent, shaking her head.*) Oh — you men — what's to become of you? All right — I'll sweep the place. Where's your broom?

BUBNOFF. Behind the door — in the hall —— (LUKA *goes into the hall.*) Nastinka!

NASTYA. Yes?

BUBNOFF. Why did Vassilisa jump on Alyoshka?

NASTYA. He told her that Vaska was tired of her and was going

to get rid of her — and that he's going to make up to Natasha —
I'll go away from here — I'll find another lodging-house ——

BUBNOFF. Why? Where?

NASTYA. I'm sick of this — I'm not wanted here!

BUBNOFF (*calmly*). You're not wanted anywhere — and, anyway,
all people on earth are superfluous ——

(NASTYA *shakes her head. Rises and slowly, quietly, leaves the cellar.*
MIEDVIEDIEFF *comes in.* LUKA, *with the broom, follows him.*)

MIEDVIEDIEFF. I don't think I know you ——

LUKA. How about the others — d'you know them all?

MIEDVIEDIEFF. I must know everybody in my precinct. But I
don't know you.

LUKA. That's because, uncle, the whole world can't stow itself
away in your precinct — some of it was bound to remain outside... (*Goes into kitchen.*)

MIEDVIEDIEFF (*crosses to* BUBNOFF). It's true — my precinct is
rather small — yet it's worse than any of the very largest.
Just now, before getting off duty, I had to bring Alyoshka, the
shoemaker, to the station house. Just imagine — there he was,
stretched right in the middle of the street, playing his concertina and yelping: "I want nothing, nothing!" Horses going
past all the time — and with all the traffic going on, he could
easily have been run over — and so on! He's a wild youngster
— so I just collared him — he likes to make mischief ——

BUBNOFF. Coming to play checkers tonight?

MIEDVIEDIEFF. Yes — I'll come — how's Vaska?

BUBNOFF. Same as ever ——

MIEDVIEDIEFF. Meaning — he's getting along —— ?

BUBNOFF. Why shouldn't he? He's able to get along all right.

MIEDVIEDIEFF (*doubtfully*). Why shouldn't he? (LUKA *goes into
hallway, carrying a pail.*) M-yes — there's a lot of talk about
Vaska. Haven't you heard?

BUBNOFF. I hear all sorts of gossip...

MIEDVIEDIEFF. There seems to have been some sort of talk concerning Vassilisa. Haven't you heard about it?

BUBNOFF. What?

MIEDVIEDIEFF. Oh — why — generally speaking. Perhaps you

know — and lie.  Everybody knows — (*Severely.*)  You mustn't lie, brother!

BUBNOFF.  Why should I lie?

MIEDVIEDIEFF.  That's right.  Dogs!  They say that Vaska and Vassilisa... but what's that to me?  I'm not her father.  I'm her uncle.  Why should they ridicule me?  (KVASHNYA *comes in.*)  What are people coming to?  They laugh at everything.  Aha — you here?

KVASHNYA.  Well — my love-sick garrison —— ?  Bubnoff!  He came up to me again on the marketplace and started pestering me about marrying him...

BUBNOFF.  Go to it!  Why not?  He has money and he's still a husky fellow.

MIEDVIEDIEFF.  Me — ?  I should say so!

KVASHNYA.  You ruffian!  Don't you dare touch my sore spot!  I've gone through it once already, darling.  Marriage to a woman is just like jumping through a hole in the ice in winter.  You do it once, and you remember it the rest of your life...

MIEDVIEDIEFF.  Wait!  There are different breeds of husbands...

KVASHNYA.  But there's only one of me!  When my beloved husband kicked the bucket, I spent the whole day all by my lonely — just bursting with joy.  I sat and simply couldn't believe it was true....

MIEDVIEDIEFF.  If your husband beat you without cause, you should have complained to the police.

KVASHNYA.  I complained to God for eight years — and he didn't help.

MIEDVIEDIEFF.  Nowadays the law forbids to beat your wife... all is very strict these days — there's law and order everywhere.  You can't beat up people without due cause.  If you beat them to maintain discipline — all right...

LUKA (*comes in with* ANNA).  Well — we finally managed to get here after all.  Oh, you!  Why do you, weak as you are, walk about alone?  Where's your bunk?

ANNA (*pointing*).  Thank you, grand-dad.

KVASHNYA.  There — she's married — look at her!

LUKA.  The little woman is in very bad shape... she was creeping along the hallway, clinging to the wall and moaning — why do you leave her by herself?

KVASHNYA. Oh, pure carelessness on our part, little father — forgive us! Her maid, it appears, went out for a walk...

LUKA. Go on — poke fun at me... but, all the same, how can you neglect a human being like that? No matter who or what, every human life has its worth...

MIEDVIEDIEFF. There should be supervision! Suppose she died suddenly — ? That would cause a lot of bother... we must look after her!

LUKA. True, sergeant!

MIEDVIEDIEFF. Well — yes — though I'm not a sergeant — ah — yet!

LUKA. No! But you carry yourself most martially!

    (*Noise of shuffling feet is heard in the hallway. Muffled cries.*)

MIEDVIEDIEFF. What now — a row?

BUBNOFF. Sounds like it?

KVASHNYA. I'll go and see...

MIEDVIEDIEFF. I'll go, too. It is my duty! Why separate people when they fight? They'll stop sooner or later of their own accord. One gets tired of fighting. Why not let them fight all they want to — freely? They wouldn't fight half as often — if they'd remember former beatings...

BUBNOFF (*climbing down from his bunk*). Why don't you speak to your superiors about it?

KOSTILYOFF (*throws open the door and shouts*). Abram! Come quick — Vassilisa is killing Natasha — come quick!

    (KVASHNYA, MIEDVIEDIEFF, and BUBNOFF *rush into hallway;*
    LUKA *looks after them, shaking his head.*)

ANNA. Oh God — poor little Natasha...

LUKA. Who's fighting out there?

ANNA. Our landladies — they're sisters...

LUKA (*crossing to* ANNA). Why?

ANNA. Oh — for no reason — except that they're both fat and healthy...

LUKA. What's your name?

ANNA. Anna... I look at you... you're like my father — my dear father... you're as gentle as he was — and as soft....

LUKA. Soft! Yes! They pounded me till I got soft!

    (*Laughs tremulously.*)

**CURTAIN**

# ACT TWO

*Same as Act I — Night.*

*On the bunks near the stove* SATINE, *the* BARON, KRIVOY ZOB, *and the* TARTAR *play cards.* KLESHTCH *and the* ACTOR *watch them.* BUBNOFF, *on his bunk, is playing checkers with* MIEDVIEDIEFF. LUKA *sits on a stool by* ANNA'S *bedside. The place is lit by two lamps, one on the wall near the card players, the other is on* BUBNOFF'S *bunk.*

THE TARTAR. I'll play one more game — then I'll stop…

BUBNOFF. Zob! Sing!        (*He sings.*)

    "The sun rises and sets…"

ZOB (*joining in*).

    "But my prison is dark, dark…"

THE TARTAR (*to* SATINE). Shuffle the cards — and shuffle them well. We know your kind ——

ZOB AND BUBNOFF (*together*).

    "Day and night the wardens
    Watch beneath my window…"

ANNA. Blows — insults — I've had nothing but that all my life long…

LUKA. Don't worry, little mother!

MIEDVIEDIEFF. Look where you're moving!

BUBNOFF. Oh, yes — that's right…

THE TARTAR (*threatening* SATINE *with his fist*). You're trying to palm a card? I've seen you — you scoundrel…

ZOB. Stop it, Hassan! They'll skin us anyway… come on, Bubnoff!

ANNA. I can't remember a single day when I didn't go hungry… I've been afraid, waking, eating, and sleeping… all my life I've trembled — afraid I wouldn't get another bite… all my life I've been in rags — all through my wretched life — and why…?

LUKA. Yes, yes, child — you're tired — never you mind!

THE ACTOR (*to* ZOB). Play the Jack — the Jack, devil take you!

THE BARON. And we play the King!

KLESHTCH. They always win.

SATINE. Such is our habit.

MIEDVIEDIEFF. I have the Queen!

BUBNOFF. And so have I!

ANNA. I'm dying...

KLESHTCH. Look, look! Prince, throw up the game — throw it up, I tell you!

THE ACTOR. Can't he play without your assistance?

THE BARON. Look out, Andrushka, or I'll beat the life out of you!

THE TARTAR. Deal once more — the pitcher went after water — and got broke — and so did I!

(KLESHTCH *shakes his head and crosses to* BUBNOFF.)

ANNA. I keep on thinking — is it possible that I'll suffer in the other world as I did in this — is it possible? There, too?

LUKA. Nothing of the sort! Don't you disturb yourself! You'll rest there... be patient. We all suffer, dear, each in our own way.... *(Rises and goes quickly into kitchen.)*

BUBNOFF *(sings)*.

"Watch as long as you please..."

ZOB. "I shan't run away..."

BOTH *(together)*.

"I long to be free, free —
Alas! I cannot break my chains...."

THE TARTAR *(yells)*. That card was up his sleeve!

THE BARON *(embarrassed)*. Do you want me to shove it up your nose?

THE ACTOR *(emphatically)*. Prince! You're mistaken — nobody — ever...

THE TARTAR. I saw it! You cheat! I won't play!

SATINE *(gathering up the cards)*. Leave us alone, Hassan... you knew right along that we're cheats — why did you play with us?

THE BARON. He lost forty kopecks and he yelps as if he had lost a fortune! And a Prince at that!

THE TARTAR *(excitedly)*. Then play honest!

SATINE. What for?

THE TARTAR. What do you mean "what for"?

SATINE. Exactly. What for?

THE TARTAR. Don't you know?

SATINE. I don't. Do you?

*(The* TARTAR *spits out, furiously; the others laugh at him.)*

ZOB (*good-naturedly*). You're a funny fellow, Hassan! Try to understand this! If they should begin to live honestly, they'd die of starvation inside of three days.

THE TARTAR. That's none of my business. You must live honestly!

ZOB. They did you brown! Come and let's have tea.... (*Sings.*)
    "O my chains, my heavy chains..."

BUBNOFF (*sings*).
    "You're my steely, clanking wardens..."

ZOB. Come on, Hassanka!    (*Leaves the room, singing.*)
    "I cannot tear you, cannot break you..."

    (*The* TARTAR *shakes his fist threateningly at the* BARON, *and follows the other out of the room.*)

SATINE (*to* BARON, *laughing*). Well, Your Imperial Highness, you've again sat down magnificently in a mud puddle! You've learned a lot — but you're an ignoramus when it comes to palming a card.

THE BARON (*spreading his hands*). The Devil knows how it happened....

THE ACTOR. You're not gifted — you've no faith in yourself — and without that you can never accomplish anything...

MIEDVIEDIEFF. I've one Queen — and you've two — oh, well...

BUBNOFF. One's enough if she has brains — play!

KLESHTCH. You lost, Abram Ivanovitch?

MIEDVIEDIEFF. None of your business — see? Shut up!

SATINE. I've won fifty-three kopecks.

THE ACTOR. Give me three of them... though, what'll I do with them?

LUKA (*coming from kitchen*). Well — the Tartar was fleeced all right, eh? Going to have some vodka?

THE BARON. Come with us.

SATINE. I wonder what you'll be like when you're drunk.

LUKA. Same as when I'm sober.

THE ACTOR. Come on, old man — I'll recite verses for you.

LUKA. What?

THE ACTOR. Verses. Don't you understand?

LUKA. Verses? And what do I want with verses?

THE ACTOR. Sometimes they're funny — sometimes sad.

SATINE. Well, poet, are you coming?    (*Exit with the* BARON.)

THE ACTOR. I'm coming. I'll join you. For instance, old man, here's a bit of verse — I forget how it begins — I forget…

(*Brushes his hand across his forehead.*)

BUBNOFF. There! Your Queen is lost — go on, play!

MIEDVIEDIEFF. I made the wrong move.

THE ACTOR. Formerly, before my organism was poisoned with alcohol, old man, I had a good memory. But now it's all over with me, brother. I used to declaim these verses with tremendous success — thunders of applause… you have no idea what applause means… it goes to your head like vodka! I'd step out on the stage — stand this way — (*Strikes a pose.*) — I'd stand there and… (*Pause.*) I can't remember a word — I can't remember! My favorite verses — isn't it ghastly, old man?

LUKA. Yes — is there anything worse than forgetting what you loved? Your very soul is in the thing you love!

THE ACTOR. I've drunk my soul away, old man — brother, I'm lost… and why? Because I had no faith…. I'm done with…

LUKA. Well — then — cure yourself! Nowadays they have a cure for drunkards. They treat you free of charge, brother. There's a hospital for drunkards — where they're treated for nothing. They've owned up, you see, that even a drunkard is a human being, and they're only too glad to help him get well. Well — then — go to it!

THE ACTOR (*thoughtfully*). Where? Where is it?

LUKA. Oh — in some town or other… what do they call it — ? I'll tell you the name presently — only, in the meanwhile, get ready. Don't drink so much! Take yourself in hand — and bear up! And then, when you're cured, you'll begin life all over again. Sounds good, brother, doesn't it, to begin all over again? Well — make up your mind!

THE ACTOR (*smiling*). All over again — from the very beginning — that's fine… yes… all over again… (*Laughs.*) Well — then — I can, can't I?

LUKA. Why not? A human being can do anything — if he only makes up his mind.

THE ACTOR (*suddenly, as if coming out of a trance*). You're a queer bird! See you anon! (*Whistles.*) Old man — *au revoir!* (*Exit.*)

ANNA. Grand-dad!

LUKA. Yes, little mother?

ANNA. Talk to me.

LUKA (*close to her*). Come on — let's chat...

    (KLESHTCH, *glancing around, silently walks over to his wife, looks at her, and makes queer gestures with his hands, as though he wanted to say something.*)

LUKA. What is it, brother?

KLESHTCH (*quietly*). Nothing...

    (*Crosses slowly to hallway door, stands on the threshold for a few seconds, and exit.*)

LUKA (*looking after him*). Hard on your man, isn't it?

ANNA. He doesn't concern me much...

LUKA. Did he beat you?

ANNA. Worse than that — it's he who's killed me ——

BUBNOFF. My wife used to have a lover — the scoundrel — how clever he was at checkers!

MIEDVIEDIEFF. Hm-hm ——

ANNA. Grand-dad! Talk to me, darling — I feel so sick...

LUKA. Never mind — it's always like this before you die, little dove — never mind, dear! Just have faith! Once you're dead, you'll have peace — always. There's nothing to be afraid of — nothing. Quiet! Peace! Lie quietly! Death wipes out everything. Death is kindly. You die — and you rest — that's what they say. It is true, dear! Because — where can we find rest on this earth?

(PEPEL *enters. He is slightly drunk, dishevelled, and sullen. Sits down on bunk near door, and remains silent and motionless.*)

ANNA. And how is it — there? More suffering?

LUKA. Nothing of the kind! No suffering! Trust me! Rest — nothing else! They'll lead you into God's presence, and they'll say: "Dear God! Behold! Here is Anna, Thy servant!"

MIEDVIEDIEFF (*sternly*). How do you know what they'll say up there? Oh, you...

    (PEPEL, *on hearing* MIEDVIEDIEFF's *voice, raises his head and listens.*)

LUKA. Apparently I do know, Mr. Sergeant!

MIEDVIEDIEFF (*conciliatory*). Yes — it's your own affair — though I'm not exactly a sergeant — yet ——

BUBNOFF. I jump two!

MIEDVIEDIEFF. Damn — play!

LUKA. And the Lord will look at you gently and tenderly and He'll say: "I know this Anna!" Then He'll say: "Take Anna into Paradise. Let her have peace. I know. Her life on earth was hard. She is very weary. Let Anna rest in peace!"

ANNA (*choking*). Grandfather — if it were only so — if there were only rest and peace...

LUKA. There won't be anything else! Trust me! Die in joy and not in grief. Death is to us like a mother to small children...

ANNA. But — perhaps — perhaps I get well...?

LUKA (*laughing*). Why — ? Just to suffer more?

ANNA. But — just to live a little longer... just a little longer! Since there'll be no suffering hereafter, I could bear it a little longer down here...

LUKA. There'll be nothing in the hereafter... but only...

PEPEL (*rising*). Maybe yes — maybe no!

ANNA (*frightened*). Oh — God!

LUKA. Hey — Adonis!

MIEDVIEDIEFF. Who's that yelping?

PEPEL (*crossing over to him*). I! What of it?

MIEDVIEDIEFF. You yelp needlessly — that's what! People ought to have some dignity!

PEPEL. Block-head! And that's an uncle for you — ho-ho!

LUKA (*to* PEPEL, *in an undertone*). Look here — don't shout — this woman's dying — her lips are already grey — don't disturb her!

PEPEL. I've respect for you, grand-dad. You're all right, you are! You lie well, and you spin pleasant yarns. Go on lying, brother — there's little fun in this world...

BUBNOFF. Is the woman really dying?

LUKA. You think I'm joking?

BUBNOFF. That means she'll stop coughing. Her cough was very disturbing. I jump two!

MIEDVIEDIEFF. I'd like to murder you!

PEPEL. Abramka!

MIEDVIEDIEFF. I'm not Abramka to you!

PEPEL. Abrashka!  Is Natasha ill?

MIEDVIEDIEFF. None of your business!

PEPEL. Come — tell me!  Did Vassilisa beat her up very badly?

MIEDVIEDIEFF. That's none of your business, either!  It's a family affair!  Who are you anyway?

PEPEL. Whoever I am, you'll never see Natashka again if I choose!

MIEDVIEDIEFF (*throwing up the game*). What's that?  Who are you alluding to?  My niece by any chance?  You thief!

PEPEL. A thief whom you were never able to catch!

MIEDVIEDIEFF. Wait — I'll catch you yet — you'll see — sooner than you think!

PEPEL. If you catch me, God help your whole nest!  Do you think I'll keep quiet before the examining magistrate?  Every wolf howls!  They'll ask me: "Who made you steal and showed you where?"  "Mishka Kostilyoff and his wife!"  "Who was your fence?"  "Mishka Kostilyoff and his wife!"

MIEDVIEDIEFF. You lie!  No one will believe you!

PEPEL. They'll believe me all right — because it's the truth!  And I'll drag you into it, too.  Ha!  I'll ruin the lot of you — devils — just watch!

MIEDVIEDIEFF (*confused*). You lie!  You lie!  And what harm did I do to you, you mad dog?

PEPEL. And what good did you ever do me?

LUKA. That's right!

MIEDVIEDIEFF (*to* LUKA). Well — what are you croaking about?  Is it any of your business?  This is a family matter!

BUBNOFF (*to* LUKA). Leave them alone!  What do we care if they twist each other's tails?

LUKA (*peacefully*). I meant no harm.  All I said was that if a man isn't good to you, then he's acting wrong...

MIEDVIEDIEFF (*uncomprehending*). Now then — we all of us here know each other — but you — who are you? (*Frowns and exit.*)

LUKA. The cavalier is peeved!  Oh-ho, brothers, I see your affairs are a bit tangled up!

PEPEL. He'll run to complain about us to Vassilisa...

BUBNOFF. You're a fool, Vassily.  You're very bold these days, aren't you? Watch out! It's all right to be bold when you go gathering mushrooms, but what good is it here? They'll break your neck before you know it!

PEPEL. Well — not as fast as all that! You don't catch us Yaroslavl boys napping! If it's going to be war, we'll fight...

LUKA. Look here, boy, you really ought to go away from here ——

PEPEL. Where? Please tell me!

LUKA. Go to Siberia!

PEPEL. If I go to Siberia, it'll be at the Tsar's expense!

LUKA. Listen! You go just the same! You can make your own way there. They need your kind out there...

PEPEL. My way is clear. My father spent all his life in prison, and I inherited the trait. Even when I was a small child, they called me thief — thief's son.

LUKA. But Siberia is a fine country — a land of gold. Anyone who has health and strength and brains can live there like a cucumber in a hot-house.

PEPEL. Old man, why do you always tell lies?

LUKA. What?

PEPEL. Are you deaf? I ask — why do you always lie?

LUKA. What do I lie about?

PEPEL. About everything. According to you, life's wonderful everywhere — but you lie... why?

LUKA. Try to believe me. Go and see for yourself. And some day you'll thank me for it. What are you hanging round here for? And, besides, why is truth so important to you? Just think! Truth may spell death to you!

PEPEL. It's all one to me! If that — let it be that!

LUKA. Oh — what a madman! Why should you kill yourself?

BUBNOFF. What are you two jawing about, anyway? I don't understand. What kind of truth do you want, Vaska? And what for? You know the truth about yourself — and so does everybody else...

PEPEL. Just a moment! Don't crow! Let him tell me! Listen, old man! Is there a God? (LUKA *smiles silently.*)

BUBNOFF. People just drift along — like shavings on a stream. When a house is built — the shavings are thrown away!

PEPEL. Well? Is there a God? Tell me.

LUKA (*in a low voice*). If you have faith, there is; if you haven't, there isn't... whatever you believe in, exists...

> (PEPEL *looks at* LUKA *in staring surprise.*)

BUBNOFF. I'm going to have tea — come on over to the restaurant!

LUKA (*to* PEPEL). What are you staring at?

PEPEL. Oh — just because! Wait now — you mean to say...

BUBNOFF. Well — I'm off.  (*Goes to door and runs into* VASSILISA.)

PEPEL. So — you...

VASSILISA (*to* BUBNOFF). Is Nastasya home?

BUBNOFF. No.  (*Exit.*)

PEPEL. Oh — you've come ——— ?

VASSILISA (*crossing to* ANNA). Is she alive yet?

LUKA. Don't disturb her!

VASSILISA. What are you loafing around here for?

LUKA. I'll go — if you want me to...

VASSILISA (*turning towards* PEPEL's *room*). Vassily! I've some business with you...

> (LUKA *goes to hallway door, opens it, and shuts it loudly, then warily climbs into a bunk, and from there to the top of the stove.*)

VASSILISA (*calling from* PEPEL's *room*). Vaska — come here!

PEPEL. I won't come — I don't want to...

VASSILISA. Why? What are you angry about?

PEPEL. I'm sick of the whole thing...

VASSILISA. Sick of me, too?

PEPEL. Yes! Of you, too!

> (VASSILISA *draws her shawl about her, pressing her hands over her breast. Crosses to* ANNA, *looks carefully through the bed curtains, and returns to* PEPEL.)

Well — out with it!

VASSILISA. What do you want me to say? I can't force you to be loving, and I'm not the sort to beg for kindness. Thank you for telling me the truth.

PEPEL. What truth?

VASSILISA. That you're sick of me — or isn't it the truth? (PEPEL *looks at her silently. She turns to him.*) What are you staring at? Don't you recognize me?

PEPEL (*sighing*). You're beautiful, Vassilisa! (*She puts her arm about his neck, but he shakes it off.*) But I never gave my heart to you.... I've lived with you and all that — But I never really liked you...

VASSILISA (*quietly*). That so? Well ——— ?

PEPEL. What is there to talk about? Nothing. Go away from me!

VASSILISA. Taken a fancy to someone else?

PEPEL. None of your business! Suppose I have — I wouldn't ask you to be my match-maker!

VASSILISA (*significantly*). That's too bad... perhaps I might arrange a match...

PEPEL (*suspiciously*). Who with?

VASSILISA. You know — why do you pretend? Vassily — let me be frank. (*With lower voice.*) I won't deny it — you've offended me... it was like a bolt from the blue... you said you loved me — and then all of a sudden...

PEPEL. It wasn't sudden at all. It's been a long time since I... woman, you've no soul! A woman must have a soul... we men are beasts — we must be taught — and you, what have you taught me ——— ?

VASSILISA. Never mind the past! I know — no man owns his own heart — you don't love me any longer... well and good, it can't be helped!

PEPEL. So that's over. We part peaceably, without a row — as it should be!

VASSILISA. Just a moment! All the same, when I lived with you, I hoped you'd help me out of this swamp — I thought you'd free me from my husband and my uncle — from all this life — and perhaps, Vassya, it wasn't you whom I loved — but my hope — do you understand? I waited for you to drag me out of this mire...

PEPEL. You aren't a nail — and I'm not a pair of pincers! I thought you had brains — you are so clever — so crafty...

VASSILISA (*leaning closely towards him*). Vassa — let's help each other!

PEPEL. How?

VASSILISA (*low and forcibly*). My sister — I know you've fallen for her....

PEPEL. And that's why you beat her up, like the beast you are! Look out, Vassilisa! Don't you touch her!

VASSILISA. Wait. Don't get excited. We can do everything

quietly and pleasantly. You want to marry her. I'll give you money... three hundred rubles — even more than that...

PEPEL (*moving away from her*). Stop! What do you mean?

VASSILISA. Rid me of my husband! Take that noose from around my neck...

PEPEL (*whistling softly*). So that's the way the land lies! You certainly planned it cleverly... in other words, the grave for the husband, the gallows for the lover, and as for yourself...

VASSILISA. Vassya! Why the gallows? It doesn't have to be yourself — but one of your pals! And supposing it were yourself — who'd know? Natalia — just think — and you'll have money — you go away somewhere... you free me forever — and it'll be very good for my sister to be away from me — the sight of her enrages me.... I get furious with her on account of you, and I can't control myself. I tortured the girl — I beat her up — beat her up so that I myself cried with pity for her — but I'll beat her — and I'll go on beating her!

PEPEL. Beast! Bragging about your beastliness?

VASSILISA. I'm not bragging — I speak the truth. Think now, Vassa. You've been to prison twice because of my husband — through his greed. He clings to me like a bedbug — he's been sucking the life out of me for the last four years — and what sort of a husband is he to me? He's forever abusing Natasha — calls her a beggar — he's just poison, plain poison, to everyone...

PEPEL. You spin your yarn cleverly...

VASSILISA. Everything I say is true. Only a fool could be as blind as you....

(KOSTILYOFF *enters stealthily and comes forward noisily.*)

PEPEL (*to* VASSILISA). Oh — go away!

VASSILISA. Think it over! (*Sees her husband.*) What? You? Following me?

(PEPEL *leaps up and stares at* KOSTILYOFF *savagely.*)

KOSTILYOFF. It's I, I! So the two of you were here alone — you were — ah — conversing? (*Suddenly stamps his feet and screams.*) Vassilisa — you bitch! You beggar! You damned hag! (*Frightened by his own screams which are met by silence and indifference*

*on the part of the others.*)    Forgive me, O Lord… Vassilisa —
again you've led me into the path of sin…. I've been looking
for you everywhere.   It's time to go to bed.   You forgot to
fill the lamps — oh, you… beggar!   Swine!

> (*Shakes his trembling fist at her, while* VASSILISA *slowly goes to
> door, glancing at* PEPEL *over her shoulder.*)

PEPEL (*to* KOSTILYOFF). Go away — clear out of here ——

KOSTILYOFF (*yelling*). What?   I?   The Boss?   I get out?   You
thief!

PEPEL (*sullenly*). Go away, Mishka!

KOSTILYOFF. Don't you dare — I — I'll show you.

> (PEPEL *seizes him by the collar and shakes him.   From the stove
> come loud noises and yawns.* PEPEL *releases* KOSTILYOFF
> *who runs into the hallway, screaming.*)

PEPEL (*jumping on a bunk*). Who is it?   Who's on the stove?

LUKA (*raising his head*). Eh?

PEPEL. You?

LUKA (*undisturbed*). I — I myself — oh, dear Jesus!

PEPEL (*shuts hallway door, looks for the wooden closing bar, but can't
find it.*) The devil!   Come down, old man!

LUKA. I'm climbing down — all right…

PEPEL (*roughly*). What did you climb on that stove for?

LUKA. Where was I to go?

PEPEL. Why — didn't you go out into the hall?

LUKA. The hall's too cold for an old fellow like myself, brother.

PEPEL. You overheard?

LUKA. Yes — I did.   How could I help it?   Am I deaf?   Well,
my boy, happiness is coming your way.   Real, good fortune I
call it!

PEPEL (*suspiciously*). What good fortune —— ?

LUKA. In so far as I was lying on the stove…

PEPEL. Why did you make all that noise?

LUKA. Because I was getting warm… it was your good luck… I
thought if only the boy wouldn't make a mistake and choke
the old man…

PEPEL. Yes — I might have done it… how terrible…

LUKA. Small wonder!   It isn't difficult to make a mistake of that
sort.

PEPEL (*smiling*). What's the matter?   Did you make the same
sort of mistake once upon a time?

LUKA. Boy, listen to me.   Send that woman out of your life!
Don't let her near you!   Her husband — she'll get rid of him
herself — and in a shrewder way than you could — yes!   Don't
you listen to that devil!   Look at me!   I am bald-headed —
know why?   Because of all these women.... Perhaps I knew
more women than I had hair on the top of my head — but
this Vassilisa — she's worse than the plague....

PEPEL. I don't understand... I don't know whether to thank
you — or — well...

LUKA. Don't say a word!   You won't improve on what I said.
Listen: take the one you like by the arm, and march out of here
— get out of here — clean out...

PEPEL (*sadly*). I can't understand people.   Who is kind and who
isn't?   It's all a mystery to me...

LUKA. What's there to understand?   There's all breeds of men...
they all live as their hearts tell them... good today, bad tomorrow!   But if you really care for that girl... take her away
from here and that's all there is to it.   Otherwise go away
alone... you're young — you're in no hurry for a wife...

PEPEL (*taking him by the shoulder*). Tell me!   Why do you say all
this?

LUKA. Wait.   Let me go.   I want a look at Anna... she was
coughing so terribly... (*Goes to* ANNA'S *bed, pulls the curtains,
looks, touches her.*  PEPEL *thoughtfully and distraught, follows him with
his eyes.*)   Merciful Jesus Christ!   Take into Thy keeping the
soul of this woman Anna, new-comer amongst the blessed!

PEPEL (*softly*). Is she dead?

        (*Without approaching, he stretches himself and looks at the bed.*)

LUKA (*gently*). Her sufferings are over!   Where's her husband?

PEPEL. In the saloon, most likely...

LUKA. Well — he'll have to be told...

PEPEL (*shuddering*). I don't like corpses!

LUKA (*going to door*). Why should you like them?   It's the living
who demand our love — the living...

PEPEL. I'm coming with you...

LUKA. Are you afraid?

PEPEL. I don't like it...

(*They go out quickly. The stage is empty and silent for a few moments. Behind the door is heard a dull, staccato, incomprehensible noise. Then the* ACTOR *enters.*)

THE ACTOR (*stands at the open door, supporting himself against the jamb, and shouts*). Hey, old man — where are you — ? I just remembered — listen... (*Takes two staggering steps forward and, striking a pose, recites.*)

> "Good people! If the world cannot find
> A path to holy truth,
> Glory be to the madman who will enfold all humanity
> In a golden dream..."

(NATASHA *appears in the doorway behind the* ACTOR.) Old man! (*Recites.*)

> "If tomorrow the sun were to forget
> To light our earth,
> Tomorrow then some madman's thought
> Would bathe the world in sunshine...."

NATASHA (*laughing*). Scarecrow! You're drunk!

THE ACTOR (*turns to her*). Oh — it's you? Where's the old man, the dear old man? Not a soul here, seems to me... Natasha, farewell — right — farewell!

NATASHA (*entering*). Don't wish me farewell, before you've wished me how-d'you-do!

THE ACTOR (*barring her way*). I am going. Spring will come — and I'll be here no longer ——

NATASHA. Wait a moment! Where do you propose going?

THE ACTOR. In search of a town — to be cured — And you, Ophelia, must go away! Take the veil! Just imagine — there's a hospital to cure — ah — organisms for drunkards — a wonderful hospital — built of marble — with marble floors... light — clean — food — and all gratis! And a marble floor — yes! I'll find it — I'll get cured — and then I shall start life anew.... I'm on my way to regeneration, as King Lear said. Natasha, my stage name is... Svertchkoff — Zavoloushski... do you realize how painful it is to lose one's name? Even dogs have their names...

(NATASHA *carefully passes the* ACTOR, *stops at* ANNA's *bed and looks.*) To be nameless — is not to exist!

NATASHA. Look, my dear — why — she's dead....

THE ACTOR (*shakes his head*). Impossible...

NATASHA (*stepping back*). So help me God — look...

BUBNOFF (*appearing in doorway*). What is there to look at?

NATASHA. Anna — she's dead!

BUBNOFF. That means — she's stopped coughing! (*Goes to* ANNA'S *bed, looks, and returns to his bunk.*) We must tell Kleshtch — it's his business to know...

THE ACTOR. I'll go — I'll say to him — she lost her name ——

(*Exit.*)

NATASHA (*in center of room*). I, too — some day — I'll be found in the cellar — dead....

BUBNOFF (*spreading out some rags on his bunk*). What's that? What are you muttering?

NATASHA. Nothing much...

BUBNOFF. Waiting for Vaska, eh? Take care — Vassilisa'll break your head!

NATASHA. Isn't it the same who breaks it? I'd much rather he'd do it!

BUBNOFF (*lying down*). Well— that's your own affair...

NATASHA. It's best for her to be dead — yet it's a pity... oh, Lord — why do we live?

BUBNOFF. It's so with all... we're born, live, and die — and I'll die, too — and so'll you — what's there to be gloomy about?

(*Enter* LUKA, *the* TARTAR, ZOB, *and* KLESHTCH. *The latter comes after the others, slowly, shrunk up.*)

NATASHA. Sh-h! Anna!

ZOB. We've heard — God rest her soul...

THE TARTAR (*to* KLESHTCH). We must take her out of here. Out into the hall! This is no place for corpses — but for the living...

KLESHTCH (*quietly*). We'll take her out ——

(*Everybody goes to the bed,* KLESHTCH *looks at his wife over the other's shoulders.*)

ZOB (*to the* TARTAR). You think she'll smell? I don't think she will — she dried up while she was still alive...

NATASHA. God! If they'd only a little pity... if only someone would say a kindly word — oh, you...

LUKA. Don't be hurt, girl — never mind! Why and how should we pity the dead? Come, dear! We don't pity the living — we can't even pity our own selves — how can we?

BUBNOFF (*yawning*). And, besides, when you're dead, no word will help you — when you're still alive, even sick, it may....

THE TARTAR (*stepping aside*). The police must be notified...

ZOB. The police — must be done! Kleshtch! Did you notify the police?

KLESHTCH. No — she's got to be buried — and all I have is forty kopecks ——

ZOB. Well — you'll have to borrow then — otherwise we'll take up a collection... one'll give five kopecks, others as much as they can. But the police must be notified at once — or they'll think you killed her or God knows what not...

(*Crosses to the TARTAR's bunk and prepares to lie down by his side.*)

NATASHA (*going to BUBNOFF's bunk*). Now — I'll dream of her... I always dream of the dead... I'm afraid to go out into the hall by myself — it's dark there...

LUKA (*following her*). You better fear the living — I'm telling you...

NATASHA. Take me across the hall, grandfather.

LUKA. Come on — come on — I'll take you across —

(*They go away. Pause.*)

ZOB (*to the TARTAR*). Oh-ho! Spring will soon be here, little brother, and it'll be quite warm. In the villages the peasants are already making ready their ploughs and harrows, preparing to till... and we... Hassan? Snoring already? Damned Mohammedan!

BUBNOFF. Tartars love sleep!

KLESHTCH (*in center of room, staring in front of him*). What am I to do now?

ZOB. Lie down and sleep — that's all...

KLESHTCH (*softly*). But — she... how about...

(*No one answers him. SATINE and the ACTOR enter.*)

THE ACTOR (*yelling*). Old man! Come here, my trusted Duke of Kent!

SATINE. Miklookha-Maklai is coming — ho-ho!

THE ACTOR. It has been decided upon! Old man, where's the town — where are you?

SATINE. Fata Morgana, the old man bilked you from top to bottom! There's nothing — no towns — no people — nothing at all!

THE ACTOR. You lie!

THE TARTAR (*jumping up*). Where's the boss? I'm going to the boss. If I can't sleep, I won't pay! Corpses — drunkards...

(*Exit quickly.*)

(SATINE *looks after him and whistles.*)

BUBNOFF (*in a sleepy voice*). Go to bed, boys — be quiet... night is for sleep...

THE ACTOR. Yes — so — there's a corpse here.... "Our net fished up a corpse...." Verses — by Béranger....

SATINE (*screams*). The dead can't hear... the dead do not feel — Scream! — Roar!... the deaf don't hear!

(*In the doorway appears* LUKA.)

### CURTAIN

# ACT THREE

"*The Waste,*" *a yard strewn with rubbish and overgrown with weeds. Back, a high brick wall which shuts out the sight of the sky. Near it are elder bushes. Right, the dark, wooden wall of some sort of house, barn or stable. Left, the grey, tumbledown wall of* KOSTILYOFF's *night asylum. It is built at an angle so that the further corner reaches almost to the centre of the yard. Between it and the wall runs a narrow passage. In the grey, plastered wall are two windows, one on a level with the ground, the other about six feet higher up and closer to the brick wall. Near the latter wall is a big sledge turned upside down and a beam about twelve feet long. Right of the wall is a heap of old planks. Evening. The sun is setting, throwing a crimson light on the brick wall. Early spring, the snow having only recently melted. The elder bushes are not yet in bud.*

NATASHA *and* NASTYA *are sitting side by side on the beam.* LUKA *and the* BARON *are on the sledge.* KLESHTCH *is stretched on the pile of planks to the right.* BUBNOFF's *face is at the ground floor window.*

NASTYA (*with closed eyes, nodding her head in rhythm to the tale she is telling in a sing-song voice*). So then at night he came into the garden. I had been waiting for him quite a while. I trembled with fear and grief — he trembled, too… he was as white as chalk — and he had the pistol in his hand…

NATASHA (*chewing sunflower seeds*). Oh — are these students really such desperate fellows…?

NASTYA. And he says to me in a dreadful voice: "My precious darling…"

BUBNOFF. Ho-ho! Precious —— ?

THE BARON. Shut up! If you don't like it, you can lump it! But don't interrupt her…. Go on…

NASTYA. "My one and only love," he says, "my parents," he says, "refuse to give their consent to our wedding — and threaten to disown me because of my love for you. Therefore," he says, "I must take my life." And his pistol was huge — and loaded with ten bullets… "Farewell," he says, "beloved comrade! I have made up my mind for good and all… I can't live without you…" and I replied: "My unforgettable friend — my Raoul…."

BUBNOFF (*surprised*). What? What? Krawl — did you call him —— ?

THE BARON. Nastka! But last time his name was Gaston….

NASTYA (*jumping up*). Shut up, you bastards! Ah — you lousy mongrels! You think for a moment that you can understand love — true love? My love was real honest-to-God love! (*To the* BARON.) You good-for-nothing!… educated, you call yourself — drinking coffee in bed, did you?

LUKA. Now, now! Wait, people! Don't interfere! Show a little respect to your neighbors… it isn't the word that matters, but what's in back of the word. That's what matters! Go on, girl! It's all right!

BUBNOFF. Go on, crow! See if you can make your feathers white!

THE BARON. Well — continue!

NATASHA. Pay no attention to them… what are they? They're just jealous… they've nothing to tell about themselves…

NASTYA (*sits down again*). I'm going to say no more! If they don't believe me they'll laugh. (*Stops suddenly, is silent for a few seconds, then, shutting her eyes, continues in a loud and intense voice, swaying her hands as if to the rhythm of far music.*) And then I replied to him: "Joy of my life! My bright moon! And I, too, I can't live without you — because I love you madly, so madly — and I shall keep on loving you as long as my heart beats in my bosom. But —" I say — "don't take your young life! Think how necessary it is to your dear parents whose only happiness you are. Leave me! Better that I should perish from longing for you, my life! I alone! I — ah — as such, such! Better that I should die — it doesn't matter... I am of no use to the world — and I have nothing, nothing at all ——"

(*Covers her face with her hand and weeps gently.*)

NATASHA (*in a low voice*). Don't cry — don't!

(LUKA, *smiling, strokes* NASTYA'S *head.*)

BUBNOFF (*laughs*). Ah — you limb of Satan!

THE BARON (*also laughs*). Hey, old man? Do you think it's true? It's all from that book "Fatal Love"... it's all nonsense! Let her alone!

NATASHA. And what's it to you? Shut up — or God'll punish you!

NASTYA (*bitterly*). God damn your soul! You worthless pig! Soul — bah! — you haven't got one!

LUKA (*takes* NASTYA'S *hand*). Come, dear! It's nothing! Don't be angry — I know — I believe you! You're right, not they! If you believe you had a real love affair, then you did — yes! And as for him — don't be angry with a fellow-lodger... maybe he's really jealous, and that's why he's laughing. Maybe he never had any real love — maybe not — come on — let's go!

NASTYA (*pressing her hand against her breast*). Grandfather! So help me God — it happened! It happened! He was a student, a Frenchman — Gastotcha was his name — he had a little black beard — and patent leathers — may God strike me dead if I'm lying! And he loved me so — my God, how he loved me!

LUKA. Yes, yes, it's all right. I believe you! Patent leathers, you said? Well, well, well — and you loved him, did you?

(*Disappears with her around the corner.*)

THE BARON. God — isn't she a fool, though? She's good-hearted — but such a fool — it's past belief!

BUBNOFF. And why are people so fond of lying — just as if they were up before the judge — really!

NATASHA. I guess lying is more fun than speaking the truth — I, too...

THE BARON. What — you, too? Go on!

NATASHA. Oh — I imagine things — invent them — and I wait —

THE BARON. For what?

NATASHA (*smiling confusedly*). Oh — I think that perhaps — well — tomorrow somebody will really appear — someone — oh — out of the ordinary — or something'll happen — also out of the ordinary.... I've been waiting for it — oh — always.... But, really, what is there to wait for? (*Pause.*)

THE BARON (*with a slight smile*). Nothing — I expect nothing! What is past, is past! Through! Over with! And then what?

NATASHA. And then — well — tomorrow I imagine suddenly that I'll die — and I get frightened... in summer it's all right to dream of death — then there are thunder storms — one might get struck by lightning...

THE BARON. You've a hard life... your sister's a wicked-tempered devil!

NATASHA. Tell me — does anybody live happily? It's hard for all of us — I can see that...

KLESHTCH (*who until this moment has sat motionless and indifferent, jumps up suddenly*). For all? You lie! Not for all! If it were so — all right! Then it wouldn't hurt — yes!

BUBNOFF. What in hell's bit you? Just listen to him yelping!

(KLESHTCH *lies down again and grunts.*)

THE BARON. Well — I'd better go and make my peace with Nastinka — if I don't, she won't treat me to vodka...

BUBNOFF. Hm — people love to lie... with Nastka — I can see the reason why. She's used to painting that mutt of hers — and now she wants to paint her soul as well... put rouge on her soul, eh? But the others — why do they? Take Luka for instance — he lies a lot... and what does he get out of it? He's an old fellow, too — why does he do it?

THE BARON (*smiling and walking away*). All people have drab-colored souls — and they like to brighten them up a bit...

LUKA (*appearing from round the corner*). You, sir, why do you tease the girl? Leave her alone — let her cry if it amuses her... she weeps for her own pleasure — what harm is it to you?

THE BARON. Nonsense, old man! She's a nuisance. Raoul

today, Gaston tomorrow — always the same old yarn, though!
Still — I'll go and make up with her. (*Leaves.*)

LUKA. That's right — go — and be nice to her. Being nice to
people never does them any harm...

NATASHA. You're so good, little father — why are you so good?

LUKA. Good, did you say? Well — call it that! (*Behind the brick
wall is heard soft singing and the sounds of a concertina.*) Someone
has to be kind, girl — someone must pity people! Christ pitied
everybody — and he said to us: "Go and do likewise!" I tell
you — if you pity a man when he most needs it, good comes
of it. Why — I used to be a watchman on the estate of an
engineer near Tomsk — all right — the house was right in the
middle of a forest — lonely place — winter came — and I
remained all by myself. Well — one night I heard a noise ——

NATASHA. Thieves?

LUKA. Exactly! Thieves creeping in! I took my gun — I went
out. I looked and saw two of them opening a window — and
so busy that they didn't even see me. I yell: "Hey there — get
out of here!" And they turn on me with their axes — I warn
them to stand back, or I'd shoot — and as I speak, I keep on
covering them with my gun, first the one, then the other —
they go down on their knees, as if to implore me for mercy.
And by that time I was furious — because of those axes, you
see — and so I say to them: "I was chasing you, you scoundrels
— and you didn't go. Now you go and break off some stout
branches!" — and they did so — and I say: "Now — one of
you lie down and let the other one flog him!" So they obey
me and flog each other — and then they begin to implore me
again. "Grandfather," they say, "for God's sake give us some
bread! We're hungry!" There's thieves for you, my dear!
(*Laughs.*) And with an ax, too! Yes — honest peasants, both
of them! And I say to them, "You should have asked for bread
straight away!" And they say: "We got tired of asking —
you beg and beg — and nobody gives you a crumb — it hurts!"
So they stayed with me all that winter — one of them, Stepan,
would take my gun and go shooting in the forest — and the
other, Yakoff, was ill most of the time — he coughed a lot...
and so the three of us together looked after the house... then

Spring came... "Good-bye, grandfather," they said — and
they went away — back home to Russia...

NATASHA. Were they escaped convicts?

LUKA. That's just what they were — escaped convicts — from a
Siberian prison camp... honest peasants! If I hadn't felt sorry
for them — they might have killed me — or maybe worse —
and then there would have been trial and prison and afterwards Siberia — what's the sense of it? Prison teaches no
good — and Siberia doesn't either — but another human
being can... yes, a human being can teach another one kindness — very simply!                                        (*Pause.*)

BUBNOFF. Hm — yes — I, for instance, don't know how to lie...
why — as far as I'm concerned, I believe in coming out with
the whole truth and putting it on thick... why fuss about
it?

KLESHTCH (*again jumps as if his clothes were on fire, and screams*). What
truth? Where is there truth? (*Tearing at his ragged clothes.*)
Here's truth for you! No work! No strength! That's the
only truth! Shelter — there's no shelter! You die — that's
the truth! Hell! What do I want with the truth? Let me
breathe! Why should I be blamed? What do I want with
truth? To live — Christ Almighty! — they won't let you live —
and that's another truth!

BUBNOFF. He's mad!

LUKA. Dear Lord... listen to me, brother ——

KLESHTCH (*trembling with excitement*). They say: there's truth!
You, old man, try to console everyone... I tell you — I hate
everyone! And there's your truth — God curse it — understand? I tell you — God curse it!

       (*Rushes away round the corner, turning as he goes.*)

LUKA. Ah — how excited he got! Where did he run off to?

NATASHA. He's off his head...

BUBNOFF. God — didn't he say a whole lot, though? As if he
was playing drama — he gets those fits often... he isn't used to
life yet...

PEPEL (*comes slowly round the corner*). Peace on all this honest
gathering! Well, Luka, you wily old fellow — still telling them
stories?

LUKA. You should have heard how that fellow carried on!

PEPEL. Kleshtch — wasn't it? What's wrong with him? He was running like one possessed!

LUKA. You'd do the same if your own heart were breaking!

PEPEL (*sitting down*). I don't like him... he's got such a nasty, bad temper — and so proud! (*Imitating* KLESHTCH.) "I'm a workman!" And he thinks everyone's beneath him. Go on working if you feel like it — nothing to be so damned haughty about! If work is the standard — a horse can give us points — pulls like hell and says nothing! Natasha — are your folks at home?

NATASHA. They went to the cemetery — then to night service...

PEPEL. So that's why you're free for once — quite a novelty!

LUKA (*to* BUBNOFF, *thoughtfully*). There — you say — truth! Truth doesn't always heal a wounded soul. For instance, I knew of a man who believed in a land of righteousness...

BUBNOFF. In what?

LUKA. In a land of righteousness. He said: "Somewhere on this earth there must be a righteous land — and wonderful people live there — good people! They respect each other, help each other, and everything is peaceful and good!" And so that man — who was always searching for this land of righteousness — he was poor and lived miserably — and when things got to be so bad with him that it seemed there was nothing else for him to do except lie down and die — even then he never lost heart — but he'd just smile and say: "Never mind! I can stand it! A little while longer — and I'll have done with this life — and I'll go in search of the righteous land!" — it was his one happiness — the thought of that land...

PEPEL. Well? Did he go there?

BUBNOFF. Where? Ho-ho!

LUKA. And then to this place — in Siberia, by the way — there came a convict — a learned man with books and maps — yes, a learned man who knew all sorts of things — and the other man said to him: "Do me a favor — show me where is the land of righteousness and how I can get there." At once the learned man opened his books, spread out his maps, and looked and looked and he said — no — he couldn't find this land anywhere... everything was correct — all the lands on earth were marked — but not this land of righteousness...

PEPEL (*in a low voice*). Well? Wasn't there a trace of it?

(BUBNOFF *roars with laughter*.)

NATASHA. Wait... well, little father?

LUKA. The man wouldn't believe it.... "It must exist," he said, "look carefully. Otherwise," he says, "your books and maps are of no use if there's no land of righteousness." The learned man was offended. "My plans," he said, "are correct. But there exists no land of righteousness anywhere." Well, then the other man got angry. He'd lived and lived and suffered and suffered, and had believed all the time in the existence of this land — and now, according to the plans, it didn't exist at all. He felt robbed! And he said to the learned man: "Ah — you scum of the earth! You're not a learned man at all — but just a damned cheat!" — and he gave him a good wallop in the eye — then another one... (*After a moment's silence.*) And then he went home and hanged himself!

(*All are silent.* LUKA, *smiling, looks at* PEPEL *and* NATASHA.)

PEPEL (*low-voiced*). To hell with this story — it isn't very cheerful...

NATASHA. He couldn't stand the disappointment...

BUBNOFF (*sullen*). Ah — it's nothing but a fairytale...

PEPEL. Well — there is the righteous land for you — doesn't exist, it seems...

NATASHA. I'm sorry for that man...

BUBNOFF. All a story — ho-ho! — land of righteousness — what an idea!                (*Exit through window.*)

LUKA (*pointing to window*). He's laughing! (*Pause.*) Well, children, God be with you! I'll leave you soon...

PEPEL. Where are you going to?

LUKA. To the Ukraine — I heard they discovered a new religion there — I want to see — yes! People are always seeking — they always want something better — God grant them patience!

PEPEL. You think they'll find it?

LUKA. The people? They will find it! He who seeks, will find! He who desires strongly, will find!

NATASHA. If only they could find something better — invent something better...

LUKA. They're trying to! But we must help them, girl — we must respect them...

NATASHA. How can I help them? I am helpless myself!

PEPEL (*determined*). Again — listen — I'll speak to you again, Natasha — here — before him — he knows everything... run away with me?

NATASHA. Where? From one prison to another?

PEPEL. I told you — I'm through with being a thief, so help me God! I'll quit! If I say so, I'll do it! I can read and write — I'll work — He's been telling me to go to Siberia on my own hook — let's go there together, what do you say? Do you think I'm not disgusted with my life? Oh — Natasha — I know... I see... I console myself with the thought that there are lots of people who are honored and respected — and who are bigger thieves than I! But what good is that to me? It isn't that I repent... I've no conscience... but I do feel one thing: One must live differently. One must live a better life... one must be able to respect one's own self...

LUKA. That's right, friend! May God help you! It's true! A man must respect himself!

PEPEL. I've been a thief from childhood on. Everybody always called me "Vaska — the thief — the son of a thief!" Oh — very well then — I am a thief —... just imagine — now, perhaps, I'm a thief out of spite — perhaps I'm a thief because no one ever called me anything different.... Well, Natasha —— ?

NATASHA (*sadly*). Somehow I don't believe in words — and I'm restless today — my heart is heavy... as if I were expecting something... it's a pity, Vassily, that you talked to me today...

PEPEL. When should I? It isn't the first time I speak to you...

NATASHA. And why should I go with you? I don't love you so very much — sometimes I like you — and other times the mere sight of you makes me sick... it seems — no — I don't really love you... when one really loves, one sees no fault.... But I do see...

PEPEL. Never mind — you'll love me after a while! I'll make you care for me... if you'll just say yes! For over a year I've watched you... you're a decent girl... you're kind — you're reliable — I'm very much in love with you...

(VASSILISA, *in her best dress, appears at window and listens.*)

NATASHA. Yes — you love me — but how about my sister...?

PEPEL (*confused*). Well, what of her? There are plenty like her...

LUKA. You'll be all right, girl! If there's no bread, you have to eat weeds...

PEPEL (*gloomily*). Please — feel a little sorry for me! My life isn't all roses — it's a hell of a life... little happiness in it... I feel as if a swamp were sucking me under... and whatever I try to catch and hold on to, is rotten... it breaks... Your sister — oh — I thought she was different... if she weren't so greedy after money... I'd have done anything for her sake, if she were only all mine... but she must have someone else... and she has to have money — and freedom... because she doesn't like the straight and narrow... she can't help me. But you're like a young fir-tree... you bend, but you don't break...

LUKA. Yes — go with him, girl, go! He's a good lad — he's all right! Only tell him every now and then that he's a good lad so that he won't forget it — and he'll believe you. Just you keep on telling him "Vasya, you're a good man — don't you forget it!" Just think, dear, where else could you go except with him? Your sister is a savage beast... and as for her husband, there's little to say of him? He's rotten beyond words ... and all this life here, where will it get you? But this lad is strong...

NATASHA. Nowhere to go — I know — I thought of it. The only thing is — I've no faith in anybody — and there's no place for me to turn to...

PEPEL. Yes, there is! But I won't let you go that way — I'd rather cut your throat!

NATASHA (*smiling*). There — I'm not his wife yet — and he talks already of killing me!

PEPEL (*puts his arms around her*). Come, Natasha! Say yes!

NATASHA (*holding him close*). But I'll tell you one thing, Vassily — I swear it before God... the first time you strike me or hurt me any other way, I'll have no pity on myself... I'll either hang myself... or...

PEPEL. May my hand wither if ever I touch you!

LUKA. Don't doubt him, dear! He needs you more than you need him!

VASSILISA (*from the window*). So now they're engaged! Love and advice!

NATASHA. They've come back — oh, God — they saw — oh, Vassily...

PEPEL. Why are you frightened? Nobody'll dare touch you now!

VASSILISA. Don't be afraid, Natalia! He won't beat you... he don't know how to love or how to beat... I know!

LUKA (*in a low voice*). Rotten old hag — like a snake in the grass...

VASSILISA. He dares only with the word!

KOSTILYOFF (*enters*). Natashka! What are you doing here, you parasite? Gossiping? Kicking about your family? And the samovar not ready? And the table not cleared?

NATASHA (*going out*). I thought you were going to church...?

KOSTILYOFF. None of your business what we intended doing! Mind your own affairs — and do what you're told!

PEPEL. Shut up, you! She's no longer your servant! Don't go, Natalia — don't do a thing!

NATASHA. Stop ordering me about — you're commencing too soon! (*Leaves.*)

PEPEL (*to* KOSTILYOFF). That's enough. You've used her long enough — now she's mine!

KOSTILYOFF. Yours? When did you buy her — and for how much? (VASSILISA *roars with laughter.*)

LUKA. Go away, Vasya!

PEPEL. Don't laugh, you fools — or first thing you know I'll make you cry!

VASSILISA. Oh, how terrible! Oh — how you frighten me!

LUKA. Vassily — go away! Don't you see — she's goading you on... ridiculing you, don't you understand...?

PEPEL. Yes... You lie, lie! You won't get what you want!

VASSILISA. Nor will I get what I don't want, Vasya!

PEPEL (*shaking his fist at her*). We'll see... (*Exit.*)

VASSILISA (*disappearing through window*). I'll arrange some wedding for you...

KOSTILYOFF (*crossing to* LUKA). Well, old man, how's everything?

LUKA. All right!

KOSTILYOFF. You're going away, they say —— ?

LUKA. Soon.

KOSTILYOFF. Where to?

LUKA. I'll follow my nose...

KOSTILYOFF. Tramping, eh? Don't like stopping in one place all the time, do you?

LUKA. Even water won't pass beneath a stone that's sunk too firmly in the ground, they say...

KOSTILYOFF. That's true for a stone. But man must settle in one place. Men can't live like cockroaches, crawling about wherever they want.... A man must stick to one place — and not wander about aimlessly...

LUKA. But suppose his home is wherever he hangs his hat?

KOSTILYOFF. Why, then — he's a vagabond — useless... a human being must be of some sort of use — he must work...

LUKA. That's what you think, eh?

KOSTILYOFF. Yes — sure... just look! What's a vagabond? A strange fellow... unlike all others. If he's a real pilgrim then he's some good in the world... perhaps he discovered a new truth. Well — but not every truth is worth while. Let him keep it to himself and shut up about it! Or else — let him speak in a way which no one can understand... don't let him interfere... don't let him stir up people without cause! It's none of his business how other people live! Let him follow his own righteous path... in the woods — or in a monastery — away from everybody! He mustn't interfere — nor condemn other people — but pray — pray for all of us — for all the world's sins — for mine — for yours — for everybody's. To pray — that's why he forsakes the world's turmoil! That's so! (*Pause.*) But you — what sort of a pilgrim are you — ? An honest person must have a passport... all honest people have passports... yes...!

LUKA. In this world there are people — and also just plain men...

KOSTILYOFF. Don't coin wise sayings! Don't give me riddles! I'm as clever as you... what's the difference — people and men?

LUKA. What riddle is there? I say — there's sterile and there's fertile ground... whatever you sow in it, grows... that's all...

KOSTILYOFF. What do you mean?

LUKA. Take yourself for instance... if the Lord God himself said to you: "Mikhailo, be a man!" — it would be useless —

nothing would come of it — you're doomed to remain just as you are...

KOSTILYOFF. Oh — but do you realize that my wife's uncle is a policeman, and that if I...

VASSILISA. (*coming in*). Mikhail Ivanitch — come and have your tea...

KOSTILYOFF (*to* LUKA). You listen! Get out! You leave this place — hear?

VASSILISA. Yes — get out, old man! Your tongue's too long! And — who knows — you may be an escaped convict...

KOSTILYOFF. If I ever see sign of you again after today — well — I've warned you!

LUKA. You'll call your uncle, eh? Go on — call him! Tell him you've caught an escaped convict — and maybe uncle'll get a reward — perhaps all of three kopecks...

BUBNOFF (*in the window*). What are you bargaining about? Three kopecks — for what?

LUKA. They're threatening to sell me...

VASSILISA (*to her husband*). Come...

BUBNOFF. For three kopecks? Well — look out, old man — they may even do it for one!

KOSTILYOFF (*to* BUBNOFF). You have a habit of jumping up like a jack-in-the-box!

VASSILISA. The world is full of shady people and crooks —

LUKA. Hope you'll enjoy your tea!

VASSILISA (*turning*). Shut up! You rotten toadstool!

(*Leaves with her husband.*)

LUKA. I'm off tonight.

BUBNOFF. That's right. Don't outstay your welcome!

LUKA. True enough.

BUBNOFF. I know. Perhaps I've escaped the gallows by getting away in time...

LUKA. Well?

BUBNOFF. That's true. It was this way. My wife took up with my boss. He was great at his trade — could dye a dog's skin so that it looked like a raccoon's — could change cat's skin into kangaroo — muskrats, all sorts of things. Well — my wife took up with him — and they were so mad about each other

that I got afraid they might poison me or something like that —
so I commenced beating up my wife — and the boss beat me...
we fought savagely! Once he tore off half my whiskers — and
broke one of my ribs... well, then I, too, got enraged.... I
cracked my wife over the head with an iron yard-measure —
well — and altogether it was like an honest-to-God war!
And then I saw that nothing really could come of it... they
were planning to get the best of me! So I started planning —
how to kill my wife — I thought of it a whole lot... but I thought
better of it just in time... and got away...

LUKA. That was best! Let them go on changing dogs into
raccoons!

BUBNOFF. Only — the shop was in my wife's name... and so I
did myself out of it, you see? Although, to tell the truth,
I would have drunk it away... I'm a hard drinker, you know...

LUKA. A hard drinker — oh...

BUBNOFF. The worst you ever met! Once I start drinking, I
drink everything in sight, I'll spend every bit of money I have —
everything except my bones and my skin... what's more, I'm
lazy... it's terrible how I hate work!

(*Enter* SATINE *and the* ACTOR, *quarreling.*)

SATINE. Nonsense! You'll go nowhere — it's all a damned lie!
Old man, what did you stuff him with all those fairy-tales for?

THE ACTOR. You lie! Grandfather! Tell him that he lies! —
I am going away. I worked today — I swept the streets...
and I didn't have a drop of vodka. What do you think of that?
Here they are — two fifteen kopeck pieces — and I'm sober!

SATINE. Why — that's absurd! Give it to me — I'll either drink
it up — or lose it at cards...

THE ACTOR. Get out — this is for my journey...

LUKA (*to* SATINE). And you — why are you trying to lead him
astray?

SATINE. Tell me, soothsayer, beloved by the Gods, what's my
future going to be? I've gone to pieces, brother — but everything isn't lost yet, grandfather... there are sharks in this world
who got more brains than I!

LUKA. You're cheerful, Constantine — and very agreeable!

BUBNOFF. Actor, come over here!

    (*The* ACTOR *crosses to window, sits down on the sill before* BUBNOFF, *and speaks in a low voice with him.*)

SATINE. You know, brother, I used to be a clever youngster. It's nice to think of it. I was a devil of a fellow... danced splendidly, played on the stage, loved to amuse people... it was awfully gay...

LUKA. How did you get to be what you are?

SATINE. You're inquisitive, old man! You want to know everything? What for?

LUKA. I want to understand the ways of men — I look at you, and I don't understand. You're a bold lad, Constantine, and you're no fool... yet, all of a sudden...

SATINE. It's prison, grandfather — I spent four years and seven months in prison... afterwards — where could I go?

LUKA. Aha! What were you there for?

SATINE. On account of a scoundrel — whom I killed in a fit of rage... and despair... and in prison I learned to play cards...

LUKA. You killed — because of a woman?

SATINE. Because of my own sister.... But look here — leave me alone! I don't care for these cross-examinations — and all this happened a long time ago. It's already nine years since my sister's death.... Brother, she was a wonderful girl...

LUKA. You take life easily! And only a while ago that locksmith was here — and how he did yell!

SATINE. Kleshtch?

LUKA. Yes — "There's no work," he shouted; "there isn't anything..."

SATINE. He'll get used to it. What could I do?

LUKA (*softly*). Look — here he comes!

    (KLESHTCH *walks in slowly, his head bowed low.*)

SATINE. Hey, widower! Why are you so down in the mouth? What are you thinking?

KLESHTCH. I'm thinking — what'll I do? I've no food — nothing — the funeral ate up all...

SATINE. I'll give you a bit of advice... do nothing! Just be a burden to the world at large!

KLESHTCH. Go on — talk — I'd be ashamed of myself...

SATINE. Why — people aren't ashamed to let you live worse than a dog. Just think... you stop work — so do I — so do hundreds, thousands of others — everybody — understand? — everybody'll quit working... nobody'll do a damned thing — and then what'll happen?

KLESHTCH. They'll all starve to death...

LUKA (to SATINE). If those are your notions, you ought to join the order of Begunes — you know — there's some such organization...

SATINE. I know — grandfather — and they're no fools...

(NATASHA *is heard screaming behind* KOSTILYOFF's *window:* "What for? Stop! What have I done?")

LUKA (worried). Natasha! That was she crying — oh, God...

(*From* KOSTILYOFF's *room is heard noise, shuffling, breaking of crockery, and* KOSTILYOFF's *shrill cry:* "Ah! Heretic! Bitch!")

VASSILISA. Wait, wait — I'll teach her — there, there!

NATASHA. They're beating me — killing me...

SATINE (shouts through the window). Hey — you there —...

LUKA (trembling). Where's Vassily — ? Call Vaska — oh, God — listen, brothers...

THE ACTOR (running out). I'll find him at once!

BUBNOFF. They beat her a lot these days...

SATINE. Come on, old man — we'll be witnesses...

LUKA (following SATINE). Oh — witnesses — what for? Vassily — he should be called at once!

NATASHA. Sister — sister dear! Va-a-a...

BUBNOFF. They've gagged her — I'll go and see...

(*The noise in* KOSTILYOFF's *room dies down gradually as if they had gone into the hallway. The old man's cry:* "Stop!" *is heard. A door is slammed noisily, and the latter sound cuts off all the other noises sharply. Quiet on the stage. Twilight.*)

KLESHTCH (seated on the sledge, indifferently, rubbing his hands; mutters at first indistinguishably, then:). What then? One must live. (Louder.) Must have shelter — well? There's no shelter, no roof — nothing... there's only man — man alone — no hope... no help...

(*Exit slowly, his head bent. A few moments of ominous silence, then somewhere in the hallway a mass of sounds, which grows in volume and comes nearer. Individual voices are heard.*)

VASSILISA. I'm her sister — let go...

KOSTILYOFF. What right have you...?

VASSILISA. Jail-bird!

SATINE. Call Vaska — quickly! Zob — hit him!

(*A police whistle. The TARTAR runs in, his right hand in a sling.*)

THE TARTAR. There's a new law for you — kill only in daytime!

(*Enter ZOB, followed by MIEDVIEDIEFF.*)

ZOB. I handed him a good one!

MIEDVIEDIEFF. You — how dare you fight?

THE TARTAR. What about yourself? What's your duty?

MIEDVIEDIEFF (*running after*). Stop — give back my whistle!

KOSTILYOFF (*runs in*). Abram! Stop him! Hold him! He's a murderer — he...

(*Enter KVASHNYA and NASTYA supporting NATASHA who is disheveled. SATINE backs away, pushing away VASSILISA who is trying to attack her sister, while near her, ALYOSHKA jumps up and down like a madman, whistles into her ear, shrieking, roaring. Also other ragged men and women.*)

SATINE (*to VASSILISA*). Well — you damned bitch!

VASSILISA. Let go, you jail-bird! I'll tear you to pieces — if I have to pay for it with my own life!

KVASHNYA (*leading NATASHA aside*). You — Karpovna — that's enough — stand back — aren't you ashamed? Or are you crazy?

MIEDVIEDIEFF (*seizes SATINE*). Aha — caught at last!

SATINE. Zob — beat them up! Vaska — Vaska...

(*They all, in a chaotic mass, struggle near the brick wall. They lead NATASHA to the right, and set her on a pile of wood. PEPEL rushes in from the hallway and, silently, with powerful movements, pushes the crowd aside.*)

PEPEL. Natalia, where are you... you...

KOSTILYOFF (*disappearing behind a corner*). Abram! Seize Vaska! Comrades — help us get him! The thief! The robber!

PEPEL. You — you old bastard!

> (*Aiming a terrific blow at* KOSTILYOFF. KOSTILYOFF *falls so that only the upper part of his body is seen.* PEPEL *rushes to* NATASHA.)

VASSILISA. Beat Vaska! Brothers! Beat the thief!

MIEDVIEDIEFF (*yells to* SATINE). Keep out of this — it's a family affair... they're relatives — and who are you...

PEPEL (*to* NATASHA). What did she do to you? She used a knife?

KVASHNYA. God — what beasts! They've scalded the child's feet with boiling water!

NASTYA. They overturned the samovar...

THE TARTAR. Maybe an accident — you must make sure — you can't exactly tell...

NATASHA (*half fainting*). Vassily — take me away ——

VASSILISA. Good people! Come! Look! He's dead! Murdered!

> (*All crowded into the hallway near* KOSTILYOFF. BUBNOFF *leaves the crowd and crosses to* PEPEL.)

BUBNOFF (*in a low voice, to* PEPEL). Vaska — the old man is done for!

PEPEL (*looks at him, as though he does not understand*). Go — for help — she must be taken to the hospital... I'll settle with them...

BUBNOFF. I say — the old man — somebody's killed him...

> (*The noise on the stage dies out like a fire under water. Distinct, whispered exclamations:* "Not really?" "Well — let's go away, brothers!" "The devil!" "Hold on now!" "Let's get away before the police comes!" *The crowd disappears.* BUBNOFF, *the* TARTAR, NASTYA, *and* KVASHNYA, *rush up to* KOSTILYOFF'S *body.*)

VASSILISA (*rises and cries out triumphantly*). Killed — my husband's killed! Vaska killed him! I saw him! Brothers, I saw him! Well — Vasya — the police!

PEPEL (*moves away from* NATASHA). Let me alone. (*Looks at* KOSTILYOFF; *to* VASSILISA.) Well — are you glad? (*Touches the corpse with his foot.*) The old bastard is dead! Your wish has been granted! Why not do the same to you?

> (*Throws himself at her.*)

> (SATINE *and* ZOB *quickly overpower him, and* VASSILISA *disappears in the passage.*)

SATINE. Come to your senses!

ZOB. Hold on!  Not so fast!

VASSILISA (*appearing*). Well, Vaska, dear friend?  You can't escape your fate... police — Abram — whistle!

MIEDVIEDIEFF. Those devils tore my whistle off!

ALYOSHKA. Here it is!    (*Whistles,* MIEDVIEDIEFF *runs after him.*)

SATINE (*leading* PEPEL *to* NATASHA). Don't be afraid, Vaska!  Killed in a row!  That's nonsense — only manslaughter — you won't have to serve a long term...

VASSILISA. Hold Vaska — he killed him — I saw it!

SATINE. I, too, gave the old man a couple of blows — he was easily fixed... you call me as witness, Vaska!

PEPEL. I don't need to defend myself... I want to drag Vassilisa into this mess — and I'll do it — she was the one who wanted it... she was the one who urged me to kill him — she goaded me on...

NATASHA (*sudden and loud*). Oh — I understand — so that's it, Vassily?  Good people!  They're both guilty — my sister and he — they're both guilty!  They had it all planned!  So, Vassily, that's why you spoke to me a while ago — so that she should overhear everything — ?  Good people!  She's his mistress — you know it — everybody knows it — they're both guilty!  She — she urged him to kill her husband — he was in their way — and so was I!  And now they've maimed me...

PEPEL. Natalia!  What's the matter with you?  What are you saying?

SATINE. Oh — hell!

VASSILISA. You lie.  She lies.  He — Vaska killed him...

NATASHA. They're both guilty!  God damn you both!

SATINE. What a mix-up!  Hold on, Vassily — or they'll ruin you between them!

ZOB. I can't understand it — oh — what a mess!

PEPEL. Natalia!  It can't be true!  Surely you don't believe that I — with her ——

SATINE. So help me God, Natasha!  Just think...

VASSILISA (*in the passage*). They've killed my husband — Your Excellency!  Vaska Pepel, the thief, killed him, Captain!  I saw it — everybody saw it...

NATASHA (*tossing about in agony; her mind wandering*). Good people —

my sister and Vaska killed him! The police — listen — this sister of mine — here — she urged, coaxed her lover — there he stands — the scoundrel! They both killed him! Put them in jail! Bring them before the judge! Take me along, too! To prison! Christ Almighty — take me to prison, too!

CURTAIN

# ACT FOUR

*Same as Act I. But* PEPEL'S *room is no longer there, and the partition has been removed. Furthermore, there is no anvil at the place where* KLESHTCH *used to sit and work. In the corner, where* PEPEL'S *room used to be, the* TARTAR *lies stretched out, rather restless, and groaning from time to time.* KLESHTCH *sits at one end of the table, repairing a concertina and now and then testing the stops. At the other end of the table sit* SATINE, *the* BARON, *and* NASTYA. *In front of them stand a bottle of vodka, three bottles of beer, and a large loaf of black bread. The* ACTOR *lies on top of the stove, shifting about and coughing. It is night. The stage is lit by a lamp in the middle of the table. Outside the wind howls.*

KLESHTCH. Yes... he disappeared during the confusion and noise...

THE BARON. He vanished under the very eyes of the police — just like a puff of smoke...

SATINE. That's how sinners flee from the company of the righteous!

NASTYA. He was a dear old soul! But you — you aren't men — you're just — oh — like rust on iron!

THE BARON (*drinks*). Here's to you, my lady!

SATINE. He was an inquisitive old fellow — yes! Nastenka here fell in love with him...

NASTYA. Yes! I did! Madly! It's true! He saw everything — understood everything...

SATINE (*laughing*). Yes, generally speaking, I would say that he was — oh — like mush to those who can't chew....

THE BARON (*laughing*). Right! Like plaster on a boil!

KLESHTCH. He was merciful — you people don't know what pity means...

SATINE. What good can I do you by pitying you?

KLESHTCH. You needn't have pity — but you needn't harm or offend your fellow-beings, either!

THE TARTAR (*sits up on his bunk, nursing his wounded hand carefully*). He was a fine old man. The law of life was the law of his heart.... And he who obeys this law, is good, while he who disregards it, perishes...

THE BARON. What law, Prince?

THE TARTAR. There are a number — different ones — you know...

THE BARON. Proceed!

THE TARTAR. Do not do harm unto others — such is the law!

SATINE. Oh — you mean the Penal Code, criminal and correctional, eh?

THE BARON. And also the Code of Penalties inflicted by Justices of the Peace!

THE TARTAR. No. I mean the Koran. It is the supreme law — and your own soul ought to be the Koran — yes!

KLESHTCH (*testing his concertina*). It wheezes like all hell! But the Prince speaks the truth — one must live abiding by the law — by the teachings of the Gospels...

SATINE. Well — go ahead and do it!

THE BARON. Just try it!

THE TARTAR. The Prophet Mohammed gave to us the law. He said: "Here is the law! Do as it is written therein!" Later on a time will arrive when the Koran will have outlived its purpose — and time will bring forth its own laws — every generation will create its own...

SATINE. To be sure! Time passed on — and gave us — the Criminal Code... It's a strong law, brother — it won't wear off so very soon!

NASTYA (*banging her glass on the table*). Why — why do I stay here — with you? I'll go away somewhere — to the ends of the world!

THE BARON. Without any shoes, my lady?

NASTYA. I'll go — naked, if must be — creeping on all fours!

THE BARON. That'll be rather picturesque, my lady — on all fours!

NASTYA. Yes — and I'll crawl if I have to — anything at all — as long as I don't have to see your faces any longer — oh, I'm so sick of it all — the life — the people — everything!

SATINE. When you go, please take the actor along — he's preparing to go to the very same place — he has learned that within a half mile's distance of the end of the world there's a hospital for diseased organons...

THE ACTOR (*raising his head over the top of the stove*). A hospital for organisms — you fool!

SATINE. For organons — poisoned with vodka!

THE ACTOR. Yes! He will go! He will indeed! You'll see!

THE BARON. Who is he, sir?

THE ACTOR. I!

THE BARON. Thanks, servant of the goddess — what's her name —? The goddess of drama — tragedy — whatever is her name —— ?

THE ACTOR. The muse, idiot! Not the goddess — the muse!

SATINE. Lachesis — Hera — Aphrodite — Atropos — oh! To hell with them all! You see — Baron — it was the old man who stuffed the actor's head full with this rot...

THE BARON. That old man's a fool...

THE ACTOR. Ignoramuses! Beasts! Melpomene — that's her name! Heartless brutes! Bastards! You'll see! He'll go! "On with the orgy, dismal spirits!" — poem — ah — by Béranger! Yes — he'll find some spot where there's no — no...

THE BARON. Where there's nothing, sir?

THE ACTOR. Right! Nothing! "This hole shall be my grave — I am dying — ill and exhausted..." Why do you exist? Why?

THE BARON. You! God or genius or orgy — or whatever you are — don't roar so loud!

THE ACTOR. You lie! I'll roar all I want to!

NASTYA (*lifting her head from the table and throwing up her hands*). Go on! Yell! Let them listen to you!

THE BARON. Where is the sense, my lady?

SATINE. Leave them alone, Baron! To hell with the lot! Let them yell — let them knock their damned heads off if they feel like it! There's a method in their madness! Don't you go and interfere with people as that old fellow did! Yes — it's he — the damned old fool — he bewitched the whole gang of us!

KLESHTCH. He persuaded them to go away — but failed to show them the road...

THE BARON. That old man was a humbug!

NASTYA. Liar! You're a humbug yourself!

THE BARON. Shut up, my lady!

KLESHTCH. The old man didn't like truth very much — as a matter of fact he strongly resented it — and wasn't he right, though? Just look — where is there any truth? And yet, without it, you can't breathe! For instance, our Tartar Prince over there, crushed his hand at his work — and now he'll have to have his arm amputated — and there's the truth for you!

SATINE (striking the table with his clenched fist). Shut up! You sons of bitches! Fools! Not another word about that old fellow! (To the BARON.) You, Baron, are the worst of the lot! You don't understand a thing, and you lie like the devil! The old man's no humbug! What's the truth? Man! Man — that's the truth! He understood man — you don't! You're all as dumb as stones! I understand the old man — yes! He lied — but lied out of sheer pity for you... God damn you! Lots of people lie out of pity for their fellow-beings! I know! I've read about it! They lie — oh — beautifully, inspiringly, stirringly! Some lies bring comfort, and others bring peace — a lie alone can justify the burden which crushed a workman's hand and condemns those who are starving! I know what lying means! The weakling and the one who is a parasite through his very weakness — they both need lies — lies are their support, their shield, their armor! But the man who is strong, who is his own master, who is free and does not have to suck his neighbors' blood — he needs no lies! To lie — it's the creed of slaves and masters of slaves! Truth is the religion of the free man!

THE BARON. Bravo! Well spoken! Hear, hear! I agree! You speak like an honest man!

SATINE. And why can't a crook at times speak the truth — since honest people at times speak like crooks? Yes — I've forgotten a lot — but I still know a thing or two! The old man? Oh — he's wise! He affected me as acid affects a dirty old silver coin! Let's drink to his health! Fill the glasses... (NASTYA fills a glass with beer and hands it to SATINE, who laughs.) The old man lives within himself... he looks upon all the world from his own angle. Once I asked him: "Grand-dad, why do people live?"

(*Tries to imitate* LUKA'S *voice and gestures.*) And he replied: "Why, my dear fellow, people live in the hope of something better! For example — let's say there are carpenters in this world, and all sorts of trash... people... and they give birth to a carpenter the like of which has never been seen upon the face of the earth... he's way above everybody else, and has no equal among carpenters! The brilliancy of his personality was reflected on all his trade, on all the other carpenters, so that they advanced twenty years in one day! This applies to all other trades — blacksmiths and shoemakers and other workmen — and all the peasants — and even the aristocrats live in the hopes of a higher life! Each individual thinks that he's living for his own Self, but in reality he lives in the hope of something better. A hundred years — sometimes longer — do we expect, live for the finer, higher life..." (NASTYA *stares intently into* SATINE'S *face.* KLESHTCH *stops working and listens. The* BARON *bows his head very low, drumming softly on the table with his fingers. The* ACTOR, *peering down from the stove, tries to climb noiselessly into the bunk.*) "Everyone, brothers, everyone lives in the hope of something better. That's why we must respect each and every human being! How do we know who he is, why he was born, and what he is capable of accomplishing? Perhaps his coming into the world will prove to be our good fortune... Especially must we respect little children! Children — need freedom! Don't interfere with their lives! Respect children!" (*Pause.*)

THE BARON (*thoughtfully*). Hm — yes — something better? — That reminds me of my family... an old family dating back to the time of Catherine... all noblemen, soldiers, originally French... they served their country and gradually rose higher and higher. In the days of Nicholas the First my grandfather, Gustave DeBille, held a high post — riches — hundreds of serfs... horses — cooks ——

NASTYA. You liar! It isn't true!

THE BARON (*jumping up*). What? Well — go on ——

NASTYA. It isn't true.

THE BARON (*screams*). A house in Moscow! A house in Petersburg! Carriages! Carriages with coats of arms!

(KLESHTCH *takes his concertina and goes to one side, watching the scene with interest.*)

NASTYA. You lie!

THE BARON. Shut up! — I say — dozens of footmen...

NASTYA (*delighted*). You lie!

THE BARON. I'll kill you!

NASTYA (*ready to run away*). There were no carriages!

SATINE. Stop, Nastenka! Don't infuriate him!

THE BARON. Wait — you bitch! My grandfather...

NASTYA. There was no grandfather! There was nothing!

(SATINE *roars with laughter.*)

THE BARON (*worn out with rage, sits down on bench*). Satine! Tell that slut — what — ? You, too, are laughing? You — don't believe me either? (*Cries out in despair, pounding the table with his fists*). It's true — damn the whole lot of you!

NASTYA (*triumphantly*). So — you're crying? Understand now what a human being feels like when nobody believes him?

KLESHTCH (*returning to the table*). I thought there'd be a fight...

THE TARTAR. Oh — people are fools! It's too bad...

THE BARON. I shall not permit anyone to ridicule me! I have proofs — documents — damn you!

SATINE. Forget it! Forget about your grandfather's carriages! You can't drive anywhere in a carriage of the past!

THE BARON. How dare she — just the same —— ?

NASTYA. Just imagine! How dare I —— ?

SATINE. You see — she does dare! How is she any worse than you are? Although, surely, in her past there wasn't even a father and mother, let alone carriages and a grandfather...

THE BARON (*quieting down*). Devil take you — you do know how to argue dispassionately — and I, it seems — I've no will-power...

SATINE. Acquire some — it's useful... (*Pause.*) Nastya! Are you going to the hospital?

NASTYA. What for?

SATINE. To see Natashka.

NASTYA. Oh — just woke up, did you? She's been out of the hospital for some time — and they can't find a trace of her...

SATINE. Oh — that woman's a goner!

KLESHTCH. It's interesting to see whether Vaska will get the best of Vassilisa, or the other way around —— ?

NASTYA. Vassilisa will win out! She's shrewd! And Vaska will go to the gallows!

SATINE. For manslaughter? No — only to jail...

NASTYA. Too bad — the gallows would have been better... that's where all of you should be sent... swept off into a hole — like filth...

SATINE (*astonished*). What's the matter? Are you crazy?

THE BARON. Oh — give her a wallop — that'll teach her to be less impertinent...

NASTYA. Just you try to touch me!

THE BARON. I shall!

SATINE. Stop! Don't insult her! I can't get the thought of the old man out of my head! (*Roars with laughter.*) Don't offend your fellow-beings! Suppose I were offended once in such a way that I'd remember it for the rest of my life? What then? Should I forgive? No, no!

THE BARON (*to* NASTYA). You must understand that I'm not your sort... you — ah — you piece of dirt!

NASTYA. You bastard! Why — you live off me like a worm off an apple! (*The men laugh amusedly.*)

KLESHTCH. Fool! An apple —— ?

THE BARON. You can't be angry with her — she's just an ass ——

NASTYA. You laugh! Liars? Don't strike you as funny, eh?

THE ACTOR (*morosely*). Give them a good beating!

NASTYA. If I only could! (*Takes a cup from the table and throws it on the floor.*) That's what I'd like to do to you all!

THE TARTAR. Why break dishes — eh — silly girl?

THE BARON (*rising*). That'll do! I'll teach her manners in half a second.

NASTYA (*running toward door*). Go to hell!

SATINE (*calling after her*). Hey! That's enough! Whom are you trying to frighten? What's all the row about, anyway?

NASTYA. Dogs! I hope you'll croak! Dogs! (*Runs out.*)

THE ACTOR (*morosely*). Amen!

THE TARTAR. Allah! Mad women, these Russians! They're bold, wilful; Tartar women aren't like that! They know the law and abide by it....

KLESHTCH. She ought to be given a sound hiding!

THE BARON. The slut!

KLESHTCH (*testing the concertina*). It's ready! But its owner isn't here yet — that young fellow is burning his life away...

SATINE. Care for a drink — now?

KLESHTCH. Thanks... it's time to go to bed...

SATINE. Getting used to us?

KLESHTCH (*drinks, then goes to his bunk*). It's all right... there are people everywhere — at first you don't notice it... but after a while you don't mind....

(*The* TARTAR *spreads some rags over his bunk, then kneels on them and prays.*)

THE BARON (*to* SATINE, *pointing at the* TARTAR). Look!

SATINE. Stop! He's a good fellow! Leave him alone! (*Roars with laughter.*) I feel kindly today — the devil alone knows the reason why...

THE BARON. You always feel kindly when you're drunk — you're even wiser at such times...

SATINE. When I'm drunk? Yes — then I like everything — right — He prays? That's fine! A man may believe or not — that's his own affair — a man is free — he pays for everything himself — belief or unbelief — love — wisdom... a man pays for everything — and that's just why he's free! Man is — truth! And what is man? It's neither you nor I nor they — oh no — it's you and they and I and the old man — and Napoleon — Mohammed — all in one! (*Outlines vaguely in the air the contour of a human being.*) Do you understand? It's tremendous! It contains the beginning and the end of everything — everything is in man — and everything exists for him! Man alone exists — everything else is the creation of his hands and his brain! Man! It is glorious! It sounds — oh — so big! Man must be respected — not degraded with pity — but respected, respected! Let us drink to man, Baron! (*Rises.*) It is good to feel that you are a man! I'm a convict, a murderer, a crook — granted! — When I'm out on the street people stare at me as if I were a scoundrel — they draw away from me — they look after me and often they say: "You dog! You humbug! Work!" Work? And what for? to fill my belly? (*Roars with laughter.*) I've always despised people who worry too much about their bellies.

It isn't right, Baron! It isn't! Man is loftier than that! Man stands above hunger!

THE BARON. You — reason things out.... Well and good — it brings you a certain amount of consolation.... Personally I'm incapable of it... I don't know how. (*Glances around him and then, softly, guardedly.*) Brother — I am afraid — at times. Do you understand? Afraid! — Because — what next?

SATINE. Rot! What's a man to be afraid of?

THE BARON (*pacing up and down*). You know — as far back as I can remember, there's been a sort of fog in my brain. I was never able to understand anything. Somehow I feel embarrassed — it seems to me that all my life I've done nothing but change clothes — and why? I don't understand! I studied — I wore the uniform of the Institute for the Sons of the Nobility... but what have I learned? I don't remember! I married — I wore a frock-coat — then a dressing-gown... but I chose a disagreeable wife... and why? I don't understand. I squandered everything that I possessed — I wore some sort of a grey jacket and brick-colored trousers — but how did I happen to ruin myself? I haven't the slightest idea.... I had a position in the Department of State.... I wore a uniform and a cap with insignia of rank.... I embezzled government funds... so they dressed me in a convict's garb — and later on I got into these clothes here — and it all happened as in a dream — it's funny...

SATINE. Not very! It's rather — silly!

THE BARON. Yes — silly! I think so, too. Still — wasn't I born for some sort of purpose?

SATINE (*laughing*). Probably — a man is born to conceive a better man. (*Shaking his head.*) — It's all right!

THE BARON. That she-devil Nastka! Where did she run to? I'll go and see — after all, she... (*Exit; pause.*)

THE ACTOR. Tartar! (*Pause.*) Prince! (*The* TARTAR *looks round.*) Say a prayer for me...

THE TARTAR. What?

THE ACTOR (*softly*). Pray — for me!

THE TARTAR (*after a silence*). Pray for your own self!

THE ACTOR (*quickly crawls off the stove and goes to the table, pours out*

*a drink with shaking hands, drinks, then almost runs to passage).*
All over!

SATINE. Hey, proud Sicambrian! Where are you going?

(SATINE *whistles.* MIEDVIEDIEFF *enters, dressed in a woman's flannel shirt-waist; followed by* BUBNOFF. *Both are slightly drunk.* BUBNOFF *carries a bunch of pretzels in one hand, a couple of smoked fish in the other, a bottle of vodka under one arm, another bottle in his coat pocket.)*

MIEDVIEDIEFF. A camel is something like a donkey — only it has no ears....

BUBNOFF. Shut up! You're a variety of donkey yourself!

MIEDVIEDIEFF. A camel has no ears at all, at all — it hears through its nostrils...

BUBNOFF (*to* SATINE). Friend! I've looked for you in all the saloons and all the cabarets! Take this bottle — my hands are full...

SATINE. Put the pretzels on the table — then you'll have one hand free ——

BUBNOFF. Right! Hey — you donkey — look! Isn't he a clever fellow?

MIEDVIEDIEFF. All crooks are clever — I know! They couldn't do a thing without brains. An honest man is all right even if he's an idiot... but a crook must have brains. But, speaking about camels, you're wrong... you can ride them — they have no horns... and no teeth either...

BUBNOFF. Where's everybody? Why is there no one here? Come on out... I treat! Who's in the corner?

SATINE. How soon will you drink up everything you have? Scarecrow!

BUBNOFF. Very soon! I've very little this time. Zob — where's Zob?

KLESHTCH (*crossing to table*). He isn't here...

BUBNOFF. Waughrr! Bull-dog! Brr-zz-zz! — Turkey-cock! Don't bark and don't growl! Drink — make merry — and don't be sullen! — I treat everybody — Brother, I love to treat — if I were rich, I'd run a free saloon! So help me God, I would! With an orchestra and a lot of singers! Come, everyone! Drink and eat — listen to the music — and rest in peace!

Beggars — come, all you beggars — and enter my saloon free of charge! Satine — you can have half my capital — just like that!

SATINE. You better give me all you have straight away!

BUBNOFF. All my capital? Right now? Well — here's a ruble — here's twenty kopecks — five kopecks — sunflower seeds — and that's all!

SATINE. That's splendid! It'll be safer with me — I'll gamble with it…

MIEDVIEDIEFF. I'm a witness — the money was given you for safe-keeping. How much is it?

BUBNOFF. You? You're a camel — we don't need witnesses…

ALYOSHKA (comes in barefoot). Brothers, I got my feet wet!

BUBNOFF. Go on and get your throat wet — and nothing'll happen — you're a fine fellow — you sing and you play — that's all right! But it's too bad you drink — drink, little brother, is harmful, very harmful…

ALYOSHKA. I judge by you! Only when you're drunk do you resemble a human being… Kleshtch! Is my concertina fixed?
(Sings and dances.)

"If my mug were not so attractive,
My sweetheart wouldn't love me at all…"

Boys, I'm frozen — it's cold…

MIEDVIEDIEFF. Hm — and may I ask who's this sweetheart?

BUBNOFF. Shut up! From now on, brother, you are neither a policeman nor an uncle!

ALYOSHKA. Just auntie's husband!

BUBNOFF. One of your nieces is in jail — the other one's dying…

MIEDVIEDIEFF (proudly). You lie! She's not dying — she disappeared — without trace…     (SATINE roars.)

BUBNOFF. All the same, brothers — a man without nieces isn't an uncle!

ALYOSHKA. Your Excellency! Listen to the drummer of the retired billygoats' brigade!     (Sings.)

"My sweetheart has money,
I haven't a cent.
But I'm a cheerful,
Merry lad!"

Oh — isn't it cold!

(*Enter* ZOB. *From now until the final curtain men and women drift in, undress, and stretch out on the bunks, grumbling.*)

ZOB. Bubnoff! Why did you run off?

BUBNOFF. Come here — sit down — brother, let's sing my favorite ditty, eh?

THE TARTAR. Night was made for sleep! Sing your songs in the daytime!

SATINE. Well — never mind, Prince — come here!

THE TARTAR. What do you mean — never mind? There's going to be a noise — there always is when people sing!

BUBNOFF (*crossing to the* TARTAR). Count — ah — I mean Prince — how's your hand? Did they cut it off?

THE TARTAR. What for? We'll wait and see — perhaps it won't be necessary... a hand isn't made of iron — it won't take long to cut it off...

ZOB. It's your own affair, Hassanka! You'll be good for nothing without your hand. We're judged by our hands and backs — without the pride of your hand, you're no longer a human being. Tobacco-carting — that's your business! Come on — have a drink of vodka — and stop worrying!

KVASHNYA (*comes in*). Ah, my beloved fellow-lodgers! It's horrible outside — snow and slush... is my policeman here?

MIEDVIEDIEFF. Right here!

KVASHNYA. Wearing my blouse again? And drunk, eh? What's the idea?

MIEDVIEDIEFF. In celebration of Bubnoff's birthday... besides, it's cold...

KVASHNYA. Better look out — stop feeling about and go to sleep!

MIEDVIEDIEFF (*goes to kitchen*). Sleep? I can — I want to — it's time —— (*Exit.*)

SATINE. What's the matter? Why are you so strict with him?

KVASHNYA. You can't be otherwise, friend. You have to be strict with his sort. I took him as a partner. I thought he'd be of some benefit to me — because he's a military man — and you're a rough lot... and I am a woman — and now he's turned drunkard — that won't do at all!

SATINE. You picked a good one for partner!

KVASHNYA. Couldn't get a better one. You wouldn't want to

live with me... you think you're too fine! And even if you did it wouldn't last more than a week... you gamble me and all I own away at cards!

SATINE (*roars with laughter*). That's true, landlady — I'd gamble...

KVASHNYA. Yes, yes. Alyoshka!

ALYOSHKA. Here he is — I, myself!

KVASHNYA. What do you mean by gossiping about me?

ALYOSHKA. I? I speak out everything — whatever my conscience tells me. There, I say, is a wonderful woman! Splendid meat, fat, bones — over four hundred pounds! But brains — ? not an ounce!

KVASHNYA. You're a liar! I've lots of brains! What do you mean by saying I beat my policeman?

ALYOSHKA. I thought you did — when you pulled him by the hair!

KVASHNYA (*laughs*). You fool! You aren't blind, are you? Why wash dirty linen in public? And — it hurts his feelings — that's why he took to drink...

ALYOSHKA. It's true, evidently, that even a chicken likes vodka...

(SATINE *and* KLESHTCH *roar with laughter.*)

KVASHYNA. Go on — show your teeth! What sort of a man are you anyway, Alyoshka?

ALYOSHKA. Oh — I am first-rate! Master of all trades! I follow my nose!

BUBNOFF (*near the* TARTAR's *bunk*). Come on! At all events — we won't let you sleep! We'll sing all night. Zob!

ZOB. Sing — ? All right...

ALYOSHKA. And I'll play...

SATINE. We'll listen!

THE TARTAR (*smiling*). Well — Bubnoff — you devil — bring the vodka — we'll drink — we'll have a hell of a good time! The end will come soon enough — and then we'll be dead!

BUBNOFF. Fill his glass, Satine! Zob — sit down! Ah — brothers — what does a man need after all? There, for instance, I've had a drink — and I'm happy! Zob! Start my favorite song! I'll sing — and then I'll cry....

ZOB (*begins to sing*).

"The sun rises and sets..."

BUBNOFF (*joining in*).

            "But my prison is all dark...."

                                    (*Doors open quickly.*)

THE BARON (*on the threshold; yells*). Hey — you — come — come
    here!   Out in the waste — in the yard... over there... The
    actor — he's hanged himself....

        (*Silence.   All stare at the* BARON.   *Behind him appears*
        NASTYA, *and slowly, her eyes wide with horror, she walks to
        the table.*)

SATINE (*in a matter-of-fact voice*). Damned fool — he ruined the
    song...!

                            CURTAIN

# THE LIFE OF MAN
## (ZHIZN CHELOVIEKA)

A PLAY IN FIVE SCENES WITH A PROLOGUE

By LEONID ANDREYEV

*Translated by THOMAS SELTZER*

TO THE BRIGHT MEMORY OF MY FRIEND, MY WIFE

I DEDICATE THIS COMPOSITION

THE LAST

ON WHICH WE WORKED TOGETHER

# LEONID ANDREYEV

LEONID NIKOLAEVITCH ANDREYEV was born at Orel, Russia, in 1871 and died in 1919 in Finland. An unpromising student he graduated at the Gymnasium and studied law at the Universities of St. Petersburg and Moscow, meanwhile earning money by painting portraits, reporting for the *Courier*, and writing sketches and stories. He was a man of melancholy temperament and early turned his interests to abnormal psychology, and in a fit of depression attempted to commit suicide. In his initial literary work, largely of an autobiographical nature, he was encouraged by Gorky. A prolific writer in all forms of composition he composed rapidly and in a creative passion with little care for construction and the orderly refinements of style. His first story to attract attention was entitled *The Abyss*; within a few years his books were best sellers in Russia. He was deeply interested in the Revolution of 1905 but was out of sympathy with the Soviet Revolution of 1917. His first play, *To the Stars*, was produced in 1905. Among the most widely admired of his non-dramatic works was *The Seven that were Hanged*; his international fame began with *The Red Laugh*, a story of the horrors of the Russo-Japanese War. Andreyev's Letters on the Theatre, 1913, were condensed and translated in the *New York Times* for October 5 and 19, 1919.

## THE LIFE OF MAN

IT IS a commonplace of dramatic criticism that the most characteristic of Russian playwrights fail in the transfer to foreign tongues.
Conversely those plays which are not strictly characteristic are
not unlikely to obtain a foreign vogue. Andreyev as a dramatist
is a product of particular conditions; extravagantly popular for
a decade and a half in Russia he was recognized to write in a manner that was untypical of the Russian genius, and was subjected
to bitter censure by Tolstoy for careless composition and for an
abstract emotionalism. *The Life of Man* is one of the few examplars
of the symbolic drama in Russia. Alone among the great dramas
of Europe the Russian theatre lacks the store of dramatic legend
and convention drawn from the drama of the mediaeval church.
In *The Life of Man*, *King Hunger*, *The Black Maskers*, *Anathema*, and
*The Ocean* Andreyev seeks his inspiration from foreign sources in
which allegory was more firmly planted as an art form than it ever
was in Russia. The inspiration of *The Life of Man* is of course
the mediaeval morality *Everyman*. Under an antique convention
the author generalizes modern life, in Periods, Birth, Love and
Marriage, Struggle for Existence, Success, Riches, and in Person-
alities concrete and abstract, the Man, the Wife, the Child, Someone in Gray. *The Life of Man* was presented at the Moscow Art
Theatre in late 1907; it had been published at the beginning of
that year. It has been several times translated into English.

# PERSONS

SOMEONE IN GRAY CALLED HE
MAN
HIS WIFE

MAN'S
{
FATHER
RELATIVES
NEIGHBORS
FRIENDS
ENEMIES
GUESTS
SERVANTS
}

MUSICIANS
PHYSICIANS
A BARTENDER
DRUNKARDS
OLD WOMEN

# PROLOGUE

## SOMEONE IN GRAY CALLED HE, SPEAKING OF THE LIFE OF MAN

*A large, rectangular space resembling a room without doors or windows and quite empty. Everything is gray, monocolored, drab — the walls gray, and the ceiling, and the floor. A feeble, even light enters from some invisible source. It too is gray, monotonous, spectral, producing neither lights nor shadows.*

SOMEONE IN GRAY *moves noiselessly away from the wall, close against which* HE *has been standing.* HE *wears a broad, gray, formless smock, vaguely outlining the contours of* HIS *body; and a hat of the same gray throws the upper part of* HIS *face into heavy shadow.* HIS *eyes are invisible. All that is seen are* HIS *cheekbones,* HIS *nose, and* HIS *chin, which is massive, heavy, and blunt, as if hewn out of rock.* HIS *lips are pressed tight together. Raising* HIS *head slightly,* HE *begins to speak in a firm, cold, unemotional, unimpassioned voice, like a reader hired by the hour reading the Book of Fate with brutal indifference.*

SOMEONE IN GRAY. Look and listen, you who have come here to laugh and be amused. There will pass before you the whole life of Man, from his dark beginning to his dark ending. Previously non-existant, mysteriously hidden in the infiniteness of time, neither feeling nor thinking, and known to no one, he will mysteriously break through the prison of non-being and with a cry announce the beginning of his brief life. In the night of non-existence a light will go up, kindled by an unseen hand. It is the life of Man. Behold the flame — it is the life of Man.

Being born, he will take the form and the name of Man, and in all things will become like other men already living. And their hard lot will be his lot, and his hard lot will be the lot of all human beings. Inexorably impelled by time, he will, with invertible necessity, pass through all the stages of human life, from the bottom to the top, from the top to the bottom. Limited in vision, he will never see the next step which his unsteady foot, poised in the air, is in the very act of taking. Limited in knowledge, he will never know what the coming day will bring, or the coming hour, or the coming minute. In his unseeing blindness, troubled by premonitions, agitated by hope and fear, he will submissively complete the iron-traced circle foreordained.

Behold him a happy youth. See how brightly the candle burns. From boundless stretches of space the icy wind blows, circling, careering, and tossing the flame. In vain. Bright and clear the candle burns. Yet the wax is dwindling, consumed by the fire. Yet the wax is dwindling.

Behold him a happy husband and father. But see how strangely dim and faint the candle burns, as if the yellowing flame were wrinkling, as if it were shivering with cold and were creeping into concealment. The wax is melting, consumed by the fire. The wax is melting.

Behold him an old man, ill and feeble. The stages of life are already ended. In their stead nothing but a black void. Yet he drags on with palsied limbs. The flame, now turned blue, bends to the ground and crawls along, trembling and falling, trembling and falling. Then it goes out quietly.

Thus Man will die. Coming from the night, he will return to the night and go out, leaving no trace behind. He will pass into the infinity of time, neither thinking nor feeling, and known to no one. And I, whom all call He, shall remain the faithful companion of Man throughout his life, on all his pathways. Unseen by him, I shall be constantly at hand when he wakes and when he sleeps, when he prays and when he curses. In his hours of joy, when his spirit, free and bold, rises aloft; in his hours of grief and despair, when his soul clouds over with mortal pain and sorrow, and the blood congeals in his heart; in the hours of victory and defeat; in the hours of great strife with the immutable, I shall be with him — I shall be with him.

And you who have come here to be amused, you who are consecrated to death, look and listen. There will pass before you, like a distant phantom echo, the fleet-moving life of Man with its sorrows and its joys.

(SOMEONE IN GRAY *turns silent. The light goes out, and* HE *and the gray, empty room are enveloped in darkness.*)

## THE FIRST SCENE

### THE BIRTH OF MAN AND THE MOTHER'S TRAVAIL

*Profound darkness; not a stir. Like a swarm of mice in hiding, the gray silhouettes of* OLD WOMEN *in strange headgear are dimly discerned; also vaguely the outline of a large, lofty room. The* OLD WOMEN *carry on a conversation in low, mocking voices.*

OLD WOMEN'S CONVERSATION

— I wonder whether it'll be a boy or a girl.

— What difference does it make to you?

— I like boys.

— I like girls. They always sit at home waiting till you call on them.

— Do you like to go visiting? (*The* OLD WOMEN *titter.*)

— He knows.

— He knows. (*Silence.*)

— Our friend would like to have a girl. She says boys are so restless and venturesome and are always seeking danger. Even when they are little, they like to climb tall trees and bathe in deep water. They often fall, and they drown. And when they get to be men, they make wars and kill one another.

— She thinks girls don't drown. I have seen many girls drowned. They look like all drowned people, wet and green.

— She thinks girls don't get killed by stones thrown at them.

— Poor woman, she has such a hard time giving birth to her child. We have been sitting here sixteen hours, and she is still crying. At first she cried out loud. Her screams pierced our ears. Then she cried more quietly, and now she is only moaning.

— The doctor says she'll die.

— No, the doctor says the child will die and she will live.

— Why do they bear children? It is so painful.

— And why do they die? It is still more painful.

(*The* OLD WOMEN *laugh suppressedly.*)

— Yes, they bear children and die.

— And bear children again.

(*They laugh. A subdued cry of the suffering woman is heard.*)

— Beginning again.

— She's recovered her voice.   That's good.

— That's good.

— Poor husband.   He's lost his head completely.   You ought to see him.   He's a sight.   At first he was glad his wife was pregnant and said he wanted a boy.   He thinks his son will be a cabinet minister or a general.   Now he doesn't want anything, neither a boy nor a girl.   He just goes about grieving and crying.

— Every time she is seized with pain he begins to labor, too, and gets red in the face.

— He was sent to the chemist's shop for medicine, and he hung about there for two hours without being able to remember what he was sent for.   He returned without it.

(*The* OLD WOMEN *titter.   The cries grow louder and die away. Silence.*)

— What's the matter with her?   Maybe she has died already.

— No.   If she had, we'd hear crying, and the doctor would come running and begin to talk nonsense.   They'd bring her husband out in a faint, and we'd have to work over him.   No, she's not dead.

— Then what are we sitting here for?

— Ask Him.   What do we know?

— He won't tell.

— He won't tell.   He never tells anything.

— He orders us about as he pleases, gets us out of bed, and makes us watch; and then it turns out that our coming wasn't even needed.

— We came of our own accord, didn't we?   We must tell the truth.   There, she's screaming again.

— Haven't you had as much of it as you want?

— Are you satisfied?

— I keep my mouth shut and wait.

— You're an angel.          (*They laugh.   The cries grow louder.*)

— Listen to her.   What fearful pain she must be suffering. Have you an idea of what the pain is like?   It's as if your insides were being torn to pieces.

— We all have borne children.

— It's just as if she were not herself.   I don't recognize our friend's voice.   It's naturally so soft and gentle.

— Her screaming is more like the roar of a wild beast.

— You feel the night in it.

— You feel the boundless black forest and hopelessness and terror.

— You feel solitude and grief.  There are other people with her.  Why can't you hear other voices beside that savage, dismal wail?

— They are talking, but you can't hear them.  Have you ever noticed how solitary man's cries are?  Any number of men will talk, and you won't hear them.  But let one human being cry, and it seems as if the others were all silent, listening.

— I once heard a man scream who had been run over by a carriage and had his leg crushed.  The street was full of people.  Yet he seemed to be the only one there.

— But this is more terrible.

— Say rather it is louder.

— I should say it is more prolonged.

— No, it's more terrible.  You feel death in it.

— You had a feeling of death then, too.  In fact, the man did die.

— Don't dispute.  It's all the same to you.      (*Silence.  Cries.*)

— How strange man's crying is!  When you yourself are ill and cry, you don't notice how strange it is.  I can't imagine the mouth that produces such sounds.  Can it be a woman's mouth?  I can't imagine it.

— It's as if it got twisted and crooked.

— As if the sound issued from some depth.  Now it's like the cry of someone drowning.  Listen, she's choking.

— A heavy person is sitting on her chest.

— Someone is choking her.           (*The crying ceases.*)

— At last she has quieted down.  You get tired of crying.  It's monotonous and not beautiful.

— You're looking for beauty here too, are you?

(*The* OLD WOMEN *titter.*)

— Hush!  Is He here?

— I don't know.

— He seems to be.

— He doesn't like laughing.

— They say He laughs Himself.

— Whoever heard Him laugh? You are simply repeating hearsay. So many lies are told about Him.

— He hears us. Let us be serious.          (*They laugh quietly.*)

— After all, I'd like to know whether it'll be a boy or a girl.

— I admit, it's interesting to know whom you'll have to deal with.

— I wish it died before it was born.

— What a kind creature you are.

— No better than you.

— I hope it turns out to be a general.          (*They laugh.*)

— You are too merry. I don't like it.

— And you are too sad. I don't like that.

— Don't wrangle. Don't wrangle. We are all both sad and merry. Let each be what she pleases.          (*Silence.*)

— When they are born, they are so funny. Babies are very funny.

— And self-satisfied.

— And very exacting. I don't like them. They begin to cry and make demands, as if they expected everything to be ready for them. Even before looking, they know there is a breast and milk, and demand them. Then they demand to be put to sleep and rocked and dandled and patted on their red backs. I like them better when they die. Then they're less exacting. They stretch out of themselves and don't ask to be rocked.

— No, they are very funny. I like to wash them when they are born.

— I like to wash them when they are dead.

— Don't dispute. Don't dispute. Each will have her way. One will wash the child when it is born, another when it dies.

— But why do they think they have a right to make demands the moment they are born? I don't like it. They don't *think* they have. It's their stomachs that make the demands.

— They're forever demanding.

— But their demands are never granted.

                    (*The* OLD WOMEN *laugh. The cries begin again.*)

— She is screaming again.

— Animals give birth to their offspring more easily.

— And they die more easily, and live more easily. I have a cat. You ought to see how fat and happy she is.

— I have a dog, and I tell him every day: "You are going to die." His only reply is to show his teeth and to wag his tail gayly.

— But they are animals.

— And these are human beings. (*They laugh.*)

— Now she'll either die or be delivered. I feel that the whole remnant of her strength is in that wail.

— Eyes wide open.

— Cold perspiration on her forehead. (*They listen.*)

— She is giving birth to the child.

— No, she is dying. (*The cries cease.*)

— I tell you ——

SOMEONE IN GRAY (*speaks in a resonant, powerful voice*). Silence! Man is born.

(*Almost simultaneously with* HIS *announcement the crying of an infant is heard and the candle in* HIS *hand lights. A tall candle. It burns hesitatingly and feebly. Gradually the flame grows stronger. The corner in which* SOMEONE IN GRAY *stands motionless is always darker than the other corners, and the yellow flame illumines* HIS *blunt chin,* HIS *tightly closed lips, and* HIS *massive, bony face. The upper part of* HIS *face is concealed by* HIS *cap.* HE *is somewhat taller than an ordinary man.*)

(HE *puts the long, thick candle in an antique candlestick.* HIS *hand comes into relief against the green bronze. It is gray, firm, with long, thin fingers.*)

(*Gradually the room grows brighter. The figures of five hunchbacked* OLD WOMEN *emerge from the gloom, and the room becomes visible. It is rectangular, with high, smooth, monotonously colored walls. Two curtainless windows in the background and two on the right. The night glooms through them. Straight, high-backed chairs against the walls.*)

THE OLD WOMEN (*Talking rapidly.*)

— Hear them running about. They're coming here.

— How bright it is! Let's go.

— Look, the candle is tall and bright.

— Let's go, let's go. Quick!

— But we'll come back. We'll come back.

(*They laugh quietly, mockingly, and disappear into the dusk with odd, zigzagging movements. As they leave, the light grows brighter, but still it remains dim, lifeless, and cold. The corner in which* SOMEONE IN GRAY *stands motionless with the burning candle is darker than the others.)*

*(Enter the* DOCTOR *in a white uniform, and* MAN'S FATHER, *whose face wears an expression of extreme exhaustion and joy. There are lines under his eyes; his cheeks are sunken and his hair is dishevelled; he is very negligently dressed. The* DOCTOR *looks very learned.)*

DOCTOR. Up to the very last moment I didn't know whether your wife would pull through or not. I used all the means at the disposal of medical skill and science. But science can do very little unless nature helps too. I was really excited. My pulse is still going hard. Though I have assisted at so many births, yet I can't rid myself of a sense of uneasiness. But you are not listening to me, sir.

MAN'S FATHER. I'm listening, but I can't hear. Her screams are still ringing in my ears, and it's hard for me to pull myself together. Poor woman, how she suffered! I was a fool, I was stupid and wanted to have children. But hereafter I will renounce. It is criminal.

DOCTOR. You will call me again when your next child comes.

FATHER. No, never. I'm ashamed to admit it, but just now I hate the child for which she suffered so. I didn't even see him. What sort of a boy is he?

DOCTOR. He's a well-fed, strong little youngster, and if I'm not mistaken he resembles you.

FATHER. Me? Fine! Now I'm beginning to love him. I always wanted a boy to look like me. Did you see — his nose is like mine, isn't it?

DOCTOR. Yes, his nose and eyes.

FATHER. His eyes too? Ah, that's good. I'll raise your fee.

DOCTOR. You'll have to pay me for using the instruments also.

FATHER (*turning to the corner where He stands motionless*). God, I thank Thee for having granted my wish and given me a son who resembles me. I thank Thee for preserving my wife from death and bringing my child into the world alive. I pray Thee that he may grow up big, healthy, and strong; that he may be wise and honest, and that he may never cause us grief, but be a constant joy to his mother and me. If Thou wilt do this, I will always believe in Thee and go to church.

(*Enter* RELATIVES, *six in number. An elderly woman, uncommonly stout, with a double chin and small, proud eyes and an air of extreme haughtiness and self-importance. An elderly man, her husband, very tall and uncommonly thin, so that his coat hangs loosely on his body; a short goatee, long, smooth hair, as if wet, reaching to his shoulders; eyeglasses; has a frightened yet pedantic expression; a low black silk hat in his hand. A young girl, their daughter, with naïvely upturned nose, blinking eyes, and open mouth. A weazened woman, with contracted features and a sour expression, in her hand a handkerchief, with which she frequently wipes her mouth. Two young men, looking absolutely alike, with extremely high collars that stretch their necks; glossy hair; a hesitating, embarrassed expression. The characteristics of each of the* RELATIVES *is exaggerated in the extreme.*)

ELDERLY LADY. Let me congratulate you on the birth of your son, dear brother. (*Kisses him.*)

ELDERLY MAN. My dear brother, I heartily congratulate you on the birth of your son, to which you have been looking forward so long. (*Kisses him.*)

THE REST. We congratulate you, dear uncle, on the birth of your son. (*They kiss him. Exit the* DOCTOR)

MAN'S FATHER (*greatly moved*). Thank you! Thank you! You are all very good, very nice, dear people, and I love you very much. I had my doubts before, and thought that you, dear sister, were a little too much rapt up in yourself and your own worth and importance; and that you, dear brother, were somewhat too pedantic. The rest of you I thought were too cold to me, and came here only for the sake of the dinners. Now I see I was mistaken. I'm very happy. I get a son who resembles me, and then all at once I see myself surrounded by so many good people who love me. (*They kiss.*)

GIRL. Uncle dear, what are you going to call your son? I hope you'll give him a lovely, poetic name. So much depends on a man's name.

ELDERLY LADY. I should advise a simple, solid name. Men with nice names are usually frivolous and rarely successful.

ELDERLY MAN. It seems to me, brother, you should name your son after some older relative. Keeping the same names in the family tends to preserve and strengthen the line.

FATHER. Yes, my wife and I have already discussed the subject, but have not been able to reach a decision. You see, there are so many new things to think of when a child comes, so many new problems to solve which never arose before.

ELDERLY LADY. It fills up your life.

ELDERLY MAN. It gives life a beautiful purpose. By properly educating a child, preventing it from making the mistakes which we had to pay for so dearly, and strengthening its mind with our own rich experiences, we produce a better man and advance slowly but surely toward the final goal of existence, which is perfection.

FATHER. You are quite right, brother. When I was little I loved to torture animals. That developed cruelty in me. I won't allow my son to torture animals. Even after I had grown up I often made mistakes in my friendships and love. I chose friends who were unworthy and women who were faithless. I'll explain to my son ——

DOCTOR (*enters and says aloud*). Your wife is feeling very bad. She wants to see you.

FATHER. Oh, my God! (HE *and the* DOCTOR *leave.*)

(*The* RELATIVES *seat themselves in a semicircle. Solemn silence for a time.* SOMEONE IN GRAY *stands motionless in the corner, His stony face turned toward them.*)

RELATIVES' CONVERSATION

— Do you think, dear, she may die?

— No, I don't think so. She is a very impatient woman and makes too much of her pains. All women bear children and none of them die. I have borne six children.

— But the way she screamed, mamma?

— Yes, her face was purple from screaming. I noticed it.

— Not from screaming, but from laboring. You don't understand about these things. My face got purple too, but I didn't scream.

— Not long ago an acquaintance of mine, the civil engineer's wife, gave birth to a child, and she scarcely made a sound.

— I know. There's no need for my brother to be so upset. One must be firm and take things calmly. And I'm afraid, too, he'll introduce a lot of his fantastic notions in the bringing up of his children and indulge their every whim.

— He's a very weak character. He has little enough money, and yet he lends it to people who don't deserve to be trusted.

— Do you know how much the child's layette cost?

— Don't talk to me of it! It gets on my nerves, my brother's extravagance does. I often quarrel with him because he's so improvident.

— They say a stork brings babies. What sort of a stork is it?

*(The young men burst out laughing.)*

— Don't talk nonsense. I gave birth to five children right in your presence, and I'm no stork, thank the Lord.

*(The young men burst out laughing again. The* ELDERLY WOMAN *eyes them long and sternly.)*

— It's only a superstition. Children are born in an absolutely natural way, firmly established by science. They've moved to new quarters now.

— Who?

— The engineer and his wife. Their old place was chilly and damp. They complained to the landlord several times, but he paid no attention.

— I think it's better to live in a small place that's warm than in a large place that's damp. You are liable to catch your death of cold and rheumatism if you live in a damp house.

— I have a friend, too, who lives in a very damp house. And I too. Very damp.

— There are so many damp places nowadays.

— Tell me, please — I've been wanting to ask you a long time — how do you remove a grease stain from light-colored material?

— Woolen?

— No, silk. *(The child's crying is heard behind the scene.)*

— Take a piece of ice and rub it on the spot hard. Then take a hot iron and press the spot.

— No? Fancy, how simple! I heard benzine was better.

— No, benzine is good for dark material. For light goods ice is better.

— I wonder whether smoking is allowed here. Somehow it

never occurred to me before whether one may or may not smoke where there is a new-born baby.

— It never occurred to me either. How strange! I know it isn't proper to smoke at funerals, but here ——

— Nonsense! Of course you may smoke.

— Smoking is a bad habit just the same. You are still a very young man and ought to take good care of your health. There are many occasions in life when good health is highly essential.

— But smoking stimulates.

— Believe me, it's a very unhealthy stimulant. When I was young and reckless, I was also guilty of using, or rather abusing, tobacco ——

— Mamma, listen to him crying. My, how he's crying! Does he want milk, mamma?

(*The young men burst out laughing. The* ELDERLY WOMAN *looks at them sternly.*)

CURTAIN

## THE SECOND SCENE

### LOVE AND POVERTY

*The entire place is filled with a warm, bright light. A large, very poor room, high walls, the color of old rose, covered here and there with beautiful, fantastic, roughly drawn designs. To the right are two lofty windows, eight panes in each, with the darkness of night glooming through them. Two poor beds, two chairs, and a bare table, on which stands a half-broken pitcher of water and a pretty bunch of flowers.*

*In the darkest corner stands* SOMEONE IN GRAY, *the candle in* HIS *hand now reduced by a third, but the flame still very bright, high, and white. It throws a powerful light on* HIS *face and chin.*

(*Enter the* NEIGHBORS, *dressed in light, gay dresses, their hands full of flowers, grasses, and fresh branches of oak and birch. They run about the room, scattering them. Their faces are merry, simple, and good-natured.*)

NEIGHBORS' CONVERSATION

— How poor they are! Look, they haven't even a single spare chair.

— And no curtains in the windows.

— And no pictures on the walls.

— How poor they are! All they eat is hard bread.

— And all they drink is water, cold water from the spring.

— They don't own any clothes at all except what they have on. She always goes about in her rosy dress with her neck bare, which makes her look like a young girl.

— And he wears his blouse and loose necktie, which makes him look like an artist, and makes the dogs bark at him.

— And makes all the respectable people disapprove of him.

— Dogs hate the poor. I saw three dogs attack him yesterday. He beat them off with a stick and shouted: "Don't you dare to touch my trousers; they're my last pair!" And he laughed, and the dogs flung themselves at him and showed their teeth and barked viciously.

— I saw two respectable people, a lady and a gentleman, meet him on the street today. They were terribly frightened and crossed to the other side. "He'll ask for money," said the gentleman. "He'll kill us," piped the lady. From the other side of the street they looked back at him and held on to their pockets. He shook his head and laughed.

— He's such a jolly good fellow.

— They're always laughing.

— And singing.

— It's he who sings. She dances.

— In her rosy dress, with her little bare neck.

— It does one good to look at them. They are so young and wholesome.

— I am sorry for them. They're starving. Do you understand? They're actually going without food.

— Yes, it's true. They had more clothes and furniture, but they sold every bit, and now they've nothing more to sell.

— I know. She had such pretty earrings, and she sold them to buy bread.

— He had a beautiful black frock-coat, the one in which he was married, and he sold that too.

— The only thing they have left is their engagement rings. How poor they are!

— That's nothing. I was once young myself, and I know what it is.

— What did you say, grandpa?

— I said it's nothing, nothing at all.

— Look, the mere thought of them makes grandpa want to sing.

— And dance. (*They laugh.*)

— He is so kind. He made my boy a bow and arrow.

— She cried with me when my daughter was ill.

— He helped me mend the rickety fence. He's strong.

— It's nice to have such good neighbors. Their youth warms our cold old age. Their jolliness drives away our cares.

— But their room is like a prison, it's so empty.

— No, it's like a temple. It's so bright.

— Look, they have flowers on the table, the flowers she picked on her walk in the country in her rosy dress with her little bare neck. Here are lilies-of-the-valley. The dew hasn't dried on them yet.

— There is the burning campion.

— And violets.

— Don't touch, don't touch the flowers, girls. Her kisses are upon them. Don't throw them on the floor, girls. Her breath is upon them. Don't blow them away with your breath. Don't touch, don't touch the flowers, girls.

— He'll come and he'll see the flowers.

— He'll take the kisses.

— He'll drink her breath.

— How poor they are! How happy they are!

— Come, let's leave.

— Haven't we brought our dear neighbors anything?

— What a shame!

— I brought a bottle of milk and a piece of white, sweet-smelling bread. (*Puts them on the table.*)

— I brought flowers. (*Scatters them.*)

— We brought branches of oak and birch with green leaves. Let's put them up around the walls. The room will look like cheerful green woods.

(*They decorate the room with the branches, concealing the dark windows and covering the pinkish nakedness of the walls with leaves.*)

— I brought a good cigar. It is a cheap one, but it's strong and fragrant and will give pleasant dreams.

— And I brought a ribbon, a red ribbon. It makes a very pretty fancy bow for the hair. It's a present my sweetheart gave me; but I have so many ribbons and she hasn't even one.

— What did *you* bring, grandpa? Did you bring anything?

— Nothing, nothing, except my cough. They don't want that, do they, neighbor?

— No more than they want my crutches. Hey, girls, who wants my crutches?

— Do you remember, neighbor?

— Do *you* remember, neighbor?

— Come, let's go to sleep, neighbor. It's late already.

(*They sigh and leave, one coughing, the other knocking the floor with his crutches.*)

— Come, come!

— May God give them happiness. They are such good neighbors.

— God grant that they may always be healthy and merry and always love each other. And may the hideous black cat never pass between them.

— And may the good man find work. It's bad when a man is out of work. (*They leave.*)

(*Enter immediately the* WIFE OF MAN, *very pretty, graceful, and delicate, wearing flowers in her luxuriant hair which is hanging loose. The expression on her face is very sad. She seats herself on a chair, folds her hands in her lap, and speaks in a sad tone, turned toward the audience.*)

MAN'S WIFE. I've just returned from the city, where I went looking for I don't know what. We are so poor, we have nothing, and it's very hard for us to live. We need money, and I don't know how in the world to get it. People won't give it to you for the asking, and I haven't the strength to take it away from them. I was looking for work, but I can't get work either. There are lots of people and little work, they say. I looked on the ground as I walked to see if some rich person hadn't lost his purse, but either nobody had lost one or somebody luckier than

I had already picked it up. I feel so sad. My husband will soon come from his search for work, tired and hungry. What am I to give him except my kisses? But you can't satisfy your hunger on kisses. I feel so sad I could cry.

I can go without eating for a long time and not feel it, but he can't. He has a large body which demands food, and when he's gone a long time without it, he gets pale, sick, and excited. He scolds me and then begs me not to be angry at him. I never *am* angry at him, because I love him dearly. It only makes me feel so sad.

My husband is a very talented architect. I even think he's a genius. He was left an orphan when a mere boy, and after his parents' death his relatives supported him for some time; but as he was always of an independent nature, sharp in his talk and prone to make unpleasant remarks, and as he showed them no gratitude, they dropped him. He continued to study, nevertheless, supporting himself by giving lessons, and so made his way through college. He often went hungry, my poor husband. Now he is an architect and draws plans of beautiful buildings, but no one wants to buy them, and many stupid persons make fun of them even. To make one's way in the world one must have either patrons or luck. He has neither. So he goes about looking for a chance, and maybe with his eyes on the ground looking for money like me. He is still very young and simple. Of course, some day fortune will come to us, too. But when will it be? In the meantime it's very hard to live. When we were married we had a little property, but we soon spent it. We went to the theatre and ate candy. He still has hopes, but I sometimes lose all hope and cry to myself. My heart breaks when I think he'll be here soon and I have nothing to give him again except my poor kisses.

O God, be a kind, merciful Father to us. You have so much of everything, bread and work and money. Your earth is so rich. She grows corn and fruit in her fields, covers the meadows with flowers, and yields gold and beautiful precious stones from her bowels. And your sun has so much warmth, and your pensive stars have so much quiet joy. Give us, I pray you, a little from your abundance, just a little, as much as you give your birds. A little bread, so that my dear good husband may not be hungry; a little warmth, so that he may not be cold; and a little work, so that he may carry his beautiful head erect. And please do not be angry with my husband because he swears so and laughs, and even sings and makes me dance. He is so young and not a bit staid or serious.

Now, after I have prayed, I feel relieved and hopeful again. Why, indeed, should God not grant one's request when one asks Him for it so earnestly? I'll go and hunt a little to see if somebody hasn't dropped a purse or a diamond. (*Exit.*)

SOMEONE IN GRAY. She knows not that her wish has already been fulfilled. She knows not that this morning two men in a rich house were bending eagerly over a sketch by Man and were delighted with it. They searched for Man the whole day; wealth was looking for him as he was looking for wealth. And to-morrow morning, after the neighbors have gone to work, an automobile will stop in front of this house, and two men bending low will enter the poor room and bring wealth and fame. But neither he nor she knows it. Thus fortune will come to Man and thus also it will go.

(*Enter* MAN *and his* WIFE. *He has a beautiful proud head, bright eyes, a high forehead, dark eyebrows parting at the root of the nose like two bold wings, and wavy black hair carelessly tossed back. A low, white, turndown collar reveals a well-formed neck and part of his chest. He is light and quick in his movements, like a young animal.*)

MAN. Nothing again. I'll lie down and remain in bed the whole day. Anyone wanting me will have to come here. I can't go to him. I'll stay in bed the whole of tomorrow too.

WIFE. Are you tired?

MAN. Yes, I'm tired and hungry. I could eat a whole ox, like the Homeric hero, but I shall have to content myself with a piece of hard bread. Don't you know that a man can't live all the time on bread alone? I want to tear, bite, chew!

WIFE. I'm sorry for you, dear.

MAN. I'm sorry for myself, but that doesn't satisfy my hunger. I stood a whole hour in front of a restaurant today, looking at the chickens, pastry, and sausages, as people look at works of art. And then the signs. They describe ham so well that you could eat sign and all.

WIFE. I like ham too.

MAN. Who doesn't like ham? How about lobster? Do you like lobster?

WIFE. Yes.

MAN. You should have seen the lobster I saw. It was a painted one, but it was even more beautiful than a live one. Red like a cardinal, majestic, stern. You could kneel down and do homage to it. I think I could eat two such cardinals and a priest of a carp besides.

WIFE (*sadly*). You didn't see my flowers, did you?

MAN. Flowers? You can't eat flowers, can you?

WIFE. You don't love me.

MAN (*kisses her*). Excuse me, but really I'm so hungry. Look, my hands are trembling and I haven't even the strength to throw a stone at a dog.

WIFE (*kisses his hand*). My poor husband!

MAN. Where do those leaves on the floor come from? They smell so good. Is that your work too?

WIFE. No, the neighbors must have done it.

MAN. Fine people our neighbors are. It's strange, there are so many good people in the world, and yet a man can die of hunger. Why is it?

WIFE. You've turned so sad. Your face is growing pale. What is the matter? Do you see anything?

MAN. Yes, as I was joking, the terrible image of poverty glided in front of me and stopped there, in the corner. Do you see it? Arms stretched out in complaint, a child abandoned in the woods, a praying voice, and the stillness of a human desert. Help! No one hears. Help, I'm dying! No one hears. Look, wife, look! See the dark, gloomy shadows there, quivering and rising like black smoke from a long, terrible chimney leading into hell. Look! And I'm in the midst of them!

WIFE. I'm afraid. I can't look in that dark corner. Did you see all that in the street?

MAN. Yes, I saw it in the street, and soon it'll be that way with us.

WIFE. No, God will not permit it.

MAN. Then why does He permit it to happen to others?

WIFE. We're better than others. We are good people. We never offend Him.

MAN. You think so? I do a lot of swearing.

WIFE. You're not bad.

MAN. Yes, I am bad. When I walk along the street and see all the things that don't belong to us, I feel as if I had tusks like a boar. Oh, how much money I haven't got! Listen, my dear wife. I was walking in the park today, that lovely park, where the paths are straight as arrows and the beech-trees like kings wearing crowns —

WIFE. And I was walking in the city streets. Shops everywhere, such beautiful shops!

MAN. I saw men, beautifully dressed, carrying canes, and I thought: "I haven't anything like that."

WIFE. I saw elegantly dressed women, wearing dainty shoes that make your feet beautiful, and pretty hats from under which your eyes shine impenetrably, and silk skirts that make such a mysterious rustle; and I thought: "I haven't a good hat or a silk skirt."

MAN. A ruffian jostled me. I showed him my tusks, and he fled in disgrace to hide himself in the crowd.

WIFE. A well-dressed lady jostled me, but I didn't even look at her, I felt so embarrassed.

MAN. Men rode by on proud, fiery horses. And I have nothing like that.

WIFE. She had diamonds in her ears. You felt like kissing them.

MAN. Red and green automobiles glided past noiselessly like phantoms with burning eyes, and people sat in them and laughed and looked lazily from one side to the other. And I have nothing like it.

WIFE. And I have no diamonds, no emeralds, no pure white pearls.

MAN. I saw a fine restaurant on the Island. It was brightly illuminated, like heaven, and they were eating there. Blackcoated monsters carried around butter and bread and wine and beer, and people ate and drank. My little wife, I'm hungry! I want something to eat!

WIFE. Dearie, you're running around all the time, and that makes you still hungrier. You'd better sit down. I'll kneel beside you, and you can take a piece of paper and draw a beautiful, beautiful building.

MAN. My inspiration is also hungry. It draws nothing but edible landscapes. My palaces are like portly cakes with fat stuffing, and my churches like sausages. But I see tears in your eyes. What is it, my dear wife?

WIFE. I feel so miserable not to be able to help you.

MAN. You make me ashamed of myself. I am a strong man with a good mind; I am able, talented, and healthy, and yet I can't do a thing. My dear wife, my little fairy is crying, and I am not able to help her. A woman's tears are her husband's disgrace. I am ashamed.

WIFE. But it isn't your fault that people don't appreciate you.

MAN. My ears are burning just as they used to when I was a boy and had had them boxed. Why, you are hungry too, and I, egoist that I am, haven't noticed it. It's mean of me.

WIFE. My dear, I don't feel hungry.

MAN. It's unfair, it's contemptible. That ruffian who jostled me was right. He saw I was a fat pig and that's all, a boar with sharp tusks but a stupid head.

WIFE. If you are going to keep on reproaching yourself, I'll cry again.

MAN. Don't, don't. No tears! Tears in your eyes frighten me. I am afraid of those shining crystal drops, as if some other, some terrible person were shedding them, not you. I won't let you cry. We have nothing, we are poor. But I'll tell you of what we are going to have. I will charm you with a bright fairy tale, my queen. I will array you in dazzling dreams as in roses!

WIFE. You mustn't be afraid. You are strong, you are a genius, you will conquer. Your momentary despair will pass away, and divine inspiration will again quicken your proud head.

MAN (assumes a challenging attitude and throws an oak leaf into the corner where the Unknown stands, saying). Ho, you, whatever your name, Fate, Devil, or Life, I fling my glove down before you, I challenge you to combat! The poor in spirit bow before your enigmatic power. Your stony face inspires them with fear; in your silence they hear the approaching tread of misery and terrible ruin. But I am strong and bold, and I challenge you to combat! Come on! Let the swords glitter, the shields clang! Deal and receive blows so that the earth trembles! Ho, come forth to battle!

WIFE (*nestling up at his left, somewhat behind, speaking solemnly*). Bolder, my husband, still bolder!

MAN. To your evil-boding inaction I oppose my living, daring strength; to your gloom my clear, resonant laugh! Ho, repel the blows! You have a stone brow, devoid of reason. I will throw the glowing balls of my sparkling thought at it. You have a stone heart, devoid of pity. Take care, I will pour into it the poison of my rebellious outcries. The dark cloud of your grim wrath overshadows the sun. We will light the darkness with our swords. Ho, repel the blows!

WIFE. Bolder, still bolder, my proud knight! Your squire is behind you.

MAN. Victorious, I will sing songs which the whole world will re-echo; fallen under your blows, my only thought shall be to rise again and rush into battle. There are weak spots in my armor, but when my red blood is flowing, I will gather my last strength and cry: "You have not conquered, evil Enemy of Man!"

WIFE. Bolder, my knight! I will wash your wounds with my tears. I will stop the flow of your red blood with my kisses.

MAN. And dying on the field of battle as the brave die, with one cry I will destroy your blind joy: "I have conquered!" I have conquered, O cruel Enemy. Unto my last breath I did not recognize your power!

WIFE. Bolder, my knight, bolder! I will die beside you.

MAN. Ho, come forth to battle! Let the swords glitter, the shields clang! Deal and receive blows to make the earth tremble! Ho, come forth!

(*For some time* MAN *and his* WIFE *remain in the same posture; then they turn around, facing each other, and kiss.*)

MAN. That's the way we'll deal with life, my dear, won't we? Let it frown like a blind owl in the sun — we'll compel it to smile.

WIFE. And to dance to our songs — so we will, we two.

MAN. We two. You're a good wife, you're my true friend, you're a brave little woman, and as long as you are with me I fear nothing. Poverty, what does it amount to? Today we're poor, tomorrow rich.

WIFE. And what is hunger? Today we are hungry, tomorrow satisfied.

MAN. Do you think so? It's quite possible. But I'll eat a lot. I shall need so much to satisfy my hunger. Tell me, do you think this will prove enough? In the morning, tea or coffee or chocolate. You can have your choice. It's free. Then a breakfast of three courses, then lunch, then dinner, then ——

WIFE. More fruit. I like fruit.

MAN. Very well. I'll buy fruit by the barrel, direct from the wholesale market. It's cheaper and fresher. Besides, we'll have our own garden.

WIFE. But we have no land.

MAN. I'll buy land. I've always wanted to have my own piece of land. By the way, I'll build a house for us and design it too. Let the rascals see what sort of an architect I am.

WIFE. I should like to live in Italy, close by the sea; in a white marble villa in a grove of lemons and cypresses, with marble steps leading straight down to the blue water.

MAN. I understand. That's all right. But I intend, besides, to build a castle in the mountains of Norway. Below, the fjord; and above, on the steep mountain, the castle. We have no paper. But look, I'll show it to you on the wall here. Here is the fjord, you see?

WIFE. Yes, beautiful.

MAN. Here, sparkling blue water gently beating against the green grass; here, beautiful cinnamon-colored stone; and there, in the recess, where this spot is, a bit of blue sky and serene white clouds.

WIFE. Look, there is a white boat floating on the water — it looks like two swans swimming side by side.

MAN. And up there rises the mountain. Bright and green below, it turns gloomier and sterner as it ascends — rugged crags, dark shadows, fallen boulders, and patches of clouds.

WIFE. Like a ruined castle.

MAN. And there, on that spot — the middle one — I'll build my royal castle.

WIFE. It's cold up there, and windy.

MAN. I'll have thick stone walls and large windows with all the panes made out of a single piece of glass. At night, when the winter snowstorms begin to rage and the fjord below to roar, we'll draw the curtains and make a fire in the huge fireplace. It is such a tremendous fireplace that it will hold a whole log. It will burn up a whole forest of pines.

WIFE. How nice and warm!

MAN. And how quiet too, if you will please notice. Carpets covering the whole floor and lots of books will make it cosy and quietly lively. And we'll be there, the two of us. The wind howling outside and we two sitting before the fireplace on a white bear-skin rug. "Wouldn't you like to have a look at what's doing outside?" you'll say. "All right!" And we'll go to the largest window and draw aside the curtain. Good heaven! What a sight!

WIFE. See the snow whirling.

MAN. Galloping like white horses, like myriads of frightened little spirits, pale with fear and seeking safety in the night. And what a howling and roaring!

WIFE. Oh, it's cold. I'm shivering.

MAN. Go back to the fireplace, quick! Hey there, fetch me grandfather's goblet — not that one, the golden one from which the vikings drank. Fill it up with sparkling wine — not that way — fill it to the brim with the burning draught. Venison is roasting on the spit. Bring it here. I'll eat some. Quick, or I'll eat you. I'm hungry as the devil.

WIFE. There, they have brought it. Now, go on.

MAN. Go on? I'll eat some, of course. What else do you expect? What are you doing to my head, little wife?

WIFE. I am the goddess of fame. I have woven a crown of the oak leaves that our neighbors scattered here, and I'm crowning you. It's Fame that has come to you, the beautiful goddess Fame.

(*Puts the wreath on his head.*)

MAN. Yes, fame; loud, noisy fame. Look at the wall. Do you

see this? It's I, walking. And who is this next to me? Do you see?

WIFE. I.

MAN. Look, they are bowing to us; they are whispering about us; they are pointing their fingers at us. There is a venerable old gentleman saying with tears in his eyes: "Happy the land that has such children!" See how pale this youth here has turned. Fame looked at him and gave him a smile. That's after I built the People's House, which is the pride of the whole country.

WIFE. You are my famous husband. The oak wreath suits you so well. A laurel wreath would become you still better.

MAN. Look, look, there come the representatives of the city where I was born. They bow to me and say: "Our city is proud of the honor ——"

WIFE. Oh!

MAN. What is it?

WIFE. I found a bottle of milk.

MAN. Impossible!

WIFE. And bread, soft, sweet-smelling bread. And a cigar.

MAN. Impossible! You are mistaken. It's the dampness from that damned wall, that's what it is. It isn't milk.

WIFE. But it is.

MAN. A cigar? Cigars don't grow on windows. They are sold for fortunes in tobacco stores. It's a black stick, a piece of a branch, I'm sure.

WIFE. Look and see. I suppose our neighbors brought it.

MAN. Our neighbors? I tell you they're people — they're not human — they're divine. But even if the devil himself brought it — quick, give it here, my sweet little wife.

> (MAN's WIFE *seats herself on his knees, and so they eat. She breaks off pieces of bread and puts them in his mouth. He feeds her the milk from the bottle.*)

MAN. Seems to be cream.

WIFE. No, it's milk. Chew better. You'll choke.

MAN. Give me the crust. It's so brown.

WIFE. I told you, you'd choke.

MAN. No, it went down. I swallowed it.

WIFE. The milk is running down my chin and neck. Oh, it's tickling me.

MAN. Lean over. I'll lick it off. We mustn't let a drop go to waste.

WIFE. You're a cunning one.

MAN. There! Quick. All good things soon come to an end. This bottle seems to have a double bottom. It looks so large. The glass manufacturers are terrible cheats.

(*He lights the cigar with the air of a man relaxing into beatific repose. His* WIFE *ties the red ribbon in her hair, looking at herself in the dark pane of the window.*)

WIFE. Don't you see?

MAN. I see everything. I see your ribbon, and I see you want me to kiss you on your dear little bare neck.

WIFE. No, sir, I won't permit that. You've grown too forward of late anyway. You take such liberties. Please go on smoking your cigar and leave my neck ——

MAN. What, isn't your neck mine? I'll be jiggered! Why, it's an attack on the sacred rights of property! (*She runs away; he catches her and kisses her.*) So, the property rights have been restored. Now, my dear, we'll dance. Imagine that this is a magnificent, a luxurious, a wonderful, a super-natural, an exquisitely beautiful palace.

WIFE. Very well, I'm imagining it.

MAN. Imagine you're the queen of the ball.

WIFE. All right. It is imagined.

MAN. And that counts, marquises, and dukes come up and ask you to dance. But you refuse. You choose that one — What's his name? — the one in uniform — the prince. What's the matter?

WIFE. I don't like princes.

MAN. Indeed? Then whom *do* you like?

WIFE. Talented artists.

MAN. Very well. Here's one for you. Why, girl, what are you doing? Are you flirting with the air?

WIFE. I am imagining.

MAN. All right. Imagine a wonderful orchestra. Here is the Turkish drum — boom, boom, boom!

(*He strikes his fist on the table as on a drum.*)

WIFE. Why, dear, it's only in the circus that they attract crowds
by beating drums, but in a palace ——

MAN. Oh, hang it! Stop imagining that, then. Now imagine
something else. The violins are playing a melodious plaint;
the flutes are singing gently; the double bass drones like a beetle.

> (MAN *sits down, still wearing his oak wreath, and strikes up*
> *a dance tune, clapping his hands in accompaniment. The*
> *melody is the same as in the next scene at* MAN's *ball. The*
> WIFE *dances. She is well-formed and graceful.*)

MAN. Oh, you darling!

WIFE. I am the queen of the ball.

> (*The song and dance grow ever jollier.* MAN *rises slowly and*
> *begins to dance lightly on the spot where he is standing; then he*
> *seizes his* WIFE *and dances with her. The oak wreath slips to*
> *one side.*)

> (SOMEONE IN GRAY *looks on indifferently, the candle burning*
> *brightly in his petrified hand.*)

CURTAIN

## THE THIRD SCENE

### A BALL AT MAN'S HOUSE

*The ball is in the drawing-room of* MAN's *large mansion. It is a very
lofty, spacious, perfectly rectangular room. The floor is bright and smooth.
There is a certain irregularity about the room due to the disproportionate
size of the parts. Thus, the doors are very small in proportion to the
windows. This produces a strange, irritating impression, as of something
disharmonious, something lacking, and also of something superfluous and
adventitious. The whole is pervaded by a chilly white, the monotony of
which is broken only by a row of windows in the rear wall. They are very
high, reaching almost to the ceiling, and dense with the blackness of night.
Not one gleam, not a bright spot shows in the black spaces between the
window frames.* MAN's *wealth shows in the abundance of gildings.
There are gilded chairs, and very wide gold frames enclose the pictures.
These constitute the only furniture as well as the only ornamentation. The
lighting is from three chandeliers shaped like rings, with a few electric*

*lights placed at a great distance apart. At the ceiling the light is bright, but considerably less so below, so that the walls seem grayish.*

*The ball is in full swing. The music is furnished by an orchestra of three pieces. The musicians resemble closely their respective instruments; the violinist, a violin — lean neck, small head, a shock of hair brushed to one side, back somewhat bent, a handkerchief correctly adjusted on his shoulder under the violin; the flute-player, a flute — very tall, with a thin, elongated face, and stiff, thin legs; the bass-violinist, a double-bass — stumpy, round-shouldered, lower part of his body very stout, wide trousers. The uncommon effort with which the musicians play is painfully evident. They beat time, swing their heads, and shake their bodies. The tune is the same throughout the ball, a short polka in two musical phrases, producing a jolly, hopping, extremely insipid effect. The three instruments do not quite keep time with one another, producing a sort of queer detachment, a vacant space, as it were, between them and the sounds which they produce.*

*Young men and girls are dancing dreamily. All are handsome, distinguished-looking, with good figures. In contrast to the piercing notes of the music, their dancing is smooth, noiseless, light. At the first musical phrase, they circle around; at the second, they gracefully part and join again. There is a slight mannerism in their dancing.*

*Along the walls, on the gilded chairs, sit the* GUESTS, *stiff and constrained. They scarcely venture to move their heads. Their conversation is also constrained. They do not whisper to one another; they do not laugh, and they scarcely look at one another. They speak abruptly, as if chopping out the words of a text. Their hands hanging superciliously over their laps make their arms look as if they had been broken at the wrists. The monotony of their faces is strongly emphasized. Every face bears the same expression of self-satisfaction, haughtiness, and inane respect for the wealth of* MAN.

*The dancing girls are all in white, the men in black. Some of the* GUESTS *wear black, white, and brightly yellow flowers.*

*In the near corner, which is darker than the rest,* SOMEONE IN GRAY *called* HE *stands motionless. The candle in his hand is reduced two-thirds and burns with a strong, yellow light, casting a yellow sheen on His stony face and chin.*

THE GUESTS' CONVERSATION

    — It is a very great honor to be a guest at Man's ball.

    — You may add, it is an honor of which very few have been deemed worthy. The whole city tried to get themselves invited, but only a very few succeeded. My husband, my children, and I are quite proud of the honor Man has showed us.

— I am really sorry for those who were not able to get here. They won't sleep the whole night from sheer envy, and to-morrow they'll say nasty things about the ball and call it a bore.

— They never saw such magnificence.

— Or such wonderful wealth and luxury.

— Or, I dare say, such charming, free and easy gayety.

— If this isn't gay, I should like to know what is.

— Oh, what's the use of talking? You can't convince people consumed by jealousy. They'll tell us we didn't sit on gilded chairs, absolutely not.

— They'll say that the chairs were of the commonest sort, bought at second hand.

— That the illumination was not by electricity, but just by tallow candles.

— Say candle stumps.

— Or dirty lamps.

— They'll have the impudence to maintain that the mouldings in Man's house are not gilded.

— And that the broad picture frames are not made of gold. It seems to me I can hear the very ring of it.

— You can see its glitter. That's quite sufficient, I should think.

— I have rarely had the pleasure of hearing such music.

— It is divine harmony. It transports the soul to higher spheres.

— I should think the music good enough, considering the money paid for it. It is the best trio in the city. They play on the most important and solemn occasions.

— If you listen awhile, it compels your absolute attention. After a ball at Man's, my children keep singing the tune a long time.

— I sometimes think I hear it in the street. I look around — no musicians, no music.

— What I like especially in these musicians is the great effort they make when they play. They know the price they're paid and don't want to get the money for nothing. That's very decent of them.

— It seems as if they became a part of their instruments, their efforts are so great.

— Or as if the instruments became part of them.

— How rich!

— How magnificent!

— How brilliant!

— How rich!

  (*For some time the two expressions, "How rich!    How magnificent!" are repeated from different parts of the room, uttered abruptly, like a bark.*)

— Beside this ballroom there are fourteen other magnificent rooms in Man's house.   I have seen them all.   The dining-room has such a huge fireplace that you can put a whole log into it.   There are magnificent guest-rooms and a beautiful boudoir. A large bedroom, and over the pillows on the beds — just fancy! — canopies!

— Why, how wonderful!   Canopies!

— Did you hear?   Canopies!

— Permit me to continue.   For their son, the little boy, they have a beautiful bright room of golden yellow wood.   It looks as if the sun were shining into it all the time.

— He is such a fine boy.   He has curly hair that looks like the rays of the sun.

— That's true.   When you look at him you wonder whether the sun has risen.

— And when you look at his eyes you think: "Autumn is gone, and the blue sky is here again."

— Man loves his son madly.   He bought him a pony for horse-back riding, a nice snow-white pony.   My children ——

— Pray, let me continue.   Have I told you yet about the swimming-pool?

— No.   No.

— A swimming-pool, a perfect marvel.

— What, a swimming-pool!

— Yes.   And further on is Man's study, full of books, books, books.   They say he's a very learned man.

— You can see it by the books.

— I have seen his garden.

— I haven't.

— It was entrancing, I must say.  Imagine an emerald-green lawn kept beautifully mowed and trimmed at the edges.  In the middle a path of fine red sand.

— Flowers — even palms.

— Yes, even palms.  And all the trees trimmed as carefully and precisely as the lawn, some cut in the shape of pyramids, others in the shape of green columns.  There's a lovely fountain and little plaster elves and deer scattered all around in the grass.

— How rich!

— How magnificent!

— How brilliant!

— How rich!

— Man did me the honor of showing me his stables and barns. I had to tell him how much I admired his horses and carriages. I was particularly impressed by his motor car.

— Think of it, he has seven servants; seven — a chef, a woman-cook, two maids, gardeners ——

— You forget the coachman and the chauffeur.

— Yes, of course, the coachman and the chauffeur.

— And they themselves do nothing at all.  They are too fine.

— You must admit, it is a great honor to have been invited to Man's ball.

— Don't you find the music somewhat monotonous?

— No, I don't, and I'm surprised you do.  Don't you see what kind of musicians they are?

— I should like to hear such music all my life.  That's what I say.  There's something in that music that stirs me.

— Me too.

— Me too.

— It is a delicious sensation to abandon oneself to dreams of happiness under the influence of this music!

— To transport oneself in fancy to the astral spheres!

— How fine!

— How rich!

— How magnificent!                    (*These phrases are repeated.*)

— I notice a stir at that door.  Man and his Wife will soon pass through the hall.

— The musicians are working away for dear life.
— There they are!
— They're coming! Look, they're coming!

(MAN, *his* WIFE, *his* FRIENDS, *and his* ENEMIES *appear in the door on the right, cross the room diagonally to the door on the left. The dancers go on dancing, but part to make way for them. The musicians play desperately loud and out of tune.*

MAN *has aged greatly. His long hair and long beard are beginning to turn gray. But his face is manly and handsome, and he walks with calm dignity and an air of coldness. He looks straight ahead of him, as if not noticing those around him. His* WIFE *has also aged, but she is still beautiful and walks leaning on his arm. She too seems not to notice the people around her, but looks straight ahead, with a rather strange, almost fixed expression. Both are richly dressed.*

*His* FRIENDS *follow directly behind* MAN. *They resemble one another very much — noble faces, high and candid foreheads, honest eyes. They walk proudly, throwing out their chests, stepping firmly and confidently, and looking, now to this side, now to that, with condescension and slight disdain. They wear white roses in their buttonholes.*

*Following them at a slight distance come* MAN'S ENEMIES, *also very much resembling one another — mean, cunning faces; low, heavy foreheads; long, ape-like arms. They walk uneasily, pushing, bending, and hiding behind one another, and casting sharp, mean, envious, sidelong glances from beneath lowered lids. Yellow roses appear in their buttonholes.*

*Thus they pass through the room, slowly and in perfect silence. The sounds of the steps, the music, and the exclamations of the* GUESTS *produce a sharply discordant noise.*)

GUESTS' CONVERSATION

— There they are. There they are. What an honor!
— How handsome he is!
— What a manly face!
— Look! Look!
— He isn't looking at us!
— He doesn't see us!
— We are his guests!

— What an honor!   What an honor!
— And his wife!   Look!   Look!
— How beautiful she is!
— How proud!
— I tell you, just look at her diamonds!
— Her pearls!   Her pearls!
— And her rubies!
— How rich!   What an honor!
— Honor!   Honor!   Honor!
                                    (*The same phrases are repeated again.*)
— Here are Man's Friends!
— Look, look, there are Man's Friends.
— Noble faces!
— Proud gait!
— They shine with the reflected splendor of his fame.
— How they love him!
— How faithful they are to him!
— What an honor to be one of Man's Friends!
— They regard everything here as their own!
— They're at home here!
— What an honor!
— Honor!   Honor!   Honor!          (*Same phrases are repeated.*)
— And there are Man's Enemies!
— Look, look, Man's Enemies!
— They walk like whipped curs!
— Man has subdued them!
— He's put a muzzle on them!
— They're wagging their tails!
— They're sneaking behind one another.
— They're pushing one another.
— Ha-ha!   Ha-ha!                   (*Everybody laughs.*)
— What mean faces!
— What greedy looks!
— Cowardly!
— Malevolent!
— They're afraid to look at us!
— They feel we're at home!
— Let's frighten them.

— Man'll be thankful to us for it.

— Ho-ho!

> (*They shout at* MAN'S ENEMIES, *mingling their shouts with
> laughter. The* ENEMIES *huddle closer together and cast sharp,
> timid, sideward glances.*)

— They're going! They're going!

— What an honor!

— They're going!

— Ho-ho! Ha-ha!

— They're gone! They're gone! They're gone!

> (*The procession disappears through the door on the left. A pause
> of silence. The music plays less loudly, and the dancers begin
> gradually to fill the hall.*)

— Where did they go?

— I believe they went to the dining-room, where supper is
being served.

— I suppose they'll soon invite us in. Do you see anybody
looking for us?

— Yes, it's time for supper. If you eat too late, you can't sleep
well.

— I always serve supper early.

— A late supper lies heavy on your stomach.

— And the music is still playing.

— And they're still dancing.

— I wonder they don't get tired.

— How rich!

— How magnificent!

— Do you know for how many guests they have prepared the
supper?

— I didn't get a chance to count all the covers. The caterer
came in, and I had to get out.

— Could they possibly have forgotten us?

— Man is so proud, and we are so unimportant.

— Don't say that. My husband says we do him an honor by
accepting his invitation. We are rich, too.

— When you consider the reputation of his wife ——

— Do you see anyone looking for us? Maybe he's looking for
us in the other rooms.

— How rich!

— If you are not careful with other people's money, it's easy to get rich, I think.

— Oh, now, it's only his enemies who say that.

— Well, after all, there are some very respectable people among them. I must admit that my husband ——

— It is late, though.

— It's clear there must be a mistake somewhere. I can't believe we've simply been forgotten.

— Evidently you know people and life very little if you think so.

— I am surprised. We are rich enough ourselves.

— It seems to me someone called us.

— You're mistaken, no one called us. I don't understand it. To be quite frank — why did we come to a house like this, with such a reputation? One should be very careful of the friends one chooses.

A LIVERIED LACKEY (*appears at the door*). Man and his Wife beg the honored guests to step into the dining-room.

GUESTS (*rising quickly*).

— What a livery!

— He asked us to come in!

— I said there must be a mistake somewhere.

— Man is so good. I'm sure he hasn't had a chance to sit down at table himself.

— Didn't I say someone was looking for us?

— What a livery!

— They say the supper is grand.

— Everything at Man's is done in a grand style.

— What music! What an honor to be at Man's ball!

— Let those envy us who ——

— How grand!

— How magnificent!

— What an honor!

(*They go out one after the other, repeating the last phrases. One couple after the other stop dancing and follow the* GUESTS *in silence. For some time a single couple remain circling on the floor, but they too join the others at last. The musicians, however, continue to play, making the same desperate effort. The lackey turns out the electric lights, leaving only one light in the farthest chandelier. The figures of the musicians are vaguely seen in the dim light, swaying to and fro with their instruments. The outline of* SOMEONE IN GRAY *is sharply visible. The flame of the candle flickers, illuminating* HIS *stony face and chin with a garish, yellow light.*

HE *turns around without raising his head, walks slowly and calmly through the whole length of the room, and disappears through the door through which* MAN *passed out.)*

CURTAIN

# THE FOURTH SCENE

## MAN'S MISFORTUNE

*A large, gloomy, quadrangular room, with dark walls, dark floor, and dark ceiling. There are two high, curtainless windows with eight panes in the rear wall, and between them a small, low door. Two similar windows appear in the right wall. Night glooms through the windows, and when the door opens, the same deep blackness of night stares into the room. In general, however bright* MAN'S *rooms may be, the vast darkness of the windows engulfs the light.*

*On the left wall there is nothing but a small, low door leading to the rest of the house. At the window on the right stands a broad sofa covered with dark oilcloth.* MAN'S *desk is very simple and poor. On it are seen a dimly burning, shaded lamp, a sheet of yellow paper with a sketch drawn on it, and a lot of toys — a little peaked cap, a wooden horse without a tail, and a red, long-nosed clown with bells. Between the windows there is an old dilapidated bookcase entirely empty. The visible lines of dust left by the books show that they must have been removed recently. The room has only one chair.*

*In the darkest corner stands* SOMEONE IN GRAY *called* HE. *The candle in his hand is now no longer than it is thick. The wax is running over a little. The stump burns with a reddish, flickering light, and casts a red sheen on* HIS *stony face and chin.*

*The only remaining servant of* MAN, *an* OLD WOMAN, *is sitting on the chair. She speaks in an even voice, addressing an imaginary companion.*

OLD WOMAN. There! Man has slipped back into poverty. He

had a lot of valuable things, horses and carriages, and even an automobile. Now he has nothing. Of all his servants I am the only one left. There are still some good things in here and in two other rooms. There's the sofa and the bookcase. But in the other twelve rooms there's not a thing. They are dark and empty. Rats run around in them day and night and fight and squeak. People are afraid, but I'm not. It's all the same to me.

An iron sign has been hanging on the gate for ever so long, saying the house is for sale. But no one wants to buy it. The sign's rusty already, and the rain has worn the letters away. But no one comes to buy the house. No one wants an old house. Yet maybe someone will buy it. Then we'll be going to look for another place to live in. It'll be a strange place. My mistress will begin to cry, and, I dare say, the old gentleman will too. But I won't. It's all the same to me.

You wonder what's become of all his riches. I don't know. Maybe it seems strange, but I've been living with other people all my life, and many is the time I've seen money disappear, quietly running off through some leak or other. That's the way it has happened to these folks too. They had a lot, then it got to be a little, and then nothing at all. People came and bought things. Then they stopped coming. I once asked my mistress how it came about. She answered: "People have stopped liking what they used to like; they have stopped loving what they used to love." "How is that possible?" says I. "How can people stop liking what they once liked?" She didn't answer and fell to crying. But I didn't. It's all the same to me. It's all the same to me.

People say they are surprised at me. It's terrible, they say, to live in this house; terrible to sit here at night with only the wind whining in the chimney and the rats squeaking and scuffling. Maybe it is terrible, I don't know; but I don't think about it. Why should I? There they sit, the two of them, in their room, looking at each other and listening to the whining of the wind; and I sit in the kitchen alone and listen to the whining of the wind. Doesn't the same wind whine in our ears? Young folks used to come to see their son, and they would all laugh and sing and go through the empty rooms to chase the rats. But nobody comes to me, and I sit alone, all alone. There's no one to talk to, so I talk to myself, and it's all the same to me.

I'm sure they had a hard enough time of it — no need of more ill luck. But three days ago another misfortune happened to them. The young gentleman went out walking, his hat cocked, his hair dressed in latest fashion. And a bad man went and threw a stone at him from behind a corner and broke his head like a nut. They brought him home, put him to bed, and now he's dying in there. Maybe he'll recover and live — who knows? The old lady and the old gentleman cried, and then they put all the books on a wagon and sold them. With the money they hired a nurse, bought medicines, and even grapes. So the books, too, were of some good. But he doesn't eat the grapes. He doesn't even look at them. They just lie there on the dish, just lie there.

DOCTOR (*enters through the outer door; his face looks red and his manner is uneasy*). Can you tell me if I am in the right place? I'm a doctor. I have many visits to pay, and I often make mistakes. I'm called here and there and everywhere, and all the houses look alike and the people in them are all sad. Have I struck the right place?

OLD WOMAN. I don't know.

DOCTOR. I'll consult my note-book. Is there a child here choking with a sore throat?

OLD WOMAN. No.

DOCTOR. Is there a man here who suddenly went insane from poverty and attacked his wife and two children with a hatchet? Four patients in all, I suppose.

OLD WOMAN. No.

DOCTOR. Is there a girl here whose heart stopped beating? Don't lie, old woman, I think she is here.

OLD WOMAN. No.

DOCTOR. Well, I believe you. You seem to speak the truth. Is there a young man here whose head was broken by a stone and who is dying?

OLD WOMAN. Yes. Go through that door on the left, but don't go any farther. The rats will eat you up!

DOCTOR. Very well. They keep ringing, ringing all the time, day and night. Here it is, late at night. All the lights in the street are out, and I am still on the run. Often I make a mistake and enter the wrong house. Yes, old woman, I do.

(*Exit through the door leading inside.*)

OLD WOMAN. One doctor has already treated him, but didn't cure him. Now there's another, and I guess he won't cure him either. Well! Then their son will die, and we'll remain alone in the house. I'll sit in the kitchen and talk to myself, and they'll sit in there keeping quiet and thinking. Another room vacated, another room for the rats to scuffle in. Let them squeak and scuffle. It's all the same to me. It's all the same to me. You ask me why that bad fellow threw the stone at our young gentleman. I don't know — how could I know why people want to kill each other? One threw a stone from behind a corner and ran away; the other one fell in a heap and is now dying — that's all I know. They say that our young gentleman was a fine chap, very brave, and very kind to poor people. I don't know anything about it — it is all the same to me. Whether they are good or bad, young or old, quick or dead, it is all the same to me. It is all the same to me.

As long as they pay, I'll stay with them; and when they stop paying, I'll go to other people to do their housework, and finally I shall stop altogether — when I get old, and my eyesight gets poor, so that I can't tell salt from sugar. Then they'll turn me out and say: "Go where you please. We'll hire another one." What of it? I'll go. It's all the same to me. Here, there, or nowhere, it's all the same to me. It's all the same to me.

(*Enter* DOCTOR, MAN *and his* WIFE. *Both have aged greatly and are completely gray.* MAN's *long bristling hair and beard give his face a leonine appearance. He walks slightly stooping, but holds his head erect and looks sternly and resolutely from beneath his gray eyebrows. When he looks at anything closely, he puts on large, silver-framed eye-glasses.*)

DOCTOR. Your son has fallen into a deep sleep. Don't wake him. It may bring on a turn for the better. You go to sleep too.

When one has a chance to sleep one should grab it and not stay up talking.

WIFE. Thank you, doctor, it's been such a relief. Will you call tomorrow again?

DOCTOR. Yes, tomorrow and the day after tomorrow. Old woman, you go to bed too. It's late, it's time for all to go to bed. Is that the door to leave by? I often make mistakes.

(*He goes out. The* OLD WOMAN *goes also.* MAN *and his* WIFE *are left alone.*)

MAN. Look, wife, I began to draw this while our son was still well. I stopped at this line and thought I'd rest and resume the work later. See what a simple, placid line it is, yet horrible to look at. It may be the last line I shall have drawn in our boy's lifetime. What malicious ignorance there is graven in its simplicity and placidity.

WIFE. Don't get excited, my dear. Don't think those evil thoughts. I believe the doctor told the truth and our son will recover.

MAN. Aren't you excited too? Look at yourself in the mirror. You're as white as your hair, my old friend.

WIFE. Of course, I am a little excited, but I'm convinced there's no danger.

MAN. Now, as always, you encourage me and fool me so sincerely, so guilelessly. My poor squire, true guardian of my dulled sword, your knight is a poor, broken-down man. He cannot hold a weapon in his feeble hand. What do I see? Our son's toys. Who put them there?

WIFE. My dear, you put them there yourself long ago. Have you forgotten? You said you found it easier to work with the child's innocent toys beside you.

MAN. Yes, I had forgotten. But now it's terrible to look at them, as terrible as it is for a convict to look at instruments of torture. If the child dies, his toys will remain as a curse to the living. Wife, wife, the sight of them is terrible to me!

WIFE. It was when we were still poor that we bought them. How touching it is to look at them, those poor, dear toys!

MAN. I can't help it, I *must* take them in my hands. Here's the horse with the tail torn off. Hop, hop, horsie! Where are you galloping off to? I'm going far, far away, papa, to where the fields are and the green woods. Take me along, horsie. Hop, hop, hop! Sit down, dear papa. And there's the soldier's cap, the cheap cap I tried on myself in fun when I bought it. Who are you? I'm a knight, papa. I'm the bravest, the strongest knight. Where are you going, my little knight? I'm going to kill the dragon, dear papa. I'm going to free the captives, papa. Go, go, my little knight. (*The* WIFE *cries.*) And there's our everlasting clown, with his kind, stupid face. But how ragged he is, as if he had come out of a hundred frays. Tinkle, friend, the way you used to tinkle. What, you can't? Only one bell left, you say? Well, I'll throw you on the floor.

(*Throws down the toy.*)

WIFE. What are you doing? Remember how often our boy kissed his funny face.

MAN. Yes, that was wrong of me. Forgive me, friend, forgive me. (*He bends down with difficulty and picks up the clown.*) Still laughing? Don't. I'll put you away, out of sight. Don't be angry, I can't bear your smile now. Go and laugh in a place where I can't see you.

WIFE. It breaks my heart to hear you speak like that. Believe me, our son will get well. It wouldn't be just if the young were to die before the old, would it?

MAN. Just? Where have you ever seen justice, wife?

WIFE. Please, dear husband, I beg you, kneel down beside me, and let us both pray to God.

MAN. It's hard for an old man to bend his old knees.

WIFE. Bend them. You should — you must.

MAN. He will not hear me, He whose ear I've never troubled with either praise or entreaty. You pray. You are the mother.

WIFE. You pray — you are the father. If a father is not to pray for his son, who is? To whom are you leaving him? Can one person tell the same things in the same way as the two of us together?

MAN. Very well. Maybe eternal justice will answer the prayers of an old man who bends his old knees.

(*Both go down on their knees, their faces turned to the corner where the* UNKNOWN *stands motionless; their arms are folded over their breasts while they pray.*)

THE MOTHER'S PRAYER. God, I beg you, let my son live. I can understand only one thing, I can say only one thing, only one thing — God, let my son live. I have no other words, all is dark around me, everything is falling. I understand nothing, and there's such a terror in my heart, O Lord, that I can say only this one thing — God, let my son live! Let him live! Forgive me for praying so poorly. But I cannot pray in any other way. You understand, O Lord, I can't. Look at me! Just look at me! Do you see? Do you see how my head shakes, do you see how my hands shake? But what are my hands, O Lord! Have pity on him. He is so young — he has a birthmark on his right hand. Let him live, even if only a little while, a little while. He is so young, such a mere foolish child — he's still fond of sweets. I bought him grapes. Pity — have pity!

*(She weeps in a subdued way, covering her face with her hands. MAN speaks without looking at her.)*

THE FATHER'S PRAYER. Here I am praying, you see. I've bent my old knees. I've prostrated myself in the dust before you. I'm kissing the ground, do you see? Maybe I have sometimes offended you. If so, forgive me, forgive me. It is true, I was haughty, arrogant. I demanded and did not beg. Often I condemned — forgive me. And if you wish, if this be your will, punish me, but spare my son. Spare him, I beg you. Not for mercy, not for pity do I pray you. I pray for justice. You are old, and I am old too. You will understand more easily than I. Bad people wanted to kill him, people who insult you by their deeds and defile your earth — bad, heartless people, who throw stones from behind corners. From behind corners, the scoundrels! Do not then, I pray you, permit the fulfilment of this evil deed. Stay the blood, give back the life — give back the life to my noble son! You took everything away from me, but did I ever ask you like a beggar: "Give me back my wealth, give me back my friends, give me back my talent"? No, never. I did not even ask you for my talent, and you know what his talent means to a man. It is more than life. I thought perhaps that's the way it ought to be, and I bore everything, bore everything with pride. But now I ask you on my knees, in the dust, kissing the earth: "Give back my son's life." I kiss your earth!

(*He rises.* SOMEONE *called* HE *listens indifferently to the father's and mother's prayers.*)

WIFE. I'm afraid your prayer was not humble enough. There was a certain tone of pride in it.

MAN. No, no, my wife, I spoke well to Him, the way a man should speak. He cannot love cringing flatterers better than brave, proud men who speak the truth. No, wife, you cannot understand. Now I believe also and feel reassured — in fact, I am happy. I feel that I too still signify something to my boy, and it makes me glad. Go and see if he's asleep. He needs a lot of good, hard sleep.

(*The* WIFE *goes out.* MAN, *with a friendly look to the corner where* SOMEONE IN GRAY *stands, picks up the toy clown, plays with it, and gives its red nose a quick kiss. At that instant his* WIFE *enters and* MAN *speaks shamefacedly.*)

MAN. I was begging his pardon. I insulted this fool. Well, how is our dear boy?

WIFE. He is so pale.

MAN. That's nothing. It'll pass away. He lost a lot of blood.

WIFE. It makes me so sad to look at his poor shorn head. He had such beautiful golden curls.

MAN. They had to be cut so that the wound could be washed. Never mind, wife, his hair will grow again and be still finer. Did you keep what was cut off? Be sure to keep it. His precious blood is on it.

WIFE. Yes, I put it away in the chest, the last one left of all our wealth.

MAN. Don't worry about wealth. Just wait until our son begins to work. He'll restore all we've lost. I feel well again, wife, and I firmly believe in our future. Do you remember our poor little rosy room? The good neighbors scattered oak leaves in it, and you made a wreath of them and put it on my head and said I was a genius.

WIFE. I say so still. Other people have ceased to appreciate you, but not I.

MAN. No, my dear little wife, you're wrong. What genius creates outlives the old dirty bundle of rags known as the body, whereas I am still living, and my productions ——

WIFE. No, they're not dead and they never will die. Do you remember that corner house you built ten years ago? Every evening at sunset you go to look at it. Is there a more beautiful building in the whole city, is there any with more depth to it?

MAN. Yes, I purposely built it so that the last rays of the setting sun should fall upon it and set its windows aglow. When the whole city is in darkness, my house is still taking leave of the sun. It was well done, and perhaps it will survive me a little while at least. What do you think?

WIFE. Of course, my friend.

MAN. The only thing that hurts, wife, is that the people have forgotten me so soon. They might have remembered me a little longer, just a little longer.

WIFE. They have forgotten what they knew, and ceased to love what they loved.

MAN. They might have remembered me a little longer, a little longer.

WIFE. I saw a young artist near that house. He studied it carefully and made a sketch of it in his sketchbook.

MAN. Ah, why didn't you tell me that before? It's highly significant, highly significant. It means that my ideas are accepted and handed down by others, and even if I am forgotten, my ideas will live. It is tremendously significant.

WIFE. Yes, my dear, you are not forgotten. Do you remember the young man who bowed so reverently to you on the street?

MAN. Yes, that's so, wife. He was a fine, very fine youth. He had such a nice young face. It's good you reminded me of his bow. It has sent a ray of brightness into my heart. But I feel sleepy. I must be tired. I am old too, my dear little gray wife. Have you noticed it?

WIFE. You're just as handsome as ever.

MAN. And my eyes are bright?

WIFE. Yes, your eyes are bright.

MAN. And my hair is black as pitch?

WIFE. It's so white, so like snow that it's even more beautiful.

MAN. And no wrinkles?

WIFE. Yes, there are little wrinkles on your face, but ——

MAN. Of course, I know I'm a beauty. Tomorrow I'll buy myself a uniform and enter the light cavalry. Yes? (*His* WIFE *laughs.*)

WIFE. There, you're joking too, as in olden times. But lie down here and sleep a little. I'll go to look after our boy. Don't worry, I won't leave him. I'll call you when he wakes. You don't care to kiss an old wrinkled hand, do you?

MAN (*kissing her hand*). Go, you're the most beautiful woman I've ever known.

WIFE. And the wrinkles?

MAN. What wrinkles? I only see a dear, kind, good, sensible face. Nothing else. Don't take offence at my stern tone. Go to the boy, watch him, stay with him like a quiet shadow of gentleness and love. And if he is disturbed in his sleep, sing him a song as you used to do. And put the grapes nearer, so that he can reach them.

> (*The* WIFE *goes out.* MAN *lies down on the sofa, his head toward the spot where* SOMEONE IN GRAY *stands immobile, so that* HIS *hand almost touches* MAN's *gray, dishevelled hair.* MAN *falls asleep quickly.*)

SOMEONE IN GRAY. Man has fallen into a sound, sweet sleep, deceived by hope. His breath is soft as a child's, his heart beats calmly and evenly, bringing him relief. He knows not that in a few moments his son will die. In mysterious dream-fancies a picture of impossible happiness arises before him.

It seems to him that he and his son are drifting in a white boat along a beautiful, quiet stream. It seems to him that it is a glorious day, and he sees the deep sky and the transparent crystal water. He hears the rustling of the reeds as they part before the boat. It seems to him that he is happy and glad. All his feelings betray him.

Suddenly he is disturbed. The terrible truth has entered through the thick veil of sleep and stung his thoughts.

"Why is your golden hair cut so short, my boy? Why?"

"I had a headache, papa, that's why."

And deceived once more, he feels happy again, sees the deep sky, and hears the rustling of the parting reeds.

He knows not that his son is already dying. He hears not how, in a last senseless hope, with a child's faith in the power of adults, his son is calling him without words, with his heart:

"Papa, papa, I am dying! Hold me!" Man sleeps soundly and sweetly, and in the deceptive, mysterious fancies there arises before him the picture of impossible happiness. Awake, Man! Your son is dead.

(MAN *lifts his head, frightened, and rises.*)

MAN. Ha! What is it? I thought I heard someone call me.

(*At that moment many women behind the scenes burst into a wail — the loud, long-drawn wail over the dead. The* WIFE *enters, frightfully pale.*)

MAN. Dead?

WIFE. Yes, he is dead.

MAN. Did he call me?

WIFE. No, he never awoke. He didn't call anyone. He is dead — my son, my dear, darling boy!

(*She falls on her knees before* MAN *and sobs, clasping his knees. * MAN *puts his hand on her hand and, turning to the corner where* SOMEONE IN GRAY *stands indifferently, speaks in a sobbing, but terrible voice.*)

MAN. You insulted a woman, scoundrel! You killed a boy! (*His* WIFE *sobs.* MAN *softly strokes her hair with his trembling hand.*) Don't cry, my dear, don't cry. He will scoff at our tears, just as He scoffed at our prayers. And you — I don't know who you are — God, Devil, Fate, or Life — I curse you!

(MAN *speaks the following in a loud, powerful voice, one arm about his wife as if to protect her, the other arm fiercely extended toward the* UNKNOWN.)

MAN'S CURSE. I curse everything that you have given. I curse the day on which I was born. I curse the day on which I shall die. I curse the whole of my life, its joys and its sorrows. I curse myself. I curse my eyes, my ears, my tongue. I curse my heart and my head, and I fling everything back at your cruel face, a senseless Fate! Be accursed, be forever accursed! With my curses I conquer you. What else can you do to me? Hurl me to the ground, I will laugh and shout in your face: "Be accursed!" Seal my mouth with the clamps of death, with my last thought I will shout into your stupid ears: "Be accursed, be accursed!" Take my body, tear at it like a dog, drag it into the darkness — I am not in it. I have disappeared, but disappearing I shall repeat: "Be accursed, be accursed!" Through the woman whom you have insulted, through the boy whom you have killed, I convey to you the curses of Man!

(*He turns in silence, with fiercely uplifted hand.* SOMEONE IN GRAY *listens passively to the curses. The flame of the candle flickers as if blown by the wind. Thus they stand for some time in tense silence confronting each other,* MAN *and* SOMEONE IN GRAY. *The wailing behind the scenes grows louder and more prolonged, passing into a doleful chant.*)

CURTAIN

# THE FIFTH SCENE

## THE DEATH OF MAN

*An uncertain, unsteady, blinking light, so dim that at first nothing is distinguishable. When the eye grows accustomed to it, the following scene becomes visible.*

*A long, wide room with a very low ceiling and windowless. The entrance is down a flight of steps from somewhere above. The walls are bare and dirty and resemble the coarse, stained hide of some huge animal. Along the entire back wall up to the stairs runs a bar with a top of smooth glass. This is covered with bottles full of differently colored liquors that are arranged in regular rows. Behind a low table sits the Bartender, immobile, with his hands folded across his paunch. His white face is blotched with red. His head is bald, and he has a large, reddish beard. He wears an expression of utter calm and indifference, which he maintains throughout, never changing his seat or his attitude.*

*Drunkards, both men and women, sit at small tables on wooden stools. Their number seems to be augmented by their shadows dancing on the walls and ceiling.*

*It is one endless monotony of repulsive ugliness and desolation. The men's faces resemble masks with the various features disproportionately magnified or reduced: big noses, or no noses at all; eyes staring savagely, almost starting from their sockets, or eyes narrowed to scarcely visible slits and points; huge Adam's apples and tiny chins. Their hair is tangled, frowzy, dirty, covering half the face on some of them. Despite their differences, a horrible sameness is stamped upon their faces: a greenish, ghastly tinge of decay and an expression that appears grotesque in some, gloomy and stupidly timid in others.*

*They are dressed in dull rags, with here a bony arm bared, there a sharp knee, and there again a frightfully sunken chest. Some are almost entirely naked. The women differ little from the men, except that they are even uglier and more uncouth. All have trembling heads and hands and walk with an uncertain step, as if on a slippery, or hilly, or sliding surface. Their voices, too, are all alike, rough and hoarse. They speak as uncertainly as they walk, as if their lips were frozen and refused to obey.*

*In the centre, at a separate table, sits* MAN, *his gray, unkempt head leaning on his arms. In this position he remains throughout the scene, except during the one moment when he speaks. He is dressed very poorly.*

*In the corner stands* SOMEONE IN GRAY, *with the candle burned nearly to the end. The slender blue flame flickers, now bending, now striving upward with its sharp little tongue. Its blue throws a ghastly glare on* HIS *face and chin.*

THE DRUNKARDS' CONVERSATION

— Oh my! Oh my!

— Look, everything is swaying so strangely. There's nothing to rest your eyes on.

— Everything is shaking as in a fever — the people, the chair, the ceiling.

— Everything is floating and rocking as on waves.

— Do you hear a noise? I hear a kind of noise, as if an iron wheel were rumbling, or stones falling from a mountain, large stones coming down like rain.

— It's the ringing in your ears.

— It's the tingling of your blood. I feel my blood. It flows heavy through my veins, thick, thick, black, smelling of rum. And when it gets to my heart, it all falls down, and it's terrible.

— It seems to me I see flashes of lightning.

— I see huge, red woodpiles and people burning on them. It's disgusting to smell the roasting flesh.

— Dark shadows circle around the piles. They are drunk, the shadows are. Hey, invite me! I'll dance with you.

— Oh my! Oh my!

— I am happy, too. Who will laugh with me? Nobody. So I'll laugh by myself.            (*He laughs.*)

— A charming woman is kissing my lips. She smells of musk and her teeth are like a crocodile's. She wants to bite me. Get away, you dirty hussy!

— I am not a dirty hussy. I am an old pregnant snake. I've been watching a whole hour to see little snakes come out of my body below and crawl around. Say, don't step on my little snakes.

— Where are you going?

— Who's walking there? Sit down. You make the whole house shake when you walk.

— I can't. I feel awful sitting down.

— I too. When I am sitting I feel a horror running through my whole body.

— So do I. Let me go.

(*Three or four* DRUNKARDS *reel aimlessly about, getting tangled up in the chairs.*)

— Look what it's doing. It's been jumping for two hours, trying to get on my knee. It just misses by an inch. I drive it away and it comes back again.

— Black cockroaches are creeping under my skull and buzzing.

— My brain is falling apart. I feel the gray matter separating. My brain is like rotten cheese. It stinks.

— There's some sort of a corpse here. I smell it.

— Oh my! Oh my!

— I'll sneak up to her tonight and cut her throat.

— The blood will flow. It's flowing already. See how red it is.

— I am constantly being followed by three men. They are calling me into a dark corner of the vacant lot, and they want to kill me. They are already at the door.

— Who is walking on the walls and ceiling?

— Good Lord! They have come to take me.

— Who?

— They.

— My tongue is getting paralyzed. I'll cry. (*Cries.*)

— My whole body is coming out. I'll soon be turned inside out, and then I'll be all red.

— Listen, listen. Ho! Somebody! A monster is going for me. He's raising his hand. Help! Ho!

— What is it?   Help!   A spider!

— Help!              (*For some time they shout "Help!" hoarsely.*)

— We are all drunkards.   Let's call down all the people from above.   It's so disgusting up there.

— No, don't.   When I leave here and go out on the street, it rampages and tears about like a wild beast and soon throws me off my feet.

— We've all come here.   We drink rum and it gives us joy

— It gives us fright.   I shiver the whole day from fright.

— Fright is better than life.   Who wants to return to life?

— I don't.

— I don't.   I'd rather croak here.   I don't want to live.

— No one!

— Oh my!   Oh my!

— Why does Man come here?   He drinks little and just sits still.   We don't want him.

— Let him go to his own house.   He has a house of his own.

— Fifteen rooms.

— Don't touch him.   He has no place to go to any more.

— He has fifteen rooms.

— They're empty.   Only rats run around and fight in them.

— And his wife.

— He hasn't any.   Seems she died.

> (*During this conversation and the following,* OLD WOMEN *in strange headgear enter quietly and replace unnoticeably the* DRUNKARDS, *who quietly depart.   The women mingle in the conversation, but in such a way that no one notices it.*)

CONVERSATION OF DRUNKARDS AND OLD WOMEN

— He'll soon die, too.   He can scarcely drag himself along, he's so weak.

— He has fifteen rooms.

— Listen to the beating of his heart.   It's uneven and faint. It'll soon stop beating altogether.

— Hey, Man, give us an invitation to your house.   You have fifteen rooms.

— It'll soon stop beating altogether, that old, sick, feeble heart of Man!

— He's asleep, the drunken fool.   It's dreadful to sleep, and yet he sleeps.   He might die in his sleep.

— Hey, there, wake him up!

— Do you remember how it used to beat when it was young and strong? (*A low laugh is heard.*)

— Who's laughing? There are some here who have no business to be here.

— It just seems so to you. We are all alone, only we drunkards.

— I'll go out on the street and start a fight. I've been robbed. I'm stark naked, and my skin is green.

— Good evening.

— The wheel is rumbling again. Oh, Lord, they'll crush me! Help! (*No one responds.*)

— Good evening.

— Do you remember his birth? I believe you were there.

— I must be dying. Good Lord! Good Lord! Who will carry me to the grave? Who will bury me? I'll be lying like a dog on the street. People will step over me, wagons will ride over me. They'll crush me. Oh, my God! Oh, my God! (*Cries.*)

— Permit me to congratulate you, my dear friend, on the birth of your child.

— I am positive there is a mistake here. For a circle to fall out of a straight line is an absurdity. I'll demonstrate it on the spot.

— You're right.

— Oh my! Oh my!

— It's only ignoramuses in mathematics who will permit it. I won't. I won't permit it, do you hear?

— Do you remember the rosy dress and the little bare neck?

— And the flowers? The lilies-of-the-valley on which the dew never dried, and the violets, and the green grass?

— Don't touch, don't touch the flowers, girls.

(*They utter a low and suppressed laugh.*)

— Oh my! Oh my!

(*The drunkards have all gone. Their places are taken by the* OLD WOMEN. *The light grows steady and very faint. The figure of the* UNKNOWN *is sharply outlined, and so is* MAN's *gray head, on which a faint light falls from above.*)

OLD WOMEN'S CONVERSATION

— Good evening.

— Good evening. What a splendid night!

— Here we are together again. How are you feeling?

— I cough a little. (*They laugh suppressedly.*)

— It won't take long now. He'll die soon.

— Look at the candle. The flame is blue and thin and spreading sideways. There's no more wax. It's only the wick that's burning.

— It doesn't want to go out.

— When did you ever see a flame that did want to go out?

— Don't dispute, don't dispute. Whether it wants to go out, or doesn't want to go out, time is flying.

— Do you remember his motor car? He once almost ran me down.

— And his fifteen rooms?

— I was there a little while ago. The rats almost ate me up, and I caught a cold in the draught. Someone had stolen the window frames, and the wind was blowing through the whole house.

— Did you try the bed in which his wife died? Isn't it soft and nice?

— Yes, I went through all the rooms and let my fancy play a little. They have such a pretty nursery. It's a pity the window frames are knocked out there too, and the wind makes a racket with the litter on the floor. And the child's bed too is so dear. Now the rats have made their nest in it and breed their children there.

— Such dear, naked little rats. (*They titter.*)

— And in his study the toys are lying on the table: a horse without a tail, a soldier's cap, and a red-nosed clown. I played a little with them. I put on the soldier's cap. It was very becoming to me. But there's such a lot of dust on the things. I got all dirty.

— But did you go into the drawing-room where the ball was given? It's so gay there.

— Yes, I did. Fancy what I saw. It was dark, the windows were broken, and the wind was playing with the wall-paper ——

— Making a sound as of music.

— And in the darkness the guests were squatting on their knees at the wall — and you should have seen how they looked!

— We know.

— And they barked: "How rich! How magnificent! How brilliant! How rich!"

— You're joking, of course.

— Of course I'm joking. You know I have a funny disposition.

— How rich! How magnificent!

— How gay!                                        (*They titter.*)

— Let's remind him of it!

— How rich! How magnificent!

— Do you remember how the music played at your ball?

— He's going to die soon.

— The dancers circled about, circled about, and the music played so gently, so beautifully. They played this way.

   (*They make a semicircle about* MAN *and hum the tune played by the musicians at the ball.*)

— Let's get up a ball. It's so long since I've danced.

— Imagine that this is a palace, a magnificent, an exquisitely beautiful palace.

— Call the musicians. Why, you can't have a ball without music.

— Musicians!

— You remember?

   (*They sing. At that instant the three musicians who played at the ball come down the stairs. The one with the violin adjusts his handkerchief on his shoulder with great precision, and all three begin to play, making an exaggerated effort. But the notes are soft and gentle as in a dream.*)

— There you have the ball.

— How rich! How magnificent!

— How brilliant!

— You remember, don't you?

   (*Singing softly to the music, they begin to circle about* MAN, *imitating in a wild, monstrous fashion the movements of the girls in the white dresses who danced at the ball. At the first musical phrase they circle, at the second they join and part gracefully and quietly, whispering:*)

— Do you remember?

— You're going to die soon — do you remember?

— Do you remember?

— Do you remember?

— You're going to die soon — do you remember?

— Do you remember?

> (*The dance grows brisker, the movements sharper. Strange, whining notes mingle into the singing of the* OLD WOMEN. *An equally strange laugh passes around the circle of dancers, suppressed and quiet at first. As each one glides past* MAN, *she flings an abrupt whisper into his ear:*)

— Do you remember?

— Do you remember?

— How gentle! How exquisite!

— What balm to the soul! Do you remember?

— You're going to die soon, you're going to die soon.

— You're going to die soon ——

— Do you remember?

> (*They circle more quickly, their movements growing still more abrupt. Suddenly there is silence and they halt. The musicians grow rigid with the instruments in their hands. The dancers remain fixed in the same position in which they were when the silence fell.* MAN *rises, straightens himself, throws back his gray, beautiful, terribly majestic head, and calls out in a surprisingly loud voice, full of sorrow and wrath. After each short phrase a brief but profound pause follows.*)

MAN. Where is my squire? Where is my sword? Where is my shield? I am disarmed! Come to me quick! Quick! Be accurs——

> (*He sinks down on the chair and dies, his head falling backward. At the same moment the candle flares up brightly and goes out. All objects are buried in a dense twilight which seems to be descending the stairs until it gradually covers everything. The face of dead* MAN *alone remains bright. Low, vague conversation, whisperings and derisive mockery are heard from the* OLD WOMEN.)

SOMEONE IN GRAY. Silence! Man has died!

> (*Profound silence. Then the same cold, indifferent voice repeats from a remote depth, like an echo:*)

Silence! Man has died!

> (*Profound silence. The twilight thickens, but the mice-like figures*

*of the* OLD WOMEN *are still seen standing rigid. Presently
they begin to circle about the dead body mutely, quietly; then they
begin to sing softly, and the musicians begin to play. The
gloom thickens, the music and the song grow louder and louder,
and the wild dance grows more unrestrained, until finally it ceases
to be a dance, the* OLD WOMEN *merely whirling about the dead
man arm in arm, stamping their feet, screeching, and laughing
a wild, prolonged laugh. Complete darkness descends. Only
the face of* MAN *is still lighted up. Then this light too is
extinguished. Black impenetrable darkness prevails.*

*In the darkness are heard the movements of the mad dancers, their
screeching and laughter, and the discordant, desperately loud
sounds of the music. Just when they have reached their highest
pitch, all the sounds and noises withdraw rapidly somewhere and
die away. Stillness.*)

**CURTAIN**

# THE CORAL

## (DIE KORALLE)

### By GEORG KAISER

*Translated from the German by WINIFRED KATZIN*

# GEORG KAISER

OF ALL playwrights of Germany who flourished between the beginning of the World War and 1932 perhaps Georg Kaiser best typifies the virtues and the excesses of the theatre. Born in Magdeburg, November 25, 1878, the son of a merchant, he first engaged in commerce, and travelled for three years in South America as a representative of an electrical company. His first play, *Rektor Kleist*, was written at the age of 25. Unconventional as has been his playwriting Kaiser was impressionable to a variety of influences, many of which were opposed and inconsistent. Among playwrights who influenced him were Shaw, Wedekind, Maeterlinck, Strindberg and Andreyev. But the influence that was decisive was the war and post-war psychology of Germany. This influence represents a temporary phase of dramatic history which is probably over not to return, one which, because of the intensity of effort that was poured into it, cannot be ignored by the student of the theatre of our day. Dramatists liked to tell themselves that they were creating an entirely new art to signalize a new day, that they had broken with a past for which they had only contempt. When it came to standards of the new art they seemed to be poverty stricken enough. Their ideas came from the cinema, the telegraph instrument, the screaming newspaper headline. Plays were based on action; thought was taboo as was literary language; clipped speech became the basis of the technique. Kaiser tells us that his plays have never been done as he wished; for that reason he was seldom seen in the theatre. In his playwriting Kaiser discards accuracy, is not bound by the facts. He deals vigorously with such concrete matters as social and industrial forces but with no effort to reflect real conditions on the stage. This utter disregard for the facts of the case is first shown in his treatment of historical material in *The Jewish Widow*, a play on Judith. It is later applied to industrial and revolutionary material. There are no living characters. Complexity of characterization is not sought. Acts and events, accidental and without significance, dominate the play. Kaiser wrote about thirty-five plays. The outstanding exponent of Expressionism in modern German drama Kaiser's vogue came to an end with the dawning power of the National Socialist government.

## THE CORAL

*The Coral* is not the best of Kaiser's plays but it is probably the one which most usefully illustrates his qualities and those of his school. Better as plays are *Von Morgen bis Mitternachts* and *Die Bürger von Calais*. *The Coral* is the first of a trilogy of plays, of which *Gas I* and *Gas II* constitute the second and third parts, in which the author seeks to symbolize the breaking of the present industrial system over into a new era with problems of another order. Perhaps influenced by Sternheim's study of three generations of a bourgeois family Kaiser spreads the action of his trilogy over three generations which represent different phases of the industrial revolution. Of the three *The Coral* represents present conditions. The other two press into the future. But the present is treated no more realistically than is the future. The author views his action in terms of large abstractions. The characters are types, not of individuals, but of regimented classman. Kaiser does not stand upon the Marxian philosophy. Therefore while he shows society going through successive convulsions, while his characters are conventionalized into puppets, his interest is still in the inner struggles and motivations of the characters. The billionaire, the great industrial parvenu, is not seeking immensity of power. He is fleeing from poverty as his son in the later play flees from riches. His daughter is motivated by the most Victorian of Humanitarianisms. The larger symbols of the play are brought out in the similarity between the Billionaire and his Secretary, the sign of a mechanistic world, and the coral, the symbol of organic life in the great machine shop the world had become. The play was produced in 1917 at the Neues Theatre, Frankfort, Germany.

# CHARACTERS

The Billionaire
The Son
The Daughter
The Secretary
The Young Woman in Taffeta
The Man in Blue
The Lady in Black
The Daughter of the Lady in Black
The Gentleman in Gray
First Servant
Second Servant
The Singer
The Doctor
The Museum Director
The Captain
First Judge
Second Judge
A Guard
A Priest

*The action takes place at the present day in an industrialized country not definitely located*

# ACT ONE

*An oval room, "The warm heart of the earth." Pale wall-panels in which the doors are invisible, two rear, one left. Only two round arm-chairs of white elephant-leather, centre, opposite and far apart. On the outer wing of the chair, right, a signal apparatus.*

*In this chair sits the* SECRETARY. *An indefinable shy energy in the profile. Reddish stubble of hair in narrow streaks from head to chin. The frame, in its suit of the roughest material, small, yet derives weight and importance from a certain ever-ready initiative, with effort suppressed. In the other chair the* YOUNG WOMAN IN TAFFETA.

SECRETARY. Would you mind...

THE YOUNG WOMAN IN TAFFETA. Oh, I understand you — will I be brief. I am not the only one waiting to be heard. The ante-room is crowded with others — and perhaps their cases are better justified. Who can tell? The wretched are in all the earth's corners. Whether the corner my fate thought fit to set me down in is an extra windy one...

SECRETARY. I should have to know what your fate has been before I could judge of that.

YOUNG WOMAN IN TAFFETA. Hell, sir. Yes, hell. I do not ex-aggerate; that is not my way. Or might I describe it better by... one is human, sir, one has a mother... believes in God... yes, one is still capable of that, in spite of everything. And I can't speak the words out loud, but I... buy my bread with my body.

SECRETARY. Do you wish to be admitted into a home?

YOUNG WOMAN IN TAFFETA. With flowers shining on the window ledges!

SECRETARY (*takes a notebook out of his pocket and writes*). You have two years' time in which to consider the foundations of a new life.

YOUNG WOMAN IN TAFFETA. Two...

SECRETARY. The doors of every home for women who have strayed stand open to you today.

YOUNG WOMAN IN TAFFETA (*taking his hand and kissing it — hysterically*).

I never sold my childhood faith. I never held God up for sale.
Now he seeks me out with his messenger... my God's messenger
... you are he. Take my burning thanks; I offer it on my knees.
More than that... more than that, it is God himself who goes
amongst us again. We are all saved... hallelujah, amen!

> (*The* SECRETARY *presses a button on the signal board. Immedi-*
> *ately two servants enter left, herculean figures in yellow livery.*
> *They raise the* YOUNG WOMAN IN TAFFETA *and lead her*
> *through the door, rear.*)

YOUNG WOMAN IN TAFFETA (*ecstatically*). A home for the fallen —
I shall become another woman there... another...

> (*She and the servants go. The servants admit the* MAN IN BLUE *and*
> *lead him to the chair, then go.*)

SECRETARY. Would you mind...

MAN IN BLUE (*speaking with difficulty*). My chest...

SECRETARY. Do you wish to be admitted to a sanatorium?

MAN IN BLUE (*burying his face in his hands*). They've turned me out
now that I have worked my strength away for them. Am I
an old man? No. I'm in the prime of life, but I look aged,
aged. My clothes flap on my bones — once I filled them out
to the very seams. The System has been the ruin of me.

SECRETARY. Are you a laborer?

MAN IN BLUE. The System ruins everyone with its inhuman using
up of all a man's capacity. And always a crowd waiting, so
that one's got to be used up quick to make room for the next one.

SECRETARY. Can you find no employment in any factory?

MAN IN BLUE. They don't even let me through the gates any more.
I've been walking the streets for a fortnight now, and I have
eaten my last penny away. Now...

SECRETARY. We have settlements on the land.

MAN IN BLUE. We have — I know. They are far off and I can't
get there on foot.

SECRETARY. They lie on the train line.

MAN IN BLUE. I... haven't the price of a ticket.

SECRETARY (*pulls out his notebook and writes. Hands the slip of paper*
*across*). Show this note outside.

MAN IN BLUE (*reads — stands up*). That is more than the train fare.

(*Stammering.*) I have a wife and children. I can take them with me — and I had meant to leave them!

(*The* SECRETARY *presses a button on the signal-board. The two servants come.*)

MAN IN BLUE (*already hastening out, left*). My wife... my children!

(*Goes.*)

(*The servants shut the door behind him, then open it again and admit the* LADY IN BLACK *and her daughter. The* DAUGHTER *carries a violin case.*)

LADY IN BLACK (*to the servants*). Thank you — I prefer to stand.

(*Servants go.*)

SECRETARY (*standing up*). Would you mind...

LADY IN BLACK (*calmly*). I decided to take this step for my daughter's sake. I lost my husband a few months ago. He left me almost nothing. For myself I have been able to find a situation which will keep me, but I know that I should never earn enough for my daughter's musical training. I have reason to believe that her talent is great enough to ensure her future. I purposely brought no testimonials to that effect. The best witness to her capability is her playing. Will you hear her?

SECRETARY. I believe your daughter also will find that more enjoyable when her training is completed.

LADY IN BLACK. Am I to assume from that, that... (*The* SECRETARY *writes. To her* DAUGHTER.) Kiss his hand.

SECRETARY (*gives the sheet to the* LADY IN BLACK). Collect this monthly until the end of her studies.

LADY IN BLACK (*without reading it*). Thanks must weary you, you hear them so often. People must seem pitiable to you, you make so many of them happy. As for us, we can but marvel at the miracle that there can exist someone who does not shut himself away from us when we come to him with our troubles. To hear us all is an act of greater courage than the fulfillment of our requests is an act of unspeakable goodness.

(*The* SECRETARY *presses a button on the signal-board. The servants come and lead the* LADY IN BLACK *and her daughter away. A signal buzzes. Immediately the* SECRETARY *presses another button. One of the servants appears, left.*)

SECRETARY. Wait. (*Servant goes.*)

(*Through the righthand door in the rear which, as it opens, is seen to be heavily padded, the* BILLIONAIRE *hastens in. The detailed description of the* SECRETARY *above aimed at the description of the* BILLIONAIRE, *for the* SECRETARY *is merely his double, identical to a hair. Even in speech and gesture the likeness is complete.*)

BILLIONAIRE. The sailing-list of the "Freedom of the Seas." Received after departure yesterday and reported this morning by radio. My son does not appear among the passengers.

SECRETARY. Only his companion.

BILLIONAIRE. The list is incomplete.

SECRETARY. They are usually perfectly accurate.

BILLIONAIRE. Where is my son if his companion is on that steamer? He must have booked on her. It was my wish. The papers published the names of every first-class passenger, and my son's was the first.

SECRETARY. I don't believe there is any error.

BILLIONAIRE. He must be on board. There is no other ship he could possibly be on. I sent express instructions to his companion that they were to come on her; she is the fastest of all steamers. The report is wrong. Get in touch with the shipping-office. Ask the source of the error. Whether on board — or in the drawing-up of the list. (SECRETARY *hesitates.*) Wait at the telephone for an answer.

SECRETARY It will keep me...

BILLIONAIRE. From what?

SECRETARY. Today is open Thursday.

BILLIONAIRE (*thoughtfully*). Open Thursday. (*The* SECRETARY *waits.*) Go and inquire. I'll stay here meanwhile. (SECRETARY *gives him the notebook.*) Say the matter is exceedingly urgent and report at once. (SECRETARY *leaves through door left.* BILLIONAIRE *sits down in chair, presses button. Servants admit the* GENTLEMAN IN GRAY, *powerful frame, in ample light-gray suit, the pockets stuffed with newspapers and pamphlets, round red head, shorn. Sandals.*)

GENTLEMAN IN GRAY (*following the servants, who indicate the chair — fanning himself with his cap*). Take it slow. Wait a minute. Breathe deep. (*Servants wait.*) Better keep 'em calm out there — this is going to take some time. (*To the* BILLIONAIRE.)

It won't be denied either. I shall have your attention riveted
with the first three words. (*To the servants.*) I'm no wild beast.
(*At a sign from the* BILLIONAIRE, *servants off.*)

BILLIONAIRE. Would you...

GENTLEMAN IN GRAY (*looking about him*). So this is the room all
the hymns are about — fountain of great compassion — holy
of holies whence love and assistance flow... (*With descriptive
gestures.*) Sweeping circle — significant form — glowing heart
of the earth.

BILLIONAIRE. Say what you have to say...

GENTLEMAN IN GRAY. Impressive bareness — two chairs — lots
of room for plaints and lamentations. Extraordinary the
paneling hasn't turned dark yet under the cries of distress
dashing against it. (BILLIONAIRE *moves his hand towards the
signal-board.* GENTLEMAN *notices the movement.*) Don't ring for
the servants. I know this open Thursday is precious for all
who wait. Each wasted moment and some human fate is
determined.

BILLIONAIRE. In what connection do you seek my help?

GENTLEMAN IN GRAY. I... (*leaning forward*) want to help you.
(BILLIONAIRE *makes another involuntary movement towards the wall.*)
No need. I'm sane, quite. I thought this over a long time.
I've studied the material — worked over it — and come to the
result — and the solution is of absurd simplicity. The whole
struggle — this gigantic fight which is waged at present with
enormous disposal of means and counter-means — collapses,
flows away, is gone.

BILLIONAIRE. What struggle do you mean?

GENTLEMAN IN GRAY. The only one which rages eternally — between poor and rich.

BILLIONAIRE. That...

GENTLEMAN IN GRAY. I can settle.

BILLIONAIRE (*with a searching look that flashes interest*). What made
you come to me?

GENTLEMAN IN GRAY. You're surprised. But I had to hold your
attention in the first moment or all was lost. The servants
wouldn't have let me through a second time. No trifling with
those two. (*Bringing out his papers with violence.*) I now proceed

to develop what I briefly mentioned before. This is material —
exhaustive assurances. Socialist newspapers, magazines, pamphlets, the entire arsenal of the fighting proletariat. Appeals,
estimates of means for stirring up success — tariffs, statistics,
tables of figures, flood of literature. Literature — nothing else.
And brings nobody a single step further, the rift gapes wider
every day. For it is built upon enmity to the knife. (*Pushing
it all back into his pockets.*) Pity for their pains. Useless wandering in blind alleys. To no purpose. Do you follow me?

BILLIONAIRE. I don't understand.

GENTLEMAN IN GRAY. What are you doing here? Giving with
both hands. Whoever asks, gets. Much or little, whatever
they want. Your billions make it possible. You declare your
open Thursday. All come and receive. Wretchedness creeps
over this threshold cowering, and dances out joy. The mouths
of the oppressed hail paradise in this oval room — here beats
the heart of the earth — glowing, merciful. Not for a moment
does it miss a beat — but spends and spends. Why do you do it?

BILLIONAIRE. My millions...

GENTLEMAN IN GRAY. No.

BILLIONAIRE. What then?

GENTLEMAN IN GRAY. Your wealth revolts you. (BILLIONAIRE
*raises one hand.*) You're not aware of it yourself, but for me there
can be no other reason I do assure you. I didn't come upon it
overnight. I've run around too in all the wearisome blind-
alleys until I found the open road that alone leads to the goal.

BILLIONAIRE. What goal?

GENTLEMAN IN GRAY. The end of the fight, the struggle between
rich and poor. A thing that no party, no parole, can bring to
pass, that you can make real with a single stroke of your pen.
And thereby render all the rest superfluous — this glowing heart
of the earth of yours, your open Thursday, the assemblage of
misery in your anteroom. For they are all mere drops you
pour into the sea of distress. Take it from me — I know. But
by the penstroke I refer to, you can proclaim eternal peace
on earth. Sign this declaration.

BILLIONAIRE (*without taking the document*). What declaration do you
want of me?

GENTLEMAN IN GRAY. That you regard the enrichment of individuals as the most monstrous of evils.

BILLIONAIRE. That I...

GENTLEMAN IN GRAY. You must. It must come from you, the billionaire of billionaires. Coming from you it will have importance, weight. Like a lightning flash it will illuminate the battlefields where the opposing forces now stand confronting each other armed to the teeth. The white flag of peaceable discussion, that is what we will run up — understanding. War will then become superfluous, the cause itself annulled. You did not desire riches — circumstances forced you. But there is a way to alter that condition, and a solution will be found and sought for in a spirit of brotherhood.

BILLIONAIRE. I hardly think...

GENTLEMAN IN GRAY. You alone, you alone can do it. You make these gifts because you have to. An inner force compels it. But it was all in little until I came to show you the greater thing — and now you will sign with joy. (*The* BILLIONAIRE *stands up.*) Surely you do not mean to call your servants?

BILLIONAIRE. I... (*Stands behind the chair thinking.*)

GENTLEMAN IN GRAY. I knew you would.

BILLIONAIRE. I am going to explain to you.

GENTLEMAN IN GRAY. Your signature.

BILLIONAIRE (*again repudiating*). Then you shall say whether I am able to sign that paper or not.

GENTLEMAN IN GRAY. You must.

BILLIONAIRE (*returning to his seat*). Since it appears to be your wish to turn the whole order of things upside down, I must try to construct for you my world as it appears to me. Do you know anything of my beginnings?

GENTLEMAN IN GRAY. Yes, your own powers.

BILLIONAIRE. My own weaknesses.

(GENTLEMAN IN GRAY *looks at him disconcerted.*)

BILLIONAIRE. Or let us say — fear... dread. Weakness and fear, then. But you will not grasp this in the space of a word or two. My career — as they say — is told in every school book. So it is a well-known story which I am about to repeat. The data will be the same, only I shall lend them a different significance. My father was an employee in the factory which now belongs to me. Whether he kept the furnace going under a cauldron or carried loads from place to place, I don't know. At any rate, he did not earn much, for we lived in wretched circumstances. One Monday — it was payday — he failed to come home. He had been given notice to quit, for he was used up — and he had taken his last money and gone off with it. He could never have provided for us any longer. On that night my mother took her own life. Somewhere in the house I heard a scream... I didn't run to see what it was, I knew already — I was eight years old. In that moment I knew what horror was, and it took root in me. It stood before me like a gray wall that I must climb over to escape the horror that pursued me. The horror made up of my father's staying off with his wages and my mother's scream set me on my way — drove me to flight. It stood at my back as I worked — I found employment in the same factory. It never left me even for a second — and I fled and fled before it — and flee still, for it stands behind me somewhere now as then.

GENTLEMAN IN GRAY. You made a bewilderingly rapid rise.

BILLIONAIRE. Tireless diligence, tireless industry, tireless flight, nothing else. I must keep the distance ever wider between the horror and myself. It drove me on. No hope of quarter, that much I have learned. It goaded me forward. The mind becomes ingenious against a dread that freezes up the limbs. There stood the machines which had sucked my father dry, hung my mother by the neck from a hook on a door, they would crush and maim me too unless I became their master first. The factory, with its machines — with its people set between me and the horror — that was the first I ever knew of rest.

GENTLEMAN IN GRAY (*brushing his hand across his forehead*). But after all... such an experience occurs a hundred times a day ... the father disappears, the mother...

BILLIONAIRE. It struck me down because I was particularly weakly. I must have been, or I should have withstood it better. Instead, I ran away as hard as I could go. Have I said enough?

GENTLEMAN IN GRAY (*staggered*). I protest...

BILLIONAIRE. Against the weakling before you?

GENTLEMAN IN GRAY. Then you have no mercy on your fellow men...

BILLIONAIRE. No fugitive may see whom he tramples underfoot.

GENTLEMAN IN GRAY (*joyfully and with a searching regard*). Nevertheless — "The warm heart of the earth."

BILLIONAIRE. Certainly. I refuse to be brought in touch with poverty — it is too powerful a reminder. I instituted the Open Thursday, therefore — I know then when to hide myself.

GENTLEMAN IN GRAY. Yet you sit here and listen to it all.

BILLIONAIRE. Error. My Secretary sits here.

GENTLEMAN IN GRAY (*after a pause — sharply*). Is that your cosmic plan?

BILLIONAIRE. Not mine — it is *the* cosmic plan.

GENTLEMAN IN GRAY. That each class is one of the stages of escape?

BILLIONAIRE. All are fugitives.

GENTLEMAN IN GRAY. And the fleetest... the...

BILLIONAIRE. Utterest cowards... yes...

GENTLEMAN IN GRAY. Triumph...

BILLIONAIRE. My sort.

GENTLEMAN IN GRAY (*groaning, then with irony*). Then I must rest my hope in a humanity without cowards.

BILLIONAIRE. Some will always be born more timid than the rest. The cause is of no consequence. It is a lever which sets itself in motion. Progress not whither but whence — your suspicions grow. Exactly. I express what you assume. And I am more familiar than you with this line of thought. Where do they come from, the great who inherit the world? They rise out of the dark because they were in the dark. And there experience the horror... this way or that... Blazing meteors that flare... and fall.

GENTLEMAN IN GRAY (*mocking*). And when... are you due to fall? (*The* BILLIONAIRE *shakes his head, smiling.*) How have you insured yourself against the fate of meteors?

BILLIONAIRE. I have a son. (*The* SECRETARY *comes back.* BILLIONAIRE *rises, goes toward* SECRETARY). Has the mistake been corrected?

THE SECRETARY. The list was complete.

BILLIONAIRE. Without my son?

SECRETARY. He is not on the "Freedom of the Seas."

BILLIONAIRE. But his companion is.

SECRETARY. They must have separated.

BILLIONAIRE. And he with orders not to stir from his side. (*The* SECRETARY *is silent.*) I will have an explanation. At this moment I do not even know where my son is. Get into touch with his companion by radio. Let him report. Something must have happened. I do not understand how he can be traveling without my son.

SECRETARY. Your son is young.

BILLIONAIRE. Tender chains that... ? We shall soon know the reason. (SECRETARY *off again. The* BILLIONAIRE *comes back to his chair.*) Did my story affect you so deeply then?

GENTLEMAN IN GRAY (*had leapt up as the* SECRETARY *entered. He is still staring at the door through which he disappeared. Now he turns to the* BILLIONAIRE). Do I see double? Is it you sitting here? Is it you who just went through that door? Is it yourself you were just speaking to?

BILLIONAIRE. No. I was arranging a piece of business with my secretary.

GENTLEMAN IN GRAY. The *Secretary* —! are you brothers? But even then it would be...

BILLIONAIRE. But possible, as you observe.

GENTLEMAN IN GRAY (*dropping into the chair*). Horrible.

BILLIONAIRE. A common prank of Nature's. You'll find a repetition of each of us, if you try, of course. I had mine looked for — and I admit that fortune favored me.

GENTLEMAN IN GRAY. Fortune —?

BILLIONAIRE. It serves many excellent purposes for me. I can be here and there without ever bestirring myself. Even at this Open Thursday I am present in my well-known person — and am perhaps on a fishing trip at some distant river.

GENTLEMAN IN GRAY. Do you still know which one you are?

BILLIONAIRE. I imagine so.

GENTLEMAN IN GRAY. But everybody else takes the Secretary for you?

BILLIONAIRE. Except the two servants who guard my personal Secretary.

GENTLEMAN IN GRAY. Otherwise you are indistinguishable?

BILLIONAIRE. Except for a small and unobtrusive sign, a coral which the Secretary wears on his watch-chain. The one of us who wears the coral is the Secretary.

GENTLEMAN IN GRAY. And only the servants know?

BILLIONAIRE. They are detectives.

GENTLEMAN IN GRAY. What if I should betray your secret?

BILLIONAIRE. Who would believe you? It would be one more legend about me.

GENTLEMAN IN GRAY (*shaking his head energetically*). You've no coral on your watch-chain — or — I didn't notice, were you wearing one before...

BILLIONAIRE. No. I've talked to you since you came in in my own person, and if you wish to hear the rest ——

GENTLEMAN IN GRAY (*laughing*). The end of your head-over-heels flight before the horror — or is there no end?

BILLIONAIRE. In my son. I have a daughter, but the stronger bond is with the son, of course. Have you children? No. Then you must allow me to know. With a son one feels his continuation — one's own continuation — in his beginning. That is a law that runs in the blood. It is my most certain conviction that it is so. Every father wishes that his son shall have it better than he did.

GENTLEMAN IN GRAY. And not know the horror, as you call it.

BILLIONAIRE. Need I say any more? It is all so obvious.

GENTLEMAN IN GRAY. And have you protected him?

BILLIONAIRE. I let him live in brightness. He has no contact with those things that scream and wail from your pamphlets. I have led him along a bypath from all that.

GENTLEMAN IN GRAY. Where do you keep him hidden?

BILLIONAIRE. I don't keep him hidden. The earth has so many sunny strands.

GENTLEMAN IN GRAY. Where the horror may be dreamt away.

BILLIONAIRE. Where one can make oneself a happier past.

GENTLEMAN IN GRAY. And have rest from flight, and blessed peacefulness.

BILLIONAIRE. In paradise.

GENTLEMAN IN GRAY. You found your outward double — the Secretary.

BILLIONAIRE. Does that still excite you?

GENTLEMAN IN GRAY. No, there's method in it.

BILLIONAIRE. How do you mean?

GENTLEMAN IN GRAY. And now you're forming an inward double — your son.

BILLIONAIRE. It may be my passion to exchange.

GENTLEMAN IN GRAY. With such reasons.

BILLIONAIRE. So fearsome.

GENTLEMAN IN GRAY. So powerful.

BILLIONAIRE. Do you still want to help me? With your declaration that I am to sign?

GENTLEMAN IN GRAY (*pushing his newspapers, etc., still deeper into his pockets, breathing heavily*). You've set me in a turmoil. The air's thick here. It presses the sweat out of one's paws.

BILLIONAIRE. Think it over at leisure.

GENTLEMAN IN GRAY. It is too crazy — the "Warm Heart of the Earth"... "Open Thursday"... the results!

BILLIONAIRE. What results?

GENTLEMAN IN GRAY. Chaos opens up.

BILLIONAIRE. It has already — therefore let whoever can, save himself on the first spot of firm ground he can find.

GENTLEMAN IN GRAY (*almost shouting*). Not you!

BILLIONAIRE. I have a son.

GENTLEMAN IN GRAY. Let me out of here. Buzz for your servants. I can't find the door. Buzz for them, I tell you. (*The* BILLIONAIRE *does so. The two servants come. The* GENTLEMAN IN GRAY *threateningly to the* BILLIONAIRE). You've dashed my world to pieces — from under the ruins I curse you — I curse you.

(*The servants seize him roughly and take him out.*)

SECRETARY (*coming in again*). A radio from your son.

BILLIONAIRE. From land?

SECRETARY. No. From shipboard.

BILLIONAIRE. Is he on his way...

SECRETARY (*reading*). "Just left..."

BILLIONAIRE. On the "Freedom of the Seas," after all. (*The* SECRETARY *shakes his head.*) Can she have a sister-ship, then, as sumptuous?

SECRETARY (*goes on reading*). "On the Albatross."

BILLIONAIRE. "Albatross?" What sort of a ship is that?

SECRETARY. A coaler.

BILLIONAIRE. A... coaler? Does he explain? (SECRETARY *hesitates — hands him a telegraph.* MILLIONAIRE *reads it through.*) As stoker... (*Collapsing against the chair.*) What does it mean — my son... on a coaler... stoker...?

## ACT TWO

*Under the awning on the deck of the* BILLIONAIRE'S *yacht. A section of the railing, rear. Heat mist over the calm sea.*

*In white-enamelled wicker armchairs —* BILLIONAIRE, *the* DAUGHTER, *the* MUSEUM DIRECTOR, *the* DOCTOR, *the* CAPTAIN, *all in white. A negro sets out iced drinks. Off, the* SINGER'S *voice.*

SINGER (*lowering her voice on a long last note, comes in from the rear and trains her kodak on the group. Breaks off as she snaps*). Thanks... (*the rest look up surprised*) for the advertisement. On the high seas — aboard the most marvellous yacht in the world — and such an audience! We must have that on the record. Every opera-house on earth will compete for a contract with me. (*Dropping into a chair beside the* BILLIONAIRE.) If *you* enjoyed hearing me — or am I mistaken? Tell me the truth — I have the picture, anyway.

BILLIONAIRE (*in some embarrassment*). No, no, on the contrary, really extraordinary... (*The others clap applause.*)

SINGER (*quickly snapping again*). Second photo — the applause. (*Handing the negro her glass.*) Hot lemonade.

DOCTOR. Just what I was going to suggest to you.

SINGER. Ah, doctor, you don't know me — I'm everything, singer, impresario, and physician.

MUSEUM DIRECTOR. Then you are depriving two people of a livelihood.

SINGER. Well, isn't that the secret of success?

MUSEUM DIRECTOR. You've good healthy nerves.

SINGER. I've the most terrible nerves.

DOCTOR. Won't you explain that to me as a medical man?

SINGER. I see ghosts.

DOCTOR. What sort of ghosts?

SINGER. Just ghosts.

DOCTOR. That's more than I ever have.

SINGER. Because you haven't an excitable temperament. Artists have — that's why they see ghosts.

DOCTOR. I see. Only artists, nobody else.

SINGER. Let's ask round. It makes an entertaining game at sea. Each in turn now. (*To the* BILLIONAIRE.) Do you see ghosts?

BILLIONAIRE. I'm afraid we've no time just now to... (*To the* CAPTAIN.) Isn't the "Albatross" about due to come within range now, Captain?

CAPTAIN. You can't quite calculate it with ships of that type.

BILLIONAIRE. Please.                    (*The* CAPTAIN *goes.*)

DOCTOR. What sort of a ship is this "Albatross" really?

BILLIONAIRE. My son discovered it. It must have some very special points. Most likely a yacht belonging to some friend he met on his journey.

DAUGHTER. We can challenge her to a race.

SINGER. Thrilling! What a shame I've so few films with me.

DAUGHTER. The loser to be rammed.

DOCTOR. Crew and all?

DAUGHTER. Five minutes rescue time. (*To the* BILLIONAIRE.) Shall I go and tell the captain to prepare for the race?

MUSEUM DIRECTOR. Suppose the unknown "Albatross" is too much for us?

DAUGHTER. I shall stay on the bridge. I'll give the orders to the engine room, and we'll pile on all the steam we can make.

DOCTOR. At this temperature.

DAUGHTER. There'll be air up there.

DOCTOR. I was thinking of the engine room.

DAUGHTER (*stamping*). The upper deck is all I know about.

BILLIONAIRE. I don't think the "Albatross" is faster than we — so the charm of the fight isn't there.

DAUGHTER. What — my brother's chosen ship?

BILLIONAIRE. We'll leave the decision to him, then. He knows both sides. (*The* CAPTAIN *comes back.*) Sighted?

CAPTAIN. Not yet.

BILLIONAIRE (*to his daughter*). You see, she's slow. (*To the others.*) Let's amuse ourselves meanwhile —

SINGER. With the ghost game — good!

BILLIONAIRE (*hastily, to the* MUSEUM DIRECTOR). Is the Tintoretto really no good at all?

MUSEUM DIRECTOR. On the contrary — it is very fine, very fine indeed.

BILLIONAIRE. But you refused it when I offered it to you.

MUSEUM DIRECTOR (*nods*). Christ carrying the cross.

SINGER. You object to the subject?

MUSEUM DIRECTOR. When I extend it to a matter of principle — yes.

DOCTOR. There'll be precious little place for old masters in your gallery in that case.

SINGER (*to the* MUSEUM DIRECTOR). Proceed with the lecture, won't you? I'll snap your audience as you arrive at the climax.

MUSEUM DIRECTOR. In the new museum I am to be the director of, my aim is to achieve a complete break with the past, however recent. I shall conduct my entire propaganda with this end in view.

DOCTOR. And what will you have left?

SINGER. Empty walls.

MUSEUM DIRECTOR. Empty walls and practically nothing to cover them.

DOCTOR. Highly original museum.

DAUGHTER. Indoor tennis-courts.

MUSEUM DIRECTOR. And that very circumstance will be a spur to new productions. Emphatically a beginning. Which means especially no more disapproving criticism based on comparisons with what has gone before. We are all sitting in that shadow — in one way or another it is a source of torment to us all. We must get into the full light of things again — and shake off these cross-carryings. At least that is how I see it. It is a burden on us — a cross that we are made to carry — this mass of the past from which we can only free ourselves by acts of violence — or even crimes, if it should come to that.

DOCTOR. And do you consider it possible then — without self-deceiving?

MUSEUM DIRECTOR. I don't know.

DOCTOR. I'm afraid the cross-carrying is inevitable.

MUSEUM DIRECTOR. One must truly desire the future.

DOCTOR. You might manage it in your gallery.

MUSEUM DIRECTOR. My ambition goes no further.

DOCTOR. But in real life I doubt very much whether anyone can jump beyond his shadow.

(*A sailor comes with a report for the* CAPTAIN, *and goes.*)

CAPTAIN (*standing up. To the* BILLIONAIRE). The "Albatross" is close by on the starboard side.

BILLIONAIRE (*excited*). Send the launch over.　　　(CAPTAIN *goes.*)

DOCTOR. Now we shall know all about the mystery-ship.

SINGER. And the matador.

MUSEUM DIRECTOR. My curiosity is at snapping-point.

DAUGHTER. I'm going up to flash the challenge across.

BILLIONAIRE (*holding her back. To the others*). Please go ahead; we'll come in a moment. (SINGER, MUSEUM DIRECTOR, *and* DOCTOR *go.*) I want to talk to you a second first.

DAUGHTER. Now?

BILLIONAIRE. It's only a question.

DAUGHTER. What is it?

BILLIONAIRE. Could you consider — marrying the Museum Director?

DAUGHTER. I — I don't know.

BILLIONAIRE. I want to urge you to decide, because...

DAUGHTER. I hardly know him.

BILLIONAIRE. Nor I...

DAUGHTER. Then how can you persuade me so?

BILLIONAIRE. I sat listening to him just now, and he impressed me as no other person ever did.

DAUGHTER. Because he rejected your gift?

BILLIONAIRE. I like his ideas. That inner independence — his philosophy which admits only the future and annihilates the past...

DAUGHTER. I wasn't listening to him.

BILLIONAIRE. You would give me great joy...

DAUGHTER. Then it's superfluous to ask me to think it over.

BILLIONAIRE (*shakes her hands*). Now let us go and meet your brother.
(*They go.*)

(*Sound of bells and sirens. Sailors open the railing rear and let down the companion. Everybody comes back and leans over the railing. Handkerchiefs wave. Helloes.*)

DOCTOR (*coming under the awning*). It's a clumsy old tub.

MUSEUM DIRECTOR (*following him*). Does credit to the name of "Albatross."

DOCTOR. Could you see any other passengers aboard?

MUSEUM DIRECTOR. That may have been the charm of the voyage.

DOCTOR. Thanks, not for me!

SINGER (*joins them, holding camera behind her back*). Discretion — family reunion!

(*The SON, in a gray suit, comes up the stairway, and the daughter falls upon him with a storm of welcome. The CAPTAIN stands by at the salute.*)

SON. Have you been lying in wait for me?

DAUGHTER. Up and down this spot for three days. Glorious bore.

BILLIONAIRE. I planned a surprise for you.

SON. Well, you've succeeded brilliantly. Your guests?

BILLIONAIRE. A few intimates, that's all.

(*The SON goes from one to the other and shakes hands in silence. Then he stands beside a chair, still without a word. The awkward silence continues.*)

DAUGHTER (*flinging herself into a chair*). Bit too solemn for me.

BILLIONAIRE (*indicating the chairs*). Please.

(*Everybody sits down, the SON last and hesitatingly. The CAPTAIN comes back and sits down too.*)

SON (*to him, astonished*). Aren't we going on?

BILLIONAIRE. I thought we might stay at sea another three or four days.

SON. Certainly, if you wished...

BILLIONAIRE. On your account.

SON. What for?

BILLIONAIRE. After your travels...

DAUGHTER. I say, I quite forgot to look at the "Albatross" in all the excitement.   Is she very swell?   How many knots?

(*The* MUSEUM DIRECTOR *and the* DOCTOR *laugh.*)

SON.  What's the matter with the "Albatross"?

DAUGHTER.  We wanted to challenge her.  Should we have had a good opponent?

SON.  You're laughing at her.  No, sister, the "Albatross" isn't an opponent at all in the way you mean.

DAUGHTER (*surprised*).  Then why didn't you come on the "Freedom of the Seas"?

BILLIONAIRE (*uneasily, trying to change the subject*).  Well, what about your impressions of the world's great cities?

SINGER.  Did you visit the opera everywhere?

SON.  We may as well define the "Albatross's" class — she's a coaler.  You must know all the ships on these roads, Captain?

CAPTAIN.  I'm afraid the "Albatross" had escaped me.

SON.  Why?  (*The* CAPTAIN *smiles.  To the others.*)  Why should it have?  Don't other people travel on such ships?

CAPTAIN.  They are not arranged for passengers.

SON.  No, not for passengers.  But what about the sailors.  Aren't stokers people?

MUSEUM DIRECTOR (*after a pause*).  You understand the refinements of pleasure.

SON.  What pleasure?

MUSEUM DIRECTOR.  It is the antithesis between the coaler and this yacht that enables you to savour its luxury as never before.

SON.  Or else to — (*Breaking off, and turning to the* BILLIONAIRE.)  Did you have a report from my companion?

BILLIONAIRE.  I did not speak to him.

SON.  But he must have got back two days ago.

BILLIONAIRE.  I've been lying out here for two days.

SON.  Are you displeased with him?  I take all the blame.  He did all he could to prevent it.

BILLIONAIRE (*avoiding the subject*).  Won't you change your clothes?

DAUGHTER.  That's a city suit you have on.

SON.  It's a better protection against the coal-dust whirling about.  And besides it was less noticeable — it's wiser to be part of the picture.

BILLIONAIRE. Do so then — go and get into white from head to foot like us.

SON. Please let me enjoy myself my own way.

SINGER (*busy with the camera*). Most interesting pictorial effect.

SON. Is that the only way it strikes you?

DOCTOR. In this extreme heat white clothing is a matter of health.

BILLIONAIRE. There spoke our careful doctor — obey him.

SON (*with repressed sharpness*). Would you expect your professional advice to be followed in the engine room too?

DOCTOR. Scarcely.

SON. Because you don't enforce it there. Because of the black coal they work with.

DOCTOR. Exactly.

SON. Therefore health down there must suffer, while up here it must be taken care of?

MUSEUM DIRECTOR. You seem to have seen more things on your tour than you...

SON. When it is the first trip, one keeps one's eyes wide open.

DAUGHTER. Did you meet any princes?

SINGER. Tell us all about it.

SON. Every day.

DAUGHTER. Have you made any friends? Is anyone coming to visit you soon?

SON. I could introduce five — ten — to you off my coaler. Come with me next time.

MUSEUM DIRECTOR. Is this another...

SON. Refinement of pleasure?

> (*A sailor comes with a report to the* CAPTAIN. *The* CAPTAIN *goes to the* DOCTOR *and whispers to him. They go.*)

SON. Aren't we going on now?

BILLIONAIRE. I have given no orders.

SON. What did the doctor go off with the captain for?

SINGER. One of the crew's had an accident, I expect.

SON. Wouldn't you like to take a snapshot of it?

DAUGHTER. We might as well start moving — it would be one way of getting some air. This heat is really becoming unbearable.

SON. And we're on deck.

SINGER. Is it cooler anywhere else?

SON. No — hotter.

SINGER. Not possible!

SON. Go below into the stoke-hole.

BILLIONAIRE. Let's start going.

MUSEUM DIRECTOR (*ironically*). Mind the stokers.

SON. Do you know what it means to be by those furnaces?

MUSEUM DIRECTOR. I have never sought the opportunity to try it.

SON. And a description would hardly interest you.

MUSEUM DIRECTOR. Oh, graphically done by an expert...

SON. I am an expert!

BILLIONAIRE (*to the* DAUGHTER). Please go and tell the captain...

DAUGHTER. Full steam ahead!

SINGER. The ladies take over the command.

DAUGHTER. Here's where we make a new record. We'll radio it to the papers tonight and tomorrow the whole world will burst with envy. (*Goes off.*)

SON. Won't you stop that wickedness?

BILLIONAIRE. The yacht has never shown her full capacity yet.

SON. Then I must ask you to drop me first.

MUSEUM DIRECTOR. The coaler has unaccustomed you to speed.

SON. No, to frivolity, perhaps.

BILLIONAIRE. You used to enjoy that sort of sport.

SON. I am ashamed to have come to a right mind so late.

BILLIONAIRE. What does that mean?

SON. That I... (*Reflecting.*) If I'm to take part in this record-making, I can only do it before the boilers.

BILLIONAIRE (*to the* MUSEUM DIRECTOR). Don't keep the ladies waiting on the bridge. (*The* MUSEUM DIRECTOR *goes. To his* SON, *slowly.*) Did you really travel on that ship as a stoker?

SON. I couldn't hold out under it, so I had to become a passenger again.

BILLIONAIRE. Did it specially attract you to...

SON. Oh, the steamer is the least important part of it.

BILLIONAIRE. You saw much to wonder at in your travels.

SON. It was as though scales fell from my eyes. The wrongs we are committing stood up clearly before me. We rich here — and there the others, strangling in want and misery — but people like ourselves. There's not a spark of right in it — why do we do it? I ask you why? Give me an answer that absolves us both, you and I.

BILLIONAIRE (*staring at him*). You ask me?

SON. Yes, and I shall never stop asking you. I have never been so grateful to you as now, never in my life. You gave me that trip, and but for it I should have stayed blind to the end of my days.

BILLIONAIRE. You will forget.

SON. Forget what is in me now, and fills me through and through? That will only disappear when I disappear too.

BILLIONAIRE. What is in you?

SON. The horror of that life which I have seen, with its toil and oppression.

BILLIONAIRE. Travel experiences are not enough to...

SON. Not enough?

BILLIONAIRE. You exaggerate superficial impressions.

SON. They burn in my blood. And the vividest picture of all is the "Freedom of the Seas" as she lay in her wharf. Flags, music, passengers in light clothes strolling up and down the decks, chattering, gay. And a few yards underneath their feet, hell. Men feeding fire-belching holes, quivering bodies burning to death. So that we may make speed, speed. I had started to sail on that ship, I had set my foot on her deck — but I had to turn back — and only on that "Albatross" I began to feel my conscience lighter.

BILLIONAIRE. And have you conquered all that now?

SON. Now I feel it more than ever. Here on this wonderful private yacht of yours. I feel the blood beating in my heart with shame. Look at us lying back in these chairs in indolence, wailing about the heat the sun pours down on us. We sip iced water for ease, and not a grain of dust irritates our throats. And underneath the soft soles of your white shoes here, there are men with boiling fever in their veins. Tear away this wall of wooden planks — see how thin it is, but yet how fearfully it divides — and look down, look down, all of you. And the words will stick in your mouths before any of you will brag before one of them down there. (*The* DOCTOR *strolls in.*)

SON (*springing toward him*). What was it, doctor?

DOCTOR. A yellow stoker collapsed.

SON. Dead?

DOCTOR (*shaking his head*). Heat-stroke.

SON. Where have you put him?

DOCTOR. I had him laid in front of a ventilator shaft.

SON. Not brought up here?

DOCTOR. No.

SON (*briefly*). Wait here. (*He goes.*)

DOCTOR (*drops into a chair. To the* NEGRO). Ice water. (*To the* BILLIONAIRE.) I find this long drifting at sea extraordinarily quieting to the nerves. I'd like to prescribe it for you five days every other month. (BILLIONAIRE *does not move.*) I promise myself success with this new diet I've put you on. (BILLIONAIRE *silent.*) Of course we can't offer you the keen and healthful excitement of meeting your son again, but your daughter will be able to invent surprises of a more moderate kind for you. I'll talk to her about it. (*Voices and footsteps approach. The* DOCTOR *puts down his glass.*) Are they playing deck games? (SAILORS *bring the half-naked yellow stoker.*)

SON. This way.

DOCTOR (*standing up*). What does this mean?

SON. Set two chairs together. Take hold, doctor, this is a life and death matter. (*To the* SAILORS.) Lay him down. (*To the* NEGRO.) Ice water. (*To the* DOCTOR.) Come over here, doctor, you understand this better than I. Wash his chest. (*To the* BILLIONAIRE.) Will you allow your personal physician to lend a hand? (*To the* DOCTOR.) Is it dangerous?

CAPTAIN (*coming in — low, to* BILLIONAIRE). I couldn't prevent him.

(*The* BILLIONAIRE *shakes his head decidedly. The* DAUGHTER *and the* SINGER *come in.*)

SON (*to the* DAUGHTER). Won't you help us here, sister? A man may be dying. (*The* DAUGHTER *goes nearer.*) Wet your hands in that ice water and lay them on his hot chest. I am only calling you to your simple duty. (*The* DAUGHTER *does so. To the* DOCTOR, *beside himself.*) Doctor, save him — you've got to, or I am a murderer!

BILLIONAIRE (*stares down at the group — his lips move — at last he mutters*). The horror!

SINGER (*focussing her kodak — to the* MUSEUM DIRECTOR). I've never had pictures like these before. (*She snaps.*)

## ACT THREE

*Square room with rear wall of glass — the* BILLIONAIRE'S *work-room. Right and left on the walls, from the floor to the ceiling, huge brown-toned photographs of factories. Broad desk with swivel-chair; another chair at the side. Smokestacks outside, close and straight like pillars of dead lava holding up cloud-mountains of smoke.*

BILLIONAIRE (*at the desk*). How many dead?

SECRETARY (*standing by the desk*). The exact number of victims could not be ascertained, for the men who were saved and brought into the light, rushed away and had not reported yesterday.

BILLIONAIRE. What did they do that for?

SECRETARY. They must have experienced untold horror the three days they were shut up under the ground.

BILLIONAIRE. And now they flee from it, farther and farther?

SECRETARY. They came up distracted as if from their graves, screaming and shuddering.

BILLIONAIRE. Whoever is absent from his place by the day after tomorrow will not be taken back again.

SECRETARY (*making a note*). By the day after tomorrow.

BILLIONAIRE. How did the meeting go? Was I contradicted? Was I allowed to speak without interruption?

SECRETARY. No.

BILLIONAIRE. Was my life in danger?

SECRETARY. It was indeed.

BILLIONAIRE. How did I protect myself?

SECRETARY. I had requisitioned troops. They were lined up before me ready to shoot.

BILLIONAIRE. Did anything happen?

SECRETARY. Only one man kept yelling interruptions.

BILLIONAIRE. What did he say?

SECRETARY. Murderer.

BILLIONAIRE. Was he not to be found?

SECRETARY. The crowd covered him.

BILLIONAIRE. Let him be found. Threaten to take steps if he is not delivered. (*The* SECRETARY *makes a note.*) Is everything quiet now?

SECRETARY. The shaft is being worked again today.

BILLIONAIRE. What means did I use?

SECRETARY. I announced the shutting down of the entire works.

BILLIONAIRE. Thanks. (*A green lamp lights on the desk.* BILLIONAIRE *takes up the receiver. Surprised.*) Who?... My daughter?... Here?... Yes, I will see her. (*To the* SECRETARY.) Replace me in Factory 24. There has been an explosion there — I said I would be down during the afternoon. (*The* SECRETARY *makes a note.*) Thanks. (*The* SECRETARY *leaves, left, through an invisible door. The* BILLIONAIRE *stands up, makes a few rapid steps toward the wall right, changes his mind, returns to his chair and plunges into his work. One of the servants opens a padded invisible door. The* DAUGHTER *enters.* SERVANT *goes. The* BILLIONAIRE *looks round.*) Your first visit to your father's business house.

DAUGHTER (*looking about*). Yes — I am seeing it for the first time.

BILLIONAIRE. Another world!... Is the matter so urgent that you couldn't keep it until this evening before the fire?

DAUGHTER. I can only explain it to you here.

BILLIONAIRE. Am I to prepare myself for the most joyful news?

DAUGHTER. What is that?

BILLIONAIRE. I asked something of you that day we were waiting for your brother... On the yacht.

DAUGHTER (*shaking her head*). I have never given that another thought.

BILLIONAIRE (*suppressing his uneasiness. Gaily*). Really not?

DAUGHTER. It was on the yacht that I first saw my way.

BILLIONAIRE. To your brightest happiness?

DAUGHTER. To my inevitable duty.

BILLIONAIRE (*lifts his hand high in protest*). Not that!

DAUGHTER (*calmly*). When I took my hands from the seething breast of that yellow stoker they were marked. The scar sank into my blood, into my deepest heart. I have no choice. I feel the call. And submit to it willingly. You will show me the place where I shall best obey it.

BILLIONAIRE. What do you want to do?

DAUGHTER. Send me where the suffering is worst, to the injured in your factories. I will nurse them.

BILLIONAIRE. You don't know what you are saying.

DAUGHTER. I do. You can at least respect my action by believing it. I want to go to the shaft where the catastrophe happened.

BILLIONAIRE. What catastrophe?

DAUGHTER. You put down the agitation yourself.

BILLIONAIRE. Who carries you these tales?

DAUGHTER. Reports in the papers are forbidden. Yes, I know you are powerful.

BILLIONAIRE (*stares at her. A pause*). Let it be. (*He gets up and goes to her.*) I shall not ask you with words. You have a hundred to every one of mine. It is an unequal fight between father and daughter. The end is a foregone conclusion. (*He takes her hands, looks intently at her.*) No... no. Such little hands... such weak hands. (*He anticipates her contradiction with a shake of the head.*) Yes, yes... strong and hard. And only I know what for — to storm fortresses, to heap up ruins, and the victims under them. Shall I tell you who the victim is?

DAUGHTER. Now I don't understand you.

BILLIONAIRE. Do you want to make me your victim? (DAUGHTER *looks at him wonderingly.*) Then turn back. You will find your task lies nearer home. Does it seem a paltry one to you? It seems important to me because it concerns your father.

DAUGHTER (*drawing her hands away*). I have no right, while others...

BILLIONAIRE. Father and Daughter... not by quarrelling! Only by asking and yielding.

DAUGHTER. I thank you today for the lovely years of youth...

BILLIONAIRE. And as lovely a future.

DAUGHTER (*strongly*). Which will be a shining memory through my new life of duty. (*She stands up and puts out her hand.*) My decision was made so easily. Would you make it hard for me by having me change it?

BILLIONAIRE (*without taking her hand*). Where are you going now?

DAUGHTER. To my sisters and brothers.

BILLIONAIRE (*in a dead voice*). So that's where you're going...

DAUGHTER. Will you still know me among the poorest of the poor?

BILLIONAIRE (*supporting himself against the desk*). You're going there... (*The* DAUGHTER *hesitates... turns to the door. The* SERVANT *opens.* DAUGHTER *goes. The* BILLIONAIRE *falters... makes a timid gesture.*) There... there... there... (*Then pulls himself together and rings. The* SECRETARY *enters.*) Shut down the shaft. (*The* SECRETARY *makes a note.*) No! (*Clutching his brow.*) It's here or there... it can't be blown away... no one has power to do that! (*Firmly to the* SECRETARY.) My daughter wishes to dedicate herself to Samaritan work. You will meet her at the shaft and wherever accidents occur in my factories. Repudiate her... I know my daughter no longer.

SECRETARY. Does your daughter know about the coral?

BILLIONAIRE. No; besides the two servants, nobody knows. (*Business-like again.*) We were interrupted...

SECRETARY (*reads from his notebook*). In the afternoon I represent you at Factory 24.

BILLIONAIRE. Tomorrow at noon I shall attend the first half of the Missions meeting myself; I am to be appointed honorary president. Come in the car at two. Under the pretext of fetching something I shall leave the hall. You return in my place and read my contribution to them. I'll give you the papers. (*He looks for it in a drawer of the desk. The green lamp flashes.*)

SECRETARY. Telephone. (*The* BILLIONAIRE *springs up — stares at the lamp.*) I'll come back later to...

BILLIONAIRE (*brusquely*). Stay here!... Go now. Yes... later. (*The* SECRETARY *goes. The* BILLIONAIRE *takes the receiver up slowly.*) Who... (*He lets it fall from his slack fingers onto the desk. His mouth quivers.*) My son... (*The* SERVANT *admits the* SON *and goes. The* BILLIONAIRE *stiffly erect goes towards him.*) I have not seen you the last few days.

SON. Since...

BILLIONAIRE. I am not asking where you were. The time is past for me to keep watch over your comings and goings. You must justify your actions to yourself now. You are grown up.

SON. You make it easy for me...

BILLIONAIRE. Perhaps it was important to tell you this. Is that what you came for?

SON. The reason...

BILLIONAIRE. I will not probe into you to find it out. Sit down. In this stern work-a-day room...

SON. Which you have always jealously kept me out of...

BILLIONAIRE. Is it your ambition to see yourself in my place?

SON. Not in yours.

BILLIONAIRE. I'll not offer it to you. I'm not tired yet. The strings are still taut in my fingers. I shall, and can, go on working. The successor arrives too early. You shall not dethrone me today, nor tomorrow either.

SON. That was not my intention.

BILLIONAIRE. It would help you to prepare your life accordingly.

SON. You narrow the field.

BILLIONAIRE. It is your only chance. The work is my share.

SON. I know how you mean to go on.

BILLIONAIRE. You see, the gates are well barred.

SON. I stand compelled, and therefore I must pacify my conscience?

BILLIONAIRE. A compulsion lies on you too.

SON (after a pause). Will you answer certain questions that burn in me like fire?

BILLIONAIRE. If our boundaries are sharply drawn and understood — yes.

SON. Such deep contradictions split all your dealings.

BILLIONAIRE. Do you concern yourself with me?

SON. I can concern myself with nothing else.

BILLIONAIRE. What has made me so unexpectedly interesting?

SON. This monstrous wealth that you have assembled...

BILLIONAIRE. I have already mentioned my working-powers.

SON. That is not working-power, it is...

BILLIONAIRE. Wherein lies the riddle?

SON. Here the ruthless profits... and there the limitless charity that you give. The "Warm Heart of the Earth"... and the stone that you must bear in your inmost soul.

BILLIONAIRE. I don't want to solve that riddle for you.

SON. Because shame of confessing it holds you back.

BILLIONAIRE. It shall remain my secret.

SON. I tear at the veil you hide behind. You know your wealth is a mortal sin, and stifle knowledge with your "Open Thursday."

BILLIONAIRE. The explanation would not suffice.

SON. No, these gifts of yours are absurd, ridiculous. You can't pay that way for the blood...

BILLIONAIRE. I shed?

SON. No, those are accidents. But you threaten with bloodshed when they dare to cry out.

BILLIONAIRE. Did you see that?

SON. Now I must confess what it nearly drove me to yesterday.

BILLIONAIRE. Why yesterday?

SON. I was at the shaft while you were speaking. You had to appear there yourself to put down that uprising. I was down below in that haggard crowd — and saw you standing there behind the menacing guns. So cold and far away. Your words cracked down upon the gathering like bits of ice. No one dared to lift his voice again. Until you said the works would be shut down, and thousands — children and women — delivered up to hunger. That tore one mouth open.

BILLIONAIRE. So it was you...

SON. Cried out murder! —— And that was not the last.

BILLIONAIRE. It was the last I heard.

SON. Could I have but forgotten that it was my father standing up there — (*He reaches into his pocket, then lays a revolver on the table.*) I do not wish to be tempted twice.

BILLIONAIRE (*shoves the gun aside*). You wouldn't have hit me.

SON. I meant to try it.

BILLIONAIRE (*shaking his head and smiling*). No, not me. So this need not stand as a shadow between us two. (*He puts out his hand.*) Don't let it bother you.

SON (*staring at him*). Do you puff it away like a grain of dust on your coat?

BILLIONAIRE. Not *my* coat.

SON. Forget and forgive?

BILLIONAIRE. So there was nothing to forgive.

SON. No, not for you. No one else can do that. Not that. One allots one's own atonement. And I will make mine so

heavy that maybe on my dying day I shall dare to raise my
eyes again.

BILLIONAIRE. To me?

SON. No, you've taken me back today.  You've got no time to
waste.

BILLIONAIRE. Then whom do you set over you as judge?

SON. The least of your workmen.

BILLIONAIRE. What does that mean?

SON. Until another's despair drives him to the same, I shall stand
down there with them.

BILLIONAIRE. In the uprising?

SON. In the peace that will be spread around if I become one
with them all, and no more than the least of them.

BILLIONAIRE (*pushes the revolver towards him*). The time is now.
                                        (*He turns his face away.*)

SON (*jumps up and runs to him*). Oh, tell me why all this should be —
tell me why.

BILLIONAIRE. Come.  (*He leads him to the photographs.*)  See there?
Gray factories.  Narrow yards.  (*Crossing to the great window
rear.*)  Do you see that?  Where is the earth here — grass
blades — bushes — ?  From such as this I came... Do you
know my life?  I have kept it hidden from you.  But it is read
in all the schools.  I had another life for you to live, and I
have let you live it.  Yours, not mine... I came up out of
nothing, so the books say... I swung myself up out of that very
poverty here — I tell you this now.  And I have never forgotten it.  Not for a single hour have I allowed myself to drowse.
I set these pictures about me — I made this wall of glass so that
none of that might be hidden — it was to goad me into wake-
fulness should I ever fall weary and seek to rest.  It was for
warning and admonition in my blood — only not down again
— not down again to that.

SON (*withdrawing from him*). You...

BILLIONAIRE. I can warn you, you'll believe me.  It swallowed up
my father and my mother.  Its arm was already grasping after
me — but I escaped.

SON. You know...

BILLIONAIRE. A single moment upset you.  I have shuddered

before it for a lifetime.    So terrible is life.... Do you wish to go
down there?

SON. You tear the very last thing out of my hands....

BILLIONAIRE. What is that?

SON. My only excuse for you — that never having known, you
could not grasp the suffering of others.

BILLIONAIRE. I bear the cry within my breast.

SON. Are you a tiger?  Worse, for the tiger knows not what he
does.  You know the torture of your victims... and...

*(He grasps the gun, but lays it down again.)*

BILLIONAIRE. I or another...

SON. Everyone is...

BILLIONAIRE. Be thankful to me.

SON. For this?

BILLIONAIRE. That you need never be who I am.

SON *(calmly)*. Your blood is mine...

BILLIONAIRE. Do you feel it too?

SON. It makes the task worth while.

BILLIONAIRE. Of saving me from the pursuing horror?

SON. Of stifling these terrible desires, and holding steadfast by the
side of the humblest of your employees.  (BILLIONAIRE *stands
stiffly.*)   You can't prevent it.   I shall take work wherever I
can find it.

BILLIONAIRE *(collapsing at his feet)*. Mercy... mercy!!

SON *(coldly)*. Upon whom?

BILLIONAIRE. Mercy!...

SON. And that may be my cry to you on the day you deny me
and my comrades bread.  *(Before the* SERVANTS *have the door
fully open, he is gone, right.)*

BILLIONAIRE *(bounding up at last.  He looks for the revolver and thrusts
it into his pocket)*. Not here... in the heart of the woods.   Green
bowers for the glazing eyes, a bit of blue heaven fluttering down,
tinkle of little birds.  *(Glancing sideways at the walls.)*   Stopped?
Cut off?... Failed in the flight?... Overtaken?...  *(Swinging his
arms about.)*   Let me go!... Don't touch me!... With a child's
terror I fear you, all of you!  *(He runs around the line of photographs, panting, beating upon them with his hands.)*   A way out....
A way out... *(Screaming.)*   A way out!

(SECRETARY *enters from left. Looks questioningly.* BILLIONAIRE *stares at him.*)

SECRETARY (*embarrassed*). Your — papers? (*The* BILLIONAIRE *is silent.*) You wish to give me some papers?

BILLIONAIRE (*staggering to the desk and collapsing in a chair*). Daughter and son... down... down. My children have deserted me. (SECRETARY *silent.* BILLIONAIRE *glances up at him.*) Do you understand what it means to have worked for your children all your life long — and then to have them come to you, their father, and knock the whole thing out of your hands?

SECRETARY. Your son?

BILLIONAIRE (*crying out*). Who will help now to pull down mountains — to cover this? (*The* SECRETARY *looks at him inquiringly.*) Will no one help me now out of the darkness of my past?

SECRETARY. Your achievements are so gigantic, your past needs no embellishment.

BILLIONAIRE. No... ?

SECRETARY. Your work stands out the greater for it.

BILLIONAIRE. I give it up — I'll pay with all my riches — I'll give my life in exchange for any other man's. (*Full of deep feeling.*) Who'll lend me a life that was bright from its first days on? In my son I can find that no more — down... Where is the exchange I have longed for and wooed in the fever of work and the rage for possession — on the heights of my mountainous riches?... In whom can I now sink myself and lose this fear, this turmoil that destroy me? Whose life — smooth and good life — for mine?

SECRETARY (*looking down at him with growing emotion*). Your son has chosen another way. No disappointment is bitterer. But as it repeats itself so many thousandfold, it is as if it were a law. Father and son strive away from each other. It is always a struggle of life and death. (*Pause.*) I opposed my father too, and although I felt the hurt it was to him, yet I was forced to hurt him.... (*After another pause.*) I don't know yet what it was that drove me to it. The desire to try out life myself — perhaps it was that. The need to stand alone is stronger than everything else. (*With heightened animation.*) There are few homes like mine. I have a wonderful youth to look back upon.

I was an only son. Mother and father lavished an infinite treasure of love upon me. And in the shelter of their care I saw and heard nothing of the wretchedness and irritations of everyday. Sunlight lay on all our quiet rooms. Even death passed us by. My parents — even today, they still live only for me. Then I passed into the little university, and the urge for independence began to possess me. I broke away and went into the world.... I have been through many a dark hour. Buffeted here and there — but deep down nothing could shake me, for I possessed the greatest riches of all, endless and inexhaustible — the living memory of a happy childhood. Whatever might come later could be only waves upon the surface of a lake whose clearness mirrored the blue of heaven. So untroubled, so calm, within me lies that perfect past.

(*The* BILLIONAIRE *has raised his face toward him. He listens with deepest intentness. The* SECRETARY *gazes into space.*)

BILLIONAIRE (*looking about the table*). The papers. (SECRETARY *gives them to him. He speaks with a great effort.*) Go. *The* SECRETARY *takes the papers, turns to the door. The* BILLIONAIRE *pulls the revolver out of his pocket and presses the trigger. His* SECRETARY, *shot through the back, falls. The* BILLIONAIRE *stands immobile.*) My life — for another's... that was bright... from the first day on.... (*Goes slowly forward to the body and bends down... slips the coral off the watch-chain. Holds it before him on his open palm.*) This is the life I thirst for... every day of this life.... I covet and long for. (*Flings back his head.*) Those bright days shall make me happy....

(*He slips the coral on his watch-chain. Then wrenches open the door and shoots again into the air. The two* SERVANTS *rush in. One remains in the doorway standing — the other bends over the* SECRETARY.)

FIRST SERVANT (*in the doorway*). The coral?

SECOND SERVANT (*kneeling upright, shaking his head*). Arrest the Secretary.

## ACT FOUR

*Room of examining magistrate — blue square with many entrances by iron-barred doors behind which narrow passages lose themselves. A hanging lamp of clear glass lights the place brightly. One small iron table at which the clerk — with eye-shade — is seated.*

*The* FIRST JUDGE *is standing in an attitude of reflection. The two* SERVANTS, *left.* GUARD *comes in, right.*

FIRST JUDGE. Put the light out.

    (GUARD *strides to switchboard, the lamp goes out. Frosted lamps glow in the corners.*)

FIRST JUDGE (*goes to the table and takes up the receiver*). Relief, please. (*To the* SERVANTS.) You may now... (*On second thoughts.*) Or wait another minute or two. (*He has the clerk give him the dossier, reads, shakes his head. To the* SERVANTS.) Did the secretary ever allow the coral to... (*Quickly.*) It is possible that the coral had been exchanged *for once*, to...

    (*The* SECOND JUDGE *comes in, rear.*)

SECOND JUDGE. No result.

FIRST JUDGE (*gives him the papers*). Nothing more than that I now have certain doubts.

SECOND JUDGE. There's something like genius in the consistency with which he persists in masking his person.

FIRST JUDGE. His silence is certainly consistent enough.

SECOND JUDGE. He does not respond to the most obvious inquiries as to his earlier life — after all the foundation of every examination. But he receives them all as though he himself did not know. We have had to gather the data all ourselves.

FIRST JUDGE. Yes, it seems as unknown to him as though he heard of his own life today for the first time.

SECOND JUDGE. Is he simply leading us on...

FIRST JUDGE. What do you mean by that?

SECOND JUDGE. Are we to preach his past to him?

FIRST JUDGE. To what end?

SECOND JUDGE. To wear us out.

FIRST JUDGE. He's almost done that to me already.

SECOND JUDGE (*reads — lets the sheet fall*). He does not argue the point about the coral having been found on him.

FIRST JUDGE. But he refuses to admit he's the secretary.

SECOND JUDGE. Then how does he explain the coral on his watch-chain. (*Reading.*) "This repeated question the prisoner consistently refuses to answer."

FIRST JUDGE (*to* SERVANTS). Was there never a plan to confuse you in the same connection for certain purposes?

FIRST SERVANT. No. Our task would have been impossible if there had been.

SECOND SERVANT. The murdered man set great store by the personal watch he set over his person.

SECOND JUDGE. It's perfectly transparent to me. Of course, it's a matter of the fellow's neck. That's a thing one rather jibs at. But we have the son's affidavit. In the conversation that had taken place just before between father and son, the son renounced his father's riches. The daughter renounced it too. The secretary had heard the excited talk next door and could not withstand the temptation to make himself their successor. So he made no bones about it and went ahead. Only the coral he hadn't time to exchange, though he would have liked to. (*To the* SERVANTS.) The shot brought you there at once.

SECOND SERVANT. I got him as he was trying to make it out of the door.

SECOND JUDGE. Did he try to get away?

FIRST SERVANT. We didn't open the door — he did.

FIRST JUDGE. Why should he run away when he gives himself out for the one who was attacked?

SECOND JUDGE (*puts the dossier down*). That very attempt at flight proves it. The report made more noise than he had reckoned with. He was bewildered and expected to get away, but the plan was knocked to pieces by the servants' watchfulness. Now he has to recall the part he first meant to play.

FIRST JUDGE. But the resemblance is extraordinary, anyway. I've never experienced such a case of doubles.

SECOND JUDGE. Yes, if it weren't for the coral, we should be groping in the dark and never find a way out. (*Seizing the papers.*) Besides, how does he account for the attack which is alleged to have been made by the secretary?

FIRST JUDGE. He says nothing.

SECOND JUDGE. Because there never was such an attack.

FIRST JUDGE. But you said he wished to put himself in the murdered man's place.

SECOND JUDGE (*wavers*). So that would be a reason, wouldn't it?

FIRST JUDGE. To prompt him to kill.

SECOND JUDGE. So he acted under stress.

FIRST JUDGE (*excited*). But he is the secretary.

SECOND JUDGE (*rubbing his eyes*). I am really worn out. The sharp light — the passiveness of that man who hardly bothers to defend himself ——

FIRST JUDGE. I am thinking of disposing of certain means to make him more active. If showing him the coral has no effect... (*He picks it up from the table.*) The thing looks like a drop of blood still hanging onto the murderer.... (*He lays it down. To the* SERVANTS.) I don't need you any longer.

SECOND SERVANT. What time tomorrow?

FIRST JUDGE. Let's hope this is the last. Ten times over the same litany. If you're needed, I'll send for you. (*They go.*)

SECOND JUDGE. Do you promise yourself better success tonight?

FIRST JUDGE. Nothing more than a full confession.

SECOND JUDGE (*taken aback*). How do you expect to bring him to that?

FIRST JUDGE. He insists he's the billionaire. Very well, I'll bring his children to face him. Now nature can be the judge. If he hesitates a single moment to approach them — for we know by their own testimony that he loved his son and daughter above everything — then he has as good as confessed. He can face the coral — it's a dead object — but before the weight of his victim's son and daughter's eyes nobody could stand up. And as he is no professional criminal, I'll have him break down like a straw.

SECOND JUDGE. Honestly, I'm completely played out.

FIRST JUDGE. Stretch out on the sofa and have a good sleep. If you don't mind my disturbing you, I'll shout the news of our deliverance from this fortnight's martyrdom across to you.

SECOND JUDGE. I'll go straight to the country for a week.

FIRST JUDGE. And I'll write a book about the case — popular

edition of several hundred thousand! (FIRST JUDGE *goes off*. SECOND JUDGE *goes towards left and rings a bell beside a door. Led in by a* GUARD, *the* SON *and* DAUGHTER *in black — left*.) It is after all necessary that I bring you actually to confront the man. Gladly as I would have spared you this painful experience, the obstinate denial which my colleague has been unable to break down in him forces me to this step. I see no other way to get a confession out of him. And we must have the confession absolutely.

SON. Instruct us how we are to behave.

SECOND JUDGE. I intend to deal a surprise blow. He must not be allowed the least time for reflection. I must ask you to come absolutely noiselessly and not in any way to betray your presence here. For the present wait there in the back of the corridor — the guard stands round about the door. That won't strike him as peculiar. (*To* GUARD.) During the hearing I shall arrange to come this side so that the prisoner will have his back to your door. As soon as I pull out my handkerchief, admit the lady and gentleman.

SON. Is our task over when we have confronted him?

SECOND JUDGE. Obviously, I shall see that it last no longer than it must. But try to look at him intently. That is important. Especially you, madam, I should like to impress this upon. Take hold of yourself. You are about to experience the most horrible thing one could well encounter. You will think you are looking at your father who is dead.

SON. But some distinction must be possible.

SECOND JUDGE. We should have had it easy, then. The resemblance is complete. No bodily mark exists. Nature has played this trick on us.

SON. Only that coral can decide?

SECOND JUDGE. And irrevocably. Therefore do not forget that you have the secretary before you. (SON *and* DAUGHTER *off left with the* GUARD. *The* GUARD *comes back and waits behind the iron-barred door. To the* FIRST GUARD.) Bring him in. (*The* GUARD *switches on the light. Off right* SECOND JUDGE *puts on blue-glass spectacles.* GUARD *lets the* BILLIONAIRE *precede him into the room and remains at the door. His hands are bound in front of him*

*with thin steel rope.   He prepares to stand as he is now accustomed to do
— without a sign of excitement.   SECOND JUDGE for the moment
does not notice him.   Then he takes the revolver from the table and
goes — merely interested in the weapon — to the BILLIONAIRE.)*
Where do you buy this make?   (BILLIONAIRE *is silent.*)   I'd
like one myself.   But I can't very well pinch one that the law
has confiscated.   (BILLIONAIRE *smiles thinly.*)   A close-kept
secret?

BILLIONAIRE.  A present.

SECOND JUDGE.  *Indeed?   Who from?*   (BILLIONAIRE *shakes his head.*)
Surely from no tender hand.

BILLIONAIRE.  From the tenderest.

SECOND JUDGE.  Oh, come, that is unnatural.

BILLIONAIRE.  Yes — it was unnatural.

SECOND JUDGE.  Was it for you to use on yourself if ever you should
be untrue?

BILLIONAIRE.  I was the target.

SECOND JUDGE.  Who wanted to shoot you?   (BILLIONAIRE *slowly
nods his head.*)   Did you tear the weapon out of his hand?

BILLIONAIRE.  He put it down on the desk.

SECOND JUDGE *(quickly).*  The Billionaire?   (BILLIONAIRE *silent.
The* SECOND JUDGE *nods with relief and goes to the right.*)   Let's
reconstruct the situation.   Turn towards me.   (BILLIONAIRE
*does so.*)   Wait a bit.   The metal's got a bit dull — it must have
shone rather before.

(*He pulls out his handkerchief and rubs it.   The* GUARD *left,
moves back from the door.*)

THE SECOND JUDGE.  Of course it's all poppy-cock about the gun
lying about on the table.   In fact your whole story is so completely muddled that there's no use trying to grope for sense
in it any more.   The long and short of the matter is this:
under some pretext or other you got behind your victim's
back, pulled the gun out of your trousers pocket, and stood all
set and ready, exactly as you see me standing now, with this
same distance between you — (*The* GUARD *has come in with
the* SON *and* DAUGHTER.   *They stand waiting.*)   Turn your back!

THE BILLIONAIRE (*turns around.   Without hesitation he goes toward
his* SON *and* DAUGHTER).  Children!   In black?   Has there

been a death — close to us? You wonder why I don't know of it. I am out of touch with you all for the present, locked up under the strictest watch. An intolerable error that must be cleared up first. I am all imaginable pains to destroy this dreadful suspicion. But the courts are conscientious. Every trifle has weight. A bit of coral that was found on me — the revolver there which I am supposed to have carried in my pocket. (*To the* SON.) Will you not explain where it came from?

SON (*mastering his agitation*). It is my property, sir.

SECOND JUDGE. How did it come into the secretary's possession?

SON. I laid it on the table by my father.

SECOND JUDGE. Valuable information. The revolver, lying on the open table-top, prompted the deed. What did you give it to your father for?

SON. I — cannot answer that question.

BILLIONAIRE. I have not betrayed you, either.

SON (*sharply*). Because you know nothing about it.

BILLIONAIRE. You seem to be talking to someone else, not to me. Have I become a stranger to you because I stand under suspicion? (*With a strangely watchful expression.*) Do you both believe I am the secretary? You — my own children — are you seeing the secretary in me?

SON (*wearily*). Sir, do you need my sister and me here any longer?
(*The* DAUGHTER *screams — covers her face with her hands.*)

SECOND JUDGE. I thank you, no. (*The* SON, *supporting the* DAUGHTER, *go. The* JUDGE *walks up and down the room.*) Monstrous. The utmost extreme of stubbornness! — Are you not ashamed? (*Disconcerted.*) Smiling, are you?

BILLIONAIRE. I saw my children ——

SECOND JUDGE. Do you take pleasure in other people's torment?

BILLIONAIRE. But they did not see me.

SECOND JUDGE. They saw the murderer of their father. You are he. You — his secretary. Don't bring your idiotic fairy-tale forward again, please — we know it. And were the coral not the powerful proof it is, this would have unmasked you — that those two whom you brazenly pretended were your children, rejected you as an utter stranger.

BILLIONAIRE (*imperviously*). That — does not suffice.

SECOND JUDGE. Are you sure? Because you refuse your confession? We excuse you that now. You may continue to shroud yourself in your monumental silence. The time has come for us to speak! (*He signs to the* GUARD *who leads the* BILLIONAIRE *away. The* JUDGE *telephones.*) Relief, please. (*Loudly.*) Yes — relief! (*Goes excitedly up and down. Stamps angrily.*) This is... (FIRST JUDGE *hastens in, rear.*) You thought you heard wrong, I expect. No, there's no change. The man is not to be caught. He confronts them without a tremor — and finds fault with them for talking coldly to him. (*The* FIRST JUDGE *reads.*) We're done now, I think.

FIRST JUDGE. No. I'm for pressing him hard — this thing interests me. (*Striking his brow.*) Simple as daylight!

SECOND JUDGE. Were you enlightened in a dream?

FIRST JUDGE. I am furious.

SECOND JUDGE. Hardly the state of mind for brilliant discoveries.

FIRST JUDGE. He's transsubstantiated himself into the billionaire.

SECOND JUDGE. And expects to stay there.

FIRST JUDGE. Therefore we must now reverse the process ——

SECOND JUDGE. Abracadabra — one, two, three.

FIRST JUDGE. And get him back into the secretary.

SECOND JUDGE. By what sleight of hand do you mean to effect this?

(*The* GUARD *comes in at the right and switches off the arc-light.*)

FIRST JUDGE. He must be born all over again! — That's it. I'll put him back in his cradle and let him kick and crow as happy as the day's long. So far the Billionaire has never entered his life — that is a later chapter not to be recalled by a single syllable. I'll set him up such a hole-proof picture of his life and wrap him so gently and gradually in childhood recollections that he shall entirely forget what he's here for. (*Searching through the papers.*) We've all the material here — not a detail missing. A strikingly bright and happy past, too; he hasn't hardened all the way through yet. I shall have him as soft as butter once I start bringing his good days back to him.

SECOND JUDGE. He didn't mind facing his victim's children ——

FIRST JUDGE. Children are something else. In the last resort it is one's own life that counts.

SECOND JUDGE. I should hate to give up the case as hopeless.

FIRST JUDGE. Everything we've tried so far has fallen through, and my attempt may do the same. But there is a certain power of suggestion in delving into the past.

SECOND JUDGE. Would you like the glasses?

FIRST JUDGE. We'll have the lights down this time. (*To* GUARD.) Don't switch on the light. Bring him in. (GUARD *goes, right.*) That alone will be a kindness to him. And for the rest I shall find the right "Now Granny will tell you a story" tone.

SECOND JUDGE. With the wicked wolf at the end.

FIRST JUDGE. That gets hold of the murderer. (*The* SECOND JUDGE *goes. The* GUARD *comes in with the* BILLIONAIRE. *The* FIRST JUDGE *is deep in the documents before him.*) This love of animals is truly beautiful. (*Glancing up at the* BILLIONAIRE.) Had it really a black spot in the middle of its forehead? (*The* BILLIONAIRE *raises his head obediently.*) The puppy you saved from drowning. The river was pretty shallow there, I daresay? One doesn't venture very far out at ten years old. (*The* BILLIONAIRE *breathes heavily.*) Just a bit of a stream running by the little town, wasn't it? No strong current, of course — or did the tides run high in spring? (*The* BILLIONAIRE *begins to sway curiously from the waist.*) Then the water would go sweeping by with all sorts of bushes and things it had uprooted, and sometimes it flooded the banks and got into the cellars. That meant saving the family stores, and what a jolly salvaging party it always was! Father and Mother at it as hard as they could go and the boy helping like a Trojan, naturally. Always in everybody's way, but convinced that he was being absolutely indispensable, eh? (*The* BILLIONAIRE *nods slowly.*) Yes — a little bit of a town like that has its catastrophes too. Every day a different one. The wind pulls the cap off a fellow's head and rushes round the corner with it —— (*Suddenly.*) What color was your school-cap — green?

BILLIONAIRE (*with a chuckling smile*). I've...

FIRST JUDGE. You don't remember the color distinctly?

BILLIONAIRE. I've... forgotten so much.

FIRST JUDGE (*sharply watching him. After a pause*). Doesn't that sort of thing last long with you? I mean one usually likes to recall one's pleasant times long after they're gone. After all, they're our only indestructible possession. You especially could refresh yourself with your remembrances, for the picture of your past is remarkably charming and bright. Yes, you had an enviable youth. (*Turning over the documents.*) It is a pleasure even to read about it. (BILLIONAIRE *stealing a look into the papers.*) Light and sunshine — sunshine and light. No trace of a shadow anywhere. (*Glancing up.*) You must be inexpressibly grateful to your parents, aren't you?

BILLIONAIRE (*in a tone almost like singing*). My parents...

FIRST JUDGE. I see them with their hands outspread over their only child in a gesture of infinite love. Did they ever once strike you?

BILLIONAIRE. Did they... never once strike me?

FIRST JUDGE. Yes, tell me.

BILLIONAIRE. Yes... you tell me.

FIRST JUDGE (*looks at him in astonishment. Then jestingly*). Very well, let us now open the Book of the Past. Chapter one — The Home. A little provincial town set in a pleasant green landscape. Father — pastor. Do you see him now?

BILLIONAIRE (*groping before him*). ... set in a green landscape... Father... pastor...

FIRST JUDGE. Chapter two — The son is born and becomes the centre of life at the parsonage. Every care is lavished on him. He waxes and thrives.... You will hardly remember your very earliest childhood?

BILLIONAIRE. Now... I remember.

FIRST JUDGE. In the next section you're fairly under way. Schooldays. The school is not large... there are few pupils, and you are the best among them. Learning comes easily to you... you encounter no obstacles... this period is a thornless path. Or perhaps you remember a cloud?

BILLIONAIRE. If you know of none...

FIRST JUDGE. Good, then there was none. Let's go on. This, then, was the frame in which your life was set. It is seldom that a young man has things made as smooth for him as they were for you... and your own inclinations met your parents' plans half way. To a rare degree you developed the capacity for becoming a happy man. I can think of nothing finer than this complete harmony between a person and his environment. No disrupting experience to poison the blood... only the quiet succession of days like flowers on the chains children weave!... (*Intensely.*) Doesn't it flood your heart with warmth to hear me recite this evangel of your past to you? It must awaken in you such wistful longing for that paradise you used to wander in... in your so cherished and favoured youth. Sheltered and loved — protected against the blows that others have to suffer even at that age. It is like looking into a crystal sea, clear down to the very bed where only bright round pebbles lie on the white sand and nothing else. Say yes to that happy past of yours — and save the most precious of all possessions.

BILLIONAIRE. ... the best... of all possessions....

FIRST JUDGE (*in growing excitement*). Do you say yes to that past?

BILLIONAIRE (*faintly breathing the words*). Yes... yes... yes!...

FIRST JUDGE. Now you will sign your deposition.

BILLIONAIRE (*already raising his hand*). Yes.

FIRST JUDGE (*to* GUARD). Undo his hand. (*To the* BILLIONAIRE.) Your acquiescence has convicted you. That past is the secretary's. You are the secretary. (*As the* BILLIONAIRE *hesitates.*) I am telling you this so that you sign correctly — with the secretary's name. (*The* BILLIONAIRE *writes in the air.*) What are you doing? Can't you remember your own handwriting any more? (*The* BILLIONAIRE *signs.*) The examination is closed. I hope that you will not return again to your former denial of your identity. From now on it would be useless. (*He signs to the* GUARD.)

THE BILLIONAIRE (*as the* GUARD *leads him out, right*).... The best... the best... (*He goes.*)

FIRST JUDGE (*stands thinking. Then telephones*). Comprehensive confession.

SECOND JUDGE (*entering*). It sounds like a fairy-tale really. (*Reads in the dossier.*) Worked like a charm. Didn't he see the trap you were decoying him into?

FIRST JUDGE (*ruminating*). Don't you think it extraordinary?

SECOND JUDGE. He was overtired.

FIRST JUDGE. That was not my impression. In fact he seemed

... to come to life as he listened to his past.   (*The* GUARD *enters,
right.   Quickly.*)  Has he anything to tell me?

SECOND JUDGE.  Hasn't he already gone back to the other?

GUARD.  No.

SECOND JUDGE.  Has he gone to pieces?

GUARD.  He stands up straight, looking upwards and muttering.

FIRST JUDGE.  Just as he did here... in a dream....

SECOND JUDGE (*after a silence*).  Well, there's a terrible awakening
in store for him.

## ACT FIVE

*Small square yard sunk between the shafts of prison-walls on four sides.
Patch of mean grass with iron bench in the centre, fastened into the ground.
A low door left and a high, narrow door rear.*

GUARD *leads* BILLIONAIRE *in from the left, a convict now in black
linen with red neckband.*

BILLIONAIRE.  The ante-yard of death?

GUARD.  You have an hour to stay here.

BILLIONAIRE (*nods*).  The last short hour has struck.   (*Looking
about.*)  A gentle custom... feet tread upon green grass and
heaven's blue streams overhead.            (*He stands motionless.*)

GUARD.  Do you wish to see your visitors?

BILLIONAIRE.  Ah — the curious have come?   I shall not resist.

(GUARD *goes.*  BILLIONAIRE *sits on the bench.*  GUARD *admits the*
MAN IN GRAY, *and goes.*)

MAN IN GRAY (*has undergone an obvious transformation.  His suit —
the same color as before — is immaculately tailored.  He wears light
spats over patent leather shoes, gray top hat with rounded crown, white
kid gloves with black stitching.  Comes rushing in at the* BILLIONAIRE,
*stretching out his hand*).  Still in time.  This is luck indeed.  I
should have put in an appearance before this, but business, you
know.... Brimstone mine... big thing.  Yearly profits of...
But for the moment you're rather out of that world of income
and dividends and so forth, of course.  Besides I didn't come
here to talk to you on that subject.  I came to thank you.

BILLIONAIRE.  I didn't know...

MAN IN GRAY. You don't mind if I sit down beside you, do you... on the bench of repentance. One can have at least a quarter of an hour's peace and quiet. Well, then, from the bottom of my heart, thanks, thanks, and thanks again.

BILLIONAIRE. I wish you would tell me.

MAN IN GRAY. I am the Man in Gray who came to you once with a manifest that was to give harmony to all the world at one single stroke — and you refused to sign it. At the same time — the thing I find most admirable about it now is that you should have taken the time; I shouldn't have — you demonstrated to me the hopelessness of my beneficent project. Your arguments struck me like the blows of a club... and I left the "Warm Heart of the Earth," hurling curses back at you strong enough to fell an ox. Is it getting dark?

BILLIONAIRE (*with a thin smile*). You are mistaken.

MAN IN GRAY. I wished you straight into the deepest pit of hell.

BILLIONAIRE. Not me....

MAN IN GRAY. You never felt the impact?

BILLIONAIRE. Because the conversation you refer to was with the Billionaire, not with me.

MAN IN GRAY (*laughs unrestrainedly*). You need not play your rôle before me. Just put your secretary in your pocket. Or perhaps you haven't one in these pyjamas they put you in for the night without end? (*Tapping him on the shoulder.*) You're still my man fleeing from the terror.

BILLIONAIRE (*taken aback*). Don't talk so loud.

MAN IN GRAY. Don't worry — I shall neither betray you nor set you free. Surely I have no cause for such an act of ingratitude. Are you satisfied with me?

BILLIONAIRE. You are the only one....

MAN IN GRAY. Your trial was a pleasure to me. I wouldn't have disturbed it at any price. It was a stroke of genius to shove yourself into the secretary's skin and lap up the candy of his bright past. I could hear your lips smacking as they kept stuffing you with that glorious grub. How does your stomach feel now — good?

BILLIONAIRE. It was salvation.

MAN IN GRAY. While the son — that rebirth you'd arranged for yourself, all peace and joy, and so forth — turned away from you.

BILLIONAIRE. Not a word of that!

MAN IN GRAY. But you have no more to fear now.  And from the safe bank one can look back over the turbulent sea with a malicious joy that is wholesome too.  You've saved yourself — and in a few minutes your head won't be in danger from it any more.  You can be sure of that.

BILLIONAIRE. What do you thank me for?

MAN IN GRAY. Does not a casual glance upon my outer man tell you that?

BILLIONAIRE. You are dressed with a sort of challenging splendour.

MAN IN GRAY. Merely to illustrate the inner structure.  I'm in flight.

BILLIONAIRE. You?  From what?

MAN IN GRAY. From the world as you made it.

BILLIONAIRE. Then are you not going to curse me again?

MAN IN GRAY. I bless you.  You took me out of my pink clouds and set me on sober earth.  Bolt upright on both feet.  Your law ruled — flight!  Woe to the stumbler, tramp him down. The flight surges over him, on and away.  No grace, no mercy. Forward — forward!... Chaos is behind!

BILLIONAIRE. And did you gain on it?

MAN IN GRAY. I was a good pupil.  I heap up riches and set that glittering hill between them and me.  Immense energy develops when once the law is known.  Even in sleep one races on and springs out of bed in the morning with new plans ready.  A wild chase.  Thank heaven you did not take your secret with you to the grave — now I can announce to all mankind its true salvation.

BILLIONAIRE. Will you do that?

MAN IN GRAY. It is already done.  My leavings set them all wildly scrambling.  All bonds snapped, the fight rages all along the line.  Each against each, no hope for quarter.

BILLIONAIRE. And what is the goal you are storming towards?

MAN IN GRAY. Nonsense, there is no goal.

BILLIONAIRE. But there is.

MAN IN GRAY (looks at him disconcerted). Don't torture me.

BILLIONAIRE. It lies in the beginning.

MAN IN GRAY. Yes — you had all the luck. You can afford to laugh at us. Besides you removed the cause that spurs on the race. But that remains a single instance — we can't all find a double in this world.... And I'll tell you something, too. (*With a gesture round his neck.*) And most of us would shy at the price too.

BILLIONAIRE. Do you call it high?

MAN IN GRAY (*standing up*). You can best estimate that yourself according to your own measure. You were never pettifogging when it came to paying the bill. I should like to stay longer, but... your time is limited too. Anyway let it be some joy to you that your great discovery will not vanish with you. (*Offering both his hands.*) Head up, then!

BILLIONAIRE. As long as it lasts.

MAN IN GRAY (*laughs. Waving his hat*). Au revoir!

BILLIONAIRE. Where?

MAN IN GRAY. Well — what is the correct leave-taking in a case like this anyway!

(*The* GUARD *opens the door rear. The* MAN IN GRAY *goes. The* BILLIONAIRE *sits on the bench without moving, his chin on the back of his hand.*)

(*The* GUARD *admits the* SON. GUARD *goes.*)

THE SON (*hesitates — then goes quickly to the* BILLIONAIRE, *reaching out his hand*). I have come — to forgive you. (*The* BILLIONAIRE *looks slowly up at him.*) Don't you recognize me?

BILLIONAIRE. Oh, yes.

SON. My decision has taken you by surprise. Perhaps it is strange that a son should do such a thing. But that is the least. I want to save you.

BILLIONAIRE. Have you climbing-irons and rope-ladder all ready?

SON. I will recognize you as my father. (*The* BILLIONAIRE *stands up and goes behind the bench.*) Don't make it harder for me than it is already. I am as guilty as you, for I had aimed that gun at him, I had meant that very bullet for him, too. It's of no importance who it was that fired.

BILLIONAIRE. This is all incomprehensible to me.

SON. Believe me guilty with you, so that I need not flounder any longer in these frightful things.

BILLIONAIRE. But have you considered what I did?

SON. You did what we must all do at the sight of madness dancing in power.

BILLIONAIRE. Was your father mad?

SON. Power is madness.

BILLIONAIRE. Yes... he was powerful.

SON. And guilty! Behind your guilt stands his — colossal and inextinguishable. You are his victim as I am — as all others who think at all.

BILLIONAIRE. And do they all desire to kill?

SON. They must — the compulsion is not to be withstood. The temptation comes from those who thrust themselves above them. By force they rise, by force they shall be torn down.

BILLIONAIRE. You make it easy for yourself...

SON. Did not my final confirmation come from you? I know your life — I read the reports breathlessly as they appeared. The sweetest childhood, the gentlest youth — where was there a sign of impulse to violence?

BILLIONAIRE. Your childhood was no less sweet...

SON. And yet I sought a weapon when the time came. I meant to punish, being swept away by my sense of justice — you meant to enrich yourself. The sight of force seduced you. My father set you the example — he always acted regardless of others — and so long as such examples are before us, so long will we be tempted.

BILLIONAIRE. Do you mean to wipe out evil example — is that it?

SON. With your help.

BILLIONAIRE. What can I do?

SON. You are to renounce your position so high above the rest of us and come down to our level.

BILLIONAIRE. Your father should do this, you mean.

SON. I shall go to the judge and declare that from this conversation with you I realized that you were my father after all.

BILLIONAIRE. And the coral?

SON. Nothing must stand in the way. We have an immense task before us. The fate of mankind is at stake. We shall unite in the heat of work — and in our untiring zeal we shall be bound together as father and son.

BILLIONAIRE (*shaking his head*). No — I could never so belie myself.

SON. When your life depends on it?

BILLIONAIRE. Because the life you offer me depends on it.

SON. It will take some overcoming. It cost me a struggle to come to you like this. But I did so for the sake of higher things. My father's shadow stands behind you now. Serve this work and you will drive it away.

BILLIONAIRE. Not that way.

SON. I swear to you...

BILLIONAIRE. What?

SON. That I will be a son to you — a son who never lost his father.

BILLIONAIRE (*comes close to him*). Shall I name my condition?

SON. Anything.

BILLIONAIRE. Will you be the son to me that your father wished you to be?

SON. What does that mean?

BILLIONAIRE. Go back again to the bank where the sun is shining — then I shall lend myself to your wish. (*The* SON *stares at him.*) Otherwise the shadow that stands behind me will never be driven away.

SON. How are you talking to me?

BILLIONAIRE. Like your father. Is this first test too hard? (*The* SON *looks at him now timidly. The* BILLIONAIRE *puts his hand on his shoulder.*) It is good of you to have come once more. One loves to look at people who are young. Have you not a sister? Was she also ready to accept me as her father? You are decoys, but there are no more bridges. I am only more convinced than ever now. Leave me in my garden here. Green, is it not? And go on to your battlefield. It may be that peace does lead to war, but the man that comes out of that bath of blood tries to save himself. You would not help me, so I took my fate into my own hands. Should you rebuke me now, then, for refusing to lend you my support? (*He leads him towards the left.*) In no hour of your active life are you to abuse me. You have made bold plans... and if one or other of them should fail... or if, in the long run, they all should fail...

don't belabour your father's memory with rage and reproaches for his not protecting you against disappointment... for reasons which it would obviously take too long to go into here. (*The* PRIEST *comes.*) There, you see — the one indispensable element is lacking — time! (*The* SON *goes. The* BILLIONAIRE *stands looking after him. The* PRIEST *has gone to the bench and looks at the* BILLIONAIRE, *who turns towards him.*) The third and last guest?

PRIEST. After what I have just seen, my task is very hard. You have received the greatest consolation your fellow-men could give you — reconciliation with the son of that unfortunate father.

BILLIONAIRE. You are mistaken. We parted at odds with each other. And if I accompanied him to the door, that was because I was the stronger of the two. I was supporting the defeated.

PRIEST. Did he not come to see you?

BILLIONAIRE. He set a trap for me to fall into. But I was on my guard.

PRIEST. Did he forgive you?

BILLIONAIRE. Had he reason to?

PRIEST. You took his father from him.

BILLIONAIRE (*sitting down*). Do you believe in the right of reprisal?

PRIEST. Earthly things must be allowed to run their course.

BILLIONAIRE. I exercised the right of reprisal, nothing more.

PRIEST. What injury had he done you?

BILLIONAIRE. The choice falls blindly... this one or another. They killed my mother and father both.

PRIEST (*shrugs his shoulders*). Your parents met a peaceful end.

BILLIONAIRE. Then what reason could I have had to kill?

PRIEST. In an incomprehensible turmoil of spirit you stretched out your hand for another man's riches.

BILLIONAIRE (*nods*). In an incomprehensible turmoil — that stamps your wisdom. You roll heaven from over me to breathe in joy beneath. You overwhelm me with your gifts.

PRIEST (*after a pause*). You wished to have the coral; I have brought it for you. (*The* BILLIONAIRE *takes it and looks at it.*) You can dismiss me, if you wish... or close your ear to my words.

BILLIONAIRE. Speak.

PRIEST (*sits down beside him*). From the refuge which is opened to us when we leave this life which is like a house with dark windows...

BILLIONAIRE. Tell me about the house with dark windows.

PRIEST. From that refuge light could enter at a wider door than...

BILLIONAIRE. Yes, that is it.

PRIEST. And there is no such thing as too late. In one second the infinite treasure may be won.

BILLIONAIRE. What treasure?

PRIEST. The new Being that waits behind this span of life.

BILLIONAIRE. Does it lie in the future?

PRIEST. That future is his who knocks with a humble hand.

BILLIONAIRE (*shaking his head*). The old error remains.

PRIEST. Safe promises are given us.

BILLIONAIRE. Flight into the kingdom of heaven. The cross and vinegar are no salvation. In the end it is not to be found — in the beginning it is there, your paradise.

PRIEST. We are dispossessed...

BILLIONAIRE. Does that darken recognition? ... I don't want to upset you or knock your tools out of your hand. But the deepest truth will never be proclaimed by you or the thousand of you. It is found always only by one man alone. And it is so enormous that it becomes incapable of all effectiveness.... You seek a refuge — I could tell you that you are on the wrong path. The goal jumps ahead of you a hundred times over and each time with a blow in your back. And your flight towards sanctuary goes ever more wildly forward. But you never arrive. Not that way... not that way.

PRIEST. Then tell me this: what is it that gives you — I can find no other word for it — your solemn tranquillity?

BILLIONAIRE. I have reached the paradise again that lies behind all of us. A deed of violence brought me through its gates — one needs that, for the angels on either side bear swords of flame. And now I stand amidst the loveliest meadow green. And the blue of heaven streams over my head.

PRIEST. Are you thinking of your pleasant childhood?

BILLIONAIRE. Simple, is it not? "Become like little children..." Wisdom is only the matter of a phrase, too.

PRIEST. Why can we not remain children always?

BILLIONAIRE. That is a riddle you will not solve today or tomorrow either! (*The* PRIEST *stares out before him.*) ... Do you see this?

PRIEST. It is the coral you asked for as your last request.

BILLIONAIRE. Do you know how it grows out of the bed of the sea? To the surface of the water — no higher. There it stands washed by the tides — moulded by the sea and bound forever to it. Fish are little events that go by in tiny tumult. Fascinating...

PRIEST. What do you mean?

BILLIONAIRE. Only to open one corner of the case the riddle is enclosed in. What would be best? Never to come out into the storm that drives towards the shore and drags us in its wake. There turmoil roars and drags us into the frenzy of life. We are all driven on... as we are all driven out of our paradise of quiet.... Bits broken off the dim coral-tree... wounded from the first day with a wound that does not heal, but burns and burns. It is the fearful pain goads us on our way.... What is that in your hand? (*He takes the* PRIEST's *hand with the black crucifix and lifts it high.*) That only dulls the pain. (*He holds the red coral to his breast with both hands.*) This delivers from sorrow! (*The high narrow door is opened. The* BILLIONAIRE *stands up.*)

PRIEST. I cannot go with you.

(*The* BILLIONAIRE *goes towards the door, walking steadily.*)


CURTAIN

# SIX CHARACTERS IN SEARCH OF
# AN AUTHOR
## (SEI PERSONAGGI IN CERCA D'AUTORE)

### A COMEDY IN THE MAKING

#### By LUIGI PIRANDELLO

*Translated by EDWARD STORER*

# SIX CHARACTERS IN SEARCH OF AN AUTHOR

IN PIRANDELLO'S playwriting two qualities stand out. The first is the persistent attitude of mind which he turns toward his world. The second is his quality of innovation in form which derives partly from a carefree creative energy and partly from an architectural ability which enables the author to create new patterns to meet his needs. Of both these qualities the play before us, *Six Characters in Search of an Author*, is the outstanding exemplar in the author's work. Pirandello's peculiar attitude is so clearly revealed in all his work, he so effectively speaks for himself, that interpretation is unnecessary. Pirandello is not so much a commentator and critic as he is the observer with keen and corrective judgment. Toward everything he turns the light of his scepticism, a scepticism that refuses to think anything is settled because men have already agreed upon the answers. His scepticism is therefore not so much nihilistic as affirmative. He does not so much deny reality as he affirms the reality of much that before had been denied. We have assumed that reality exists in certain places, that certain positions are right. Why not assume the opposite? It need not be said that such an attitude as this greatly enlarges the area of vital experience open to the dramatist. We come now to the matter of form. Pirandello has called this play "A Comedy in the Making." As such it is to be compared with the first play in this book, Echegaray's *The Great Galeoto*. Both authors pose themselves difficult problems which lie outside the range of usual authorship. Whereas Echegaray seeks to explore the relationship between the world of the individual and the mass world Pirandello explores the question of identity between real and fictive characters. When an author invents a character how long does that character remain his own? When does it take on an identity apart from the author? "I wrote *Six Characters* in order to free myself from a nightmare," he writes. "Why, I asked myself, do I not represent the absolutely novel situation of an author who refuses to give life to certain of his personages, born living in his imagination, and who already having life refused to them, will not resign themselves to remain outside the world of art?" Given this problem it was of course necessary to create a play the action of which moved back and forth between two worlds. The play has neither acts nor scenes; the action is partly on the stage and partly in the audience chamber; the rôles of the play are taken once by the characters themselves, again by the actors assigned to these rôles. Manifestly such a play offers opportunity for satire on the theatre itself but the author does not limit himself to this satire. It is a play to make one think but not a play of ideas. Produced with acclaim in Rome in 1921 it was foreign recognition that has raised *Six Characters in Search of an Author* to commanding place among the plays of the era. It was first translated into English by E. Storer and published in *Broom* in 1922. In February of the same year it was produced at the Kingsway Theatre, London, and in October by Brock Pemberton at the Princess Theatre, in New York. It has been produced frequently by Max Reinhardt in Germany and Austria, and was played at the Comédie des Champs Elysées, Paris, in 1923.

"I see, as it were, a labyrinth wherein our soul wanders through countless, intricate, conflicting paths, without ever finding a way out. In this labyrinth I see a two-faced Hermes which with one face laughs and with the other weeps; it laughs with one face at the other's weeping." — Pirandello.

# LUIGI PIRANDELLO

AFTER Strindberg the outstanding figure in the theatre of the modern world is Luigi Pirandello. To Shaw's intellectual grasp of the spirit of modernity, his irony and comic spirit, Pirandello adds a mastery of dramatic technique by means of which he has immensely extended the conventions of dramatic form. While many of his experiments are tours de force, the authority with which he has handled play form, making it serve the uses of a searching intellect, establishes Pirandello not alone as a stimulating critic of his age but as one who will leave an impress on the structure and standards of his art. Born at Girgenti, Sicily, in 1867, Pirandello was a student of philosophy and philology at Bonn. In 1907 he became Professor at the Istituto Superiore di Magestero Femminile, Rome. He began his literary career as a novelist, and is a leader in the grotesque and futuristic school of Italy which has thrown aside the restraints of realism. Among Pirandello's contemporaries in this movement are F. T. Marinetti, Luigi Chiarelli, Rosso di San Secondo, L. Antonelli, and C. Veneziani. Pirandello's plays are often dramatizations of his short stories of which he has written hundreds. His plays, which he often revises, are issued under the general title of *Maschere Nude* (*Naked Masks*) of which more than 30 volumes have been published. Pirandello was awarded the Nobel prize in 1934. Like Chekhov and Schnitzler, Pirandello is a great story teller who cares little for form, and views human life with a fresh eye. He has made two fields his own: the field of primitive Sicilian nature, and the sophisticated world of thought. He has written 5 novels, 30 plays, and 400 *novelle*. His stories, published as *Novelle per un anno*, covering one *novella* a day for a year, were published in 21 volumes.

# CHARACTERS OF THE COMEDY IN THE MAKING

THE FATHER

THE MOTHER

THE STEPDAUGHTER

THE SON

THE BOY

THE CHILD

MADAME PACE

(*The Boy and The Child do not speak.*)

## ACTORS OF THE COMPANY

THE MANAGER

LEADING LADY

LEADING MAN

SECOND LADY LEAD

L'INGÉNUE

JUVENILE LEAD

OTHER ACTORS AND ACTRESSES

PROPERTY MAN

PROMPTER

MACHINIST

MANAGER'S SECRETARY

DOORKEEPER

SCENE-SHIFTERS

*Daytime. The Stage of a Theatre*

# ACT I

*N.B.  The Comedy is without acts or scenes.  The performance is interrupted once, without the curtain being lowered, when the* MANAGER *and the chief characters withdraw to arrange the scenario.  A second interruption of the action takes place when, by mistake, the stage hands let the curtain down.*

*The spectators will find the curtain raised and the stage as it usually is during the daytime.  It will be half dark, and empty, so that from the beginning the public may have the impression of an impromptu performance.*

PROMPTER'S *box and a small table and chair for the* MANAGER. *Two other small tables and several chairs scattered about as during rehearsals.*

*The* ACTORS *and* ACTRESSES *of the company enter from the back of the stage: first one, then another, then two together: nine or ten in all. They are about to rehearse a Pirandello play:* Mixing It Up. *Some of the company move off towards their dressing rooms.  The* PROMPTER *who has the "book" under his arm, is waiting for the* MANAGER *in order to begin the rehearsal.*

*The* ACTORS *and* ACTRESSES, *some standing, some sitting, chat and smoke.  One perhaps reads a paper; another cons his part.*

*Finally, the* MANAGER *enters and goes to the table prepared for him. His* SECRETARY *brings him his mail, through which he glances.  The* PROMPTER *takes his seat, turns on a light, and opens the "book."*

THE MANAGER (*throwing a letter down on the table*).  I can't see. (*To* PROPERTY MAN.)  Let's have a little light, please!

PROPERTY MAN.  Yes sir, yes, at once.

(*A light comes down onto the stage.*)

THE MANAGER (*clapping his hands*).  Come along!  Come along! Second act of "Mixing It Up."                 (*Sits down.*)

(*The* ACTORS *and* ACTRESSES *go from the front of the stage to the wings, all except the three who are to begin the rehearsal.*)

THE PROMPTER (*reading the "book"*).  "Leo Gala's house.  A curious room serving as dining-room and study."

THE MANAGER (*to* PROPERTY MAN). Fix up the old red room.

PROPERTY MAN (*noting it down*). Red set. All right!

THE PROMPTER (*continuing to read from the "book"*). "Table already laid and writing desk with books and papers. Book-shelves. Exit rear to Leo's bedroom. Exit left to kitchen. Principal exit to right."

THE MANAGER (*energetically*). Well, you understand: The principal exit over there; here, the kitchen. (*Turning to actor who is to play the part of Socrates.*) You make your entrances and exits here. (*To* PROPERTY MAN.) The baize doors at the rear, and curtains.

PROPERTY MAN (*noting it down*). Right oh!

PROMPTER (*reading as before*). "When the curtain rises, Leo Gala, dressed in cook's cap and apron, is busy beating an egg in a cup. Philip, also dressed as a cook, is beating another egg. Guido Venanzi is seated and listening."

LEADING MAN (*to* MANAGER). Excuse me, but must I absolutely wear a cook's cap?

THE MANAGER (*annoyed*). I imagine so. It says so there anyway.
(*Pointing to the "book."*)

LEADING MAN. But it's ridiculous!

THE MANAGER (*jumping up in a rage*). Ridiculous? Ridiculous? Is it my fault if France won't send us any more good comedies, and we are reduced to putting on Pirandello's works, where nobody understands anything, and where the author plays the fool with us all? (*The actors grin. The* MANAGER *goes to* LEADING MAN *and shouts.*) Yes sir, you put on the cook's cap and beat eggs. Do you suppose that with all this egg-beating business you are on an ordinary stage? Get that out of your head. You represent the shell of the eggs you are beating! (*Laughter and comments among the actors.*) Silence! and listen to my explanations, please! (*To* LEADING MAN.) "The empty form of reason without the fullness of instinct, which is blind." — You stand for reason, your wife is instinct. It's a mixing up of the parts, according to which you who act your own part become the puppet of yourself. Do you understand?

LEADING MAN. I'm hanged if I do.

THE MANAGER. Neither do I. But let's get on with it. It's sure to be a glorious failure anyway.  (*Confidentially.*)  But I say, please face three-quarters.  Otherwise, what with the abstruseness of the dialogue, and the public that won't be able to hear you, the whole thing will go to hell.  Come on! come on!

PROMPTER. Pardon sir, may I get into my box?  There's a bit of a draught.

THE MANAGER. Yes, yes, of course!

*At this point, the* DOORKEEPER *has entered from the stage door and advances towards the* MANAGER'S *table, taking off his braided cap. During this manoeuvre, the Six Characters enter, and stop by the door at back of stage, so that when the* DOORKEEPER *is about to announce their coming to the* MANAGER, *they are already on the stage.  A tenuous light surrounds them, almost as if irradiated by them — the faint breath of their fantastic reality.*

*This light will disappear when they come forward towards the actors. They preserve, however, something of the dream lightness in which they seem almost suspended; but this does not detract from the essential reality of their forms and expressions.*

*He who is known as the* FATHER *is a man of about 50: hair, reddish in color, thin at the temples; he is not bald, however; thick moustaches, falling over his still fresh mouth, which often opens in an empty and uncertain smile.  He is fattish, pale; with an especially wide forehead.  He has blue, oval-shaped eyes, very clear and piercing.  Wears light trousers and a dark jacket.  He is alternatively mellifluous and violent in his manner.*

*The* MOTHER *seems crushed and terrified as if by an intolerable weight of shame and abasement.  She is dressed in modest black and wears a thick widow's veil of crêpe.  When she lifts this, she reveals a wax-like face.  She always keeps her eyes downcast.*

*The* STEPDAUGHTER *is dashing, almost impudent, beautiful.  She wears mourning too, but with great elegance.  She shows contempt for the timid half-frightened manner of the wretched* BOY (*14 years old, and also dressed in black*); *on the other hand, she displays a lively tenderness for her little sister, the* CHILD (*about four*), *who is dressed in white, with a black silk sash at the waist.*

*The* SON (*22*) *tall, severe in his attitude of contempt for the* FATHER, *supercilious and indifferent to the* MOTHER.  *He looks as if he had come on the stage against his will.*

DOORKEEPER (*cap in hand*). Excuse me, sir...

THE MANAGER (*rudely*). Eh? What is it?

DOORKEEPER (*timidly*). These people are asking for you, sir.

THE MANAGER (*furious*). I am rehearsing, and you know perfectly well no one's allowed to come in during rehearsals! (*Turning to the characters.*) Who are you, please? What do you want?

THE FATHER (*coming forward a little, followed by the others who seem embarrassed*). As a matter of fact... we have come here in search of an author...

THE MANAGER (*half angry, half amazed*). An author? What author?

THE FATHER. Any author, sir.

THE MANAGER. But there's no author here. We are not rehearsing a new piece.

THE STEPDAUGHTER (*vivaciously*). So much the better, so much the better! We can be your new piece.

AN ACTOR (*coming forward from the others*). Oh, do you hear that?

THE FATHER (*to* STEPDAUGHTER). Yes, but if the author isn't here... (*To* MANAGER.)   ... unless you would be willing...

THE MANAGER. You are trying to be funny.

THE FATHER. No, for Heaven's sake, what are you saying? We bring you a drama, sir.

THE STEPDAUGHTER. We may be your fortune.

THE MANAGER. Will you oblige me by going away? We haven't time to waste with mad people.

THE FATHER (*mellifluously*). Oh sir, you know well that life is full of infinite absurdities, which, strangely enough, do not even need to appear plausible, since they are true.

THE MANAGER. What the devil is he talking about?

THE FATHER. I say that to reverse the ordinary process may well be considered a madness: that is, to create credible situations, in order that they may appear true. But permit me to observe that if this be madness, it is the sole *raison d'être* of your profession, gentlemen. (*The actors look hurt and perplexed.*)

THE MANAGER (*getting up and looking at him*). So our profession seems to you one worthy of madmen then?

THE FATHER. Well, to make seem true that which isn't true... without any need... for a joke as it were... isn't that your mission, gentlemen: to give life to fantastic characters on the stage?

THE MANAGER (*interpreting the rising anger of the company*). But I would beg you to believe, my dear sir, that the profession of the comedian is a noble one. If today, as things go, the playwrights give us stupid comedies to play and puppets to represent instead of men, remember we are proud to have given life to immortal works here on these very boards!

(*The actors, satisfied, applaud their* MANAGER.)

THE FATHER (*interrupting furiously*). Exactly, perfectly, to living beings more alive than those who breathe and wear clothes: beings less real perhaps, but truer! I agree with you entirely.

(*The actors look at one another in amazement.*)

THE MANAGER. But what do you mean? Before, you said...

THE FATHER. No, excuse me, I meant it for you, sir, who were crying out that you had no time to lose with madmen, while no one better than yourself knows that nature uses the instrument of human fantasy in order to pursue her high creative purpose.

THE MANAGER. Very well — but where does all this take us?

THE FATHER. Nowhere! It is merely to show you that one is born to life in many forms, in many shapes, as tree, or as stone, as water, as butterfly, or as woman. So one may also be born a character in a play.

THE MANAGER (*with feigned comic dismay*). So you and these other friends of yours have been born characters?

THE FATHER. Exactly, and alive as you see!

(MANAGER *and actors burst out laughing.*)

THE FATHER (*hurt*). I am sorry you laugh, because we carry in us a drama, as you can guess from this woman here veiled in black.

THE MANAGER (*losing patience at last and almost indignant*). Oh, chuck it! Get away please! Clear out of here! (*To* PROPERTY MAN.) For Heaven's sake, turn them out!

THE FATHER (*resisting*). No, no, look here, we...

THE MANAGER (*roaring*). We come here to work, you know.

LEADING ACTOR. One cannot let oneself be made such a fool of.

THE FATHER (*determined, coming forward*). I marvel at your incredulity, gentlemen. Are you not accustomed to see the characters created by an author spring to life in yourselves and face each other? Just because there is no "book" (*pointing to the* PROMPTER's *box*) which contains us, you refuse to believe...

THE STEPDAUGHTER (*advances toward* MANAGER, *smiling and co-quettish*). Believe me, we are really six most interesting characters, sir; side-tracked however.

THE FATHER. Yes, that is the word! (*To* MANAGER *all at once.*) In the sense, that is, that the author who created us alive no longer wished, or was no longer able, materially to put us into a work of art. And this was a real crime, sir; because he who has had the luck to be born a character can laugh even at death. He cannot die. The man, the writer, the instrument of the creation will die, but his creation does not die. And to live forever, it does not need to have extraordinary gifts or to be able to work wonders. Who was Sancho Panza? Who was Don Abbondio? Yet they live eternally because — live germs as they were — they had the fortune to find a fecundating matrix, a fantasy which could raise and nourish them: make them live forever!

THE MANAGER. That is quite all right. But what do you want here, all of you?

THE FATHER. We want to live.

THE MANAGER (*ironically*). For Eternity?

THE FATHER. No, sir, only for a moment... in you.

AN ACTOR. Just listen to him!

LEADING LADY. They want to live, in us...!

JUVENILE LEAD (*pointing to the* STEPDAUGHTER). I've no objection, as far as that one is concerned!

THE FATHER. Look here! look here! The comedy has to be made. (*To the* MANAGER.) But if you and your actors are willing, we can soon concert it among ourselves.

THE MANAGER (*annoyed*). But what do you want to concert? We don't go in for concerts here. Here we play dramas and comedies!

THE FATHER. Exactly! That is just why we have come to you.

THE MANAGER. And where is the "book"?

THE FATHER. It is in us! (*The actors laugh.*) The drama is in us, and we are the drama. We are impatient to play it. Our inner passion drives us on to this.

THE STEPDAUGHTER (*disdainful, alluring, treacherous, full of impudence*). My passion, sir! Ah, if you only knew! My passion for him! (*Points to the* FATHER *and makes a pretence of embracing him. Then she breaks out into a loud laugh.*)

THE FATHER (*angrily*). Behave yourself! And please don't laugh in that fashion.

THE STEPDAUGHTER. With your permission, gentlemen, I, who am a two months' orphan, will show you how I can dance and sing.

> (*Sings and then dances* Prenez garde à Tchou-Tchin-Tchou.)
>> Les chinois sont un peuple malin,
>> De Shangaî à Pekin,
>> Ils ont mis des écriteux partout:
>> Prenez garde à Tchou-Tchin-Tchou.

ACTORS AND ACTRESSES. Bravo! Well done! Tip-top!

THE MANAGER. Silence! This isn't a café concert, you know! (*Turning to the* FATHER *in consternation.*) Is she mad?

THE FATHER. Mad? No, she's worse than mad.

THE STEPDAUGHTER (*to* MANAGER). Worse? Worse! Listen! Stage this drama for us at once! Then you will see that at a certain moment I... when this little darling here... (*Takes the* CHILD *by the hand and leads her to the* MANAGER.) Isn't she a dear? (*Takes her up and kisses her.*) Darling! Darling! (*Puts her down again and adds feelingly.*) Well, when God suddenly takes this dear little child away from that poor mother there; and this imbecile here (*seizing hold of the* BOY *roughly and pushing him forward*) does the stupidest things, like the fool he is, you will see me run away. Yes, gentleman, I shall be off. But the moment hasn't arrived yet. After what has taken place between him and me (*indicates the* FATHER *with a horrible wink*), I can't remain any longer in this society, to have to witness the anguish of this mother here for that fool... (*Indicates the* SON.) Look at him! Look at him! See how indifferent, how frigid he is, because he is the legitimate son. He despises me, despises him (*pointing to the* BOY), despises this baby here; because... we are bastards (*goes to the* MOTHER *and embraces her*). And he doesn't want to recognize her as his mother — she who is

the common mother of us all. He looks down upon her as if
she were only the mother of us three bastards. Wretch!

(*She says all this very rapidly, excitedly. At the word "bastards"*
*she raises her voice, and almost spits out the final "Wretch!"*)

THE MOTHER (*to the* MANAGER, *in anguish*). In the name of these
two little children, I beg you... (*She grows faint and is about*
*to fall.*) Oh God!

THE FATHER (*coming forward to support her as do some of the actors*).
Quick, a chair, a chair for this poor widow!

THE ACTORS. Is it true? Has she really fainted?

THE MANAGER. Quick, a chair! Here!

(*One of the actors brings a chair, the others proffer assistance.*
*The* MOTHER *tries to prevent the* FATHER *from lifting the veil*
*which covers her face.*)

THE FATHER. Look at her! Look at her!

THE MOTHER. No, no; stop it please!

THE FATHER (*raising her veil*). Let them see you!

THE MOTHER (*rising and covering her face with her hands, in desperation*).
I beg you, sir, to prevent this man from carrying out his plan
which is loathsome to me.

THE MANAGER (*dumbfounded*). I don't understand at all. What is
the situation? Is this lady your wife? (*To the* FATHER.)

THE FATHER. Yes, gentlemen: my wife!

THE MANAGER. But how can she be a widow if you are alive?

(*The actors find relief for their astonishment in a loud laugh.*)

THE FATHER. Don't laugh! Don't laugh like that, for Heaven's
sake. Her drama lies just here in this: she has had a lover,
a man who ought to be here.

THE MOTHER (*with a cry*). No! No!

THE STEPDAUGHTER. Fortunately for her, he is dead. Two
months ago as I said. We are in mourning, as you see.

THE FATHER. He isn't here you see, not because he is dead. He
isn't here — look at her a moment and you will understand —
because her drama isn't a drama of the love of two men for
whom she was incapable of feeling anything except possibly
a little gratitude — gratitude not for me but for the other.
She isn't a woman, she is a mother, and her drama — powerful
sir, I assure you — lies, as a matter of fact, all in these four
children she has had by two men.

THE MOTHER. I had them? Have you got the courage to say that I wanted them? (*To the company.*) It was his doing. It was he who gave me that other man, who forced me to go away with him.

THE STEPDAUGHTER. It isn't true.

THE MOTHER (*startled*). Not true, isn't it?

THE STEPDAUGHTER. No, it isn't true, it just isn't true.

THE MOTHER. And what can you know about it?

THE STEPDAUGHTER. It isn't true. Don't believe it. (*To MANAGER.*) Do you know why she says so? For that fellow there (*indicates the* SON). She tortures herself, destroys herself on account of the neglect of that son there; and she wants him to believe that if she abandoned him when he was only two years old, it was because he (*indicates the* FATHER) made her do so.

THE MOTHER (*vigorously*). He forced me to it, and I call God to witness it. (*To the* MANAGER.) Ask him (*indicates husband*) if it isn't true. Let him speak. You (*to* DAUGHTER) are not in a position to know anything about it.

THE STEPDAUGHTER. I know you lived in peace and happiness with my father while he lived. Can you deny it?

THE MOTHER. No, I don't deny it...

THE STEPDAUGHTER. He was always full of affection and kindness for you. (*To the* BOY, *angrily*.) It's true, isn't it? Tell them! Why don't you speak, you little fool?

THE MOTHER. Leave the poor boy alone. Why do you want to make me appear ungrateful, daughter? I don't want to offend your father. I have answered him that I didn't abandon my house and my son through any fault of mine, nor from any wilful passion.

THE FATHER. It is true. It was my doing.

LEADING MAN (*to the company*). What a spectacle!

LEADING LADY. We are the audience this time.

JUVENILE LEAD. For once, in a way.

THE MANAGER (*beginning to get really interested*). Let's hear them out. Listen!

THE SON. Oh yes, you're going to hear a fine bit now. He will talk to you of the Demon of Experiment.

THE FATHER. You are a cynical imbecile. I've told you so already a hundred times. (*To the* MANAGER.) He tries to make fun of me on account of this expression which I have found to excuse myself with.

THE SON (*with disgust*). Yes, phrases! phrases!

THE FATHER. Phrases! Isn't everyone consoled when faced with a trouble or fact he doesn't understand, by a word, some simple word, which tells us nothing and yet calms us?

THE STEPDAUGHTER. Even in the case of remorse. In fact, especially then.

THE FATHER. Remorse? No, that isn't true. I've done more than use words to quieten the remorse in me.

THE STEPDAUGHTER. Yes, there was a bit of money too. Yes, yes, a bit of money. There were the hundred lire he was about to offer me in payment, gentlemen...

(*Sensation of horror among the actors.*)

THE SON (*to the* STEPDAUGHTER). This is vile.

THE STEPDAUGHTER. Vile? There they were in a pale blue envelope on a little mahogany table in the back of Madame Pace's shop. You know Madame Pace — one of those ladies who attract poor girls of good family into their ateliers, under the pretext of their selling *robes et manteaux*.

THE SON. And he thinks he has bought the right to tyrannise over us all with those hundred lire he was going to pay; but which, fortunately — note this, gentlemen — he had no chance of paying.

THE STEPDAUGHTER. It was a near thing, though, you know!

(*Laughs ironically.*)

THE MOTHER (*protesting*). Shame, my daughter, shame!

THE STEPDAUGHTER. Shame indeed! This is my revenge! I am dying to live that scene... The room... I see it... Here is the window with the mantles exposed, there the divan, the looking-glass, a screen, there in front of the window the little mahogany table with the blue envelope containing one hundred lire. I see it. I see it. I could take hold of it... But you, gentlemen, you ought to turn your backs now: I am almost nude, you know. But I don't blush: I leave that to him (*indicating* FATHER).

THE MANAGER. I don't understand this at all.

THE FATHER. Naturally enough. I would ask you, sir, to exercise

your authority a little here, and let me speak before you believe
all she is trying to blame me with.  Let me explain.

THE STEPDAUGHTER.  Ah yes, explain it in your own way.

THE FATHER.  But don't you see that the whole trouble lies here.
In words, words.  Each one of us has within him a whole
world of things, each man of us his own special world.  And
how can we ever come to an understanding if I put in the
words I utter the sense and value of things as I see them;
while you who listen to me must inevitably translate them
according to the conception of things each one of you has
within himself.  We think we understand each other, but we
never really do.  Look here!  This woman (*indicating the*
MOTHER) takes all my pity for her as a specially ferocious form
of cruelty.

THE MOTHER.  But you drove me away.

THE FATHER.  Do you hear her?  I drove her away!  She believes
I really sent her away.

THE MOTHER.  You know how to talk, and I don't; but, believe me
sir, (*to* MANAGER) after he had married me... who knows
why?... I was a poor insignificant woman...

THE FATHER.  But, good Heavens! it was just for your humility
that I married you.  I loved this simplicity in you.  (*He stops
when he sees she makes signs to contradict him, opens his arms wide in
sign of desperation, seeing how hopeless it is to make himself understood.*)
You see she denies it.  Her mental deafness, believe me, is
phenomenal, the limit (*touches his forehead*): deaf, deaf, mentally
deaf!  She has plenty of feeling.  Oh yes, a good heart for the
children; but the brain — deaf, to the point of desperation —— !

THE STEPDAUGHTER.  Yes, but ask him how his intelligence has
helped us.

THE FATHER.  If we could see all the evil that may spring from
good, what should we do?

(*At this point the* LEADING LADY *who is biting her lips with rage
at seeing the* LEADING MAN *flirting with the* STEPDAUGHTER,
*comes forward and says to the* MANAGER.)

LEADING LADY.  Excuse me, but are we going to rehearse today?

MANAGER.  Of course, of course; but let's hear them out.

JUVENILE LEAD.  This is something quite new.

L'INGÉNUE. Most interesting!

LEADING LADY. Yes, for the people who like that kind of thing.
(*Casts a glance at* LEADING MAN.)

THE MANAGER (*to* FATHER). You must please explain yourself
quite clearly. (*Sits down.*)

THE FATHER. Very well then: listen! I had in my service a poor
man, a clerk, a secretary of mine, full of devotion, who became
friends with her (*indicating the* MOTHER). They understood
one another, were kindred souls in fact, without, however, the
least suspicion of any evil existing. They were incapable even
of thinking of it.

THE STEPDAUGHTER. So he thought of it — for them!

THE FATHER. That's not true. I meant to do good to them — and
to myself, I confess, at the same time. Things had come to
the point that I could not say a word to either of them without
their making a mute appeal, one to the other, with their eyes.
I could see them silently asking each other how I was to be
kept in countenance, how I was to be kept quiet. And this,
believe me, was just about enough of itself to keep me in a
constant rage, to exasperate me beyond measure.

THE MANAGER. And why didn't you send him away then — this
secretary of yours?

THE FATHER. Precisely what I did, sir. And then I had to watch
this poor woman drifting forlornly about the house like an
animal without a master, like an animal one has taken in out
of pity.

THE MOTHER. Ah yes...!

THE FATHER (*suddenly turning to the* MOTHER). It's true about the
son anyway, isn't it?

THE MOTHER. He took my son away from me first of all.

THE FATHER. But not from cruelty. I did it so that he should
grow up healthy and strong by living in the country.

THE STEPDAUGHTER (*pointing to him ironically*). As one can see.

THE FATHER (*quickly*). Is it my fault if he has grown up like this?
I sent him to a wet nurse in the country, a peasant, as *she* did
not seem to me strong enough, though she is of humble origin.
That was, anyway, the reason I married her. Unpleasant all
this maybe, but how can it be helped? My mistake possibly,

but there we are! All my life I have had these confounded aspirations towards a certain moral sanity. (*At this point the* STEP-DAUGHTER *bursts out into a noisy laugh.*) Oh, stop it! Stop it! I can't stand it.

THE MANAGER. Yes, please stop it, for Heaven's sake.

THE STEPDAUGHTER. But imagine moral sanity from him, if you please — the client of certain ateliers like that of Madame Pace!

THE FATHER. Fool! That is the proof that I am a man! This seeming contradiction, gentlemen, is the strongest proof that I stand here a live man before you. Why, it is just for this very incongruity in my nature that I have had to suffer what I have. I could not live by the side of that woman (*indicating the* MOTHER) any longer; but not so much for the boredom she inspired me with as for the pity I felt for her.

THE MOTHER. And so he turned me out ——

THE FATHER. — well provided for! Yes, I sent her to that man, gentlemen... to let her go free of me.

THE MOTHER. And to free himself.

THE FATHER. Yes, I admit it. It was also a liberation for me. But great evil has come of it. I meant well when I did it; and I did it more for her sake than mine. I swear it. (*Crosses his arms on his chest; then turns suddenly to the* MOTHER.) Did I ever lose sight of you until that other man carried you off to another town, like the angry fool he was? And on account of my pure interest in you... my pure interest, I repeat, that had no base motive in it... I watched with the tenderest concern the new family that grew up around her. She can bear witness to this. (*Points to the* STEPDAUGHTER.)

THE STEPDAUGHTER. Oh yes, that's true enough. When I was a kiddie, so so high, you know, with plaits over my shoulders and knickers longer than my skirts, I used to see him waiting outside the school for me to come out. He came to see how I was growing up.

THE FATHER. This is infamous, shameful!

THE STEPDAUGHTER. No. Why?

THE FATHER. Infamous! infamous! (*Then excitedly to* MANAGER *explaining.*) After she (*indicating* MOTHER) went away, my house seemed suddenly empty. She was my incubus, but she filled my house. I was like a dazed fly alone in the empty rooms. This boy here (*indicating the* SON) was educated away from home, and when he came back, he seemed to me to be no more mine. With no mother to stand between him and me, he grew up entirely for himself, on his own, apart, with no tie of intellect or affection binding him to me. And then — strange but true — I was driven, by curiosity at first and then by some tender sentiment, towards her family, which had come into being through my will. The thought of her began gradually to fill up the emptiness I felt all around me. I wanted to know if she were happy in living out the simple daily duties of life. I wanted to think of her as fortunate and happy because far away from the complicated torments of my spirit. And so, to have proof of this, I used to watch that child coming out of school.

THE STEPDAUGHTER. Yes, yes. True. He used to follow me in the street and smiled at me, waved his hand, like this. I would look at him with interest, wondering who he might be. I told my mother, who guessed at once. (*The* MOTHER *agrees with a nod.*) Then she didn't want to send me to school for some days; and when I finally went back, there he was again — looking so ridiculous — with a paper parcel in his hands. He came close to me, caressed me, and drew out a fine straw hat from the parcel, with a bouquet of flowers — all for me!

THE MANAGER. A bit discursive this, you know!

THE SON (*contemptuously*). Literature! Literature!

THE FATHER. Literature indeed! This is life, this is passion!

THE MANAGER. It may be, but it won't act.

THE FATHER. I agree. This is only the part leading up. I don't suggest this should be staged. She (*pointing to the* STEPDAUGHTER), as you see, is no longer the flapper with plaits down her back ——

THE STEPDAUGHTER. — And the knickers showing below the skirt!

THE FATHER. The drama is coming now, sir; something new, complex, most interesting.

THE STEPDAUGHTER. As soon as my father died...

THE FATHER. — There was absolutely misery for them. They came back here, unknown to me. Through her stupidity (*pointing to the* MOTHER)!  It is true she can barely write her own name; but she could anyhow have got her daughter to write to me that they were in need...

THE MOTHER.  And how was I to divine all this sentiment in him?

THE FATHER.  That is exactly your mistake, never to have guessed any of my sentiments.

THE MOTHER.  After so many years apart, and all that had happened...

THE FATHER.  Was it my fault if that fellow carried you away? It happened quite suddenly; for after he had obtained some job or other, I could find no trace of them; and so, not unnaturally, my interest in them dwindled.  But the drama culminated unforeseen and violent on their return, when I was impelled by my miserable flesh that still lives... Ah! what misery, what wretchedness is that of the man who is alone and disdains debasing *liaisons!*  Not old enough to do without women, and not young enough to go and look for one without shame.  Misery?  It's worse than misery; it's a horror; for no woman can any longer give him love; and when a man feels this... One ought to do without, you say?  Yes, yes, I know. Each of us when he appears before his fellows is clothed in a certain dignity.  But every man knows what unconfessable things pass within the secrecy of his own heart.  One gives way to the temptation, only to rise from it again, afterwards, with a great eagerness to re-establish one's dignity, as if it were a tombstone to place on the grave of one's shame, and a monument to hide and sign the memory of our weaknesses.  Everybody's in the same case.  Some folks haven't the courage to say certain things, that's all!

THE STEPDAUGHTER.  All appear to have the courage to do them though.

THE FATHER.  Yes, but in secret.  Therefore, you want more courage to say these things.  Let a man but speak these things out, and folks at once label him a cynic.  But it isn't true. He is like all the others, better indeed, because he isn't afraid to reveal with the light of the intelligence the red shame of human bestiality on which most men close their eyes so as not to see it.  Woman — for example, look at her case!  She turns tantalizing inviting glances on you. You seize her. No sooner does she feel herself in your grasp than she closes her eyes. It is the sign of her mission, the sign by which she says to man: "Blind yourself, for I am blind."

THE STEPDAUGHTER. Sometimes she can close them no more: when she no longer feels the need of hiding her shame to herself, but dry-eyed and dispassionately, sees only that of the man who has blinded himself without love. Oh, all these intellectual complications make me sick, disgust me — all this philosophy that uncovers the beast in man, and then seeks to save him, excuse him... I can't stand it, sir. When a man seeks to "simplify" life bestially, throwing aside every relic of humanity, every chaste aspiration, every pure feeling, all sense of ideality, duty, modesty, shame... then nothing is more revolting and nauseous than a certain kind of remorse — crocodiles' tears, that's what it is.

THE MANAGER. Let's come to the point. This is only discussion.

THE FATHER. Very good, sir! But a fact is like a sack which won't stand up when it is empty. In order that it may stand up, one has to put into it the reason and sentiment which have caused it to exist. I couldn't possibly know that after the death of that man, they had decided to return here, that they were in misery, and that she (*pointing to the* MOTHER) had gone to work as a modiste, and at a shop of the type of that of Madame Pace.

THE STEPDAUGHTER. A real high-class modiste, you must know, gentlemen. In appearance, she works for the leaders of the best society; but she arranges matters so that these elegant ladies serve her purpose... without prejudice to other ladies who are... well... only so so.

THE MOTHER. You will believe me, gentlemen, that it never entered my mind that the old hag offered me work because she had her eye on my daughter.

THE STEPDAUGHTER. Poor mamma! Do you know, sir, what that woman did when I brought her back the work my mother had finished? She would point out to me that I had torn one of my frocks, and she would give it back to my mother to mend. It was I who paid for it, always I; while this poor creature here believed she was sacrificing herself for me and these two children here, sitting up at night sewing Madame Pace's robes.

THE MANAGER. And one day you met there...

THE STEPDAUGHTER. Him, him. Yes sir, an old client. There's a scene for you to play! Superb!

THE FATHER. She, the mother arrived just then...

THE STEPDAUGHTER (*treacherously*). Almost in time!

THE FATHER (*crying out*). No, in time! in time! Fortunately I recognized her... in time. And I took them back home with me to my house. You can imagine now her position and mine: she, as you see her; and I who cannot look her in the face.

THE STEPDAUGHTER. Absurd! How can I possibly be expected — after that — to be a modest young miss, a fit person to go with his confounded aspirations for "a solid moral sanity"?

THE FATHER. For the drama lies all in this — in the conscience that I have, that each one of us has. We believe this conscience to be a single thing, but it is many-sided. There is one for this person, and another for that. Diverse consciences. So we have this illusion of being one person for all, of having a personality that is unique in all our acts. But it isn't true. We perceive this when, tragically perhaps, in something we do, we are as it were, suspended, caught up in the air on a kind of hook. Then we perceive that all of us was not in that act, and that it would be an atrocious injustice to judge us by that action alone, as if all our existence were summed up in that one deed. Now do you understand the perfidy of this girl? She surprised me in a place, where she ought not to have known me, just as I could not exist for her; and she now seeks to attach to me a reality such as I could never suppose I should have to assume for her in a shameful and fleeting moment of my life. I feel this above all else. And the drama, you will see, acquires a tremendous value from this point. Then there is the position of the others... his... (*Indicating the* SON.)

THE SON (*shrugging his shoulders scornfully*). Leave me alone! I don't come into this.

THE FATHER. What? You don't come into this?

THE SON. I've got nothing to do with it, and don't want to have;

because you know well enough I wasn't made to be mixed up in all this with the rest of you.

THE STEPDAUGHTER. We are only vulgar folk! He is the fine gentleman. You may have noticed, Mr. Manager, that I fix him now and again with a look of scorn while he lowers his eyes — for he knows the evil he has done me.

THE SON (scarcely looking at her). I?

THE STEPDAUGHTER. You! you! I owe my life on the streets to you. Did you or did you not deny us, with your behaviour, I won't say the intimacy of home, but even that mere hospitality which makes guests feel at their ease! We were intruders who had come to disturb the kingdom of your legitimacy. I should like to have you witness, Mr. Manager, certain scenes between him and me. He says I have tyrannized over everyone. But it was just his behaviour which made me insist on the reason for which I had come into the house — this reason he calls "vile" — into his house, with my mother who is his mother too. And I came as mistress of the house.

THE SON. It's easy for them to put me always in the wrong. But imagine, gentlemen, the position of a son, whose fate it is to see arrive one day at his home a young woman of impudent bearing, a young woman who inquires for his father, with whom who knows what business she has. This young man has then to witness her return bolder than ever, accompanied by that child there. He is obliged to watch her treat his father in an equivocal and confidential manner. She asks money of him in a way that lets one suppose he must give it her, must, do you understand, because he has every obligation to do so.

THE FATHER. But I have, as a matter of fact, this obligation. I owe it to your mother.

THE SON. How should I know? When had I ever seen or heard of her? One day there arrive with her (indicating STEPDAUGHTER) that lad and this baby here. I am told: "This is your mother too, you know." I divine from her manner (indicating STEPDAUGHTER again) why it is they have come home. I had rather not say what I feel and think about it. I shouldn't even care to confess to myself. No action can therefore be hoped for from me in this affair. Believe me, Mr. Manager, I am an "unrealized" character, dramatically speaking; and I find myself not at all at ease in their company. Leave me out of it, I beg you.

THE FATHER. What? It is just because you are so that...

THE SON. How do you know what I am like? When did you ever bother your head about me?

THE FATHER. I admit it. I admit it. But isn't that a situation in itself? This aloofness of yours which is so cruel to me and to your mother, who returns home and sees you almost for the first time grown up, who doesn't recognize you but knows you are her son... (*Pointing out the* MOTHER *to the* MANAGER.) See, she's crying!

THE STEPDAUGHTER (*angrily, stamping her foot*). Like a fool!

THE FATHER (*indicating* STEPDAUGHTER). She can't stand him you know. (*Then referring again to the* SON.) He says he doesn't come into the affair, whereas he is really the hinge of the whole action. Look at that lad who is always clinging to his mother, frightened and humiliated. It is on account of this fellow here. Possibly his situation is the most painful of all. He feels himself a stranger more than the others. The poor little chap feels mortified, humiliated at being brought into a home out of charity as it were. (*In confidence.*) He is the image of his father. Hardly talks at all. Humble and quiet.

THE MANAGER. Oh, we'll cut him out. You've no notion what a nuisance boys are on the stage...

THE FATHER. He disappears soon, you know. And the baby too. She is the first to vanish from the scene. The drama consists finally in this: when that mother re-enters my house, her family born outside of it, and shall we say superimposed on the original, ends with the death of the little girl, the tragedy of the boy and the flight of the elder daughter. It cannot go on, because it is foreign to its surroundings. So after much torment, we three remain: I, the mother, that son. Then, owing to the disappearance of that extraneous family, we too find ourselves strange to one another. We find we are living in an atmosphere of mortal desolation which is the revenge, as he (*indicating* SON) scornfully said of the Demon of Experiment, that unfortunately hides in me. Thus, sir, you see when faith is lacking, it becomes impossible to create certain states of happiness, for we lack the necessary humility. Vaingloriously, we try to substitute ourselves for this faith, creating thus for the rest of the world a reality which we believe after their fashion, while, actually, it doesn't exist. For each one of us has his own reality to be respected before God, even when it is harmful to one's very self.

THE MANAGER. There is something in what you say. I assure you all this interests me very much. I begin to think there's the stuff for a drama in all this, and not a bad drama either.

THE STEPDAUGHTER (*coming forward*). When you've got a character like me.

THE FATHER (*shutting her up, all excited to learn the decision of the* MANAGER). You be quiet!

THE MANAGER (*reflecting, heedless of interruption*). It's new... hem... yes...

THE FATHER. Absolutely new!

THE MANAGER. You've got a nerve though, I must say, to come here and fling it at me like this...

THE FATHER. You will understand, sir, born as we are for the stage...

THE MANAGER. Are you amateur actors then?

THE FATHER. No. I say born for the stage, because...

THE MANAGER. Oh, nonsense. You're an old hand, you know.

THE FATHER. No, sir, no. We act that rôle for which we have been cast, that rôle which we are given in life. And in my own case, passion itself, as usually happens, becomes a trifle theatrical when it is exalted.

THE MANAGER. Well, well, that will do. But you see, without an author... I could give you the address of an author if you like...

THE FATHER. No, no. Look here! You must be the author.

THE MANAGER. I? What are you talking about?

THE FATHER. Yes, you, you! Why not?

THE MANAGER. Because I have never been an author: that's why.

THE FATHER. Then why not turn author now? Everybody does it. You don't want any special qualities. Your task is made much easier by the fact that we are all here alive before you...

THE MANAGER. It won't do.

THE FATHER. What? When you see us live our drama...

THE MANAGER. Yes, that's all right. But you want someone to write it.

THE FATHER. No, no. Someone to take it down, possibly, while we play it, scene by scene! It will be enough to sketch it out at first, and then try it over.

THE MANAGER. Well... I am almost tempted. It's a bit of an idea. One might have a shot at it.

THE FATHER. Of course. You'll see what scenes will come out of it. I can give you one, at once...

THE MANAGER. By Jove, it tempts me. I'd like to have a go at it. Let's try it out. Come with me to my office. (*Turning to the actors.*) You are at liberty for a bit, but don't stop out of the theatre for long. In a quarter of an hour, twenty minutes, all back here again! (*To the* FATHER.) We'll see what can be done. Who knows if we don't get something really extraordinary out of it?

THE FATHER. There's no doubt about it. They (*indicating the characters*) had better come with us too, hadn't they?

THE MANAGER. Yes, yes. Come on! come on! (*Moves away and then turning to the actors.*) Be punctual, please!

(MANAGER *and the six characters cross the stage and go off. The other actors remain, looking at one another in astonishment.*)

LEADING MAN. Is he serious? What the devil does he want to do?

JUVENILE LEAD. This is rank madness.

THIRD ACTOR. Does he expect to knock up a drama in five minutes?

JUVENILE LEAD. Like the improvisers!

LEADING LADY. If he thinks I'm going to take part in a joke like this...

JUVENILE LEAD. I'm out of it anyway.

FOURTH ACTOR. I should like to know who they are. (*Alludes to characters.*)

THIRD ACTOR. What do you suppose? Madmen or rascals!

JUVENILE LEAD. And he takes them seriously!

L'INGÉNUE. Vanity! He fancies himself as an author now.

LEADING MAN. It's absolutely unheard of. If the stage has come to this... well I'm...

FIFTH ACTOR. It's rather a joke.

THIRD ACTOR. Well, we'll see what's going to happen next.

(*Thus talking, the actors leave the stage; some going out by the little door at the back; others retiring to their dressing-rooms. The curtain remains up. The action of the play is suspended for twenty minutes.*)

## ACT II

*The stage call-bells ring to warn the company that the play is about to begin again.*

*The* STEPDAUGHTER *comes out of the* MANAGER'S *office along with the* CHILD *and the* BOY. *As she comes out of the office, she cries:* Nonsense! nonsense! Do it yourselves! I'm not going to mix myself up in this mess. (*Turning to the* CHILD *and coming quickly with her onto the stage.*) Come on, Rosetta, let's run!

*The* BOY *follows them slowly, remaining a little behind and seeming perplexed.*

THE STEPDAUGHTER (*stops, bends over the* CHILD *and takes the latter's face between her hands*). My little darling! You're frightened, aren't you? You don't know where we are, do you? (*Pretending to reply to a question of the* CHILD.) What is the stage? It's a place, baby, you know, where people play at being serious, a place where they act comedies. We've got to act a comedy now, dead serious, you know; and you're in it also, little one. (*Embraces her, pressing the little head to her breast, and rocking the* CHILD *for a moment.*) Oh darling, darling, what a horrid comedy you've got to play! What a wretched part they've found for you! A garden... a fountain... look... just suppose, kiddie, it's here. Where, you say? Why, right here in the middle. It's all pretence you know. That's the trouble, my pet: it's all make-believe here. It's better to imagine it though, because if they fix it up for you, it'll only be painted cardboard, painted cardboard for the rockery, the water, the plants... Ah, but I think a baby like this one would sooner have a make-believe fountain than a real one, so she could play with it. What a joke it'll be for the others! But for you, alas!

not quite such a joke: you who are real, baby dear, and really play by a real fountain that is big and green and beautiful, with ever so many bamboos around it that are reflected in the water, and a whole lot of little ducks swimming about... No, Rosetta, no, your mother doesn't bother about you on account of that wretch of a son there. I'm in the devil of a temper, and as for that lad... (*Seizes* BOY *by the arm to force him to take one of his hands out of his pockets.*) What have you got there? What are you hiding? (*Pulls his hand out of his pocket, looks into it and catches the glint of a revolver.*) Ah! where did you get this? (*The* BOY, *very pale in the face, looks at her, but does not answer.*) Idiot! If I'd been in your place, instead of killing myself, I'd have shot one of those two, or both of them: father and son.

(*The* FATHER *enters from the office, all excited from his work. The* MANAGER *follows him.*)

THE FATHER. Come on, come on, dear! Come here for a minute! We've arranged everything. It's all fixed up.

THE MANAGER (*also excited*). If you please, young lady, there are one or two points to settle still. Will you come along?

THE STEPDAUGHTER (*following him towards the office*). Ouff! what's the good, if you've arranged everything.

(*The* FATHER, MANAGER *and* STEPDAUGHTER *go back into the office again (off) for a moment. At the same time, the* SON, *followed by the* MOTHER, *comes out.*)

THE SON (*looking at the three entering office*). Oh, this is fine, fine! And to think I can't even get away!

(*The* MOTHER *attempts to look at him, but lowers her eyes immediately when he turns away from her. She then sits down. The* BOY *and the* CHILD *approach her. She casts a glance again at the* SON, *and speaks with humble tones, trying to draw him into conversation.*)

THE MOTHER. And isn't my punishment the worst of all? (*Then seeing from the* SON'S *manner that he will not bother himself about her.*) My God! Why are you so cruel? Isn't it enough for one person to support all this torment? Must you then insist on others seeing it also?

THE SON (*half to himself, meaning the* MOTHER *to hear, however*).

And they want to put it on the stage! If there was at least a reason for it! He thinks he has got at the meaning of it all. Just as if each one of us in every circumstance of life couldn't find his own explanation of it! (*Pauses.*) He complains he was discovered in a place where he ought not to have been seen, in a moment of his life which ought to have remained hidden and kept out of the reach of that convention which he has to maintain for other people. And what about my case? Haven't I had to reveal what no son ought ever to reveal: how father and mother live and are man and wife for themselves quite apart from that idea of father and mother which we give them? When this idea is revealed, our life is then linked at one point only to that man and that woman; and as such it should shame them, shouldn't it?

> (*The* MOTHER *hides her face in her hands. From the dressing-rooms and the little door at the back of the stage the actors and* STAGE MANAGER *return, followed by the* PROPERTY MAN *and the* PROMPTER. *At the same moment, the* MANAGER *comes out of his office, accompanied by the* FATHER *and the* STEP-DAUGHTER.)

THE MANAGER. Come on, come on, ladies and gentlemen! Heh! you there, machinist!

MACHINIST. Yes sir?

THE MANAGER. Fix up the white parlor with the floral decorations. Two wings and a drop with a door will do. Hurry up!

> (*The* MACHINIST *runs off at once to prepare the scene, and arranges it while the* MANAGER *talks with the* STAGE MANAGER, *the* PROPERTY MAN, *and the* PROMPTER, *on matters of detail.*)

THE MANAGER (*to* PROPERTY MAN). Just have a look, and see if there isn't a sofa or divan in the wardrobe...

PROPERTY MAN. There's the green one.

THE STEPDAUGHTER. No, no! Green won't do. It was yellow, ornamented with flowers — very large! and most comfortable!

PROPERTY MAN. There isn't one like that.

THE MANAGER. It doesn't matter. Use the one we've got.

THE STEPDAUGHTER. Doesn't matter? It's most important!

THE MANAGER. We're only trying it now. Please don't interfere.

(*To* PROPERTY MAN.) See if we've got a shop window — long and narrowish.

THE STEPDAUGHTER. And the little table! The little mahogany table for the pale blue envelope!

PROPERTY MAN (*to* MANAGER). There's that little gilt one.

THE MANAGER. That'll do fine.

THE FATHER. A mirror.

THE STEPDAUGHTER. And the screen! We must have a screen. Otherwise how can I manage?

PROPERTY MAN. That's all right, Miss. We've got any amount of them.

THE MANAGER (*to the* STEPDAUGHTER). We want some clothes pegs too, don't we?

THE STEPDAUGHTER. Yes, several, several!

THE MANAGER. See how many we've got and bring them all.

PROPERTY MAN. All right!

(*The* PROPERTY MAN *hurries off to obey his orders. While he is putting the things in their places, the* MANAGER *talks to the* PROMPTER *and then with the characters and the actors.*)

THE MANAGER (*to* PROMPTER). Take your seat. Look here: this is the outline of the scenes, act by act. (*Hands him some sheets of paper.*) And now I'm going to ask you to do something out of the ordinary.

PROMPTER. Take it down in shorthand?

THE MANAGER (*pleasantly surprised*). Exactly! Can you do shorthand?

PROMPTER. Yes, a little.

MANAGER. Good! (*Turning to a stage hand.*) Go and get some paper from my office, plenty, as much as you can find.

(*The stage hand goes off, and soon returns with a handful of paper which he gives to the* PROMPTER.)

THE MANAGER (*to* PROMPTER). You follow the scenes as we play them, and try and get the points down, at any rate the most important ones. (*Then addressing the actors.*) Clear the stage, ladies and gentlemen! Come over here (*pointing to the left*) and listen attentively.

LEADING LADY. But, excuse me, we...

THE MANAGER (*guessing her thought*). Don't worry! You won't have to improvise.

LEADING MAN. What have we to do then?

THE MANAGER. Nothing. For the moment you just watch and listen. Everybody will get his part written out afterwards. At present we're going to try the thing as best we can. They're going to act now.

THE FATHER (*as if fallen from the clouds into the confusion of the stage*). We? What do you mean, if you please, by a rehearsal?

THE MANAGER. A rehearsal for them.   (*Points to the actors.*)

THE FATHER. But since we are the characters...

THE MANAGER. All right: "characters" then, if you insist on calling yourselves such. But here, my dear sir, the characters don't act. Here the actors do the acting. The characters are there, in the "book" (*pointing towards* PROMPTER's *box*) — when there is a "book"!

THE FATHER. I won't contradict you; but excuse me, the actors aren't the characters. They want to be, they pretend to be, don't they? Now if these gentlemen here are fortunate enough to have us alive before them...

THE MANAGER. Oh, this is grand! You want to come before the public yourselves, then?

THE FATHER. As we are...

THE MANAGER. I can assure you it would be a magnificent spectacle!

LEADING MAN. What's the use of us here anyway then?

THE MANAGER. You're not going to pretend that you can act? It makes me laugh! (*The actors laugh.*) There, you see, they are laughing at the notion. But, by the way, I must cast the parts. That won't be difficult. They cast themselves. (*To the* SECOND LADY LEAD.) You play the mother. (*To the* FATHER.) We must find her a name.

THE FATHER. Amalia, sir.

THE MANAGER. But that is the real name of your wife. We don't want to call her by her real name.

THE FATHER. Why ever not, if it is her name?... Still, perhaps, if that lady must... (*Makes a slight motion of the hand to indicate the* SECOND LADY LEAD.) I see this woman here (*means the* MOTHER) as Amalia. But do as you like. (*Gets more and more confused.*) I don't know what to say to you. Already, I begin to hear my own words ring false, as if they had another sound...

THE MANAGER. Don't you worry about it. It'll be our job to find the right tones. And as for her name, if you want her Amalia, Amalia it shall be; and if you don't like it, we'll find another! For the moment though, we'll call the characters in this way. (*To* JUVENILE LEAD.) You are the Son. (*To the* LEADING LADY.) You naturally are the Stepdaughter...

THE STEPDAUGHTER (*excitedly*). What? what? I, that woman there? (*Bursts out laughing.*)

THE MANAGER (*angry*). What is there to laugh at?

LEADING LADY (*indignant*). Nobody has ever dared to laugh at me. I insist on being treated with respect; otherwise I go away.

THE STEPDAUGHTER. No, no, excuse me... I am not laughing at you...

THE MANAGER (*to* STEPDAUGHTER). You ought to feel honored to be played by...

LEADING LADY (*at once contemptuously*). "That woman there"...

THE STEPDAUGHTER. But I wasn't speaking of you, you know. I was speaking of myself — whom I can't see at all in you! That is all. I don't know... but... you... aren't in the least like me...

THE FATHER. True. Here's the point. Look here, sir, our temperaments, our souls...

THE MANAGER. Temperament, soul, be hanged! Do you suppose the spirit of the piece is in you? Nothing of the kind!

THE FATHER. What, haven't we our own temperaments, our own souls?

THE MANAGER. Not at all. Your soul or whatever you like to call it takes shape here. The actors give body and form to it, voice and gesture. And my actors — I may tell you — have given expression to much more lofty material than this little drama of yours, which may or may not hold up on the stage. But if it does, the merit of it, believe me, will be due to my actors.

THE FATHER. I don't dare contradict you, sir; but, believe me, it is a terrible suffering for us who are as we are, with these bodies of ours, these features to see...

THE MANAGER (*cutting him short and out of patience*). Good heavens! The make-up will remedy all that, man, the make-up...

THE FATHER. Maybe. But the voice, the gestures...

THE MANAGER. Now, look here! On the stage, you as yourself, cannot exist. The actor here acts you, and that's an end to it!

THE FATHER. I understand. And now I think I see why our author who conceived us as we are, all alive, didn't want to put us on the stage after all. I haven't the least desire to offend your actors. Far from it! But when I think that I am to be acted by... I don't know by whom...

LEADING MAN (*on his dignity*). By me, if you've no objection!

THE FATHER (*humbly, mellifluously*). Honored, I assure you, sir. (*Bows.*) Still, I must say that try as this gentleman may, with all his good will and wonderful art, to absorb me into himself...

LEADING MAN. Oh, chuck it! "Wonderful art!" Withdraw that, please!

THE FATHER. The performance he will give, even doing his best with make-up to look like me...

LEADING MAN. It will certainly be a bit difficult! (*The actors laugh.*)

THE FATHER. Exactly! It will be difficult to act me as I really am. The effect will be rather — apart from the make-up — according as to how he supposes I am, as he senses me — if he does sense me — and not as I inside of myself feel myself to be. It seems to me then that account should be taken of this by everyone whose duty it may become to criticize us...

THE MANAGER. Heavens! The man's starting to think about the critics now! Let them say what they like. It's up to us to put on the play if we can. (*Looking around.*) Come on! come on! Is the stage set? (*To the actors and characters.*) Stand back — stand back! Let me see, and don't let's lose any more time! (*To the* STEPDAUGHTER.) Is it all right as it is now?

THE STEPDAUGHTER. Well, to tell the truth, I don't recognize the scene.

THE MANAGER. My dear lady, you can't possibly suppose that we can construct that shop of Madame Pace piece by piece here? (*To the* FATHER.) You said a white room with flowered wall-paper, didn't you?

THE FATHER. Yes.

THE MANAGER. Well then. We've got the furniture right more or less. Bring that little table a bit further forward. (*The stage hands obey the order. To* PROPERTY MAN.) You go and find an envelope, if possible, a pale blue one; and give it to that gentleman. (*Indicates* FATHER.)

PROPERTY MAN. An ordinary envelope?

MANAGER AND FATHER. Yes, yes, an ordinary envelope.

PROPERTY MAN. At once, sir. (*Exit.*)

THE MANAGER. Ready, everyone! First scene — the young lady. (*The* LEADING LADY *comes forward.*) No, no, you must wait. I meant her (*indicating the* STEPDAUGHTER). You just watch —

THE STEPDAUGHTER (*adding at once*). How I shall play it, how I shall live it!...

LEADING LADY (*offended*). I shall live it also, you may be sure, as soon as I begin!

THE MANAGER (*with his hands to his head*). Ladies and gentlemen, if you please! No more useless discussions! Scene I: the young lady with Madame Pace: Oh! (*Looks around as if lost.*) And this Madame Pace, where is she?

THE FATHER. She isn't with us, sir.

THE MANAGER. Then what the devil's to be done?

THE FATHER. But she is alive too.

THE MANAGER. Yes, but where is she?

THE FATHER. One minute. Let me speak! (*Turning to the actresses.*) If these ladies would be so good as to give me their hats for a moment...

THE ACTRESSES (*half surprised, half laughing, in chorus*). What? Why? Our hats? What does he say?

THE MANAGER. What are you going to do with the ladies' hats? (*The actors laugh.*)

THE FATHER. Oh, nothing. I just want to put them on these pegs for a moment. And one of the ladies will be so kind as to take off her mantle...

THE ACTORS. Oh, what d'you think of that? Only the mantle? He must be mad.

SOME ACTRESSES. But why? Mantles as well?

THE FATHER. To hang them up here for a moment. Please be so kind, will you?

THE ACTRESSES (*taking off their hats, one or two also their cloaks, and going to hang them on the racks*). After all, why not? There you are! This is really funny! We've got to put them on show.

THE FATHER. Exactly; just like that, on show.

THE MANAGER. May we know why?

THE FATHER. I'll tell you. Who knows if, by arranging the stage for her, she does not come here herself, attracted by the very articles of her trade? (*Inviting the actors to look towards the exit at back of stage.*) Look! Look!

(*The door at the back of stage opens and* MADAME PACE *enters and takes a few steps forward. She is a fat, oldish woman with puffy oxygenated hair. She is rouged and powdered, dressed with a comical elegance in black silk. Round her waist is a long silver chain from which hangs a pair of scissors. The* STEPDAUGHTER *runs over to her at once amid the stupor of the actors.*)

THE STEPDAUGHTER (*turning towards her*). There she is! There she is!

THE FATHER (*radiant*). It's she! I said so, didn't I? There she is!

THE MANAGER (*conquering his surprise, and then becoming indignant*). What sort of a trick is this?

LEADING MAN (*almost at the same time*). What's going to happen next?

JUVENILE LEAD. Where does *she* come from?

L'INGÉNUE. They've been holding her in reserve, I guess.

LEADING LADY. A vulgar trick!

THE FATHER (*dominating the protests*). Excuse me, all of you! Why are you so anxious to destroy in the name of a vulgar, common-place sense of truth, this reality which comes to birth attracted and formed by the magic of the stage itself, which has indeed more right to live here than you, since it is much truer than you — if you don't mind my saying so? Which is the actress among you who is to play Madame Pace? Well, here is Madame Pace herself. And you will allow, I fancy, that the actress who acts her will be less true than this woman here, who is herself in person. You see my daughter recognized her and went over to her at once. Now you're going to witness the scene!

(*But the scene between the* STEPDAUGHTER *and* MADAME PACE *has already begun despite the protest of the actors and the reply of the* FATHER. *It has begun quietly, naturally, in a manner impossible for the stage. So when the actors, called*

*to attention by the* FATHER, *turn round and see* MADAME
PACE, *who has placed one hand under the* STEPDAUGHTER'S
*chin to raise her head, they observe her at first with great atten-
tion, but hearing her speak in an unintelligible manner their
interest begins to wane.*)

THE MANAGER. Well? well?

LEADING MAN. What does she say?

LEADING LADY. One can't hear a word.

JUVENILE LEAD. Louder! Louder please!

THE STEPDAUGHTER (*leaving* MADAME PACE, *who smiles a sphinx-like
smile, and advancing toward the actors*). Louder? Louder? What
are you talking about? These aren't matters which can be
shouted at the top of one's voice. If I have spoken them out
loud, it was to shame him and have my revenge (*indicates*
FATHER). But for Madame it's quite a different matter.

THE MANAGER. Indeed? indeed? But here, you know, people
have got to make themselves heard, my dear. Even we who
are on the stage can't hear you. What will it be when the
public's in the theatre? And anyway, you can very well speak
up now among yourselves, since we shan't be present to listen
to you as we are now. You've got to pretend to be alone in a
room at the back of a shop where no one can hear you.

(*The* STEPDAUGHTER *coquettishly and with a touch of malice
makes a sign of disagreement two or three times with her finger.*)

THE MANAGER. What do you mean by no?

THE STEPDAUGHTER (*sotto voce, mysteriously*). There's someone who
will hear us if she (*indicating* MADAME PACE) speaks out loud.

THE MANAGER (*in consternation*). What? Have you got someone
else to spring on us now? (*The actors burst out laughing.*)

THE FATHER. No, no sir. She is alluding to me. I've got to be
here — there behind that door, in waiting; and Madame Pace
knows it. In fact, if you will allow me, I'll go there at once,
so I can be quite ready. (*Moves away.*)

THE MANAGER (*stopping him*). No! Wait! wait! We must observe
the conventions of the theatre. Before you are ready...

THE STEPDAUGHTER (*interrupting him*). No, get on with it at once!
I'm just dying, I tell you, to act this scene. If he's ready, I'm
more than ready.

THE MANAGER (*shouting*). But, my dear young lady, first of all, we must have the scene between you and this lady... (*Indicates* MADAME PACE.) Do you understand?...

THE STEPDAUGHTER. Good Heavens! She's been telling me what you know already: that mamma's work is badly done again, that the material's ruined; and that if I want her to continue to help us in our misery I must be patient...

MADAME PACE (*coming forward with an air of great importance*). Yes indeed, sir, I no wanta take advantage of her, I no wanta be hard...

(*Note.* MADAME PACE *is supposed to talk in a jargon half Italian, half Spanish.*)

THE MANAGER (*alarmed*). What? What? She talks like that?
(*The actors burst out laughing again.*)

THE STEPDAUGHTER (*also laughing*). Yes, yes, that's the way she talks, half English, half Italian! Most comical it is!

MADAME PACE. Itta seem not verra polite gentlemen laugha atta me eef I trya best speaka English.

THE MANAGER. *Diamine!* Of course! Of course! Let her talk like that! Just what we want. Talk just like that, Madame, if you please! The effect will be certain. Exactly what was wanted to put a little comic relief into the crudity of the situation. Of course she talks like that! Magnificent!

THE STEPDAUGHTER. Magnificent? Certainly! When certain suggestions are made to one in language of that kind, the effect is certain, since it seems almost a joke. One feels inclined to laugh when one hears her talk about an "old signore" "who wanta talka nicely with you." Nice old signore, eh, Madame?

MADAME PACE. Not so old my dear, not so old! And even if you no lika him, he won't make any scandal!

THE MOTHER (*jumping up amid the amazement and consternation of the actors who had not been noticing her. They move to restrain her*). You old devil! You murderess!

THE STEPDAUGHTER (*running over to calm her* MOTHER). Calm yourself, mother, calm yourself! Please don't...

THE FATHER (*going to her also at the same time*). Calm yourself! Don't get excited! Sit down now!

THE MOTHER. Well then, take that woman away out of my sight!

THE STEPDAUGHTER (*to* MANAGER). It is impossible for my mother to remain here.

THE FATHER (*to* MANAGER). They can't be here together. And for this reason, you see: that woman there was not with us when we came... If they are on together, the whole thing is given away inevitably, as you see.

THE MANAGER. It doesn't matter. This is only a first rough sketch — just to get an idea of the various points of the scene, even confusedly... (*Turning to the* MOTHER *and leading her to her chair.*) Come along, my dear lady, sit down now, and let's get on with the scene...

(*Meanwhile, the* STEPDAUGHTER, *coming forward again, turns to* MADAME PACE.)

THE STEPDAUGHTER. Come on, Madame, come on!

MADAME PACE (*offended*). No, no, *grazie*. I not do anything witha your mother present.

THE STEPDAUGHTER. Nonsense! Introduce this "old signore" who wants to talk nicely to me. (*Addressing the company imperiously.*) We've got to do this scene one way or another, haven't we? Come on! (*To* MADAME PACE.) You can go!

MADAME PACE. Ah yes! I go'way! I go'way! Certainly!
(*Exit furious.*)

THE STEPDAUGHTER (*to the* FATHER). Now you make your entry. No, you needn't go over here. Come here. Let's suppose you've already come in. Like that, yes! I'm here with bowed head, modest like. Come on! Out with your voice! Say "Good morning, Miss" in that peculiar tone, that special tone...

THE MANAGER. Excuse me, but are you the manager, or am I? (*To the* FATHER, *who looks undecided and perplexed.*) Get on with it, man! Go down there to the back of the stage. You needn't go off. Then come right forward here.

(*The* FATHER *does as he is told, looking troubled and perplexed at first. But as soon as he begins to move, the reality of the action affects him, and he begins to smile and to be more natural. The actors watch intently.*)

THE MANAGER (*sotto voce, quickly to the* PROMPTER *in his box*). Ready! ready? Get ready to write now.

THE FATHER (*coming forward and speaking in a different tone*). Good afternoon, Miss!

THE STEPDAUGHTER (*head bowed down slightly, with restrained disgust*). Good afternoon!

THE FATHER (*looks under her hat which partly covers her face. Perceiving she is very young, he makes an exclamation, partly of surprise, partly of fear lest he compromise himself in a risky adventure*). Ah... but... ah... I say... this is not the first time that you have come here, is it?

THE STEPDAUGHTER (*modestly*). No sir.

THE FATHER. You've been here before, eh? (*Then seeing her nod agreement.*) More than once? (*Waits for her to answer, looks under her hat, smiles, and then says.*) Well then, there's no need to be so shy, is there? May I take off your hat?

THE STEPDAUGHTER (*anticipating him and with veiled disgust*). No sir... I'll do it myself. (*Takes it off quickly.*)

(*The* MOTHER, *who watches the progress of the scene with the* SON *and the other two children who cling to her, is on thorns; and follows with varying expressions of sorrow, indignation, anxiety, and horror the words and actions of the other two. From time to time she hides her face in her hands and sobs.*)

THE MOTHER. Oh, my God, my God!

THE FATHER (*playing his part with a touch of gallantry*). Give it to me! I'll put it down. (*Takes hat from her hands.*) But a dear little head like yours ought to have a smarter hat. Come and help me choose one from the stock, won't you?

L'INGÉNUE (*interrupting*). I say... those are our hats you know.

THE MANAGER (*furious*). Silence! silence! Don't try and be funny, if you please... We're playing the scene now I'd have you notice. (*To the* STEPDAUGHTER.) Begin again, please!

THE STEPDAUGHTER (*continuing*). No thank you, sir.

THE FATHER. Oh, come now. Don't talk like that. You must take it. I shall be upset if you don't. There are some lovely little hats here; and then — Madame will be pleased. She expects it, anyway, you know.

THE STEPDAUGHTER. No, no! I couldn't wear it!

THE FATHER. Oh, you're thinking about what they'd say at home if they saw you come in with a new hat? My dear girl, there's always a way round these little matters, you know.

THE STEPDAUGHTER (*all keyed up*). No, it's not that. I couldn't wear it because I am... as you see... you might have noticed...
(*Showing her black dress.*)

THE FATHER. ... in mourning! Of course: I beg your pardon: I'm frightfully sorry...

THE STEPDAUGHTER (*forcing herself to conquer her indignation and nausea*). Stop! Stop! It's I who must thank you. There's no need for you to feel mortified or specially sorry. Don't think any more of what I've said. (*Tries to smile.*) I must forget that I am dressed so...

THE MANAGER (*interrupting and turning to the* PROMPTER). Stop a minute! Stop! Don't write that down. Cut out that last bit. (*Then to the* FATHER *and* STEPDAUGHTER.) Fine! it's going fine! (*To the* FATHER *only*.) And now you can go on as we arranged. (*To the actors.*) Pretty good, that scene, where he offers her the hat, eh?

THE STEPDAUGHTER. The best's coming now. Why can't we go on?

THE MANAGER. Have a little patience! (*To the actors.*) Of course, it must be treated rather lightly.

LEADING MAN. Still, with a bit of go in it!

LEADING LADY. Of course! It's easy enough! (*To* LEADING MAN.) Shall you and I try it now?

LEADING MAN. Why, yes! I'll prepare my entrance.
(*Exit in order to make his entrance.*)

THE MANAGER (*to* LEADING LADY). See here! The scene between you and Madame Pace is finished. I'll have it written out properly after. You remain here... oh, where are you going?

LEADING LADY. One minute. I want to put my hat on again.
(*Goes over to hat-rack and puts her hat on her head.*)

THE MANAGER. Good! You stay here with your head bowed down a bit.

THE STEPDAUGHTER. But she isn't dressed in black.

LEADING LADY. But I shall be, and much more effectively than you.

THE MANAGER (*to* STEPDAUGHTER). Be quiet please, and watch!

You'll be able to learn something. (*Clapping his hands.*) Come on! come on! Entrance, please!

(*The door at rear of stage opens, and the* LEADING MAN *enters with the lively manner of an old gallant. The rendering of the scene by the actors from the very first words is seen to be quite a different thing, though it has not in any way the air of a parody. Naturally, the* STEPDAUGHTER *and the* FATHER, *not being able to recognize themselves in the* LEADING LADY *and the* LEADING MAN, *who deliver their words in different tones and with a different psychology, express, sometimes with smiles, sometimes with gestures, the impression they receive.*)

LEADING MAN. Good afternoon, Miss...

THE FATHER (*at once unable to contain himself*). No! no!

(*The* STEPDAUGHTER *noticing the way the* LEADING MAN *enters, bursts out laughing.*)

THE MANAGER (*furious*). Silence! And you please just stop that laughing. If we go on like this, we shall never finish.

THE STEPDAUGHTER. Forgive me, sir, but it's natural enough. This lady (*indicating* LEADING LADY) stands there still; but if she is supposed to be me, I can assure you that if I heard anyone say "Good afternoon" in that manner and in that tone, I should burst out laughing as I did.

THE FATHER. Yes, yes, the manner, the tone...

THE MANAGER. Nonsense! Rubbish! Stand aside and let me see the action.

LEADING MAN. If I've got to represent an old fellow who's coming into a house of an equivocal character...

THE MANAGER. Don't listen to them, for Heaven's sake! Do it again! It goes fine. (*Waiting for the actors to begin again.*) Well?

LEADING MAN. Good afternoon, Miss.

LEADING LADY. Good afternoon.

LEADING MAN (*imitating the gesture of the* FATHER *when he looked under the hat, and then expressing quite clearly first satisfaction and then fear*). Ah, but... I say... this is not the first time that you have come here, is it?

THE MANAGER. Good, but not quite so heavily. Like this (*acts

*himself*). "This isn't the first time that you have come here"...
(*To* LEADING LADY.) And you say: "No, sir."

LEADING LADY. No, sir.

LEADING MAN. You've been here before, more than once.

THE MANAGER. No, no, stop! Let her nod "yes" first. "You've been here before, eh?"

(*The* LEADING LADY *lifts up her head slightly and closes her eyes as though in disgust. Then she inclines her head twice.*)

THE STEPDAUGHTER (*unable to contain herself*). Oh my God!
(*Puts a hand to her mouth to prevent herself from laughing.*)

THE MANAGER (*turning round*). What's the matter?

THE STEPDAUGHTER. Nothing, nothing!

THE MANAGER (*to* LEADING MAN). Go on!

LEADING MAN. You've been here before, eh? Well then, there's no need to be so shy, is there? May I take off your hat?

(*The* LEADING MAN *says this last speech in such a tone and with such gestures that the* STEPDAUGHTER, *though she has her hand to her mouth, cannot keep from laughing.*)

LEADING LADY (*indignant*). I'm not going to stop here to be made a fool of by that woman there.

LEADING MAN. Neither am I! I'm through with it!

THE MANAGER (*shouting to* STEPDAUGHTER). Silence! for once and all, I tell you!

THE STEPDAUGHTER. Forgive me! forgive me!

THE MANAGER. You haven't any manners: that's what it is! You go too far.

THE FATHER (*endeavoring to intervene*). Yes, it's true, but excuse her...

THE MANAGER. Excuse what? It's absolutely disgusting.

THE FATHER. Yes, sir, but believe me, it has such a strange effect when...

THE MANAGER. Strange? Why strange? Where is it strange?

THE FATHER. No, sir; I admire your actors — this gentleman here, this lady; but they are certainly not us!

THE MANAGER. I should hope not. Evidently they cannot be you, if they are actors.

THE FATHER. Just so: actors! Both of them act our parts exceedingly well. But, believe me, it produces quite a different effect on us. They want to be us, but they aren't, all the same.

THE MANAGER. What is it then, anyway?

THE FATHER. Something that is... that is theirs — and no longer ours...

THE MANAGER. But naturally, inevitably. I've told you so already.

THE FATHER. Yes, I understand... I understand...

THE MANAGER. Well then, let's have no more of it! (*Turning to the actors*): We'll have the rehearsals by ourselves, afterwards, in the ordinary way. I never could stand rehearsing with the author present. He's never satisfied! (*Turning to* FATHER *and* STEPDAUGHTER): Come on! Let's get on with it again; and try and see if you can't keep from laughing.

THE STEPDAUGHTER. Oh, I shan't laugh any more. There's a nice little bit coming for me now: you'll see.

THE MANAGER. Well then: when she says "Don't think any more of what I've said. I must forget, etc.," you (*addressing the* FATHER) come in sharp with "I understand, I understand"; and then you ask her...

THE STEPDAUGHTER (*interrupting*). What?

THE MANAGER. Why she is in mourning.

THE STEPDAUGHTER. Not at all! See here: when I told him that it was useless for me to be thinking about my wearing mourning, do you know how he answered me? "Ah well," he said, "then let's take off this little frock."

THE MANAGER. Great! Just what we want, to make a riot in the theatre!

THE STEPDAUGHTER. But it's the truth!

THE MANAGER. What does that matter? Acting is our business here. Truth up to a certain point, but no further.

THE STEPDAUGHTER. What do you want to do then?

THE MANAGER. You'll see, you'll see! Leave it to me.

THE STEPDAUGHTER. No sir! What you want to do is to piece together a little romantic sentimental scene out of my disgust, out of all the reasons, each more cruel and viler than the other, why I am what I am. He is to ask me why I'm in mourning; and I'm to answer with tears in my eyes, that it is just two months since papa died. No sir, no! He's got to say to me; as he did say: "Well, let's take off this little dress at once." And I; with my two months' mourning in my heart, went there behind that screen, and with these fingers tingling with shame...

THE MANAGER (*running his hands through his hair*). For Heaven's sake! What are you saying?

THE STEPDAUGHTER (*crying out excitedly*). The truth! The truth!

THE MANAGER. It may be. I don't deny it, and I can understand all your horror; but you must surely see that you can't have this kind of thing on the stage. It won't go.

THE STEPDAUGHTER. Not possible, eh? Very well! I'm much obliged to you — but I'm off!

THE MANAGER. Now be reasonable! Don't lose your temper!

THE STEPDAUGHTER. I won't stop here! I won't! I can see you've fixed it all up with him in your office. All this talk about what is possible for the stage... I understand! He wants to get at his complicated "cerebral drama," to have his famous remorses and torments acted; but I want to act my part, *my part!*

THE MANAGER (*annoyed, shaking his shoulders*). Ah! Just *your* part! But, if you will pardon me, there are other parts than yours: His (*indicating the* FATHER) and hers (*indicating the* MOTHER)! On the stage you can't have a character becoming too prominent and overshadowing all the others. The thing is to pack them all into a neat little framework and then act what is actable. I am aware of the fact that everyone has his own interior life which he wants very much to put forward. But the difficulty lies in this fact: to set out just so much as is necessary for the stage, taking the other characters into consideration, and at the same time hint at the unrevealed interior life of each. I am willing to admit, my dear young lady, that from your point of view it would be a fine idea if each character could tell the public all his troubles in a nice monologue or a regular one hour lecture (*good humoredly*). You must restrain yourself, my dear, and in your own interest, too; because this fury of yours, this exaggerated disgust you show, may make a bad impression, you know. After you have confessed to me that there were others before him at Madame Pace's and more than once...

THE STEPDAUGHTER (*bowing her head, impressed*). It's true. But remember those others mean him for me all the same.

THE MANAGER (*not understanding*). What? The others? What do you mean?

THE STEPDAUGHTER. For one who has gone wrong, sir, he who was responsible for the first fault is responsible for all that follow. He is responsible for my faults, was, even before I was born. Look at him, and see if it isn't true!

THE MANAGER. Well, well! And does the weight of so much responsibility seem nothing to you? Give him a chance to act it, to get it over!

THE STEPDAUGHTER. How? How can he act all his "noble remorses" all his "moral torments," if you want to spare him the horror of being discovered one day — after he had asked her what he did ask her — in the arms of her, that already fallen woman, that child, sir, that child he used to watch come out of school? (*She is moved.*)

(*The* MOTHER *at this point is overcome with emotion, and breaks out into a fit of crying. All are touched. A long pause.*)

THE STEPDAUGHTER (*as soon as the* MOTHER *becomes a little quieter, adds resolutely and gravely*). At present, we are unknown to the public. Tomorrow, you will act us as you wish, treating us in your own manner. But do you really want to see drama, do you want to see it flash out as it really did?

THE MANAGER. Of course! That's just what I do want, so I can use as much of it as is possible.

THE STEPDAUGHTER. Well then, ask that Mother there to leave us.

THE MOTHER (*changing her low plaint into a sharp cry*). No! No! Don't permit it, sir, don't permit it!

THE MANAGER. But it's only to try it.

THE MOTHER. I can't bear it. I can't.

THE MANAGER. But since it has happened already... I don't understand!

THE MOTHER. It's taking place now. It happens all the time. My torment isn't a pretended one. I live and feel every minute of my torture. Those two children there — have you heard them speak? They can't speak any more. They cling to me to keep my torment actual and vivid for me. But for themselves, they do not exist, they aren't any more. And she (*indicating* STEPDAUGHTER) has run away, she has left me,

and is lost.   If I now see her here before me, it is only to renew
for me the tortures I have suffered for her too.

THE FATHER.  The eternal moment!   She (*indicating the* STEP-
DAUGHTER) is here to catch me, fix me, and hold me eternally
in the stocks for that one fleeting and shameful moment of my
life.   She can't give it up!   And you sir, cannot either fairly
spare me it.

THE MANAGER.  I never said I didn't want to act it.   It will form,
as a matter of fact, the nucleus of the whole first act right up
to her surprise.                      (*Indicates the* MOTHER.)

THE FATHER.  Just so!   This is my punishment: the passion in all
of us that must culminate in her final cry.

THE STEPDAUGHTER.  I can hear it still in my ears.   It's driven me
mad, that cry! — You can put me on as you like; it doesn't
matter.   Fully dressed, if you like — provided I have at least
the arm bare; because, standing like this (*she goes close to the*
FATHER *and leans her head on his breast*) with my head so, and my
arms round his neck, I saw a vein pulsing in my arm here; and
then, as if that live vein had awakened disgust in me, I closed
my eyes like this, and let my head sink on his breast.   (*Turning
to the* MOTHER.)   Cry out mother!   Cry out!   (*Buries head in*
FATHER'S *breast, and with her shoulders raised as if to prevent her
hearing the cry, adds in tones of intense emotion.*)   Cry out as you
did then!

THE MOTHER (*coming forward to separate them*).  No!   My daughter,
my daughter!   (*And after having pulled her away from him.*)
You brute! you brute!   She is my daughter!   Don't you see
she's my daughter?

THE MANAGER (*walking backwards towards footlights*).  Fine! fine!
Damned good!   And then, of course — curtain!

THE FATHER (*going towards him excitedly*).  Yes, of course, because
that's the way it really happened.

THE MANAGER (*convinced and pleased*).  Oh, yes, no doubt about it.
Curtain here, curtain!

> (*At the reiterated cry of the* MANAGER, *the* MACHINIST *lets the
> curtain down, leaving the* MANAGER *and the* FATHER *in front of
> it before the footlights.*)

THE MANAGER.  The darned idiot!   I said "curtain" to show the

act should end there, and he goes and lets it down in earnest.
(*To the* FATHER, *while he pulls the curtain back to go on to the stage
again*.)   Yes, yes, it's all right.   Effect certain!   That's the
right ending.   I'll guarantee the first act at any rate.

## ACT III

*When the curtain goes up again, it is seen that the stage hands have
shifted the bit of scenery used in the last part, and have rigged up instead
at the back of the stage a drop, with some trees, and one or two wings.
A portion of a fountain basin is visible.   The* MOTHER *is sitting on
the right with the two children by her side.   The* SON *is on the same side,
but away from the others.   He seems bored, angry, and full of shame.
The* FATHER *and the* STEPDAUGHTER *are also seated towards the
right front.   On the other side (left) are the actors, much in the positions
they occupied before the curtain was lowered.   Only the* MANAGER *is
standing up in the middle of the stage, with his hand closed over his mouth
in the act of meditating.*

THE MANAGER (*shaking his shoulders after a brief pause*).  Ah yes:
the second act!   Leave it to me, leave it all to me as we arranged, and you'll see!   It'll go fine!

THE STEPDAUGHTER.  Our entry into his house (*indicates* FATHER)
in spite of him (*indicates* SON)...

THE MANAGER (*out of patience*).  Leave it to me, I tell you!

THE STEPDAUGHTER.  Do let it be clear, at any rate, that it is in
spite of my wishes.

THE MOTHER (*from her corner, shaking her head*).  For all the good
that's come of it...

THE STEPDAUGHTER (*turning towards her quickly*).  It doesn't matter.
The more harm done us, the more remorse for him.

THE MANAGER (*impatiently*).  I understand!   Good Heavens!
I understand!   I'm taking it into account.

THE MOTHER (*supplicatingly*).  I beg you, sir, to let it appear quite
plain that for conscience sake I did try in every way...

THE STEPDAUGHTER (*interrupting indignantly and continuing for the
MOTHER*).  ... to pacify me, to dissuade me from spiting him.
(*To* MANAGER.)  Do as she wants: satisfy her, because it is

true! I enjoy it immensely. Anyhow, as you can see, the meeker she is, the more she tries to get at his heart, the more distant and aloof does he become.

THE MANAGER. Are we going to begin this second act or not?

THE STEPDAUGHTER. I'm not going to talk any more now. But I must tell you this: you can't have the whole action take place in the garden, as you suggest. It isn't possible!

THE MANAGER. Why not?

THE STEPDAUGHTER. Because he (*indicates the* SON *again*) is always shut up alone in his room. And then there's all the part of that poor dazed-looking boy there which takes place indoors.

THE MANAGER. Maybe! On the other hand, you will understand — we can't change scenes three or four times in one act.

THE LEADING MAN. They used to once.

THE MANAGER. Yes, when the public was up to the level of that child there.

THE LEADING LADY. It makes the illusion easier.

THE FATHER (*irritated*). The illusion! For Heaven's sake, don't say illusion. Please don't use that word, which is particularly painful for us.

THE MANAGER (*astounded*). And why, if you please?

THE FATHER. It's painful, cruel, really cruel; and you ought to understand that.

THE MANAGER. But why? What ought we to say then? The illusion, I tell you, sir, which we've got to create for the audience...

THE LEADING MAN. With our acting.

THE MANAGER. The illusion of a reality.

THE FATHER. I understand; but you, perhaps, do not understand us. Forgive me! You see... here for you and your actors, the thing is only — and rightly so... a kind of game...

THE LEADING LADY (*interrupting indignantly*). A game! We're not children here, if you please! We are serious actors.

THE FATHER. I don't deny it. What I mean is the game, or play, of your art, which has to give, as the gentleman says, a perfect illusion of reality.

THE MANAGER. Precisely —— !

THE FATHER. Now, if you consider the fact that we (*indicates him-*

*self and the other five characters*), as we are, have no other reality outside of this illusion...

THE MANAGER (*astonished, looking at his actors, who are also amazed*). And what does that mean?

THE FATHER (*after watching them for a moment with a wan smile*). As I say, sir, that which is a game of art for you is our sole reality. (*Brief pause. He goes a step or two nearer the* MANAGER *and adds*:) But not only for us, you know, by the way. Just you think it over well. (*Looks him in the eyes.*) Can you tell me who you are?

THE MANAGER (*perplexed, half smiling*). What? Who am I? I am myself.

THE FATHER. And if I were to tell you that that isn't true, because you are I...?

THE MANAGER. I should say you were mad —— !
(*The actors laugh.*)

THE FATHER. You're quite right to laugh: because we are all making believe here (*to* MANAGER). And you can therefore object that it's only for a joke that that gentleman there (*indicates the* LEADING MAN), who naturally is himself, has to be me, who am on the contrary myself—this thing you see here. You see I've caught you in a trap! (*The actors laugh.*)

THE MANAGER (*annoyed*). But we've had all this over once before. Do you want to begin again?

THE FATHER. No, no! That wasn't my meaning! In fact, I should like to request you to abandon this game of art (*looking at the* LEADING LADY *as if anticipating her*) which you are accustomed to play here with your actors, and to ask you seriously once again: who are you?

THE MANAGER (*astonished and irritated, turning to his actors*). If this fellow here hasn't got a nerve! A man who calls himself a character comes and asks me who I am!

THE FATHER (*with dignity, but not offended*). A character, sir, may always ask a man who he is. Because a character has really a life of his own, marked with his especial characteristics; for which reason he is always "somebody." But a man — I'm not speaking of you now — may very well be "nobody."

THE MANAGER. Yes, but you are asking these questions of me, the boss, the manager! Do you understand?

THE FATHER. But only in order to know if you, as you really are now, see yourself as you once were with all the illusions that were yours then, with all the things both inside and outside of you as they seemed to you — as they were then indeed for you. Well, sir, if you think of all those illusions that mean nothing to you now, of all those things which don't even *seem* to you to exist any more, while once they *were* for you, don't you feel that — I won't say these boards — but the very earth under your feet is sinking away from you when you reflect that in the same way this *you* as you feel it today — all this present reality of yours — is fated to seem a mere illusion to you tomorrow?

THE MANAGER (*without having understood much, but astonished by the specious argument*). Well, well! And where does all this take us anyway?

THE FATHER. Oh, nowhere! It's only to show you that if we (*indicating the Characters*) have no other reality beyond the illusion, you too must not count overmuch on your reality as you feel it today, since, like that of yesterday, it may prove an illusion for you tomorrow.

THE MANAGER (*determining to make fun of him*). Ah, excellent! Then you'll be saying next that you, with this comedy of yours that you brought here to act, are truer and more real than I am.

THE FATHER (*with the greatest seriousness*). But of course; without doubt!

THE MANAGER. Ah, really?

THE FATHER. Why, I thought you'd understand that from the beginning.

THE MANAGER. More real than I?

THE FATHER. If your reality can change from one day to another...

THE MANAGER. But everyone knows it can change. It is always changing, the same as anyone else's.

THE FATHER (*with a cry*). No, sir, not ours! Look here! That is the very difference! Our reality doesn't change: it can't change! It can't be other than what it is, because it is already fixed forever. It's terrible. Ours is an immutable reality which should make you shudder when you approach us if you are really conscious of the fact that your reality is a mere transitory and fleeting illusion, taking this form today and that tomorrow, according to the conditions, according to your will, your sentiments, which in turn are controlled by an intellect that shows them to you today in one manner and tomorrow... who knows how?... Illusions of reality represented in this fatuous comedy of life that never ends, nor can ever end! Because if tomorrow it were to end... then why, all would be finished.

THE MANAGER. Oh, for God's sake, will you *at least* finish with this philosophizing and let us try and shape this comedy which you yourself have brought me here? You argue and philosophize a bit too much, my dear sir. You know you seem to me almost, almost... (*Stops and looks him over from head to foot.*) Ah, by the way, I think you introduced yourself to me as a — what shall... we say — a "character," created by an author who did not afterward care to make a drama of his own creations.

THE FATHER. It is the simple truth, sir.

THE MANAGER. Nonsense! Cut that out, please! None of us believes it, because it isn't a thing, as you must recognize yourself, which one can believe seriously. If you want to know, it seems to me you are trying to imitate the manner of a certain author whom I heartily detest — I warn you — although I have unfortunately bound myself to put on one of his works. As a matter of fact, I was just starting to rehearse it, when you arrived. (*Turning to the actors:*) And this is what we've gained — out of the frying-pan into the fire!

THE FATHER. I don't know to what author you may be alluding, but believe me I feel what I think; and I seem to be philosophizing only for those who do not think what they feel, because they blind themselves with their own sentiment. I know that for many people this self-blinding seems much more "human"; but the contrary is really true. For man never reasons so much and becomes so introspective as when he suffers; since he is anxious to get at the cause of his sufferings, to learn who has produced them, and whether it is just or unjust that he should have to bear them. On the other hand, when he is happy, he takes his happiness as it comes and doesn't analyse it, just as if happiness were his right. The animals suffer without reasoning about their sufferings. But take the case of a man who suffers and begins to reason about it. Oh no! it can't be allowed! Let him suffer like an animal, and then — ah yes, he is "human!"

THE MANAGER. Look here! Look here! You're off again, philosophizing worse than ever.

THE FATHER. Because I suffer, sir! I'm not philosophizing: I'm crying aloud the reason of my sufferings.

THE MANAGER (*makes brusque movement as he is taken with a new idea*). I should like to know if anyone has ever heard of a character who gets right out of his part and perorates and speechifies as you do. Have you ever heard of a case? I haven't.

THE FATHER. You have never met such a case, sir, because authors, as a rule, hide the labor of their creations. When the characters are really alive before their author, the latter does nothing but follow them in their action, in their words, in the situations which they suggest to him; and he has to will them the way they will themselves — for there's trouble if he doesn't. When a character is born, he acquires at once such an independence, even of his own author, that he can be imagined by everybody even in many other situations where the author never dreamed of placing him; and so he acquires for himself a meaning which the author never thought of giving him.

THE MANAGER. Yes, yes, I know this.

THE FATHER. What is there then to marvel at in us? Imagine such a misfortune for characters as I have described to you: to be born of an author's fantasy, and be denied life by him; and then answer me if these characters left alive, and yet without life, weren't right in doing what they did do and are doing now, after they have attempted everything in their power to persuade him to give them their stage life. We've all tried him in turn, I, she (*indicating the* STEPDAUGHTER) and she (*indicating the* MOTHER).

THE STEPDAUGHTER. It's true. I too have sought to tempt him, many, many times, when he has been sitting at his writing table, feeling a bit melancholy, at the twilight hour. He would sit in his armchair too lazy to switch on the light, and all the shadows that crept into his room were full of our presence coming to tempt him. (*As if she saw herself still there by the writing table, and was annoyed by the presence of the actors.*) Oh, if you would only go away, go away and leave us alone — mother here with that son of hers — I with that child — that boy there always alone — and then I with him (*just hints at the* FATHER) — and then I alone, alone... in those shadows! (*Makes a sudden movement as if in the vision she has of herself illuminating those shadows she wanted to seize hold of herself.*) Ah! my life! my life! Oh, what scenes we proposed to him — and I tempted him more than any of the others!

THE FATHER. Maybe. But perhaps it was your fault that he refused to give us life: because you were too insistent, too troublesome.

THE STEPDAUGHTER. Nonsense! Didn't he make me so himself? (*Goes close to the* MANAGER *to tell him as if in confidence.*) In my opinion he abandoned us in a fit of depression, of disgust for the ordinary theatre as the public knows it and likes it.

THE SON. Exactly what it was, sir; exactly that!

THE FATHER. Not at all! Don't believe it for a minute. Listen to me! You'll be doing quite right to modify, as you suggest, the excesses both of this girl here, who wants to do too much, and of this young man, who won't do anything at all.

THE SON. No, nothing!

THE MANAGER. You too get over the mark occasionally, my dear sir, if I may say so.

THE FATHER. I? When? Where?

THE MANAGER. Always! Continuously! Then there's this insistence of yours in trying to make us believe you are a character. And then too, you must really argue and philosophize less, you know, much less.

THE FATHER. Well, if you want to take away from me the possibility of representing the torment of my spirit which never gives me peace, you will be suppressing me: that's all. Every true man, sir, who is a little above the level of the beasts and plants does not live for the sake of living, without knowing how to live; but he lives so as to give a meaning and a value of his own to life. For me this is *everything*. I cannot give up this, just to represent a mere fact as she (*indicating the* STEPDAUGHTER) wants. It's all very well for her, since her "vendetta" lies in the "fact." I'm not going to do it. It destroys my *raison d'être*.

THE MANAGER. Your *raison d'être*. Oh, we're going ahead fine! First she starts off, and then you jump in. At this rate, we'll never finish.

THE FATHER. Now, don't be offended! Have it your own way — provided, however, that within the limits of the parts you assign us each one's sacrifice isn't too great.

THE MANAGER. You've got to understand that you can't go on arguing at your own pleasure. Drama is action, sir, action and not confounded philosophy.

THE FATHER. All right. I'll do just as much arguing and philosophizing as everybody does when he is considering his own torments.

THE MANAGER. If the drama permits! But for Heaven's sake, man, let's get along and come to the scene.

THE STEPDAUGHTER. It seems to me we've got too much action with our coming into his house (*indicating* FATHER). You said, before, you couldn't change the scene every five minutes.

THE MANAGER. Of course not. What we've got to do is to combine and group up all the facts in one simultaneous, close-knit, action. We can't have it as you want, with your little brother wandering like a ghost from room to room, hiding behind doors and meditating a project which — what did you say it did to him?

THE STEPDAUGHTER. Consumes him, sir, wastes him away!

THE MANAGER. Well, it may be. And then at the same time, you want the little girl there to be playing in the garden... one in the house, and the other in the garden: isn't that it?

THE STEPDAUGHTER. Yes, in the sun, in the sun! That is my only pleasure: to see her happy and careless in the garden after the misery and squalor of the horrible room where we all four slept together. And I had to sleep with her — I, do you understand? — with my vile contaminated body next to hers; with her folding me fast in her loving little arms. In the garden, whenever she spied me, she would run to take me by the hand. She didn't care for the big flowers, only the little ones; and she loved to show me them and pet me.

THE MANAGER. Well then, we'll have it in the garden. Everything shall happen in the garden; and we'll group the other scenes there. (*Calls a stage hand.*) Here, a backcloth with trees and something to do as a fountain basin. (*Turning round to look at the back of the stage.*) Ah, you've fixed it up. Good! (*To* STEPDAUGHTER.) This is just to give an idea, of course. The boy, instead of hiding behind the doors, will wander about here in the garden, hiding behind the trees. But it's going to be rather difficult to find a child to do that scene with you where she shows you the flowers. (*Turning to the* YOUTH.) Come forward a little, will you please? Let's try it now! Come along! come along! (*Then seeing him come shyly forward, full of fear and looking lost.*) It's a nice business, this lad here. What's the matter with him? We'll have to give him a word or two to say. (*Goes close to him, puts a hand on his shoulders, and leads him behind one of the trees.*) Come on! come on! Let me see you a little! Hide here... yes, like that. Try and show your head just a little as if you were looking for someone... (*Goes back to observe the effect, when the* BOY *at once goes through the action.*) Excellent! fine! (*Turning to* STEPDAUGHTER.) Suppose the little girl there were to surprise him as he looks round, and run over to him, so we could give him a word or two to say?

THE STEPDAUGHTER. It's useless to hope he will speak, as long as that fellow there is here... (*Indicates the* SON.) You must send him away first.

THE SON (*jumping up*). Delighted! delighted! I don't ask for anything better. (*Begins to move away.*)

THE MANAGER (*at once stopping him*). No! No! Where are you going? Wait a bit!

(*The* MOTHER *gets up alarmed and terrified at the thought that he is really about to go away. Instinctively she lifts her arms to prevent him, without, however, leaving her seat.*)

THE SON (*to* MANAGER *who stops him*). I've got nothing to do with this affair. Let me go please! Let me go!

THE MANAGER. What do you mean by saying you've got nothing to do with this?

THE STEPDAUGHTER (*calmly, with irony*). Don't bother to stop him: he won't go away.

THE FATHER. He has to act the terrible scene in the garden with his mother.

THE SON (*suddenly resolute and with dignity*). I shall act nothing at all. I've said so from the very beginning (*to the* MANAGER). Let me go!

THE STEPDAUGHTER (*going over to the* MANAGER.) Allow me? (*Puts down the* MANAGER's *arm which is restraining the* SON.) Well, go away then, if you want to! (*The* SON *looks at her with contempt and hatred. She laughs and says.*) You see, he can't, he can't go away! He is obliged to stay here, indissolubly bound to the chain. If I, who fly off when that happens which has to happen, because I can't bear him — if I am still here and support that face and expression of his, you can well imagine that he is unable to move. He has to remain here, has to stop with that nice father of his, and that mother whose only son he is. (*Turning to the* MOTHER.) Come on, mother, come along! (*Turning to* MANAGER *to indicate her.*) You see, she was getting up to keep him back. (*To the* MOTHER, *beckoning her with her hand.*) Come on! come on! (*Then to* MANAGER.) You can imagine how little she wants to show these actors of yours what she really feels; but so eager is she to get near him that... There, you see? She is willing to act her part.

(*And in fact, the* MOTHER *approaches him; and as soon as the* STEPDAUGHTER *has finished speaking, opens her arms to signify that she consents.*)

THE SON (*suddenly*). No! no! If I can't go away, then I'll stop here; but I repeat: I act nothing!

THE FATHER (*to* MANAGER *excitedly*). You can force him, sir.

THE SON. Nobody can force me.

THE FATHER. I can.

THE STEPDAUGHTER. Wait a minute, wait... First of all, the baby has to go to the fountain...

(*Runs to take the* CHILD *and leads her to the fountain.*)

THE MANAGER. Yes, yes of course; that's it. Both at the same time.

(*The* SECOND LADY LEAD *and the* JUVENILE LEAD *at this point
separate themselves from the group of actors. One watches the*
MOTHER *attentively; the other moves about studying the movements and manner of the* SON *whom he will have to act.*)

THE SON (*to* MANAGER). What do you mean by both at the same
time? It isn't right. There was no scene between me and
her. (*Indicates the* MOTHER.) Ask her how it was!

THE MOTHER. Yes, it's true. I had come into his room...

THE SON. Into my room, do you understand? Nothing to do
with the garden.

THE MANAGER. It doesn't matter. Haven't I told you we've got
to group the action?

THE SON (*observing the* JUVENILE LEAD *studying him*). What do you
want?

THE JUVENILE LEAD. Nothing! I was just looking at you.

THE SON (*turning towards the* SECOND LADY LEAD). Ah! she's at it
too: to re-act her part! (*Indicating the* MOTHER.)

THE MANAGER. Exactly! And it seems to me that you ought to
be grateful to them for their interest.

THE SON. Yes, but haven't you yet perceived that it isn't possible
to live in front of a mirror which not only freezes us with the
image of ourselves, but throws our likeness back at us with a
horrible grimace?

THE FATHER. That is true, absolutely true. You must see that.

THE MANAGER (*to* SECOND LADY LEAD *and* JUVENILE LEAD). He's
right! Move away from them!

THE SON. Do as you like. I'm out of this!

THE MANAGER. Be quiet, you, will you? And let me hear your
mother! (*To* MOTHER.) You were saying you had entered...

THE MOTHER. Yes, into his room, because I couldn't stand it
any longer. I went to empty my heart to him of all the anguish
that tortures me... But as soon as he saw me come in...

THE SON. Nothing happened! There was no scene. I went
away, that's all! I don't care for scenes!

THE MOTHER. It's true, true. That's how it was.

THE MANAGER. Well now, we've got to do this bit between you
and him. It's indispensable.

THE MOTHER. I'm ready... when you are ready. If you could

only find a chance for me to tell him what I feel here in my heart.

THE FATHER (*going to* SON *in a great rage*). You'll do this for your mother, for your mother, do you understand?

THE SON (*quite determined*). I do nothing!

THE FATHER (*taking hold of him and shaking him*). For God's sake, do as I tell you! Don't you hear your mother asking you for a favor? Haven't you even got the guts to be a son?

THE SON (*taking hold of the* FATHER). No! No! And for God's sake stop it, or else...

   (*General agitation. The* MOTHER, *frightened, tries to separate them.*)

THE MOTHER (*pleading*). Please! please!

THE FATHER (*not leaving hold of the* SON). You've got to obey, do you hear?

THE SON (*almost crying from rage*). What does it mean, this madness you've got? (*They separate.*) Have you no decency, that you insist on showing everyone our shame? I won't do it! I won't! And I stand for the will of our author in this. He didn't want to put us on the stage, after all!

THE MANAGER. Man alive! You came here...

THE SON (*indicating* FATHER). *He* did! I didn't!

THE MANAGER. Aren't you here now?

THE SON. It was his wish, and he dragged us along with him. He's told you not only the things that did happen, but also things that have never happened at all.

THE MANAGER. Well, tell me then what did happen. You went out of your room without saying a word?

THE SON. Without a word, so as to avoid a scene!

THE MANAGER. And then what did you do?

THE SON. Nothing... walking in the garden...

   (*Hesitates for a moment with expression of gloom.*)

THE MANAGER (*coming closer to him, interested by his extraordinary reserve*). Well, well... walking in the garden...

THE SON (*exasperated*). Why on earth do you insist? It's horrible!
   (*The* MOTHER *trembles, sobs, and looks towards the fountain.*)

THE MANAGER (*slowly observing the glance and turning towards the* SON *with increasing apprehension*). The baby?

THE SON. There in the fountain…

THE FATHER (*pointing with tender pity to the* MOTHER). She was following him at the moment…

THE MANAGER (*to the* SON *anxiously*). And then you…

THE SON. I ran over to her; I was jumping in to drag her out when I saw something that froze my blood … the boy there standing stock still, with eyes like a madman's, watching his little drowned sister, in the fountain! (*The* STEPDAUGHTER *bends over the fountain to hide the* CHILD. *She sobs.*) Then…

(*A revolver shot rings out behind the trees where the* BOY *is hidden.*)

THE MOTHER (*with a cry of terror runs over in that direction together with several of the actors amid general confusion*). My son! My son! (*Then amid the cries and exclamations one hears her voice.*) Help! help!

THE MANAGER (*pushing the actors aside while they lift up the* BOY *and carry him off*). Is he really wounded?

SOME ACTORS. He's dead! dead!

OTHER ACTORS. No, no, it's only make believe, it's only pretence!

THE FATHER (*with a terrible cry*). Pretence? Reality, sir, reality!

THE MANAGER. Pretence? Reality? To hell with it all! Never in my life has such a thing happened to me. I've lost a whole day over these people, a whole day!

CURTAIN

# L'INVITATION AU VOYAGE

## A PLAY IN THREE ACTS AND FIVE SCENES

### By JEAN–JACQUES BERNARD

*Translated by ERNEST BOYD*

*Reprinted by permission of Ernest Boyd*

## JEAN–JACQUES BERNARD

JEAN-JACQUES BERNARD, the son of the famous dramatist Tristan Bernard, was born at Enghien-les-Bains, July 30, 1888. He is one of the leading members of that after-the-war group in France which has devoted itself to refining and subtilizing the mediums of dramatic expression. Among the more important of Bernard's contemporaries are H. R. Lenormand, Charles Vildrac, Paul Géraldy, Paul Reynal, Jean Sarment, Denys Amiel and André Obey. Turning alike aside from force and from an obtrusive craft Bernard seeks to give voice to the unspoken, to dramatize the intangible overtones of experience. In addition to writing plays and novels he has contributed to *Figaro*, *Le Matin*, *Gil Blas* and *La Revue Française*. His plays reveal the tragic undercurrent of simple and undistinguished life. There is a classical quality in his economy of means and in his concentration, that almost, but not quite, conceals the fact that his plays are indeed exquisite works of artifice.

"The theatre has no worse enemy than literature. It expounds and dilutes that which it should only suggest." J. J. BERNARD.

# L'INVITATION AU VOYAGE

THOUGH he has identified himself with the drama of silence, and with the idea that literature is the greatest enemy of drama, Bernard protests against the supposition that he represents one style alone. "I always protest when, seeing me flee from outmoded formulas, people wish to confine me in new formulas. Whether one is prisoner of others or prisoner of himself the danger is the same," he says. *L'Invitation au Voyage*, in three acts and five scenes, was first produced at the Odeon in Paris, February 15, 1924; it was repeated at the Studio des Champs-Elysées, March 28, 1924. A new version in three acts and four scenes was produced at the Comédie de Genève by the company of the Studio des Champs-Elysées, October 17, 1926. Translated as *Glamour* by Winifred Katzin it was published in *Eight European Plays*, New York, 1927. The present translation by Ernest Boyd of the earlier form of the play was produced by the Civic Repertory Theatre, New York, October, 1928. It has not before been printed.

# CAST OF CHARACTERS

Marie Louise

Olivier, *her husband*

Jacqueline, *her sister*

Monsieur Landreau, *her father*

Gerard, *her son*

Monsieur Galais

# ACT I

*The present time. In the Vosges Mountains. A circular room, almost all windows, through which on every side a pine forest can be seen.*

*There are only two small panels without windows, in the foreground to the right and to the left. To the right is a door, and to the left, opposite the door, is a large Sarrequemines porcelain stove, in front of which are three low armchairs.*

*The rest of the room consists of a series of tall windows, against which is a divan.*

*To the left from the audience is a broad, massive desk with a chair. To the right a baby grand piano, with the keyboard turned away from the audience.*

*A small table, a little bookshelf. Papers on the desk. Flowers on the piano and table. The atmosphere is suggested, not so much by the arrangement of the room as by the pine forest, deep and overflowing.*

## FIRST SCENE

*The windows are all wide open on the forest. The pink light of a fine afternoon in September, on the wane. MARIE LOUISE, 26 years old, is at the piano playing a Chopin nocturne. After a while a clock outside strikes six. Then a factory whistle blows for a few seconds. MARIE LOUISE stops playing. To the left men's voices and footsteps can be heard, and two men, in the sixties, pass slowly talking in front of the windows. One has a light colored suit and straw hat. He is obviously at home. The other has a dark suit and a derby hat — a chance visitor.*

FIRST MAN. Yes. The factory is closing for the day. At six now. Look, down there are some of the men getting back to the village.

SECOND MAN. We seem to have got back to our starting point.

FIRST MAN. We are at the west end of the house. We have made the grand tour. Before we go in, I want you to see this apartment... it is my favorite.

SECOND MAN. Ah! My dear Landreau, what a pleasant life you lead.

*(They exit at right. MARIE LOUISE leaves the piano. Soon the door opens and the two men enter.)*

LANDREAU. Yes. My life is properly regulated. That constitutes its charm. Hello! My daughter is here.... Come here, Marie Louise.... This is my elder daughter, Madame Olivier Mailly, my partner's wife... M. Galais, a business acquaintance who happened to be in the neighborhood.

MARIE LOUISE. How do you do?

GALAIS. Delighted to meet you.

LANDREAU. M. Galais was at the Ecole Centrale with me.

GALAIS. We were both younger then.

LANDREAU. I'm so sorry you can't stay a while. My daughter would have displayed all her talents.... She's a... an artist, a musician.... She knows everything. She and her sister have had a good education.... Presently you'll see the younger girl. She isn't married... There's five years between them... You'd never take them for sisters, they're so unlike. We are in the apartment which I had arranged when Marie Louise got married. As a matter of fact, it was in such a state that it had to be almost entirely rebuilt.... This is my son-in-law's desk. He takes refuge here when he doesn't want to be disturbed. He never receives people here. It's too far from the factory. Don't you think it's nice? The desk, the piano? Just look out of this window and you'll get a better idea of my property.

(*They look out of window at right.* MARIE LOUISE, *who is slightly irritated, has sat down with a book, which she is not reading.*)

GALAIS. I see the factory is separated from the house.

LANDREAU. Exactly. My great-grandfather, who began building, arranged that very well. The factory is down there to the east fifteen hundred yards from the village. The hands don't have to pass this way when they're going home. My family life is quite separate from my business life. Not that it has prevented my wife and daughters from helping when it was necessary. But there's no compulsion. If they want to work, they work. If they want to dream, they dream.

GALAIS (*looking politely at* MARIE LOUISE). That's very nice for the ladies.

LANDREAU (*pointing to the right*). Look, on the way here, after the factory and the office, you come to my garage, which was the stable in my father's time. After the garage, come the outhouses,

and after the outhouses, my house, with my orchard, my green-
houses, my tennis court, or rather, my children's tennis court.
Then there's that gallery you see, fifteen yards long, which I had
built eight years ago to connect this apartment with the house.
That's the end of my property, I mean, of course, my buildings.
... Beyond that is the pine forest. You can walk for an hour
and a half in any direction and see nothing but pines, pines,
pines....

GALAIS. In the north we haven't anything to compare with this.
You manufacturers in the Vosges are well off.

LANDREAU. If you'd had time, I'd have taken you for a walk.
There are some views in the neighborhood which are greatly
admired.

GALAIS. I'll be back some other time. And I hope to see you at my
place. It's very good for us to see what each of us is doing.

LANDREAU. Very... very good. Especially for the young folk.
By the way, this year we have with us the son of one of our biggest
Paris customers. You must know them.... Valbeille & Com-
pany.

GALAIS. Yes, I know them.... They have an excellent reputation.
If you have Valbeille as well as Huchard and Santerre, I can
understand why you are satisfied.

(*A voice is heard shouting:* "MARIE LOUISE!")

A YOUNG GIRL (*appearing at a window*). I say, Marie Louise. What
about that game of tennis?

MARIE LOUISE. Not this evening. I don't feel like it.

LANDREAU (*going to the window*). Jacqueline, my younger daughter
... M. Galais, who happened to be passing through.

JACQUELINE. How do you do?

GALAIS. Delighted to meet you.

LANDREAU (*pinching* JACQUELINE's *cheek*). A clever youngster.
Not as artistic, I'll admit, even though her sister *is* present. My
daughters are not vain. She's got brains, but she's not so
artistic.

JACQUELINE (*to* MARIE LOUISE). Why won't you play? Philippe
and I have been waiting for you for the past half hour.

LANDREAU. Oh! Philippe. That's the young fellow I was talking
about. He's working for a spell with each of his father's big

customers. He helps the children to pass the time. Why won't you play tennis, Marie Louise?

MARIE LOUISE. Because I don't want to, father.

LANDREAU. You're wrong, dear. I had the court made for you. M. Valbeille will only be here for a few days more. You ought to play while you have a partner.

(*Meanwhile* JACQUELINE *has left the window and come into the room.*)

GALAIS. I'm very sorry, but it's getting late, and I have to be in Epinal for dinner.

LANDREAU. You can't go like that. Won't you have a cup of tea? No? Well, a glass of port? I'm sure my wife has ordered tea. Come along! Are you coming children?

(JACQUELINE *looks at* MARIE LOUISE.)

MARIE LOUISE. I... don't want any port.

JACQUELINE. We're going to play tennis, father.

LANDREAU (*going towards the door*). Very well.

GALAIS (*bowing*). Good-bye....

LANDREAU. I'll show you the way. (*Exit with* GALAIS.)

JACQUELINE. Well, are you coming?

MARIE LOUISE. Where?

JACQUELINE. To play tennis.

MARIE LOUISE. I told you I wasn't.

JACQUELINE. Then I must tell Philippe. He's not at the factory. He's waiting for us.

MARIE LOUISE. Oh, he can always find something to do.

JACQUELINE. We've got to be polite to Father's and Olivier's guest.

MARIE LOUISE. Olivier doesn't bother about such things, thank heaven.

JACQUELINE. But Father does! I'm sure he'd have been delighted if we had poured tea for that man. He was very sweet about it. He saw you didn't want to, so he didn't insist.

MARIE LOUISE. Mother is here. If we have to be all smiles every time Father receives an ironmonger....

JACQUELINE. I was thinking of *him*. He's proud of us.

MARIE LOUISE. Oh! I know only too well how proud he is of us. A while ago he showed me to that man and said "My daughter," just as he said "my house," "my garage," "my orchard." Do you know what we are? Annexes to the factory.

JACQUELINE. What is the matter with you?

MARIE LOUISE. Nothing. Father irritated me, that's all.

JACQUELINE. You're most unreasonable.

MARIE LOUISE. I suppose I am. You're so reasonable. You really ought to be my elder sister.

JACQUELINE. At least, Olivier's all right.

MARIE LOUISE. Olivier? Why, of course. What makes you think that?

JACQUELINE. He's the most important....

MARIE LOUISE. He's everything. Olivier and I are one person.

JACQUELINE. You talk like a young wife. It's charming.

MARIE LOUISE. Am I not a young wife?

JACQUELINE. Eight years.

MARIE LOUISE. They've passed quickly.

JACQUELINE. Your happiness is a great example for me.

MARIE LOUISE. Olivier deserves all the credit. You see, my feeling is more than love, it's esteem and admiration. Why do you smile?

JACQUELINE. I'm not smiling.

MARIE LOUISE. Look what he has done with the factory in eight years. Not that I want to belittle Father. But he's getting old and without Olivier.... And consider his standing in the district.

JACQUELINE. Yes. You have everything to make you happy. A good husband and a fine child. I can't see what you have to complain of.

MARIE LOUISE. But, Jacqueline, I wasn't complaining....

(*She walks up stage and stands for a moment in reverie, her eyes fixed on the forest.*)

JACQUELINE. What are you looking at?

MARIE LOUISE. Those trees....

JACQUELINE. What's wrong with them?

MARIE LOUISE. Oh! Just an idea I had. Have you never thought that, instead of those trees that never change, we might have others that lose their leaves in the autumn and have new ones in the spring?

JACQUELINE. If we had other trees, you'd be longing to have those back.

MARIE LOUISE. That's possible.  A while ago Father said to that man: "You can walk for an hour and a half in any direction and see nothing but pines, pines, pines... (*to herself*)pines... pines....

JACQUELINE. Why do you say that?

MARIE LOUISE. I don't know.  For no reason.  (*Comes down front.*) That man wasn't very entertaining.

JACQUELINE. I didn't notice him.

MARIE LOUISE. It hasn't been very lively here for some time.

JACQUELINE. Yet lots of people drop in.

MARIE LOUISE. I'd just as soon not see them.

JACQUELINE. You're too quick at judging people.  One gesture, one look, and they're either perfect or terrible.  What an imagination you have!

MARIE LOUISE. I see more than you give me credit for.  But I have a curious impression of all these people who come and go.  It's like a little window opening onto the world, then shutting immediately.... What we have seen is not meant for us.

JACQUELINE. Apparently you regret it.

MARIE LOUISE. I?  Not at all!  All those people love me.

JACQUELINE. Even Philippe?

MARIE LOUISE. Just like the others.

JACQUELINE. But, he's better....

MARIE LOUISE. Don't be absurd!  I'll tell you what Philippe is — a nail merchant's son.  What did he come here for?  To see how nails are made.  And what will he do when he leaves?  Go and see other nails being made.  And so on eternally.  In the end, he'll be exactly like his father.

JACQUELINE. There you go!  If he were not the son of one of father's customers, you'd think him charming.

MARIE LOUISE. Don't be silly!  Why should I take Philippe so seriously?  Because he plays a good game of tennis and likes music and poetry?  Oh! Jacqueline... I admit he's not a bad sort, but he's every inch an ironmonger.

JACQUELINE. That's not his fault.

MARIE LOUISE. Even when he plays tennis, he has a way of hitting the balls which reminds you of the machine that flattens out the heads of nails.

JACQUELINE. I've never noticed that.

MARIE LOUISE. Well, I have.... He lacks a certain something that I can't describe, but it's something you can't pick up so easily. ... When he recites verse he always makes me think of the hum of a sawmill. (*She laughs.*)

JACQUELINE. You mean, he gets on your nerves?

MARIE LOUISE. Not even that. I can see his good qualities, his good manners. For instance, those fans he gave us. I thought that was nice of him. (*Takes up a fan from the piano and smiles.*) Mine, obviously... inlaid ivory... cherubs... as for taste... And this Baudelaire he brought me from Epinal.... (*Takes a book off the table.*) Of course, he couldn't guess that my favorite poet was Chenier. I don't understand Baudelaire. He's too obscure, too complicated. (*Puts down book.*) However, he meant well.

JACQUELINE. Well, what does Olivier think of him?

MARIE LOUISE. Did you ever hear Olivier speaking ill of anyone?... The worst of it is that he can't defend himself. You know that Philippe sometimes comes back here with us after dinner. He sits there — (*points to the three armchairs*) — the whole evening long, there, between us.... And do you think Olivier would try to get rid of him? Not at all. They tell each other stories for hours. I have to beg for mercy. Last night I fell asleep listening to them. Olivier would go on all night. He's such a child! But you can imagine how amusing it is for me.

JACQUELINE. Why not explain all that?

MARIE LOUISE. It's not worth while for the few days that Philippe still has here. The truth is, I am only too pleased that he looks on the bright side of life. After all, we get over these little worries.

JACQUELINE. You have one thing that is a great help: you love each other.

MARIE LOUISE. Yes, I admit I am not unhappy.

JACQUELINE. I wish I could discover an Olivier ——

MARIE LOUISE. There can't be another man just like him.

JACQUELINE. There isn't another woman just like you.

MARIE LOUISE. I am what he has made me. (*Door opens.*) Hello! Here he is.

(*Enter* OLIVIER.    *Thirty-five years old.*)

JACQUELINE. We've just been slandering you, Olivier....

OLIVIER. Really?... What for, may I ask?

MARIE LOUISE. No, you mustn't.... (*Goes to his arms.*) Good evening, big darling.  I haven't seen you for two hours.

OLIVIER. Good evening, little darling.... It *has* been a long time....

JACQUELINE. Well, I'll be off and leave you two turtle-doves.

OLIVIER. Don't go, Jacqueline.  I'll have to leave in a couple of seconds.

MARIE LOUISE. Leave?  What an idea!

OLIVIER. There was a M. Galais here a while ago...

MARIE LOUISE. Yes, I saw him....

OLIVIER. ... And he submitted an interesting scheme to your father which I must look into at once.

MARIE LOUISE. Well, look into it here while we're talking.

OLIVIER (*smiling*).  I wish I could, but your father is waiting for me.... (*Goes to desk and takes papers.*)  Why don't you have a game of tennis?

MARIE LOUISE (*looking at* JACQUELINE).  We don't feel like it.... You know, I was astonished to find you were still at the factory.... Very soon I should have been worried.

OLIVIER. Silly child!  (*Returns with papers.*)  Listen to this, pitiful wife: as I was coming across the yard, I met your son all alone.

MARIE LOUISE. Gerard alone?

OLIVIER. All alone in the main yard.  And you'll never guess what he was doing.

MARIE LOUISE. No.  Tell me.

OLIVIER. Unscrewing a hose.  You'll admit that this was a strange occupation for a boy of seven.  He was looking for — guess what — the pressure!

MARIE LOUISE. Oh!

JACQUELINE (*laughing*).  The pressure!  Who on earth told him about that?

OLIVIER. It must have been Philippe.  Of course the child got it all wrong.  I tried to explain it to him, but I don't think I was any more successful.

MARIE LOUISE. What did Philippe want to...

OLIVIER. Oh! It's not so very serious. Rather nice, even...
By the way, he leaves the day after tomorrow.

JACQUELINE. Philippe?

MARIE LOUISE. Bon Voyage!

JACQUELINE. Did he suddenly decide to go? He never mentioned
it to me.

OLIVIER. A letter came from his father a few moments ago. I've
just seen it. He must sail for America on Wednesday....

MARIE LOUISE (*astonished*). For America?...

OLIVIER. Yes. To the Argentine, on a big deal about which he
had spoken to me. The thing has been hanging fire for months.
It has gone through. And he's in luck.

MARIE LOUISE (*her tone changed*). To the Argentine?

OLIVIER. Yes. To the Argentine... Buenos Ayres... the large
cities... Well, he'll tell us all about it tonight.

MARIE LOUISE. But... will he be away for long?

OLIVIER. How do you mean... for long?

MARIE LOUISE. Will his business keep him... away over there?

OLIVIER. Why, of course.

MARIE LOUISE. But, for how long?

OLIVIER. You never can tell. Perhaps for the rest of his life...
if everything goes well.... In any case, there's plenty to be
done in those new countries, as you can imagine.

JACQUELINE. That's just what Father was saying the other day.

MARIE LOUISE. What? did you know about it?

JACQUELINE. Yes, I heard some talk of it.

OLIVIER. And there'll be more talk about it for the next two days!
We'll have out the atlases and gazetteers. That will fill up his
evenings until he leaves. (*Laughs.*) Well, I'll see you later.

MARIE LOUISE (*abstractedly*). See you later. (*Exit* OLIVIER.)

JACQUELINE. If I were in his shoes, I'd be rather upset at the idea
of crossing the ocean, and perhaps never coming back. It must
make a difference to him.... But when a man's a bachelor...
(*Sees that* MARIE LOUISE *is not listening.*) What's wrong with you?

MARIE LOUISE (*dreamily*). The Argentine... How strange!

JACQUELINE. Why strange?

MARIE LOUISE. I don't know. It doesn't seem to suit him.... The
Argentine... I suppose he's lucky.

JACQUELINE. That may or may not be the case.

MARIE LOUISE. ... The Argentine... Yes, it's strange to hear that word when one is buried somewhere.

JACQUELINE. Buried?

(MARIE LOUISE *does not reply. She goes up stage and looks at the forest. Suddenly, as she turns to the right, her face is lit up by a ray of light from outside.*)

MARIE LOUISE. What is that? (*She turns her head to escape from the beam of light that follows her.*) Who is amusing himself reflecting the sun in my face?

JACQUELINE (*who has gone to the window*). It's Philippe. He has a mirror in one hand and is waving his racket in the other.

MARIE LOUISE. He certainly is keen on that game of tennis. But I won't go. (*Advancing.*) You hear? I won't go. Why, he's blinding me. I can't see a thing.

JACQUELINE. All you have to do is to get out of the ray.

MARIE LOUISE (*not listening*). You may do what you please. I won't come.

(*She moves her head from side to side as if playing with the ray.*)

JACQUELINE. But, why don't you step to one side.

MARIE LOUISE. You're going too far! Can't you stop? What a fool you are! What a fool! (*She grows more and more excited and talks while laughing and moving her head.*) Isn't he silly, Jacqueline? You're a fool, do you hear? A fool, a fool... An absolute fool, do you hear?...

(*During this, the curtain falls.*)

END OF SCENE I

## SECOND SCENE

*Six weeks later. The windows are closed. The light coming through the windows is more sombre. It is a gray November morning. The stove is lit.* MARIE LOUISE *is alone. She is sitting on the divan, reading.* OLIVIER *enters. She is absorbed in her book and does not hear him. He looks at her for a moment, then steps towards her.*

OLIVIER. What are you reading?

MARIE LOUISE (*looks around, jumps up suddenly, frightened*). You here!

OLIVIER. Did I frighten you?

MARIE LOUISE. Oh... it doesn't matter.

OLIVIER. What were you reading?

MARIE LOUISE. Baudelaire... a poem of Baudelaire's.

*(She goes quickly and puts her book on the little table.)*

OLIVIER. By Jove! Your tastes *have* changed.

MARIE LOUISE. What?

OLIVIER *(sitting down)*. You know, I really can't get over that postcard. It was so unexpected.

MARIE LOUISE. But... why?

OLIVIER. Doesn't it surprise you? A man who spent several months here, on such an intimate footing — and then not a sign of life. Suddenly, after six weeks, a postcard from Dakar... *(MARIE LOUISE doesn't answer.)* Yes, it's true, he has an excuse... the rush of getting away. We're very quiet here.... Well, that card saves him. If I cared to be nasty, I might say that he had another excuse. You were never very cordial to him.

MARIE LOUISE. I?

OLIVIER. I remember that you refused to accompany him to Epinal because it bored you.

MARIE LOUISE. I never said that.

OLIVIER. Oh yes, you did .... At least, that is my impression.... And that evening when you imitated his way of eating and speaking...

MARIE LOUISE. I don't remember.... Perhaps I did.

OLIVIER. Unless you were trying to conceal the fact that you were upset.

MARIE LOUISE. Upset?... You're quite mistaken, Olivier.

OLIVIER. Why not? I am like that, too. After all it always *is* upsetting to see someone go away. *(Reflectively.)* If that card was from Dakar, he can't be far from Buenos Ayres now. *(Silence.)* Don't you think so?

MARIE LOUISE. What?

OLIVIER. That it always *is* upsetting to see someone go away.

MARIE LOUISE. Yes.... *(Suddenly.)* Oh, you're exaggerating....

OLIVIER. Not a bad chap, Philippe. We *did* get along all right together. He wasn't, of course, a close friend, but a good companion.... Don't you think so?

MARIE LOUISE. Yes.

OLIVIER. You know, it's rather funny to think that this man, whom we shall probably never see again, was sitting in that chair joking with us only six weeks ago.

MARIE LOUISE (*staring at the armchair between the two others in front of the stove*). That's true... in that chair... How long ago it seems....

OLIVIER. No. It's not long ago... or, if you like, it is, like everything that will never return. Even then... That's only an impression.... We'd scarcely have given Philippe a thought now, if we hadn't spent those evenings together when he amused us both. Probably in the end he'd have bored us and it's a good thing he has gone.... Yet, it seems as if we had turned a page of our happiness. Do you understand? In that sense you can say that people never completely go away.

MARIE LOUISE. Do you think so? (*Looks around with a forced smile.*) What you say is rather terrifying.

OLIVIER (*going to her*). 'Pon my word, you actually look terrified.... (*Laughs.*) Don't worry, tender heart, Philippe Valbeille is not the piano.

MARIE LOUISE. How do you mean?

OLIVIER. Don't you remember? The time they took the piano away to repair it, you could hardly bear to live. That empty place made you ill.

MARIE LOUISE. You silly! (*Leans her head on his shoulder.*) Oh, I love you... hold me very tight, very close.

OLIVIER (*holding her in his arms*). There, there... what is the matter with you? I didn't expect this burst of emotion.

MARIE LOUISE. Tighter, tighter... As if you wanted to keep me and protect me... Ah! Now I feel better.... (*Breaks away.*) Oh, tell me... (*She hesitates.*) What are you doing this morning?

OLIVIER. I'll just go to the factory for a moment. Before lunch I may need your advice about a couple of letters. Shall you be free?

MARIE LOUISE. Oh, I am only too delighted when you need me. I have to correct the child's exercises.... That won't take long. (*Silence.*) Oh!...

OLIVIER. What?

MARIE LOUISE. I wanted to... ask you something.

OLIVIER. Go on...

MARIE LOUISE. I was still thinking about... since you were talking about letters... Have you ever thought... if you answer M. Valbeille... where will you write?...

OLIVIER. Care of his father. They'll forward the letter.... It would be very difficult to reach him in South America.

MARIE LOUISE. In Buenos Ayres...

OLIVIER. Buenos Ayres... You know, that's a city of one million people....

MARIE LOUISE. Of course, I know. Don't be silly.... But he might have told you...

OLIVIER. He doesn't know himself where he's going to live.

MARIE LOUISE. ... I know, but won't he stay at an hotel?

OLIVIER. He'll make his way out there.

MARIE LOUISE. Yes... Did he... Did he tell you very much about his business?

OLIVIER. You were present every time he spoke of it, usually at meals.

MARIE LOUISE. I thought... you might have...

OLIVIER. I doubt if he knows any more about it than what we've heard.

MARIE LOUISE. Yes.... (*Goes up stage. Opens the window, then turns around and notices that he is looking at her.*) It is very close.

OLIVIER. What are you doing this afternoon?

MARIE LOUISE (*absent-mindedly*). This afternoon?

OLIVIER. It's Saturday, and my work is all done. What about a walk?

MARIE LOUISE. Perhaps.... We can settle that at lunch.

OLIVIER. As you like.

(*A knock at door. Enter* JACQUELINE.)

JACQUELINE. May I come in?

OLIVIER. Why, of course, Jacqueline.

JACQUELINE. I didn't mean to disturb you. I thought Marie Louise was alone....

MARIE LOUISE. Don't be silly....

JACQUELINE. Your spouse is in a bad humour.... What have you been doing to her?

OLIVIER. Nothing very serious. We were still talking about Philippe Valbeille.... So, you see...

JACQUELINE. Oh! That explains it. She certainly never could stand Philippe.

OLIVIER. You see, dear. I'm not the only person who...

JACQUELINE. I'm surprised that you didn't put away this fan the moment his back was turned.

*(Takes fan from piano, opens and shuts it.)*

MARIE LOUISE. Leave that fan alone! *(Notices* JACQUELINE's *look.)* What's the use of breaking something that may have some value?... Don't you agree, Olivier?

OLIVIER. There is no use breaking anything.

JACQUELINE. Oh! All right! *(Puts fan down carefully.)* By the way, look... Philippe's postcard reminded me. I have his photo. It was in a book he left behind.

OLIVIER. Oh! That's funny. We were just saying we hadn't a souvenir of him.

*(*JACQUELINE *goes to sit down in the centre arm chair in front of the stove.)*

MARIE LOUISE *(impetuously).* Stop!... *(With a forced smile.)* Sit there....

*(She points vaguely at the corner of the desk.* JACQUELINE *sits down.* OLIVIER *approaches. All three look at the photo.)*

JACQUELINE. What do you think of it?... Do you remember how you used to complain of playing tennis with the nail machine? *(*MARIE LOUISE *does not reply.)* Or listening to a sawmill reciting poetry? *(She laughs.)*

OLIVIER. It's funny.

MARIE LOUISE. What's funny about it?

JACQUELINE. Don't you think he looks very well?

OLIVIER. It's rather like him.

JACQUELINE. Very like him.

MARIE LOUISE. I don't think so at all.

OLIVIER. Well, you'd recognize him.

JACQUELINE. It's the image of him.

MARIE LOUISE. Only the faintest resemblance. It's not a good photo.

OLIVIER. It's very good, I assure you.

JACQUELINE. It certainly is.

MARIE LOUISE (*looking dreamily at photo*). Have it your own way....

OLIVIER. Isn't it curious. There's a man who hasn't been gone two months, and yet we can't agree whether his photo is like him. At least one of us has too much imagination.

MARIE LOUISE (*moving away impatiently*). All right. I am wrong. Let us say no more about it.

OLIVIER. Oh! The simple explanation is that we don't see things with the same eyes. That is usually the case. (*Looks at photo.*) Obviously, his features seemed finer when he used to sit there near the stove talking. The camera is not so indulgent as the eye. Yet... look at it closely... (*Hands her photo.*)

MARIE LOUISE (*takes it without looking at it*). I assure you I have seen it properly.

JACQUELINE. Well, in any case, he'll be in the Argentine in a few days.

OLIVIER. He may be there already.

JACQUELINE. That's a journey I'd rather like to make. Wouldn't you, Olivier?

OLIVIER. All journeys sound attractive, especially when you can't make them. (*He laughs.*) Don't you think so, Marie Louise?

MARIE LOUISE. Please, don't laugh like that....

OLIVIER (*after a moment of surprise*). I didn't think...

MARIE LOUISE (*approaching impatiently*). Stop talking!... I am impossible.... Listen, go the factory, You'll be late.

OLIVIER. I'm not late. But I'll do as you say. (*Looks at her.*) No, you silly child. You're not impossible. Smile. Come on... but you must admit the photo is like him.

MARIE LOUISE (*with a forced smile*). Oh! very well. Be off with you....

OLIVIER. She's driving me away, and I am going. I am not conceited.... See you later, Jacqueline. (*In the doorway he throws a kiss to MARIE LOUISE.*) There!

MARIE LOUISE (*returning the kiss*). There!

(*But as soon as he is gone, MARIE LOUISE's hand drops dejectedly. She looks at the door for a moment, then goes back to the window and looks out dreamily.*)

JACQUELINE (*sings softly*).

> Sous le ciel bleu de l'Argentine,
> Toutes les femmes sont divines...

MARIE LOUISE (*exasperated, turns around*). Jacqueline!

JACQUELINE. Well?

MARIE LOUISE. You're very irritating!

JACQUELINE. Does my singing irritate you? I was still thinking about the Argentine and... Don't you remember, at Epinal all the soldiers used to sing...

> Sous le ciel bleu...

MARIE LOUISE. Please, stop! (JACQUELINE *looks surprised*.) I don't care about your song.... But you look as if... Oh! Well. Sing, if it amuses you. After all, what do I care?

JACQUELINE. Yes, but I'll sing somewhere else. You don't seem to be in a joking mood today.

MARIE LOUISE. Please yourself.

JACQUELINE (*looks at her for a moment, shakes her head and murmurs*). Hello! Hello... (*She goes out singing*.) Sous le ciel bleu de l'Argentine...

> (MARIE LOUISE *again shows signs of irritation. When she is alone she stands still staring at the photo. Suddenly she tears it up and watches the pieces scattering.*)

CURTAIN

## ACT II

*Eighteen months later. Towards the end of an April afternoon. Nothing in the room has changed. The three chairs are still in front of the stove, the fan is on the piano and the Baudelaire on the little table.*

*As the curtain rises,* OLIVIER *is arranging papers at his desk and making notes.* MARIE LOUISE *is seated near the piano. She is doing some needlework, rather absent-mindedly.*

OLIVIER (*without stopping*). What are you doing?

> (MARIE LOUISE *does not even turn around. She does not seem to have heard. A long silence. Both of them behave the same way.*)

MARIE LOUISE (*without raising her head, like a distant echo*).  What are you doing?

OLIVIER.  Arranging some papers.  I've just finished.  (*But* MARIE LOUISE *seems to have forgotten the question.  She does not continue the conversation.  After putting the last letter under a paper weight, it is* OLIVIER *who leaves the desk.  He goes towards her and looks at her.*)  What about you?

MARIE LOUISE.  Me?          (*She puts down her work in a tired manner.*)

OLIVIER.  That doesn't seem very thrilling.

MARIE LOUISE.  You wanted me to do this, but I am not a sewing woman.

OLIVIER.  I don't want you to do anything that bores you.

MARIE LOUISE.  You are very kind.

OLIVIER.  Don't make fun of me.

MARIE LOUISE.  I am not making fun of you.  You really are frightfully kind.

OLIVIER.  Frightfully?

MARIE LOUISE (*after a pause*).   ... You haven't told me what to reply to your tailor.

OLIVIER.  Tell him not to bother.  I don't need anything.  Next month... Thanks for attending to it.

MARIE LOUISE.  Isn't it my duty?

OLIVIER.  ... Yes....

MARIE LOUISE (*rising*).  I'm going to take a walk in the forest.

OLIVIER.  Listen....

MARIE LOUISE.  What?

OLIVIER.  Don't you remember... what we promised my sister and her husband?...

MARIE LOUISE.  Oh! yes.  We're to spend the rest of the afternoon together.  (*Sits down again.*)  Very well.  We'll spend the rest of the afternoon together... as we did yesterday, and the day before yesterday....

OLIVIER (*after a silence*).  It's not very nice of you to say that.

MARIE LOUISE.  You are right.  It's not very nice.... I'm sorry.

OLIVIER.  The Jauberts are only going to be here a week.

MARIE LOUISE.  Yes, I know.  I was wrong.  Sorry....

OLIVIER.  After all... we don't see them so often.... What I like about them is not only is she my sister, but they are a couple so very much like us.

MARIE LOUISE. Do you really think so?

OLIVIER. They're married eleven years and we nine and a half....
You understand?

MARIE LOUISE. Why should I not understand?

OLIVIER (*gently*). And you make me very happy when you are nice
to them.

MARIE LOUISE. Am I not nice to them?

OLIVIER. I'm sure you'll be very nice to them for the few more
days they'll be here.

MARIE LOUISE. For your sake, I promise.... As you know, I am not
particularly attracted to them.

OLIVIER. Once upon a time you were more indulgent.

MARIE LOUISE. One can't argue about such things. However, you
can rely on me. When you ask me nicely...

OLIVIER. You often say that to me. And sometimes you forget.
You are nervous, and when people irritate you...

MARIE LOUISE. I? You're exaggerating....

OLIVIER. You must admit that if a thing is a bore, I always hate
to ask you to do it, and go about it as tactfully as possible.

MARIE LOUISE. Always.... I have nothing to complain about. No.
Really. I have nothing to complain about.

OLIVIER. Then you can easily understand that I... worry a little
about you?

MARIE LOUISE. Worry? Why?

OLIVIER. I can't quite make you out lately. You are sad.

MARIE LOUISE. Sad? Nervous, sad? Oh! Come now, I assure
you I'm not.... See how calm I am.

OLIVIER. At this moment, yes... That's why I am talking to you....
You will say that you are all right.... But I'd like to know what
is wrong.

MARIE LOUISE. Why, really... Nothing. Am I not a very happy
woman?

OLIVIER. How sorry I am for you!...

MARIE LOUISE. Because I say I'm happy?

OLIVIER. What you give me would be enough for any other man —
faithful, respectable, a good housewife... Everything to satisfy
a man with no ideals... I cannot explain, but you understand...

MARIE LOUISE (*weakly*). But... I don't...

OLIVIER (*taking her head between his hands and smiling*). You strange little woman!

MARIE LOUISE. Why do you say that to me?

OLIVIER (*seriously, after looking at her for a second*). How reasonable you've become!

MARIE LOUISE. Reasonable?

OLIVIER. Yes... let me see... for more than a year I've had that impression. Life seems to have matured you, darling. Yes, life has matured my little girl.... You are serious, very.... What were you when I married you? A child, weren't you? And our happiness kept you a child.... There were no caves in those dear eyes.... But now... (*Touches her forehead.*) What is behind there? I can feel lots of thoughts... profound... hidden thoughts...

MARIE LOUISE (*breaking away*). No, Olivier. Not at all. Why do you say that?

OLIVIER. Once I thought I knew you. Now I'm not sure.

MARIE LOUISE. You are wrong to let your imagination get worked up about... absolutely nothing. What's the use? You know me better than you think. Remember it's my nature, that's all....

OLIVIER. When you speak like that I am tempted to believe you. If I could be sure, at least, that you are sincere....

MARIE LOUISE (*making an effort*). But, dearest, I am.... (*She comes and leans against him, looks at him, and smiles.*) Can't you feel that I am?

OLIVIER (*hesitatingly*). Do I... Are you disappointed in me?

MARIE LOUISE. Olivier! How can you ask such a question?

OLIVIER. You're not?... Really?

MARIE LOUISE. Why, of course not, darling. Where did you get such an idea?

OLIVIER. I don't know.... I had the feeling that I was losing something.... So I just wondered if it wasn't I... who...

MARIE LOUISE. You mustn't say that.

(*Now she is behind him and covers his face with her two hands. Her eyes are full of tears.*)

OLIVIER (*breaking away after a couple of seconds*). Witch, there are no replies to your arguments.... I'm just stupid....

MARIE LOUISE. You are not.....

(*She quickly dries her eyes. She doesn't look at him.*)

OLIVIER. I don't know how to make you happy.

MARIE LOUISE. What more *could* you do?

OLIVIER. A thousand things... spoil you... give you...er... more jewelry... more clothes... would you like that?

MARIE LOUISE. Oh yes, if you want to.....

OLIVIER. A car... a little car all for you...

MARIE LOUISE. Yes... (*Indifferently.*)

OLIVIER. Friends... other friends... more often... parties...

MARIE LOUISE. Yes...

OLIVIER. Or perhaps books... You like books... knick-knacks... old ornaments... pictures...

MARIE LOUISE. Yes...

OLIVIER. Or, if you are bored, a trip to Paris... That's it. A week in Paris... theatres, the races... What do you say?

MARIE LOUISE. Yes...

OLIVIER (*changing his tone*). And not one of those thousand things is what you really want.

MARIE LOUISE. Please don't worry like that. The best thing you can offer me is... in yourself.

OLIVIER. That's probably true. A lesson, perhaps: Our happiness is within ourselves, isn't that what you mean?...

MARIE LOUISE (*absent-mindedly*). Yes... I think so.... What time is it?

OLIVIER. Ten to six...

MARIE LOUISE. And we have an engagement...

OLIVIER. In ten minutes.

MARIE LOUISE (*resignedly*). We'll be there.... Tell me, Olivier, have you ever been late in your life?

OLIVIER. Not very often.....

MARIE LOUISE. Do you know... (*Hesitates.*) what Jacqueline called you the other day in fun?

OLIVIER. Out with it!

MARIE LOUISE. The chronometer.

OLIVIER (*smiling*). Quite funny...

MARIE LOUISE (*dreamily*). The chronometer... (*A pause.*)

OLIVIER. Coming?

MARIE LOUISE. What time is it by you?

OLIVIER. Cruel.

MARIE LOUISE. Not really... I was only joking.... Suppose you were three minutes late for once in your life... Aren't the Jauberts with Jacqueline?

OLIVIER. Very likely. She's always with them....

MARIE LOUISE. They're going to take her for a week to Epinal. Arthur's younger brother stands a very good chance of becoming my brother-in-law.

OLIVIER. Would you like that?

MARIE LOUISE. The main thing is that Jacqueline shall be happy.... (*Thoughtfully.*) She *will* be. Her husband will give her everything she can desire: a home, domestic peace, a good bank balance, children, Paris twice a year, friends in their own circle, gossip.... Jacqueline is not very... ambitious...

(*An uncomfortable pause. She goes to window and looks at forest.*)

OLIVIER. Come on. Now let us go.

(*At this moment a child of nine appears outside the window.*)

GERARD. Heh! Heh!

MARIE LOUISE (*gives a start*). Gerard! Is it you? What a way to frighten mother.

GERARD. I beg your pardon, mother. May I sit here and go over my lesson?

OLIVIER. If you like.

GERARD. I'll sit in front of the window. I won't make any noise.

(*He sits outside the window, with his back turned. Only his head can be seen. MARIE LOUISE approaches, bends over, looks at his book, and draws back at once, ill at ease.*)

MARIE LOUISE (*suddenly to* OLIVIER). Oh! Listen. Go by yourself. Say I have a headache and need a rest.

OLIVIER. Do you?...

MARIE LOUISE. I'd rather stay with Gerard.

OLIVIER. Very good... I'll excuse you.

MARIE LOUISE. I'll see you later. (*Exit* OLIVIER. MARIE LOUISE *stands motionless for a moment. Outside the window the head of* GERARD *is still visible as he learns his lesson.* MARIE LOUISE *approaches and whispers:*) Gerard. (*The child does not hear. She repeats more loudly:*) Gerard...

GERARD. Yes, mother?

MARIE LOUISE.  What are you learning?   Why don't you come in?
It's not easy to talk like this.   Come through the window.
(*The child looks in surprise.*)  Yes, I'll allow you this once.   Get
up on the chair.   (*She helps him to get onto the chair and then onto
the window-sill.*)   There!  How heavy you are for eight years old.

GERARD.  Nine, mother.

MARIE LOUISE (*holding him*).  That's true!  Excuse me... My little
man is nine now.   (GERARD *jumps into the room.*)   Aren't you
strong!... Look, you're forgetting your book.   You won't know
your lesson on my account, and Mlle. Andre will scold you.

GERARD.  Oh!  I know it.

MARIE LOUISE (*the book in her hand*).  Is it difficult?

GERARD.  We're repeating old lessons.   Mlle. Andre thinks that
during the Easter holidays...

MARIE LOUISE.  She's right.   Shall I hear your lesson?

GERARD.  Oh yes, mother.   Won't Mlle. Andre be surprised!

MARIE LOUISE.  Why?

GERARD.  Because I'll know it still better if you hear me....

MARIE LOUISE (*turning the pages*).  You're not very good at geography?

GERARD.  Oh... fair.

MARIE LOUISE.  How far have you got?... I noticed just now you
were learning... what's this it was?

GERARD.  America.

MARIE LOUISE.  America?... North... or South?

GERARD.  Both, since I'm repeating old lessons.

    (*While* MARIE LOUISE *is looking for the page, he turns the leaves
    of the Baudelaire on the table.*)

MARIE LOUISE (*uneasily*).  Put down that book... (*Looks around her.*)
Don't sit there.   It's too dark.   It's better here.   Come.

    (*The light has been gradually fading.   She goes downstage and
    lights a little lamp.   GERARD stands beside her.*)

GERARD (*looks at the book in her hand and begins to laugh*).  Mother,
you're holding it upside down.

MARIE LOUISE (*turning it round*).  Well, now.   Go on.

GERARD.  But... won't you ask me questions?

MARIE LOUISE.  Oh!  I see.... What are the principal countries of
South America?

GERARD. South America?... Then it's the next page.

MARIE LOUISE. I know. Come on... answer the question.

GERARD (*repeating the question*). The principal countries of South America? (*In monotonous recital.*) The principal countries of South America are: Brazil, Chile, the Argentine Republic, Columbia... Bolivia... Peru...

MARIE LOUISE. No, no, Gerard. You mustn't answer in that stupid way. You don't understand what you are saying. Do you even know where all those countries are?

GERARD. Why, yes, mother.

MARIE LOUISE. Then, tell me... for example... where is the Argentine?...

GERARD. I don't know.... (*Quickly.*) In America...

MARIE LOUISE. Darling, there's no use learning your lessons like that. If they are not explained to you, you might just as well close your books. You've just rattled off the names of countries and you seem to have no idea that they are huge countries, with fields, forests, rivers, and large cities with houses, people, tramways, noise, trees.... Don't you understand?

GERARD. Are the towns larger than Epinal?

MARIE LOUISE. There are some larger... oh, very much larger.

GERARD. Which that you know?

MARIE LOUISE. I don't know them, but I've heard about them. It's very far away, you know, far, far from here... as far away as a fairy tale.

GERARD. Are we going there? (*A long pause. It grows darker.*)

MARIE LOUISE. No, no... we're not going. It's impossible... you know that

GERARD. When I'm grown up?

MARIE LOUISE. Yes... you... perhaps.

GERARD. And the rivers, mother? Won't you tell me them?

MARIE LOUISE. The rivers?

GERARD. Can they be seen?

MARIE LOUISE. Of course, they can be seen... they're the most important thing. But for those rivers... rich in legends, would one have the same? (*She stops.*)

GERARD. The same what?

MARIE LOUISE. I'll explain that later.

GERARD. Then, you're going to tell me the rivers....

MARIE LOUISE. But what, Gerard?

GERARD. Everything.

MARIE LOUISE. It is difficult.... You have to have seen...

GERARD. Are they the largest?

MARIE LOUISE. I don't know about the largest, but certainly the most beautiful. I read somewhere that everything over there is much more extraordinary than anywhere else. The plants, the flowers are fantastic, ten times the size of ours.

GERARD. Ten times! My!

MARIE LOUISE. The tree trunks are so thick that several people cannot encircle them. And the animals! There are gigantic kinds that we never see in France. So you can imagine what the forests, mountains and waterfalls are like. There are rivers so wide that you can't see from one bank to the other. And it seems... I forget where I read that... they take on all the colors of the rainbow.

GERARD. All the colors?

MARIE LOUISE (*now quite remote*). There are moments — it must be in the morning just after sunrise — when they are all pink, you know, really rose-colored.... There are other times, when it is very fine, when they're all blue. When mist is on the surface of the water, they're white... real rivers of milk. On certain days, when the sky is overcast, stormy, they become all gray, metallic... like rivers of lead....   (*A silence. She does not move.*)

GERARD (*timidly*). And then?

MARIE LOUISE (*starts as if snatched from her dream*). And then?...
(*She looks at the child and suddenly seizes his head between her hands.*)
Oh! Perhaps you can still understand...Oh! What am I saying?
(*She lets him go and gets up, trembling. The amazed child watches her. She goes to the piano and slumps onto the stool in front of the keys and dreams a moment. She begins to play very softly and then sings Duparc's music to L'Invitation au Voyage.*)
            Mon enfant, ma soeur,
            Songe a la douceur
        D'aller la-bas vivre ensemble;
            Aimer a loisir,
            Aimer et mourir
        Au pays qui te ressemble.

(OLIVIER *enters on this last line. Stands in the doorway looking at* MARIE LOUISE. *It is now almost dark. The music grows fainter and seems to die beneath her fingers.* MARIE LOUISE *is lost in silent reverie. Then* OLIVIER *turns on the switch. Bright light.* MARIE LOUISE *jumps up, shuts down the piano, leans on it with her body and both hands. She is all upset, like a woman caught in a guilty action.*)

OLIVIER. L'Invitation au Voyage... of course, Baudelaire...

MARIE LOUISE (*with an effort, trying to smile*). Why, no... I... I was going over Gerard's lesson.

OLIVIER (*surprised*). Gerard's lesson?

GERARD. She heard my geography, father... South America.

(OLIVIER *and* MARIE LOUISE *exchange a long look.*)

OLIVIER (*in a colorless voice*). Run along, sonny. (*Exit* GERARD.) (*Silence. They are facing each other. He looks at her intently. She meets his glance. Obviously, he expects her to speak, but she says nothing. She hesitates, breathes deeply, then suddenly lowers her head, crosses the stage and goes out without a word. He follows her with his glance, amazed. As soon as she is gone, he runs towards the door, calling:*) Marie Louise!... Marie Louise!... (*In a moment she reappears at the door. He takes her hand and draws her trembling into the middle of the room.*) Listen... I want... you to... I am so... tormented...

MARIE LOUISE (*in colorless tones*). Torment...

(*Looks at him and cannot go on.*)

OLIVIER. You have... nothing you want to say to me?...

MARIE LOUISE (*with bowed head*). What?

OLIVIER. Really nothing?

MARIE LOUISE. But... Olivier... no...

OLIVIER. Yet...

MARIE LOUISE. What?

OLIVIER. I don't know...

MARIE LOUISE. Then... (*Moves to leave. But outside a bell is heard. They listen motionless. Then look at each other... a pause. She goes toward him.*) The dinner bell... calling us... which will always call us... Come, come...

(*She catches him by the shoulder and pushes him gently. Furtively, behind his back she wipes away a tear.*)

CURTAIN

# ACT III

*Eight months later.   December.   The windows are closed.   Snow outside.*

## FIRST SCENE

(MARIE LOUISE *and* JACQUELINE *enter after a few moments.*)

MARIE LOUISE.  At last we can have a little peace.

JACQUELINE.  Are you sure I didn't offend mother by leaving so soon?

MARIE LOUISE.  You'll see her presently.   She knows that we two like to chat when you come.   We've been exchanging polite nothings for the past three-quarters of an hour.   I think we're entitled to a quiet moment.

JACQUELINE (*smiling*).   That's not very polite to our parents and your husband.

MARIE LOUISE.  Our parents have never been very strict.   As for Olivier, he couldn't be angry with me.   In any case, he's busy.   And you, in spite of your love for your husband, you must be rather relieved to get away from him for an hour or so, from time to time.

JACQUELINE.  No, I'm not, really.   As a matter of fact, the only reason I came over today from Epinal to see you was because he had to be away the whole afternoon.

MARIE LOUISE.  Yes, you are a good wife...

JACQUELINE.  Well, so are you...

MARIE LOUISE (*after a pause*).   Yes — so am I... obviously...

JACQUELINE.  Aren't you curious?

MARIE LOUISE.  About what?

JACQUELINE.  I have things to tell you.

MARIE LOUISE.  Tell me quickly.   I have things to tell you.... It's been quite a while since I've seen you.

JACQUELINE.  What I have to tell doesn't interest you much.

MARIE LOUISE.  You have a new cook; you've had the Prefect to dinner...

JACQUELINE.  You tease!   I shouldn't wait to be alone with you to tell you that sort of thing.   No.   I have a most amusing piece of news for you, and I've been looking forward to telling it to you in private.

MARIE LOUISE. Go on. I'm dying of curiosity.

JACQUELINE. Philippe Valbeille is in Epinal... Well! — What's the matter with you?

MARIE LOUISE. Listen, Jacqueline. What have you just said?

JACQUELINE. That Philippe Valbeille is in Epinal...

MARIE LOUISE. How do you know?

JACQUELINE. I've seen him.

MARIE LOUISE. Where? When?

JACQUELINE. Yesterday.

MARIE LOUISE. What did he say to you?

JACQUELINE. I didn't speak to him, but I shall see him, I'm sure. He's in Epinal for two days and the Chaulieux, with whom we're dining tonight, have asked him to dinner.

MARIE LOUISE. But, where did you see him? What was he doing? How did he look?

JACQUELINE. I was with Berthe Chaulieux. He was coming out of the post office. I gave an exclamation. Berthe said: "Do you know M. Valbaille?" While we were talking, he had turned the corner and disappeared without seeing us.

MARIE LOUISE (*overcome*). My God!... My God!...

JACQUELINE. You're certainly in a nice state.... If I had known...

MARIE LOUISE. What news, Jacqueline! What news!...

JACQUELINE. What's extraordinary about it? We thought Philippe was in America. He is in France. He has come to Epinal... That's all.

MARIE LOUISE (*brokenly*). What on earth shall I do?

JACQUELINE. What will you do?

MARIE LOUISE. To know that he is in Epinal. It's... Oh! It's unbearable...

JACQUELINE. Unbearable?... Why, may I ask?

MARIE LOUISE. Why?... an... impression... that you couldn't possibly understand.

JACQUELINE. Thank you...

MARIE LOUISE. Don't mind me... You know, we feel differently about things, especially since your marriage.

JACQUELINE. I assure you I understand more than you think.

I have eyes to see. And I know very well that you've been dreaming of nothing but the Argentine.

MARIE LOUISE. How dare you say that! It isn't true.

JACQUELINE. Oh! You can't fool me.... Would I have taken you aside to tell you that news, if I hadn't thought it would produce a certain effect?

MARIE LOUISE. You have a strange sense of humor!

JACQUELINE. Not any stranger than your crush.

MARIE LOUISE. What do you mean by that stupid word?

JACQUELINE. Well, what can I call it?

MARIE LOUISE. Oh, you don't understand. You don't understand.

JACQUELINE. Then, explain.

MARIE LOUISE. Explain what?

JACQUELINE. Don't look at me like that, you frighten me.

MARIE LOUISE. No, you have a way of...

JACQUELINE. Of what?... (*Seizing her hand.*) Come, dear. I didn't mean to hurt you. I am your little sister, after all.

MARIE LOUISE. But you say... such things to me...

JACQUELINE. Well, all I want is to understand you.

MARIE LOUISE. Honestly?

JACQUELINE. I swear it...

MARIE LOUISE (*with tears in her eyes*). I want you and me to be nice to each other. Perhaps we are very remote from one another. But, after all, I have only you, Jacqueline.

JACQUELINE. I had no idea of disturbing you so, when I told he was back.

MARIE LOUISE. If you only knew...

JACQUELINE. Tell me....

MARIE LOUISE. It is... much more serious than you think....

JACQUELINE. Than I think? Oh! Come now!

MARIE LOUISE. My whole life... yes, my whole life is at stake.

JACQUELINE. Your whole life?

MARIE LOUISE. Perhaps I have missed real happiness... all through my own fault....

JACQUELINE. Your own fault! What an idea!

MARIE LOUISE. All because of an unspoken word... a simple reply to him.... But I didn't dare.

JACQUELINE. Reply to him... But he never asked you for anything.

MARIE LOUISE. Never asked me for anything!

JACQUELINE. What?

MARIE LOUISE. Well, it was just as if he had. Some questions tremble on one's lips. It depended only on me to have them spoken....

JACQUELINE. Are you dreaming?

MARIE LOUISE. Oh! My memories do not deceive me.... Words, looks, handshakes, ways of passing things at table, of sending me the ball at tennis... a hundred other things you know nothing about....

JACQUELINE. Well, tell me what they are?...

MARIE LOUISE. Can such things be explained?... Intangible things that I now understand. What's the use of thinking of them?... (*Looks about her.*) I have no right to.... But what tears my heart, darling, is to hear that he is so near and is going away again... who knows where?... Back to the Argentine again... Ah! If only once more I could have...

JACQUELINE. Seen him?... If that is your only worry, it's very simple. Come to my place over night....

MARIE LOUISE (*agitated*). What are you saying? What are you saying?

JACQUELINE. Yes. I'll take you back. It wouldn't be the first time you spent a night at Epinal. You'll come with us to the Chaulieux this evening and you can talk to him. He will say: "my life is settled." You will reply: "I am glad." And you will part good friends, at peace, and happy.

MARIE LOUISE. You arrange it all very calmly. Ah! No. You don't understand.

JACQUELINE. Won't you come?

MARIE LOUISE. It is impossible.

JACQUELINE. Why? Do you want to live regretting that you never had this conversation? That won't help you. I'm beginning to understand you. Besides, it's perfectly safe. He's going back to the Argentine, someone told me. And if you... were in love with him....

MARIE LOUISE. Jacqueline!...

JACQUELINE. I repeat: if you were in love with him, you're not now, are you? (*She does not reply.*) ... if so, poor Olivier...

MARIE LOUISE (*echoes*). Poor Olivier....

JACQUELINE (*after a pause*). Ah! You're not sure of yourself?...

MARIE LOUISE. Oh! No... I'm not.... Now do you understand?

JACQUELINE. Oh!... Well, in that case, consider that I've said nothing. You had better stay here.

MARIE LOUISE (*reflects for a moment, then suddenly decides*). Yes! Yes! You're right. I'll come.

JACQUELINE. Listen, I'm not so sure. Now I have doubts....

MARIE LOUISE. No. I insist. What I am doing is dreadful. But it must be. If you love me you won't stand in my way.

JACQUELINE. What have I started?

MARIE LOUISE. Olivier must still be in the drawing-room. Go at once and tell him you're taking me back this evening. But be sure to say it is you who want me to come. And don't let Olivier know that... *he* is in Epinal....

JACQUELINE. Better be frank....

MARIE LOUISE. Impossible. Precisely on that account there has been a cloud between us since a certain evening... we never completely explained things because we couldn't. If he knew... Run along. I'll wait for you.... (*Shoves her towards the door.*)

JACQUELINE. You can be obstinate when you want to.

> (*Exit.* MARIE LOUISE *remains in a state of anxious agitation, then, trembling, she goes to the little table and, without sitting down, she mechanically turns the pages of the Baudelaire.... Silence. Suddenly, hearing a voice, she closes the book and moves away with assumed indifference.* JACQUELINE *enters with* OLIVIER.)

OLIVIER (*going to the desk to collect some papers*). So you're going to Epinal?

MARIE LOUISE (*in a toneless voice*). Yes... Olivier... I am....

OLIVIER (*without looking up from his papers*). Why?

MARIE LOUISE. But... Jacqueline....

> (*Looks imploringly at her sister.*)

JACQUELINE. Yes, as I told you, we thought it would be a good chance of seeing each other properly. We haven't seen much of one another lately. But Marie Louise was afraid you mightn't like it....

OLIVIER. Why, what an idea! I understand perfectly. Go, of

course... I am always glad to know you are together. When do you leave?...

JACQUELINE. In half an hour....

OLIVIER. And you'll be back... when?... in the morning?

MARIE LOUISE. Yes, Olivier, yes, I suppose....

OLIVIER. Very good... I don't know if I shall see you before you leave.

MARIE LOUISE (*impulsively*). Why, yes, Olivier. I'll look in on my way and... give you a kiss.

OLIVIER. But you know, I have to go with father in a minute and look at those trees they've cut down. It may take some time....

MARIE LOUISE. Then....

OLIVIER. Then, give me a kiss now, at once.... (*Goes to her, takes her head in his hands and smiles.*) Have a good time, fickle woman!

MARIE LOUISE (*rising suddenly*). Olivier!...

OLIVIER (*laughing*). Can't one even joke?... Remember me to your husband, Jacqueline. See you soon, I hope.... (*Looks at* MARIE LOUISE.) Till tomorrow... (*She has a forced smile.*) Till tomorrow.                                                              (*Exit.*)

MARIE LOUISE. My God!... (*Hesitating.*) Jacqueline....

JACQUELINE. Well?

MARIE LOUISE. Olivier... what must he think?

JACQUELINE. What could he think? When I told him I wanted to take you along, he thought it very natural.

MARIE LOUISE. Wasn't he at all surprised?

JACQUELINE. You're spending the night with your sister. What a fuss about nothing!... Now, my dear, if you have any scruples, my advice is: stay here.

MARIE LOUISE (*after a silence*). ... But what would he think?

JACQUELINE. That you changed your mind.

MARIE LOUISE. No... I don't mean Olivier....

JACQUELINE. What?

MARIE LOUISE. He...

JACQUELINE. Philippe?

MARIE LOUISE. Yes...

JACQUELINE. He won't even know you thought of coming.

MARIE LOUISE. Do you think so?

JACQUELINE. I certainly shan't tell him.

MARIE LOUISE. It's not a question of his being told....

JACQUELINE. What then?

MARIE LOUISE. Suppose he were expecting me?

JACQUELINE. What! Philippe expecting *you*?

MARIE LOUISE. Why not?

JACQUELINE. Well, if he'd wanted to see you, he'd have come.

MARIE LOUISE. Oh! No....

JACQUELINE. Oh! Yes, he would....

MARIE LOUISE. You don't know him....

JACQUELINE. As well as you do.

MARIE LOUISE. No!

JACQUELINE. So, you imagine....

MARIE LOUISE. I imagine nothing whatever. All you have to do is think. What could be more natural than to come here? A simple politeness... To the house where he has stayed... Yet, he hasn't come....

JACQUELINE. Well?

MARIE LOUISE. He expects me, Jacqueline. I'm certain of it....

JACQUELINE. If he expected you, he'd have found some means of getting in touch with you.

MARIE LOUISE. His unnatural silence is enough.

JACQUELINE. What a strange idea! Not to see you because he wants to see you! You might not have known he was in Epinal.

MARIE LOUISE. He knows how quickly things get around. He probably also knows that you live in Epinal. Perhaps he arranged to meet you by chance, you say he didn't see you. Suppose he only pretended not to?

JACQUELINE. That's all too complicated.

MARIE LOUISE. Life is always more complicated than you think.

JACQUELINE. But what would be the sense in all this mystery?

MARIE LOUISE. What if it were a test?

JACQUELINE. A test?

MARIE LOUISE. He said to himself: "She will know I am there and I shall not make a move towards her. Either she'll come or she won't."

JACQUELINE. But that's absurd! Even granting that he played such a game, why should be set all the odds against him?

MARIE LOUISE. He's a good gambler, that's all! If he did that, it was daring, you must admit.... And I shall stay here!

(*Walks up and down in distress.*)

JACQUELINE (*after looking at her a moment*). Come, come!... Listening to you I don't know where I am.... But we mustn't be foolish. You shan't move from here. Now I am certain it's better not.

MARIE LOUISE. I absolutely refuse... to let him go away like that! What would he think of me?

JACQUELINE. But what do you propose to do?

MARIE LOUISE. Can't you understand that this is the greatest day in my life?

JACQUELINE. I understand that you attach to the whole thing an importance which....

MARIE LOUISE. Be silent.

JACQUELINE. But what you are saying is madness.

MARIE LOUISE. That is possible. I feel mad.... Unless I have been mad up till now, and am sane only today.

JACQUELINE. Listen.... Listen.... Be reasonable....

MARIE LOUISE. Reasonable! Reasonable! Haven't I been that all my life?... If I can call such an existence life! See where I am.... I am no further advanced than when I was ten. My gilded prison has simply got another jailer. First father, then Olivier.

JACQUELINE. But, you have nothing to complain about....

MARIE LOUISE. No. I have nothing to complain about, and that makes it all the worse, do you see?

JACQUELINE. Stay here, I beg you.

MARIE LOUISE. That's out of the question. I'll go alone, on foot, if necessary. I must see him, Jacqueline. I must see him.

JACQUELINE. No. No.

MARIE LOUISE. What! He comes from the other end of the world to me — yes, to me — and he is to go away like that.... It's monstrous....

JACQUELINE. What's monstrous?...

MARIE LOUISE. Stop! It shall not be said that I refused the opportunity of not being a coward, for once. He is waiting for me.

JACQUELINE. He is not...

MARIE LOUISE. Well, at least, I shall have seen him. I shall not have been afraid....

JACQUELINE. You're going to certain disappointment.

MARIE LOUISE. That's not true....

JACQUELINE. This man's life is settled. Haven't you thought of that?

MARIE LOUISE. That can't be possible!

JACQUELINE. You talk as if he loved you.

MARIE LOUISE. Nothing suggests that he doesn't.

JACQUELINE. Yet...

MARIE LOUISE. Well, I'll find out...

JACQUELINE. What a fool I was to mention it. Now I'm responsible.

MARIE LOUISE. You're responsible for nothing. Don't destroy my courage. That's all I ask you.

JACQUELINE. But courage would mean not giving way to what draws you there.

MARIE LOUISE. No. No...

JACQUELINE. Do you realize what will happen?

MARIE LOUISE. What does that matter?

JACQUELINE. Obviously you don't want to think.

MARIE LOUISE. What is the use?

JACQUELINE. All the same...

MARIE LOUISE. I have been thinking too much....

JACQUELINE. Look around you...

MARIE LOUISE. Spare me, Jacqueline...

JACQUELINE. Your home, mine, our parents', a peaceful life, happiness...

MARIE LOUISE. Stop!... Stop!

JACQUELINE. Do you want to destroy all that for a whim?

MARIE LOUISE. Stop!...

JACQUELINE. This house where you were born, where you learnt all your happiness, where you were a young wife...

MARIE LOUISE. Stop!

JACQUELINE. Where you became a mother.

MARIE LOUISE (*stopping up her ears*). Jacqueline!...

JACQUELINE. It can't be strong enough to overcome all that.

MARIE LOUISE. Will you, please, stop! It is cruel to talk to me like that. For years I have been stifling — you know it well! You ought to understand. I can't go on like this! I can't go on....

(*Weeps.*)

JACQUELINE (*after a silence*). Sh! Listen.... (*The noise of voices to the right grows louder. Soon* OLIVIER *and* LANDREAU *appear outside.* JACQUELINE *murmurs entreatingly.*) Marie Louise... look... look...

(*The two men pass slowly before the closed windows. Only a confused murmur is heard. They disappear into the forest.* MARIE LOUISE *looks at them a moment, hesitates, suddenly averts her head and runs off.*)

## SECOND SCENE

(*The curtain rises at once. It is the next morning.* OLIVIER *and* LANDREAU *are at the desk bending over the papers.*)

OLIVIER. You see, November shows a net increase over October, and December promises to be even better. All our customers' orders are increasing. We have supplies to meet demand for some months. But it is wiser to provide for the purchase of the new machines for next July.

LANDREAU. Magnificent, my dear Olivier. The factory has prospered every year since you became my son-in-law and partner.

OLIVIER. It is following the impetus you gave it.

LANDREAU. Don't belittle yourself. I've seen you at work. I can retire quietly.... Not for some time, I hope.... But the work of my fathers is in decidedly good hands.

OLIVIER. You are too kind....

LANDREAU. Give me one or two grandsons more and all my wishes will be fulfilled.

OLIVIER. But...

LANDREAU. Oh! I'm not finding fault with you. Our little man is a fine piece of work.... By the way, when does that wicked wife of yours get back?

OLIVIER. I don't know.... At any moment now...

LANDREAU. What on earth took her to Epinal?

OLIVIER. It was Jacqueline who...

LANDREAU. Yes. I know. No use ever trying to understand women, especially yours. I, her own father, could never make out her ideas. But what does that matter? We know she's all right at heart. That's the main thing...

OLIVIER (*after a silence*). What do you mean exactly?

LANDREAU. Why... nothing at all.... Oh! You think I know something... If I did I shouldn't be so foolish as to talk to you like this.... No. You know as well as I do that Marie Louise is romantic, a dreamer. That's all.... Just like her grandmother.... (*Lowers his voice.*) My late mother-in-law... Thank God, Marie Louise is more serious. Just imagine, when she was eighteen my mother-in-law got a crush on an acrobat.

(*He laughs.*)

OLIVIER (*uncomfortably*). That's very funny.

LANDREAU. Oh! Everything happened for the best, you know. It didn't last. It's just to show you that Marie Louise has someone to inherit imagination from. My wife has always been more settled. Jacqueline takes after her mother.... Come now, don't frown. You're better off, believe me.... Have you anything else to show me?

OLIVIER. No. No. I wanted to show you that the balance was satisfactory. Now, if you like, we can go through the letters.

LANDREAU. Oh! You can do that yourself. You've made me lazy. When you're my age you will rest like me. By Jove, I believe I have earned it.

OLIVIER. You certainly have earned it. (*Opens letters which he puts under a paper weight.*) Nothing very interesting today.

LANDREAU. Why do you trouble to open all that stuff? Can't you rely on your stenographer?

OLIVIER (*goes on opening them*). Yes. But I like to see everything for myself.

LANDREAU. I don't know quite why I asked you that, because I was just like you. Before your marriage, I never really relied on anyone. (OLIVIER *has opened a letter which he reads anxiously. The paper trembles in his hands.*) What's wrong with you?

OLIVIER (*controlling himself*). I say... Look....

LANDREAU (*takes letter and reads*) ... Gentlemen, I am passing through Epinal and regret I cannot come as far as Ambrosay. But in case you... (*He goes on in silence, then looks at* OLIVIEP.) Well?

OLIVIER. Well?

LANDREAU. Why, I knew he was at Epinal.

OLIVIER. You knew it?

LANDREAU. Gustave telephoned me yesterday....

OLIVIER (*in a choking voice*). Gustave did?

LANDREAU. Why, yes. Gustave, Jacqueline's husband. He 'phoned me yesterday at eleven. Amongst other things, he told me Valbeille Junior was in Epinal. It went completely out of my head.

OLIVIER. It went completely out of your head...

LANDREAU. I never believed we could do business in the Argentine. German competition is too strong. If he has come to the Vosges it's for tacks and brass-headed nails, as he says. That doesn't interest us. That letter confirms what I thought. (OLIVIER *leaves desk and walks up and down.*) Well, what's the matter?

OLIVIER. The matter? (*Looks at him and sits down again.*) Nothing.

LANDREAU. That's no answer.

OLIVIER (*trying to control himself*). Gustave knew that he was in Epinal.... Then Jacqueline knew it, too.

LANDREAU. Very probably.

OLIVIER. She must have told Marie Louise.

LANDREAU. Well? (*Looks at him.*) Are you angry because she didn't tell you?

OLIVIER (*lost in thought*). No.... No. Not at all.

LANDREAU (*after a pause*). If you attach importance to such things, my dear fellow, you're mad.... (*He reflects a moment, then in a changed tone, a little uneasy.*) You are mad....

OLIVIER (*picking up his papers*). Oh! Let us change the subject....

LANDREAU. Not until....

OLIVIER (*gets up suddenly and opens the window at the right and after a moment turns round*). Did you hear anything?

LANDREAU. No....

OLIVIER (*shutting the window again*). I thought I heard... (*Sits down again and absent-mindedly opens a letter.*) A reply from the Comite des Forges about our dispute with... Not very important. (*Opens another letter.*) A letter from the Huchart people. Hello! This *is* important. They want to know if we can in-

crease our consignments by twenty per cent. Well, I should say
so!... Don't you agree? (*Looks at him and sees that* LANDREAU *is
dreaming and not listening. He leans over to him.*) You... agree...
don't you... Huchart's....

LANDREAU (*startled*). Huchart!... Yes, yes.... A big house... reliable, very reliable.... What do they want? Increased consignments.... Oh! Certainly. Huchart. I should say so....
(*Now* OLIVIER *is not listening. He is looking at his watch and
winding it mechanically.*)

OLIVIER (*after a pause*). What time have you?

LANDREAU (*pulling out his watch*). Ten to eleven....

OLIVIER. That's correct... (*Listens and raises his finger.*) What's
that?... (*After a pause.*) No....

LANDREAU (*keeping his watch in his hand and winding it as he speaks*).
I knew old Huchart well, the founder of the firm. He had
some property near Saint-Die. A fine man. He used to drop
in once in a while. After he died his children went into partner-
ship with his son-in-law, Santerre, whose people made money in
the agricultural belting business... I never see them now except
on business.... (*He looks at* OLIVIER *and puts back his watch.*)
Well, I'll be off. You don't seem to be in the mood either to
work or to talk....

OLIVIER (*pointing to the table*). I'll finish up presently....

LANDREAU. Yes. You don't need me. Anyhow, there's nothing
very urgent.

(*The door opens noisily. Both men turn suddenly, but it is only
GERARD, who rushes in.*)

GERARD (*throwing himself into* LANDREAU's *arms*). Good-morning,
grandpa!

LANDREAU. Good-morning, little man!

GERARD. Grandpa, do you know what father promised me!

LANDREAU. What did he promise you, young man?

GERARD. To take me for a walk this morning.

LANDREAU. Lucky boy.... (*He looks at* OLIVIER.) But....

GERARD. Will you hear me my fable, grandpa?

LANDREAU. Not now. I have to go. (*Trying to shake* GERARD *off.*)
Be careful, young man....

OLIVIER. Don't be annoying your grandfather, Gerard.

LANDREAU. No. Not at all. That's all right.... Well, Olivier, I'll leave this fellow to you. You have both lots of things to talk about, I'm sure.

(OLIVIER *is abstracted and seems not to have heard.*)

GERARD (*whispering and pulling* LANDREAU *by the sleeve*). Grandpa....

LANDREAU. What?

GERARD. Tell me a story....

LANDREAU. Your father knows more and better ones than I do.

GERARD. I want yours. One about when you were small.

LANDREAU. Ah! That's a long time ago....

GERARD. It was before the day we went fishing....

LANDREAU. Long before that, certainly.

GERARD. Grandpa, when will you be a hundred?

LANDREAU. Let me see... oh... in thirty-two and a half years.

GERARD. Oh! That'll be grand!

LANDREAU. Think so?

GERARD. Unless you die before that.

LANDREAU. Sh!... Stop.... (*Looks at* OLIVIER *whose thoughts are far away.*) You mustn't say such things. I ought to scold you.

GERARD (*frightened*). I'm glad Father didn't hear me.

LANDREAU. Sh! You silly child.

GERARD. What's Father thinking about?

LANDREAU. Lots of things... you, perhaps....

GERARD (*staring at his father*). But why does he look as if he was crying?

LANDREAU (*impatiently*). Come now!... That'll do!... (*He coughs.* OLIVIER *turns around. He goes to him.*) Listen... can I?... Would you like me to finish all that work... and leave you free? ... (OLIVIER *cannot control a gesture of impatience.*) No.... Very well. I'll be off. It's all right. You needn't explain.... See you later, my son. (*Exit rapidly.*)

GERARD (*after a pause*). Papa... we are going out?...

OLIVIER (*startled*). No. Not this morning.... Later, if you like.

GERARD. Father, tell me something.

OLIVIER. What?

GERARD. Why don't you take me for a walk every day?

OLIVIER. Why? (*Looks at his watch and goes to the window.*)

GERARD. Are you going, Father?

OLIVIER (*coming back*). No. I'm not going.... (*Sits down.*) What were you saying? You want to go for a walk with me every day? That's impossible.

GERARD. But you will sometimes?

OLIVIER. Sometimes, yes.... We'll see about that... tomorrow....

GERARD. Oh! Where shall we go?

OLIVIER. Where?... (*Looks at his watch.*)

GERARD. Are you waiting for someone?

OLIVIER. Why?

GERARD. You keep looking at your watch.

OLIVIER (*rather harshly*). Gerard, you're too curious. (*The child lowers his head.* OLIVIER *is seized with remorse.*) I'm waiting for mother, child.

GERARD. Why did she go to Epinal?

OLIVIER. She's coming back.

GERARD. If she doesn't will you explain my lesson to me?

OLIVIER (*gets up, a little irritated*). Yes, yes. We'll see.... There's no hurry. Mlle. Andre is not coming today.... (*With his hands in his pockets he walks about in every direction.* GERARD *looks at him anxiously.* OLIVIER *suddenly notices him. Sits down and draws the child towards him.*) What is this lesson? Tell me about it.

GERARD. An arithmetic lesson.

OLIVIER. Hard?

GERARD. Very!

OLIVIER. Well, be a good boy and try it by yourself. When it's finished, show it to me.

GERARD. Yes, father.... Shall I at once?...

OLIVIER (*again lost in thought*). What?... Whenever you like.

GERARD. Now, will you hear me my fable?

OLIVIER (*far away*). If you like.

GERARD. I know it, you'll see. Listen.... *The Lion and the Rat.* "To show all " — No... *The Lion and the Rat: A Fable.* "To show all your kindness, it behoves "... (*He tries to remember.*) Are you listening, father?

OLIVIER. Yes, go on.

"To show all your kindness, it behoves:
There's none so small but you his aid may need.

I quote two fables for this weighty creed,
Which either of them fully proves.

(MARIE LOUISE *has come in. She remains in the doorway watching them.* GERARD *goes on without seeing her.*)

From underneath the sward
A rat, quite off his guard,
Popped out between a lion's paw." (*He turns around.*)

Oh! Mother!

OLIVIER (*gets up, agitated*). Marie Louise....

MARIE LOUISE (*to* GERARD, *without moving*). Go on....

GERARD. Shall I?

OLIVIER. Leave us....

(GERARD *reluctantly takes his book and goes towards the door.*)

MARIE LOUISE (*sharply*). No. No. Gerard. Stay here.

OLIVIER. Marie Louise....

MARIE LOUISE. Well?

OLIVIER. I want to... talk to you.

MARIE LOUISE (*to* GERARD). Go to your room.... (*Suddenly, as he passes her, she embraces him and holds him for some time. Then she pushes him away. Exit* GERARD. *She begins to take off her gloves without looking at* OLIVIER.) Why... why interrupt the lesson?

OLIVIER. But, I can't listen to that fable when... anyhow, you're back... we have things to talk over.

MARIE LOUISE. Pooh! What could be more important than Gerard's fable?

OLIVIER. What do you say?

MARIE LOUISE. Well, aren't you even going to...

(*She offers her cheek.*)

OLIVIER (*taken aback*). But...

(*Comes up, kisses her mechanically and moves away quickly.*)

MARIE LOUISE (*takes off her hat and coat with affected calm, but without looking at him*). Am I late? You didn't expect me earlier, I hope. It's half past eleven. Jacqueline sent me back in the car. She wouldn't let me take the train. Anyway, if I had taken the train, I shouldn't be here yet. Anything new?... I saw father and mother as I came in. (*Meeting his look.*) Why are you looking at me like that?

OLIVIER (*in a colorless tone*). So you've really nothing to tell me?

MARIE LOUISE. To tell you?... why.... I'm glad to be back.... Is that it?

OLIVIER. Is that all?

MARIE LOUISE. What more can there be? After all, I've only been away one day.

OLIVIER. Yes, but in... Epinal.... What did you do there?

MARIE LOUISE. There?... Oh, you know well what I did.... I... dined at Jacqueline's, of course. Just the three of us.... Just the three of us.... After dinner we went out. We went to the Chaulieux.... You know, Berthe Chaulieux. I... we got home early.... There were some people... a fair crowd... I... (*His stare causes her to lose her assurance. She hesitates. She sits down. Suddenly, with as detached an air as possible.*) Oh! I forgot to tell you.... Do you know who I saw? Philippe Valbeille.

OLIVIER (*staggering*). Oh!

MARIE LOUISE. Yes, at the Chaulieux, where I was, I told you,... last night with Jacqueline... and Gustave... Gustave was really very nice. We talked a lot about you. He apologized for not coming over more often.

OLIVIER. ... Did you know... that Valbeille was in Epinal?

MARIE LOUISE. ... Yes...

OLIVIER. Did you know it... before you left here?

MARIE LOUISE. Why.... Yes... I think so.

OLIVIER. Don't say: "I think so."

MARIE LOUISE. Very well, yes. Jacqueline... told me.

OLIVIER. ... Why did you go to Epinal?

MARIE LOUISE. Why? (*They look at each other.*)

OLIVIER. ... So you saw Philippe Valbeille?

MARIE LOUISE (*forcing a smile*). Why, yes. I saw him.

OLIVIER (*irritated*). Oh! Answer me....

MARIE LOUISE. I am answering you. What do you want to know?

OLIVIER. Tell me what happened. Tell me what he said.

MARIE LOUISE. Oh! It isn't very interesting.

OLIVIER. Not interesting?

MARIE LOUISE. My goodness!... a person we once used to know... whom one meets again like that.... I recognized him at once, you know.... That's all!

OLIVIER. But, he must have been glad to see you again. After all those months he spent here.... How did he receive you? What did you talk about?...

MARIE LOUISE. Do you really want to know? Well, it's very simple.... He told me he had eight hundred employees, and that he turned out six hundred thousand nails a day.... He told me he had a partner named Dupont, and that their only serious competitor was a German firm, Beckmann or Stockmann, something ending in "mann."... He told me he was vice-president of the Buenos Ayres Chamber of Commerce, and that he had founded something or other for workmen's insurance.... He told me the streets of Buenos Ayres were all ruled out in straight lines and that he never went to the theatre.... He told me... he told me the foreign trade of the Argentine... of the Argentine Republic.... Well, you know... all that sort of thing....

   (*While she is speaking her voice, at first calm, becomes slightly emotional. She remains lost in thought.*)

OLIVIER. Then what?

MARIE LOUISE. Why, that's all. Polite nothings, stupid nothings. (*Repressing a sigh.*) What on earth interest has it? Does it matter? A dead man....

OLIVIER. Dead?

MARIE LOUISE (*as if talking to herself*). Dead as far as we're concerned, certainly. Do you understand? I felt so remote from him. Could it be the same man? Yes and no.... One thing I did realize, in any case, was how little he ever interested me....

OLIVIER (*looks at her for a moment without moving, then he goes and takes her hand, sits beside her and says softly*). You mustn't cry.

MARIE LOUISE (*stiffening*). I'm not....

OLIVIER. Sh!... Tell me... when do you see him again?

MARIE LOUISE. Why, never.... (OLIVIER *tries to get up, but sits down again, his hand on his heart.*) Olivier?

OLIVIER. Stop! It's nothing.... It's over.... You see, sometimes one's heart is too full and then... (*She tries to speak.*) No, no, not today! (*Restraining his joy.*) Don't tell me anything. Marie Louise.... You look at me.... Perhaps I seem happy, but I'm not happy when you are sad.... You seem surprised because I smiled.... But don't pay any attention. I don't want to smile....

That... that will be some days hence... when I see joy in those eyes of yours....

MARIE LOUISE (*with tears in her voice*). But I am very happy, Olivier....

OLIVIER. No. No.... Don't say that now....

MARIE LOUISE. It is good to hear you talk to me nicely.

OLIVIER. Haven't I always done so?

MARIE LOUISE (*lowers her head and murmurs*)... Darling, I need you so....

OLIVIER. Honestly?

MARIE LOUISE. Honestly....

OLIVIER (*choking with emotion*). Marie Louise.... Then.... (*He stops.*)

MARIE LOUISE. Then?

(OLIVIER *represses his feelings. His glance rests on the little table.* MARIE LOUISE's *glance follows his and stops at the same point. Suddenly she takes the Baudelaire and puts it in the bookcase. Then she takes the fan from the piano and puts it away in the table drawer. Finally, she goes to one of the armchairs and draws it away from the stove.... As she walks backwards she reaches* OLIVIER *who has not ceased to watch her with repressed emotion.... A long embrace....* MARIE LOUISE *is the first to break away. Lightly she goes over to the piano and begins the piece she was playing at the beginning of Act I.*)

OLIVIER (*in a choking voice*). Ah! Yes. That Nocturne of Chopin's... that you loved so much.... (*He leans over her.*) Thanks....

**CURTAIN**

# GENERAL BIBLIOGRAPHIES

## BOOKS ON CONTINENTAL DRAMA

### GENERAL SURVEYS

#### In English

CHANDLER, F. W., *Aspects of Modern Drama* (New York, 1914); *Modern Continental Playwrights* (New York, 1931); CLARK, B. H., *The Continental Drama of To-day* (New York, 1914); *A Study of the Modern Drama* (New York, 1928); DICKINSON, T. H., *An Outline of Contemporary Drama* (Boston, 1927); DUKES, A., *Modern Dramatists* (Chicago, 1912); HENDERSON, A., *European Dramatists* (New York, 1926); HUDDLESTON, S., *Those Europeans; Studies in Foreign Faces* (New York, 1924); HUNEKER, J. G., *Iconoclasts, a Book of Dramatists* (New York, 1912); GOLDBERG, I., *The Drama of Transition* (Cincinnati, 1922); JAMESON, S., *The Modern Drama in Europe* (New York, 1920); LEWISOHN, L., *The Modern Drama* (New York, 1915); PHELPS, W. L., *Essays on Modern Dramatists* (New York, 1921); VERNON, F., *The Twentieth Century Theatre* (Boston, 1924).

#### In German

ARNOLD, R. F., *Das Moderne Drama* (Strassburg, 1908); BAB, J., *Das Theater der Gegenwart* (Leipzig, 1928); BUSSE, B., *Das Drama*, vol. 3 (Leipzig, 1914); FREYHAN, M., *Das Drama der Gegenwart* (Berlin, 1922); KERR, A., *Das neue Drama* (Berlin, 1909); STEIGER, E., *Das Werden des neueren Dramas* (2 vols., Berlin, 1898–1903); ZABEL, E., *Zur modernen Dramaturgie*, vol. 3 (Oldenburg, 1903).

#### In Italian

RUBERTI, G., *Il teatro contemporaneo in Europa* (2 vols., Bologna, 1920–21); *Storia del teatro contemporaneo* (3 vols., Bologna, 1928); TILGHER, A., *Studi sul teatro contemporaneo* (Rome, 1923).

### THEORY AND TECHNIQUE OF DRAMA

ANDREWS, C., *The Technique of Playmaking* (Springfield, Mass., 1915); ARCHER, W., *The Old Drama and the New* (Boston, 1923); *Playmaking*, (New York, 1924); BAB, J., *Schauspieler und Schauspielkunst* (Berlin, 1926); BULTHAUPT, H. A., *Dramaturgie des Schauspiels* (4 vols., Oldenburg, 1918–24); CLARK, B. H., *European Theories of the Drama* (New York, 1925); FLEMMING, W., *Das Wesen der Schauspielkunst* (Rostock, 1927); FREYTAG, G., *The Technique of the Drama* (Chicago, 1900); PRICE, W. T., *Analysis of Play Construction and Dramatic Principle* (New York, 1908); *Technique of the Drama* (New York, 1892); NICOLL, A.,

*An Introduction to Dramatic Theory* (New York, 1924); SCHLAG, H., *Das Drama, Wesen, Theorie, und Technic* (Essen, 1909); STUART, D. C., *The Development of Dramatic Art* (New York, 1928).

## THE ONE-ACT PLAY

GANNON, R. L., *The Technique of the One-Act Play* (New York, 1925); HILLEBRAND, H. N., *Writing the One-Act Play* (New York, 1925); LEWIS, R. B., *The Technique of the One-Act Play* (Boston, 1918); WILDE, P., *The Craftsmanship of the One-Act Play* (Boston, 1923).

## STAGING AND THE ARTS OF THE THEATRE

BAKSHY, A., *The Theatre Unbound* (London, 1923); CARTER, H., *The New Spirit in Drama and Art* (New York, 1913); CHENEY, S., *The Art Theatre* (New York, 1925); *Stage Decoration* (New York, 1928); COURNOS, J., *Gordon Craig and the Theatre of the Future* (London, 1913); CRAIG, G., *On the Art of the Theatre* (New York, 1925); *Scene* (London, 1923); *The Theatre — Advancing* (Boston, 1923); *Towards a New Theatre* (New York, 1913); FISCHEL, O., *Das moderne Bühnenbild* (Berlin, 1923); FLANAGAN, A., *Shifting Scenes* (New York, 1928); FUERST, W. R., and HUME, S. J., *Twentieth Century Stage Decoration* (London, 1928); GAMBLE, W. B., *The Development of Scenic Art and Stage Machinery: a List of References* (New York, 1928); HAGEMANN, C., *Moderne Bühnenkunst* (2 vols., Berlin, 1916–18); ISAACS, E. J. R., Editor, *Thirty-One Essays on the Arts of the Theatre* (New York, 1927); JONES, R. E., *Drawings for the Theatre* (New York, 1925); MACGOWAN, K., *The Theatre of Tomorrow* (New York, 1921); MACGOWAN, K., and ROSSE, H., *Masks and Demons* (New York, 1923); MACGOWAN, K., and JONES, R. E., *Continental Stagecraft* (New York, 1922); MODERWELL, H. K., *The Theatre of To-Day* (New York, 1927); MOUSSINAC, L. C., *La Décoration Théâtrale* (Paris, 1922); ROUCHÈ, J., *L'Art Théâtral* (Paris, 1924); SIMONSON, L., *The Stage is Set* (New York, 1932).

## CONTINENTAL DRAMA AFTER THE WAR

CARTER, H., *The New Spirit in the European Theatre* (New York, 1926); DIEBOLD, B., *Anarchie im Drama* (Frankfurt a. M., 1921); DUKES, A., *The Youngest Drama* (Chicago, 1924); EULENBERG, H., *Der Krieg und die Kunst* (Oldenburg, 1915); LAVRIN, Y., *Studies in European Literature* (London, 1929).

## BOOKS ON THE NATURALISTIC MOVEMENT

BERG, L., *Der Naturalismus* (Berlin, 1892); BENOIST-HANAPPIER, L., *Le drame naturaliste en Allemagne* (Paris, 1905); BYTKOWSKI, S., *Gerhart Hauptmanns Naturalismus und das Drama* (Hamburg, 1908); DOELL, O., *Die Entwicklung der naturalistischen Form in Jungstdeutschen Drama* (Halle, 1910); FRIED, A., *Der Naturalismus; seine Entstehung und Berechtigung*

(Leipzig, 1890); ELLIS, H., *The New Spirit* (Boston, 1926); HOLZ, A., *Die Kunst, ihr Wesen und ihre Gesetze* (Berlin, 1891); STOECKIUS, A., *Naturalism in Recent German Drama* (New York, 1909); ZOLA, E., *Le naturalisme au théâtre; les théories et les exemples* (Paris, 1898).

## BOOKS ON FUTURISM, EXPRESSIONISM, AND NEWER MOVEMENTS

AMICO, S. D', *Il teatro dei Fantocci* (Florence, 1920); BAHR, H., *Expressionism* (translated by R. F. Gribble, London, 1925); DAHLSTRÖM, C., *August Strindberg, the Father of Dramatic Expressionism* (Michigan Academy of Science, Arts and Letters, Ann Arbor, 1929); *Strindberg's Dramatic Expressionism* (University of Michigan Publications in Language and Literature, Ann Arbor, 1930); DIEBOLD, B., *Anarchie im Drama* (Frankfurt a. M., 1921); FECHTER, P., *Der Expressionismus* (Leipzig, 1919); FLORA, F., *Dal romanticismo al futurismo* (Milan, 1925); EDSCHMID, K., *Ueber den dichterischen Expressionismus* (Berlin, 1919); GOLDBERG, I., *The Drama of Transition* (Cincinnati, 1922); JELLIFFE, S. E., and BRINK, L., *Psychoanalysis and the Drama* (New York, 1922); PFISTER, O. R., *Expressionism in Art; its Psychological and Biological Basis* (trans., London, 1922); POUPEYE, C., *Les dramaturges exotiques* (Brussels, 1926); SCHNEIDER, M., *Expressionism in Drama* (Stuttgart, 1920); WALZEL, O., *Gerhart Hauptmann und der Expressionismus* (Preussische Jahrbücher, Berlin, 1922).

## GENERAL WORKS ON RECENT RUSSIAN DRAMA

CARTER, H., *The New Theatre and Cinema of Soviet Russia* (London, 1924); *The New Spirit in the Russian Theatre, 1917–28* (London, 1929); GREGOR, J., and FÜLÖP-MILLER, R., *Das Russische Theater* (Vienna, 1928); GOURFINKEL, N., *Théâtre russe contemporain* (Paris, 1931); SAYLER, O. M., *The Russian Theatre* (New York, 1922); STANISLAVSKY, C., *My Life in Art* (Boston, 1927); WIENER, L., *The Contemporary Drama of Russia* (Boston, 1924).

## GENERAL WORKS ON RECENT GERMAN DRAMA

ARNOLD, R. F., *Das deutsche Drama* (Munich, 1925); BAB, J., *Die Chronik des deutschen Dramas* (5 vols., Berlin, 1926); FREYHAN, M., *Das Drama der Gegenwart* (Berlin, 1922); FRIEDMANN, S., *Das deutsche Drama des 19 Jahrhunderts*, vol. 2 (Leipzig, 1900–03); HELLER, O., *Studies in Modern German Literature* (Boston, 1905); HOLL, K., *Geschichte des deutschen Lustspiels* (Leipzig, 1923); KERR, A., *Gesammelte Schriften* (7 vols., Berlin, 1917–20); LAURET, R., *Le Théâtre allemande d'aujourdhui* (Paris, 1934).

## GENERAL WORKS ON RECENT SPANISH DRAMA

BASTINOS, A. J., *Arte dramatico español contemporaneo* (Barcelona, 1914); BELL, A. F. G., *Contemporary Spanish Literature* (New York, 1925);

BUENO, M., *Teatro español contemporaneo* (Madrid, 1909); FORD, J. D. M., *Main Currents in Spanish Literature* (New York, 1919); FRANCOS-RODRIGUEZ, J., *El teatro en Espagna* (Madrid, 1909); GONZALES-BLANCO, A., *Los dramaturgos españoles contemporaneos* (Valencia, 1917); WARREN, L. A., *Modern Spanish Literature* (New York, 1929).

## GENERAL WORKS ON RECENT FRENCH DRAMA

BENOIST, A., *Le théâtre d'aujourdhui* (2 vols., Paris, 1911–12); BORDEAUX, H., *La vie au théâtre* (3d and 4th Series, Paris, 1913, 1919); BRISSON, A., *Le théâtre* (Paris, 1918); *La théâtre pendant la guerre* (Paris, 1919); CAPUS, A., *Le théâtre* (Paris, 1913); CHANDLER, F. W., *The Contemporary Drama of France* (Boston, 1925); CLARK, B. H., *Contemporary French Dramatists* (Cincinnati, 1915); DUBECH, L., *Le théâtre, 1918–23* (Plon, 1925); DOUMIC, R., *Le théâtre nouveau* (Paris, 1908); FILON, A., *De Dumas à Rostand* (Paris, 1911); KAHN, A., *Le théâtre social en France de 1870 à nos jours* (Paris, 1907); LALOU, R., *Histoire de la littérature française* (Paris, 1923); MORTIER, A., *Dramaturgie de Paris* (Paris, 1917); SÉCHÉ, A., and BERTRAUT, J., *L'Evolution de théâtre contemporain* (Paris, 1908); SÉE, E., *Le théâtre français contemporain* (Paris, 1933); SMITH, H. A., *Main Currents of Modern French Drama* (New York, 1925); SOLVAY, L., *L'Evolution théâtrale* (Brussels, 1922); THALASSO, A., *Le Théâtre-Libre* (Paris, 1909); WAXMAN, S. M., *Antoine and the Théâtre-Libre* (Cambridge, Mass., 1924).

## GENERAL WORKS ON RECENT ITALIAN DRAMA

D'AMICO, S., *Il teatro italiano* (Milan, 1932); GORI, G., *Il teatro contemporaneo* (Torino, 1924); MACCLINTOCK, L., *The Contemporary Drama of Italy* (Boston, 1923); PHELPS, R., *Italian Silhouettes* (New York, 1924); STARKIE, W., *Some Italian Dramatists of To-day* (*Nineteenth Century*, vol. 99); TONELLI, L., *L'Evoluzione del teatro contemporaneo in Italia* (Milan, 1908); *Il teatro Italiano dalle origini ai giorni nostri* (Milan, 1924).

## JOSÉ ECHEGARAY

BUENO, M., *El Teatro Español contemporaneo* (Madrid, 1909); CURZON, H. DE, *Le théâtre de José Echegaray, étude analytique* (Paris, 1912); KENNEDY, R., *The Indebtedness of Echegaray to Ibsen* (*Sewanee Review*, 1926); LYNCH, H., Preface to translation of *The Great Galeoto* and *Folly or Saintliness* (Boston, 1905); MORLEY, S. G., *José Echegaray* (California University Chronicle, Berkeley, 1925); ZACHER, A., *Don José Echegaray, der Verfasser des Galeoto* (Berlin, 1892).

## CHIEF PLAYS OF JOSÉ ECHEGARAY

*La esposa del vengador*, produced 1875.

*Cóme empreza cóma acaba*, produced 1876.

*O locura ó sanidad*, produced 1877. Translated as *Folly or Saintliness* by

Hannah Lynch, London, 1895. Translated as *Madman or Saint* by Ruth Lansing, Boston, 1912.

*En el seno de la muerte*, produced 1879.

*El gran Galeoto*, produced 1881.

*Vida alegre y muerte triste*, produced 1885.

*Siempre en ridículo*, produced 1890. Translated as *Always Ridiculous* by T. Walter Gilkyson, *Poet Lore*, 1916.

*El hijo de Don Juan*, produced 1892. Inspired by Ibsen's *Ghosts*. Translated as *The Son of Don Juan* by James Graham, 1895.

*Mariana*, produced 1892. Translated by James Graham, Boston, 1895; by F. Sardi and C. D. S. Wuppermann, New York, 1909.

*El poder de la impotencia*, produced 1893.

*Mancha que limpia*, produced 1895.

*La calumnia por castigo*, produced 1898.

*El hombre negro*, produced 1898. Translated as *The Man in Black* by E. Watson in *Universal Anthology*, London, 1899.

*El loco Dios*, produced 1900. Translated as *The Madman Divine* by Elizabeth Howard West, *Poet Lore*, 1908.

## FRANK WEDEKIND

KUTSCHER, A., *Frank Wedekind, sein Leben und seine Werke* (3 vols., Munich, 1922–31); FECHTER, P., *Frank Wedekind; der Mensch und das Werk* (Jena, 1920); KAPP, J., *Frank Wedekind; seine Eigenart und seine Werke* (Berlin, 1909); KEMPNER, H., *Frank Wedekind als Mensch und Kunstler* (Berlin, 1911); BLEI, F., *Ueber Wedekind, Sternheim und das Theater* (Leipzig, 1915); ELIOT, S. A., Jr., Introduction to *Tragedies of Sex* (New York, 1923); ELSTER, H. M., *Frank Wedekind und seine besten Bühnenwerke* (Berlin, 1922); FAY, F. C., *Frank Wedekind* (*The Drama*, Chicago, 1915); FRIEDENTHAL, J., editor, *Das Wedekindbuch* (Munich, 1914); HAGEMANN, F., *Wedekinds Erdgeist und Die Büchse der Pandora* (Neustrelitz, 1926); PINEAU, L., *Frank Wedekind* (*Revue Germanique*, Paris, 1913); WEDEKIND, F., *Schauspielkunst; ein Glossarium* (Munich, 1910).

### PLAYS BY FRANK WEDEKIND

*Der Schnellmaler, oder Kunst und Mammon*, published 1899.

*Die junge Welt*, written 1889; published 1890.

*Frühlings Erwachen, ein Kindertragödie*, published 1891; produced 1906. Translated as *The Awakening of Spring* by F. J. Ziegler, Philadelphia, 1909; and under the same title by S. A. Eliot, Jr., in *Tragedies of Sex*, New York, 1915.

*Die Flöhe, oder Der Schmerzenstanz*. A ballet in three scenes. Published 1892.

*Der Mückenprinz*. A dance pantomime. Published 1894.

*Die Kaiserin von Neufundland*. Pantomime in three scenes. Published 1897.

*Erdgeist*, First Part of *Lulu*. Published 1895; produced 1898. Translated as *The Earth Spirit* by S. A. Eliot, Jr., in *Tragedies of Sex*, New York, 1915.

*Der Kammersänger*, produced 1897; published 1899. Translated as *The Court Singer* in *The German Classics*, vol. 20, 1913–14.

*Fritz Schwigerling, oder Der Liebestrank*, published 1899.

*Der Marquis von Keith*, published 1900; produced 1901.

*So ist das Leben (König Nikolo)* published 1902; produced 1903. Translated as *Such is Life* by F. J. Ziegler, Philadelphia, 1912.

*Die Büchse der Pandora*, Second Part of *Lulu*. Written 1892–1901; published 1904; produced 1905 in Vienna. Translated as *Pandora's Box* by S. A. Eliot, Jr., in *Tragedies of Sex*, New York, 1915.

*Karl Hetman, Der Zwergriese (Hidalla)*, published 1904; produced 1912.

*Tod und Teufel (Totentanz)*, published 1905. Translated as *Damnation* by S. A. Eliot, Jr., New York, 1923.

*Musik, Sittengemälde in vier Bildern*, published 1907; produced 1912.

*Zensur, Theodizee in drei Scenen*, published 1908.

*Der Stein der Weisen*, published 1909.

*Oaha (Till Eulenspiegel)*, published 1909.

*Schloss Wetterstein* (in three parts: *In Allen Sätteln gerecht; Mit allen Hunden gehetzt; In allen Wassern gewaschen*), published 1910.

*Franzisca, ein Mysterium*, published 1912; produced 1913.

*Simson, oder Scham und Eifersucht*, published 1914.

*Bismarck*, published 1915.

*Herakles* (posthumous), published 1919.

*Sonnenspektrum* (posthumous), published 1921.

In addition to the above there is an early poetic play, *Elins Erweckung*, of about 1887, published in part in 1894; and various fragments published in 1924; *Bethel*, a pantomime, *Die Jungfrau*, and *Kitsch*.

See *Tragedies of Sex*, translated by S. A. Eliot, Jr., New York, 1923, for *Spring's Awakening, Earth Spirit, Pandora's Box*, and *Damnation*.

## EDMOND ROSTAND

LIFE AND WORK:

ALBERT, C., *A travers l'oeuvre d'Edmond Rostand* (Paris, 1919); FAURE, P., *Vingt ans d'intimité avec Edmond Rostand* (Paris, 1928); HARASZTI, J., *Edmond Rostand* (Paris, 1913); LAUTIER, A., and KELLER, F., *Edmond Rostand; son oeuvre* (Paris, 1924); SUBERVILLE, J., *Le Théâtre d'Edmond Rostand* (Paris, 1919); *Edmond Rostand* (Paris, 1921).

CRITICISM:

AUBRY, G. J., *Edmond Rostand* (*Fortnightly Review*, New York, 1919); CHESTERTON, G. K., *Varied Types: a Book of Essays* (New York, 1905); LAROUGE, R., *Edmond Rostand intime* (*Revue des deux Mondes*, Paris, 1930); RENOUARD, D., *Le romantisme d'Edmond Rostand* (*Nouvelle Revue*, Paris, 1931).

WORKS ON CYRANO DE BERGERAC:

BERNARD, J., *Savinien de Cyrano et M. Edmond Rostand* (Paris, 1903);
PLATOW, H., *Die Personen von Rostand's Cyrano de Bergerac in der
Geschichte und in der Dichtung* (Berlin, 1902); RICTUS, J., *Un Bluff
littéraire, le cas Edmond Rostand* (Paris, 1903); SCHENCK, F. A., *Études
sur la rime dans Cyrano de Bergerac* (Kiel, 1900); SCHMIDT, E., *Cyrano
de Bergerac* (in *Charakteristiken*, vol. 2, Berlin, 1901).

## PLAYS OF EDMOND ROSTAND

*Le Gant Rouge*, published 1888.

*Les deux Pierrots*, published 1891.

*Les Romanesques*, published and produced 1894. Translated as *The
Romancers* by Mary Hendee, 1899; by B. H. Clark, 1915; by Anna E.
Bagstad, *Poet Lore*, 1921. Translated as *The Fantasticks*, 1900; as
*The Romantics* by H. D. Norman, New York, 1921.

*La Princesse Lointaine*, published 1897. Translated as *The Princess Far-
Away* by C. Renould, New York, 1899 and by H. D. Norman, New
York, 1921; as *The Lady of Dreams*, 1912; as *The Far Princess* by John
Heard, Jr., 1925.

*Cyrano de Bergerac*, published and produced 1897.

*La Samaritaine*, published and produced 1898. Translated as *The
Woman of Samaria* by H. D. Norman, New York, 1921.

*L'Aiglon*, published and produced 1900. Translated by L. N. Parker,
New York, 1900; by Basil Davenport, New Haven, 1927; as *The
Eaglet* by H. D. Norman, New York, 1921.

*Chantecler*, published and produced 1910. Translated by Gertrude
Hall, New York, 1910; by H. D. Norman, New York, 1921.

*Le Bois sacré*, published 1910.

*Le Dernière Nuit de Don Juan*, dramatic poem, published 1922. Translated as *The Last Night of Don Juan* by T. L. Riggs, Yellow Springs,
Ohio, 1929.

## COLLECTED EDITION OF ROSTAND IN ENGLISH

The Plays of Edmond Rostand, translated by Henderson Danger-
field Norman, in 2 volumes, New York, 1921, contains *The Romantics*,
*The Princess Far-Away*, *The Woman of Samaria*, *Cyrano de Bergerac*, *The
Eaglet*, and *Chantecler*.

## EUGÈNE BRIEUX

BENOIST, A., *Le théâtre de Brieux* (Toulouse, 1907); BERTRAND, A.,
*Eugène Brieux, biographie critique* (Paris, 1910); CHANDLER, F. W.,
*The Contemporary Drama of France* (Boston, 1921); *Aspects of Modern
Drama* (New York, 1914); SCHEIFLEY, W. H., *Brieux and Contemporary
French Society* (New York, 1917); THOMAS, P. V., *The Plays of Eugene
Brieux* (Boston, 1925); BRIEUX, E., Introduction to Clark's *Four Plays*

*of the Free Theatre* (Cincinnati, 1914); Introduction to *Woman on Her Own, False Gods, The Red Robe* (New York, 1916); KAHN, A., *Le théâtre social en France* (Paris, 1907); MENCKEN, H. L., Introduction to *Blanchette* and *The Escape* (Boston, 1913); SÉCHÉ, A., and BERTRAUT, J., *L'Evolution du Théâtre contemporain* (Paris, 1908); SHAW, G. B., Introduction to *Three Plays by Brieux* (New York, 1914).

## THE PLAYS OF EUGÈNE BRIEUX

*Bernard Palissy*, published 1879.   (In collaboration with G. Salandri.)

*Le Bureau des Divorces*, published 1880.   (In collaboration with G. Salandri.)

*Sténio*, published 1888.

*Ménage d'Artistes*, published 1890.   Translated as *Artists' Families* by B. H. Clark, Garden City, 1918.

*La Fille de Duramé*, published 1890.

*Corneille á Petit-Couronne*, published 1890.

*M. de Reboval*, published 1892.

*Blanchette*, published 1892.   Translated by F. Eisemann, Boston, 1913.

*La Couvée*, published 1893.

*L'Engrenage*, published 1894.

*La Rose bleue*, published 1895.

*Le Soldat Graindor*, published 1895.

*L'Évasion*, published 1896.   Translated as *The Escape*, by F. Eisemann, Boston, 1913.

*Les Bienfaiteurs*, published 1896.

*Les trois Filles de M. Dupont*, published 1897.   Translated as *The Three Daughters of M. Dupont* by St. John Hankin in *Three Plays by Brieux*, New York, 1911.

*L'Ecole des belles-mères*, published 1898.   Translated as *The School for Mothers-in-Law* by W. H. Wright in *Smart Set*, New York, 1913.

*Résultat des Courses!* published 1898.

*Le Berceau*, published 1898.

*La Robe rouge*, published 1900.   Translated as *The Red Robe* by F. O. Reed, in *Chief Contemporary Dramatists*, Boston, 1915; and by A. B. Miall, New York, 1916.

*Les Remplaçantes*, published 1901.

*La Petite Amie*, published 1902.

*Les Avariés*, published 1902.   Translated as *Damaged Goods* by John Pollock, London, 1914.

*Maternité*, published 1903.   Translated as *Maternity* by Mrs. Bernard Shaw, New York, 1911.

*La Deserteuse*, published 1904.   (In collaboration with Jean Sigaux.)

*L'Armature*, published 1905.   Dramatized from Hervieu.

*Les Hannetons*, published 1906.   Produced in English as *Madame Pierre*.

*La Française*, published 1907.

*Simone*, published 1908.

*Suzette*, published 1909.

*La Foi*, published 1909. Translated as *False Gods* by J. B. Fagan, New York, 1916.

*La Femme seule*, published 1912. Translated as *Woman on Her Own* by Mrs. Bernard Shaw, New York, 1916.

*Le Bourgeois aux Champs*, published 1914.

*Les Américains chez nous*, published 1920.

*Les trois bons Amis*, published 1921.

*L'Avocat*, published 1922.

*L'Enfant (Pierrette et Galaor)*, published 1923.

# AUGUST STRINDBERG

LIFE AND WORK:

CAMPBELL, G. A., *Strindberg* (London, 1933); ERDMANN, N., *August Strindberg* (German translation, Leipzig, 1924); HEDÉN, E., *Strindberg* (Stockholm, 1921); JOLIVET, A., *Le Théâtre de Strindberg* (Paris, 1931); LIND-AF-HAGEBY, L., *August Strindberg, the Spirit of Revolt* (London, 1913); *August Strindberg, a Study* (London, 1928); McGILL, V. J., *August Strindberg, the bedevilled Viking* (New York, 1930); UDDGREN, C. G., *Strindberg the Man* (translated by A. J. Uppvall, Boston, 1920).

CRITICISM:

BRETT, A., *Psychological Abnormalities in August Strindberg (Journal of English and Germanic Philology*, Urbana, 1921); BULMAN, J., *Strindberg and Shakespeare* (London, 1933); DAHLSTRÖM, C., *August Strindberg, the Father of Dramatic Expressionism* (Michigan Academy of Science, Art and Letters, Ann Arbor, 1929); *Strindberg's Dramatic Expressionism* (University of Michigan Publications in Language and Literature, 1930); HAYWARD, I. N., *Strindberg's Influence on Eugene O'Neill (Poet Lore*, Boston, 1928); LAMM, M., *Strindberg's Dramer* (2 vols., Stockholm, 1924); MARCUS, C. D., *August Strindbergs Dramatik* (Munich, 1918); MARCUSE, L., *Strindberg, das Leben der Tragischen Seele* (Berlin, 1920).

SELF-CRITICISM:

See *Strindberg's Dramaturgie* (German translation by E. Schering, Munich, 1911); *Dramatische Charakteristiken* (German translation by E. Schering, Munich, 1914); see *Lettres inédites de Friedrich Nietzsche et A. Strindberg (Revue*, Paris, 1913); see Strindberg's Preface to *Miss Julia* and *The Dream Play*.

## PLAYS OF AUGUST STRINDBERG

(List based on Carl Dahlstrom, *Strindberg's Dramatic Expressionism*. A Dissertation. University of Michigan Publications, Language and Literature, 1930, vol. 7.)

*Den fredlöse (The Outlaw)*, produced 1871; published 1876. Translated by M. Harned, *Poet Lore*, 1906; E. and W. Oland, Boston, 1912.

*Mäster Olof*, prose versions, written 1871, published and produced 1881. Translated as *Master Olof* by E. Björkman, New York, 1915; by C. D. Locock, London, 1931.

*Anno fyrtia åtta* (*The Year Forty-Eight*), written 1875, published 1881.

*Gillets hemlighed* (*The Secret of the Guild*), written 1879–80; published and produced 1880.

*Lycko Pers resa* (*Lucky Peter's Journey*), written 1881–82; published 1882; produced 1883. Translated as *Lucky Pehr* by V. S. Howard, Chicago, 1922; as *Lucky Peter's Travels* by E. Classen, London, 1930.

*Herr Bengts hustru* (*Sir Bengt's Wife*), written 1882; produced and published the same year. Translated into French as *Marget*, 1898.

*Marodörer* (early form of *Comrades*), written 1886.

*Fadren* (*The Father*), written and published 1887; produced in Denmark 1887, at Stockholm 1888, at the Freie Bühne in Berlin, 1890. Translated by E. and W. Oland, Boston, 1912; N. Erichsen, London, 1898; G. D. Locock, London, 1931.

*Kamraterna* (*Comrades*), written 1887 in collaboration with Axel Lundegård; published 1888; produced 1910. Translated by E. and W. Oland, Boston, 1913; H. B. Samuel, London, 1914.

*Fröken Julie* (*Lady Julia*), written and published in 1888; produced in 1892 by the Freie Bühne in Berlin; not until 1906 in Stockholm.

*Fordringsägare* (*Creditors*), written 1888; published and produced in 1890. Translated by M. Harned, Boston, 1911; E. Björkman, New York, 1912.

*Hemsöborna* (*Hemso Folk*), written 1888; produced 1889; published in German 1905.

*Paria* (*Pariah*), written 1888; published 1890; produced 1908. Translated by E. Björkman, New York, 1912; E. and W. Oland, Boston, 1913; H. B. Samuels, London, 1914.

*Den starkare* (*The Stronger*), written 1888–89; produced 1889; published 1890. Translated in *Poet Lore*, 1906; by E. and W. Oland, Boston, 1912; Charles Wangel, New York, 1923.

*Samum* (*Simoon*), written 1889; published 1890; produced 1892. Translated by M. Harned in *Poet Lore*, 1906; E. Björkman, New York, 1914; H. B. Samuel, London, 1914.

*Himmelrikets nycklar* (*The Keys of the Kingdom of Heaven*), written 1891–92; published 1892.

*Debet och Kredit* (*Debit and Credit*), written 1892; published 1893. Translated [by M. Harned, *Poet Lore*, 1906; E. Björkman, New York, 1914.

*Första varningen* (*The First Warning*), written 1892; published 1893; produced 1910. Translated by E. Björkman, New York, 1916.

*Inför döden* (*Facing Death*), written 1892; published 1893; produced 1910. Translated by E. and W. Oland, Boston, 1913.

*Moderskärlek* (*Motherlove*), written 1892; published 1893. Translated by F. J. Ziegler, Philadelphia, 1910.

*Leka med elden* (*Playing with Fire*), written 1892; published 1893; produced 1908. Translated by E. Classen, London, 1930.

*Bandet* (*The Link*), written 1892; published 1893; produced 1908. Translated as *The Link* by E. Björkman, New York, 1912; E. Sprigge and Claude Napier, London, 1930.

*Till Damaskus*, First Part (*To Damascus*), written 1897–98; published 1898; produced 1900; Second Part, written and published 1898.

*Advent, ett mysterium* (*Advent*), written 1898; published 1899. Translated by E. and W. Oland, Boston, 1914; E. Björkman, New York, 1914; Claude Field, London, 1921.

*Broch och Brott* (*Crimes and Crimes*), written 1898; published 1899; produced 1900. Translated as *There are Crimes and Crimes* by E. Björkman, New York, 1912.

*Folkungasagan* (*The Folkung Saga*), written and published 1899; produced 1901. Translated as *The Saga of the Folkungs* by C. D. Locock, London, 1931.

*Gustav Vasa*, written, published and produced 1899. Translated by E. Björkman, New York, 1916; C. D. Locock, London, 1931.

*Erik XIV*, written, published and produced 1899. Translated by Joan Bulman, London, 1931.

*Gustav Adolf*, written 1899; published 1900; produced 1912.

*Kaspers Fet-Tisdag* (*Caspar's Shrove Tuesday*), written 1900; produced 1901; published 1915.

*Midsommar* (*Midsummer*), written 1900; published and produced 1901.

*Påsk* (*Easter*), written 1900; published and produced 1901. Translated by V. S. Howard, Cincinnati, 1912; E. and W. Oland, Boston, 1913; E. Classen, London, 1929.

*Dödsdansen* (*The Dance of Death*), First Part, written and published 1901; produced 1909; Second Part written and published 1901; produced 1909. Translated by E. Björkman, New York, 1912; C. D. Locock, 1929.

*Kronbruden* (*The Crown Bride*), written 1901; published 1902; produced 1907. Translated as *The Bridal Crown* by E. Björkman, New York, 1916.

*Svanevit* (*Swanwhite*), written 1901; published 1902; produced 1908. Translated by F. J. Zeigler, Philadelphia, 1909; E. and W. Oland, Boston, 1914; E. Björkman, New York, 1914.

*Carl XII*, written and published 1901; produced 1902.

*Engelbrakt*, written, published, and produced 1901.

*Kristina* (*Christina*), written 1901; published 1903; produced 1908.

*Ett dromspel* (*A Dream Play*), written 1901–02; published 1902; produced 1907. Translated by E. Björkman, New York, 1912; C. D. Locock, London, 1929.

*Gustav III*, written 1902; published 1903; produced 1916.

*Näktergalen i Wittenberg* (*The Nightingale in Wittenberg*), written 1903; published 1904.

*Genom öknar till arfland, eller, Moses* (*Through the Wilderness to the Promised Land, or Moses*), written 1903; published 1918.

*Hellas, eller, Sokrates* (*Ellas or Socrates*), written 1903; published 1918.

*Lammet och vilddjuret, eller, Kristus* (*The Lamb and the Wild Beast, or Christ*), written 1903; published 1918.

*Till Damaskus*, Third Part, written 1900–04; published 1904.

*Förspel till ett drömspel* (*Prologue to a Dream Play*), written 1906; produced 1907; published 1920.

*Oväder* (*The Thunderstorm*), written, published, and produced 1907. Translated as *The Storm* by E. and W. Oland, Boston, 1914; as *The Thunderstorm* by E. Björkman, New York, 1914.

*Brände tomten* (*After the Fire*), written, published, and produced 1907. Translated by E. Björkman, New York, 1914.

*Spöksonaten* (*The Spook Sonata*), published 1907; produced 1908. Translated by E. Björkman, New York, 1916; as *The Ghost Sonata* by E. Palmstierna and J. B. Fagan, London, 1929.

*Pelikanen* (*The Pelican*), written, published, and produced 1907.

*Siste riddaren* (*The Last Knight*), written 1908; published and produced 1909.

*Riksföreståndaren* (*The Regent*), written 1908; published 1909; produced 1911.

*Abu Casems toffler* (*Abu Casem's Slipper*), written, published, and produced 1908.

*Bjälbo-Jarlen* (*The Earl of Bjälbo*), written 1908; published and produced 1909.

*Svarta handsken* (*The Black Glove*), written 1908; published 1909; produced 1911.

*Stora landsvägen* (*The Great Highway*), written and published 1909; produced 1910.

## Collected Translations of Strindberg in English

*Plays*, vol. 1, by Edith and Warner Oland, Boston, 1912, contains *Comrades, Pariah, Facing Death*, and *Easter*, New York, 1913.

*Plays*, vol. 2, by Edith and Warner Oland, Boston, 1912, contains *The Father, Countess Julie, The Outlaw*, and *The Stronger*, New York, 1912.

*Plays*, vol. 3, by Edith and Warner Oland, Boston, 1914, contains *Swanwhite, Advent*, and *The Storm*, New York, 1914.

*Plays*, 1st Series, translated by E. Björkman, contains *The Dream Play, The Link*, and *The Dance of Death*, New York, 1912.

*Plays*, 2d Series, translated by E. Björkman, contains *There are Crimes and Crimes, Miss Julia, The Stronger*, and *Creditors*, New York, 1913.

*Plays*, 3d Series, translated by Edwin Björkman, New York, 1913, contains *Swanwhite, Simoon, Debit and Credit, Advent, The Thunderstorm*, and *After the Fire*, New York, 1913.

*Plays*, 4th Series, translated by Edwin Björkman, New York, 1916, contains *Bridal Crown, Spook Sonata, The First Warning*, and *Gustavus Vasa*, New York, 1916.

*Plays*, 5th Series, translated by Edwin Björkman, contains *The Father*, *The Black Glove*, *The Pelican*, and *Moses*, New York, 1917.

*Miss Julia and Other Plays*, in Modern Library Series, New York, 1918, contains *Miss Julia*, *The Creditors*, *The Stronger Woman*, *Motherly Love*, *Pariah*, and *Simoon*.

*Lucky Peter's Travels and Other Plays*, Anglo-Swedish Literary Foundation, London, 1931, contains *Lucky Peter's Travels*, *The Father*, *Lady Julia*, *Playing with Fire*, and *The Bond*.

*Easter and Other Plays*, Anglo-Swedish Literary Foundation, London, 1931, contains *Easter*, *The Dance of Death*, *The Ghost Sonata*, and *A Dream Play*.

Translations of *Outcast*, *Simoon*, and *Debit and Credit* by Mary Harned were published by *Poet Lore*, Boston, 1906.

## MAXIM GORKY

DILLON, E. J., *Maxim Gorky; his Life and Writings* (London, 1902); DUESEL, F., *Maxim Gorky and Anton Chekhov* (Berlin, 1922); KAUN, A. S., *Maxim Gorky and his Russia* (New York, 1931); *Tolstoy and Gorky* (California University Chronicle, Berkeley, 1930); OSTWALD, H. O. A., *Maxim Gorky* (translated by F. A. Welby, New York, 1907); CLARK, B. H., *Conversations with Maxim Gorky* (*Fortnightly Review*, New York, 1923); GORKY, M., *My Childhood* (translation, New York, 1914); *In the World* (translated by G. M. Foakes, New York, 1917); *My University Days* (translation, New York, 1923); *Reminiscences of My Youth* (translated by V. Dewey, London, 1924).

### PLAYS OF MAXIM GORKY

*The Middle Class*, produced 1901; published 1903. Translated as *The Smug Citizen* in *Poet Lore*, 1906.

*The Lower Depths*, produced 1902; published 1903.

*Summer Folk*, produced 1903; published 1904. Translated by A. Delano in *Poet Lore*, 1905.

*Children of the Sun*, produced and published 1905. Translated by A. J. Wolfe in *Poet Lore*, 1906.

*Barbarians*, produced 1905; published 1906.

*Enemies*, produced and published 1906.

*The Last Ones*, produced 1908; published 1906.

*Odd Folk*, produced and published 1910.

*Children*, published 1910.

*The Meeting*, published 1910.

*The Zykovs*, published 1914.

*The Judge* (*The Old Man*), published 1915. Translated by B. H. Clark, New York, 1924.

*The Counterfeit Coin*, published 1926.

The following of Gorky's tales have been adapted for the stage: *Fora Gordyev* (1901); *The Three* (1911); *Malva* (1911).

## LEONID ANDREYEV

KAUN, A., *Leonid Andreyev: a Critical Study* (New York, 1924); *Tolstoy and Andreyev* (*California University Chronicle*, Berkeley, 1924); GORKY, M., *Leonid Andreyev at Capri* (*Living Age*, New York, 1922); *Reminiscences of Leonid Andreyev* (*Adelphi*, London, 1924); *More Reminiscences of Leonid Andreyev* (*Dublin Magazine*, Dublin, 1925); SELTZER, T., *Life and Works of L. Andreyev* (*The Drama*, Chicago, 1914); ANDREYEV, L., *The Confessions of a Little Man During Great Days*, London, 1923; see *Translations of Andreyev's Letters on the Theatre*, 1912–13, by Manart Kippen, in the *New York Times*, October 5 and 19, 1919.

### THE PLAYS OF LEONID ANDREYEV

*To the Stars*, published 1905.  Translated by A. Goudiss, *Poet Lore*, 1907.

*Savva*, published 1906.  Translated by Thomas Seltzer, New York, 1914.

*The Life of Man*, published 1906.  Translated by Thomas Seltzer, New York, 1914; C. J. Hogart, London, 1915; Meader and Scott, New York, 1923.

*Tsar Hunger*, published 1907.  Translated as *King Hunger* by E. M. Kayden, *Poet Lore*, 1911.

*The Death of Man*, published 1908.  Variant of the last act of *The Life of Man*.

*The Black Maskers*, published 1908.  Translated by S. M. Meader and F. N. Scott, New York, 1915.

*Days of Our Life*, published 1908.

*Love of your Neighbor*, published 1908.  Translated as *Love of One's Neighbor* by T. Seltzer, New York, 1914; as *The Dear Departing* by T. West, London, 1916.

*The Bat*, published 1908.

*Anathema*, published 1909.  Translated by Herman Bernstein, New York, 1910.

*Anfisa*, published 1909.

*Gaudeamus*, published 1910.

*The Ocean*, published 1911.

*Honor*, published 1912.

*The Pretty Sabine Women*, published 1912.  Translated under this title in *The Drama*, Chicago, 1914; as *The Sabine Women* by Meader and Scott, New York, 1923.

*Professor Storitsyn*, published 1912.

*Katherina Ivanovna*, published 1912.  Translated as *Katerina* by H. Bernstein, New York, 1923.

*Thou Shalt Not Kill*, published 1913.

*Thought*, published 1914.

*An Event*, published 1914.  Translated as *An Incident* by L. Paslovsky, *Poet Lore*, 1916.

*Samson Enchained*, written in 1914. Translated as *Samson in Chains* by H. Bernstein, New York, 1923.

*The Waltz of the Dogs*, written in 1914; published in Paris, 1922. Translated by H. Bernstein, New York, 1922.

*The Parrot*, published 1914.

*War's Burden*, published 1915. Translated as *The Sorrows of Belgium*, by H. Bernstein, New York, 1915.

*He Who Gets Slapped*, published 1915. Translated by Gregory Zilboorg, *The Dial*, 1921.

*Dear Phantoms*, published 1916.

*Requiem*, published 1917.

See *Plays*, translated by C. L. Meader and F. N. Scott, New York, 1915, containing *The Black Maskers*, *The Life of Man*, *The Sabine Women*.

## GEORG KAISER

FRUCHTER, M. J., *Georg Kaiser's Dramatic Works* (Philadelphia, 1933); FREYHAN, M., *Georg Kaisers Werk* (Berlin, 1926); KOENIGSGARTEN, H. F., *Georg Kaiser* (with a Bibliography, Potsdam, 1928); OMAN-KOWSKI, W., *Georg Kaiser und seine besten Bühnenwerke* (Berlin, 1922); KNUDSEN, H., *Georg Kaiser in der Zeit* (Masken, Berlin, 1929); LEWIN, L., *Dus Erlebnis bei Georg Kaiser* (Masken, Berlin, 1922).

### PLAYS BY GEORG KAISER

*Rektor Kleist*, written 1905; published and produced 1918.

*Claudius, Friedrich und Anna, Juana*, one-act plays, published 1914; produced 1918.

*Die Sorina* (earlier *Der Bethlehemistische Kindermord*), published 1917.

*Konstantin Strobel* (*Der Zentaur*), published 1916; produced 1917.

*Die jüdische Witwe*, written and published 1911; produced 1921.

*Die Bürger von Calais*, written and published 1914; produced 1917.

*König Hahnrei*, written 1913; published 1916; produced 1917.

*Europa*, published 1915; produced 1920.

*Von Morgen bis Mitternachts*, published 1916; produced 1917. Translated as *From Morn to Midnight* by Ashley Dukes, 1920.

*Die Koralle*, published and produced 1917. Translated as *The Coral* by Winifred Katzin, New York, 1927.

*Der Brand im Opernhaus*, published 1919; produced 1918. Translated as *The Fire in the Opera House* by Winifred Katzin, New York, 1927.

*Hölle, Weg, Erde*, published and produced 1919.

*Gas I*, published 1918; produced 1919. Translated by H. Scheffauer, 1924.

*Gas II*, published 1919; produced 1920. Translated by Winifred Katzin, 1931.

*Der gerettete Alkibiades*, published and produced 1920.

*Das Frauenopfer*, published 1920; produced 1922.
*David und Goliath*, published and produced 1921.
*Noli me Tangere*, published and produced 1922.
*Kanzlist Krehler*, published and produced 1922.
*Gilles und Jeanne*, published and produced 1923.
*Nebeneinander*, published and produced, 1923.
*Die Flucht nach Venedig* (after A. de Musset), published and produced
    1923.
*Der Geist der Antike*, published and produced 1923.
*Kolportage*, published and produced 1924.
*Der Protagonist*, one-act opera, published 1925; produced 1926.
*Zweimal Oliver*, published and produced 1926.
*Der Praesident*, published and produced 1927.
*Die Lederkoepfe*, published and produced 1928.
*Oktobertag*, published and produced 1928.    Translated as *The Phantom
    Lover* by H. Bernstein and A. E. Meyer, New York, 1928.
*Papiermuehle*, published and produced 1928.
*Hellserei*, published 1929.
*Zwei Krawatten*, revue in 9 pictures, published 1930.

# LUIGI PIRANDELLO

BOOKS ON THE MAN AND WORK:
> MATHEWS, G. W., *Pirandello: a Study in the Psychology of the Modern
> Stage* (Liverpool, 1928); PASINI, F., *Luigi Pirandello (Come mi pare)*
> (Trieste, 1927); SICILIANO, ITALO, *Il Teatro di Luigi Pirandello*
> (Torino, 1929); STARKIE, W., *Luigi Pirandello* (London, 1926).

CRITICAL ARTICLES:
> CHIMINEZ, S. A., *Il Teatro di Luigi Pirandello* (*Nuova Antologia*, Rome,
> 1921); GREY, J. C., *Luigi Pirandello* (*Theatre Arts Magazine*, New
> York, 1922); GILLET, L., *Littérature étrangères; un humoriste Sicilien*
> (*Revue des deux Mondes*, Paris, 1923); LEO, ULRICH, *Pirandello,
> Kunsttheorie and Maskensymbol* (*Deutsche Vierteljahrsschrift für Literatur-
> wissenschaft*, Halle, 1933); PHELPS, RUTH S., *Italian Silhouettes* (New
> York, 1924); ROPS, D., *Luigi Pirandello* (*Grande Revue*, Paris, 1927);
> SAN SECONDO, ROSSI DI, *Luigi Pirandello* (*Nuova Antologia*, Rome,
> 1916); STORER, E., *Luigi Pirandello, Dramatist* (*Fortnightly Review*,
> New York, 1924); WILLIAMS, ORLA, *Luigi Pirandello, Dramatist*
> (*Cornhill Magazine*, London, 1923).

PIRANDELLO SELF-REVEALED:
> PIRANDELLO, LUIGI, *Comment et pourquoi j'ai écrit Six Personnages en
> Quête d'Auteur* (*Revue de Paris*, Paris, 1925); *The Late Mattia Pascal*
> (translated by A. Livingston, New York, 1923).

See Introductions by Arthur Livingston to the translated plays by
Luigi Pirandello.

## ONE-ACT PLAYS BY LUIGI PIRANDELLO

*La patente*, produced 1918. Translated as *The Judgment of Court* by E. Abbott, New York, 1928.

*La sagra del Signore della nave*, produced 1925. Translated as *Our Lord of the Ship* by B. V. Mitchell, New York, 1928.

*Il dovere del medico*, early play. Translated as *The Doctor's Duty* by B. V. Mitchell, New York, 1928.

*Cecè*, early play. Translated as *Chee-Chee* by E. Abbott, New York, 1928.

*L'uomo dal fiore in bocca*, produced 1923. Translated as *The Man with a Flower in his Mouth* by Arthur Livingston, New York, 1928.

*All'uscita (At the Door)*, produced 1924. Translated as *At the Gate* by B. V. Mitchell, New York, 1928.

*La morsa*, produced 1912. Translated as *The Vise* by E. Abbott, New York, 1928.

*L'altro figlio*, produced 1925. Translated as *The House with the Columns* by E. Abbott, New York, 1928.

*Lumie di Sicilie*, published 1911. Translated as *Sicilian Limes* by E. Abbott, New York, 1928; by I. Goldberg, 1921.

*La giara*, produced 1925. Translated as *The Jar* by Arthur Livingston, New York, 1928.

## LONGER PLAYS BY LUIGI PIRANDELLO

*Se non così (If Not Thus)*, an early form of *La Ragione degli Altir*, produced 1915; published 1916.

*Liolà* (first written in Sicilian), produced 1916; published 1917.

*Pensaci, Giacomino (Just Think, Jimmy)*, comedy in three acts from a *novella*, produced 1916; published 1918.

*Così è (se vi pare)*, a parable in three acts from a *novella*, first published in the *Nuova Antologia*, Rome, 1918; produced, 1916. Translated as *Right You Are! (If You Think So)* by Arthur Livingston, 1923.

*Il piacere dell'onestà*, a comedy, produced 1917; published 1918. Translated into English as *The Pleasure of Honesty* by Arthur Livingston, 1925; and into French as *La Volupté de l'honneur*, Paris, 1923.

*Il Berretto a Sonagli (Cap and Bells)*, a comedy in three acts, produced 1917; published 1921.

*Il Giuoco delle parti*, a comedy in three acts, produced 1918; published 1919.

*L'innesto*, a comedy in three acts, produced 1917; published 1921.

*Ma non è una cosa seria*, a comedy in three acts from a *novella*, published 1919.

*L'uomo, la bestia e la virtù*, an apology in three acts from a *novella*, produced 1919; published 1922.

*La Signora Morli Una e Due*, a comedy in three acts revised from *Due in Una*, produced 1920; published 1925.

*Tutto per bene*, a comedy in three acts from a *novella*, published 1920; produced 1921. Translated as *Tant pour le mieux!* Paris, 1929.

*Come prima, meglio di prima*, a comedy, produced 1920; published 1921.

*Sei Personaggi in cerca d'Autore*, a comedy in the making from the *novella*, *La Tragedia d'un Personnagio*, published and produced 1921. Translated as *Six Characters in Search of an Author* by Edward Storer, and first published in Broom, Rome, 1922; New York, 1923; produced in New York, 1923.

*Vestire gl'ignudi*, a comedy in three acts, produced 1922; published 1923. Translated as *Naked* by Arthur Livingston, New York, 1925.

*Enrico IV*, a tragedy in three acts, produced and published 1922. Translated by Edward Storer, 1923.

*La Ragione degli Altri* (*The Rights of Others*), produced 1921; published 1926. This is a revised form of *Se non così*, produced 1915.

*La Vita che ti Diedi*, a tragedy in three acts, produced 1923; published 1924.

*Ciascuno a suò Modo*, a comedy with choral interludes, published and produced 1924. Translated as *Each in His Own Way* by Arthur Livingston, New York, 1925.

*La nuova colonia*, produced 1926; published 1927.

*L'amica delle mogli*, a comedy in three acts, published and produced 1927.

*Diana e la Tuda*, a tragedy, published 1927.

*Scamandro*, published 1929.

*O di uno o di nessuno*, a comedy, published 1929.

*Questa sera si recita a soggetto*, produced 1930; published 1932. Translated as *Tonight We Improvise* by S. Putnam, New York, 1932.

*Lazzaro*, a play in three acts, published 1930.

*Come tu mi vuoi*, a play in three acts, published and produced 1930. Translated as *As You Desire Me* by Samuel Putnam, and published and produced, New York, 1931.

*I fantasmi*, published 1931.

## JEAN–JACQUES BERNARD

BILLY, A., *La Littérature française contemporaine* (Paris, 1927); BLANCHART, P., *Jean-Jacques Bernard* (*Masques*, May, 1928); CHARPENTIER, J., *Les tendresses menacées* (*Mercure de France*, 1925); DUBECH, L., *Jean-Jacques Bernard*, *L'Ecole du Silence* (*Revue Universelle*, 1924); HOMMEL, L., *Le Théâtre de Jean-Jacques Bernard* (*Revue Générale*, Brussels, 1925); LEMONNIER, L., *Le Théâtre de Jean-Jacques Bernard* (*La Revue Mondiale*, 1925); MORNET, D., *Histoire de la littérature et da la pensée française contemporaine* (Paris, 1927); PALMER, JOHN, *Jean-Jacques Bernard and the Theory of Silence* (*Fortnightly Review*, January, 1927).

## PLAYS BY JEAN-JACQUES BERNARD

*Le voyage à deux*, a play in one act, produced 1909; published 1910.

*La joie du sacrifice*, a play in one act, produced and published 1912.

*La maison épargnée*, a play in three acts, produced 1919; published 1920.

*Le feu qui reprend mal*, a play in three acts, published and produced 1921.

*Martine*, a play in five scenes, produced and published 1922. Translated by Winifred Katzin in *Eight European Plays*, New York, 1927.

*L'Invitation au voyage*, a play in three acts and five scenes, produced and published 1924. Translated as *Glamour* by Winifred Katzin in *Eight European Plays*, New York, 1927.

*Le printemps des autres*, a play in three acts, produced and published 1924.

*Le secret d'Arvers*, a play in one act, produced and published 1926.

*L'Ame en peine*, a play in three acts, produced 1926; published 1927.

*Denise Marette*, a play in three acts, produced 1925; published 1927.

*La grande B. A.*, a play in one act, published and produced 1930.

*Les sœurs Quédonec*, a play in two acts, published and produced 1931.

*Jeanne de Pantin*, produced and published 1933.

*Le Roi de Malousie*, produced 1928; published 1933.

Le Jeu qui expand mat, a play in three acts, published and produced 1921.
Manette, a play in five scenes, produced and published 1921. Translated
  by Winifred Katzin in Eight European Plays, New York, 1927.
L'Invitation au voyage, a play in three acts and two scenes, produced and
  published 1924. Translated as Glamour by Winifred Katzin in Eight
  European Plays, New York, 1927.

Le printemps des autres, a play in three acts, produced and published 1924.
Le secret d'Arvers, a play in one act, produced and published 1926.
Prends ta prise, a play in three acts, produced 1926, published 2027.
Dardamelle, a play in three acts, produced 1927, published 1927.
La gentille Dariel, a play in one act, published and produced 1929.
Le jour, Vaillant, a play in two acts, published and produced 1931.
Jeanne de France, produced and published 1933.
La Fleur de Malaga, produced 1928, published 1933.

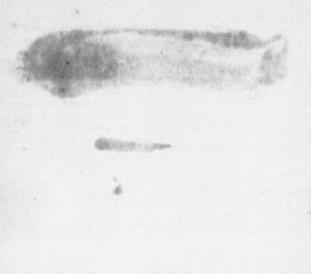